ONLINE BUSINESS COMPUTER APPLICATIONS

Third Edition

Alan L. Eliason
University of Oregon

MACMILLAN PUBLISHING COMPANY
New York

COLLIER MACMILLAN CANADA
Toronto

MAXWELL MACMILLAN INTERNATIONAL
New York   Oxford   Singapore   Sydney

Copyright © 1991 by Macmillan Publishing Company, a division of
Macmillan, Inc.

Printed in the Republic of Singapore

Macmillan Publishing Company
866 Third Avenue, New York, NY 10022

Collier Macmillan Canada, Inc.
1200 Eglinton Avenue East
Suite 200
Don Mills, Ontario, M3C 3N1

Library of Congress Cataloging-in-Publication Data

Eliason, Alan L.
Online business computer applications/Alan L. Eliason.–3rd ed.
p.   cm.
Includes index.
1. Business–Data processing. I. Title.
HF5548.2.E427 1991   90-43499
658'.05–dc20   CIP
ISBN 0-02-332481-3 (Hardcover Edition)
ISBN 0-02-946508-7 (International Edition)

IE Printing: 1 2 3 4 5   Year: 1 2 3 4 5

ISBN 0-02-946508-7

Preface

This book explores the design characteristics of the most common types of business computer applications. Written for a large audience, it should interest students of business and computer science. It will be useful in the fields of data processing, management information systems, accounting, and systems analysis and design. Besides the university and college audience, the book should appeal to practicing computer programmers, systems analysts and designers, accountants, and business managers. They will find it a valuable reference, particularly when faced with the challenge of beginning to develop an online design. The book's practical approach should be especially attractive.

The text follows a two-section format and is divided into five main parts. The first section, Part I, introduces the student to concepts important to online systems. Chapter 1 examines the business computing environment and compares batch and online processing. Chapter 2 continues this introduction by describing the common properties of online business computer applications, and Chapter 3, even more applied in its orientation, describes the main features of online systems design.

The second section of the text, Parts II through V, describes features specific to the design of twelve online business computer applications. The initial three-chapter part, entitled "Receivables Applications," examines the ways in which customer invoices, cash receipts, and accounts receivable are processed by computer. The next three-chapter part, "Payables Applications," describes the online processing associated with the payment of suppliers and employees and with the management of fixed assets. Part IV, "Materials-control Applications," deals with the online processing of customer orders, inventory receipts, purchase orders, and receiving receipts. It explains how computer technology assists in managing inventory levels in a company. The last three chapters, in Part V, examine "Financial and Marketing Applications"—the use of the computer to analyze cost, revenue, budget, profit, sales, and market information.

The twelve application chapters in Parts II through V are organized similarly. Following a brief introduction, a section entitled "Preliminary Overview of Processing" provides a logical view of processing and introduces concepts and terms important to the chapter. It explains the makeup of computer files and describes the main inputs to processing and the outputs, or products, that follow from processing. The more detailed features of applications processing are explained next. This section examines the computer programs important to the application and explains the interactive and the batch features of processing. Most chapters include a section entitled "Processing Controls." These sections underscore the importance of control in applications processing. Each chapter concludes with a brief section entitled "Management Implications," which explores the impact of the application on the internal workings of a business organization.

Materials described early on in the book are used in subsequent chapters. For example, the product master file introduced in the discussion of customer invoicing (Chapter 4) is featured again in the chapters dealing with materials control, payables, and financial and market planning.

Another important feature is the explanation of the way online designs are developed. All designs presented in the book, for example, feature program- and file-processing menus; they require users of an application to signify what specific step in processing is to be executed. This menu-driven, step-by-step approach helps clarify the component parts of each online application.

Other important features include a wide range of visual aid materials, sets of self-testing review questions, end-of-chapter summaries, lists of key words, sets of exercises, discussion questions, a software-supported case study, and a complete glossary of key terms. The visual aid materials were selected to provide a better comprehension of terms, concepts, and design features and ideas. The sets of review questions help in testing understanding of key concepts, and exercises and discussion questions provide practice in thinking about solutions to systems problems. The software-supported case study provides actual practice in processing transactions for a company.

The most major change for this third edition is the addition of the 4-in-1 case study. The 4-in-1 case is an integrated basic accounting software package. It covers four areas of accounting: general ledger, accounts receivable, accounts payable, and payroll. By working through the case lessons, students learn how a company is defined in financial terms. Students learn to process sales, receipts, payables, disbursements, and payroll transactions; this information is then brought together in the chapter on the general ledger. After students complete the fifteen case study lessons, they should have an appreciation of how computer-based accounting systems work to simplify the accounting procedures in a company.

Other changes in this edition include the addition of structure charts showing the functional organization of each application and interactive- and batch-processing menus. The chapter on inventory control was revised to add materials on methods of costing finished-goods inventory. The chapter on the general ledger was revised to demonstrate the relationship between the general journal and application-specific G/L subsidiary journals.

I wish to thank the many companies and people who helped me in preparing this book. I am indebted to a number of companies that supplied me with computer display and graphics materials, preprinted forms, and computer-printed reports. In particular, I wish to thank the RealWorld Corporation for allowing me to use the promotional version of 4-in-1. This version is robust. It allows students to test the full functionality of this software product. I also wish to thank the many reviewers of this third edition. They were able to suggest ways of improving the text, given the changes in the computing industry during the past four years. I wish to thank the editorial team at Macmillan and the production group at Publication Services, Inc. Special thanks to Kristina Williamson and Jan Fisher at Publication Services for coordinating all the last-minute details associated with publishing a book. Finally, I wish to thank all the students who have commented on the text materials, adding clarity to weaker sections and enriching my understanding of the materials.

Alan L. Eliason

Contents

ACKNOWLEDGMENTS

Figure 1–9: courtesy of Schlage Electronics

Figure 1–10: courtesy Chase Manhattan Bank, N.A.

Figures 1–11, 5–14, 5–15: photo courtesy of NCR Corporation

Figures 1–12, 3–11: Realworld Corporation

Figure 3–3: courtesy of Digital Communication Associates, Inc.

Figure 3–5: courtesy Microsoft

Figures 3–16, 3–17, 9–7: courtesy of Standard Register

Figures 4–10, 4–20, 4–21, 5–2, 9–9, 9–10, 13–5, 13–6, 14–10, 14–19, 15–11, 15–13: courtesy of Checkmark Software, Inc.

Figures 5–17, 5–18: courtesy of Emporium, Inc.

Figure 6–1: courtesy of Eugene Hospital and Clinic

Figures 7–7, 12–4: courtesy of North Coast Electric Company

Figures 7–8, 8–16, 9–6, 10–19: courtesy of MCBA

Figures 7–18, 9–5: courtesy of Manzanita Software Systems Corporation

Figure 8–15: courtesy of Computype, Inc.

Figure 9–3: © 1989 Kronos Incorporated, 62 Fourth Avenue, Waltham, MA 02154 U.S. and Foreign Patents

Figure 9–11: courtesy of Software AG of North America

Figures 9–18, 9–19: courtesy of TLS Co.

Figure 10–4: courtesy of Digital Equipment Corporation

Figure 12–5: courtesy of Dun and Bradstreet Software

Figure 12–17: courtesy of Weber Marking Systems, Inc.

Figures 13–7, 13–16, 14–4, 14–5: courtesy of Global Software, Inc.

The following figures are reprinted by permission from the listed publications © by International Business Machines Corporation: Figure 2–8, GX20-8020-1; Figure 3–6, IBM System/370 Record Layout Worksheet GX20-1711-0; Figure 7–15, Business Information for the Executive GH30-0593-1, p. 52; Figure 9–17, Payroll Managing System Program No. 5798—CYP, GB21-2399-0; Figure 11–4, COPICS Implementation, Inventory Management (GE20-0616-1), Fig. 65; Figure 11–12, Business Information for the Executive GH30-0593-1, p. 42; Figure 11–13, Order Processing and Accounting Applications GH30-0330-1, File No S34-72, p. 2–37; Figure 11–14, Business Information for the Executive GH30-0593-1, p. 23; Figure 11–15, Order Processing and Accounting Applications GH30-0220-1 File No S34-72, p. 2–42; Figure 11–21, COPICS Implementation, Inventory Management (GE20-0616-1), Fig. 8; Figure 11–22, COPICS Implementation, Inventory Management (GE20-0616-1), Fig. 29; Figure 11–24, COPICS Implementation, Inventory Management (GE20-0616-1), Fig. 30; Figure 12–11, COPICS Implementation, Inventory Management (GE20-0616-1), Fig. 63; Figure 12–12, COPICS Implementation, Inventory Management (GE20-0616-1), Fig. 64; Figure 13–17, Graphical Data Display Manager GC33-0100-1 5478-XXH, p. 8; Figure 14–15, IBM 3279 Color Display Station, Financial Analysis GK 10-6292-0; Figure 15–9, Introducing IBM System/34 GH30-0185-4, p. 2–106; Figure 15–8, Introducing IBM System/34 GH30-0185-4, p. 2–108; Figure 15–12, Introducing IBM System/34 GH30-0185-4, p. 2–100; Figure 15–10, Introducing IBM System/34 GH30-0185-4, p. 2–103; Figure 15–14, Introducing IBM System/34 GH30-0185-4, p. 2–99; Figure 15–15, Business Information for the Executive GH30-0593-1, p. 40; Figure 15–16, Introducing IBM System/34 GH30-0185-4, p. 2–102.

PART

I

INTRODUCTION

Most business firms currently use interactive methods of data processing. Interactive processing offers two important advantages: first, business transactions can be processed one at a time, as they occur, and, second, the person using the computer, the *user*, can communicate directly with it. This second advantage, known as being *online* to the computer, permits the user to command the attention of the computer. He or she is able to direct the computer to process instructions entered into processing, to retrieve and display information immediately, and to modify directly the information stored on computer files.

This initial three-chapter introductory section provides a brief overview of the purpose, scope, and makeup of online business computer applications. In a review, the attention given to any one topic is necessarily limited. The intent was to consider beginning concepts essential to understanding online business computer applications and to examine properties of online applications and of online systems design. In so doing, we set out to answer the following questions:

- Why do most business firms process the majority of their transactions by computer and why are online systems important to this process?
- How are business computer applications related to one another and why do they feature both interactive and batch methods of data processing?
- Which tasks must be undertaken by computer specialists in preparing written specifications for an online business computer application?
- How are online systems designed and what are the essential parts of the design process?
- How are online systems organized and how do they provide an integrated approach to data processing?

CHAPTER

1

Beginning Concepts

Most large business firms currently process the majority of their routine business transactions by computer. The greater efficiency of the computer, compared to human processing, has been a principal factor in the movement to automate clerical, managerial, and administrative applications. Business firms are often introduced to computing once they decide to design and install everyday computer-based financial and accounting applications, such as payroll, invoicing, and accounts payable. After these applications have become operational, more complex materials control and management information systems applications are designed and installed.

An interesting result of this continuing developmental process is the fact that business firms become increasingly dependent on computer-based applications and systems. Another result is that business firms begin to welcome the development of new applications capable of performing different types of work. Besides the processing of large numbers of everyday accounting transactions, computers are viewed to be quite capable of preparing a wide variety of managerial reports and summaries and of storing large quantities of business information. Some firms believe that one end result is to use the computer in perfecting *decision support systems* (DSS). These systems utilize information prepared by online computer applications to assist managers directly in making complex business decisions.

This evolutionary process of designing increasingly wide-ranging and complex computer applications is due to many factors. In part, increased computer usage is a result of more economical and sophisticated computer *hardware* (the physical and functional properties of computing equipment) and computer *software* (the logical instructions that tell the computer what to do). As this book demonstrates, one of the most significant changes in hardware and software in recent years has been the development of easy-to-use *online computing systems*. The hardware and software designed for these systems permit human beings to communicate directly with the *central processing unit* (CPU) of the computer and permit the CPU to communicate directly with human beings.

Besides sophisticated hardware and software, the involvement of large numbers of skilled people has contributed to both ever-increasing systems understanding and design advancements. Many more people today understand how computers work and how computer software can be effectively applied. These people acknowledge that the potential of computing is great and that the applications and systems developed thus far represent only the very beginning. They contend that the future will undoubtedly reveal more foolproof types of automated business systems. It should be pointed out, however, that more advanced systems do not mean increased business complexity. On the contrary, future systems designers will develop systems that *simplify* the internal workings of the administrative process. These future systems will add greater clarity to the types of information needed by management for planning and controlling most of the routine activities of a business and for decision making.

The prospect of reduced business complexity is consistent with the applications described in this book. As you will come to appreciate, online business computer applications help to simplify and clarify the tasks associated with obtaining, improving, and using business information.

1-1   BUSINESS COMPUTER APPLICATIONS

Before we examine specific features of an online computing application, it is important to understand what is meant by a business computer application. We begin with a definition, followed by an example.

The term *business computer application* describes how a computer is used to process a particular type of business transaction and to prepare specific types of management information. Since a business must process several types of transactions and prepare several different types of management reports, there must necessarily be several of these applications. To further this description (see Figure 1–1), each application consists of one or more *computer programs* (coded instructions that tell the computer how to process data). The term to describe the nature of the work of developing and implementing these types of programs is *applications programming*. This work is performed by people who are called *applications programmers*.

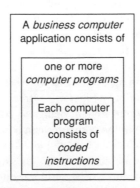

Figure 1–1   Structure of a business computer application

To help you remember these concepts, imagine that you are assigned the task of processing the company payroll. You might begin by observing that the payroll department must process payroll transactions and produce payroll summary information. Next, you might describe this application in terms of its functions, such as "get employee time cards" and "produce employee paychecks." Once the various functions are known, you or another applications programmer might write computer programs to tell the computer how to perform these functions. These "employee payroll computer programs" would be written for the "employee payroll computer application." Finally, you would need to explain to others the payroll-processing procedures you have designed, written, and implemented. Such an explanation would describe how the computer is used to process employee time cards in order to produce employee paychecks, maintain employee records, and document payments made to employees.

Two functions of most business computer applications are paperwork processing and management-information processing. *Paperwork processing* consists of using the computer to process the different types of paperwork associated with *business transactions*—the agreements made between a business and its employees, stockholders, customers, vendors, and so on. Customer orders, shipping papers, and customer billing statements are three types of paperwork that must be processed. Each of these documents is printed to verify transaction details—the terms of the transaction, the action taken, and the responsible party. *Management information processing* involves using the computer to provide detailed and summary information required by managers. For example, a report showing the fifty most active customers is one type of management information; so is a collections summary report, which shows what customers are slow in making payments.

Generally, both paperwork processing and management-information processing are built into an online business computer application. The paperwork-processing part of the application deals with checking each business transaction for correctness, adding additional supporting information to each transaction, listing each processed transaction, and producing business documents (such as paychecks and invoices). The management-information-processing part of the application stores, compares, and summarizes information needed by managers. An *exception report* might be required, for example. This type of report shows information that is the exception from normal conditions. An exception report might be designed to show the names of all employees who have been paid for more than a hundred hours of overtime, for instance. These records represent exceptions from the norm, which in this case is 100 hours or less of overtime pay.

1-2 THE COMPUTER PROCESSING ENVIRONMENT

Various computer hardware components and types of software are combined in processing online business computer applications. The computer hardware must be capable both of processing data and of communicating the results of processing to and from remote locations. Different types of computer software must instruct the computer how to process data, how to transmit data to remote locations, and how to store data awaiting transmission or processing.

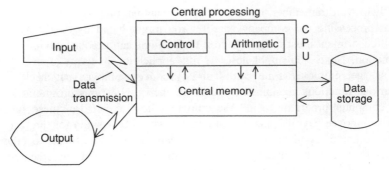

Figure 1–2 Simplified computer processing environment

Computer Hardware

Figure 1–2 illustrates a simplified computer-processing environment to show five processing functions; input, output, data transmission, central processing, and data storage (external).

Input consists of reading and transmitting data to the computer. Before data processing can begin, data must be read by an input device and transformed into machine-readable form. Key-entry and direct entry input devices perform this processing function. As we will see, key-entry terminals are of particular importance in the design of online computer applications.

Output consists of transmitting and distributing data processed by the computer. Output is the reverse of input. It involves the translation of machine-readable data to a form that people can easily understand. Processed results can be printed or displayed on an output device. As with input devices, a variety of output devices are commercially available. The most common one, the printer, produces both formal business documents and formal and informal business reports. Computer terminals are commonly used output devices. Terminals permit output to be displayed on a screen for immediate review by the user.

Data transmission is the flow of data to and from the central processing unit (CPU). The hardware used in this part of processing might be viewed as a switching station: data flowing into processing must not interfere with data leaving processing. The hardware units designed to regulate data transmission include front-end processors and network processors. They coordinate and control slow-speed input/output data transmission and high-speed central-processing data transmission.

Central processing performs numerical calculations, stores data internally, and integrates the activities of input, output, data storage, and data transmission. The *central processing unit* (CPU) performs arithmetic and controls the various parts of the computer system. The *central memory* (primary storage) stores data waiting to be processed, data being processed, data already processed, and, finally, computer program instructions used to tell the computer how to process data.

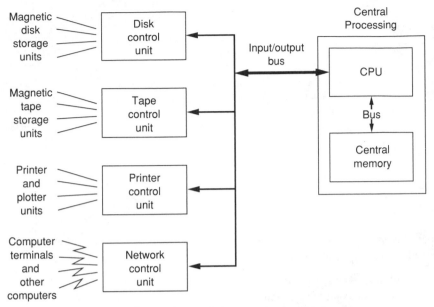

Figure 1–3   Connecting central processing to other hardware

Data storage (external) stores data in machine-readable form in a location external to the CPU. From this location, data are read from storage in processing or written to storage following processing. The capability to store data externally permits input data to be transmitted to central memory and combined with previously stored data, then entered into processing. Likewise, not all processed results need be printed or displayed: portions of processed results—or all of them—can be written to data storage devices. Much like input and output units, data storage devices can take several forms. The two most popular are magnetic disk and magnetic tape storage devices. We will discuss only these two types in this book.

Figure 1–3 shows the effects of combining input/output (I/O) devices with a single central processor. A high-speed *input/output bus* transfers data from slower speed magnetic disk, magnetic tape, computer printer and plotters, and computer terminal devices. Network and control unit processors regulate the low- and high-speed data transfers. In some computing systems, an I/O unit will have full access to memory, as does the central processor. By having separate processors regulate I/O traffic, the CPU is free to concentrate on its main job of computation. In addition, I/O processors permit the computer to work on several tasks simultaneously. The CPU can work on a job submitted by one I/O processor while it waits for a second I/O processor to transfer data to be completed for a second job.

Computer Software

Figure 1–4, a second simplified processing environment, highlights the main types of software used by an online computer system. These types include

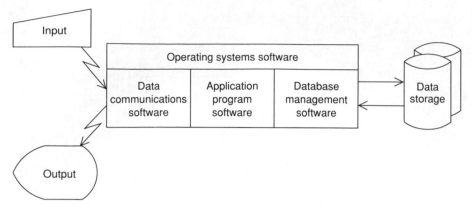

Figure 1–4   Types of computer software

operating-systems software, data communications software, database management software, and application program software.

Operating-systems software allocates, schedules, and assigns computer resources to specific jobs submitted for processing. Computer memory and peripheral computing equipment, for example, are assigned to each job. Following the completion of a job, the operating system assigns its computing resources to other jobs.

Data communications software controls the transmission of messages back and forth from the computer, between the CPU and a large number of slow-speed I/O devices. It is required, first, to *multiplex* the data—to intermix messages from several I/O devices to create what appears to be simultaneous data communications—and, second, to *regulate* the data by keeping track of each message being transmitted, so that each retains its identity.

Database management software (DBMS) handles the organizing, cataloging, locating, storing, and retrieving of data stored on magnetic disk files. In a data-base setting, software is designed to integrate a collection or large "pool" of data. Through this integration, duplication of stored data can be avoided; data can be retrieved from storage and used by more than one business computer application.

Application program software instructs the CPU how to process data. This type of software, unlike the other types, is typically prepared by applications programmers employed by the business firm that is doing the computing. (The other three types of software are written by the computer vendor or by a software development firm.) Application program software is designed to perform the functions called for by a computer application. It consists of sets of instructions, usually written in a symbolic language code, or *source code*, such as COBOL, FORTRAN, C, or BASIC.

Computer Systems

Figure 1–5 shows the functions of an online computer system. This particular system, like all others, consists of hardware and software. The hardware includes a typewriter-like keyboard, a video display screen, a magnetic disk storage unit, and

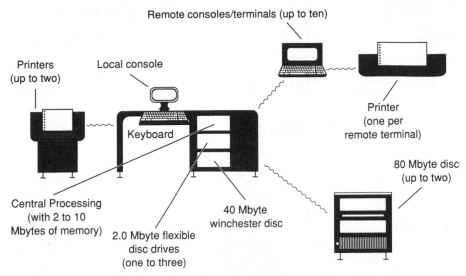

Figure 1–5 Schematic diagram of a commercial computer system

a processing unit containing from two to ten Mbytes of memory, where an *Mbyte* represents a megabyte, or one million bytes. All equipment is *online*; that is, all input, output, and data storage devices are connected and controlled by the CPU. The software, the invisible part of a computer system, unfortunately cannot be illustrated; here it consists of an operating system, data communications software, database management software, compiler programs such as COBOL compiler, and application programs.

Figure 1–5 also shows how a single computer is able to distribute processing in order to disperse the processing power of the machine to geographically separated locations. Up to ten remotely located I/O terminals can be added to this computer system. These terminals, in turn, permit up to ten users to access the computer using different (or similar) sets of processing instructions, which are transmitted directly to the CPU. Likewise, processed results are transmitted back to the user as video displays or printed results.

The computer system illustrated in Figure 1–5 is a small business computer, often referred to as a *minicomputer*. This particular system can accept input either locally, that is, from the local console, or remotely. Even so, this computer is small by comparison with many now in use. Medium- to large-scale computer systems can be accessed by hundreds of computer terminals or by several minicomputers. Then, too, at the other end of the spectrum, a variety of computers are smaller than minicomputers. These *microcomputers* typically accept input from a single terminal. Because they are usually purchased for individual rather than shared use, microcomputers are often called *personal computers*.

REVIEW QUESTIONS

1. Explain the difference between paperwork processing and management information processing.

2. Name the five processing functions associated with computer hardware.

3. What types of computer software are used in an online computer system?

4. What is a computer system?

5. How is a computer able to distribute processing?

1-3   METHODS OF PROCESSING

The ability to connect large numbers of remote computer terminals online to a single CPU has led to different methods of processing. One of these methods, *real-time processing*, enables the CPU to respond immediately to a request to transmit and process data. The high speed of response, measured in milliseconds, is the crucial element in real-time processing: in military defense environments, for example, response must be as nearly instantaneous as possible. Likewise, in many business environments, response must be close to real-time immediacy to resolve the decision facing the user. Two popular real-time processing applications are airline reservation and stock market inquiry systems. With each, computer terminals are used to transmit short messages that inquire about the status of an event—the availability of an airplane seat or the price of a stock. Very fast response, indicating processing of the inquiry and communication of the processed result, allows the user to make a decision based on the latest information. The decision might be to reserve a seat on an airplane or to purchase a hundred shares of stock at the listed price.

Online systems are associated with another method of processing known as *time sharing*. In this method, a small amount of time is allocated for processing each of several jobs submitted simultaneously; the CPU works on one job for a brief period, or *time slice*, which is defined in milliseconds. If a job is not completed during the time slice allocated to it, it is placed at the end of a *job queue* to await further attention by the CPU. This method of processing makes it possible for several end users to share the available processing time of a single CPU. Although fast response is still a requirement, it need not be as immediate as in a real-time environment. A one-second response is generally adequate.

Besides real-time processing and time sharing, three other important processing methods require clarification. The first, *batch processing*, preceded the development of online systems. Batch processing requires that data be initially grouped (as a batch) before they are processed serially. The batch might be a group of customer orders or a set of employee time cards. Following its preparation, a batch is read into processing by an input device. Each transaction in the batch is processed in serial order. For example, data relating to the first customer order in a batch are processed first, followed by data relating to the second, and so on, until the data relating to the last customer order have been processed.

The second method, *transaction processing*, does not require data to be initially batched. Instead, a single transaction (such as a single customer order) is processed as it is received by the CPU. Computer terminals connected directly to the CPU serve as input devices to feed individual transactions into processing one at a time.

The third method, *interactive processing*, should be viewed as a modified version of transaction processing. It represents a "conversational mode of processing," in which users enter into a "conversation" with the computer in order to process single business transactions, using computer terminals to send and receive messages. For example, following the terminal entry and transmission of a message, the computer processes the message, displays the results on the terminal, and typically asks for a response. One response sequence might be:

```
ARE THE RESULTS ACCURATE?
ENTER Y OR N
```

By entering a Y (for yes), the terminal operator informs the computer that the results are accurate and that it is safe to continue processing. Entering an N (no) leads to a different computer response. For example, the computer might respond with the message

```
DO YOU WISH TO TERMINATE PROCESSING? Y OR N
```

or

```
DO YOU WISH TO BACK UP TO IDENTIFY THE ERROR? Y OR N
```

The capability to communicate directly with the computer in English explains why interactive methods of processing are so popular. People find it easier to work with a computer if they can monitor the steps in processing. This step-by-step procedure permits them to go from one transaction to another with greater assurance that their actions are correct. People also find it more enjoyable to be able to command the computer to take a particular action. We believe that we are able to control the machine, rather than the reverse.

1-4 INTERACTIVE VERSUS BATCH PROCESSING

The majority of online computer systems support multiple methods of processing simultaneously. In many larger scale processing environments, for example, interactive processing occurs while batch processing is also taking place. In other processing environments, interactive processing occurs during normal business hours and batch processing is restricted to the hours before and after normal business hours.

This mixing of processing methods is advantageous because interactive and batch processing are each especially suited to certain kinds of activities. Interactive methods, with which transactions are processed one at a time, are especially suited for

- entering and transmitting small amounts of data to the computer;
- visually reviewing data to verify that processing is correct;
- making adjustments to business records stored on computer files;

- asking questions to determine the contents of data stored on computer files; and
- displaying different combinations of data before deciding which data to print.

Interactive methods are not always superior, however. Batch methods are better for

- printing long listings or registers of large numbers of business transactions;
- printing sets of formal business documents, such as paychecks;
- printing lengthy business summary listings and reports; and
- backing up computer files to permit processing to be continued if files were lost or destroyed.

More Efficient Use of the Computer

A dilemma associated with a batch-only approach to processing is that it makes efficient use of the computer but often leads to inefficient use of people. As an example, consider the steps required in creating an approved purchase order file when batch processing is used. (See Figure 1–6 to help you understand this work flow.)

Step 1   Prepare forms for data entry (transfer information by hand from purchase orders to special forms).

Step 2   Key-enter and verify purchase order information recorded on data-entry forms.

Step 3   Read the batch of transactions stored on magnetic tape into the computer.

Step 4   By computer, read and verify each transaction in the batch. If errors exist, print the error on a purchase order error report and go to step 5. If no errors are found, jump to step 6.

Step 5   Correct the errors printed on the purchase order error report. Repeat steps 1 through 5 until no errors are found, rewriting the approved input transaction file each time until it is correct.

Step 6   Sort by computer the approved input transaction file to arrange it by vendor-number sequence. This sorting places all numbers in an ascending (but not necessarily continuous) sequence, such as vendors 10026, 10027, 10043, and 10078.

Step 7   Enlarge the sequenced file by adding the vendor name and address to each transaction. If processing cannot be completed because of an incorrect or missing vendor number, list the transaction in error on a missing-vendor report. Place all correctly processed transactions on an approved purchase orders computer file. Place all transactions in error in a second file, the disapproved purchase orders computer file.

Steps 8–12   Correct reported errors (the steps needed to do this are not shown in Figure 1–6).

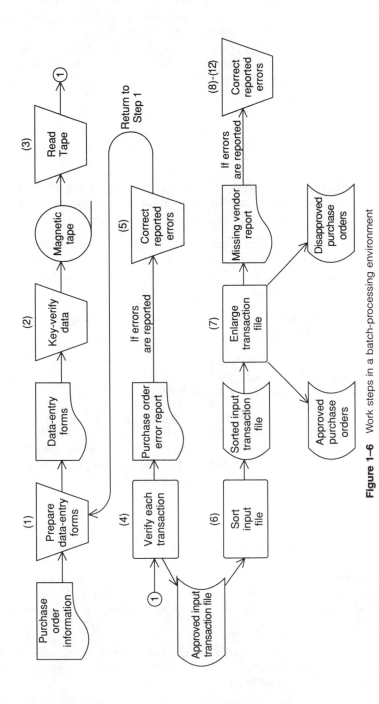

Figure 1–6 Work steps in a batch-processing environment

This example helps to demonstrate that, with batch methods, processing is efficient as long as data are error free. When errors are encountered, however, processing becomes long and involved. What may not be evident is that several people must work together to monitor batch-processing activities. People in purchasing, for example, are responsible for preparing data-entry forms for purchase orders and for reviewing purchase order error reports and missing-vendor reports. People in data processing are responsible for key-entering data, scheduling computer processing, running computer programs in the correct order, loading computer files, and distributing the results of processing.

The problem of managing large amounts of paperwork is also associated with batch processing. Consider the following cycle in resolving errors appearing on an edit report.

1. Data-entry forms are prepared for each transaction. These forms must be saved. They are used in resolving errors and in reporting what data were actually keyed to processing.

2. Each time an error is discovered in processing, it is printed on a purchase order error report that is distributed to an administrative office for review. When the report is received, administrative personnel are required to identify the cause of each error and to make corrections.

3. Corrected errors are recorded on data-entry forms that are routed to data processing for key entry.

4. Errors discovered in processing are printed on a second error report that, again, must be reviewed by people in an administrative office. This cycle continues until all data-entry errors have been resolved.

5. Errors discovered in attempting to enlarge the file are printed on a missing-vendor report, which must also be distributed to an administrative office for review. Once again, the reason for each error must be found and corrected, and the corrected version must be recorded on data-entry forms—this leads to a repeat of the processing cycle.

More Efficient Use of People

Interactive processing makes better use of people but less efficient use of the computer. Let's compare the work steps for the same processing environment using an interactive method. As shown by Figure 1–7, the first step is to key data directly to processing. What is most important is that the users, rather than data-processing personnel, are responsible for this data entry. With this in mind, we review the five interactive steps:

Step 1   Key data directly into processing using a computer terminal. (Special data-entry forms are not needed if the spaces showing where data are to be keyed appear on the screen of the terminal.)

Step 2   Verify each transaction with the help of the computer. If an error is found, the computer will print the error and, where possible, the reason for the

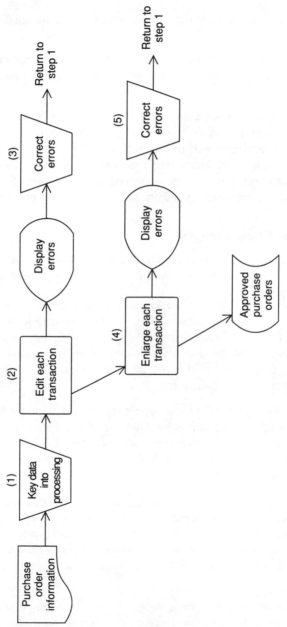

Figure 1–7 Work steps in an interactive-processing environment

error on the screen of the terminal. The computer will ask the terminal operator to enter the correct data. If the error is not corrected, the transaction in error is not permitted to be entered into processing (and hence added to the approved purchase order transaction file).

Step 3   Correct the error shown on the screen of the terminal and process again.

Step 4   Enlarge each transaction by computer immediately following the edit of the transaction. Write the approved transaction to an approved purchase orders computer file.

Step 5   Correct any update error shown on the screen of the terminal. For example, if a transaction cannot be correctly processed because of an incorrect vendor number, the computer will inform the user of this problem and ask that the correct vendor number be entered. If the correct number is not entered, the transaction in error is not written to the approved purchase order file. Instead, the update program blocks the transaction from being entered into processing.

Advantages and Disadvantages

A comparison of interactive processing with batch processing should make it clear why interactive methods are favored. Consider the following advantages:

- Interactive methods make it easier to integrate the work performed by administrative and operational groups in an organization with the work performed by data-processing groups. For example, an interactive application permits members of the user staff to prepare and enter data directly into processing, to review keyed input data for errors, and to make changes when instructed by the computer.

- Interactive methods simplify the paperwork needed to support processing. Not only are data-entry forms eliminated, but edit and missing-record reports (such as missing-vendor reports) are no longer needed. Direct retrieval of data stored on computer files also eliminates looking up account information printed on lengthy file listings.

- Interactive methods eliminate special error files, such as the disapproved purchase order file. This streamlining is accomplished by *trapping* errors at their source, before they can be entered into processing. For example, if a vendor number is found to be in error, it is displayed for the user to act on. Until the error is corrected, the transaction is blocked from further processing.

- Interactive methods reduce the number of job steps required in a processing run. Combining editing with enlarging a transaction, for instance, eliminates one job step. Eliminating a sort program saves another job step. Eliminating the distribution and routing of reports to and from administrative offices saves several other steps.

- Interactive methods are easier to understand. With batch processing, it is difficult to explain to others how input data are processed after the data leave an administrative office. Because online terminals permit the display of information at the user's location, with interactive methods, it becomes possible to explain each step in the processing of user data.

Along with these considerable advantages, several disadvantages are associated with interactive methods of processing.

- Interactive methods are more expensive. They require the purchase or lease of communications equipment, including computer terminals, I/O processors, and direct-access computer files.

- Interactive computer programs tend to be more difficult to write than batch application programs. Besides recording how data are to be processed by the CPU, interactive programs must include *conversational dialogue*, permitting the user to communicate directly with the computer.

- Interactive methods require that the CPU be always ready to handle incoming data. Because transactions are processed one at a time, rather than as a batch, CPU time is used less efficiently.

- Interactive methods of processing are slow. Users must process each transaction separately, which can present a major problem when hundreds of transactions must be processed within a short time. In severe cases, it may be necessary to substitute batch for interactive methods even though interactive methods are believed to be superior.

REVIEW QUESTIONS

6. Explain the difference between batch processing, transaction processing, and interactive processing.

7. For what tasks are interactive methods of processing especially suited? For what tasks are batch methods especially suited?

8. What are the advantages of interactive methods of processing? Of batch methods of processing?

9. Why do interactive methods of processing make more efficient use of people?

1-5 DATABASE MANAGEMENT

The collection and organization of logically related sets of business information stored on computer files constitutes the *database* of a business. The management of this database is one of the most important functions of online business computer applications. *Database management software* consists of programmed procedures for creating, updating, and backing up information stored on computer files. It includes a special high-level query language for retrieving and displaying data once they have been stored. In addition, this type of software includes file-management programs designed to simplify the storing of data on files. Taken in combination, database management software is designed to provide near immediate access to stored data. It is able to respond to user queries, or questions, in seconds.

With online systems, database management and applications program software are integrated so that data stored on computer files can be inspected and, where necessary, altered prior to processing. Consider, once again, the processing of purchase orders.

To begin, assume that there is a problem with Account 10023 and that, as a consequence, it must be inspected. In a batch-processing environment, a listing showing the contents of the account would first have to be examined to discover what information was stored. An interactive-processing environment, by contrast, permits the direct examination of the account. Following the keying of the account number into processing, the computer retrieves the account and displays it directly on the computer terminal screen.

Next, assume that Account 10023 cannot be found. Suppose that a data-input error has established Account 10032 instead. In a batch environment, this type of error might be difficult to find and would take several hours to correct, as the following procedure suggests:

1. A listing of the contents of the file would be printed and inspected. This review would indicate that Account 10023 did not exist.

2. A second search would have to be undertaken. This search might begin by requesting that another listing be prepared, sequencing all accounts by alphabetic name.

3. Error correction would be necessary once the second search revealed that Account 10023 was improperly listed. A change of account form would be filled out and sent to data entry.

4. The data-entry staff would be required to process the change instructions needed to create Account 10023 and to delete Account 10032.

Now, compare those steps to the steps required in an interactive environment:

1. An online account-inquiry procedure tells the terminal operator that Account 10023 does not exist.

2. The terminal operator begins to search for the name of the vendor, using a *search routine*. For example, most online systems feature interactive search capabilities that permit a terminal operator to locate any string of characters for an attribute stored on a computer file. Suppose the attribute is the vendor name and the characters for this attribute in this account is *FEERSON SUPPLY*. Using the search capability, the operator would find the vendor name *FEERSON SUPPLY* and, in so doing, discover that the name was actually assigned to Account 10032.

3. The terminal operator would add the correct account and delete the incorrect account. Some interactive systems also contain interactive *search-and-replace* capabilities. These permit the operator to search the database for an account and, once it is found, to rename the account.

Capabilities such as search, and search and replace, greatly simplify writing application programs and revising data stored on computer files. Although estimates vary, the availability of commonly needed precoded routines can lead to a two- to fivefold increase in programmer productivity. Savings in user time are even greater. These savings result from easy-to-follow methods of retrieving, examining, and modifying data stored within the database.

1-6 ONLINE DATA COMMUNICATIONS

The ways in which data are transmitted to and from the computer are also of primary importance in designing online business computer applications. The term *data communications* implies both telecommunications and the use of remote computer terminals. The transmission of data as signals—generally by conventional wire or cable—is one type of *telecommunications*. With telecommunications equipment, it becomes possible to send messages from several remote terminal locations to a single receiver—a single CPU. These messages can be as short as a single bit (a 0 or 1) or can consist of several thousand characters. Remote computer terminals function as sending and receiving stations in a telecommunications network. When the terminals are designed to both send and receive data, *two-way communications* takes place: the user is able to transmit data to the computer and to receive processed instructions and output in return. Because users are able to converse directly with the CPU, they are said to be *online* (or on a direct line) to the computer.

The data communication devices that are sold commercially comprise six classes of computer terminals: keyboard/printer terminals, display terminals, remote job-entry terminals, banking terminals, point-of-sale terminals, and data-collection terminals.

Keyboard/Printer Terminals

Keyboard/printer terminals are hard-copy terminal devices that act as small-scale printers. Smaller keyboard/printer terminals look much like typewriters, whereas larger units look like stand-alone computer printers. With these units, an alphanumeric keyboard is used to key data into processing; output, known as *hard copy*, is printed character by character. The terminal itself can be connected to the computer via a cable connection or by a built-in acoustic coupler or modem. An acoustic coupler, for example, permits the connection of a terminal to a standard circuit, such as a telephone circuit. In this way the terminal can be connected to a remote computer.

GOOD MORNING!
ARE YOU READY
   TO GET STARTED?
PLEASE ENTER
   (Y)ES OR (N)O.

Figure 1–8   Display terminal

Display Terminals

Display terminals feature visual review of data as *soft copy* (see Figure 1–8). These devices use an alphanumeric keyboard; however, keyed input, computer instructions, and processed results are displayed on a screen instead of printed as hard copy. Display terminals consist of several types: data-entry terminals, multipurpose display terminals, intelligent display terminals, and computer graphics terminals.

Data-entry terminals are limited-use devices, generally restricted to entering and displaying the details associated with business transactions. These terminals permit data to be keyed directly into the computer and displayed. If errors are then found, they can be corrected online.

Multipurpose display terminals are similar to data-entry terminals but are used for a variety of purposes, including entering and displaying transaction input; entering, reviewing, and testing computer programs; and retrieving and displaying data stored on computer files. Some multipurpose terminals, known as *page readers*, allow the user to display, page by page, the contents of a large document stored on computer files.

Intelligent display terminals are typically microcomputers that are used for limited-scale data processing as well as data communications (see Figure 1–9).

They are often designed to operate independently from the computer to which they are connected. Besides being used to transmit and receive data, these units are able to test and store processed data. As such, they take over some of the duties normally performed by the CPU.

Computer graphics terminals are intelligent display terminals with color monitors. They are used to prepare and display two- and three-dimensional line drawings as well as charts and tables. With these units, users are able to analyze data, picture by picture. Because many individuals prefer to work with pictures rather than tables and lists of data, computer graphics are becoming increasingly popular. Leading authorities predict that color graphics will become the preferred way of presenting many types of business information.

Remote Job-Entry Terminals

Remote job-entry (RJE) terminals are typically minicomputers that are linked to a larger CPU. There are two types of RJE terminals: *remote batch terminals*, which limit processing to data entry, data storage, and printed output, and *remote interactive terminals*, which support both interactive and batch methods of processing. Besides sending individual instructions to the CPU for processing, remote interactive terminals are used to enter data into processing, transaction by transaction, until an entire batch is assembled. Once formed, the batch can be transmitted to a larger CPU.

Figure 1–9 Intelligent display terminal

Banking Terminals

Banking terminals consist of automated tellers and teller-controlled devices. *Automated tellers* accept as input a *personal identification number (PIN)* and an account number printed on a plastic card (see Figure 1–10). If the terminal finds both numbers acceptable, it will permit and process a banking transaction such as the withdrawal of cash from the customer's account. In contrast, *teller-controlled terminals* are limited-use keyboard/printer terminals that allow the teller to revise and print a customer's account balance.

Point-of-Sale Terminals

Point-of-sale (POS) terminals look much like cash registers; however, they accept and transmit sales data to record the time of sale, as well as hold cash (see Figure 1–11). These terminals can be used in several ways: besides registering cash, they keep track of sales and inventory data. Sales clerks are required to key in product-line-item numbers, quantity sold totals, and dollar totals or to enter these data with a hand-held optical-scanning device. This information is transmitted to a larger computer that will revise in-store inventory counts and dollar amounts and summarize daily sales totals. A major advantage of these systems is their ability to capture data at its source (see Chapter 5). This eliminates the need to enter the same data later by a data-entry staff.

Figure 1–10   Bank terminal

Figure 1–11   Point-of-sale (POS) terminal

Data-Collection Terminals

Data-collection terminals are more limited in function than are POS terminals. These typically provide for the entry and transmission of small amounts of data, such as the count of inventory available for sale or an employee's identification number and the number of a workstation. Data-collection terminals feature *one-way data communications*: they send messages from the user to the CPU. Some data-collection terminals are called *badge readers*. They are limited-use terminals designed only to read a plastic badge, much like an automatic teller. Other data-collection terminals are limited-use data-entry terminals. These terminals are used to enter counts and amounts; data can be stored locally and later read to a larger computer once all data have been collected.

REVIEW QUESTIONS

10. What is a search routine? How does it differ from a search and replace routine?

11. Name the six classes of computer terminals.

12. How does a keyboard/printer terminal differ from a display terminal?

13. What is the difference between remote batch and remote interactive processing?

14. Why is point-of-sale (POS) processing important?

REVIEW OF IMPORTANT IDEAS

Most large firms process the majority of their business transactions by computer. Online computing systems simplify this process. They permit people to communicate directly with the central processing unit.

A business computer application describes how a computer is used to process business transactions and prepare management information. The processing of business transactions, known as *paperwork processing*, documents the details of business dealings. The processing of business information, known as *management information processing*, provides information to managers for decision making.

A computer system consists of hardware and software. Hardware is the *electronic* and *mechanical* aspect of the computer and provides the functions of input, output, data transmission, central processing, and data storage. Software is the *logical* aspect of the computer. Different types of software are required to make the computer operate, to transmit and store data, and to run applications programs.

Different methods of processing include real time, time sharing, batch, transaction, and interactive. Of these, interactive methods are of greatest importance in the design of online business computer applications. With interactive processing, transactions are processed one at a time; the user is able to enter into a conversation with the computer. This ability to communicate directly helps to explain the popularity of online systems.

Interactive processing provides more efficient use of people than does batch processing; however, it makes for less efficient use of the computer. Advantages of interactive processing include better integration of computing and administrative activities, reduced paperwork processing, better methods of trapping data-entry errors, fewer processing job steps, and better user understanding of how applications processing works.

With online systems, operating-systems software, database management software, and applications program software are integrated. This integration provides such capabilities as the direct examination of an account or the direct analysis of accounts stored on file.

Two-way communication is required by online computer systems. With two-way communication, the user is able to transmit messages to the computer and to receive computer output. Of the six classes of computer terminal devices that support online data communications—keyboard/printer terminals, display terminals, remote job-entry terminals, banking terminals, point-of-sale terminals, and data-collection terminals—intelligent display terminals are typically required by online computer systems.

KEY WORDS

Decision support systems (DSS)	Real-time processing
Hardware	Time sharing
Software	Batch processing

Online computer system	Transaction processing
Business computer application	Interactive processing
Applications programming	Database management
Computer programs	Conversational dialogue
Paperwork processing	Data communications
Management information processing	Telecommunications
Central processing unit (CPU)	Hard copy
Peripheral computing equipment	Soft copy
Minicomputer	Remote job-entry (RJE) terminals
Microcomputer	Point-of-sale (POS) terminals

EXERCISES

1. Visit a store in your area that uses POS equipment. Report on how the five processing functions (input, output, data transmission, central processing, and data storage) are accomplished in this environment.

2. Review the flow of data and processing steps shown in Figure 1–7, then answer the following:

   (a) What are the system inputs?

   (b) What are the system outputs?

   (c) What processing steps are done by hand?

   (d) What processing steps are done by computer?

   (e) What happens if errors cannot be corrected? (See step 5 in Figure 1–7.)

3. Even though interactive methods of processing lead to more efficient use of people, a number of business firms continue to use only batch methods of processing. Give several reasons to explain why this practice continues.

4. Why is it important for business firms to reduce the number of job steps in an administrative process? Study Figures 1–6 and 1–7. Does computing always lead to fewer job steps? Explain.

5. With interactive processing and remote job entry, it is possible to introduce data processing in different departments of a business. For example, sales and marketing are able to process information from remote locations, as are other departments such as manufacturing, personnel, accounting, and finance. What are the advantages of distributing the processing of data in an organization? What are the disadvantages?

6. A review of the six classes of computer terminals indicates that there are a number of ways in which telecommunications can take place in organizations. What factors would be important in deciding which types of terminals are best?

DISCUSSION QUESTIONS

For the study of business computer applications, explain why it is important to know something about the following:

(a) the computer processing environment

(b) the different methods of processing

(c) the differences between interactive and batch processing

(d) database management

(e) online communications

4-IN-1 CASE STUDY—AN INTRODUCTION

In this text, you are asked to use the 4-in-1 Accounting Software demonstration package produced by the RealWorld Corporation. As shown by Figure 1–12, 4-in-1 covers four areas of accounting: general ledger, accounts receivable, accounts payable, and payroll. In the next chapter, we will discuss each of these areas. This demonstration version of 4-in-1 is a complete package, subject only to the amount of data you can enter into processing and a date restriction. These restrictions by application are as follows:

AREA	MAXIMUM SIZE
Accounts payable and accounts receivable	A combined total of 20 vendors and customers
Payroll	5 employees, plus date restrictions
General ledger	Date restrictions only. You are allowed to enter only dates from 1/1/97 to 12/31/99.

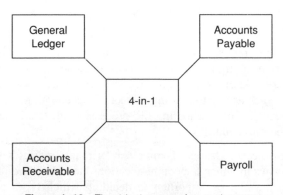

Figure 1–12   The 4-in-1 processing environment

Computer Requirements

This 4-in-1 software is written for the IBM PC/XT/AT, IBM PS/2, Tandy 1000/2000/3000, and true IBM/Tandy compatibles. At least 192,000 (192KB) of memory is required. A hard disk with one floppy diskette is recommended. Otherwise, two floppy disk drives are required.

Installation Procedure

The installation procedure can be complex. We suggest you have your instructor help you if you are required to install the software by yourself. The time it takes to install the software will depend on the type of computing equipment you are using.

Blank Diskettes Requirements

You will need blank diskettes to work with the 4-in-1 software. Once again, your instructor will determine the exact number you will need. For the first set of exercises, you will need a minimum of three blank diskettes if you are working with 360KB diskettes or one blank diskette if you are working with either 1.2M or 720KB diskettes.

Starting 4-in-1

After 4-in-1 is installed, you can activate it by following a set of steps. These steps differ depending on whether the software is installed on a hard disk or not.

The hard disk start-up procedure   When 4-in-1 is installed on a hard disk, do the following.

1. Turn your computer on.
2. From the C drive, type **CD\4IN1** and press ENTER. This changes the working directory to 4IN1, the directory where 4-in-1 programs are stored.
3. Type **4IN1** and press ENTER to load the software. Next jump to step 4 below.

The diskette procedure   When 4-in-1 is kept on diskettes, do the following.

1. Turn your computer on.
2. Insert the *master diskette* in drive A and the *data diskette* in drive B. The data diskette is a blank disk to be used in storing data.
3. From the A drive type **4IN1** and press ENTER to load the software. Keep all other diskettes handy. If you need another, a message will appear telling you to remove a diskette and insert another. Continue by doing step 4 below.

Reviewing the Main Menu

The successful loading of the software into your computer will lead to the display of the title and copyright screen. Do the following to advance to the main menu.

4. Press ENTER to remove the title and copyright screen.

5. If you are required by your instructor to use a password, enter your password and press ENTER. Likewise, if passwords are required, but you cannot remember what the password is, type **user** as an initial test. If this does not work, ask your instructor. Finally, if a password is not needed, go to the next step.

6. Enter the date **010197**. This step is important because 4-in-1 will not accept a date earlier than this.

7. Press ENTER when asked, *Any change?*

8. The 4-in-1 main menu will appear. Study this menu and answer the questions below. Do not make menu selections at this time. The next chapter will ask you to change, delete, and add accounts.

9. Press the F10 key.

10. Press the TAB key (end END key or double arrow (⇆) key on other keyboards).

11. Press the TAB key again to exit 4-in-1.

QUESTIONS

1. As shown by the main menu, how many menu choices can be made for the general ledger? Accounts receivable? Accounts payable? Payroll?

2. What happens when you press the F10 key? What is the purpose of this key?

3. What happens when you press the TAB key in step 10? In step 11?

2

Properties of Online Applications

Before we consider specific types of online business computer applications, a review of their general properties is useful. We begin by examining four properties.

- Business computer applications are related to one another. Output from one application often is used to provide input to another application for a linking of applications. This linking integrates various administrative and operational activities in a business and leads to what are known as *integrated information systems*.

- Business computer applications consist of common input, processing, storage, output, and control functions. Besides these functions, common types of computer files and computer programs are used in applications processing.

- Business computer applications can be designed to follow a batch, an interactive, or a combined interactive/batch method of processing. Typically, interactive methods are used to enter and to process data stored on computer files. Batch methods are used to print business documents, listings, and standard management reports.

- Business computer applications are relatively easy to understand, provided that a uniform method of systems documentation is adopted. Documentation includes an overview of the flow of information through a system and a detailed description of the contents of the computer files important to the system.

Even though the properties of business computer applications and systems are similar, most business firms find their description difficult. What is often missing is a systematic method that depicts, in an easy-to-follow way, what online applications are designed to accomplish. Those who begin the task of providing descriptions quickly discover that most systems documentation is highly technical, if it exists at all. Many business firms, for example, tend to document only the programming features of a design. They give little attention to the logical features of an application or to the relationships between applications.

This chapter considers ways in which business computer applications are interrelated and how they might be documented using data-flow diagrams. We begin with a look at business information systems and cycles. Later on we examine types of systems documentation and systems-flow diagrams.

2-1   BUSINESS INFORMATION SYSTEMS AND CYCLES

Business information systems consist of sets of procedures for processing business transactions and for providing a written record of processing. Within a business, four main information systems can be identified: the revenue system, the expenditure system, the conversion system, and the cash management system.

The revenue system processes financial transactions associated with the sale and delivery of goods and services. It includes the processing steps needed by a business to exchange its goods or services for cash from its customers.

The expenditure system processes financial transactions associated with the acquisition of and payment for property, labor, and goods and services. The reverse of the revenue system, it includes the processing steps needed by a business to exchange its cash with vendors and employees for goods and services.

The conversion system processes material, labor, and financial transactions associated with production (the transformation of raw materials into finished goods). This information system includes the processing steps that account for the acquisition, use, and movement of resources (property, material, labor, and dollars).

The cash management system processes financial transactions associated with the management of capital funds. This information system includes the processing steps used to determine the cash requirements of a business for internal purposes and for repayment of funds to creditors and investors.

Business information systems can be described logically by their transaction-processing or management information–processing cycles. Business computer applications, the components of these systems, are designed for each major function or set of activities within a cycle. Applications are designed to transform information into a more usable form and to comply with the terms and conditions of business agreements. Figure 2–1 illustrates a revenue-collection information-processing cycle. As shown by this data-flow diagram, the cycle begins with (is *triggered* by) the notification that goods were shipped to customers. A shipping summary provides the details of the shipment. Such a summary includes, at a minimum, the name of the customer and the quantity of merchandise shipped.

Once shipping summary information is received, processing begins. As shown by Figure 2–1, three functions are essential to the revenue-collection cycle: *produce customer invoice, process customer payment*, and *process customer receivable*

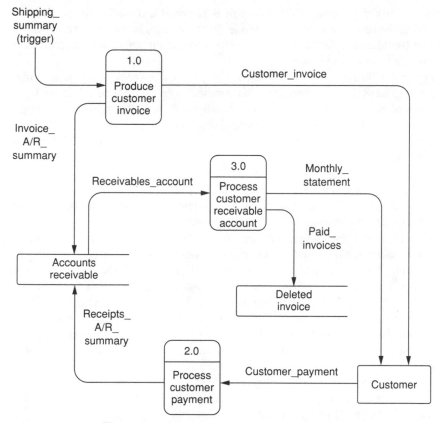

Figure 2–1 Revenue-collection data-flow diagram

account. Each of these functions can be described in terms of exact processing requirements. This description, or *system specification*, in turn leads to the design and development of three business computer applications.

The customer-invoice computer application (produce customer invoice) transforms quantity-shipped totals into customer charges, prints the customer invoice, and prepares summary data for the accounts receivable computer application. The computer-printed invoice is mailed to the customer; the summary data processed are written to an accounts receivable file or data store.

The cash-receipts computer application (process customer payment) then transforms payments received from customers into summary data for the accounts receivable computer application. As with invoicing, summary data are written to the accounts receivable file or data store.

The accounts-receivable computer application (process customer receivable account) compares outstanding invoice charges with customer cash payments and attempts to reduce to zero all customer receivable accounts. When an account does reduce to zero, it is written to a deleted-invoice file. However, when an account fails to reduce to zero and when charges are older than a specified cutoff point, such as thirty days, a monthly statement is prepared and mailed to the customer, notifying the customer of the balance due. In those cases in which account balances cannot be collected, the accounts-receivable application must write off outstanding account balances (not shown).

Figure 2–1 illustrates that a business information cycle consists of several (linked) processing steps. It also shows how a *data-flow diagram* (DFD) describes the logical features of an information system. Only four symbols are important in drawing a DFD: the *transform* symbol, the *source* or *sink* symbol, the *data-store* symbol, and the *data-flow* symbol. "Process customer invoice" is placed within a rounded, numbered transform symbol. Shipping summary information is shown as being transformed into a customer invoice and an invoice accounts-receivable (A/R) summary. "Customer" is enclosed by a rectangular source or sink symbol. The customer is shown to *receive* information (as a *sink*) from the system and to *send* information (as a *source*) back to the system. "Accounts receivable," enclosed in an open-ended data-store symbol, is a place where data are "at rest" (that is, stored). These stores act as internal buffers within a system. Data can be read to or written from a data store; data cannot be transformed within a data store. Finally, all data flows are represented by arrows. The data flow "customer_invoice" is shown to flow from the transform 1.0, "Produce customer information," to the sink labeled "Customer." Thus, "customer_invoice" is an external output of the system. "Invoice_A/R_summary," a second data flow produced by the transform 1.0, leads to a data store. This data flow represents an output that is important to the internal operation of the system.

Figure 2–2 provides a DFD to demonstrate the linking of two expenditure cycles. In this example, one expenditure cycle deals with the purchasing and receiving of goods from vendors, while another cycle concerns the payment of the vendor for goods and services.

The first cycle shown on Figure 2–2 is triggered by a low inventory level. Once this condition is spotted, processing is needed to prepare a purchase requisition (see step 1.0) and to prepare a purchase order (see step 2.0). The purchase order is the formal document mailed to the vendor.

The second half of this first cycle follows the shipment of goods from the vendor. Processing is required to record the ordered goods (see step 3.0). This step transforms the vendor shipment into a receipts summary, which is written to the pending-payables data store, and to a new quantity on hand, which is written to the product inventory data store. However, prior to either output, it is necessary to match the goods ordered (as shown on the purchase order summary) with the goods received (as shown on the vendor shipment). Once this information is reconciled, the quantity-received totals can be written as output to the two data stores.

The second expenditure cycle, the accounts payable cycle, is triggered by the receipt of the invoice from the vendor. Once the invoice is approved (see step 4.0), it is possible to pay the vendor (see step 5.0). The products of processing are a payment that is mailed to the vendor and a record of the payment that is written to the pending-payables checks data store.

Four computer applications, rather than two, support these two expenditure cycles. They are the purchasing computer application, the receiving computer

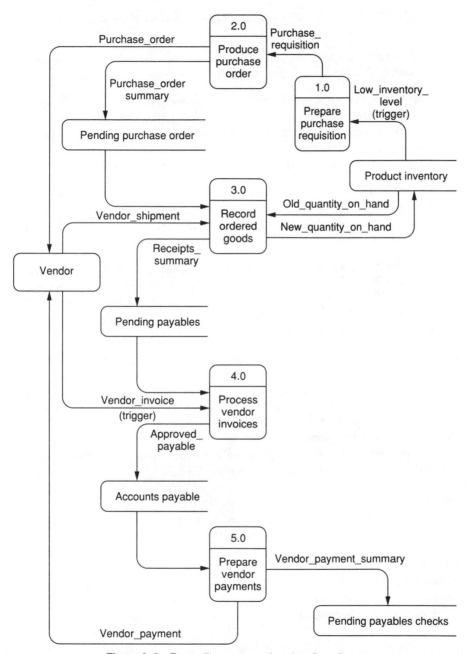

Figure 2–2 Expenditure-processing data-flow diagram

application, the inventory computer application, and the accounts payable computer application.

The purchasing computer application processes the data necessary to prepare a purchase order. This formal business document is mailed to the vendor.

The receiving computer application compares the quantity received from the vendor with the quantity ordered. This application is activated following the actual receipt of the merchandise. Once goods are received, they must be inspected to determine if they are acceptable. The result of this activity is the preparation of a receiving slip, which serves as an input to the receiving application.

The inventory computer application does at least two things: it shows what items are low in quantity and need to be added to inventory, and it records the quantity of merchandise that is added to inventory. In the latter case, the application must be designed to revise inventory records to show a new on-hand quantity.

The accounts payable computer application determines whether the vendor invoice charge is consistent with the quantity ordered and the quantity received. It keeps track of when and how the invoice must be paid, it produces the vendor payment to be mailed to the vendor, and it stores a summary of the payment in a pending-payables checks data store.

Processing cycles, such as the revenue-collection cycle and the expenditure-processing cycles, are similar in design; however, the reasons for their implementation differ. Revenue cycles, for example, are designed to speed the processing of invoices and statements to customers, thus helping to minimize the average accounts-receivable collection period and to reduce receivable write-offs. Expenditure cycles, in contrast, determine whether vendor charges are legitimate and which vendor to pay, in what amount, and when. These cycles permit correct and prompt payment of vendor invoices and reduce the use of internal cash.

Besides differing in purpose, processing cycles differ in their frequency of use. With revenue cycles, customer invoice and cash receipts computer applications are scheduled more frequently than is the accounts receivable computer application. Generally, customer invoices and cash receipts are processed daily; accounts receivable are processed weekly or monthly. Expenditure cycles also differ in processing frequency: the purchasing and receiving computer applications are scheduled daily, whereas the accounts-payable computer application in smaller companies is often scheduled either weekly or twice each month.

2-2   COMMON BUSINESS COMPUTER APPLICATIONS

Business computer applications, unlike business information cycles, are designed to automate specific information-processing activities. Each application is designed to accomplish a limited set of processing tasks. Most applications, for example, are designed to prepare

- formal business documents, to be used in conducting the affairs of the business (paychecks, purchase orders, financial statements);

- summary information, to aggregate facts important to transaction processing (such as current and year-to-date amounts paid to each employee individually and to all employees);

- summary information, to analyze business conditions (such as payroll costs by department as a percentage of total departmental costs); and

- computer files of processed information, to be used in printing formal business documents and in preparing summary information as well as for reference by other computer applications.

Approximately twenty-five business computer applications can be classified as belonging to either the revenue, expenditure, conversion, or cash-management information systems (see Figure 2–3). Observe the characteristics of this listing of applications. Revenue-related applications deal with the processing of customer orders, the management of customer accounts, and the analysis of sales. Observe next that these twenty-five applications collectively automate the information-processing cycles common to almost any business. Many of these applications are designed to process business transactions and to produce formal business documents, such as employee paychecks. These might be called *transaction-based applications*. Other applications are designed to provide important types of management information. The sales analysis and market analysis applications, for example, assist management in the development of sound business strategies by identifying the types of products and markets most profitable and the types of products and markets expected to be the most profitable. These are more appropriately called *management-based applications*.

These four classes of information systems depend on one single application more than any other. This is the *general ledger application*. The word "general," in this context, means pertaining to many areas, and "ledger" is a place where accounting records are recorded. As shown by Figure 2–4, the main inputs to the general ledger (G/L) system are the chart of accounts, journal vouchers, and G/L summaries. The application produces a balance sheet, a profit and loss statement, a consolidated G/L, and a report known as a trial balance as outputs.

The *chart of accounts* establishes the codes against which all other coded numbers will be evaluated. For example, one or more accounts are required for sales, accounts receivable, accounts payable, and payroll transactions. Once the chart of accounts is defined, the account numbers can be used by other accounting systems in the organization. *Journal vouchers*, for example, are used to debit and credit financial amounts to G/L accounts. (The terms debit and credit will be made clear to you in later chapters of this book.) These vouchers are prepared by hand,

---

Revenue-Related Business Computer Applications

1. Order entry
2. Customer invoicing
3. Cash receipts
4. Accounts receivable
5. Sales analysis
6. Customer and product analysis
7. Market analysis

Expenditure-Related Business Computer Applications

1. Employee payroll
2. Accounts payable
3. Check reconciliation
4. Fixed assets
5. Purchasing
6. Receiving
7. Personnel
8. Cash disbursements

Conversion-Related Business Computer Applications

1. Product inventory
2. Work in process
3. Labor distribution
4. Job costing
5. Property accounting

Cash-Management-Related Business Computer Applications

1. General ledger
2. Budget planning and control
3. Profit planning and control
4. Cash management
5. Portfolio management

Figure 2–3   Twenty-five business computer applications

unless summaries from computer applications can be entered instead. As shown by Figure 2–4, *G/L summaries* can be provided from all transaction-based computer applications, beginning with the customer invoice G/L summary. Chapter 4 will explain what this summary contains.

Once all financial totals are brought together into a single ledger, three important management summary reports can be prepared: the *consolidated G/L*, the company *balance sheet*, and the company *profit and loss statement*. These statements compare sales to revenues and contrast what is owned by the company to what

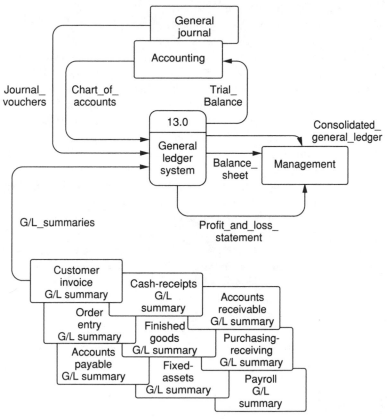

Figure 2–4   The general ledger system

is owed. By comparing financial totals a company is able to determine whether it is earning a profit and whether it is financially viable.

REVIEW QUESTIONS

1. Name the four main business information systems.

2. Explain the following statement: A business information system consists of several linked processing cycles.

3. What is accomplished by the revenue-collection cycle? By the expenditure-processing cycle?

4. How do business computer applications differ from information-processing cycles? How do they differ from business information systems?

5. Why are data-flow diagrams helpful in describing information-processing cycles?

2-3   SIX TYPES OF COMPUTER FILES

A primary purpose of business computer applications is the creation, improvement, and use of files of business information. Computer files store logically related sets of business information. If these sets are accurate, complete, and easily accessed, a business has at its disposal both detailed and summary information that is important for business record keeping and for management decision making.

Computer files store business records. A *record* is made up of a set of facts, known as *data elements*, that are logically related. Each record describes an event, an object, or a person. For example, a record describing your background might begin with your Social Security number (the first data element), your name (the second data element), and your home address (the third data element). Each of these facts is important in identifying and describing you as a person.

Business firms must create and maintain several types of business records. Almost all firms create and maintain employee records, vendor records, customer records, and product records. Firms must also create and maintain records of their receivables, payables, assets, and liabilities. In each case, a computer file can be used to store these types of records. Within each file there is one record for each event, object, or person. The collection of a firm's files makes up the database of the organization (see Chapter 1).

Six types of computer files are used in the design of online business computer applications. Each type stores business records; however, as the following discussion makes clear, each is created and maintained for a different purpose.

The Transaction File

A transaction file contains records that describe the details of business dealings, such as information used in printing a customer invoice. Most transaction files are created for a specific processing run. When the run has been completed, there is little need to retain the file: at that point the information to be retained has been stored elsewhere. Thus, a transaction file contains *temporary* business records. It is saved long enough to provide a backup to processing—to permit rerunning steps in processing, if necessary. Then the storage space required by the file can be released.

The Master File

A master file contains records that describe the details of an event, object, or person. Unlike a transaction file, a master file contains *relatively permanent* records. A product master file, for example, contains records that describe the products carried in inventory by a business. These records change only if a product is dropped from inventory, a product is added to inventory, or the information describing a product carried in inventory needs to be modified. During a processing run, information stored on a master file can be updated (or otherwise modified)or extracted and transferred to a transaction file. Figure 2–5 shows the advantage gained by the transfer of information from one file to another. Each logical record

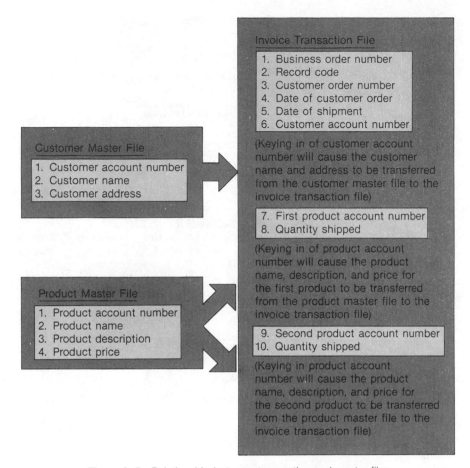

Figure 2–5   Relationship between transaction and master files

stored on the invoice transaction file need contain only ten data elements, which are either keyed to processing or are calculated by the computer. Three elements, number 6 (the customer account number), number 7 (the first product account number), and number 9 (the second product account number) are *data-extraction keys*. These keys permit record keys stored on master files to be matched with record keys keyed to processing. Following a match, the entire record associated with the stored key can be transferred from the master file into processing.

Figure 2–6 shows the user's view of this transfer of information. As shown, the customer number printed on the source document is keyed to processing and displayed. If it can be matched to the corresponding record key stored on file, the customer name and address are bought into processing and displayed. At the end of processing, these same data are written to the invoice transaction file. Likewise, for each product shipped, a match of product account numbers leads to the transfer of the product name, product description, and product price from the product master file to processing, where the information is displayed. In processing, customer

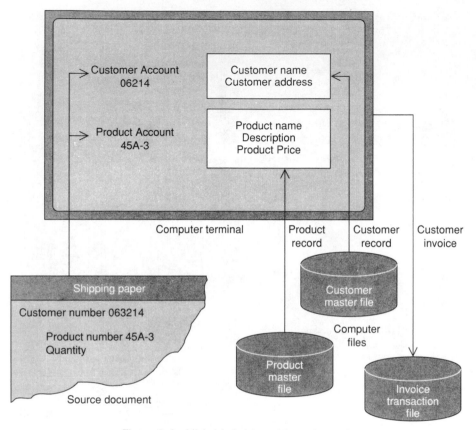

Figure 2–6   Minimizing data-entry requirements

information is combined with product information. This leads to the creation of a customer invoice that is written to the invoice transaction file.

The Summary File

A summary file contains condensed versions of transaction or master file data. Summary files are used in preparing management summary reports and in linking together computer applications. They are products of processing, created by a processing run. Figure 2–7 shows the relationship between a transaction file and a summary file. When the invoice summary file in Figure 2–7 is created, only eight out of the twenty-four data elements contained in the invoice transaction file are saved. Even so, this considerably smaller file allows a business to summarize the financial totals associated with preparing invoices. The summary file is now suitable as input to the accounts-receivable application. If the salesperson number were added to this summary, it would also be suitable as input to the sales-analysis computer application.

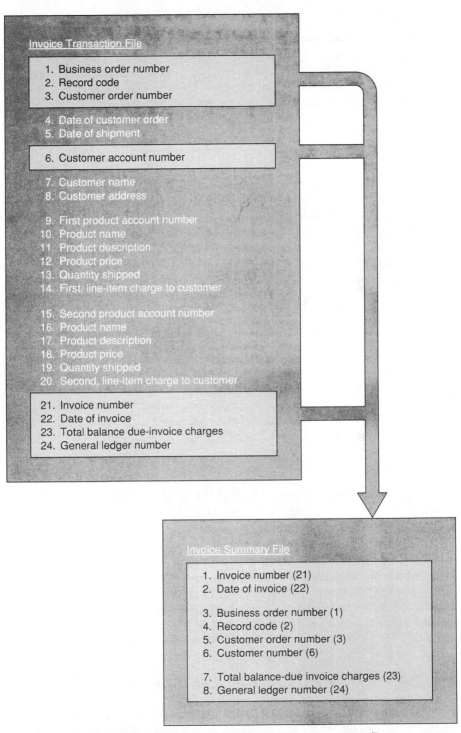

Figure 2–7 Relationship between transaction and summary files

The Suspense File

A suspense file contains records that have been found to be in error. Because online business computer applications block or trap errors before they can be entered into processing, suspense files can often be omitted from an online design. There are, however, some exceptions. As an example, suppose that, in keying data for a customer shipment, a data-entry operator notices that, although the first twenty product numbers have been accepted by the computer, the twenty-first number is rejected as incorrect. Two alternatives then exist. The operator could stop processing and disallow the data for the first twenty products entered successfully; when the questionable number is corrected, the operator would resubmit the data for all other product numbers as well. This duplication of effort is obviously undesirable, however. In the second alternative, the operator could halt processing and transfer the transaction-in-error to a suspense file. This would avoid rekeying the data for the first twenty items. Once the problem with the twenty-first item is identified, the transaction-in-error could be removed from the suspense file to be corrected and tested. If the tests are successful, the transaction is entered into processing. If the tests indicate another problem, the type of error is identified, and the troublesome transaction is transferred a second time to the suspense file. Here it remains until the error can be resolved.

The Backup File

A backup file is a copy of a transaction, master, summary, or suspense file. Copies of files are made for security reasons. If a file is destroyed or tampered with, the copy of the file can be used to restore processing. File-backup procedures are required by all online business computer applications. They protect a business against natural disasters and from human failings.

The Change File

A change file is a special type of backup file. It contains all adjustments made online to records. Most change files log the date and time of change and the account number of the user making the change. In addition, change files usually store two versions of the same record: one showing the contents of the record before a change and a second showing the contents after a change. This *before-after recording* is done for security reasons. If the legitimacy of a change to a file is questioned, the contents of the change file can be listed to determine what changes were made and who made the change. Before-after recording also has a backup purpose: the change file can be used as an input file, should it be necessary to restore changes made to a file.

2-4 SEVEN TYPES OF COMPUTER PROGRAMS

Besides six types of computer files, seven types of computer programs are used in the design of online business computer applications. These are the edit, up-date, display, register, action-document, summary, and change-report programs.

Understanding these programs together with the six types of computer files will help you follow the notation used in describing online business computer applications.

The Edit Program

Almost all online business computer applications begin with either an edit program or, as we will see later, a combined edit and update program. An edit program tests for errors in key-entered data. It is written to ensure proper input of data to the computer and to block or trap input errors. Two types of tests are made by edit programs: computer-controlled edit tests and human-controlled edit tests.

Computer-controlled edit tests consist of individual record-checking and file-balancing procedures. Because records in an online environment are entered into processing transaction by transaction, records must be checked individually. Each data element keyed into processing is subjected to one or more edit tests. These tests can include *mixed-mode* tests (for example, an alphabetic character in a numeric field), *limit* tests (for example, overtime hours too high), *reasonableness-of-data* tests (for example, a wage code of 85, apparently too high), and *check-digit* tests (see the following for an example). When a test identifies an error or a possible error, the terminal operator is notified. Suppose that an operator erroneously keys in Account 65032 instead of 60532. A check-digit test would trap this *transposition error*. The computer might respond by telling the terminal operator to rekey the number.

A *file-balance procedure* is a special type of computer-controlled edit test. This procedure creates and maintains control records placed at the beginning of a computer file. The records store beginning and ending balances of record counts and amounts, as well as the number of changes to these counts and amounts. The interpretation of these control records is accomplished by simple equations. For example, one file-balance equation used in an online payroll computer application keeps track of the number of employees on file:

Old count of employees + Employee additions − Employee deletions
= New count of employees.

Here, four record counts are required: the old count of employees, the number of additions, the number of deletions, and the new count of employees. Each time the employee master file is changed, either the number of employee additions or the number of employee deletions is increased; the new count of employees is therefore either increased or decreased. When all changes are completed, these counts are matched to determine if they are in balance. The new count of employees is matched against a listing of all employees stored on file. If the count differs from the listing, the contents of the entire file may be in error.

Human-controlled edit tests are designed to require the terminal operator to review visually and verify the correctness of keyed data. This type of test also takes a wide variety of forms. For example, the computer might produce the following display:

```
ACCOUNT NUMBER : 354778
   THE NEW BUILDING ADDRESS FOR MARTIN J. JOHNSON IS

   JOHNSON'S BUILDING SUPPLY
   2555 BROWN AVENUE
   SAN CRUSES, CA 94302

   IS THIS BUILDING ADDRESS CORRECT (Y OR N)?
```

This display requires the operator to verify the new building address visually. If the address is incorrect, the operator enters the letter **N**. The computer responds by telling the operator the steps to follow to modify the address.

The Update Program

An update program either creates or modifies one or more files of business records. In online systems, transaction files are generally created (that is, records are only written to a file) and master files are modified (that is, records are read from as well as written to a file). Creating a record to be stored on a transaction file is a multistep process. First, some data are extracted from one or more master files and transferred to enlarge the contents of the transaction-file record. Third, some data are computed directly and stored. If, as an example, the computer calculates the line-item charge for merchandise shipped to a customer, the calculation is based on the quantity ordered, which is keyed to processing, times the unit price of the item, which is extracted from the product master file and transferred into processing (review Figure 2–5 if this procedure is not clear).

Modifying master-file records involves revising data elements either before or during transaction processing. The address of a customer, for example, would be changed *before* processing. Current data (the current sales total) would be added to a historical sales total (the year-to-date sales total) *during* transaction processing. This second type of modification involves the reading of data to processing (the old year-to-date total), adding current sales to the total, and writing the revised total back to the master file.

In database processing, a single update program may consult, revise, and transfer data from several files. Besides creating one or more transaction files, the program may extract data from several master files and modify data stored on several other master or summary files. Typically, one set of file-balance control records must be developed for each file affected by processing. This procedure helps determine that processing is correct. It provides a formal *audit trail*—a method of tracing output back through the various steps in processing, which eventually leads all the way back to the original source documents.

The Display Program

A display program extracts records from computer files for display on a video display terminal. It may also produce a hard copy of information shown on the display screen, following the user command to print the display. Unlike update programs, which modify file records, display programs permit retrieved records to be examined but not changed.

Display programs are generally written to limit access to portions of a record, so that information judged as sensitive cannot be displayed or can be displayed but not changed. Fields that cannot be displayed are known as *restricted fields*. Fields that can be displayed but not changed are *protected fields*. An employee's salary, for example, is usually considered sensitive information. In designing a display of an employee's record, a firm might define salary as a restricted field and limit display information to less sensitive facts, such as name, address, home telephone, business telephone extension, department, and job title.

Display programs clearly separate online from batch methods of processing. These programs allow search activities to be performed by the person needing information. With batch methods, in contrast, the search must be delegated to a member of the data-processing staff.

The Register Program

A register program provides a printed listing of information stored on a transaction, master, suspense, summary, or backup file. These listings serve a number of important uses. They can be inspected to determine whether actions taken by the computer were correct. They permit information to be looked up when it cannot be displayed. They provide a permanent record of processing. If a question arises concerning the details of a transaction, for example, the transaction-file register can be examined to find out the contents of the record in question.

Most register listings are *ordered listings*. This means that they are arranged in a prescribed order, such as in account number sequence or in alphabetic order. Ordered listings generally take more time to prepare than unordered listings, but they save people time in their search for a specific account. *Sort programs* are typically used to prepare ordered listings.

An alternative to printing a register on computer paper is to write the register print file to a magnetic-tape file initially and to input this file to computer output microfile (COM) processing. A product of COM is *microfiche*, a card-sized film on which photographic images of information are placed. Microfiche processing is less costly than printing registers on paper and storing these bulky documents for long periods. A single four-by-six-inch microfiche card, for instance, costs about 35 cents and can store up to 270 pages of printed material. The equivalent cost for paper is approximately $2.50.

The Action-Document Program

An action-document program produces formal business documents, such as payroll checks, customer invoices, and vendor voucher-checks—materials that require action by parties external to data processing. Most transaction-processing computer applications contain an action-document program. Their preparation is often a major reason for developing an application.

The Summary Program

A summary program extracts information from transaction files in order to create summary files and print summary displays and reports. These programs tend to feature management information processing rather than transaction processing. Some business firms use summary programs to create a management information database for use in online spreadsheet and color graphics applications. A requirement of many of these analysis and reporting systems is that the database be limited to only essential information.

The Change-Report Program

A change-report program is a special type of register program that provides a listing of information stored on a change file. A change-report listing is commonly referred to as an *is/was report*. It shows the contents of records stored on a master file after a change (the "is" condition) and the contents of records before the change (the "was" condition); it reports the beginning file-balance-control totals and the ending file-balance-control totals and compares these totals to the printed list of changes.

REVIEW QUESTIONS

6. Why are computer files important to a business?

7. What is the difference between a transaction file and a master file? Between a summary file and a suspense file? Between a backup file and a change file?

8. What is the difference between a computer-controlled and a human-controlled edit test?

9. What does an update program do?

10. What is the difference between a register program and a change-report program?

11. Why is an ordered listing important?

2-5   SYSTEMS DOCUMENTATION

To be understood and used successfully, online business computer applications must be properly documented. A *systems specification* documents what a system will accomplish. It includes a statement of purpose, systems data-flow diagrams, systems organization charts, systems flowcharts, and processing menus. Collectively, these materials provide a clear picture of the logical properties of an application.

   The statement of purpose clarifies the reasons for developing the computer application. It includes an explanation of why the application was designed and what results should follow its implementation.

Systems data-flow diagrams show the logical functions of a system. These diagrams illustrate how data flow in a system, how data are transformed by the system, where data are stored within a system, and who receives or sends information from outside the system. Collectively, these functions include sets of activities to be performed by the computer and by people.

Systems organization charts show the interactive and batch functions performed by a business computer application and the specific computer programs written for that application.

Systems flowcharts illustrate the movement of data through the computer programs in a business computer application. Standard flowcharting symbols depict the component parts of processing and their functions.

Processing menus describe the processing selections that can be made from a computer terminal to activate interactive and batch processing functions. *Program processing menus* are program specific: they show which computer programs can be brought into processing. *File-processing menus* are file specific: they show how records stored on computer files can be processed.

In addition to the logical properties of an application, a systems specification must include a detailed, technical description of processing. These materials are prepared as part of online systems design (see Chapter 3). They include printed report layouts, video-screen report layouts, video-screen input layouts, file-coding structures, data-element dictionary specifications, computer program structure charts, and processing-control specifications.

Printed report layouts describe the registers, action-documents, summary reports, and change reports that are to be printed by a business computer application. Each report must be documented. Report layouts show how the design will be fitted to common stock paper or to special-order custom business forms.

Video-screen report layouts include report and message formats to be transmitted as displays during processing. Each display must be documented. Video-screen layouts show how the design is fitted to the display screen.

Video-screen input layouts consist of data-entry instructions to be followed in transmitting data from the video terminal into processing. Instructions must be prepared for each type of input. Video-screen input layouts show how data will be keyed into processing.

File-coding structures explain the meaning of the various numeric, alphabetic, and alphanumeric codes used in processing. Coding worksheets explain the significance of each digit or character of a code.

Data-element dictionary specifications include the field name, field type, field length, and description of each data element in a computer file. Record format analysis sheets define all data elements to be contained in a record.

Computer program structure charts show the internal structure of each computer program to explain how the various functions of processing are sequenced and interrelated. Besides structure charts, program specifications explain the internal logic of a computer program. These specifications are especially critical when complex programmed decision rules require clarification. Other specifications, such as program run-time estimates and memory requirements, must also be stated.

Processing-control specifications clarify how each step in processing is to be controlled. Computer- and human-controlled edit and update tests must be described. The equations used in file-balance procedures must be explained.

2-6   SYSTEMS FLOWCHARTING

Because systems flowcharts are used throughout this book, it is essential to understand their purpose, the symbols used in their design, and the guidelines to be followed in their actual construction. Once they are understood, it becomes possible to visualize the movement of data through the various processing stages of an online application. Unlike data-flow diagrams, *systems flowcharts* depict the main parts of a business computer application. They are limited to showing inputs to processing, outputs from processing, and computer programs written for processing.

Flowchart Symbols

The standard symbols used in designing systems flowcharts are available on specially prepared flowcharting templates. One such template—there are several different types—features twenty-three standard symbols (see Figure 2–8). These twenty-three are more than adequate to describe the features of online computer applications. In fact, to describe the important features of the online applications developed for this text, only seven are needed: the *process* symbol, the *manual input* symbol, the *document* symbol, the *display* symbol, the *communication link* symbol, the *online storage* symbol, and the *magnetic tape* symbol.

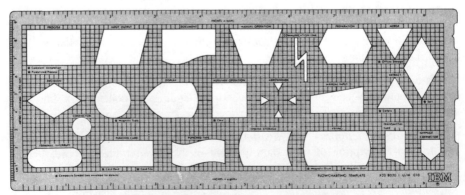

Figure 2–8   Template of flowchart symbols

Process

The most prominent symbol in a systems flowchart is the process symbol. It represents a computer program and shows the point at which information is brought into and altered by processing. In a systems flowchart, only one process symbol is used to show the different processing steps in any one computer program. Only a single symbol is required even though the program may do several things: check keyed input data for errors, enlarge the input transaction file, display messages to the terminal operator, and maintain file-balance equations. Computer structure charts, not systems flowcharts, are used to illustrate program details.

Manual Input

In most online environments, input to processing is entered directly from a terminal keyboard. This direct entry of data is indicated by the manual input symbol.

Document

The document symbol represents either source documents or computer-printed material. *Source documents*—those that have been prepared by users prior to processing—include customer orders, purchase requisitions, and employee-change forms. Information is extracted from these documents and entered into processing. *Computer-printed documents* consist of listings and reports, such as registers and summary reports, and of formal business documents.

Display

The display symbol indicates that data are to be displayed on screen: either a single screen (a single display page) or multiple screens (several display pages). Most online applications require the terminal operator to use several display pages to enter, modify, or retrieve data.

Communication Link

The communication-link symbol represents the transmission of data back and forth between the computer and remote locations. It is used together with the manual input symbol to show the transmission of data to the computer or together with the document or display symbol to illustrate the transmission of data from the computer.

Online Storage

The online storage symbol represents a computer file that can be read from or written to directly. In an online processing environment, online file storage generally means direct, indexed, or sequential access magnetic disk storage. Direct- and indexed-access permit individual records to be read directly into processing, examined, updated, and written back to the disk. Sequential access does not encourage the reading, writing, or updating of individual records. Instead, this method is used primarily in writing several records at a time to a disk, where they are stored in the order in which they were written.

Magnetic Tape Storage

The symbol for magnetic tape storage can also represent online storage. Compared with magnetic disks, however, tape cannot be used efficiently either to access or to insert individual records in a file. In online computer applications, magnetic-tape storage is mainly used for backing up computer files.

Flowchart Layout   Besides using standard symbols, it is important to follow a set of guidelines for describing the sequence of events illustrated by systems flowcharts. The more standard the layout, the more information the chart will convey. The following six guidelines are used in designing system flowcharts.

1. A systems flowchart should be simple enough to be placed on one $8\frac{1}{2}$-by-11-inch page.

2. The flow of information in the chart should move from the top of the page to the bottom. Edit, update, display, register, action-document, summary, and change-report computer programs should be placed in sequence whenever possible.

3. Inputs to processing, including computer files, should appear on the left side of the main flow of processing. A single arrow from a computer file to a computer program shows that information is read into processing. A double arrow indicates that information is both read from and written to a computer file.

4. Outputs from processing should appear on the right side of the main flow of processing. Note two exceptions, however: if a file of records is created by processing, this output file can be placed at the bottom of the computer program symbol; and if a file of records is updated by processing, the placement of the output file is the same as the placement of the input file. As before, a double arrow indicates that data are to be read from the file into processing and to be written to the file at some later point in processing.

5. Clear labels should be given to each symbol placed on the flowchart. For computer programs, the title for each process should consist of a verb followed by one or two adjectives followed by an object—for example, "print customer credit report."

6. Short descriptive statements can be appended to a flowchart to clarify how information is passed between programs. We will use a wide variety of these statements in describing the systems flowcharts contained in the chapters that follow.

Figures 2–9 and 2–10 illustrate the layouts of two different processing designs. The flowchart in Figure 2–9 shows the steps required in the batch processing of purchase order requisitions, up to the point of creating an approved purchase order transaction file. The steps required in processing were described in Chapter 1 (see Figure 1–6). The systems flowchart now clarifies the relationships between the three required programs: the edit purchase order requisitions program, the sort purchase order transactions program, and the update purchase requisitions program. Each computer program can be described as follows:

Step 1   The *edit purchase order requisitions program* accepts a serially read batch of key-verified purchase order transactions. As each transaction is brought into processing, it is edited by the edit purchase order requisitions program for correctness; if an error is found, the transaction in error is printed on a purchase order edit report. After all errors have been printed, processing is discontinued, to permit the errors to be corrected. Following this, transactions in error are corrected and resubmitted to be checked a second time by the edit program. If no errors are found, the purchase order transactions file created by processing is considered error free.

Step 2   The *sort purchase order transactions program* arranges all transactions stored on the purchase order transactions file sequentially by vendor number. (The sorted file must be in the same sequence as the vendor master file, which is used next.)

Step 3   The *update purchase requisitions program* enlarges the contents of sorted purchase order transactions file. In processing, the update program must

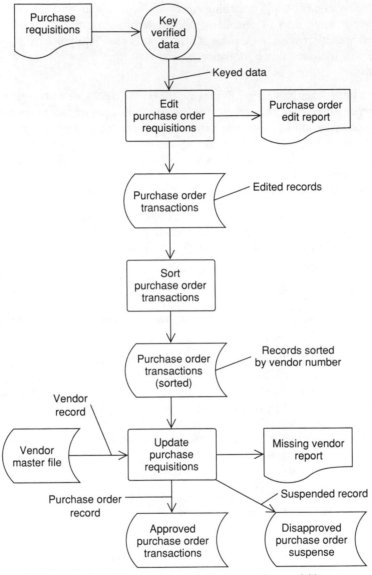

Figure 2–9 Batch processing of purchase order requisitions

first match vendor numbers. A record stored on the purchase order transaction file is read to obtain a vendor number. Once obtained, the vendor master file is searched until the same vendor number is found. Following the match, the vendor's name and address are added to the purchase order transaction. Next, the enlarged record is written to the approved purchase order output transaction file. If a match cannot be made, however, a transaction in error is printed on the missing-vendor report.

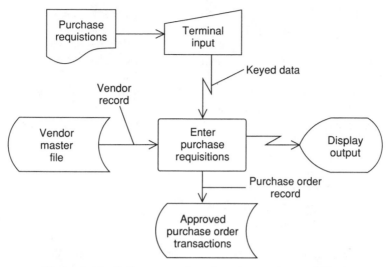

Figure 2–10   Online processing of purchase order requisitions

The transaction is also suspended by being written to a disapproved purchase order suspense file.

Figure 2–10 flowcharts this same procedure for an interactive processing environment (see Figure 1–7). Only one program, the *enter purchase requisitions program*, is now needed. This program edits keyed transactions and creates an approved purchase order transaction file, one transaction at a time. The steps important to processing are as follows:

Step 1   Information describing a purchase order requisition is keyed and edited for correctness by the edit portion of the program. If an error is identified, the terminal operator is notified. If some data had not been transmitted, for example, the computer might notify the operator with a message reading:

```
THE QUANTITY ORDERED WAS NOT INDICATED.
WHAT QUANTITY IS DESIRED?
```

Step 2   The update portion of the program enlarges the transaction by transferring name and address information from the vendor master file into processing. A successful update leads to the creation of an approved purchase order transaction. If problems with the update are encountered, the terminal operator is notified. For instance:

```
VENDOR ACCOUNT 10023 CANNOT BE FOUND.
DO YOU WISH TO SUBMIT A NEW VENDOR NUMBER? (Y OR N)
```

Comparing batch processing and interactive processing gives the impression that, since fewer programs are required in an interactive environment, it will be more machine-efficient. This is a false impression: actually, the interactive edit and update of each transaction take considerably more computer time than is used to read and process all transactions as a batch. The clearest advantage of the interactive approach is that transactions are more carefully edited by people and by the computer prior to their storage as "approved." The careful human inspection and machine checking save time and ensure accuracy. Both factors are vital in processing business information.

Another comparison of batch processing to interactive processing reveals that, in an online environment, both types of processing are advantageous but in very different ways. Typically, interactive methods are used to create or update a file, and batch methods are required to produce various types of listings and reports, such as a listing of the contents of computer files. Printing a master list of vendors, for example, is accomplished by the batch program entitled "print vendor register." As the flowchart in Figure 2–11 shows, this report can be produced directly, provided that records of the file are arranged in the correct sequence. In a second example, we see that a slightly different processing arrangement is needed to print the approved purchase order register (see Figure 2–12). Before the register can be printed, the approved purchase order transactions file is sorted by purchase order number to arrange all transactions in serial order. After the sort, a second batch program, appropriately entitled "print purchase order register," produces the register.

Finally, Figure 2–13 features another interactive processing procedure to show the relationship between the master file and a change file. In this instance, new vendor information must be added to the vendor master file. As the double arrow indicates, the vendor master file is updated by reading into processing the old vendor record, updating the record, and writing the revised record back to the master file. At the same time, the change to the vendor master file is written to the vendor change file. This logging of the update provides a record of all types of changes (additions, modifications, deletions) to the master file, subject to review once the contents of the change file are printed.

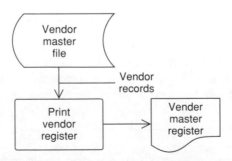

Figure 2–11   Printing the vendor master register

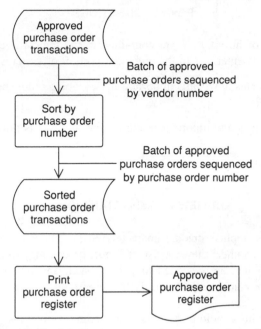

Figure 2–12 Printing the approved purchase order register

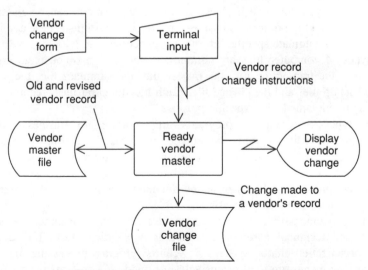

Figure 2–13 Updating the vendor master file

REVIEW QUESTIONS

12. What types of information are contained in the logical overview portion of systems documentation? In the technical portion of systems documentation?

13. Why are systems flowcharts important in describing online business computer applications?

14. What guidelines are important in the design of systems flowcharts?

15. Explain why online processing requires some type of direct-access storage.

REVIEW OF IMPORTANT IDEAS

Business computer applications are characterized by four general properties: they are related to one another; they consist of input, processing, storage, output, and control functions; they are designed to permit batch and interactive methods of processing; and they are relatively easily to understand if systems documentation is logical and complete.

Four business information systems are common to most business firms: the revenue system, the expenditure system, the conversion system, and the cash-management system. Each of these information systems can be broken down into information-processing systems and cycles. Each cycle consists of several business computer applications.

Approximately twenty-five business computer applications can be classified as belonging to one of the four main business information systems. These applications are designed to automate specific information-processing activities.

Six types of computer files are common to the design of business computer applications: the transaction file, the master file, the summary file, the suspense file, the backup file, and the change file. Each file stores business records; each is created and maintained for a specific purpose.

Seven types of computer programs are common to business computer applications: the edit program, the update program, the display program, the register program, the action-document program, the summary program, and the change-report program. Edit, update, and display programs are generally used in interactive processing. Register, action-document, summary, and change-report programs are used in batch processing.

Systems documentation is required to describe and illustrate the systems overview and technical parts of a computer application. Data-flow diagrams, systems organization charts, systems flowcharts, program-processing menus, and file-processing menus are used extensively in providing a systems overview. More technical documentation specifies input and output requirements and explains how processing is accomplished.

Systems flowcharts are of importance in preparing a systems overview. These diagrams chart the flow of data through various computer programs in a business computer application.

KEY WORDS

Business information system	Before-after recording
System specification	Edit program
Business computer applications	File-balance procedure
Transaction-based applications	Update program
Management-based applications	Audit trail
Record	Display program
Data element	Register program
Fields	Action-document program
Transaction file	Summary program
Data-extraction keys	Change-report program
Master file	Is/was report
Summary file	Systems specification
Suspense file	Systems data flow diagram
Backup file	Systems flowchart
Change file	Source document

EXERCISES

1. Individuals as well as business firms require information systems. Discuss the information system you require in

    (a) handling your personal income;

    (b) managing your personal expenses.

2. Suppose you know the following about your personal check system:

    (a) You deposit a paycheck. After you receive a paycheck from your employer, you fill out a deposit slip and deposit the paycheck at the bank. In addition, you enter the deposit amount in your checkbook register, revising the ending checkbook balance as you record your entry in the register.

    (b) You write checks. This procedure involves obtaining the beginning checkbook balance from the checkbook register, writing the check, and revising the checkbook-register balance to show the ending balance. Each personal check contains a unique check number. Personal checks are sent to several sources.

    (c) You reconcile your checkbook register. This procedure is triggered by the receipt of the bank monthly statement and the canceled checks sent to you by the bank. In processing, you match canceled checks against outstanding checks shown in the checkbook register to determine whether each check is still outstanding or has been cashed. A cashed check is marked off in the checkbook register.

    Draw a data-flow diagram describing this system.

3. Suppose a computer application is designed to process and store personal check information. The design includes a check-register master file and a check/deposit transaction file. Data entered into processing for each check consist of a check number, record code (type of record), date of check, check description, and amount of check. Deposit information would also be entered into processing. Data entered for each deposit includes a deposit number, record code, date of deposit, and amount of deposit. The checking account balance would always be calculated and kept by the computer.

    (a)   Using the symbols described in this chapter, design an online systems flowchart to show how this personal checking application works.

    (b)   After your design is completed, answer the following questions:

        (i)   Why is a record code required?
        (ii)   What information would be contained in master file records?
        (iii)   When are edit procedures required in processing?
        (iv)   What changes are made to the master file when it is updated?
        (v)   How must your design in part (a) be modified to permit checks to be shown as outstanding or canceled (checked off as being correctly processed)?

4. Why should systems documentation include a logical description of processing? Give several reasons. Why should it include a technical description of processing? Give several reasons.

5. Some business computer applications are transaction based, and others are management based. How would you characterize the general ledger application? Explain your answer.

DISCUSSION QUESTIONS

In review of the properties of online applications, why is it important to be familiar with

(a) the four main information systems in an organization?

(b) the wide mix of business computer applications?

(c) the design of the general ledger application?

(d) the six types of computer files?

(e) the seven types of computer programs?

(f) differences between the logical and technical descriptions of processing?

(g) the design of systems flowcharts?

4-IN-1 CASE STUDY—MODIFYING GENERAL LEDGER ACCOUNTS

When 4-in-1 was installed, several decisions were made for you and keyed into processing. These included the name, address, and telephone number of the fic-ticious company you will be asked to deal with in the case study that runs the length of the book. Unless changed by your instructor, this company information is as follows:

Name:	A and J Enterprises, Inc.
Address:	1169 Student Way
	Collegeville, OR 97000
Telephone:	503-686-5000

In addition to this information, the general ledger coding format was selected, as was the type of business. Specifically, a two-part general ledger code was selected; the type of business was that of a wholesaler, namely, a company that purchases goods in larger lots from manufacturers and sells goods in smaller lots to a large number of retailers.

Printing the Predefined Chart of Accounts

4-in-1 provides a predefined chart of accounts for a wholesale business. Do the following to review and print this chart of accounts:

1. Log on using the instructions in Chapter 1. Remember that the starting date is 010197.

2. Type **1** from the main menu and press ENTER.

3. Type **4**, *Print out accounts*, from the maintain chart of accounts menu.

4. Press F1 (the function key) to indicate that you want to begin printing with the first account.

5. Press F1 to indicate that you want to end printing with the last account.

6. Press ENTER.

7. Type **Y** when asked, *Display this report?* The entire report will be scrolled across the screen. Press ENTER.

8. Repeat steps 3 through 7, except this time print the report. If you experience problems in printing, press the F1 key.

9. Press TAB (the END or double arrow key on some keyboards) to return to the main menu.

Changing a General Ledger (G/L) Account

4-in-1 allows you to add, change, or delete a G/L account from the predefined chart of accounts. In this way, you can tailor account numbers for specific types of businesses. Do the following to change an account:

1. From the main menu, type **1**, maintain chart of accounts, and press ENTER.

2. From the maintain chart of accounts menu, type **2**, change accounts, and press ENTER.

```
┌─────────────────────────────────────────────────────────────────────────┐
│  Maintain chart of accounts                        A and J Enterprises, Inc. │
│  Change accounts                                                          │
│                                                                           │
│                                                                           │
│              1. Account #                                                 │
│              2. Description                                               │
│              3. Fin statement type                                        │
│              4. Paren control code                                        │
│              5. Compression code                                          │
│                                                                           │
│                                                                           │
│                                                                           │
│  Enter account, or press F1 for next account                              │
└─────────────────────────────────────────────────────────────────────────┘
```

Figure 2–14   Reviewing Change Account Menu

3. From the change account menu (see Figure 2–14), type **1010** and press ENTER twice. Even though the account code reads *1010-000*, only four digits are required at this time. By pressing ENTER, the last three digits default to zero.

4. Type **2** when asked *Field number to change?* Press ENTER.

5. Type **CASH RECEIPTS—Checking #1** and press ENTER.

6. Do not make any other changes at this time. Instead, type ENTER when asked *Field number to change?* a second time. This will allow you to press TAB and exit the change account process.

Deleting a G/L Account

Deleting an account is easier than modifying one. Do the following to remove accounts from the G/L:

1. From the maintain chart of accounts menu, type **3**, *Delete accounts*, and press ENTER.

2. Type **2380** when asked to enter the account number. Press ENTER twice. The account number for Local W/H Tax Payable will be displayed. Local withholding taxes are not required by our fictitious wholesaler.

3. Answer **Y** when asked, *Ok to delete account?* Press ENTER twice.

4. Repeat steps 2 and 3 to delete accounts 2460 and 7600. Write down the names of these accounts before you delete them.

5. Press TAB to exit the deletion of account process.

Adding a G/L Account

Adding a G/L account is similar to changing a G/L account. In this instance, the data for all fields must be key-entered. To add an account to the G/L, do the following:

1. From the maintain chart of accounts menu, type **1**, *Add accounts*, and press ENTER.

2. Type **4030** and press ENTER to indicate the first part of the new account number.

3. Press ENTER to add the 000 subcode to the new account number.

4. Type **Sales—product C** to add a field description to the new account. In later chapters, you will be asked to group sales by product.

5. Type **P** to indicate that this account is to be printed on the profit and loss sheet.

6. Type **D** to indicate that parentheses are to be added when a debit is to be added to this account.

7. Type **D** to indicate that you would like to compress transactions for this account number. By compressing transactions, the result is a single transaction for each date when there is activity for this G/L account.

8. Press ENTER when asked *Field number to change?* This will add the new account to the chart of accounts.

9. Repeat steps 2 through 5 to add account 5030, description Purchases—product C, to the first two fields.

10. Type **P** to indicate profit and loss.

11. Type **C** to indicate that parentheses are to be added when a credit is to be added to this account.

12. Type **P** to indicate that you would like to compress transactions by period for this account number. The result is a single transaction for each accounting period when there is activity for this G/L account.

13. Press ENTER when asked *Field number to change?* This will add the new account to the chart of accounts.

14. Press TAB to return to the maintain chart of accounts menu.

Printing the Revised G/L

Print the revised general ledger to document the changes you have made. Follow the instructions in part 1.

QUESTIONS

1. How many G/L account numbers have been predefined for you by 4-in-1?

2. What are the names of the three accounts that you deleted?

3. Why is it important to be able to add, change, and delete G/L account numbers?

4. Suppose you wanted to collect sales data on twenty-four different products. What changes to the chart of accounts are required?

5. What type of file (for example, transaction, master, summary, and so forth) is needed to store the chart of accounts list?

3

Online Systems Design

Once a logical overview of processing has been developed, fully documented, and approved by management, it must be translated into a detailed technical description. This process is *systems design*. The work associated with design is assigned to an individual known as a *systems designer*. The designer translates the logical overview of processing into a fully operational computer application. Viewed in a broader perspective, the systems designer builds information processing systems.

In preparing a systems design, the designer must include written specifications for five areas: systems inputs, computer files, systems outputs, computer programs, and processing controls. Completion of these areas leads to the development and documentation of the technical features of processing: video-screen input and report layouts, computer-printed report layouts, file-coding structures, data-element definitions, program structure charts, and specifications for both computer programs and processing controls. In other words, systems design defines the way in which a business computer application is actually to be processed by the computer.

Systems design encompasses both the technical and human factors of processing and seeks to make them clear and accessible. *Technical factors* include a variety of items: the sets of instructions to be translated into code, the types of data to be stored on computer files, the data to be keyed in or retrieved from computer files, and the equations to bring about control in processing. *Human factors* deal with the use of the completed computer application. They stress items important to the design from the user's perspective, such as the display of error messages and user-help instructions.

3-1 DESIGNING SYSTEMS INPUT

A major advantage of online business computer applications is the capability to make a visual review and to edit the input of data into processing. In design, the systems designer must determine what data must be entered into processing, how these data are to be physically entered, and what checks are necessary to determine if data have been entered correctly. In addition, the designer must provide a variety of user aids; this includes making sure that the instructions for entering and correcting data are clear and can be followed by the user with little difficulty and that messages produced by the program and displayed are consistent with these input instructions.

Data-Element Requirements

In deciding what data are to be entered into processing, the designer reviews the list of required data elements and separates those to be keyed directly to processing from those to be stored on computer files in advance of processing. Data stored in advance on master files can be transferred rather than keyed.

The documentation describing data to be keyed typically includes the name of the field, the description of the field (for example, whether the field is numeric, alphabetic, or alphanumeric), the number of characters in the field, the source of the data, and other important comments. The data element name and the field name may differ, however. For example, the data element name might be DATE_OF_CUSTOMER_SHIPMENT, compared to the field name SHIPDATE. With many programming languages, the length of a field name must be limited to a maximum number of characters, such as eight. In the examples that follow, field-length restrictions are not imposed. However, underscores are added (as in order_number) to make each field name a single string of characters.

Input-analysis forms record data element descriptions (see Figure 3–1). These forms, combined with copies of all source documents, show the specific pieces of information to be keyed directly to processing.

SYSTEM DOCUMENTATION				
NAME OF APPLICATION Customer Invoice		DATE October 15, 19XX	PAGE 1 OF 2	
PROGRAMMER/ANALYST B. Thompson		TYPE OF ANALYSIS Input Analysis		
Field *Name*	*Field* *Description*	*No. of* *Characters*	*Source*	*Comments*
Order_Number	Numeric	7	Packing Slip	4 bytes
Record_Code	Numeric	1	Packing Slip	1 byte
Customer_Number	Numeric	5	Packing Slip	3 bytes
Date_of_Order	Numeric	6	Packing Slip	4 bytes
Date_of_Shipment	Numeric	6	Packing Slip	4 bytes
Product_Number	Numeric	5	Packing Slip	3 bytes
Quantity_Shipped	Numeric	5	Packing Slip	3 bytes

Figure 3–1   Input-analysis form

SYSTEM DOCUMENTATION			
NAME OF APPLICATION Customer Invoice		DATE October 15, 19XX	PAGE 2 OF 2
PROGRAMMER/ANALYST B. Thompson		TYPE OF ANALYSIS Customer Master Record Format Analysis	

Field Name	Field Description	No. of Characters	Source	Comments
Customer_Number	Numeric	5	New Customer Form	3 bytes
Customer_Name	Alphabetic	30	New Customer Form	Last, First, M.I.
Bill_to_Street	Alphanumeric	18	New Customer Form	
Bill_to_City	Alphabetic	8	New Customer Form	
Bill_to_State	Alphabetic	2	New Customer Form	
Bill_to_Zip	Numeric	5	New Customer Form	3 bytes

Figure 3–2   Record format analysis form

The documentation describing data to be stored on computer files is similar to the documentation for data entered directly (see Figure 3–2). *Record analysis forms* define each field name, field description (numeric, alphabetic, or alphanumeric), the number of characters in the field, the source of the data, and data storage comments. These forms, combined with copies of all source documents, show how computer fields are to be developed for processing.

Data-Entry Procedures

Data-entry procedures are designed after data-element requirements are set. These procedures show how data will be entered into processing, edited by the data-entry operator and by the computer, and corrected by the operator if data are found to be in error.

An important data-entry rule requires the operator to key into processing as little as possible, using the computer to interpret and fill in as much as possible. The objective is to reduce the number of *keystrokes*—the number of times a terminal operator must strike the keys of a keyboard. One method of reducing the number of keystrokes is to require numeric codes. Assume, for example, that a five-digit code is used to identify company employees. If the number 92189 (five keystrokes) is used to replace the name Barbara J. Wilson (seventeen keystrokes, including spaces), twelve keystrokes are saved. As importantly, one way of improving the efficiency of data entry is to make all input data numeric. This permits the data-entry operator to use only the *numeric pad* at the right of a terminal keyboard (see Figure 3–3). The numeric pad contains the ten number keys plus decimal-point and comma keys, a minus-sign key, and an enter (value) key.

Another design solution to improve efficiency is to use special purpose keys called *function keys* (see the top row of keys in Figure 3–3). These allow the

Figure 3–3 Terminal keyboard with numeric pad and function keys

data-entry operator to execute processing functions. In practice, function keys provide for many possibilities. Striking a key function marked *CLERK*, for instance, tells the computer to enter the pre-entered "clerk number" into processing. Striking a key marked *VOID* tells the computer to cancel the data transmitted for a transaction.

Light pens and optical character readers are also used to speed the entry of data into processing. A *light pen* is a small pencil-like instrument that is designed to activate positions on the face of a video display screen. Most pens are able to pick, move, and construct lines as well as to point to a specific set of X and Y coordinates.

A hand-held *mouse* is also used to increase the speed of moving from one point on a video display screen to another. The user is able to move the cursor from one point (X, Y coordinate) to another and to activate processing instructions by pressing a button or the mouse. For example, in a windows environment (where users can pull down menus), a report can be printed by selecting the File Print command and the OK button. All this can be done without ever touching the terminal keyboard.

An *optical scanner* is similar to a light pen; however, a scanner reads input data as well. The design of the scanner features a light-sensitive cell that permits it to "read" characters optically. The cell distinguishes between patterns of black and white, thus allowing it to match black-and-white patterns or images against character-recognition circuits.

Display Screen Design

Video display screens for data entry should be designed with operator efficiency in mind. Many key-entry designs begin with the layout of easy-to-use processing menus and processing commands. These menus are typically defined early on as part of the logical description of processing. A *processing menu* defines the different parts of processing that can be selected by an operator. A *program-processing menu*, for example, shows the computer programs available to be run. Such a menu for a membership accounts-receivable application might read as follows:

```
MEMBERSHIP PROCESSING

ENTER CHARGES/CREDITS
ENTER MEMBER PAYMENTS
CHANGE MEMBER ACCOUNTS
DISPLAY MEMBER ACCOUNTS
DISPLAY FILE-BALANCES

RETURN
```

This menu would be followed by a *prompt*, such as *Enter program number*, signaling the operator to select from the menu and enter a command. Entering the number 3, for example, commands the computer to execute the programmed instructions designed to *Change member accounts*. A *command* is thus a clear order from the user. It illustrates a direct mode of processing in which an instruction (an order) is entered and executed without delay.

Many online designs are both menu-driven and language-driven. A *menu-driven design* requires the user to move from one menu to another in making processing decisions. The advantage of this approach is that the system is more or less self-teaching (all one has to do is to make a choice). For this reason, this type of design is ideal for systems that are not used frequently, are used by many different people for short intervals, or are being used for the first time. The major disadvantage of this design is that it is slow. For example, the user may have to make several menu selections to perform a simple processing function, such as *Add a member account*.

A *language-driven design* requires the user to issue a key command to perform a processing function. The user executes the command by depressing either a function key or two keys on the terminal keyboard. *Control-C*, for example, is a common key command to interrupt and stop processing. This command is executed by depressing the control key and the letter *C* at the same time. Likewise, a key command to allow the user to *Add a member account* might be designed to *Control + A*. In this case, Control followed by the letter *A* signifies that the function to be performed is to add an account. The main advantage of a language-driven design is greater efficiency. The main disadvantage is that this approach is more difficult for most users. This is especially so if there are many different commands to memorize.

Video display layouts help in designing screen displays. As Figure 3–4 shows, a display layout sizes and arranges information to be displayed. Screen displays must be designed with care, because of their small size. Screens, such as those with 24 lines and 80 characters per line, restrict an input design to 1,920 characters. If additional lines are required beyond the screen maximums, multiple screens, or pages, become necessary. A *page* is a display formatted to fit the screen of a video display terminal. In designing data-entry procedures, designers often use several pages to enter data into processing. As you will observe in later chapters, some pages contain program-processing menus, others contain file and self-help menus, and still others display business forms to be completed by the terminal operator.

```
PART NUMBER: 9999999              DESCRIPTION: AAAAAAAAAAAAAAAAAAAAAA

     ORDER POLICY        99999999999    WAREHOUSE          999999
     REORDER POINT       99999999999    LOCATION           999999
     SAFETY STOCK        99999999999    CONTROL CENTER     999999
     ORDER QUANTITY      99999999999
     SHRINKAGE           99999999999    COUNT IN           999999
     YIELD               99999999999    COUNT OUT          999999
     AGING POLICY        99999999999    CURRENT LEVEL      999999

 PART SUBSTITUTES

     NUMBER (1):  9999999   DESCRIPTION:  AAAAAAAAAAAAAAAAAAAAAA
     NUMBER (2):  9999999                 AAAAAAAAAAAAAAAAAAAAAA
     NUMBER (3):  9999999                 AAAAAAAAAAAAAAAAAAAAAA
 - - - - - - - - - - - - - - - - - - - - - - - - - - - - - - - - - - - -
                     (MESSAGE AREA ON SCREEN)
 - - - - - - - - - - - - - - - - - - - - - - - - - - - - - - - - - - - -
```

Figure 3–4 Video display layout

New frame-based systems feature software that allows the user to display and manipulate several *windows*, or *pads*, on a single video display screen. A *frame* is a two-dimensional area of any size and is used to enclose a window, much like a window frame or a picture frame. A *window* is a viewpoint within the screen that permits one view of a system to be shown, using a portion of the screen. As shown by Figure 3–5, a window might contain a table of values or a chart of these values. Each provides a different view of processed data. In most frame-based systems, a window can be opened or closed, changed in size, and stacked or overlayed on top of another window. In addition, data within windows can be edited, and graphics or text too large for the window can be scrolled both horizontally and vertically. Frame-based systems feature a *cut-and-paste* option. It is possible to *cut* from one window and to *paste* the cutting to another window. Some systems also allow the user to *pop* and *push* windows in a stack. To review the contents of the second window, for example, the top window is popped from the stack.

Specific design techniques are used to highlight data-entry requirements and to identify problems in processing. These include prompts by the computer to check keyed information, blinking lights to show accounts to be inspected, soft sounds to indicate when an error has been made, underlining, and reverse video (shaded areas on a terminal screen) to emphasize what data to enter.

REVIEW QUESTIONS

1. What is systems design?

2. What written specifications must be prepared in systems design?

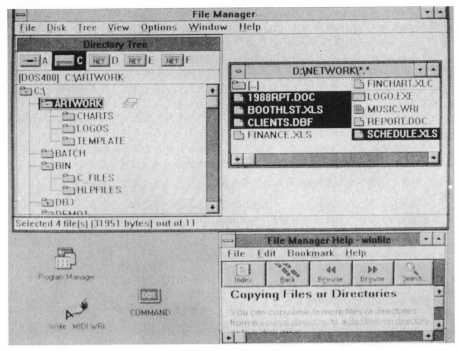

Figure 3–5 A multiwindow display

3. How does an input-analysis form differ from a record analysis form?

4. Explain why the following statement is true: An important objective of systems design is to reduce the number of keystrokes.

5. What is the difference between a menu-driven and a language-driven screen design?

6. Video displays often consist of several pages. Why?

7. What features are provided by frame-based systems?

3-2 DESIGNING COMPUTER FILES

Although a major reason for creating online business computer applications is the capability to edit and review the entry of data into processing visually, it is the computer files rather than the data-entry procedures that represent the most sizable investment in business computer applications. Computer files are dominant in business information processing. Businesses use computer files to store information required for both record keeping and management decision making.

Like data entry, computer files are designed following basic rules, some of which are simply good common sense. For instance:

- Do not place data in a computer file unless file maintenance is easy. As an example, suppose a manager decides that it is important to know the age of each employee. In this situation, each employee record should contain the date of the employee's birth rather than the age of the employee, since the date of birth can be used to calculate an employee's age and does not need to be changed.

- Do not place data in a computer file unless the cost of storage space can be justified. Continuing with the example, we should raise the following questions: How much will it cost to maintain the date of each person's birth in the file? How often will the age of employee value be used by a business? How valuable is this use?

- Do not place data in a computer file unless the accuracy of the stored information can be checked periodically by people able to detect errors. For example, the accuracy of an employee's beneficiary in a file is often questionable unless the employee is periodically asked to review the name.

File Design Guidelines

Besides these commonsense rules, several file design guidelines aid the systems designer.

- *Account codes* should be used to sequence business accounts and identify events, objects, and persons. Each customer of a business should be assigned a unique account code, for example, as should each product carried in inventory by the business.

- *Record codes* should be used to distinguish between different types of financial transactions, such as credits, debits, and adjustments. Properly designed record codes simplify the process by which dollar amounts are added to or subtracted from business accounts.

- *Sort keys* should be placed in a common location in a record. These keys permit a file to be sequenced in an order different from the account-code sequence. Placing them in a common location simplifies the design of sort procedures.

- Data elements in a record should be arranged by *common characteristic*. Each customer's name should be followed by his or her address, for example; it would be confusing if instead the customer's name were followed by the salesperson's name, which was then followed by the customer's address.

- File records should be divided into *header* and *trailing sections*. The header section should contain the relatively permanent elements of a record, such as the customer's account code and name. The trailing section should contain variable elements, whose values change as a result of processing. Year-to-date product sales, for example, would be revised each time a product is sold to a customer. In a database processing environment, header and trailing sections should be stored in different files.

- *Change* or *addition records* should be kept separate from transaction records. These update the records stored on master files. In contrast, transaction records, as discussed in Chapter 2, are enlarged during processing by transferring information from computer files and by entering information directly from the keyboard.

- Records should be blocked to save file space and to improve the efficiency of processing. *Blocking* is the grouping of logical records to form a single physical record (the record read into or written from central memory). The *blocking factor* specifies the number of logical records placed within a physical record.

Figure 3–6 shows record layouts for the fields specified by the input analysis form and the record format analysis form in Figures 3–1 and 3–2. These layouts help clarify how design rules are applied in practice. The top half of Figure 3–6 shows that the invoice transaction file contains an order number code, a record code (to indicate a credit or debit), the customer number, date of order, date of shipment, product number, and quantity shipped. The customer and product numbers are used as sort keys. The length of the record is 22 characters.

The bottom half of Figure 3–6 shows the customer master file record. It too contains an account code (customer number) as well as two sort keys (state and ZIP code). The fields on this record are arranged by common characteristic so that the customer's name is followed by the customer's bill-to address. As the figure shows, the master record contains only a header section. If a new field were added to store year-to-date customer sales, a trailing section would exist.

With database management systems, the concept of header and trailer sections takes on even more significance. Generally, header information is placed in one file, and trailing information is stored in another file. In the application chapters of the text we will illustrate the significance of this approach.

File Organization

After file records have been designed, the systems designer must determine how the various files containing these records are to be organized. Usually the designer will choose one of the two main types of file organization: *direct* organization, which gives immediate access to records stored on external storage devices, or *sequential* organization, which stores records in a file in sequence, generally in numeric order. Only magnetic disk storage devices permit direct file organization, but both magnetic tape and magnetic disk storage devices permit sequential storage of data.

Direct-access storage is common in online systems. This type of storage permits individual records to be read from and written directly to files. The database management software supplied with interactive computer systems contains

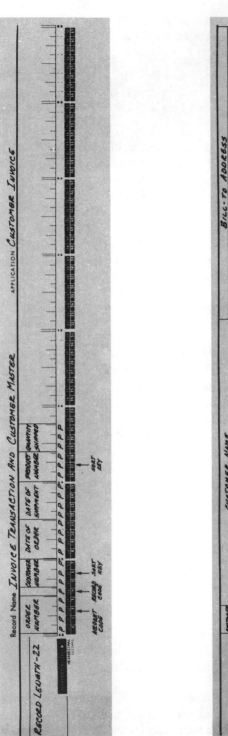

Figure 3-6 Record layout worksheet

a number of features that simplify this movement of data in and out of processing. These systems include software to create indexes on record-keys, for example. Indexes simplify the search for individual records. In addition, database management software allocates file storage space. This provision frees the programmer from having to specify exact data storage locations.

Indexed-sequential file organization is utilized when records must be accessed one by one and processed in sequence. With this method, individual records can be added, changed, or deleted from a file directly. Also, all records contained on the file can be printed in sequence, such as by customer order number, when all records follow a customer-order-number sequence, or by product number, when all records follow a product-number sequence.

Direct-access file organization is especially important when several files are to be opened at the same time in processing. As Figure 3–7 shows, a multiple file approach to processing leads to reading from two master files, updating (reading from and writing to) a salesperson master file, and writing to an invoice transaction file. In this example, an invoice record is enlarged by transferring information from customer and product master files, both of which are direct-access disk files. After the transfer is made, the enlarged record is added to the invoice transaction file. The updating of the salesperson master file is another result of processing. In this instance, the customer master file indicates the number of the salesperson assigned to the customer's account. This information, combined with the dollar amount of the sale, is used to update the salesperson master file.

Updating several files concurrently requires that some files be organized to permit direct access to stored records. However, it does not mean that all files must be

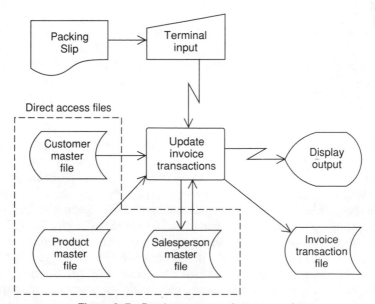

Figure 3–7 Database approach to processing

organized in this way. In the last example, the reading of a single customer record and a single product record requires direct-access organization, as does the update of the salesperson master file. The mere writing of a record to the invoice transaction file, however, suggests that this file can be organized sequentially.

Relational database management systems have an added condition that all records stored in files be of fixed length. This condition simplifies the direct access and manipulation of individual records. Later in the text we provide examples of the relational system.

File-Updating Procedures

After determining what types of data are to be stored on computer files and how files are to be organized, the systems designer must prepare file-updating procedures. These are similar to data- entry procedures. They feature easy-to-use file-processing menus, combined with sets of commands. A *file-processing menu* is much like a program-processing menu, except that it shows what actions can be taken to change the contents of a direct-access file. The following menu, for example, was developed to modify a membership master file.

```
MEMBERSHIP FILE PROCESSING

INSERT NEW MEMBER ACCOUNT
MOVE TO MEMBER ACCOUNT
MOVE TO NEXT ACCOUNT
CHANGE MEMBER ACCOUNT
DELETE MEMBER ACCOUNT

RETURN
```

This menu is activated by highlighting one of the choices shown. If the operator responds with *Move to a member account*, this selection commands the computer to ask initially for an account number. Once the number is known, the computer either locates and displays the account or indicates that the account cannot be found.

Besides file-processing procedures, the systems analyst must design *file-backup procedures*, which make it possible to restore processing in case of a total or partial systems failure. As Figure 3–8 shows, three different processing runs are associated with backing up a master file. The first run updates the member master file and creates a change file. The second run creates a member change tape backup file and a change listing that shows the contents of master-file records before and after they were modified. Finally, the third run creates a tape backup file and a master-file register that lists all records currently stored on the master file. Together, the tape backup of the master file and the change file permit a fourth processing run to be scheduled, if needed. This run restores processing—it permits another member master direct-access file to be built.

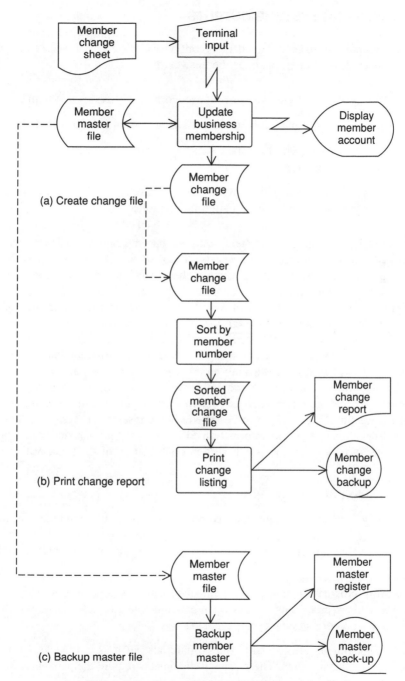

Figure 3–8 File-backup processing procedures

3-3   DESIGNING SYSTEMS OUTPUTS

Systems outputs must be designed to permit visual review of processed results. With outputs, several questions must be answered:

- What types of information will be needed by the users of a system?

- How should information be presented? How should it be distributed?

- Will specialized forms of output, such as computer-output microfilm or audio response, be required?

- Is any information sensitive? Who should receive sensitive information? How will access to sensitive information be controlled?

Historically, the design of systems outputs has meant the design of printed business listings, documents, and reports. Today, however, video display output is being used with increasing frequency. The advantage of a soft-copy display over hard-copy is that information can be retrieved from computer files, inspected, manipulated, and then discarded or saved, depending on the importance of the display. In some information retrieval systems, such as a customer shipping inquiry system, an inquiry is made to determine if a customer's shipment has been made. Once the answer to the inquiry has been displayed, the information is discarded. In other retrieval systems, such as a hotel-motel reservation system, an inquiry is made to determine the availability of a room. If a room is available, it can be assigned to a customer, and the information associated with the reservation (customer name, room number, and room rate) can be saved. Some reservation systems allow the terminal operator to transmit information to a computer printer stationed nearby. The printer provides customers with written confirmation of their reservations.

Classification of Output

In defining output requirements, computer-printed and computer-displayed reporting requirements must be kept separate. Three primary classifications for computer-printed information are registers, action documents, and summary reports.

Registers provide a complete, printed, historical record of all transactions that are generated by processing. A payroll register is one example. It shows all the detail used in preparing employee paychecks.

Action documents are formal business materials, such as paychecks, customer invoices, and packing slips. These printed documents require the persons receiving them to do something—to take some action.

Summary reports show consolidated totals. These reports *aggregate* (pull together) the detail provided in registers to highlight important features, such as exceptions, or to show subtotals and totals.

Run Date: XX/XX/XX   Billing Analysis
Group Business Analysis Summary

------------- Activity -------------		--- Month-To-Date ---		----- Year-To-Date -----	
No.	Description	Amt-Billed	%-Total	Amt-Billed	%-Total
10	Civil Litigation				
10-1	Matrimonial	$26,544	27%	$178,264	29%
10-2	Contracts	8,554	09	48,324	08
10-3	Bankruptcies	12,102	13	68,612	11
10-4	Arbitration	4,600	05	28,900	05
	Total Civil Litigation	$51,800	54%	$324,100	53%
20	Real Estate				
20-1	Commercial	$3,250	03%	$23,000	04%
20-2	Residential	1,230	01	7,440	01
	Total Real Estate	$4,480	04%	$30,440	05%
30	Criminal Litigation				
30-1	Felonies	$ 9,560	10%	$ 52,335	09%
30-2	Juvenile	3,210	03	24,635	04
30-3	Mental Commitment	530	01	2,260	00
	Total Criminal Estates	$13,300	14%	$79,230	13%
40	Estates				
40-1	Estate Planning	$10,496	11%	$ 67,976	11%
40-2	Estate Administration	13,560	14	87,352	14
	Total Estates	$24,056	25%	$155,328	25%
50	Corporate				
50-1	Contracts	$ 895	01%	$ 6,872	11%
50-2	Bankruptcies	2,143	02	14,858	03
	Total Corporate	$ 3,038	03%	$ 21,730	04%
	Company Totals	$96,674	100%	$610,828	100%

Figure 3–9 Summary report with subtotals

Figure 3–9 illustrates a report with subtotals summary report. Transaction details are aggregated by month-to-date and year-to-date to show types of litigation, real estate, estates, and corporate activities. These activities represent different departments of a legal firm. Besides showing subtotals by type of activity, the report shows company totals at the bottom of the form. This particular report can be interpreted in several ways. For example, civil, rather than criminal, litigation provides the greater level of billable dollar totals.

Besides computer-printed output classifications, there are different classes of computer-displayed information. Two of these are fixed-form and free-form displays.

Fixed-form displays are permanent parts of a processing design. They are used when hard copy is not required and when managers prefer visual results. Figure 3–10 illustrates three display pages to show how the computer-printed summary report with subtotals might be displayed. Displays (a) and (b) provide the user with two summary pages, showing month-to-date and year-to-date billable totals. Display screen (c) shows the first of six more detailed pages. These pages provide a more detailed breakdown of departmental billable totals. The user is able to move from one page to another by pressing the keyboard Return key.

Free-form displays are variable parts of a processing design. These ad hoc displays are designed by the user rather than by a systems designer. The user retrieves and manipulates information, visually reviewing the results on the screen. With a free-form display option, for example, the user might perform different types of billing analyses. Consider the following output instructions:

```
WOULD YOU LIKE TO PERFORM A BILLING ANALYSIS? (Y OR N) Y
WHAT TYPE OF BILLING ANALYSIS?

     A. BY DEPARTMENT
     B. BY ATTORNEY
     C. BY CLIENT
     D. EXIT

ENTER SELECTION HERE: A
```

```
WHICH ACTIVITIES ARE TO BE DISPLAYED?

     A. GROUP HEADINGS ONLY
     B. ALL ACTIVITIES
     C. SELECTED ACTIVITIES
     D. EXIT

ENTER SELECTION HERE: C
```

```
WHAT TYPE OF OUTPUT IS DESIRED?

     A. TABULAR
     B. GRAPHIC
     C. EXIT

ENTER SELECTION HERE: B
```

```
RUN DATE:  XX/XX/XX                        BILLING ANALYSIS
                                             PAGE 1 OF 2
GROUP BUSINESS ANALYSIS SUMMARY
------------ ACTIVITY ------------     ----- MONTH-TO-DATE -----
  NO.          DESCRIPTION            AMT-BILLED      %-TOTAL

   10     CIVIL LITIGATION             $51,800         54%
   20     REAL ESTATE                    4,480         04
   30     CRIMINAL LITIGATION           13,300         14
   40     ESTATES                       24,056         25
   50     CORPORATE                      3,038         03

          COMPANY TOTALS               $96,674        100%

PRESS RETURN TO CONTINUE
```

(a)   Summary display page 1

```
RUN DATE:  XX/XX/XX                        BILLING ANALYSIS
                                             PAGE 2 OF 2
GROUP BUSINESS ANALYSIS SUMMARY
------------ ACTIVITY ------------     -------YEAR-TO-DATE-------
  NO.          DESCRIPTION            AMT-BILLED      %-TOTAL

   10     CIVIL LITIGATION            $324,100         53%
   20     REAL ESTATE                   30,440         05
   30     CRIMINAL LITIGATION           79,230         13
   40     ESTATES                      155,328         25
   50     CORPORATE                     21,730         04

          COMPANY TOTALS              $610,828        100%

PRESS RETURN TO CONTINUE
```

(b)   Summary display page 2

```
RUN DATE:  XX/XX/XX                        BILLING ANALYSIS
                                             PAGE 1 OF 6
ITEM BUSINESS ANALYSIS SUMMARY
---------------- ACTIVITY ----------------  ----- MONTH-TO-DATE -----
  NO.          DESCRIPTION            AMT-BILLED      %-TOTAL

   10     CIVIL LITIGATION

  10-1    MATRIMONIAL                  $26,544         27%
  10-2    CONTRACTS                      8,554         09
  10-3    BANKRUPTCIES                  12,102         13
  10-4    ARBITRATION                    4,600         05

          TOTAL CIVIL LITIGATION       $51,800         54%

PRESS RETURN TO CONTINUE
```

(c)   Detail display page 1

Figure 3–10 Summary report display pages

As this interactive dialogue suggests. each user response tells the computer what to do next. When the user enters *C* for *Selected activities*, the computer brings into processing a list of activities and asks the user to make a selection from the list. Likewise, when selection *B*, for *Graphic*, is indicated, the computer displays the existing types of graphic manipulation. The user might be required to specify whether a pie chart, a bar chart, or a distribution curve is desired.

Output Procedures

Like data-entry procedures, systems outputs are designed by using special layout sheets or by printing mockups of display-screen pages. As an example, Figure 3–11 illustrates a mockup of a customer list register. This report shows that space will be provided to print the customer name and contact, up to three addresses, the sales-person code, the customer phone number, and other customer comments. The date the customer started doing business with the company ("First-date") and the frequency with which statements are to be mailed ("Stmt-freq") are also to be printed.

```
Date: 99/99/99        *Your company name prints here*      #9999  Page 9999
                         C  U  S  T  O  M  E  R

Starting customer:  "First"
Ending customer:    "Last"
------------------------------------------------------------------------------
Name                    Address-1              Sales        First-date
Contact                 Address-2              Phone        Stmnt-freq
                        Address-3              Comment
------------------------------------------------------------------------------

XXXXXXXXXXXXXXXXXXXXXXXX XXXXXXXXXXXXXXXXXXXXXXXX XXX              99/99/99
XXXXXXXXXXXXXXX          XXXXXXXXXXXXXXXXXXXXXXXX 999-999-9999    XXXXXXXXX
                         XXXXXXXXXXXXXXXXXXXXXXXX XXXXXXXXXXXXXXXXXXXXXXXX

XXXXXXXXXXXXXXXXXXXXXXXX XXXXXXXXXXXXXXXXXXXXXXXX XXX              99/99/99
XXXXXXXXXXXXXXX          XXXXXXXXXXXXXXXXXXXXXXXX 999-999-9999    XXXXXXXXX
                         XXXXXXXXXXXXXXXXXXXXXXXX XXXXXXXXXXXXXXXXXXXXXXXX

XXXXXXXXXXXXXXXXXXXXXXXX XXXXXXXXXXXXXXXXXXXXXXXX XXX              99/99/99
XXXXXXXXXXXXXXX          XXXXXXXXXXXXXXXXXXXXXXXX 999-999-9999    XXXXXXXXX
                         XXXXXXXXXXXXXXXXXXXXXXXX XXXXXXXXXXXXXXXXXXXXXXXX

XXXXXXXXXXXXXXXXXXXXXXXX XXXXXXXXXXXXXXXXXXXXXXXX XXX              99/99/99
XXXXXXXXXXXXXXX          XXXXXXXXXXXXXXXXXXXXXXXX 999-999-9999    XXXXXXXXX
                         XXXXXXXXXXXXXXXXXXXXXXXX XXXXXXXXXXXXXXXXXXXXXXXX

XXXXXXXXXXXXXXXXXXXXXXXX XXXXXXXXXXXXXXXXXXXXXXXX XXX              99/99/99
XXXXXXXXXXXXXXX          XXXXXXXXXXXXXXXXXXXXXXXX 999-999-9999    XXXXXXXXX
                         XXXXXXXXXXXXXXXXXXXXXXXX XXXXXXXXXXXXXXXXXXXXXXXX

XXXXXXXXXXXXXXXXXXXXXXXX XXXXXXXXXXXXXXXXXXXXXXXX XXX              99/99/99
XXXXXXXXXXXXXXX          XXXXXXXXXXXXXXXXXXXXXXXX 999-999-9999    XXXXXXXXX
                         XXXXXXXXXXXXXXXXXXXXXXXX XXXXXXXXXXXXXXXXXXXXXXXX

    99 customers

                       --End of Report--
```

Figure 3–11   Mockup of customer list register

Besides printed mockups, *printed-spacing charts* are used to illustrate the layout of a printed listing, document, or report. This type of chart indicates the print positions for each item to be printed and the various document headings and subheadings. It provides room to indicate carriage-control requirements for printing continuous forms.

Most computer-printed output can be produced directly from a transaction or summary file, provided that the sequence of the file is suitable. When this is not the case, an output procedure is required to specify how the file is to be sorted. The procedure defines the steps leading to the creation of a *print file*—a file organized in the same sequence as that of a printed report.

Because a print-processing run can require several hours to complete, print procedures include provisions to guard against delays and *reruns* (the rerunning of the entire processing run). One such provision is the ability to *restart* printing from a point shortly before where an error occurred, instead of beginning the process running again from the very start. This provision saves several hours of computer time and helps to minimize the investment in computer printing. Besides restart, another provision is to establish *checkpoints* in processing. Checkpoints are points at which printed subtotals are to be reviewed to determine if they are correct. If they are, processing is continued.

In designing video-display output, system designers must lay out the headings and typical content of each display. In this instance, video display mockups of screen mats can be made (see Figure 3–4). Mockups involve designing the display on the computer terminal and printing the entire screen once the design is complete.

Besides restart provisions, discontinue-output-processing provisions are built into each output processing selection. For example, each set of processing instructions generally contains either the commands *Exit* or *Return to main menu*. Either choice returns processing to an earlier point or discontinues processing. Likewise, most output procedures provide for some emergency command sequence. The command *Control-Q* (meaning to quit), for example, is a common discontinue-processing command.

Output procedures must also be designed to limit access to processing. These restrictions are accomplished with user account codes and passwords. To receive output, the user is required to *log on*, following a specific series of steps. First, he or she is required to key in an *account code*—a numeric code that has been previously assigned. This code is checked against a master-account-code file to verify that the user's code is legitimate. Second, the user is required to key in a *password*—an alphanumeric or alphabetic code. This second code is checked against a password master file. If the password does not agree with the password on file and assigned to the account code, the user is prohibited from gaining access to the computer.

REVIEW QUESTIONS

8. What three commonsense rules should be followed in the design of computer files?

9. What file design guidelines are important to the systems designer?

10. What is the difference between direct and sequential file organization?

11. How does a program-processing menu differ from a file-processing menu?

12. Why are file-backup procedures needed?

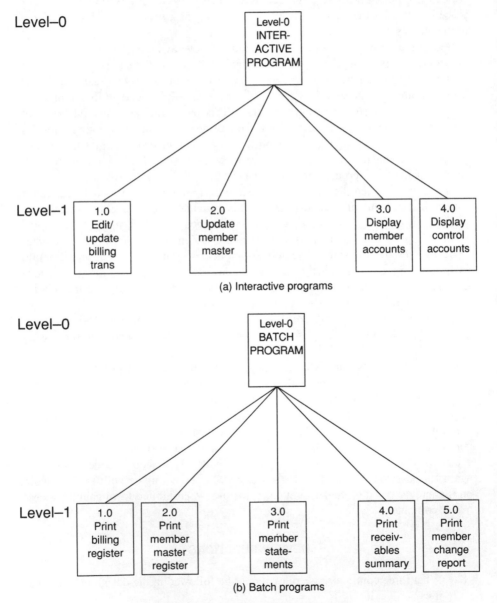

(a) Interactive programs

(b) Batch programs

Figure 3–12 Systems organization chart

13. Name the three classes of computer-printed output.

14. What is the difference between fixed-form and free-form displays?

3-4 DESIGNING COMPUTER PROGRAMS

Prior to the design of the processing runs for an online business computer application, the systems analyst must identify the types of computer programs required by the interactive and by the batch portions of processing and the functional parts or *modules* of each program. As stated in Chapter 2, seven types of computer programs are placed in various combinations in the construction of a business computer application. Three of these seven are used primarily for interactive processing; four of the seven are used for batch processing. Edit and update programs, for example, are typically designed for the interactive portion of processing; display programs are used exclusively in interactive processing. Register, action-document, summary, and change-report programs represent different types of computer-print programs common to the batch portion of processing.

Systems Organization Chart

A systems organization chart shows the type of computer programs to be written for a business computer application, the function of each in relation to processing, and whether a program is to be written for the interactive or the batch portion of processing. As Figure 3–12 shows, a systems organization chart consists of three levels. Level 0 indicates whether processing is interactive or batch. Level 1 provides the names of the computer programs designed for the application. The interactive portion consists of four programs, beginning with edit/update billing transactions; the batch portion consists of five programs, beginning with print billing register.

Program-Processing Menu

The design of the program-processing menu is based on the completed systems organization chart. It shows how a specific computer program is selected and executed. Using the chart in Figure 3–12, a systems designer would prepare the following menus:

MEMBERSHIP TRANSACTION

    ENTER MEMBER CHARGES
    UPDATE MEMBER MASTER
    DISPLAY MEMBER ACCOUNT
    DISPLAY CONTROL TOTALS

    RETURN

```
MEMBERSHIP REPORTS

    BILLING REGISTER
    MEMBER REGISTER
    STATEMENTS
    RECEIVABLES SUMMARY
    MEMBER CHANGE REPORT

    RETURN
```

Program Structure Charts

The final component of program design is the creation of detailed structure charts. These charts show the modules to be designed, coded, and documented for each computer program. Figure 3–13 illustrates a simplified program structure chart for program 1, *Print billing register*. At level 1.0, the top level, one module represents the entire computer program. Level 1.1, the next lower level, divides the *Print transaction totals* function into three finer modules: *Read billing transaction*, *Sum transaction*, and *Print report lines*. Finally, level 1.1.3 contains the modules needed to print the report lines.

A structure chart, such as the one shown, is sometimes called a *visual table of contents*, or VTOC. Its development features a *top-down design*. The system of charts divides a computer application into processing functions followed by computer programs for each function. Each computer program is further defined by functions, such as *Print transaction totals*. These functions are divided into sets of subordinate modules.

3-5 DESIGNING PROCESSING CONTROLS

A difficult yet most important phase of systems design is the preparation of processing controls. Consider a few of the reasons for processing controls:

- to verify that all data have been processed
- to block or trap faulty data from entry into processing
- to be able to reconstruct information if computer files are destroyed
- to prohibit tampering with information by unauthorized individuals
- to prevent employee fraud, embezzlement, and theft

With online systems, the need for controls in processing is especially critical. Since data input, processing, and output are oftentimes directed by users at remote locations, control techniques must determine that all records (and only the intended records) are processed and that only authorized people are able to gain access to processing.

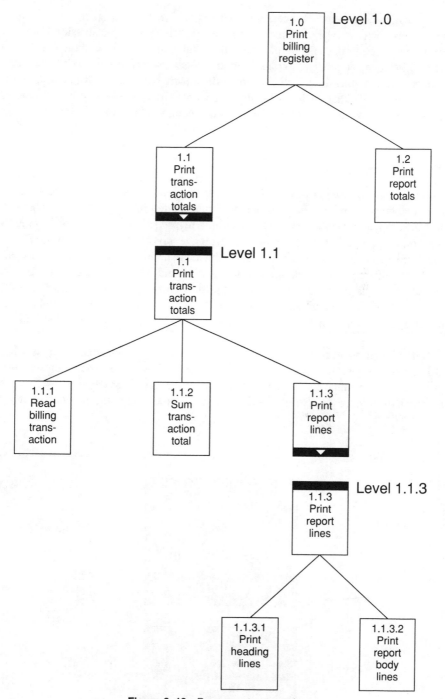

Figure 3–13 Program structure chart

In designing a set of processing controls, a systems designer must include provisions for four types: source-document controls, input transmission controls, programmed controls, and output controls. With online designs, both batch and transaction control procedures are needed. *Batch control procedures* verify that counts and amounts in a batch of records are in balance. *Transaction control procedures* verify that each transaction is accurate and complete. Where possible, these controls test to verify that counts and amounts within the transaction are in balance.

Source-Document Controls

Source-document controls involve matching the counts and amounts recorded on source documents with the counts and amounts entered into processing. Both batch and interactive transaction control procedures help verify that counts and amounts are correct. For example, assume that the five invoice totals shown in Figure 3–14 are to be entered into processing. Next assume that, before these invoice totals are entered, the *batch-balance totals* of 5 and $1,561.15 are keyed in. By keying in the batch-balance totals first, the data-entry operator is able to sum the individual invoice counts and amounts and to compare these summed totals to the batch-balance totals. In effect, the computer "balances back" to the batch-balance totals.

Batch balances work well with groups of transactions, but what happens when only a single transaction is entered into processing? Another example helps answer this question. Assume that five line items are to be keyed (see Figure 3–15). Two *transaction-balance totals* become important in processing: the number of items

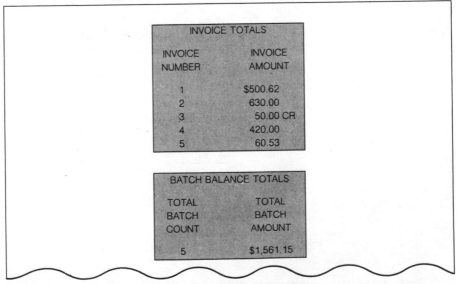

Figure 3–14   Batch balance control

ordered (5) and the total quantity ordered (1,560). In this case, the data-entry operator would key in both the line-item amount and the total item amount. Unless the computer is able to balance back the summed line item totals to the transaction-control totals, the keyed-in data will be seen to be in error.

Input Transmission Controls

Input transmission controls include procedures to verify that data transmission is accurate and complete. Most input controls are built into the computer system, as integral parts of computer terminals and of data communications software. Pressing the terminal key marked Return, for example, tells the computer that a message has ended.

Additional input controls are usually designed for such purposes as protecting against unauthorized access to the computer. As was discussed earlier, user account codes and passwords are common methods of attempting to stop unauthorized access to processing. Unless both the account code and the password agree with an on-file code and password, access to processing is prohibited.

Logging data transmission is another form of input control. Online computer systems keep a journal tape or disk of all transactions entered into processing from remote locations. Should problems in processing or transmission be detected, this procedure—known as *journaling*—permits recovery of transmission, from the file copy. Online cash registers similarly feature small cassette tapes to record daily sales transactions. After the cash register has been closed for the day, the tape is sent to the company's internal audit group, where it is used to isolate the reasons for any differences that appear in the daily cash audit.

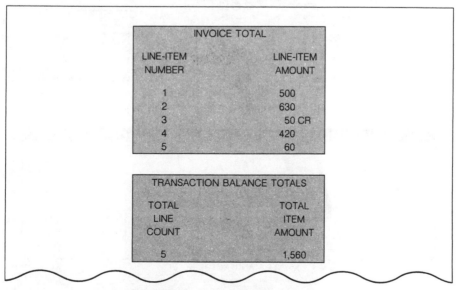

Figure 3–15 Transaction balance control

Programmed Controls

Programmed controls are procedures written into computer programs. Some programmed controls block or trap data in error from entering processing. These controls are generally written into edit and update programs, where tests such as mixed-mode tests, limit tests, and check-digit tests are conducted on data transmitted as input. Other programmed controls verify that files can be opened and the correct types of data can be read. Finally, programmed controls maintain file-balance procedures that store beginning and ending balances of record counts and amounts. Similar to batch-balance totals (see Figure 3–14), *file-balance totals* indicate the number of records stored on a file and the summed value of a particular field, such as the number of courses taken or the current payroll total. These totals allow those responsible for controlling a business computer application to determine whether the records stored on file are fully and accurately accounted for.

Output Controls

Output Controls are designed to prevent unauthorized access to computer output and to ensure that output transmission is accurate and complete. Once again, typical output control techniques employ user account codes and passwords. A special type of output control uses printed registers and voided action documents. An example helps clarify the importance of these printed materials.

Figure 3–16   Safety II check

Imagine that you are designing a computer system to process personal checks. After all outstanding bills are entered, your design permits you to decide which bills to pay. Before writing checks for these bills, however, you find it necessary to produce a check register. The register shows the beginning check balance, the name of the person or company and the check amount for each check to be written, the ending check balance, and the total dollar amount for which checks are to be written. After printing the register, it must be reviewed to make sure that all check data have been processed fully. Only following this review are checks printed.

In the design of the check print procedure, the first step produces a *voided check* to show the beginning check balance. The word *void* is clearly printed across the face of the check. Next, personal checks are printed. After the last check is printed, a second voided check is produced. This check shows the ending check balance, the number of checks written, and the total dollar amount for which checks were written. These totals, together with the beginning check balance, are compared with those printed on the check register. Before any personal checks are endorsed and mailed, the number of checks printed (the total batch count) and their dollar amount (the total batch amount) must be in balance.

Still another type of output control involves the use of output materials that contain special properties. For example, Figure 3–16 shows a check that cannot be photocopied for fraudulent use. If a person does photocopy the check, the word

Figure 3–17 Photocopy of Safety II check

COPY becomes visible on the copy (see Figure 3–17). Special output materials such as these discourage attempts by employees to embezzle funds from a company.

REVIEW QUESTIONS

15. With online systems, explain the procedures designed to control access to the computer.

16. What information is placed on a systems organization chart?

17. How does a program structure chart differ from a systems organization chart?

18. Why must different types of processing controls be designed?

19. Name the four types of processing controls.

20. Why is journaling important?

REVIEW OF IMPORTANT IDEAS

Several tasks are undertaken by a systems designer in preparing written specifications for an online business computer application. Designing systems input, for instance, requires that the designer first determine which data elements are required in processing. Following this, the designer must decide which data must be keyed into processing, stored on computer files, and computed. An important objective in designing input procedures is to minimize the number of keystrokes. This is done by designing data-entry display screens with operator efficiency in mind and by properly using special data-input instruments, such as light pens and hand-held optical scanners.

Designing computer files is based on the knowledge of what data are to be stored. In design, several rules and guidelines should be followed. The designer should not attempt to place in a computer file data that cannot be easily revised, justified, or reviewed. The designer must use care in record layout. He or she must determine how each file is to be organized and develop efficient file-processing menus and file-backup procedures.

Designing systems output requires that the designer deal with computer-printed and computer-displayed materials. Computer-printed information includes registers, action documents, and summary reports. These are developed using report mockups and printer-spacing charts. Computer-displayed information includes fixed- and free-form displays. These designs are developed by making screen mockups and printing these screens.

Designing computer programs requires that the designer specify the interactive and batch features of the design. Following this, the systems organization chart is constructed to show the computer programs to be written and their functions relative to the overall design. The designer also shows the computer program modules to be designed. Program structure charts illustrate the hierarchy of modules within a computer program.

Designing processing controls requires an appreciation of what numeric and logical checks are needed to verify the accuracy of processed data and to prevent unauthorized use of computer systems. Source-document and programmed procedures are most effective in determining whether processed data are accurate and complete. Input and output control procedures are used extensively to prevent unauthorized use of computer systems.

KEY WORDS

Systems design

Systems designer

Input-analysis form

Record-analysis form

Function key

Program-processing menu

Command

Window

Account code

Record code

Sort key

Blocking

Direct file organization

Sequential file organization

Indexed-sequential file organization

File-processing menu

File-backup procedure

Fixed-form display

Free-form display

Printer spacing chart

Print file

Restart

Password

Systems organization chart

Program structure chart

Batch-control procedure

Transaction-control procedure

Journaling

EXERCISES

1. For each of the following, indicate what systems design feature has been overlooked.

   (a) A business discovers that a change can be made to a customer's billing account online, but once added, it cannot be corrected or adjusted. This situation has contributed to large suspense files. For example, if an incorrect charge is added to a customer's account, the account must be transferred from a customer master file to a suspended records file. To correct this problem, a batch processing run is required. This run restores the account to its original amount.

   (b) Cash totals transmitted from a remote processing station to a central office look suspicious. Normally, cash sales should be higher than the totals indicated. Unfortunately, there is no way to determine whether someone is stealing from the company.

   (c) The instructions for a video-display program-processing menu have tended to cause problems. If the terminal operator makes an incorrect selection, several additional pages must be t̲   ̇ the computer program finally returns to the menu a seco

2. Systems designers are often criticized for giving too much emphasis to technical factors and too little to human factors. Suppose this criticism is true. How might designers give more emphasis to human factors?

3. Batch- and transaction-balance controls, such as those shown on Figures 3–14 and 3–15, are often criticized because they require too much clerical work. Suppose a supervisor asks: "Why do we need to total by hand the line-items ordered? Why not have the computer do this instead?" How would you respond to these questions?

4. Compare menu-driven designs to language-driven designs. Describe several real-life settings in which a menu-driven design is more appropriate. Describe several settings in which a language-driven design is more appropriate. Should some software products be both menu- and language-driven? Explain.

5. Using the backup files shown in Figure 3–8, draw a system flowchart to depict how a new master file can be built if the old file is lost or destroyed.

6. Suppose the lower and side portions of Figure 3–4 can be used to open up two additional windows to help with data entry. What types of information might be placed in these additional windows?

7. Most interactive designs make provisions for both fixed- and free-form screen designs. Why are both types required?

8. Study the program shown in Figures 3–12 (a) and (b). Which programs are the edit programs? Update programs? Display programs? Register programs? Action-document programs? Summary programs? Change-report programs?

DISCUSSION QUESTIONS

1. In preparing the design of an online business computer application, what factors become important in

(a) designing systems input?

(b) designing computer files?

(c) designing systems output?

(d) designing computer programs?

(e) designing processing controls?

2. In the study of online business computer applications, why is it important to understand the steps that are central to these five design tasks?

4-IN-1 CASE STUDY—LOADING DATA FILES

Now that you have a better understanding of what 4-in-1 is all about, it is time to begin loading master files. An important rule to remember is that master files must be ready before processing can begin.

Adding Customer Master File Information

Information must be added to the customer master file before customers can be billed. To add customer data to 4-in-1, do the following:

1. From the main menu, type **7** and press ENTER.

2. From the maintain customer data menu, type **1**, *Add customers*. Press ENTER.

3. Using the customer data shown in Figure 3–18, follow the steps shown below. If you make a mistake, you can use the ↑ on your keyboard to go back to a previous field or the ↓ to move forward.

   a. Type the first business name shown and press ENTER. Use only capital letters in typing this name.

   b. Enter the address next. Place the street name on one line, the city on the second line, and the state and zip code on the third line.

   c. Type the name of the person to contact at the customer's location.

   d. Type the phone number of the customer.

   e. Type the date when you first started doing business with the customer. (Press return.)

   f. Enter additional information about the customer (up to 25 characters) in the comment field.

   g. Enter the initials of the salesperson.

A and J Enterprises Customer List		
1 Name	LAWNS-ARE-GREEN	FARMERS-COOP
2 Address-1	1225 Fairview Lane	P.O. Box 6700
3 Address-2	Prettyville	Junction City
4 Address-3	CA 95000	OR 97000
5 Contact	Mary Rodgers	Larry Contrary
6 Phone #	408-777-9999	503-686-9999
7 First date	10197	10197
8 Comment	Good potential customer	Start up business
9 Salesman	JPR	JPR
10 Statement frequency	M	M

Figure 3–18 The A and J Enterprise

h. Enter **M** to designate that you plan to bill the customer on a monthly basis. The choices are W for weekly, B for biweekly, M for monthly, Q for quarterly, and O for other.

4. After the statement frequency field is keyed, the message *Field number to change?* will appear. Press ENTER to add the new customer to the customer master file.

5. Add the second customer shown on Figure 3–18 to the file using the same procedure.

6. Press TAB to return to the maintain customer data menu.

Changing Customer Master File Information

After adding customer information to a file, you can review and change it, if necessary, using the change function. Do the following:

1. From the maintain customer data menu, type **2**, *Change customers*, and press ENTER. A screen appears, asking you to enter the name of the customer.

2. Type **LAWNS** and press ENTER to display the LAWNS-ARE-GREEN account.

3. Type **6** when asked, *Field number to change?* Press ENTER.

4. Type a new telephone number, **408-787-9999**, and press ENTER.

5. Press ENTER when asked, *Field number to change?*

6. Press TAB to return to the maintain customer data menu.

Printing the Contents of the Customer Master File

Once all accounts have been added to the customer master file, its contents can be printed. To print the customer master file register, do the following:

1. From the maintain customer data menu, type **4**, *Print customer list*, and press ENTER. A screen appears, asking you to enter the name of the first customer to print.

2. Press F1 and ENTER to indicate the first customer on file.

3. Press F1 and ENTER to indicate the last customer on file.

4. When asked, *Any change?* press ENTER.

5. When asked, *Display this report?* press ENTER.

6. After the report is printed, press TAB to return to the main menu.

Adding Company Supplier (Vendor) Master File Information

Vendors (companies that supply goods to a company) must be added to the vendor master file before goods and services can be ordered. To add vendor information to 4-in-1, do the following:

1. From the main menu, type **13** and press ENTER.

2. From the maintain vendor data menu, enter **1**, *Add vendors*. Press ENTER.

3. Using the vendor data shown in Figure 3–19, follow the steps shown below. If you make a mistake, you can use the ↑ on your keyboard to go back to a previous field or the ↓ to move forward.

   a. Type the first vendor name shown and press ENTER. Use only capital letters in typing this name.

   b. Enter the address next. Place the street name on one line, the city on the second line, and the state and zip code on the third line.

   c. Type the name of the person to contact at the vendor's location.

   d. Type the phone number of the vendor.

   e. Type the date when you first started doing business with the vendor.

   f. Enter additional information about the vendor (up to 25 characters) in the comment field.

   g. Enter the G/L number so that you automatically assign purchases from this vendor to this account at the time purchases enter processing. Type the first four digits and press ENTER. Then add the last three digits.

A and J Enterprises Vendor List

1 Name	A AND P CHEMICALS	JXX TOOLS AND SUPPLIES
2 Address-1	1662 Route 66	Franklin Building
3 Address-2	Carsonville	Daysroad
4 Address-3	NH 03000	NJ 07600
5 Contact	Marty Ford	Joan Fairday
6 Phone #	603-224-9999	201-590-9999
7 First date	10197	10197
8 Comment	Solid supplier	Temporary supplier
9 Default exp acct	5010-000	5020-000

Figure 3–19   The A and J Enterprises vendor list

4. After the G/L number is keyed, the message *Field number to change?* will appear. Press ENTER to add the new vendor to the vendor master file.

5. Add the second vendor shown on Figure 3–19 to the file using the same procedure.

6. Press TAB to return to the main menu.

Printing the Contents of the Vendor Master File

Once all accounts have been added to the vendor master file, its contents can be printed. To print the vendor master file register, do the following:

1. From the maintain vendor data menu, type **4**, *Print vendor list*, and press ENTER. A screen appears, asking you to enter the name of the first vendor to print.

2. Press F1 and ENTER to indicate the first vendor on file.

3. Press F1 and ENTER to indicate the last vendor on file.

4. When asked, *Any change?* press ENTER.

5. When asked, *Display this report?* press ENTER.

6. After the report is printed, press TAB to return to the main menu.

7. Press TAB to exit the software.

QUESTIONS

1. Compare the add customer data procedure to the add vendor data procedure. In what ways are they similar? How do they differ?

2. Compare the customer and vendor file-processing commands provided by 4-in-1 to the file-processing command described in the chapter. In what ways are they similar? How do they differ?

3. Why is it important to create master files in advance of processing?

4. Suppose you need to change a vendor's record. What procedure is required?

5. Examine the chart of accounts printed for the last chapter. Why were accounts 5010-000 and 5020-000 selected as G/L accounts for the two suppliers? What would happen if there were 50 suppliers?

⫿⫿

RECEIVABLES
APPLICATIONS

Most businesses carry their customers "on account." That is, when a sale is made, credit is extended to the customer and the dollar amount of the credit is added to the customer's account. This practice of extending credit to customers requires careful management. A business cannot permit its outstanding receivables (customer account balances) to reach levels that place the firm in a *cash poor* position. Instead, a business must constantly work to reduce its receivables to a reasonable level. This level should be consistent with the terms and conditions specified by the credit arrangements the business sets for its customers.

Besides carrying customers on account, most business firms use the *accrual method* of accounting for sales. With this method, a sale is counted as soon as goods and services are delivered, not when actual payment is received from the customer. The accrual method contrasts with the *cash method*. Under the cash method, a sale is counted only when a cash payment is received from the customer.

In Part II, the first of four sets of three computer applications, we will examine the processing of accounts-receivable (A/R) information. This part of the business cycle begins with billing customers for goods shipped and continues with processing customer payments. As this section demonstrates, online designs shorten the time required to bill customers, to process customer payments, and to reconcile outstanding account balances. Moreover, these receivables applications improve the accuracy of receivables processing, standardize the processing of account collections, reduce clerical and administrative costs, and permit transactions to be processed where they occur, at the time of sale.

CHAPTER

Customer Invoicing

An *invoice* is a billing statement. It informs customers of the charges for goods and services supplied to them and specifies when payment is due. Whenever a business extends credit to a customer, an invoice must be prepared. The invoice documents the date of sale, the name and address of the customer, the items purchased, the charges for the merchandise, and the terms and condition of payment. If these charges are not paid within the period specified by the invoice, a second billing statement, the *monthly statement*, is prepared. This second statement is a summary billing statement. It reminds a customer that an invoice has not been paid. Whereas an invoice provides a complete description of the charges of each item shipped to a customer, a monthly statement provides only a summary of outstanding invoice charges.

An invoice is not required when a company receives cash for merchandise at the time of the sale or when it accepts a bank or company credit card instead of cash payment. When cash is received, a sales receipt is usually prepared. Handing the receipt to the customer completes a cash sales transaction. When a credit card is accepted, a *sales draft* (a draw on an established line of personal credit) is prepared. Customers are not expected to make payment on the sales draft. Instead, they are to wait until a monthly statement is sent. Credit card monthly statements list, in summary form, all outstanding charges. These cards are used almost exclusively in retailing, however; they are not common to wholesaling or to manufacturing, where invoices are used. This distinction should clarify why customer invoicing is so important to many large business firms.

This first application chapter describes the features of an online customer invoice application that has been developed for a wholesaler, a business that sells merchandise to a large number of retail establishments. (An online credit card computer application is discussed in the next chapter.) Businesses develop an invoicing application for a variety of reasons other than to produce a printed record of processing and formal invoice statements. For instance, this application can shorten the time between the shipment of goods to customers and the mailing of invoices, reduce the cost of customer billing, cut the number of billing errors, improve processing controls, help to determine sales patterns, and create files for determining which customers and products are the most profitable to a business.

An online design permits checks and balances to be built into the interactive parts of processing. Besides reducing the number of billing errors, these checks and balances block input data in error from entering processing. In addition, an online design typically avoids the problems of transporting billing information to and from a company data center. With distributed processing, for example, data are keyed, inspected, and corrected directly from customer sales and invoicing centers.

4-1   PRELIMINARY OVERVIEW OF PROCESSING

Understanding the primary data flows of the customer invoice system is critical in the study of this computer application. As Figure 4–1 shows, the main inputs to processing consist of shipping summary, product pricing, and customer information; the main outputs are the customer invoice and the invoice accounts receivable (A/R) summary. Let's consider each of these inputs and outputs in more detail.

Inputs to Processing

Of the three main inputs to the customer-invoicing computer application, shipping summary information is the most complex and difficult to understand. For normal shipments, shipping summary documents consist either of a packing slip and a bill of lading or of a document that combines these two features. The *packing slip* is the document packed with the shipment. It shows which items were packed and provides references to the customer order. Consider the five types of information printed on the packing slip:

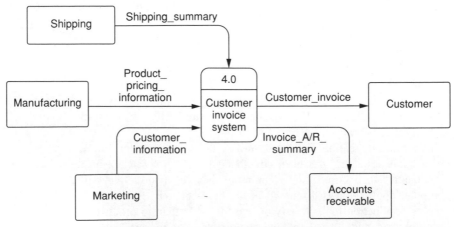

Figure 4–1   The customer invoice system

- *Business order information* documents the business order number (the number assigned by the business to a customer order) and the date of the order.

- *Customer order information* identifies the customer number, customer purchase order (P.O.) number, and any special instructions.

- *Packing information* identifies each product number, and the quantity ordered, shipped, back-ordered, or canceled.

- *Customer information* shows the customer's name and address, customer credit terms, and the salesperson and distributor assigned to a customer's account.

- *Product information* identifies each product by name and describes each product.

As illustrated, some of this information is sent directly from shipping, and other information is collected and sent from manufacturing and from marketing. It is common for information to flow from more than one source in processing a business transaction.

In contrast to a packing slip, the *bill of lading* shows how goods were shipped (UPS, Express Mail, etc.), the charges for shipment and insurance, and the date of the shipment. This document may also summarize the contents of shipment by indicating the number of boxes, parcels, or bags.

Figure 4–2 illustrates a combined packing slip and bill of lading. As indicated, five size-$6\frac{1}{2}$ Little Foxes (Item number 3924) and four size-$8\frac{1}{2}$ Speed Trims (Item number 4410) were ordered and shipped. The completed form is handled as follows: the original copy of this form is sent with the shipping papers that accompany the shipment; and a second copy is packed with the shipment. The business also retains a copy. This copy becomes the main source of input to customer-invoice processing.

Another input to this application (one not shown in Figure 4–1) is *customer return slips*. Return slips resemble packing slips, except that they record the return of merchandise from customers or show differences between the quantity reported as shipped and the quantity indicated by the customer as received. Customer return slips generally provide coded responses to tell why merchandise is being returned. These reasons are often limited to a fixed set of responses, such as wrong color, incorrect size, defective item, or incorrect count. For example, if the five Little Foxes shoes ordered were supposed to be size $9\frac{1}{2}$, not size $6\frac{1}{2}$, the customer would probably return them. Following their return, the business would indicate *incorrect size* as the reason. Return information such as this can be extremely valuable. It tells the business what went wrong and (sometimes) why. The customer-invoicing application is the point in processing to capture this relevant information.

Another input consists of information sorted on computer files. This information is required in calculating invoice charges. It also simplifies the entry of data into processing. Examine Figure 4–3. In creating the invoice record, information from

SOLD TO
Kid Togs
1526 Pearl
Eugene, OR   97402

SHIP TO
Kid Togs
1526 Pearl
Eugene, OR   97402

OUR ORDER NO.
4635

SHIP DATE
11-6-9X

SHIPPED VIA
Truck

CUSTOMER NO.
5264

CUST. P.O. NO.
P32456

SHIPPING WEIGHT
12.4

SHIPPING CHARGES
6.25

ITEM NO.	DESCRIPTION			ORDERED	SHIPPED	B.O.	1	1½	2	2½	3	3½	4	4½	5	5½	6	6½	7	7½	8	8½	9	9½	10	10½	11
				QUANTITY														SIZE RUN										
3924	Little Foxes	B	M	5	5													5										
4410	Speed Trims	R	M	4	4																	4						

TOTALS THIS PAGE

ALL CLAIMS MUST BE MADE WITHIN TEN
(10) DAYS AFTER RECEIPT OF GOODS.

SPECIAL INSTRUCTIONS:

Figure 4–2 Shipping document

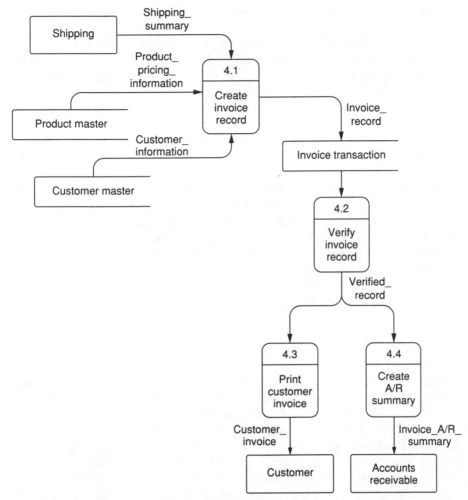

Figure 4–3 Steps required in producing the customer invoice

two files is required: customer information from the customer master file and product pricing information from the product master file.

The *customer master file* contains information on every customer that conducts business with a company. In the processing of customer invoices, the file is used to transfer into processing such information as customer name and address, customer credit terms, and salesperson and distributor numbers. The transfer of information follows the input of the customer account number: the *primary record key*. The advantage of such a transfer should be evident: it is easier to transfer information from a file than to key the information into processing.

A second input file, the *product master file*, contains information on every product sold by a business. The transfer of information such as product name, description, and product price and discount information also simplifies processing.

This transfer follows the entry of the product number: a *second primary record key*.

Before beginning to develop the computer programs required by an application, the systems designer must carefully define the types of data to be keyed into processing, the types to be transferred into processing from computer files, and the types to be computed. Figure 4–4 illustrates the relationships between data sets that are important to customer invoicing. Keyed information begins with the entry of *business order information*: the business order number, the date of the order, and the record code. The *business order number* is a unique number assigned by the business that documents the fact that an order has been received. The date of the shipment provides additional information: it tells when the goods left the business. The record code is used to indicate whether the sale represents a regular or a recurring transaction. A *regular transaction* becomes effective immediately and is limited to a single shipment. A *recurring transaction*, in contrast, occurs over and over again, such as a sale made on the fifth of each month for 10 units of a product. The record code serves another important purpose: it indicates whether a charge or a credit is to be processed.

Next, customer order information, packing information, and general ledger data are brought into processing. Customer order information begins with the customer account number—the key to the customer's records stored on the customer master file. Other customer order information consists of the number and date of the customer's purchase order. Packing information consists of one or more sets of data, as determined by the number of products ordered. Data elements to be keyed include the product number and the breakdown of the quantity ordered versus the quantity shipped. Similar to the customer number, the product number is the key to product records stored on the product master file. After product information, freight charges and insurance charges are keyed to processing. The general ledger distribution indicates how the sale is to be recorded in the general ledger. For example, some companies group sales by product and others group sales by location or division. In addition, there are account codes for such things as sales allowances and miscellaneous sales. Chapters 7 and 15 deal with the subject of distribution of sales information in more detail.

Consider the organization of these two master files. The customer master file begins with the customer account number followed by three record segments. The first, the customer name and address segment, contains identifiers for both sold-to and ship-to names and addresses. In business, goods are often shipped to one location and bills mailed to another location. The second contains customer credit terms: credit limit code, last revision of the customer's credit, and terms of payment. Under terms of payment, one subcode separates retail accounts from commercial accounts. Typically, retail accounts are expected to make payment on receipt of the invoice, whereas commercial accounts are expected to make payment within 30 days. The third segment consists of salesperson/distributor keys. These permit salesperson and distributor numbers to be printed on an invoice or a credit memo. They are better known as *secondary keys* because they allow invoice charges and credits to be transferred to sales summary files, in which data are organized by salesperson and by distributor numbers.

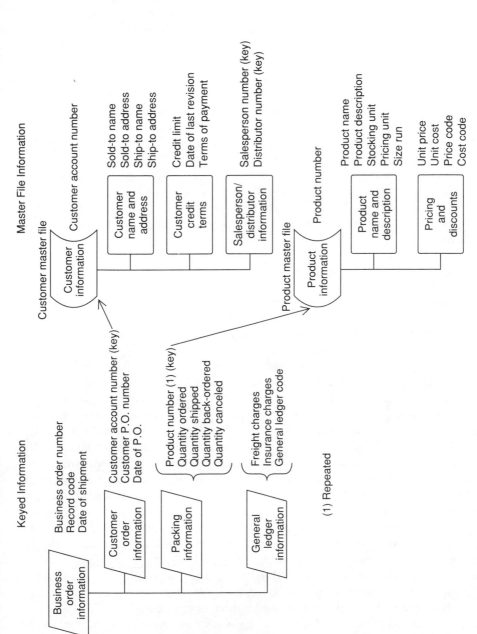

Figure 4-4 Relationships between invoice data sets

The product master file begins with the product number and two record segments. The first segment is the product name and description. The description includes the stocking unit and the pricing unit which refer to the unit of measure (dozen, pound, barrel) for stocking the product and for selling the product. For example, items might be purchased by the ton and sold by the pound. The size run (size S, M, L; 34, 38, and so forth) might also be needed to describe the product fully. The second segment, the pricing and discount segment, contains unit price, cost, and quantity discount information. The quantity discount is based on a price code. For example, price breaks are often provided for larger orders—the larger the order, the lower the unit price. A price code determines how the discount will be made, and a cost code specifies how the product is costed. In chapter 8, four different methods of costing inventory are discussed.

Storing retrievable information in the customer and product master files reduces data-entry activity considerably. For all new customer accounts, however, the complete customer record must be keyed to processing prior to the entry of shipping details. Special data-entry procedures are required for adding new customers to the master file.

Outputs from Processing

Two types of output follow from processing: transaction documents (customer invoices and credit memos) and processing summaries (for example, the back order summary and the invoice A/R summary). Figure 4–5 illustrates a typical customer invoice. It contains information previously recorded on shipping papers and shows how line-item invoice charges are calculated. A number of business firms use the invoice to show differences between the quantity ordered by the customer and the quantity that was actually shipped. This difference is explained by the terms *back order* and *cancel*. *Back order* (B.O.) means that another shipment will follow once sufficient stock is available. *Cancel* means that a second shipment will not follow; if additional merchandise is required, the customer is expected to reorder.

Any discounts or penalty charges included in the *terms of sale* are printed on the invoice. If a *cash discount* is permitted, the invoice will provide terms such as 2% 10, *net* 30, or 3% 20, *net* 31. The percentage indicates the amount discounted if the invoice is paid within the first time period specified (that is, 10 or 20 days). If payment is not received during this time, full (*net*) payment is due by the end of the second time period specified (30 or 31 days). The invoice may also specify a *service charge*—a cash penalty to be added to all past-due accounts. Most business firms provide a grace period of 60 days or more before adding a service charge amount to a customer's account. Practices vary, however; some companies add a charge whenever an invoice is past due by more than 30 days.

Like many other business documents, the invoice is a two-part form. The upper portion serves as the *customer copy:* it documents the charges and is retained by the customer. The lower portion is the *customer remittance slip*. Customers are requested to detach and return this part with their cash payment. Another design alternative is to send customers two copies of the invoice. The first copy is kept by customers for their records; the second is the return copy (the remittance slip).

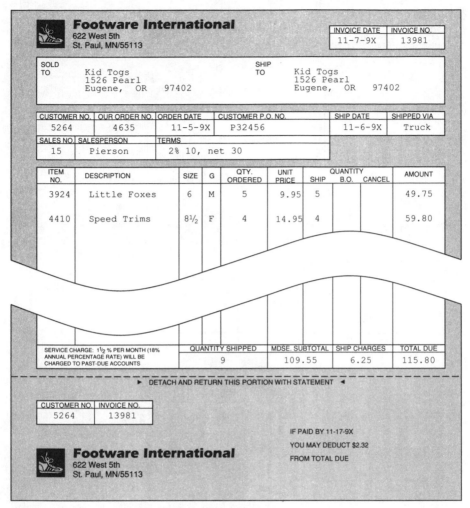

Figure 4–5 Customer invoice

Duplicate forms have become more common with the introduction of carbonless business forms.

Figure 4–6 illustrates a *customer credit memo*. This document informs the customer that a cash credit has been applied to offset outstanding invoice charges. It is similar in design to the customer invoice, with the following exceptions: the credit memo number and date are printed together with the original invoice number and invoice date. Credit numbers are much like invoice numbers: they permit a business to locate a specific credit memo, should the information appearing on it be questioned by the customer. The invoice information is needed to apply the credit to an outstanding invoice. In this sense, a credit and a customer payment both serve to reduce the invoice balance to zero.

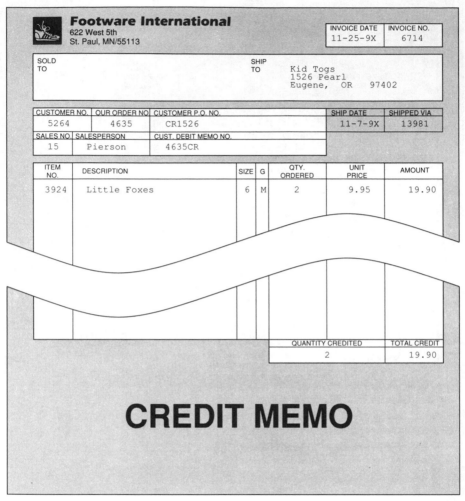

Figure 4–6   Customer credit memo

There are several reasons for crediting a customer's account. If an error is made in a customer's bill, for example, it is often necessary to issue a business credit. If the customer finds shipped merchandise unacceptable and returns it, a customer credit is given. Finally, for some businesses a cash credit is given to a customer if the price of a product drops within 30 days of purchase and the customer asks to be given the lower price. This practice is currently used by a number of retail businesses.

Outputs other than customer invoices and credit memos can include a variety of processing lists and summaries. One of these, an *invoice register*, lists all invoice and credit transactions. Another output, an *invoice A/R summary*, is a condensed version of the invoice register. It shows the invoice charges and customer credits to be posted to a customer's account during A/R processing. The term *posting* means to transfer an amount from one ledger to another. With invoicing, this posting is performed by the computer.

The *invoice A/R summary file* contains the condensed version of the records created during processing. It is used to produce the A/R summary and is retained for accounts-receivable processing.

REVIEW QUESTIONS

1. Why is the invoice so important to large business firms?

2. List the benefits of the customer-invoice computer application.

3. What types of information are printed on the packing slip?

4. How does a bill of lading differ from a packing slip?

5. Name the master files required by this computer application.

6. Describe the main types of output produced by this computer application.

7. Why is an invoice generally a two-part form?

8. What is the difference between the customer invoice and the customer credit memo?

4-2 INVOICE-PROCESSING PROGRAMS

Figure 4–7 (a) and (b) illustrate the systems organization of the customer invoice computer application. The interactive portion consists of five processing functions. The first enters invoice and credit transactions into processing, and the second and third add, delete, and revise records stored on the customer and product master files. The fourth and fifth functions display individual accounts stored on the customer and product master files.

The batch portion of the application is made up of six functions. In this design, all programs lead to some type of printed output. The first two functions produce three registers: the invoice register, the customer master register, and the product master register. The third function leads to the printing of the customer invoices and credit memos. The remaining three functions—*Print back order report*, *Print invoice-A/R summary*, and *Print change reports*—lead to the printing of items placed on back order; input to accounts receivable processing; and two change reports, one to show changes to the customer master file and the other to show changes to the product master file.

The systems organization charts illustrated represent a minimal processing design. *Processing summaries*, for example, could be expanded to produce a list of canceled orders or a report showing daily sales by distributor.

The invoice-processing program menu, shown in Figure 4–8 (a) and (b), follows from the systems organization charts. Processing is activated by choosing from one of these interactive or batch programs.

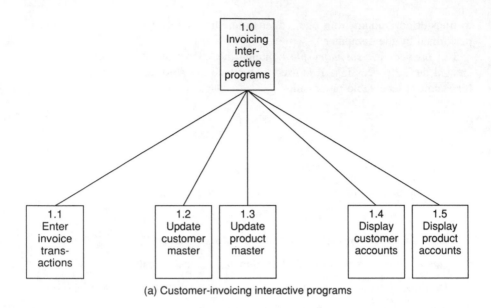

(a) Customer-invoicing interactive programs

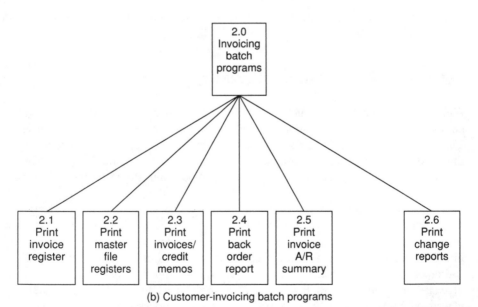

(b) Customer-invoicing batch programs

Figure 4–7   Invoice systems organization chart

The Enter Invoice Transactions Program

The flowchart in Figure 4–9 shows the main steps associated with the daily processing of invoice charges and credit transactions (see also Figure 4–3). Inputs
to processing are shipping documents and customer return slips. Once activated,
the program performs a variety of processing functions: it edits keyed data, transfers

```
┌─────────────────────────────────┐
│ CUSTOMER INVOICING      │       │
│                         └───────┤
│                                 │
│      ENTER INVOICE TRANSACTIONS │
│      UPDATE CUSTOMER MASTER     │
│      UPDATE PRODUCT MASTER      │
│      DISPLAY CUSTOMER ACCOUNT   │
│      DISPLAY PRODUCT ACCOUNT    │
│                                 │
│                                 │
│      RETURN                     │
│                                 │
└─────────────────────────────────┘
```

(a) Customer invoicing interactive
processing menu

```
┌─────────────────────────────────┐
│ CUSTOMER INVOICING      │       │
│                         └───────┤
│                                 │
│      PRINT INVOICE REGISTER     │
│      PRINT CUSTOMER REGISTER    │
│      PRINT PRODUCT REGISTER     │
│      PRINT CUSTOMER INVOICES    │
│      PRINT BACKORDER REPORT     │
│      PRINT INVOICE A/R SUMMARY  │
│      PRINT CHANGE REPORTS       │
│                                 │
│      RETURN                     │
│                                 │
└─────────────────────────────────┘
```

(b) Computer invoicing batch
processing menu

Figure 4–8 Invoice processing menu

data from the customer and product master files, calculates line item invoice charges and the total invoice charge, and adds the completed transaction to the invoice transaction file.

Program processing is designed around a data-entry display, such as the *split-screen display* shown in Figure 4–10. This display requires customer and order information to be keyed to the top half of the screen and product information to be keyed to the lower half. With a split-screen format, a variable number of items can be ordered. If the number exceeds the space provided, the open window set aside for entering product information scrolls downward. After the last product is entered, another window must be opened to record bill of lading information: the total quantity shipped, the date of the shipment, and the insurance and freight charges.

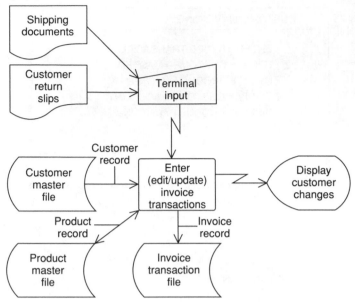

Figure 4–9 Building the invoice transaction file

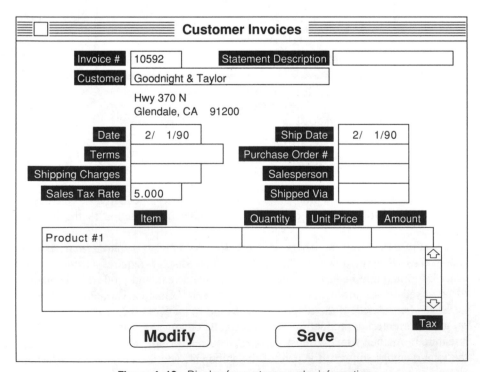

Figure 4–10 Display for customer order information

Control totals are checked line item by item to ensure that data entry is correct. For each line item, the following condition must be true:

Quantity ordered = Quantity shipped + Quantity back ordered
+ Quantity canceled

Unless this condition is met, an error message will be displayed. For example:

QUANTITY TOTALS ARE NOT IN BALANCE

When this happens the user must edit quantity totals to make them balance. A second control total is based on the quantity-shipped total. This control equation is:

Total quantity shipped = (Quantity shipped, line 1)
+ (Quantity shipped, line 2) + $\cdots$ +(Quantity shipped, last line)

If the key-entered total does not match the computed total, the computer will respond with a message, such as:

QUANTITY SHIPPED TOTAL NOT IN BALANCE

Once all line items have been entered into processing and all control totals have been approved, the program computes the total invoice charge and transfers the completed invoice transaction record to the *invoice transaction file*. After the transfer, the computer returns to await input of another business order number.

The process of entering packing-slip information continues throughout the business day or until the decision is reached to process the invoice transaction file. At this point, the file is closed, and batch programs are selected for processing.

The Print Invoice Register Program

The first batch program called into processing prints the invoice register—the list of invoice and credit transactions contained in the invoice transaction file. Because this file is not arranged in any particular order, it is necessary to sort the file before printing it. The sort separates invoices from credit memos and numerically sequences each set.

Figure 4–11 illustrates a small section of an invoice register. The upper portion of each invoice entry gives the invoice number and information important to each shipment: customer number, customer sold-to and ship-to name and address, salesperson and distributor numbers, and so forth. The lower portion of each entry lists the line item entries to be printed on the invoice, the extended line item price, and the total invoice charge. At the bottom are invoice control totals: quantity ordered, shipped, back ordered, and canceled. These totals must balance to the quantity totals entered into processing. The program also computes the invoice gross dollar total, cash discount dollar total, and invoice net dollar total. These totals establish the dollar controls for the print customer invoices program.

Invoice Register   Date 15-May-9X   Page 1

Invoice No.	Cust No.	Cust Sold To/Ship To Name and Address	State	Zip	Sales/GL No.	Cust P.O./Date of P.O.
11532	44831	International Supply	Seattle	WA 98166	064-014	Z03489
		S and P Stores	Burian	WA 98164	4000-010	05-13-9X

No	Line Code	Ord	Ship	B/O	Canc	Price	Disc	Ext Price	Prod $	Tax $	Fht $	Ins $	Gross $	C.D. $	Net $
1	37813	10	10			4.50		45.00							
2	42164	5	5			8.30		41.50							
3	52132	120	120			5.95	.45	660.00							
4	33117	25	25			8.20	.06	203.50	950.00	0.00	45.00	0.00	995.00	29.85	965.15

Invoice detail

Invoice No.	Cust No.	Cust Sold To/Ship To Name and Address	State	Zip	Sales/GL No.	Cust P.O./Date of P.O.
11538	39662	Home Stores, Inc.	Kent	WA 98172	064-014	1362
		—Same as Above—	Burian	WA 98164	4000-010	05-14-9X

No	Line Code	Ord	Ship	B/O	Canc	Price	Disc	Ext Price	Prod $	Tax $	Fht $	Ins $	Gross $	C.D. $	Net $
1	22661	15	15			9.85		147.75							
2	44132	12		12											
3	55419	5	5			39.00	1.55	187.25	335.00	0.00	25.00	5.00	365.00	7.30	357.70

Invoice detail

	Ord	Ship	B/O	Canc		Prod $	Tax $	Fht $	Ins $	Gross $	C.D. $	Net $
Totals	546	492	36	18		3973.50	76.55	256.50	33.00	4339.55	111.14	4228.41

Total Invoices Processed   5
Total Credit Memos Processed   0
Total Count   5

Register summary

Figure 4–11 Invoice register

The Print Customer Invoices Program

Another batch program produces customer-formatted customer invoices and credit memos similar in design to those previously illustrated (see Figures 4–5 and 4–6). Processing is scheduled after the invoice register has been visually inspected and approved. As you might imagine, the running time of this statements program is determined by the number of statements, the number of line items per statement, and the speed of the computer printer. Typically, several hours are needed to complete printing, so the program should contain a *restart* provision. With restart, control subtotals are maintained for groups of printed statements. These subtotals permit printing to be restarted at a point prior to the occurrence of an error (the most recent subtotal).

Besides restart, the program must contain a provision for computing control totals, to ensure that invoice and credit memo dollar counts and amounts are in balance. The usual operating procedure is to print the computed invoice count and dollar amount on a blank invoice, following the printing of the last invoice, and to print the computed credit count and dollar amount on a blank credit memo, following the printing of the last credit memo. If these counts and amounts differ from those on the invoice register, the program must be rerun, but without producing custom forms. The purpose of the rerun is to list, by invoice number, running invoice gross and net dollar totals. This listing is compared with the invoice register to determine where discrepancies in processing occurred.

The Print Back Order Report Program

The back order report is designed to list customer orders that could not be filled because of temporarily insufficient stock. Besides showing the business order number and the customer account number and name, the report should include the number and date of the customer order and the number and quantity of each product reported as a back order. This information greatly assists the order processing staff: for example, it enables them to write or call people whose orders are more than 30 days old, to determine if the ordered merchandise is still wanted. The back-order listing also helps the purchasing staff identify where product demand is greater or product shipments from vendors are slower than expected. To provide this information in a useful form, the back order report should ideally be printed in produce-number sequence instead of in business order-number sequence. This means an additional processing step: the computer must be instructed to create a separate back order file during the printing of the invoice register. Once readied, the additional file is sorted prior to beginning the back order program.

Besides listing back orders, back order reports are used to show different types of summary sales statistics, which are usually prepared according to the following common formulas:

$$\text{Average invoice dollar total} = \frac{\text{Invoice gross dollar total}}{\text{Number of invoices}}$$

$$\text{Average invoice line item dollar total} = \frac{\text{Invoice gross dollar total}}{\text{Number of invoice line items}}$$

Invoice A/R Sales Summary							Date 15-May-9X	
Invoice	Product $	Tax $	Freight $	Ins $	Invoice Gross $	Cash Discount	Invoice Net $	G.L. Code
11532	950.00	0.00	45.00	0.00	995.00	29.85	965.15	4000
11538	335.00	0.00	25.00	5.00	365.00	7.30	357.70	4000
11539	436.50	21.83	57.00	15.00	530.33	10.61	519.72	4000
11542	1340.00	0.00	87.00	13.00	1440.00	43.20	1396.80	4000
11546	912.00	54.72	42.50	0.00	1009.22	20.18	989.04	4000
Totals	3973.50	76.55	256.50	33.00	4339.55	111.14	4228.41	

Total invoice processed	5
Total credit memos processed	0
Total count	5

Figure 4–12 Invoice A/R summary

$$\text{Percentage of back orders} = \frac{\text{Number of line items back ordered}}{\text{Number of invoice line items}}$$

$$\text{Percentage of canceled orders} = \frac{\text{Number of line items canceled}}{\text{Number of invoice line items}}$$

By themselves, these summary statistics may not be very meaningful. When examined over the long term, however, they usually show some interesting trends. In Chapter 15 we will examine sales analysis in more detail.

The Print Invoice A/R Summary Program

Still another batch program is required to produce an *invoice A/R summary file* and to list the information placed on file. The invoice A/R summary produced by this processing step separates product charges from nonproduct charges, determines total allowable cash discounts, and calculates dollar control totals, much as the invoice register does. Figure 4–12 illustrates an abbreviated invoice A/R summary. This listing separates product charges from sales tax charges, freight charges, and insurance charges. It shows the maximum cash discount allowed if customers take advantage of the terms printed on the invoices. Finally, the invoice gross dollar total and invoice net dollar total are printed. These figures form one set of input control totals for the accounts receivable computer application.

4-3 INVOICE TRANSACTION AND SUMMARY FILE PROCESSING

Two files are created as a result of invoice processing: the invoice transaction file and the invoice A/R summary file. As suggested by Figures 4–3 and 4–8, the invoice transaction file is created one transaction at a time. As a result, its over-all size is determined by the number of customer shipments processed by the billing department on a given day. The invoice A/R summary file is a condensed version of the invoice transaction file. This file is required by the A/R application in posting charges to a customer's account.

Invoice Transaction File

The combining of data keyed into processing with data transferred from computer files defines in large part the contents of the invoice transaction file. As the listing of the file contents in Figure 4–13 shows, only a few data elements must be added to complete the transaction record:

- An *invoice number* must be assigned to the record. This is true unless the business order number always leads to the printing of a single invoice. In this case, it is best to allow the business order number to be the same as the invoice number. Using the same number simplifies paperwork processing.

- The *invoice date* must be assigned to the record. In this instance, the date is usually obtained from the computer operating system.

- The *line item extensions* and the *total invoice charge* must be calculated and added to the record. Line item extensions result from multiplying the unit price of the product by the quantity shipped. The total invoice charge is the sum of the line-term extensions plus the charge for insurance and freight.

- *Sales tax* might also need to be calculated and added to the record. If so, it is a percentage of the total invoice charge.

Once completed, the invoice transaction record consists of a header and a trailing portion. The *header portion*, the fixed part of the record, consists of business order information and customer information. The *trailing portion*, the variable part of the record (see boxed area), is made up of product information that must be appended to the record for each product ordered. Thus, the transaction record will be much shorter for a customer ordering one product from stock than for a customer ordering twenty products.

Because invoice records vary in length, the invoice transaction file is typically a sequential file or two relations rather than an indexed sequential file. The problem with a sequential file is that it must generally be sorted into a desired sequence before it can be used. In addition, once a record is stored on a sequential file, it is difficult to modify.

Invoice A/R Summary File

The invoice A/R summary file (see Figure 4–14) is produced by the *Print invoice A/R summary* program. Since accounts receivable summarizes only outstanding invoice charges, the information placed in the summary file is limited to invoice identification information and the total invoice charge. To meet the requirements of A/R processing, the file is sequenced by customer account number.

The invoice A/R summary file may contain data elements other than those shown in Figure 4–14 and may be used in applications other than accounts receivable.

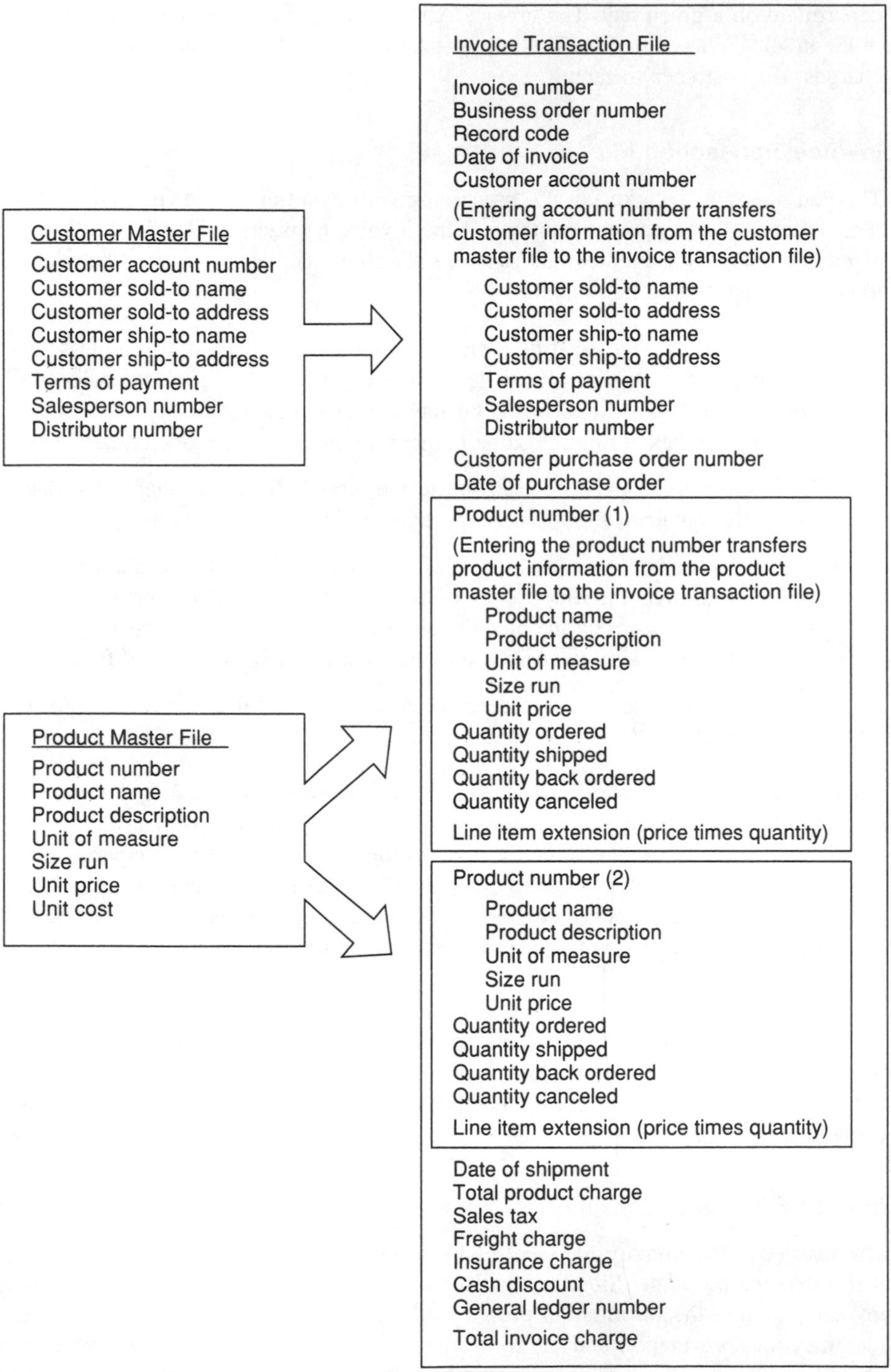

Invoice Transaction File

Invoice number
Business order number
Record code
Date of invoice
Customer account number
(Entering account number transfers customer information from the customer master file to the invoice transaction file)

    Customer sold-to name
    Customer sold-to address
    Customer ship-to name
    Customer ship-to address
    Terms of payment
    Salesperson number
    Distributor number

Customer purchase order number
Date of purchase order

Customer Master File

Customer account number
Customer sold-to name
Customer sold-to address
Customer ship-to name
Customer ship-to address
Terms of payment
Salesperson number
Distributor number

Product number (1)
(Entering the product number transfers product information from the product master file to the invoice transaction file)
    Product name
    Product description
    Unit of measure
    Size run
    Unit price
Quantity ordered
Quantity shipped
Quantity back ordered
Quantity canceled
Line item extension (price times quantity)

Product Master File

Product number
Product name
Product description
Unit of measure
Size run
Unit price
Unit cost

Product number (2)
    Product name
    Product description
    Unit of measure
    Size run
    Unit price
Quantity ordered
Quantity shipped
Quantity back ordered
Quantity canceled
Line item extension (price times quantity)

Date of shipment
Total product charge
Sales tax
Freight charge
Insurance charge
Cash discount
General ledger number

Total invoice charge

Figure 4–13 Invoice transaction file

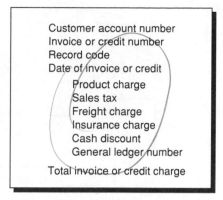

Figure 4-14   Invoice A/R summary file

After salesperson numbers are added to the file, for example, the summary file can be used to analyze customer sales by salesperson. An inversion of the file by salesperson number forms an interesting spreadsheet. It permits a company to determine the sales dollar totals attributed to each member of the sales force. Similarly, the summary file can be used to analyze sales by distributor, provided the distributor number is added to the summary file. An inversion by distributor number distributes the sales dollar totals by distributor.

REVIEW QUESTIONS

9. Name the three interactive processing functions of this application.

10. What does a split-screen design accomplish?

11. What types of control information are printed on the invoice register?

12. Why is restart important in printing customer invoices?

13. What information is listed on a back order report?

14. What information is contained on the header portion of an invoice transaction record? On the trailing portion of the record?

15. How does the invoice A/R summary file differ from the invoice transaction file?

4-4 INVOICE MASTER FILE PROCESSING

Adjustments to customer and product master files are generally completed before invoice processing. This practice permits file records to be corrected and verified prior to entering customer-invoice details and allows the different tasks associated with file updating to be assigned to individuals who are the most familiar with the

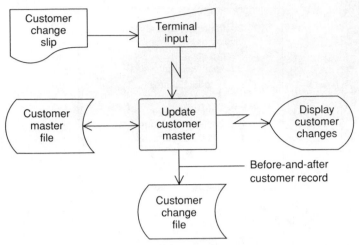

Figure 4–15   Updating customer records

types of changes needed. The customer order department for instance, can be made responsible for spotting new customer orders and changes to customer names and addresses—information that is generally supplied by customers when they call in an order or by salespersons assigned to customers' accounts. Likewise, merchandising departments can be responsible for supplying new product information and for approving product price changes and discounts. These departments are best able to determine if product prices and discount schedules are competitive.

The flowcharts in Figures 4–15 and 4–16 show the processing steps required to update the customer and product master files. Interactive processing leads to the updating of these two master files; display procedures describe the way in which the operator is to alter the individual master file records. Besides updating the file

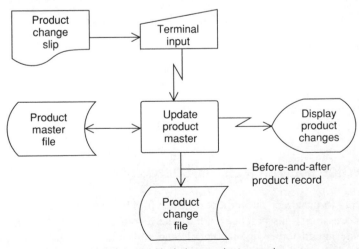

Figure 4–16   Updating product records

and displaying the results of processing, each update program produces a change file. The customer and product change files store the before-and-after effects of processing.

Batch processing is required to print master file registers and change reports. As Figure 4–17 illustrates, two batch programs are associated with each interactive file-update program. These programs print the contents of the master files and the contents of the change files. The programs *Print customer master register* and *Print product master register*, for example, are designed to list the contents of the customer and product master files; the programs *Print customer change report* and *Print product change report* are designed to list the contents of the customer and the product change files.

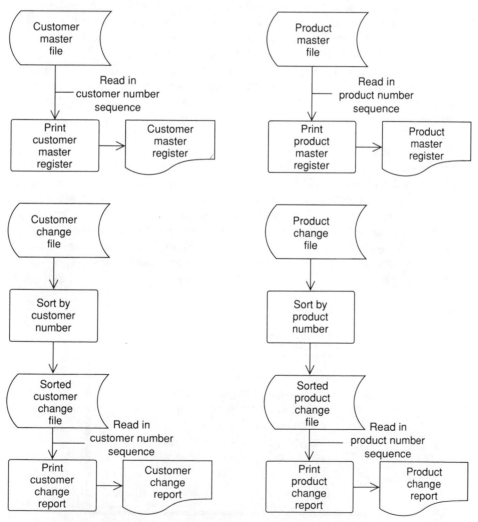

Figure 4–17 Printing registers and file-change reports

The Update Customer Master Program

The program to update the customer master file must be designed to add, change, or delete records stored on the file. After the operator calls the program into processing using the main processing menu, a secondary, file-processing menu is activated. Figure 4–18 shows a typical file menu for a customer master file. This menu permits the operator to add a record to the file, to change a record currently on file, and to delete a record from the file. It makes it possible to move to the next or the previous customer record, to display only a record, and to exit from the program and return to the main program menu.

Figure 4–19 illustrates a display for adding a customer account to the customer master file. To begin processing, the terminal operator assigns a seven-digit customer account number. Following input, the cursor jumps to the sold-to name line on the screen; the computer waits for the customer's sold-to name to be keyed and transmitted. Data entry continues until the *Attention* line is reached. This final line is reserved for entering a person's name, if one has been specified on the customer order. If no name is indicated, the line is left blank.

The second half of the display is similar to the first. The headings now refer to the ship-to name and address. If the sold-to and ship-to information are identical, a special input code, such as *SA* (same address), informs the computer to skip these lines and to return control to the file-processing menu.

Other display information associated with the update of the customer master file deals with entering customer credit terms and salesperson and distributor information on file. Customer credit terms must be assigned before an order is filled by a business. To add these terms to an account, a special terms display may be requested (see Figure 4–20). Frequently the credit department will contact a credit-rating service, such as Dun and Bradstreet, for a composite credit appraisal and estimate of the customer's financial strength. In most cases, customers will have been successfully screened by salespersons. Thus, verifying customer credit information is often routine. When a customer's credit is suspect, however, a business may decide to refuse to sell merchandise to the customer or to require

```
┌─────────────────────────────────────────┐
│ ┌──────────────────────────┐            │
│ │  SETUP CUSTOMER MASTER   │            │
│ └──────────────────────────┘            │
│                                          │
│         ADD CUSTOMER ACCOUNT             │
│         CHANGE CUSTOMER ACCOUNT          │
│         DELETE CUSTOMER ACCOUNT          │
│         NEXT CUSTOMER ACCOUNT            │
│         PREVIOUS CUSTOMER ACCOUNT        │
│         DISPLAY CUSTOMER ACCOUNT         │
│                                          │
│                                          │
│         RETURN                           │
│                                          │
└─────────────────────────────────────────┘
```

Figure 4–18   Processing menu for a customer master file

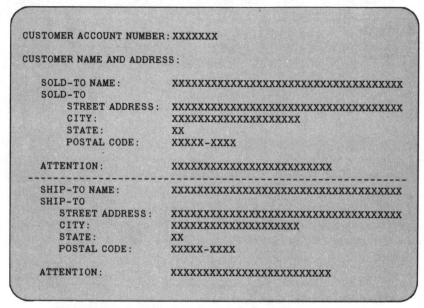

```
CUSTOMER ACCOUNT NUMBER: XXXXXXX

CUSTOMER NAME AND ADDRESS:

   SOLD-TO NAME:        XXXXXXXXXXXXXXXXXXXXXXXXXXXXXXXXXXXX
   SOLD-TO
       STREET ADDRESS:  XXXXXXXXXXXXXXXXXXXXXXXXXXXXXXXXXXXX
       CITY:            XXXXXXXXXXXXXXXXXXXX
       STATE:           XX
       POSTAL CODE:     XXXXX-XXXX

   ATTENTION:           XXXXXXXXXXXXXXXXXXXXXXXX
-------------------------------------------------------------
   SHIP-TO NAME:        XXXXXXXXXXXXXXXXXXXXXXXXXXXXXXXXXXXX
   SHIP-TO
       STREET ADDRESS:  XXXXXXXXXXXXXXXXXXXXXXXXXXXXXXXXXXXX
       CITY:            XXXXXXXXXXXXXXXXXXXX
       STATE:           XX
       POSTAL CODE:     XXXXX-XXXX

   ATTENTION:           XXXXXXXXXXXXXXXXXXXXXXXX
```

Figure 4–19   Name-and-address display for customer master file

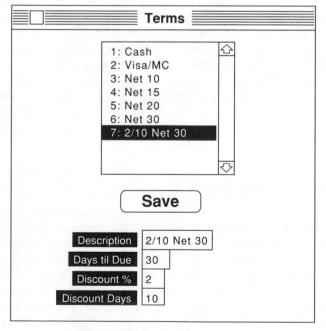

Figure 4–20   Customer terms display

cash payment before a shipment is made. Selling on a cash-only basis means that a cash code must be added to the credit segment of the customer record. Finally, it is common to adjust credit terms periodically. If a customer is slow in making payments, credit terms are often adjusted to be less liberal. Very slow-paying customers are often placed on a cash-only basis.

Compared with customer credit terms, salesperson and distributor information is easier to add to the customer master file if one salesperson and distributor, not several, are assigned to a customer's account. When one salesperson and distributor are assigned, unique code numbers are added to the customer master file. In processing, the computer is instructed either to add these numbers to the invoice or, using the numbers, to look up the names of the salesperson and the distributor from a table and to add these names to the invoice. When more than one salesperson and distributor are assigned to an account, multiple salesperson and distributor code numbers must be appended to customer records. In addition, the salesperson and distributor number for each customer order must be keyed and verified. Verification consists of matching a keyed number against the same number stored on file. If a match cannot be made, the error is displayed and the operator must either enter a different number or change one of the code numbers stored on the computer file.

The Update Product Master Program

The program to update the product master file is similar in design to the update customer master program. It too must be able to add, change, and remove records from a file. It should permit the terminal operator to move to the next product record, to display a record, and to exit and return to the main processing menu.

Figure 4–21 illustrates a multipurpose product display. By clicking on a product number, such as Product #4, the name, unit price, quantity on hand, unit cost, and month-to-day and year-to-date totals are displayed. Likewise, the general ledger sales account for the product can be selected at this time. The possible choices are shown in the open window. Also, whether product sales are taxable or commissionable can be checked. Displays such as this simplify making changes to records stored on master files; it becomes easy to understand how to find a specific record and to make changes and assignments.

Master File Backup and Reporting

After all changes have been made to the customer and product master files, file-backup procedures must be scheduled. Although operating practices differ, file backup usually occurs during the late evening or early morning hours. A common practice is to produce a daily backup copy of all master files stored on magnetic disks and to print weekly master file registers. For this application, a *customer register* and a *product register* are required (see Figure 4–17). These registers show what information is contained on the customer and product master files. An alternative to printing the registers on computer stock paper is to use the tape file

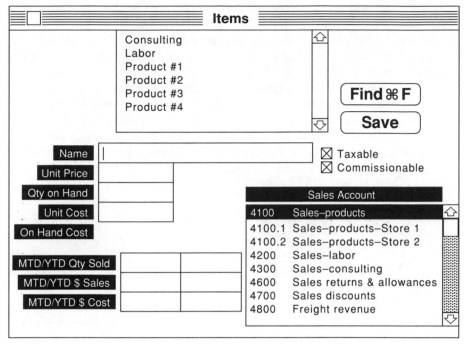

Figure 4–21   A multi-purpose product display

copies as input to create microfiche. As a storage medium, microfiche not only is less costly but also is often easier to work with than lengthy printed listings.

In addition to registers, two change reports must be produced (see Figure 4–17). The *customer change report* shows all new customer accounts, all updates to customer accounts, and all customer accounts to be removed from the file as a result of deletion instructions. Likewise, the *product change report* shows all new product accounts, all updates to product accounts, and all product accounts to be removed from the file. Both change reports are printed daily. This practice permits all file changes to be visually reviewed and approved. If the review indicates an improper update, new change instructions must be keyed into processing.

Master File Display Programs

Programs to display customer accounts and product accounts utilize data stored in master files. They are designed to allow users to examine (but not alter) information stored on master files. Each is written to answer ad hoc questions. The display customer accounts program, for example, answers such questions as: "What is the name of the salesperson assigned to the S and P Stores account?" A search of the customer file reveals that the salesperson assigned to this account is 064; a lookup procedure then finds and displays the name of the salesperson. The display program might be used to answer the question, "Are the ship-to and sold-to addresses the same for S and P Stores?" A search of the account indicates that they are not the same.

The product display program can also answer ad hoc questions; however, its main purpose is the display of product pricing and discount information. Assume that a customer calls to find out the price and price breaks for a product. In times past, the only way to find this information was to look through a catalog for the product number. If this search required several minutes, either the customer was placed on hold or the representative had to take the customer's name and call back with the pricing information. With an online design, the slow catalog look-up procedure has been eliminated. Keying in the product number locates pricing information in seconds; the response to customer inquiries can thus be close to immediate.

4-5 PROCESSING CONTROLS

The design of processing controls for the customer-invoicing computer application is relatively straightforward, provided that the differences between transaction and batch controls are understood. The quantity ordered must be the same as the sum of the quantity shipped, back ordered, or canceled. Checking this information illustrates a *transaction control procedure:* it verifies that each transaction keyed into processing is accurate. Once transaction processing is completed, batch controls are used. The *Invoice register* program (see Figure 4–11), for example, provides three types of batch-balance controls: counts of invoice and credit memos processed, quantity totals, and invoice dollar totals. When transactions are batched, the quantity-total balance consists of equating the total quantity ordered to the total quantities shipped, back ordered, and canceled. The invoice dollar total balances are slightly different. In this instance, the equations are

Total invoice charge (gross dollar amount)
         = Product dollars + Tax dollars + Freight dollars + Insurance dollars

Total invoice receipts (net dollar amount)
         = Total invoice charge (gross dollar amount) − Cash discount

These dollar amounts are carried forward in processing to ensure that customer invoices and credit memos are printed for the correct dollar amounts and that the correct dollar amounts have been transferred to the invoice A/R summary file. Carried one step further, these same dollar totals become the file-balance control totals for the accounts receivable computer application.

The design of dollar control totals requires great care. Typically, all dollar control totals will be used later on in processing other types of business information. The tax dollar total, for example, is required in filing state and federal tax returns. Freight and insurance dollar totals must be accounted for and are shown separately on end-of-month summaries. The cash discount total shows the maximum allowable dollar amount that can be taken by customers for prompt payment of invoices. This total is for particular importance in the cash receipts computer application.

File-balance control totals must also be developed for the customer and product master files. At a minimum, a count of the records stored in each file should be maintained. The change reports produced by the two master file backup programs then verify these counts. The equation is simply

New record count = Old record count + Additions − Deletions

Although transaction and batch control totals help ensure accurate processing, checking a sample of invoices by hand before they are mailed to customers helps make certain that all data to be printed appear on each invoice and that processing totals are correct. In a manual test of processing, the invoice dollar total amount should be computed and checked against the computer-determined dollar total. Unless this is done, problems such as rounding errors will not be discovered. For example, it would be wrong for 2 percent times $6.98 ($.02 \times 6.98 = .1396$) to be truncated to $.13 instead of rounded to $.14.

4-6 MANAGEMENT IMPLICATIONS

To most business people, a customer invoice computer application means one thing: producing an accurate and professional-looking invoice document. This, however, is a short-term benefit. In the long term, the application yields improved management of customer billing and customer credit. Such an improvement can be traced to several factors.

First, the customer invoice application reduces the time between the shipment of goods and the delivery of the invoice to the customer. Business firms have discovered that customers are often 20 percent faster in making their payments when bills are delivered promptly. Moreover, faster customer payment means that firms can dramatically reduce the total dollar amount owed to them.

Second, the application improves the overall accuracy of processing and, correspondingly, the clerical costs of processing. With manual and even with batch methods of processing invoices, a sizable amount of clerical time is spent working with customers to clarify their bills. With an online design, clerical cost savings are substantial. Much of the savings results from the capability to find a customer's record quickly to correct a simple mistake, such as an incorrect product charge.

Third, the application reduces paperwork, so fewer source documents showing shipments to be billed are lost. With this single application, a business is able to streamline its billing procedures by routing all shipping documents to a designated billing center where they are processed quickly and accurately.

Fourth, the application standardizes customer and product records. The importance of standardizing business data will be emphasized throughout this book. For now, a brief look at the procedures for pricing products will help clarify why standards are needed. Consider a business in which prices can be adjusted by sales personnel. Then suppose that the salesperson decides to shave a price slightly at first and sharply later on, in order to make a sales quota. If this practice of making price concessions is permitted to continue, the unit selling price may become lower than the unit cost of the merchandise. Much to the surprise of management, this practice frequently goes unchecked, because people preparing bills by hand have little idea of the recommended selling price of merchandise. With master files storing standard prices, quantity discounts, and terms of payments, however, any price concessions can be closely monitored. Attempts by members of the sales force to shave prices and promise especially favorable terms, such as 5 to 10 percent cash discounts, can be quickly spotted and stopped.

Fifth, the application decentralizes the authority and responsibility for producing customer invoices, for revising company records, and for preparing invoice summary data. With an interactive system, departmental rather than data-processing personnel are able to control what information is entered into processing. In times past, with either manual methods or batch-computing methods, people in departments were responsible for passing along needed changes to billing or data-processing departments; however, they were never given the authority to make these changes. With an online design, responsibility and authority are brought more into balance. Besides being responsible for determining changes to customer and product files, departments now have the authority to make changes. To some managers this is the most significant aspect of the online customer-invoicing computer application.

REVIEW QUESTIONS

16.   Why are file-processing menus required by this application?

17.   What registers and reports are produced in maintaining master files?

18.   Why are display programs important in invoice processing?

19.   Why should some invoices be checked by hand before they are mailed to customers?

20.   What are the long-term management implications of this computer application?

REVIEW OF IMPORTANT IDEAS

A basic objective of invoice processing is to speed the delivery of invoices to customers. An online design streamlines processing procedures. Interactive methods of processing permit data to be keyed, inspected, and corrected by order-processing and billing personnel.

Information that must be keyed as input to processing is contained on shipping documents and customer return slips. Shipping documents show what merchandise is ordered and what is actually shipped to customers. Customer return slips explain why merchandise is being returned for credit.

Outputs from customer invoicing include printed invoices and credit memos and several processing lists and reports. Because customer invoices and credit memos are sent to customers, they must be prepared on custom business forms. Internal working documents such as the invoice register and the invoice A/R summary provide a detailed record of processing.

The interactive portion of invoice processing consists of entering invoices into processing, adjusting and revising the customer and product master files, and displaying records stored on these two master files.

Interactive processing transfers customer and product information from master files where it is combined with data from shipping that has been keyed to processing. Throughout processing, transaction controls are maintained to ensure that the data keyed and transmitted are correct.

Following the building of the invoice transaction file, batch programs are used to produce the invoice register, customer invoices, and special reports, such as the back order report. A batch-processed step is the creation of an invoice A/R summary file, suitable as input to accounts receivable processing.

Each record written to the invoice transaction file contains a header and trailing portion. The trailing portion is variable: it varies by the number of products shipped. The invoice A/R summary file is a condensed version of the transaction file. It contains fixed-length records and is limited to invoice identification information and the total invoice charge.

The customer and product master files must be readied before data from shipping are keyed into processing. Interactive methods permit file records to be added, changed, and deleted, using easy-to-follow master file processing menus. Each time a record is changed, the change must be reported. Change reports produced by file-backup programs provide this information.

Online display programs permit the ad hoc search of stored data. They greatly improve a business's capability to respond to customer inquiries.

Both transaction and batch-processing controls are required by the invoicing computer application. Initially, quantity-only totals are compared. When dollars are computed, both total quantity and total dollar controls are maintained.

The long-term implication of processing customer invoices by computer is improved management of customer billing and of credit. Invoices are processed much more quickly, at less cost, with improved methods of control. Distributed processing provides departmental personnel with the capabilities to effect change directly.

KEY WORDS

Customer invoice	Terms of sale
Monthly statement	Cash discount
Sales draft	Service charge
Packing slip	Customer remittance slip
Bill of lading	Customer credit memo
Customer return slips	Invoice A/R summary
Customer master file	Invoice transaction file
Primary record key	Customer register

Product master file   Product register
Secondary key   Transaction-control procedure
Back order

EXERCISES

1. On inspection of the invoice register (see Figure 4–11), it is discovered that the sold-to address for the International Supply Company is in error. The correct address is *5610 NW Ferris* and not *5160 SW Ferris*. How should this error be corrected at this point in processing?

2. A customer complains that he was billed twice for a shipment. How could this problem be checked by a customer representative? If the customer's claim is correct, what corrective actions should be taken?

3. Study the shipping document shown in Figure 4–2.

   (a) Identify and list the types of information placed on a packing slip, namely, business order information, customer order information, packing information, customer information, and product information.

   (b) Identify and list the bill-of-lading information.

4. Suppose credit memo processing is to be kept separate from invoice processing.

   (a) What new computer programs will be required?

   (b) How must the program-processing menu be modified?

   (c) What new computer files will be created?

   (d) What new reports will be printed?

   (e) How will file-backup and reporting procedures change?

5. "Invoicing could be simplified if we could eliminate some of the numbers," remarked Rose. "Why do we need the customer number, the customer P.O. number, the business order number, and the invoice number?"

   (a) Answer Rose's question. Assume that back orders are processed by this company.

   (b) Would your answer be different if no back orders or split orders were processed?

6. Suppose you decide to create a separate back order file during the printing of the invoice register. Draw the systems flowchart to show how this is done.

DISCUSSION QUESTIONS

1. Why is understanding the primary data flows of the customer invoice system so important to understanding the design of this business computer application?

2. Explain what processing tasks are assigned to each of the following programs.

   (a) the *Enter invoice transaction* program

   (b) the *Print invoice register* program

   (c) the *Print customer invoice* program

   (d) the *Print back order report* program

   (e) the *Print invoice A/R summary* program

3. Why is it necessary to create an A/R summary file? Why can't the invoice transaction file be used instead?

4. Why must the customer master file and the product master file be created in advance of processing invoice transactions? What happens if they are not created in advance?

4-IN-1 CASE STUDY—PROCESSING CUSTOMER INVOICES

In this set of exercises using 4-in-1, you are asked to perform a variety of tasks. These include

- adding a balance-forward amount to customer records
- processing a sales transaction
- processing a sales credit
- printing an invoice transaction register
- printing an invoice and a customer credit and
- posting invoice transactions to the general ledger.

In working on these tasks, you will handle only a regular transaction. You might observe, however, that 4-in-1 is also able to process a recurring transaction.

Adding a Balance-forward Amount to Customer Records

To process a sales transaction, do the following.

1. Type **8** from the main menu and press ENTER.

2. Type **1**, *Add transactions*, from the process sales and DR/CR memos menu, where *DR* means debit and *CR* means credit.

3. Type **LAWNS** when asked to enter the full or partial name of the customer. (If you cannot remember the name of a customer when using 4-in-1, press the F1 key. Pressing the F1 key repeatedly allows you to scroll through the customer list.) Press ENTER.

4. Press ENTER when asked *Right customer?*

5. Type **B** and press ENTER to place a balance-forward amount in the LAWNS-ARE-GREEN account.

6. Press ENTER when the transaction date is displayed.

7. Type **0.00** and press ENTER when asked to indicate the amount of money that this customer owes you.

8. Press ENTER when the reference *Balance forward* is displayed.

9. Press ENTER to record this amount and to return to the add transactions menu.

Processing an Invoice (Sales) Transaction

To ready an invoice transaction do the following:

10. Type **LAWNS** again and press ENTER.

11. Press ENTER when asked *Right customer?*

12. Press ENTER to indicate that you want to process a sale.

13. Type **010597** to change the date. Press ENTER.

14. Press ENTER to leave the document number blank.

15. Type **100.00** to indicate the total amount of the sale. Press ENTER.

16. Press ENTER for the reference.

17. Press ENTER when asked, *Payment with sale?*

18. Press ENTER when asked, *Debit A/R?*

19. Press ENTER to record the sale.

20. Press F1 when asked to enter the G/L number.

21. Press F1 to distribute the entire amount.

22. Press ENTER when asked, *Any change?*

23. Press TAB to end.

Entering Invoice Information

After recording the sale, the remaining information to place on the invoice can be entering into processing. Figure 4–22 shows the invoice created by the following steps.

24. Type **Y** and press ENTER when asked, *Do you wish to prepare an invoice for this transaction?*

25. Press F1 to enter the ship-to name and address.

26. Type **100** and press ENTER when asked for the customer's purchase order (P.O.) number.

```
A and J Enterprises, Inc.   I N V O I C E        Inv-date  Inv-#  Pg
1169 Student Way                                 01/05/97  1111   1
Collegeville, OR 97000


Sold to: LAWNS-ARE-GREEN              Ship to: LAWNS-ARE-GREEN
         1225 Fairview Lane                    1225 Fairview Lane
         Prettyville                          Prettyville
         CA 95000                             CA 95000
```

Prch-ord-#	Ship-via	Ship-dat	Terms
100	Truck	01/05/97	Net 30 days

Item		Cost
3 units microgrow plus		30.00
10 units growth-additive		50.00
	Sale amount	80.00
	Misc. charges	.00
	Sales tax	6.00
	Freight	14.00
	Total	100.00

Figure 4–22   A 4-in-1 invoice

27. Type **Truck** and press ENTER when asked, *Shipped via?*

28. Type **Net 30** days and press ENTER when asked, *Terms?*

29. Type **010597** and press ENTER to enter the ship date.

30. Press ENTER for miscellaneous charges.

31. Type **6.00** and press ENTER to record the sales tax.

32. Type **14.00** and press ENTER to record the freight charges.

33. Press ENTER when asked, *Field number to change?*

34. Type **1** when asked to enter the line number. Press ENTER.

35. Type **3 units microgrow plus** to add the units sold and the product description. Press ENTER.

36. Press ENTER twice.

37. Type **30.00** to add the sales amount. Press ENTER.

38. Press ENTER.

39. Type **2** to enter the line number and repeat steps 35 to 38 to add 10 units of growth addition and a sales amount of 50.00.

40. Press TAB to end the line-by-line description.

Processing a Credit Transaction

Suppose one of the goods shipped is damaged and returned for a credit. A credit is processed as follows:

41. Type **LAWNS** and press ENTER.

42. Press ENTER when asked, *Right customer?*

43. Type **C** and press ENTER to indicate that you want to apply a credit to the LAWNS-ARE-GREEN account.

44. Type **011097** to add the date of the credit. Press ENTER.

45. Press ENTER to leave the document number blank.

46. Type **12.50** and press ENTER to indicate the amount of the credit.

47. Type **Damaged goods** and press ENTER when asked for a reference.

48. Press ENTER when asked, *Credit A/R?*

49. Press ENTER when asked, *Field number to change?*

50. Press F1 when asked to enter the G/L number.

51. Press F1 to distribute the entire amount.

52. Press ENTER when asked, *Any change?*

53. Press TAB to end.

Entering Credit Memo Information

After recording the credit, the remaining information to place on the credit can be entered into processing. Figure 4–23 shows the credit the following steps create.

54. Type **Y** and press ENTER when asked, *Do you wish to prepare an invoice (credit memo) for this transaction?*

55. Press F1 to enter the ship-to name and address.

56. Type **101C** and press ENTER when asked for the customer's purchase order (P.O.) number.

57. Type **Truck** and press ENTER when asked, *Shipped via?*

58. Press ENTER when asked, *Terms?*

59. Press ENTER when asked, *Ship date?*

60. Press ENTER for miscellaneous charges.

61. Type **.75** and press ENTER to record the sales tax.

62. Type **1.75** and press ENTER to record the freight charges.

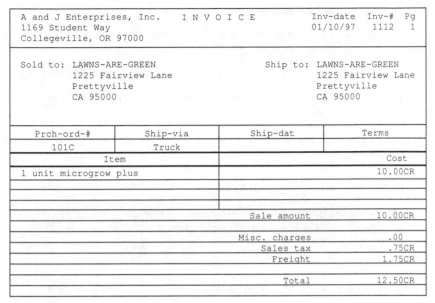

```
A and J Enterprises, Inc.    I N V O I C E         Inv-date  Inv-#  Pg
1169 Student Way                                   01/10/97  1112    1
Collegeville, OR 97000


Sold to: LAWNS-ARE-GREEN                 Ship to: LAWNS-ARE-GREEN
         1225 Fairview Lane                        1225 Fairview Lane
         Prettyville                               Prettyville
         CA 95000                                  CA 95000
```

Prch-ord-#	Ship-via	Ship-dat	Terms
101C	Truck		

Item		Cost
1 unit microgrow plus		10.00CR
	Sale amount	10.00CR
	Misc. charges	.00
	Sales tax	.75CR
	Freight	1.75CR
	Total	12.50CR

Figure 4–23 A 4-in-1 credit

63. Press ENTER when asked, *Field number to change?*

64. Type **1** when asked to enter the line number. Press ENTER.

65 Type **1 unit microgrow plus** to add the units returned and the product description. Press ENTER.

66. Press ENTER twice.

67. Type **10.00** to add the credit amount. Press ENTER.

68. Press ENTER.

69. Press TAB to end the line-by-line description

70. Press TAB to return to the process sales and DR/CR memos menu.

Printing the Transaction Edit List

The transaction edit list is easily prepared. Do the following:

71. Type **4** and press ENTER from the process sales and DR/CR memos menu.

72. Press ENTER when asked, *Display this report?* This step leads to the printing of the sales edit list. The list contains a detail page and a summary page.

Printing an Invoice and a Credit

The invoices and credits will be batched for printing. To print these action documents, do the following:

73. Type **5** and press ENTER from the process sales and DR/CR memos menu.

74. Type **P** (for plain paper) and press ENTER when asked to specify the invoice format.

75. Type **1111** and press ENTER to specify the starting invoice number.

76. Press F1 for the starting customer.

77. Press F1 for the ending customer.

78. Press ENTER when asked, *Field number to change?* This step leads to the printing of the LAWNS-ARE-GREEN invoice (see Figure 4–22) and the LAWNS-ARE-GREEN credit. Press TAB to exit.

Posting Invoice and Credit Transactions to the General Ledger

Posting invoice and credit transactions is often done immediately after they are printed. Do the following:

79. Type **6** and press ENTER from the process sales and DR/CR memos menu. Before moving to the next step, make sure your printer is turned on.

80. Type **Y** when asked, *Are sales transaction OK to print*? This leads to the printing of the sales register. The register shows all postings to the general ledger.

81. Press TAB to return to the main menu.

82. Press TAB to log off if you do not plan to begin the next exercise.

QUESTIONS

Compare the design of the 4-in-1 invoicing application to the application described in the chapter. Then do the following:

1. Draw the data flow diagram required by 4-in-1 in producing the customer invoice. Use Figure 4–3 as a guide in drawing this DFD.

2. Draw the 4-in-1 systems organization chart. Use Figure 4–7 as a guide.

3. List the contents of the 4-in-1 invoice transaction file. Use Figure 4–14 in preparing this list.

4. Compare the 4-in-1 invoice to the 4-in-1 credit. How do these document differ? How do they differ from the documents described by the chapter?

5. Compare the 4-in-1 sales edit list to the 4-in-1 sales register. How do they differ? Why must both documents be printed? How do these documents differ from those described by the chapter?

6. Examine the 4-in-1 postings to the general ledger. Why is $12.50 credited to Trade Accounts Receivable and debited to Sales—Product A?

5

Customer Cash Receipts

A *cash receipt* is a payment from a customer. As we will discuss in this chapter, cash receipts are processed when payments are made by customers at the time of sale or when payments are received from customers by mail. In most instances, customer payments received by mail are made to offset a single outstanding, or *open*, invoice balance. By making a payment against a specific invoice, the customer removes the invoice charge from his or her account. In other instances, payments are made with the understanding that they be applied to a customer's account. These *payment-on-account* transactions may reduce to zero several outstanding invoices. They are not difficult to process, provided that the rules of processing have been clearly thought out in advance.

The design of an online customer cash-receipts computer application is very similar to the design for customer-invoice processing. It uses three types of input to processing: information contained on remittance slips from invoices or monthly statements, information shown on customer checks, and information stored on the customer master file. Only the customer master file is required because dollars rather than quantities must be accounted for; the product master file is not needed in processing cash receipts.

The online customer cash-receipts design is more complex when a business accepts payments at the time of purchase *and* accepts payments by mail. Cash payments received at the time of purchase require *point-of-sale* (POS) equipment, such as online cash registers. In contrast, cash payments received by mail generally are processed interactively by video display terminals. This chapter is divided into two parts to compare these two methods of processing. The first part examines a cash-receipts application designed to operate in parallel with the customer-invoicing computer application. The second part shows what is required to process POS transactions.

The objectives of the cash-receipts application are actually very much like those associated with customer invoicing. This application can help a business to shorten the time between the receipt of a customer payment and the deposit of the payment in the bank, cut the number of clerical errors, improve processing controls, and project the amount of cash available to offset business expenses and other liabilities. As with invoicing, time is a critical factor. If a business is able to process customer receipts faster, dollars can be immediately applied to meet business expenses. This improved cash flow reduces the need by a business to obtain short- or long-term loans.

Improved processing control is also critical. Large business firms, in particular, require a method of processing that verifies that cash discounting by customers is done properly and that all cash-discount funds can be accounted for. If customers are taking discounts larger than authorized or much later than the date permitted (as shown on the invoice), this situation must be brought to the attention of management.

5-1   PRELIMINARY OVERVIEW OF PROCESSING

Figure 5–1 illustrates the context of the cash-receipts computer application. Compared with customer invoicing, receipts processing is relatively easy. Inputs to processing are limited to a customer payment and customer information. The main outputs are a cash receipts register sent to auditing for cash discount verification, a receipts A/R summary, and a bank deposit slip, which is to be taken with customer checks to the bank.

Figure 5–2, the level-0 DFD, highlights the main steps in processing. As in invoicing, the first step is to verify the incoming transaction and build a transaction file—the receipts transaction file, in this instance. Several batch-processing steps are then required to utilize the data placed on the transaction file.

The advantage of this design is that it is simple. It allows a business to process all incoming receipts quickly and produce a cash-receipts register. The register indicates the cash payment amounts that are to be added during accounts receivable processing and the cash deposit to be made at the bank. You will notice that the design does not attempt to match a payment against an outstanding customer invoice. This step is accomplished by the accounts receivable application.

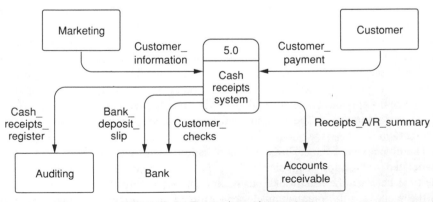

Figure 5–1   The cash receipts system

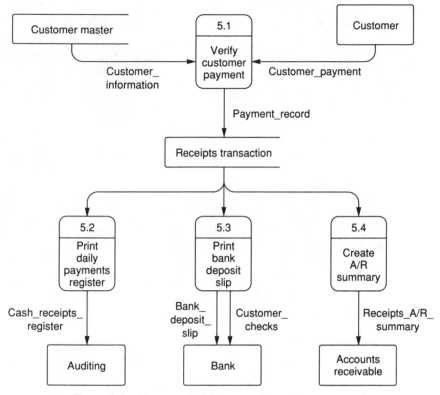

Figure 5–2 Steps required in processing customer payments

Inputs to Processing

Inputs to the cash receipts application are limited to payment information from invoice remittance and monthly statement remittance slips, the customer check, and the customer master file designed for processing customer invoices. Figure 5–3 shows the difference between invoice remittance and monthly statement remittance slips. As indicated, the invoice remittance offsets a single invoice, whereas the monthly statement remittance typically offsets several outstanding invoices. In addition, the invoice remittance indicates any cash discount taken by the customer for prompt payment; the monthly statement remittance does not indicate a discount amount. Other than these differences, both remittances contain the following types of information.

- *customer invoice number* to identify the invoice to be paid
- *customer account number* to identify the customer
- *customer payment information* to show the dollar amount due, the date when the payment is due, and the cash discount if one applies

As in customer invoicing, the cash receipts application requires several code numbers to permit documents to be identified and related to other business

INVOICE

REMIT TO
ELIASON AND ASSOCIATES
2520 CHARNELTON
EUGENE, OR 97405

Customer acct. no.	Invoice no.
35214	26205

If paid by	07-12-9X
You may deduct	2.97
From total due	148.72

To issue proper credit to
your account, please return
this portion with your payment

Thank you

Invoice remittance stub

STATEMENT

REMIT TO
ELIASON AND ASSOCIATES
2520 CHARNELTON
EUGENE, OR 97405

Return this protion with payment by
09-15-9X

Customer acct. no.	Month ending
35214	08-31-9X

Invoice no.	Amount	Date
24636	$135.40	06-20-9X
25810	69.20	07-05-9X
26123	93.42	07-10-9X
26205	148.72	07-12-9X
Total Due	$446.74	

Monthly statement remittance stub

Figure 5–3   Customer remittance stubs.

documents. Five numbers important to customer cash receipts are the remittance number, record code number, invoice reference number, general ledger number, and customer check number.

- The *remittance number* keeps each cash receipt unique. It must be different from the invoice number because the customer may make several payments before the outstanding invoice charge is fully paid.

- The *record code number* separates invoice remittances from monthly statement remittances and from other types of cash payments. Another purpose of the record code is to permit a customer payment to be adjusted. If a payment is entered into processing incorrectly, for example, there must be some method for correcting the error.

- The *invoice reference number* is the number of the invoice mailed to the customer. It is needed to match the receipt against an open invoice.

- The *general ledger number* separates different types of cash receipts. For example, companies typically have a number of deposit and checking accounts at a bank. Some accounts are limited-use accounts—they are limited to storing funds needed to cover specific business activities. Other accounts are more general in terms of their purpose. When several accounts are active, each account must be identified by a unique general ledger code. In cash receipts processing, this code must be entered to deposit the cash in the correct bank account.

- The *check number* provides a point of reference if the customer questions whether a particular check has been processed.

At times, a customer payment will be received without a remittance. When this occurs, a business must identify the customer by number and prepare a remittance slip. The processing of this information together with the amount of payment is controlled by a record code and interpreted by the computer as a *payment on account*. The payment is applied to outstanding invoice charges. The computer is instructed to follow prescribed decision rules, such as these:

1. Continue to offset outstanding charges until the entire payment has been applied.

2. Use the cash payment to offset the oldest outstanding charge first.

Combining these two rules then works as follows:

```
IF A CASH BALANCE REMAINS
    AND THERE ARE OTHER INVOICES TO BE PAID
        THEN APPLY THE REMAINDER TO OFFSET THE
        OLDEST INVOICE CHARGE. CONTINUE TO APPLY THE
        CASH
        UNTIL THERE ARE NO REMAINING INVOICES TO BE PAID.
    END-IF
APPLY ANY REMAINING CASH AS A CREDIT ON ACCOUNT.
```

Figure 5–4 shows that the data keyed into processing consist of customer remittance information, customer account information, and payment information. A close inspection of keyed information shows that only numerics are keyed and that a total of approximately forty-five keystrokes are used. For a remittance that follows from a customer invoice, the data-entry operator is required to key in all data shown. For a remittance that follows from a monthly statement, the operator is required to key each invoice number and the payment to be applied to each invoice in addition to keying in all other data shown.

The customer master file is required by the cash-receipts application. The file segments and data elements shown for this file are identical to those used in the customer-invoicing application. Thus, once the file is readied for customer invoicing, it is also readied for customer cash receipts. As you will observe in later chapters, the sharing of information between applications is not unusual. It means that the application files must be carefully designed for further use, however.

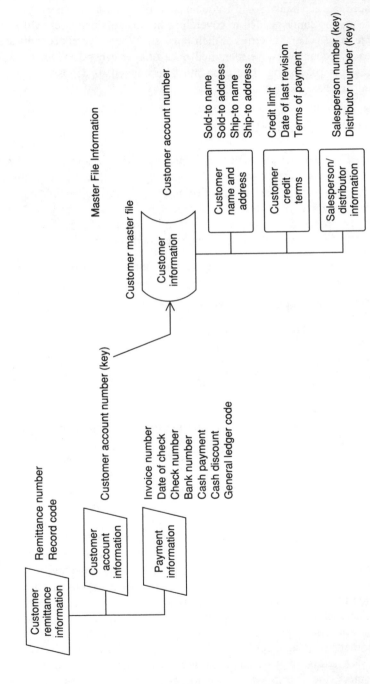

Figure 5-4 Relationships between cash receipts data sets

Outputs from Processing

Because it does not produce formal business documents, the customer cash-receipts application differs from many other business computer applications. For this application the only feedback to processing lies outside the system, namely, the return of the cancelled check to the customer by the customer's bank and the approving of the bank deposit. Within the system, the single output file produced, the *receipts A/R summary file*, contains a condensed version of the records created by processing. Its contents are printed on the *receipts A/R summary*. The contents of transaction records are shown on two other output documents: the *cash receipts register* and the *bank deposit slip*.

Because the cash receipts register shows all customer payments received and verified, some firms see little need to prepare a separate bank deposit slip or even a receipts A/R summary. However, there are good reasons for printing three listings. The cash receipts register clearly documents each cash amount, each discount taken, and how these amounts were distributed to the general ledger. The bank deposit slip, in contrast, does not need to show the same amount of information. It is often limited to a listing of checks for deposit and their amount. The receipts A/R summary is more limited than the cash receipts register and follows a different sequence. The summary is generally prepared by customer number sequence, which makes it easier to locate a customer account. This sequence is usually required in processing receivable accounts (see Chapter 6).

REVIEW QUESTIONS

1. Why should a business develop the cash-receipts computer application?

2. What are the three types of input to processing?

3. What is the difference between an invoice remittance and a monthly statement remittance?

4. How is a customer payment processed if it is received without a remittance?

5. What outputs are printed by processing?

5-2 CASH RECEIPTS PROCESSING

Figure 5–5 (a) and (b) illustrate the systems organization chart for the cash receipts application. The four new programs to be designed for this application are the programs to enter cash receipts transactions, print the cash receipts register, print the bank deposit slip, and print the receipts A/R summary.

Figure 5–6 (a) and (b) show the corresponding processing menu. Three interactive programs must be developed to enter transaction data into processing, to update the customer master file, and to display accounts stored on the customer master file. The single update program is particularly important. It alters customer records stored

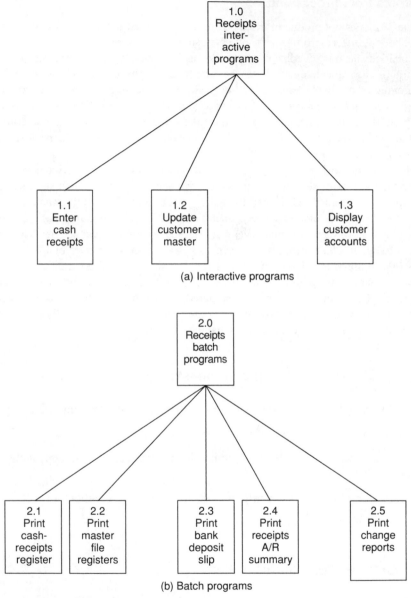

(a) Interactive programs

(b) Batch programs

Figure 5–5   Cash receipts systems organization chart

on file—in particular, customer name and address information. These changes are often reported by customers making their cash payments.

Besides three interactive programs, five batch programs are needed in processing cash receipts: two of these print registers; one prints a deposit slip; one prints a summary report; and one prints a change report. The printing of the customer master register and customer change report were discussed in Chapter 4, so they need not

```
┌─────────────────────────────────────────┐
│ CASH RECEIPTS            │               │
│ ─────────────────────────               │
│                                         │
│      ENTER CUSTOMER RECEIPTS            │
│      UPDATE CUSTOMER MASTER             │
│      DISPLAY CUSTOMER ACCOUNTS          │
│                                         │
│                                         │
│                                         │
│                                         │
│      RETURN                             │
│                                         │
└─────────────────────────────────────────┘
```

(a)

```
┌─────────────────────────────────────────┐
│ CASH RECEIPTS            │               │
│ ─────────────────────────               │
│                                         │
│      PRINT RECEIPTS REGISTER            │
│      PRINT CUSTOMER REGISTER            │
│      PRINT BANK DEPOSIT SLIP            │
│      PRINT RECEIPTS A/R SUMMARY         │
│      PRINT CHANGE REPORT                │
│                                         │
│                                         │
│      RETURN                             │
│                                         │
└─────────────────────────────────────────┘
```

(b)

Figure 5–6 Cash receipts processing menu

be described again. The programs designed to print the cash-receipts register, the bank deposit slip, and the receipts A/R summary, however, are different. These produce an internal control and a bank-deposit register of all customer payments and a receipts A/R summary file.

The Enter Cash-Receipts Program

The flowchart segment in Figure 5–7 shows the main steps associated with the program to enter and verify customer payments. As indicated, data from invoice and monthly statement remittance slips are keyed into processing. At this point, the program edits remittance details and permits the terminal operator to verify keyed data visually. Once data are verified as correct, the completed transaction is written to the *receipts transaction file*, which remains open until all receipts have been processed.

A split-screen display is often used in entering cash-receipt transactions. This screen format requires the operator to key in the cash receipts remittance number,

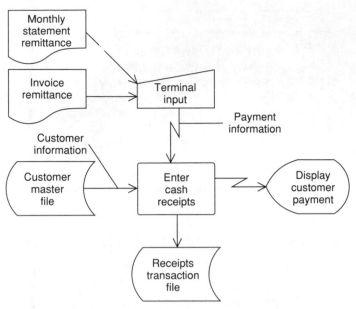

Figure 5–7   Building the cash receipts file

the record code, and the customer number (see the top part of Figure 5–8). A record code of 1, for example, could indicate that an invoice remittance is to be processed. Once a 1 is entered, the computer responds by completing the display screen. As Figure 5–8 shows, the bottom portion of the screen is designed for the entry of an invoice remittance. Input requirements are thus minimal: keyed data

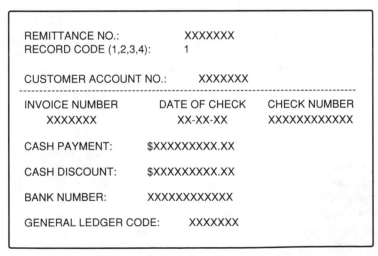

Figure 5–8   Invoice remittance display

consist of the invoice number, the date of the customer check, the customer check number, the cash payment amount, the cash discount (if taken), the bank number shown on the check, and the general ledger code. A record code of 2 instructs the computer to accommodate the entry of a monthly statement remittance (see Figure 5–9). The keystroke requirements for this display consist of the invoice number, cash payment amount, and general ledger code for each invoice to be paid by the customer check. This information is supplied in addition to the date of the customer check, the check number, the bank number, and the total cash payment.

Besides serving as a way of entering data into processing, the program to enter cash receipts verifies the correctness of the customer number and confirms the correctness of transaction control totals for each transaction keyed into processing. To check transaction-control totals for each invoice remittance, the computer determines the balance due by adding the cash payment to the cash discount; it then compares the computed balance-due total to the balance-due total keyed into processing. If a difference is found, an error message is displayed, so that the terminal operator can visually determine why the error occurred and make the necessary corrections. To check control totals for each monthly statement remittance, a balance test is advised. In performing this test, the computer adds the cash payment amount keyed for each invoice and compares this sum to the cash payment total, which must also be keyed. If the two are not in agreement, the computer responds:

THE CASH PAYMENT TOTAL IS NOT IN BALANCE.

The computer then waits for payment line entries to be corrected or for the cash payment total to be changed.

```
REMITTANCE NO.:              XXXXXXX
RECORD CODE (1,2,3,4):   2

CUSTOMER ACCOUNT NO.:   XXXXXXX  CHECK NO.: XXXXXXXXXXXX
DATE OF CHECK:  XX-XX-XX              BANK NO.:   XXXXXXXXXXXX
-----------------------------------------------------------------------------------------------
   INVOICE NUMBER          CASH PAYMENT         GENERAL LEDGER CODE
      XXXXXXX              $XXXXXXXXX.XX              XXXXXXX
      XXXXXXX              $XXXXXXXXX.XX              XXXXXXX
      XXXXXXX              $XXXXXXXXX.XX              XXXXXXX
      XXXXXXX              $XXXXXXXXX.XX              XXXXXXX
      XXXXXXX              $XXXXXXXXX.XX              XXXXXXX
      XXXXXXX              $XXXXXXXXX.XX              XXXXXXX
      XXXXXXX              $XXXXXXXXX.XX              XXXXXXX
      XXXXXXX              $XXXXXXXXX.XX              XXXXXXX
-----------------------------------------------------------------------------------------------
   TOTAL CASH PAYMENT                            $XXXXXXXXX.XX
```

Figure 5–9 Monthly statement remittance display

The last function of the enter receipts program is to establish control balances for the receipts transaction file. The file control totals consist of the number of invoices to be fully or partially paid and their dollar amounts as well as the uncommitted dollar amounts to be applied as payments on account. In addition to these file balance totals, invoice and monthly statement remittance dollar totals are carried forward in processing. For invoice remittances, the number of receipts processed is saved, as are the dollar amounts of the cash payments and cash discount. For monthly statements, the number of receipts processed is saved, as are the number of invoices to be paid and their dollar amount.

The Print Cash Receipts Register Program

After control totals have been approved, the records stored on the receipts transaction file are processed as a batch. The first batch-processing program produces the *cash-receipts register*, a listing of the records stored on the transaction file (see Figure 5–10). To make this listing easier to read, the records on file are generally sorted to separate monthly statement remittances from invoice remittances and to place each type of remittance in numerical sequence. One way to simplify this process is to presort remittances as much as possible before keying in data to the computer. If two receipts are to be keyed, for example, the one with the lower remittance number should be keyed first. Another way to simplify the sort requirement is to create two online receipts transaction files—monthly statement remittances would be written to one, invoice remittances to the other. The difficulty with this option is maintaining two sets of control totals.

Although the main purpose of the cash receipts register program is to provide a listing of the contents of the receipts transaction file, an important second purpose is to print receipts control totals. Figure 5–10 shows that the register program counts the number of invoice remittances, the number of monthly statement remittances, and the number of invoices to be partially or fully paid by both types of remittance. In addition, the program separates the monthly statement dollar amounts from the invoice dollar amounts, accumulates the cash discounts taken by customers, and adds cash receipts to show total dollars including and excluding cash discounts. These figures are compared with the receipts transaction file control totals. If they are the same, the correctness of the receipts audit trail is preserved.

The Print Bank Deposit Slip Program

The cash receipts register program contains too much information to be suitable for the *bank deposit register*, and, for this reason, a batch program is written to print this register (see Figure 5–11). This new register is a condensed version of the first. Its purpose is to document the number of checks and the total dollar amount of the checks taken to the bank for deposit. If the bank discovers that the sum of the individual checks differs from the total deposit amount shown at the bottom of the register, the checks must be matched against the register to determine if all checks have been accounted for and properly recorded.

Cash Receipts Register			Date 05-June-9X		Page 1
Remit. No	*Cust No*	*Cust Sold To Name*	*Date of Check*	*Check No.*	*Bank No.*
6321	39662	Home Stores, Inc.	03-06-9X	139214	22-12/111
No.	*Invoice No.*	*Cash Payment*	*Net $*		*General Ledger Code*
1	11345	365.42			2000
2	11390	121.60			2000
3	11491	89.45	576.47		2000
Remit. No.	*Cust No.*	*Cust Sold To Name*	*Date of Check*	*Check No.*	*Bank No.*
11532	44831	International Supply	01-06-9X	368-9240	16-15/510
No.	*Invoice No.*	*Cash Payment*	*Cash Discount*	*Balance Due*	*General Ledger Code*
1	11345	995.00	29.85	995.00	2000
Remit. No	*Cust No*	*Cust Sold To Name*	*Date of Check*	*Check No.*	*Bank No.*
11535	34522	Parsons and Sons	03-05-9X	169423	22-14/910
No.	*Invoice No.*	*Cash Payment*	*Cash Discount*	*Balance Due*	*General Ledger Code*
1	09332	89.14	0.00	89.14	2000

Monthly Statement Transaction

Invoice Transactions

Invoice Transactions

Total Monthly Statement Remittances   3
Total Invoices Processed   72
Total Invoice Remittances   10   72

Total Monthly Statement Cash Receipts   3,489.02
Total Invoice Cash Receipts $29,480.00
Total Cash Discounts   1,070.60
Total Cash Receipts (Including Discounts) $34,039.62
Total Cash Receipts (Excluding Discounts) $32,969.02

Figure 5–10 Cash-receipts register

Bank Deposit Register				Account Number: 96-5434			Page 1
No.	Remit No.	Bank No.	Cust Sold To Name	Date	Check No.	Amount
006	6321	22-12/111	Home Stores Inc.	03-06-9X	139214	576.47
007	6355	24-15/910	Franklin and Masters	25-05-9X	7264	1044.56
145	11532	16-15/510	International Supply	01-06-9X	368-9240	965.15
146	11535	22-14/910	Parsons and Sons	30-05-9X	169423	89.14

Total Checks   75

Total Deposits $32,969.02

Figure 5–11   Bank deposit register

The Print Receipts A/R Summary Program

Another batch program prints a *receipts A/R summary*, which shows the cash receipts and cash discounts to be applied to outstanding customer receivables. Before the summary is printed, the customer name, check number, and bank number are deleted from the receipts transaction file. In addition, the file is sorted by customer number and invoice number within customer number. This sort is necessary because customers may submit more than one cash payment.

The layout of the receipts A/R summary helps explain some of the previous processing steps. As Figure 5–12 shows, the summary lists the lowest invoice number for a customer, followed by the next lowest number, and so forth. Because these lower numbers are found on monthly statement remittances rather than invoice remittances, monthly statement remittances are placed first in the receipts transaction file. Placing the lowest numbers first allows large numbers such as 99999 to be assigned to show another type of transaction, such as a payment on account. Because the large number will always be greater than an invoice-related number, a payment on account would not be mistakenly applied to a customer account before all invoice-directed dollar amounts. At the bottom of the report are control totals to be carried forward to accounts receivable processing. These totals must be identical to those for the cash receipts and the bank deposit registers; for example, the dollar amount placed in the summary file must be the same as the dollar amount to be deposited.

Receipts Transaction and A/R Summary Files

Figure 5–13 shows the typical contents of the receipts transaction and A/R summary files. When monthly statement remittances are entered into processing, variable length receipts transaction records are created. The first invoice number is stored after the check number, followed by the cash payment amount and the general ledger number. After the information for the first invoice is stored, information

Receipts Summary

Cust No	Invoice No	Remit. No	Record	Remit Date	Check Date	Cash Payment	Cash Discount	GL Code
26877	10764	6355	2	05-06-9X	25-05-9X	544.66	0.00	2000
26877	10814	6355	2	05-06-9X	25-05-9X	199.00	0.00	2000
26877	10998	6355	2	05-06-9X	25-05-9X	300.90	0.00	2000
34522	11535	11535	1	05-06-9X	30-05-9X	89.14	0.00	2000
39662	11345	6321	2	05-06-9X	03-06-9X	365.42	0.00	2000
39662	11390	6321	2	05-06-9X	03-06-9X	121.60	0.00	2000
39662	11491	6321	2	05-06-9X	03-06-9X	89.45	0.00	2000
44831	11532	11532	1	05-06-9X	01-06-9X	965.15	29.85	2000

Total Monthly Statement Remittances   3
Total Invoices Processed   72
Total Invoice Remittances   10   72

Total Monthly Statement Cash Receipts   3,489.02
Total Invoices Cash Receipts $29,480.00
Total Cash Discounts   1,070.60
Total Cash Receipts (Including Discounts) $34,039.62
Total Cash Receipts (Excluding Discounts) $32,969.02

Figure 5–12 Receipts A/R summary

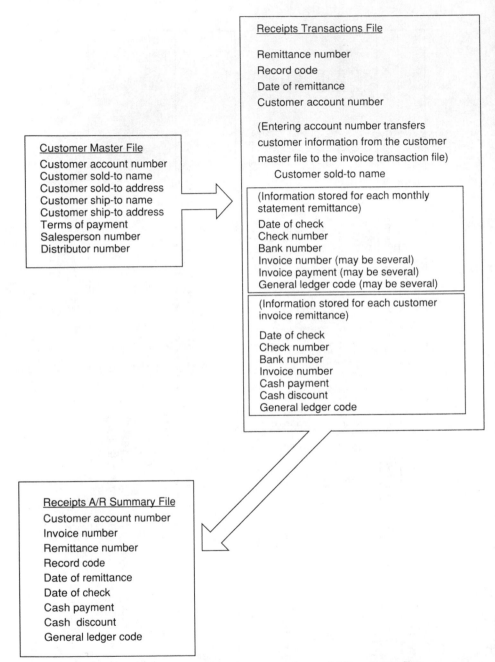

Figure 5–13 Contents of receipts transaction and A/R summary files

for each additional invoice follows, until the entire cash payment amount has been placed in the transaction file. In contrast, when invoice remittances are processed, each record has a fixed length and contains a cash discount amount as well as a cash payment amount.

The records in the receipts A/R summary file are similar to those in the receipts transaction file, except that all variable length records become fixed-length records. This is accomplished by deleting the customer sold-to name and the customer check number from the file and adding the remittance number, record code, date of remittance, and date of check to each invoice identified as being paid. The summary file is also arranged differently from the transaction file. Instead of being arranged by remittance number, the file is arranged by customer number, followed by invoice number. This sequence often leads to several summary records for a monthly statement remittance.

REVIEW QUESTIONS

6. What processing tasks are accomplished by the *Enter cash receipts* program?

7. How are transaction control totals checked during data entry?

8. What is the purpose of the cash receipts register?

9. What is the purpose of the bank deposit slip?

10. What record layout is recommended in the design of the receipts A/R summary?

11. Why are monthly statement receipt records variable in length and invoice receipt records fixed in length?

5-3   CASH RECEIPTS AND POINT-OF-SALE (POS) PROCESSING

Besides processing customer checks received by mail, most business firms accept cash payment at the time of sale. This is especially true of retail establishments and businesses that combine store sales with mail-order sales. Having to deal only with cash at the time of sale greatly simplifies the processing of cash receipts information. With cash, the need to prepare an invoice is avoided; applying customer payments to outstanding invoices is not required. In practice, most POS systems provide for a variety of payment options besides cash. Customers can charge either part or the total amount of the sale, with one of several credit options. One option is the use of a bank credit card in lieu of cash payment. Payment by *bank credit*, a line of personal credit provided to the customer by the customer's bank, requires more complex processing than a cash payment: each transaction involves preparing a sales draft, which is handed to the customer, and, later on, preparing a bank credit deposit slip. One advantage of this payment alternative is that a business avoids billing its customers. The customer's bank is responsible for this activity.

Another billing option is the use of store credit. In contrast to bank credit, *store credit* consists of a line of credit provided by the store or business. Consequently, the store must bill its customers directly. Still other customer payment possibilities include the 30-day or 30/60/90-day interest-free payment plans, revolving charge plans, and unique types of customer installment payment plans.

Because of the complexity brought about by several payment options and the large number of transactions to be handled daily, POS processing systems often employ large numbers of online cash register terminals. Figure 5–14 shows how terminals might be distributed throughout a large retail store: besides being located at each checkout lane, terminals are placed within each major department. As cash registers, these terminals must be able to store cash safely as well as to process and transmit the details of cash receipts processing directly to the computer.

POS terminals permit interactive processing to take place, much like video display terminals. Some POS terminals feature multiple-line displays, but others display only a single line of information. Still other POS terminals do not include a display screen; instead, they feature a light-emitting display panel designed to show the terminal operator the required sequence of processing steps (see Figure

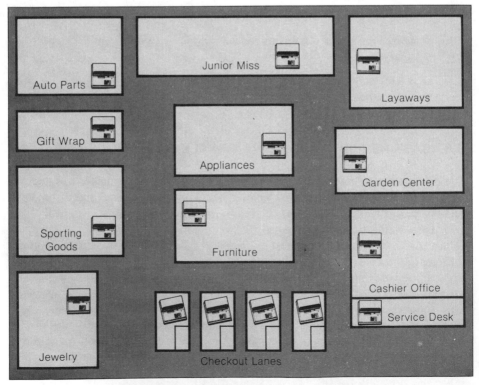

Figure 5–14 Distributed cash-receipts processing

Figure 5–15   Point-of-sale (POS) terminal, terminal keyboard, and qualification codes

5–15). Regardless of the type of POS terminal, the terminal operator is required to follow a standard set of instructions in entering the customer sale.

Most POS terminals are programmable. With programming capabilities, special keyboard operating codes, called *qualification codes*, can be developed. These codes simplify the entry of data into processing and qualify the type of transaction to be processed. For example, after the terminal operator indicates that the details of a sale are to be transmitted, the computer will ask that a qualification code be keyed into processing. Each code defines a specific set of processing instructions. Code 1 might mean a cash sale, and code 7 might indicate a bank credit card sale. Special purpose codes can also be specified. The designer might reserve code 21 for gift wrap and code 32 for gift certificates.

Besides qualification codes, *function keys* help simplify the processing of POS information. Usually located on either side of the ten-key numeric pad, function keys can be reserved to perform specific tasks, such as *Enter data into processing, Process cash payment,* or *Enter customer discount.* Programming capabilities also make it possible to define different payment options or to substitute one payment option for another. This flexibility explains why function keys designed for one retail store differ considerably from those designed for another. When the instructions are determined by the business rather than preset by the equipment manufacturer, a business can tailor its procedures for handling a sale or a return.

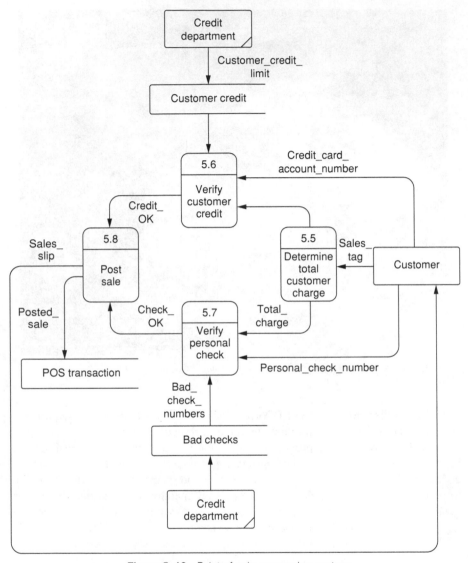

Figure 5–16   Point-of-sale processing system

POS Processing Options

The data-flow diagram in Figure 5–16 shows two different processing options that can be performed by a POS system in processing a customer sale. One option is to verify a customer's credit (see step 5.6). The procedure followed by the operator in seeking verification is as follows:

1. The operator enters the qualification code to tell the computer that the purchase is to be charged to a customer's store credit account. This instruction activates the process to *verify customer credit.*

2. When the credit card account number is keyed into processing, the computer matches it against the customer's credit record to determine if the customer's credit limit is higher or lower than the balance-due amount stored on file, plus the dollar amount to be charged. If the credit limit is higher, the computer responds by telling the operator *Credit OK*. If lower, the computer indicates a credit problem—the credit limit is exceeded or will be exceeded with the additional charge.

3. The operator calls the credit department for further clarification when a credit problem is indicated.

Another processing option is to use the POS system to verify personal checking account numbers (see step 5.7). The procedure used is as follows:

1. The operator enters the qualification code to indicate that a cash sale is to be made and that a personal check has been tendered. This activates the process *Verify personal check*.

2. The checking account number is keyed into processing, and the computer compares it against a file of bad accounts (accounts that the store has experienced problems with in the recent past). If the customer's account matches one stored on file, the computer informs the terminal operator that there is a problem with the personal check; otherwise, the computer tells the operator **Check OK**.

3. The operator calls the credit department for further clarification when the computer signals a potential problem.

Besides verifying customer credit and personal checks, the POS computer system keeps a running record of all cash receipts transactions. Regardless of the type of transaction, the terminal operator is required to key into processing his or her clerk and department number, the transaction code, and the dollar amounts of the transaction—the dollar charges for goods and services, the sales tax (if appropriate), and the final amount of the sale. In addition, the clerk must indicate how payment is to be made. All of this information is stored on the POS transaction file.

Another important step in POS receipts processing is the creation of a tape and a paper backup file. A tape copy is made of all data transmitted from an in-store terminal to a central computer. Should data be lost in transmission or otherwise destroyed, the tape copy becomes the backup to processing. Likewise, a paper copy of all information transmitted is saved. At each terminal, a small sales journal is revised with each customer sale. This is in addition to the sales receipt handed to the customer (see Figure 5-17). The journal, located inside the POS terminal, is better known as a *journal tape*. It can be seen by the clerk and checked, should a question in processing be raised by the customer. For example, the transaction number printed on the sales receipt can be compared to the sales journal entry with the same number to check a particular transaction.

Once POS transmissions are completed and the POS transaction file is closed, a *sales recap* program is activated. This program is designed to audit and summarize cash receipts processing. It sequences all transactions for the day within a store by

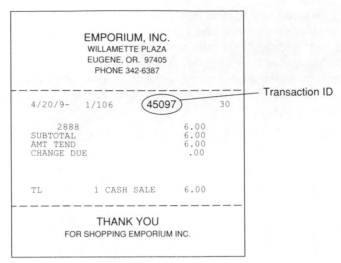

Figure 5–17   Sales receipt

terminal number. Once transactions are sorted, the cash register close-out dollar total is compared to the POS dollar total.

The *daily audit report* is the main output of the sales recap program. As Figure 5–18 shows, this report contains several summary reports: cash report, credit report, fees report, miscellaneous credits report, adjusted sales totals, miscellaneous data report, and terminal balance report. The cash and the credit reports show sales, returns, exchanges, discounts and payments, voids (no sale), aborts (cancel sale), and sales return amounts. The fees and miscellaneous credits reports show the amounts associated with special services, and the adjusted sales total report shows the sales tax collected. The last two reports are control reports. The *miscellaneous data report* indicates if any transactions are missing and the *terminal balance report* shows the difference between sales, returns, and cash.

The POS Transaction File

In marked contrast to the daily audit report, the contents of the POS transaction file are quite easy to understand. As Figure 5–19 shows, each record in the file must include several types of identification: store number, terminal number, clerk number, department number, and transaction number. Neither the store number nor the terminal number needs to be keyed. These are added by the POS program, once the cash register is active. Besides this header information, each record must include a qualification code. If you examine the daily audit report closely, you will be able to count nineteen different codes, beginning with the cash sale code of 01. These codes show how cash receipts information is classified. Dollar amounts are also included in each record. When sales tax is calculated, nontaxable dollar amounts must be kept separate from taxable dollar amounts. The dollar sales tax total and the total POS dollar amount then complete the information to be stored on file.

TERMINAL TOTALS RECAPS

EMPORIUM, INC.

STORE NO 2101
ALL TERMINALS

DATE   10/7/9-
PAGE 211
COLLECTOR 0001

CASH REPORT	QUAL CODE	SALES (TOT) CNT $ AMOUNT	RETURNS (TOT) CNT $ AMOUNT	EXCHANGES (NET) CNT $ AMOUNT	DIC/PYMT CNT $ AMOUNT	VOIDS CNT $ AMOUNT	ABORTS + REJ. CNT $ AMOUNT	SLE-RTN $ AMOUNT
CASH SALE	01	0 0.00	0 0.00	0 0.00	0 0.00	0 0.00	0 0.00	0.00
BANK CRD SALE	7	0 0.00	0 0.00	0 0.00	0 0.00	0 0.00	0 0.00	0.00
GIFT CERT-CA	14	0 0.00	0 0.00	0 0.00	0 0.00	0 0.00	0 0.00	0.00
PAID ON ACCT	09	0 0.00	0 0.00	0 0.00	0 0.00	0 0.00	0 0.00	0.00
LAYAWAY DEP	11	0 0.00	0 0.00	0 0.00	0 0.00	0 0.00	0 0.00	0.00
LAYAWAY PYMT	8	0 0.00	0 0.00	0 0.00	0 0.00	0 0.00	0 0.00	0.00
CASH TOTALS		0	0	0	0	0	0	

CASH REPORT	QUAL CODE	SALES (X=0) CNT $ AMOUNT	RETURNS (X=2) CNT $ AMOUNT	EXCHANGES (X=3) CNT $ AMOUNT	DIC/PYMT CNT $ AMOUNT	VOIDS CNT $ AMOUNT	ABORTS + REJ. CNT $ AMOUNT	SLE-RTN $ AMOUNT
CHARGE SALE	3	0 0.00	0 0.00	0 0.00	0 0.00	0 0.00	0 0.00	0.00
LWY PYMT SALE	40	0 0.00	0 0.00	0 0.00	0 0.00	0 0.00	0 0.00	0.00
STORE CREDIT	26	0 0.00	0 0.00	0 0.00	0 0.00	0 0.00	0 0.00	0.00
GIFT CERT CH	41	0 0.00	0 0.00	0 0.00	0 0.00	0 0.00	0 0.00	0.00
LAYAWAY	11	0 0.00	0 0.00	0 0.00	0 0.00	0 0.00	0 0.00	0.00
CHARGE TOTOLS		0	0	0	0	0	0	
CASH$CHG TOTALS		0 0.00	0	0	0	0	0	0.00

FEES REPORT

TYPE	QTY	$ AMOUNT
ALTERNATIONS	20	0 0.00
GIFT-WRAP	21	0 0.00
CURRENCY DIS	22	0 0.00
POSTAGE	23	0 0.00
TOTALS		0 0.00

MISC CREDITS

TYPE	QTY	$ AMOUNT
GIFT CERT	32	0 0.00
COUPONS	33	0 0.00
STORE CREDIT	34	0 0.00
LAYAWAY CR	35	0 0.00
TOTALS		0 0.00

ADJUSTED SALES TOTALS

	SALES	RETURNED
NON-TAXABLE	0.00	0.00
TAXABLE	0.00	0.00
TAX COLLECTED	0.00	0.00
TOTALS		

MISC DATA REPORT

	QTY
NO SALES	0
TOTAL TRANSACTIONS	1
MISSING TRANSACTIONS	0
NUMBER OF ERRORS	0

TERMINAL BALANCE REPORT

	SALES	RETURNS	CASH
TERMINAL RESET TOTALS	0.00	0.00	0.00
COMPUTED TOTALS	0.00	0.00	0.00
DIFFERENCE	0.00	0.00	0.00

Figure 5–18 Daily audit report

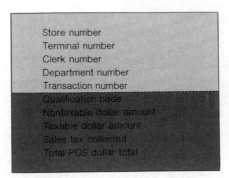

Store number
Terminal number
Clerk number
Department number
Transaction number
Qualification code
Nontaxable dollar amount
Taxable dollar amount
Sales tax collected
Total POS dollar total

Figure 5–19   Point-of-sale (POS) transaction file

5-4   PROCESSING CONTROLS

As was pointed out earlier in this chapter, different types of processing controls must be designed for monitoring cash receipts. The first type consists of control totals to monitor customer payments that are accompanied by customer invoice or monthly statement remittance stubs. For invoice remittances, control totals are the cash payment, cash discount, and balance-due amounts. For monthly statement remittances, control totals include committed and uncommitted cash payment amounts. In processing uncommitted cash payments, a control total is needed only for the dollar amount of the remittance; in processing committed cash payments, however, control totals are maintained both for the amount and for the number of invoices to be paid.

Another type of processing control monitors POS processing totals. In this environment, dollar control totals must be maintained for both cash and charge sales. *Cash sale totals* document the amount of cash contained in company cash registers. A count of the money is compared with the dollar total shown on the sales journal and the daily audit report. If the difference is significant, the people responsible for maintaining the register are held accountable. To resolve any discrepancy, either the journal tape for the day must be reviewed, transaction by transaction, or further testing by computer is required. A common test is to check for duplicate entries (double payments, returns, and so forth). *Charge sale control totals* include dollar totals for several charge categories, including bank credit, store credit, and employee credit totals. Each of these totals is used differently. Bank credit control totals, for example, should be identical to the amount shown on the *merchant summary deposit ticket*, the deposit slip taken to the bank to document bank credit card sales drafts and credit vouchers. Store credit totals are the same as monthly statement totals. When customer bills are prepared, store charge dollar control totals should be identical to the totals printed on the daily audit reports and the monthly billing register. Last, *employee credit* allows employees to charge for store purchases. Instead of billing employees, however, the dollar amount charged is deducted from an employee's paycheck. Accordingly, employee credit control totals should be identical to the total for employee purchase deductions that appears on the summary page of the employee payroll register (see Chapter 12).

POS processing systems require several sets of cash controls to deter employees from embezzlement. Shortages in cash, for example, can be hidden if an employee rings up a customer sale as a charge when the sale was for cash and pockets the cash. Later on, the fictitious charge can be removed from the receipts file by entering a fictitious customer return. Comparing a record of merchandise with a record of sales should point up missing items for which there is no record of sale. Typically, however, these discrepancies are explained as shoplifting losses. One way to stop this type of embezzlement is for customers to question any fictitious charges or returns printed on their monthly statement. Even then, the more inventive embezzler can protect against discovery by using a "safe account"—a personal account or an account held by an accomplice.

Customer charge slips (sales drafts) and return slips (credit vouchers) made out by hand and processed separately from POS processing help guard against employee embezzlement. For the charge slip to be valid, it must contain the customer's account number and signature, a description of the sale, and the dollar amount of the charge or return. Moreover, copies of these slips should be audited periodically. The counts and amounts shown on the slips should be compared to the counts and amounts entered into the computer. Any pattern or significant difference should lead to a larger scale audit of POS processing.

5-5   MANAGEMENT IMPLICATIONS

Cash receipts computer applications have become much more important in recent years because of the increasing use of customer credit in place of cash. Widespread use of credit has led to what is commonly known as the "cashless society." This chapter should make it clear, however, that "cashless" does not mean "paperless" and does not lead to greater simplicity in processing. Quite the contrary. Credit sales add complexity to processing and increase the chance of employee embezzlement and human error. Business firms have thus found it necessary to give greater management attention to receipts processing. Management is required to see that the time between the delivery and deposit of cash payments from customers is reduced as much as possible and that all receipts are accounted for.

There are several ways to gain even faster use of cash receipts than those discussed thus far. Commercial banks feature *lockbox* systems, for example. These systems instruct the customers of a business to send their payments directly to the seller's bank (or to one of its branches), instead of to the seller's business address. Once the bank receives payment, it credits the amount to the seller's account. Soon thereafter, the bank supplies the seller with a tape of the customer remittances and bank deposit information. This information is needed to process cash receipts by computer; however, because customer payments have already been deposited, there is no need to print a bank deposit register.

Another commercial banking service provides for automatic withdrawal of customer payments. In this system, customers are requested to authorize their bank to pay a bill. By written agreement, a bank might be instructed to withdraw a designated amount, say $100, and to send this amount to the seller's bank on a designated date, such as the first of the month. This type of transaction is called a *recurring charge*—a quarterly insurance premium, a monthly loan, or a lease payment. To the customer, the advantage of automatic withdrawal is that the bank does the work of transferring funds. The real advantage is the seller's, however. With automatic withdrawal, the amount and date of a cash payment are known in advance; the payment is deposited immediately in the seller's account.

POS receipts-processing systems provide vital cash-management information in addition to keeping track of daily cash and charge transactions. Week-to-week comparisons of cash-to-charge sales, for example, clarify how customers are planning to pay for their purchases. If the ratio of cash sales to credit sales is changing over time, say from 3:2 to 2:3, this information suggests one of two things: either customers are forced to use credit (because times are tight) or they prefer to use credit (because credit is cheap). In terms of cash management, the most important information is the ability to anticipate the level of cash and credit sales in the near term. If the level of cash sales can be estimated with a high degree of reliability, a business knows the amount of money that will be made available for payment of business expenses and for financing business receivables. Likewise, if the level of charge sales can be estimated, a business knows the amount of money that will be needed to finance its sales on credit.

REVIEW QUESTIONS

12.   What types of transactions must online cash registers process?

13.   How do function keys simplify the entry of data in a POS processing environment?

14.   Name three POS processing options.

15.   In a POS system, what reports are contained on the daily audit report?

16.   How do POS systems guard against employee embezzlement?

17.   How does a lockbox system work?

18.   How are POS systems able to provide vital cash-management information?

REVIEW OF IMPORTANT IDEAS

The way in which customer cash receipts are received depends upon how customers are billed. The most clear and least expensive method of billing is to disallow charge sales: to require customers to pay cash at the time of the sale. The most complex method of billing permits customers to select from one of many customer credit plans if they choose not to pay cash. Online point-of-sale systems permit both cash and credit sales transactions to be processed. They separate sales from returns and returns from exchanges.

The processing of customer payments that follow from customer invoices requires customers to return remittance slips to document how payments are to be applied. An invoice remittance slip shows how a payment will offset a single invoice, and a monthly statement remittance slip shows how a payment will offset several outstanding invoices. Besides inputting data printed on a remittance slip, the cash receipts application must accept payments for which a remittance slip is not included. These are treated as payments on account.

The cash receipts computer application is neither complicated nor involved. The products of processing consist of two registers, a bank deposit slip and the receipts A/R summary. Only the customer master file is needed to support processing. If this file was designed for customer invoice processing, it can be used without modification in receipts processing.

POS systems are designed to process cash and charge sales transactions. Most POS systems are designed to permit online checking of customer credit and verification of personal checks. Both of these options are designed to stop transactions in which the customer's credit is suspect. The most complex part of POS processing is the design and analysis of the daily audit report. This report balances cash register close-out totals to computer-calculated totals and summarizes the dollar volumes of various sales activities processed during the day.

Receipts processing requires careful attention by management. Because of the added complexity brought on by various cash and credit payment options, management must develop safeguards to be able to account for all receipts. Management must pay careful attention to changing customer payment trends. If credit sales begin to increase, management must be able to project the amount of money needed to finance this increase.

KEY WORDS

Cash receipt	Bank credit
Payment on account	Store credit
Point-of-sale (POS) system	Qualification code
Credit on account	Function key
Receipts A/R summary	Journal tape
Cash receipts register	Daily audit report
Receipts transaction file	Merchant summary deposit ticket
Bank deposit slip	Employee credit
Service charge	

EXERCISES

1. Some POS environments are designed to update a customer's store credit balance.

    (a) Using Figure 5–16 as a guide, design a flowchart of the function *Verify customer credit*.

    (b) Explain any changes to the customer master file that would be required to implement this design.

(c) Explain what type of processing control (if any) is needed.

(d) List the advantages and disadvantages of this more complex processing design.

2. An argument for using POS receipts processing states that this method makes it more difficult for employees to steal from a company. How would you respond to this evaluation?

3. The POS transaction file created by the POS system contains a minimum of ten items, beginning with the store number and ending with the POS dollar total. Why is each item stored in the file?

4. Mark Fellows, lead designer, comments: "We need to revise the processing control totals shown on the cash receipts register. Besides the counts and amounts shown, some provision must be made to indicate the number of invoices fully paid, the number of invoices partially paid, and the uncommitted dollar amount to be applied as payment on account."

Revise the control totals shown in Figure 5–10 to add Mark's new requirements. You can assume the following: first, of the 10 invoices paid by the three monthly statement remittances, all but one were fully paid. Second, of the 72 invoices paid by the 72 invoice remittances, all but six were fully paid. Third, the total uncommitted dollar amount was $1,302.00.

5. Suppose a lockbox system is used to speed the collection of customer payments. With such a system, the bank sends the customer remittances and the bank deposit slip to the business, showing the funds deposited in the lockbox account.

How will a lockbox system change the data-flow diagram shown in Figure 5–1? How will a lockbox system change the data-flow diagram shown in Figure 5–2?

6. Suppose that a company must handle only cash sales. How will cash sales change the data-flow diagram shown in Figure 5–1? How will cash sales change the data-flow diagram shown in Figure 5–2?

DISCUSSION QUESTIONS

1. Why do companies provide so many payment options, when cash payment at the time of the sale is so easily administered? Name several types of businesses that restrict their payment options to cash. How can these companies get away with placing this restriction on their customers?

2. Many companies currently provide a cash discount if a cash payment is made at the time of sale. Why is it advantageous for a business to provide such a discount? Give several reasons.

3. The cash receipts register can be used to provide different types of management information as well as a listing of cash receipts transactions. List and explain the

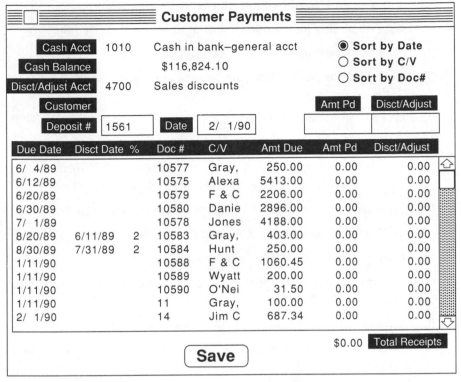

Figure 5–20   Online receipts register

different types of management summary totals that can be calculated in processing and placed on a separate summary report. Some of these totals are already shown at the bottom of Figure 5–10.

4. An online cash receipts register, such as the register shown in Figure 5–20, is advantageous for a variety of reasons. What are these reasons?

4-IN-1 CASE STUDY—PROCESSING CASH RECEIPTS

In this exercise, using 4-in-1, you will perform several tasks important to processing cash receipts. These include

- processing a cash receipt
- printing a cash receipts register
- printing a bank deposit slip, and
- posting cash receipts to the general ledger.

In working through these tasks, compare the similarities and differences between processing cash receipts and processing customer invoices and credit memos.

Processing a Cash Receipt Using an Invoice Remittance

To process a cash receipt, log on using a date of **012097** and do the following:

1. Type **9** from the main menu and press ENTER.

2. Type **1,** add transactions from the process cash receipts menu, and press ENTER.

3. Type **LAWNS** when asked to enter the name of the customer. Press ENTER.

4. Press ENTER when asked, *Right customer?*

5. Press ENTER (or type **012097** and press ENTER) to record the receipt date—the date the cash receipt was received in the mail.

6. Type **12554** and press ENTER to log the customer check number.

7. Type **100.00** and press ENTER to indicate the amount received.

8. Press ENTER to indicate that no discount was allowed.

9. Type **1111** and press ENTER to indicate that payment is made in reference to invoice 1111.

10. Type **53-16/110** and press ENTER to record the bank number.

11. Press ENTER (or type **1** and press ENTER) to place this receipt in bank checking account 1.

12. Press ENTER when asked, *Credit this transaction to the accounts receivable G/L account?*

13. Press ENTER when asked, *Field number to change?*

14. Press TAB twice to return to the main menu.

Adding Another Balance-forward Amount to a Customer's Account

To add a balance-forward amount at this time, do the following:

15. Type **8** from the main menu and press ENTER.

16. Type **1,** *Add transactions*, from the process sales and DR/CR memos menu.

17. Type **FARMERS** when asked to enter the full or partial name of the customer. If you cannot remember the name of a customer when using 4-in-1, press the F1 key. This allows you to scroll through the customer list repeatedly. Press ENTER.

18. Press ENTER when asked, *Right customer?*

19. Type **B** and press ENTER to place a balance-forward amount in the FARMERS-COOP account.

20. Press ENTER (or type **012097** and press ENTER) when the transaction date is displayed.

21. Type **200.00** and press ENTER when asked to indicate the amount of money that this customer owes you.

22. Press ENTER when the *Balance forward* reference is displayed.

23. Press ENTER to record this amount and to return to the add transactions menu.

24. Press TAB to return to the process sales and DR/CR memos menu.

25. Type **6** and press ENTER to post this transaction.

26. Ready your printer before this next step. Type **Y** when asked, *Are sales transactions OK to post?*

27. Press TAB to return to the main menu.

Processing a Payment on Account

To process a cash receipt for a payment on account, do the following:

28. Type **9** from the main menu and press ENTER.

29. Type **1**, *Add transactions*, from the process cash receipts menu. Press ENTER.

30. Type **FARMERS** when asked to enter the name of the customer. Press ENTER.

31. Press ENTER when asked, *Right customer?*

32. Press ENTER (or type **012097** and press ENTER) to record the receipt date—the date the cash receipt was received in the mail.

33. Type **1306** and press ENTER to log the customer check number.

34. Type **150.00** and press ENTER to indicate the amount received.

35. Press ENTER to indicate that no discount was allowed.

36. Type **Payment on account** and press ENTER to reference the receipt.

37. Type **55-18/990** and press ENTER to record the bank number.

38. Press ENTER to place the receipt in checking account 1.

39. Press ENTER when asked, *Credit this transaction to the accounts receivable G/L account?*

40. Press ENTER when asked, *Field number to change?*

41. Press TAB to return to the process cash receipts menu.

Printing the Cash Receipts Register

The cash receipts edit list is easily prepared. Do the following:

42. Type **4** and press ENTER from the process cash receipts menu.

43. Press ENTER when asked, *Display this report?* This step leads to the printing of the cash receipts edit list. The list contains a detail page and a summary page.

Printing the Bank Deposit Slip

The printing of a bank deposit slip is also easy. From the process sales and DR/CR memos menu, do the following:

44. Type **5** and press ENTER from the process cash receipts menu.

45. Press ENTER (or type **012097** and press ENTER) when asked to enter the deposit date.

46. Ready your printer and press ENTER when asked, *Any change?* This leads to the printing of the bank deposit slip.

Posting Cash Receipt Transactions to the General Ledger

Posting cash receipts to the G/L is often done immediately after printing bank deposit slips. From the process sales and DR/CR memos menu, do the following:

47. Type **6** and press ENTER from the process cash receipts menu.

48. Type **Y** when asked, *Are cash transactions OK to post?*

49. Press ENTER when asked to enter the date of posting.

50. Ready your printer and press ENTER when asked, *Any change?* This leads to the printing of the cash receipts register. The register shows all postings to the general ledger.

51. Press TAB to return to the main menu.

52. Press TAB to log off if you do not plan to begin the next exercise.

QUESTIONS

Compare the design of the 4-in-1 cash receipts application to the application described in the chapter. Then do the following:

1. List the contents of the 4-in-1 cash receipts transaction file. Use Figure 5–13 in preparing this list.

2. How does the 4-in-1 cash receipts edit list differ from the 4-in-1 bank deposit slip? How do they differ from the same documents described by the chapter?

3. What new information is found on the 4-in-1 cash receipts register, compared to the cash receipts register and receipts A/R summary described in the chapter?

4. Why are cash receipts credited to trade accounts receivable instead of debited? Why are cash receipts debited to cash receipts, checking #1?

Accounts Receivable

Besides billing customers for goods that are shipped and processing payments received in return, business firms must keep accurate records of all paid invoices and those that remain to be paid. This record keeping is accomplished by the accounts receivable computer application. By definition, *accounts receivable* represent legal claims against customers for amounts due. Receivables are also defined as *current assets*, where the assets of a business specify what is owned. At first glance, the mixing of legal claims and current assets may seem contradictory. However, assets can take either a physical form, such as an adding machine or a product in inventory, or a legal form, such as an outstanding customer invoice. Since receivables are current assets, all amounts due are expected to be converted into cash within a period of less than one year.

An online accounts receivable application does considerably more for a business than keep a record of legal claims against customers. This application can provide greater accuracy in processing, timely release of attractive monthly statements, improved handling of customer account inquiries, and better account-collection procedures. It can improve a business's ability to calculate the age of customer accounts and to determine customer payment patterns. Viewed in total, the accounts receivable application is designed to improve customer service and administrative control of customer accounts. It furthers the objective of effective cash management—namely, to hold customer credit balances to a minimum—while making credit sales and providing accurate and prompt delivery of goods and services.

6-1 TYPES OF ACCOUNTS RECEIVABLE SYSTEMS

There are three main types of accounts receivable systems: *balance only, balance forward,* and *open item.* The most complex of these is the open-item system of billing and processing customer payments. This type has been described in the text materials thus far. The moderately complex balance-forward system has been featured by the 4-in-1 case study. Let's examine the differences in these three types of systems.

Balance-only System

The most simple accounts-receivable system is the balance-only system. This system is designed to process minimal amounts of billing information; it produces a customer bill that shows the current amount due, past-due charges, and the current balance. Most utility companies produce balance-only customer statements. A utility bill typically contains a current statement of charges, the previous balance, and the payments received. Current charges are generally explained in terms of kilowatt hours of electricity or thousands of gallons of water consumed. Finally, the statement contains customer account information (customer number, name, and home address) but little else. The past-due amount is rarely broken down to show the number of months the charges have been outstanding.

Balance-forward System

The balance-forward system is similar to the balance-only system, except that it provides considerably more information about current charges and typically *ages* past-due amounts. Commercial banks, retail stores, and wholesalers that feature credit cards utilize *revolving* balance-forward systems. With a revolving system, a company does not expect a bill to be paid in full each month. Instead, the customer is expected to make partial payment of, at the very least, the minimum amount due. For example, a bank credit-card statement lists, by date of transaction, each sales draft, credit voucher, and payment. The statement also contains an account summary section and a minimum amount-due section. The account summary is represented by the following formula:

$$\text{Past-due balance} - \text{Payments} - \text{Returns} + \text{Purchases} + \text{Cash advances} + \text{Finance charges} = \text{New balance}$$

The minimum amount-due section is printed without explanation. If, for example, the new balance were \$569.71, the minimum payment shown might be only \$39.00—approximately 7 percent of the outstanding balance.

   Another type of balance-forward system is designed to give customers 20 or 30 days to pay an outstanding balance. This system is appropriate if customers are expected to pay their bills in full. Medical clinics and legal firms, for example, are typical users of 20- and 30-day balance-forward systems. Figure 6–1 shows a balance-forward monthly statement prepared by a medical clinic. The credit policy of the clinic is printed at the top of the description of charges. It reads

ALL CHARGES OVER 1 MONTH, WITHOUT PRIOR ARRANGEMENTS FOR PAYMENT, ARE PAST-DUE AND PAYABLE, IN FULL, BY THE 20TH.

Besides credit-policy details, the statement itemizes current charges and totals past-due charges: it shows the previous balance and ages all other past-due amounts. As indicated at the bottom of this statement, current charges are \$77.85, and charges over a month (30 days) are \$102.55. Finance charges are applied to past-due amounts. Any amount outstanding by more than 90 days will be subjected to a

STATEMENT

ANY CHARGES OR PAYMENTS RECEIVED AFTER
THE DATE BELOW WILL APPEAR ON YOUR NEXT STATEMENT

ACCOUNT NUMBER   00825–   PAGE   1 OF 1   CC • CLOSING DATE   05/31/9–

EUGENE HOSPITAL & CLINIC
EUGENE HOSPITAL COMPANY
1162 WILLIAMETTE STREET
EUGENE, OREGON 97401
F.I.D. NO. 93-0349770

TOTAL BALANCE   180.40

AMOUNT REMITTED

SEND INQUIRIES TO

ALAN L ELIASON

EUGENE OR 97405

EUGENE HOSPITAL & CLINIC
EUGENE HOSPITAL COMPANY
1162 WILLIAMETTE STREET
EUGENE, OREGON 97401

IMPORTANT! SEE REVERSE SIDE

DETACH AND RETURN THIS PORTION WITH
YOUR REMITTANCE TO THE ABOVE ADDRESS

BILLED FROM
EUGENE HOSPITAL & CLINIC

• CLOSING DATE
05/31/9–

BILLED TO
ALAN L ELIASON

ACCOUNT NUMBER

MO. DAY YR.	DR. NO.	DESCRIPTION	PROCEDURE NUMBER	CHARGE	CREDIT
********** PAYMENT–INSURANCE BILLING NOTIFICATION **********					
ALL CHARGES OVER 1 MONTH, WITHOUT PRIOR ARRANGEMENTS FOR					
PAYMENT, ARE PAST DUE AND PAYABLE, IN FULL, BY THE 20TH.					
PRIMARY INSURANCES BILLED ON ACCOUNTS SET-UP FOR AUTOMATIC					
BILLING. ATTACHED FORM FOR SECONDARY INSURANCES OR ACCOUNTS					
NOT SET-UP. BUSINESS HOURS FOR CALLS, 10AM TO 5PM MON–FRI.					
MEDICARE ACCOUNTS WILL RECIVE MEDICARE FORMS TO BILL WITH.					
		PREVIOUS BALANCE		102 55	
05299–	73	LAB CULTURE BETA-STREP	87999	11 50	
05299–	73	OFFICE VISIT LIMITED	90050	20 65	
05019–	22	OFFICE VISIT LIMITED	90050	20 65	
05059–	22	CAST MATERIAL	99070	5 00	
05059–	22	CAST REPAIR	29799	5 00	
05229–	22	OFFICE VIST BRIEF	90040	15 05	
05229–	22	CAST REMOVAL	29700		
		SERVICES PERFORMED BY			
	73	H W			
	22	R E			

DATE OF LAST PAYMENT 04/16/9–

FINANCE CHARGE is computed by a periodic rate of 1.38% per month. **ANNUAL PERCENTAGE RATE 18%.** Before next month's closing date• pay the portion of your new balance which has been outstanding more than 90 days in order to avoid additional FINANCE CHARGE
CREDIT OR INSURANCE INFORMATION (503) 678- 6231.   Keep this portion of statement for tax and record purposes.

CURRENT MO.	OVER 1 MO.	OVER 2 MO.	OVER 3 MO.	OVER 4 MO.	TOTAL AMOUNT	TOTAL BALANCE
77 85	102 55				180 40	180 40

Figure 6–1   Balance-forward statement

finance charge of 1.38 percent per month. Thus, even though this is a monthly balance-forward statement, a finance charge is not levied unless a past-due amount is older than 90 days. A third version of a balance-forward system is designed to produce invoices, record the details of a sales transaction, and complete a monthly statement of all invoice charges during the month with all cash payments. This approach also shows the previous balance and ages all other past amounts. Finance charges are not likely to be applied in this version. Instead, the invoice offers a cash discount for prompt payment. If the customer decides not to pay in time, the penalty becomes the loss of the discount.

Open-item System

In contrast to the balance-forward accounts receivable system, the open-item system does not summarize past-due charges but instead continues to list any invoice that has not been completely paid. Then, to add even more billing information, each outstanding invoice is aged. The aging categories, or *aging buckets*, show when an invoice is less than 30 days old, 30 or more but less than 60 days old, 60 or more but less than 90 days old, and over 90 days old. This aging procedure provides the customer with a clear reminder of the length of time an invoice has been outstanding. It permits business firms to determine which particular invoices are excessively past due. For long-overdue accounts, special reminder letters, know as *dunning letters*, are printed by computer. These letters become more demanding as the account balance gets older. Besides letters, overdue reminders by telephone are becoming more popular. The computer assists in this instance also: billing-collection operators use online displays to find all needed calling information for delinquent accounts. This information includes the name of the customer, the telephone number and the name of the person to contact, recent billing information, and the payment history for the customer's account. Automatic dialing of the telephone number is even possible, with some systems.

The value of an open-item system, compared with others, is that a complete accounting is provided for each sales transaction. Both customers and businesses benefit from this complete picture. Customers, for example, are able to decide which invoices to pay and whether to take advantage of a cash discount; they are able to contest a single charge and ask that the paperwork supporting the charge be reviewed. Businesses, likewise, are able to apply a customer payment, credit, or exchange to a specific invoice; they are able to bring a single invoice balance due or credit amount to the attention of the customer. Indeed, the most important advantage of an open-item system is that a clear audit trail is maintained for each sales transaction. The system provides a record of every invoice and how it is offset—by a payment, credit, or billing adjustment.

6-2   PRELIMINARY OVERVIEW OF PROCESSING

This chapter describes an open-item accounts receivable application. As shown by Figure 6–2, two inputs to processing, the invoice and the receipts A/R summary

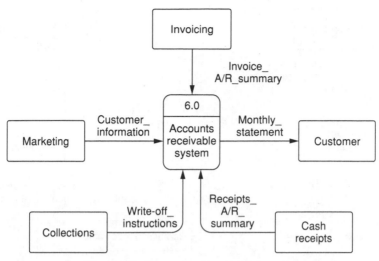

Figure 6–2 The accounts receivable system

files, follow from the customer-invoicing and the cash receipts applications. Two other inputs are customer information and write-off instructions. Customer information adds the customer name and address to processing once again, and write-off instructions permit an outstanding charge to be written off when customers refuse to pay or when the balance is too small to collect.

The main output from processing is the *monthly statement*. This statement shows which invoices are outstanding and their age. It is printed only when an outstanding invoice is past due and payable, that is, when the date of payment printed on the invoice is past and full payment has not been received.

In practice, the accounts receivable application is more complicated than the context diagram suggests. As shown by Figure 6–3, five processing steps are the *Post A/R summary*, *Post receipts summary*, *Delete A/R transactions*, *Age customer accounts*, and *Print customer statements*. The first and second steps (see 6.1 and 6.2 in the figure) update the accounts receivable file. This file is better known as a *consolidated A/R master file* because it combines billing with payment transactions. The third step (see 6.3) follows the update of the file. This step matches charges with payments, to delete paid invoices. In so doing, the receivables file is split into two smaller files: the deleted invoices file and the remaining receivables file. The fourth step (see 6.4) utilizes the remaining receivables file to print a schedule of all past-due invoices and their age. The fifth step (see 6.5) produces customer monthly statements.

The Consolidated A/R Master File

Updating the consolidated A/R master file is a major undertaking in accounts receivable processing. Before any invoice can be removed from the file or any monthly statement can be printed, the A/R master file must be in proper sequence

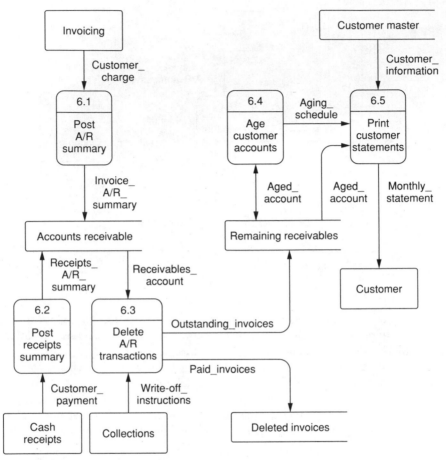

Figure 6–3   Five steps in processing accounts receivable information

and in balance. Figure 6–4 shows the arrangement of invoice, credit, and payment (cash receipts) summary information in the file, sequenced according to the following rules:

- All records are arranged by account number, such as by customer account number.

- Within each account number, customer invoice information is stored first, credit information is stored second, and payment information is stored third.

- Within each account number, the lowest invoice number (the oldest outstanding invoice) is stored first, the next lowest invoice number is stored second, and so forth.

- Each record contains one invoice summary segment; none, one, or more credit segments; and none, one, or more payment segments.

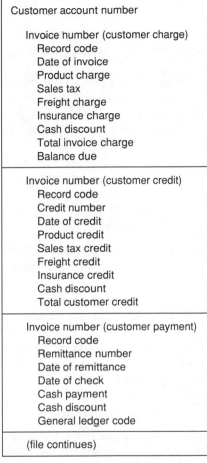

Customer account number

    Invoice number (customer charge)
        Record code
        Date of invoice
        Product charge
        Sales tax
        Freight charge
        Insurance charge
        Cash discount
        Total invoice charge
        Balance due

    Invoice number (customer credit)
        Record code
        Credit number
        Date of credit
        Product credit
        Sales tax credit
        Freight credit
        Insurance credit
        Cash discount
        Total customer credit

    Invoice number (customer payment)
        Record code
        Remittance number
        Date of remittance
        Date of check
        Cash payment
        Cash discount
        General ledger code

(file continues)

Figure 6–4 Accounts receivable master file

- Each record segment is headed by the same unique identification number, such as the invoice number, to tie together the record segments.

- Record codes identify the different record segments.

You might observe that the record segments designed for the consolidated A/R master file follow from the records contained in the invoice A/R summary file and the receipts A/R summary file (See Figures 4–14 and 5–13). Thus, no new data elements need to be added in creating this file. Second, the file is organized so that credits are applied first to offset an invoice charge. If credits do not exist, customer payments are applied. Finally, if neither credits nor payments exist, only the invoice record segment is stored.

The consolidated A/R master file must be in balance before it is used. Both total dollar amounts and total transaction counts must be accounted for. For example, the total dollar amount equation is

Old A/R dollar total + Invoice dollar total − Credit dollar total
  − Payment dollar total − Cash discounts = New A/R dollar total

In this equation, the old A/R dollar total represents the amount that was stored in the A/R master file before the invoice dollar totals were added and the credit, payment, and cash discount totals were subtracted. These last four totals—the invoice, credit, payment, and cash discount totals—represent the amounts previously stored on the invoice and receipts A/R summary files.

As another example, the first equation used in balancing the count of transactions is similar to the equation used for cash, except that all parts of the equation are positive. The equation reads

Transaction Count 1

Old number of transactions + Invoice transactions + Credit transactions
  + Payment transactions = New number of transactions

At this stage in processing, no attempt is made to apply credit and payment dollars to outstanding invoices. The important facts to retain are the counts of all transactions stored on the A/R master file. Later on, when invoices are deleted from the file, the number of transactions reported as being deleted from the file must be balanced against the number of transactions remaining on file. This second transaction-count balance equation reads

Transaction Count 2

Old number of transactions − Invoice transactions deleted
− Credit transactions deleted − Payment transactions deleted
  = New number of transactions

Thus, the first transaction count verifies that all transactions from the A/R summary files have been accounted for; the second count verifies that the correct number of transactions have been successfully deleted from the A/R master file.

Outputs from Processing

Besides monthly statements, the information printed by the A/R computer application includes one or more printed registers and one or more receivables summary reports. The purpose of each can be summarized as follows:

- The *accounts receivable register* lists the contents of the A/R master file.

- The *deleted invoice report* shows invoices that net to zero (that have been paid in full) and invoices, credits, and payments removed from the A/R master file:

- The *aging schedule* shows the balance-due amount and the aged subtotals for each customer.

Unlike previous applications, this one does not create a summary file for still another computer application. Rather, the file that becomes important is the remaining receivables file. After it is used to print customer statements (see Figure 6–3), the file becomes the *new consolidated A/R master file*, to which invoice and receipts A/R summary records are added.

Besides printed documents and files, several visual displays must be designed. Among these are the *consolidated customer receivable display*, which shows the customer's complete receivable record, and the *aged customer receivable display*, which shows the current balance-due amount and amounts past due by 31 to 60 days, 61 to 90 days, and over 90 days. The consolidated customer receivable display can be used in adjusting customer accounts, the most frequent adjustment being the removal of small invoice balances from a customer's account. In contrast, the aged customer receivable display can be used for inquiries, the most frequent of which determines whether a credit or a payment has been applied to an account. Such an inquiry generally follows a customer's request to check his or her payment history.

Figure 6–5 shows one possible design for a *customer monthly statement*. In many ways this design is very similar to the customer invoice (See Figure 4–5). It shows the customer account number, statement date, remittance (statement) number, and customer sold-to name and address; provides a brief description of each transaction; and shows the dollar amount of each transaction. A monthly statement differs from a customer invoice, however. First, it provides only a reference to the original invoice, credit, or payment. Second, it may use codes to separate different types of transactions. (The letter *A*, for example, might indicate *Discount allowed*, and the letter *F* may denote *Finance charge*.) Third, the description part of the statement supplements the reference number with a brief description such as *Payment—Thank you*.

REVIEW QUESTIONS

1. Besides keeping a record of current assets, why should a company develop an online A/R application?

2. What are the three types of A/R systems, and how do they differ?

3. What is an *aging bucket?*

4. What is a *dunning letter?*

5. How are invoice, cash payment, and customer credit records arranged in the consolidated A/R master file?

6. Explain the equation needed to balance the total dollar amount stored on the A/R master file.

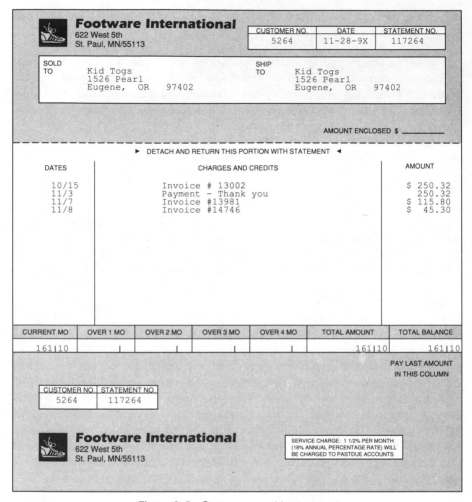

Figure 6–5   Customer monthly statement

7. Name the four types of printed output produced by this application.

8. How does a monthly statement differ from a customer invoice?

6-3   ACCOUNTS RECEIVABLE PROCESSING

Figures 6–6(a) and 6–6(b) illustrate the system organization chart for accounts receivable processing. Compared with the previous charts, the batch portion of this application is somewhat complex. A new function, *Sort/merge files*, has been added to acknowledge that processing must merge data from different files into a sequenced *consolidated A/R master file*. Other than this new function, the remaining batch functions should be familiar. They are identical to those required in invoice processing.

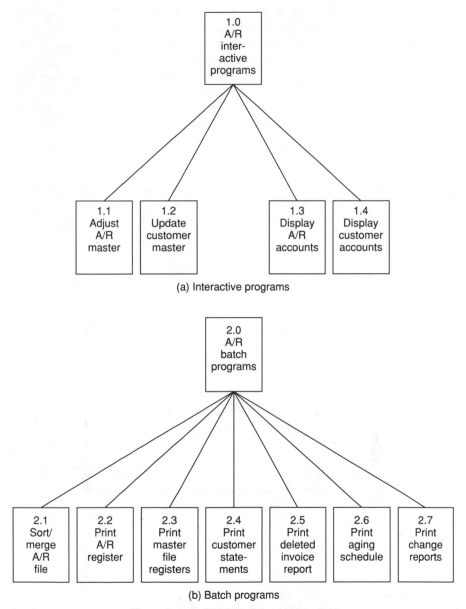

(a) Interactive programs

(b) Batch programs

Figure 6-6   A/R system organization chart

The interactive portion of processing contains two new programs: *Adjust A/R master* and *Display A/R accounts*. Of particular interest is the program designed to adjust the A/R master file. One kind of adjustment eliminates small balances from the file (such as all invoices with a balance of $.50 or less). Another is generally a credit that follows from a review of an account. Suppose a customer claims, correctly, that a debit rather than a credit has been applied to his or her account. A review in this situation should spot the difficulty immediately. Once the problem is spotted, a credit adjustment to the account can be made. There are also times when accounts simply need review. A review is needed to examine all accounts when the current and past-due amounts exceed customer credit limits. In this way, a business is able to determine which customer accounts require special attention.

The A/R systems organization chart should be viewed as a minimal processing design. Several other print programs, such as intermediate file-balance reports, error handling reports, and automatic dunning letters, could be added to the design. Even though the design is minimal, however, it should not be considered deficient. It is several times more advanced than designs common to many smaller business firms.

Parts (a) and (b) of Figure 6–7 illustrate the processing menus that follow from this chart of organization. The four interactive programs and the eight batch programs permit an operator to examine accounts stored in the consolidated A/R master file and to schedule the batch processing of accounts receivable information. In times past, processing would be scheduled once each month, leading to the production of what are commonly known as month-end customer statements. With computer processing, *cycle billing* has tended to replace month-end billing. With

```
┌─────────────────────────────────────────┐
│ ACCOUNTS RECEIVABLE                      │
├──────────────────────┘                   │
│                                          │
│      ADJUST RECEIVABLE MASTER            │
│      UPDATE CUSTOMER MASTER              │
│                                          │
│      DISPLAY A/R ACCOUNTS                │
│      DISPLAY CUSTOMER ACCOUNTS           │
│                                          │
│                                          │
│      RETURN                              │
│                                          │
└─────────────────────────────────────────┘
```

(a) Interactive processing menu

```
┌─────────────────────────────────────────┐
│ ACCOUNTS RECEIVABLE                      │
├──────────────────────┘                   │
│                                          │
│      SORT/MERGE A/R FILE                 │
│      PRINT A/R REGISTER                  │
│      PRINT MASTER FILE REGISTERS         │
│      PRINT CUSTOMER STATEMENTS           │
│                                          │
│      PRINT DELETED INVOICES              │
│      PRINT AGING SCHEDULE                │
│      PRINT CHANGE REPORTS                │
│                                          │
│      RETURN                              │
│                                          │
└─────────────────────────────────────────┘
```

(b) Batch processing menu

Figure 6–7   A/R processing menu

cycle billing, statements for groups of accounts are produced at different times, including daily, weekly, monthly, or quarterly. For example, a business might divide its accounts receivable into six groups and produce monthly statements six times each month. Likewise, a company with a large number of accounts might produce monthly statements daily. In this instance, either the customer account number, the postal code, or a specific billing-cycle code appended to the account determines the *account cycle time* (the time during the month when a monthly statement is to be prepared). With computer processing, it is also possible to produce customer monthly statements one at a time or on demand. Here the processing cycle is modified by the operator. Typically, on-demand production of statements follows the adjustment of an account. Once adjusted, the customer is supplied with a revised billing statement.

The *Sort/merge receivable files* Program

The sort/merge receivable files program is required to update the consolidated A/R master file. As Figure 6–8 shows, the update is acomplished by combining invoice, credit, and payment transactions stored on the invoice and the receipts A/R summary files with transactions stored on the old consolidated A/R master file. A new consolidated A/R master file is created as a result of processing. The records stored on this file are sequenced first by customer number and second by type of transaction.

Because sort/merge utility software packages exist for most computer systems, business firms are able to avoid designing complex custom sort/merge computer programs. As with any type of computer program, however, problems in processing are usually experienced. Thus, the sort/merge program must be carefully monitored. At a minimum, batch balance control totals of counts and amounts should be printed to verify that all records have been accounted for.

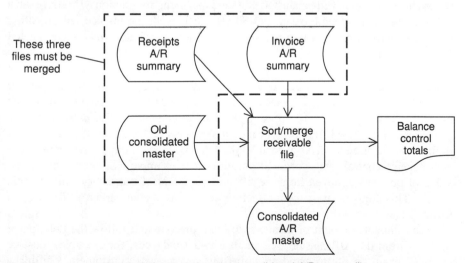

Figure 6–8 Updating the consolidated A/R master file

The *Print receivable register* Program

Figure 6–9 shows an abbreviated *accounts receivable register*. Besides listing the invoice, customer credit, and customer receipts activity for each customer account, the register shows the invoice to which a cash receipt is applied. The register also prints dollar and transaction count control totals. For example, the totals on the right-hand side of the register illustrate total dollar controls. The beginning A/R balance represents the old A/R dollars total, whereas the ending A/R balance now represents the new A/R dollar total. Likewise, beginning and ending transactions shown on the left-hand side indicate the change in the number of transactions following the update of the file. These totals follow from the file-balance control equation previously shown as Transaction Count 1.

Close review of the accounts receivable register reveals one additional processing feature: the program determines the remaining balance on any invoice older than 30 days and any balance following the application of a customer credit or payment. In Figure 6–9, a remaining balance of $29.85 is shown for customer account number 44831 (see the middle part of the figure). On examination, this balance exists because the customer took the cash discount; however, the computer determined that the discount should not have been taken. How could this happen? Suppose the terms of payment provide for the discount of $29.85 if the bill is paid within 10 days. In processing, the computer adds 10 to the date of the invoice (the invoice-posting date) and compares this date with the date of the cash receipt (the receipt-posting date). In this example, such a comparison shows that the receipt was posted 20 days after the posting of the invoice (June 5, 1990). Thus, the discount was not approved.

The *Print deleted-invoice report* Program

Before customer monthly statements are printed, invoices that net to zero must be deleted from the consolidated A/R master file. During processing, invoice transactions are matched against credit and payment transactions to arrive at a balance-due total. When a balance of $0.00 is achieved, the invoice, all offsetting credit and payment record segments, and all other record adjustments are deleted from the master file.

As illustrated by Figure 6–10, deleting invoices changes the consolidated A/R master file once again. Instead of being enlarged, as is the case when files are merged, the consolidated A/R master file is now made smaller. As with other file updates, the effects of the processing must be documented. The *deleted invoice report* meets this need. It shows all record segments deleted from the file and the dollar amounts used to arrive at each $0.00 balance. In addition, the report provides new balance control totals for audit purposes. For example, it provides the dollar value of invoices removed from the file and the count of transactions that remain on file. This adjustment of the transaction count was shown earlier as Transaction Count 2 (see page 178).

A considerable amount of detail work must precede and follow the deletion of invoices from the A/R master file. Small account balances, for example, must be removed from the file to avoid embarrassing statements to customers. (Billing a

Accounts Receivable Register   Date 16-May-9X   Page 1

No	Cust No.	Type	Number	Apply To	Posted	Check	Charge	Discount	G.L.	Payment	Discount	Balance
0131	39662	Inv.	11345		180490		346.47	7.31	4000			
0132	39662	C.R.	6321	11345	050690	03068			2000	346.47	0.00	0.00
0133	39662	Inv.	11390		200490		121.60	2.43	4000			
0134	39662	C.R.	6321	11390	050690	03068			2000	121.60	0.00	0.00
0135	39662	Inv.	11491		280490		89.45	1.79	4000			
0136	39662	C.R.	6321	11491	050690	03068			2000	89.45	0.00	0.00
0137	39662	Inv.	11538		100590		365.00	7.30	4000			
0138	39662	Inv.	11573		060590		430.60	8.61	4000			
0139	39662	Inv.	11680		150590		82.14	1.64	4000			
0187	44831	Inv.	11532		150590		995.00	29.85	4000			
0188	44831	C.R.	11532	11532	050690	01068			2000	965.15	29.85	29.85

Beginning Transactions   1076
Total Invoices Processed   241
Total Credits Processed   12
Total Payments Processed   233
Ending Transactions   1562

Beginning Accounts Receivable $159,643.26
Plus: Invoice Charges   48,326.42
Less: Customer Credits   532.16
      Customer Payments   46,842.16
      Cash Discounts   389.76
Ending Accounts Receivable $160,205.60

Figure 6-9   Accounts receivable register

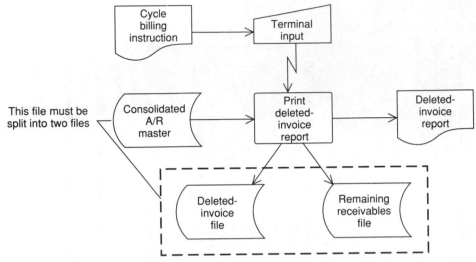

Figure 6–10   Deleting paid-in-full invoices

customer for six cents would be embarrassing; moreover, the cost to prepare the bill is more than the balance due.) To eliminate these balances, the amounts to be removed must be entered into processing as credit adjustments. Likewise, some cash discounts are allowed, even though they are taken by customers later than the date shown in the terms of payment. Writing off the discount is another type of credit adjustment.

The problem with making adjustments after the deleted-invoice program has been run is that a change will reduce invoices stored on file to zero. If they are allowed to remain on file, they lead to the printing of $0.00 balance-due monthly statements—another type of statement to avoid. The way to treat this particular problem is to rerun the deleted-invoice program. The rerun in turn produces another deleted-invoice report and a revised set of file-control balances.

The *Adjust receivable master* Program

Interactive methods of processing are especially useful in making adjustments to the consolidated A/R master file. To begin processing, the program *Adjust receivable master* is selected. As Figure 6–11 shows, this program permits the operator to review both the customer and receivable account and to adjust the consolidated A/R master file accordingly. In processing, a customer's account is displayed page by page to show how invoices will be reduced to zero. The entire customer account can thus be examined before invoices have been deleted from the file.

Figure 6–12 shows the first page of a consolidated customer receivable display. Suppose that this account is being examined to determine if the cash discount for invoice number 11225 has been allowed. On inspection it can be determined that it has: there is a discount taken of $1.03 and a balance due of $0.00.

A file-processing menu controls the types of adjustments that can be made to a customer's account (see Figure 6–13). Typical selections provide options to adjust

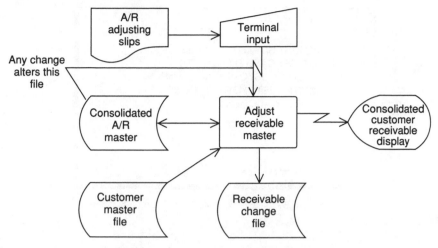

Figure 6–11   Adjusting receivable accounts

small-balance totals, adjust cash discounts, credit customer account, debit customer account, display account, and return to main menu. The first two selections deal with the analysis of receivable accounts. Selection 1, *Adjust small-balance totals*, determines the number and total dollar value of invoices that are less than a specified amount.

Processing instructions might include:

1. WHAT SMALL-BALANCE AMOUNT IS TO BE EXAMINED? $xx.xx
   (Enter the dollar amount.)

2. WHAT ACCOUNTS ARE TO BE EXAMINED? _____
   (Enter "All" or specify "Account cycle number.")

```
CUSTOMER NUMBER:     48316                                          DATE:   06-30-9X
                                                                   PAGE:   1

CUSTOMER NAME:       INTERNATIONAL PAPER PRODUCTS, LTD.

INVOICE     DATE     INVOICE    RECEIPT     DATE     PAYMENT    DISC.    BALANCE
NO.        POSTED    CHARGE      NO.       POSTED     MADE      TAKEN      DUE

07712     02-18-9X   762.00                                              762.00

10354     05-04-9X    54.00     6632      06-20-9X    54.00     0.00       0.00

10822     05-15-9X    66.00     9945      06-25-9X    66.00     0.00       0.00

10873     05-15-9X    86.40     6699      06-25-9X    50.00     0.00      36.40

11225     05-18-9X    51.40     7224      06-25-9X    50.37     1.03       0.00


TOTAL               1019.80                          220.37    1.03     798.40
```

Figure 6–12   Consolidated customer receivable display

```
┌─────────────────────────────────────┐
│  ┌──────────────────────────┐       │
│  │ CONSOLIDATED A/R FILE     │       │
│  └──────────────────────────┘       │
│                                     │
│       ADJUST SMALL-BALANCES         │
│       ADJUST CASH DISCOUNTS         │
│       CREDIT CUSTOMER ACCOUNT       │
│       DEBIT CUSTOMER ACCOUNT        │
│       DISPLAY ACCOUNT               │
│                                     │
│                                     │
│                                     │
│       RETURN                        │
│                                     │
└─────────────────────────────────────┘
```

Figure 6–13 Consolidated A/R file menu

Following a summary showing the effects of making all adjustments, the computer will ask,

3. SHOULD THE SMALL-BALANCE·ADJUSTMENT BE MADE (Y or N)? ─

Thus, if $0.50 is entered initially, this amount becomes small-balance *cutoff point*. If all accounts are to be analyzed, the computer will search through the entire A/R master file to identify the invoices whose balance-due amounts are less than the cutoff. After summarizing the effects of deleting these small-balance invoices, the computer will ask whether to go ahead. If a *Y* is entered, the small-balance invoices of $0.50 or less will be adjusted, setting their balance to zero.

Selection 2, *Adjust cash discounts*, identifies all invoices with balance-due amounts equaling the cash discount amount. Such invoices usually result when the computer has disallowed the discount taken when processing the payment. Each case must be investigated to determine that the action taken is correct. Suppose, for example, that the terms of an invoice are 2 percent 10, net 30; that the invoice was posted on June 1; that the customer check was written on June 9; and that the payment was posted by the company on June 15. As these figures show, the customer payment was made seven working days after the invoice was posted; however, the payment was posted eleven working days afterwards. In such a situation, the cash discount is usually allowed and a credit adjustment is made.

Selections 3 and 4, *Credit customer account* and *Debit customer account*, make subtractions from or additions to customer accounts. Removing a small balance, such as $0.40, for instance, is an example of a credit adjustment. A *debit adjustment* is the reverse of a credit adjustment: it adds a dollar amount to an outstanding account. Suppose a customer's check is returned to a business because of insufficient funds in the customer's checking account. By now, the payment information would have passed through the cash-receipts computer application and would show up as a payment to be applied to delete an invoice from the file. In this case, a debit adjustment is required. The adjustment offsets the payment and reinstates the invoice.

Selections 5 and 6 are similar to those discussed in earlier chapters. *Display account* permits an account to be examined but not changed. Following an examination, the operator usually enters additional instructions to show whether the account requires adjustment. *Return to main menu* is self explanatory. This option provides an exit from the file-processing menu and returns control to the main processing menu.

The *Print aging schedule* Program

One additional file-processing selection generally associated with the interactive update of the receivable file is *Age customer account*. Figure 6–14 illustrates the display that might follow this command. For each outstanding invoice, it shows the invoice number, date, and charge; any payment and the date of payment; and the balance due. At the bottom of the display, the amount due is subdivided into one or more aging buckets: current, 31–60 (days past due), 61–90 (days past due), and over 91 (days past due). The purpose of aging is to show the length of time that different dollar amounts are past due. As shown, the International Paper Products, Ltd., is slow in making payment. Invoice 07712 has a remaining balance of $762.00. It is past due by more than 90 days.

Besides aging accounts on request, a batch program is used to age each account stored on file. The purpose of processing is twofold: to print a *receivable aging schedule*, a report used to show accounts past due, and to create a print file suitable for printing customer statements. Figure 6–15 illustrates an aging schedule entitled *Accounts receivable aged trial balance*. The term *trial balance* is a carryover from precomputer days: controls are designed to ensure that all accounts are in balance. To arrive at a balance, all aged subtotals are summed for each customer account, to arrive at a balanced total for each customer. Following this, the aged subtotals are summed for *all* customer accounts, to arrive at a balanced total for all customers. Thus, the balance of $6010.13, as illustrated, is the sum of current charges of $2485.68, charges 31–60 days old ($1451.77), charges 61–90 days old ($956.98), charges 91–120 days old ($622.12), and all charges over 120 days old ($493.58). If a balance is not achieved, adjustments must be made and a second trial conducted.

CUSTOMER NUMBER:		48316				DATE:	06-30-9X
						PAGE:	2
CUSTOMER NAME:		INTERNATIONAL PAPER PRODUCTS, LTD.					
INVOICE NO.	DATE POSTED	INVOICE CHARGE	RECEIPT NO.	DATE POSTED	PAYMENT MADE	DISC. TAKEN	BALANCE DUE
07712	02-18-9X	762.00					762.00
10354	05-04-9X	54.00	6632	06-20-9X	54.00	0.00	0.00
10822	05-15-9X	66.00	9945	06-25-9X	66.00	0.00	0.00
10873	05-15-9X	86.40	6699	06-25-9X	50.00	0.00	36.40
11225	05-18-9X	51.40	7224	06-25-9X	50.37	1.03	0.00
AGED TOTALS:		CURRENT		31 - 60 DAYS	61 - 90 DAYS		OVER 90 DAYS
		$36.40		0.00	0.00		$762.00

Figure 6–14   Aged accounts receivable display

ACCOUNTS RECEIVABLE AGED TRIAL BALANCE
GENERAL OFFICE PRODUCTS
5/31/9-

6/ 2/9-
PAGE 1

CUSTOMER NUMBER	CUSTOMER NAME	BALANCE	CURRENT	31-60 DAYS	61-90 DAYS	91-120 DAYS	OVER 120 DAYS	CREDIT LIMIT	PHONE
11257	NORTH STAR SPECIALTI	463.19			203.27	173.45	86.47	2000.00	715-898-5805
11258	CROSBY MANUFACTURING	410.07	135.72**	162.02	112.33			1000.00	608-435-5960
11259	AWARD REALTY	1704.18*	289.95	397.04	178.26	431.82	407.11**	1500.00	507-447-4700
11260	STANDBY SYSTEMS INC.	300.10	244.40	55.70				2500.00	612-564-2315
11261	EDINA LAWN & LANDSCA	958.48	958.48					2000.00	612-874-3900
11262	SENTRY ENAMELING CO.	887.18	462.80	286.51	137.87			2500.00	612-882-8673
11263	ART WILLIAM & SON TRU	154.05	154.05					1500.00	612-333-6431
11265	SEASONAL CONTROL INC.	825.89	7.84	475.95	325.25	16.85		2000.00	612-854-7838
11267	BLACK & KUEHN	70.24	55.12	15.12				1000.00	612-371-4504
11268	BROCK - WHITE CO.	236.75	177.32	59.43				2000.00	612-646-4008
	TOTALS	6010.13	2485.68	1451.77	956.98	622.12	493.58		

* - Indicates problem

Figure 6-15 Receivable aging schedule

The aging schedule is used in several ways: to determine whether outstanding receivables are becoming more or less past due, to spot problem and delinquent accounts, and to project the amount of money that should be received by a business in the short term. Of these, consider how the schedule is used to spot problem accounts. In processing, several rules are followed to mark accounts to be examined—for example, accounts in which the total amount due exceeds the credit limit. As illustrated, account number 11259, the Award Realty account, has exceeded its credit limit. When this occurs, the credit department must decide whether to forbid future sales to these customers until payment is made or to increase their credit limits. Another rule is to identify all accounts whose past-due total exceeds current sales. Account 11258 would be identified if this rule were enforced. Current sales of $137.72 are less than past-due sales of $410.07. Still another rule is to identify all accounts whose past-due balance is over 60 days and above a dollar amount such as $1,000. Account 11259 would be flagged again using this rule.

The *Print customer statements* Program

The *Print aging schedule* program creates a *receivable print file* in addition to printing the receivable aging schedule. Once the aging schedule is approved, the next step is to begin printing customer statements.

Figure 6–16 shows the layout of the receivables print file. Although it is similar to the customer invoice print file, there are several small but important differences. First, only customer sold-to information is needed in printing the monthly statement, whereas both sold-to and ship-to information must be printed on the customer invoice. Second, the description of each invoice is optional. Generally, the invoice-reference number is all that is needed for the customer to be able to identify a specific transaction. Third, aging information is important to the statement. This information is calculated by the aging schedule program and explains why this program is run before customer statements are produced. As Figure 6–16 illustrates, each customer account is aged. An alternative (not shown) is to age each invoice and to print this information on the statement.

Even with cycle billing, the printing of customer statements requires considerable time to complete. Some business firms, for example, must set aside several hours to complete this processing step; others use more than one eight-hour shift. Because of the time requirements, it is essential that the program include a restart provision. With restart, it is possible to begin a rerun and to resume printing customer statements at the point at which a problem in processing was identified.

It should be possible to print statements on demand as well as in a batch, if a customer requests that a statement be sent in advance. On-demand printing adds another selection on the file-processing menu developed for updating the A/R master file. This selection is entitled *Print customer statement*. Continuous computer forms that allow the removal of one or more forms from a terminal printer without loss or waste of the next form have contributed to the increase in on-demand printing. Even then, caution is advised. Because of the high labor cost of on-demand printing, judgment is needed to determine when to use this option.

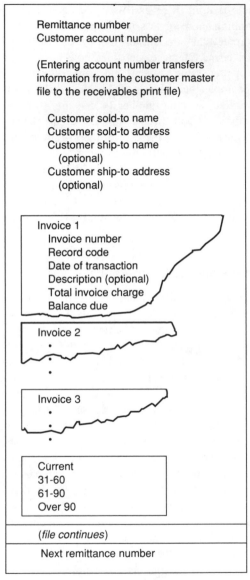

Remittance number
Customer account number

(Entering account number transfers
information from the customer master
file to the receivables print file)

    Customer sold-to name
    Customer sold-to address
    Customer ship-to name
      (optional)
    Customer ship-to address
      (optional)

Invoice 1
    Invoice number
    Record code
    Date of transaction
    Description (optional)
    Total invoice charge
    Balance due

Invoice 2

Invoice 3

Current
31-60
61-90
Over 90

(*file continues*)

Next remittance number

Figure 6–16   Receivable print file

REVIEW QUESTIONS

9. What is cycle billing and how does it work?

10. What is account cycle time and how does it work?

11. What processing function is performed by the sort/merge receivable files program?

12. How does the deleted-invoice report differ from the accounts receivable register?

13. Why do some customer accounts require adjustment prior to printing monthly statements?

14. What types of customer account adjustments can be made online?

15. What new information is printed on the receivable aging schedule?

16. How does the receivable print file differ from the print file used in producing customer invoices?

17. What is on-demand printing?

6-4   ADDING COMPLEXITY TO RECEIVABLES PROCESSING

The accounts receivable computer application, as discussed thus far, is not very complex or difficult to understand. The major conceptual difficulties perhaps lie in seeing how records are placed in the consolidated A/R master file and how these records are adjusted and eventually deleted. In this section, we will consider two areas that contribute to making receivables processing more complex. The first of these, automatic cash application, is required for customers who make payments on their accounts. The second of these, month-end closing, was developed because of conflicting choices. One choice is to print customer statements well in advance of the end of the month in order to maximize payments by customers. Another choice is to delay printing as long as possible—close to the the end of the month—in order to include as many outstanding invoices as possible on each customer statement.

Automatic Cash Application

As we saw in the last chapter, some customers make payments on account instead of indicating how a payment is to be applied. Typically, automatic cash application processing instructions are included in the *print receivable register* program or a separate cash application program is added to processing. This new program is placed between the *Sort/merge receivable files* program and the *Print receivable register* program.

Automatic cash application can best be understood by using an illustration. Figure 6–17 shows how a $780 payment on account is applied to the International Paper Products, Ltd., account illustrated earlier. Notice that the lowest invoice number (07712) is paid first, followed by the next lowest (10873), at which point the entire payment has been exhausted. It was assumed in this case that the lowest invoice number is that of the oldest invoice. This assumption holds, provided invoice numbers follow a date-ordered sequence.

A problem with automatic cash application is that it is difficult to explain to customers how a payment has been applied—especially if a customer decides to make a payment on account early in the month and another, later payment in which a

```
CUSTOMER NUMBER:   48316                          DATE:   06/30/99
                                                 PAGE:   3
CUSTOMER NAME:  INTERNATIONAL PAPER PRODUCTS, INC.

INVOICE   DATE    INVOICE RECEIPT   DATE    PAYMENT  DISC  BALANCE
  NO.    POSTED   CHARGE    NO.    POSTED    MADE   TAKEN    DUE
```

INVOICE NO.	DATE POSTED	INVOICE CHARGE	RECEIPT NO.	DATE POSTED	PAYMENT MADE	DISC TAKEN	BALANCE DUE
07712	02/18/99	762.00	POA		(762.00)	0.00	0.00
10354	05/04/99	54.00	6632	06/20/99	54.00	0.00	0.00
10822	05/15/99	66.00	9945	06/25/99	66.00	0.00	0.00
10873	05/15/99	36.40	POA		(18.00)	0.00	18.40
POA			99442	06/27/99	780.00		
11225	05/18/99	51.40					51.40
TOTAL		1019.80			950.00	0.00	69.80

Figure 6–17 Automatic cash application display

remittance stub is enclosed. (In this instance, the customer usually attempts to make payment on an invoice that has been reduced to zero.) To make payment-on-account information more understandable to all, a POA (payment on account) is appended to each related transaction. This tells where cash was applied. Even then the customer may not understand. Situations in which the customer disagrees with the way in which payment is applied are even more difficult. Suppose that, as before, a cash discount of $1.03 is permitted if invoice 11225 is paid first. As illustrated, invoice 11225 is the newest invoice. According to the oldest-invoice-paid-first rule, this invoice would always be paid last—much to the displeasure of the customer.

Obviously one way to deal with many of the problems that result from automatic cash application is to use only one method of applying a payment on account and never to deviate from this method. If a customer attempts to pay an invoice that already has been reduced to zero, the payment would be treated as yet another payment on account. If a customer complains that a discount was not allowed when it might have been, he or she is simply informed of the oldest-invoice-paid-first rule.

Interactive routines permit adjustment to be made quickly. For example, if a payment on account has reduced an outstanding invoice balance to zero and another payment instructs the company to do the same, the double payment can be flagged for online review. During the review, the account is usually adjusted so that the application of payments is consistent with the customer's instructions.

Month-End Closing

As with automatic cash application, month-end closing decisions must be set carefully to minimize internal conflict and friction. When sales commissions are based on invoices paid in full, marketing and sales personnel want to see receivables month-end closing dates delayed as long as possible so that the maximum number of outstanding invoices will be included in customer statements. Financial officers and data-processing managers, on the other hand, both view any cutoff date as the absolute deadline. To protect their interests, they like to see processing completed well in advance of the closing deadline. By processing in advance, financial officers can be sure that bills will reach customers as scheduled. Likewise, processing in advance protects the data-processing manager by providing recovery time if errors turn up. Sufficient time should remain so that reruns of programs can be made before a month-end deadline.

To avoid the conflict inherent in this situation, business firms restrict the time between closing the A/R master file and printing customer statements. This makes it necessary to assign a high priority to the printing of customer statements. Another method of reducing conflict is to establish different closing dates for different groups of customers or for different types of accounts. For example, it is common to divide accounts by store or by regional sales office. This division defines the way in which cycle billing is performed. With cycle billing, massive runs of month-end statements are avoided and recovery problems are simplified. The only area more difficult to manage is the audit of financial controls.

6-5 INTEGRATED ACCOUNTS RECEIVABLE PROCESSING

Instead of designing separate applications for customer invoicing, customer cash receipts, and accounts receivable, many business firms design all three at once. This design is know as an *integrated accounts-receivable system*. An integrated design offers several advantages. Only a single organization chart and one set of system flowcharts are needed. Likewise, the system requires a single program-processing menu, unified sets of file-processing menus for the customer and product master files, and unified file-balance control procedures. Fewer programs need to be written and fewer summary files processed. File backup procedures are simplified, as is online updating of the consolidated A/R master file. Finally, as perhaps the most important advantage, an integrated design makes it easier to understand how the system works.

Figure 6–18 shows the main processing steps of an integrated accounts receivable system. Twenty-two programs complete both the interactive and batch portions of the design. Close inspection reveals that neither the print invoice nor the cash-receipts A/R summary program is required. With an integrated system, the *Enter invoice transactions* and *Enter receipts transactions* programs update the consolidated A/R master file directly. Following this update, each transaction is added to the invoice transaction file or to the receipts transaction file. Thus, these three files must be online: the consolidated A/R master, the invoice transaction, and the receipts transaction files. Other than this major difference, the design of the integrated system is much the same as the design of the three separate applications.

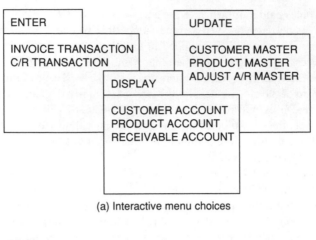

(a) Interactive menu choices

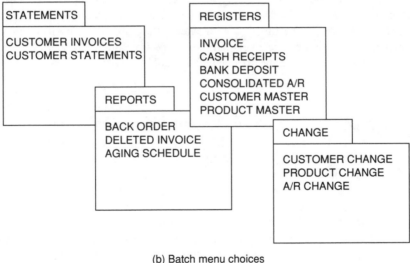

(b) Batch menu choices

Figure 6–18 Main processing menu of an integrated A/R system

6-6 MANAGEMENT IMPLICATIONS

In recent years business firms have realized that efficient use of current assets is a key factor in determining profitability. As a consequence, the management of accounts receivable has received considerable attention. With receivables, a closely watched activity ratio is the *average collection period*:

$$\text{Average collection period} = \frac{\text{Average accounts receivable in dollars}}{\text{Sales per day in dollars}}$$

To clarify how this ratio is applied, assume that the accounts receivable average is $1,000,000 and that total sales per day is $40,000. These figures permit the financial manager to compute the average collection period. In this example, the period is twenty-five days ($1,000,000 ÷ $40,000 per day = 25 days). Now suppose that the collection period considered normal for the industry within which the company belongs is thirty-five days. Since twenty-five days is clearly better than thirty-five, the financial manager is able to state that collections are well within the normal time frame.

The amount of money saved by lowering the average collection period can be substantial. Suppose all receivables must be financed with short-term loans at an interest rate of 12 percent per year. Suppose further that the average collection period is reduced by ten days, from thirty-five days to twenty-five days, but that sales remain constant at $40,000 per day. From these data, yearly interest savings of $48,000 are possible. Instead of having to finance an average receivables of $1,400,000 (35 days × $40,000 per day), the company need finance only average receivables totaling $1,000,000 (25 days × $40,000). Annual interest costs are thus reduced from $168,000 to $120,000.

With savings as high as twenty cents on the dollar (depending on the cost of short-term financing), companies have been willing to invest large amounts in automating their accounts-receivable operations. Some of these investments have produced even larger gains than expected. One firm, ranked near the bottom (sixty-first out of seventy firms) by a public accounting firm in managing its receivables, realized a complete turnaround following the installation of an online accounts receivable application. At a cost of less than $200,000 for equipment and personnel, the company automated all receivables processing. With this system in operation, the firm was able to improve its industry ranking from sixty-one to twelve. It lowered its average collection period by eighteen days and, in so doing, reduced average receivables by more than $850,000.

Besides direct dollar savings, an online accounts-receivable system leads to improved customer service. A major form of improvement is the capability to respond quickly to the questioning of an account. Suppose that a customer payment must be received before an additional sale can be made. In a strictly batch-processing environment, it can take several days to report customer payment information to district sales offices. In an interactive-processing environment, however, information is reported as it becomes known. For instance, a company can determine the status of a customer's account immediately after a cash payment has been applied. It can provide a daily display of customer accounts that have been suspended, as well as accounts that are no longer suspended.

Last, improved collection procedures typically follow from a modern, online accounts receivable system. A major collections stumbling block with batch-processed receivables is that aging reports are not designed for ease of use by collections personnel. What collections people are most concerned about is the capability to let customers know that payments are past due and to stop further sales from taking place before an even larger amount becomes past due. With online processing, these concerns are dealt with directly. If a customer account is to be limited to cash-only sales, this information can be placed immediately in the customer master file. This file must be checked before a credit sale is permitted, so the cash-sale requirement takes place immediately—not several days or weeks after the decision to change a customer's terms of payment.

REVIEW QUESTIONS

18.   Explain automatic cash application.

19.   Why must business firms use care in setting month-end closing deadlines?

20.   What is an integrated accounts receivable system?

21.   What is an average collection period? Why should it receive close attention by management?

22.   How can an online A/R system improve customer service?

REVIEW OF IMPORTANT IDEAS

The main objective of accounts receivable processing is to hold customer credit balances to a minimum, consistent with the prompt delivery of goods and services. This objective is achieved in part by the timely release of customer monthly statements and by improved customer collection procedures.

There are three types of accounts receivable systems: balance only, balance forward, and open item. The simplest of these is the balance-only system; the most complex is the open-item system. Both the balance-forward and the open-item systems age past-due amounts; however, the open-item system is the only type that lists each invoice past due until it is paid. An important advantage of the open-item system is that it provides a complete accounting of each sales transaction.

The five steps required in accounts receivable processing are post A/R summary, post receipts summary, delete A/R transactions, age customer accounts, and print customer statements. Before processing can begin, the consolidated A/R master file must be in proper sequence and in balance. After the file is consolidated, invoices that net to zero can be identified and later removed from the file. Following this, the remaining invoices are aged and month-end statements are printed. Because the consolidated A/R master file is first expanded and later reduced in size, different file-balance control equations are used to verify that all transactions are accounted for.

Different registers are needed in monitoring accounts-receivable processing. The accounts receivable register lists all transactions stored on the consolidated A/R master file and prints dollar and transaction count file-balance totals. The deleted-invoice register lists all invoices that net to zero and that have been deleted from the consolidated A/R master file. Several copies of this report may have to be prepared to account for all file adjustments.

Receivable accounts are aged to remind the customer of past-due amounts and to identify customers who are slow in making payments. Accounts can be aged both on request and as a batch. Programmed rules are used to pinpoint problem accounts.

Deleting invoices from the A/R master file, making account adjustments, and aging accounts should occur before month-end statements are prepared. Doing this work in advance protects against having to rerun the statements program. Although the statements program itself is not difficult, it takes considerable time to complete and is expensive because of custom forms.

Automatic cash application and month-end closing represent two areas that add complexity to accounts receivable processing. Automatic cash application requires programmed rules to show how payments on account are to be applied. With month-end closing, management must clearly specify receivable cutoff dates. Failure to do so leads to internal conflict and friction.

An integrated accounts receivable system is made up of the customer-invoicing, customer cash receipts, and accounts receivable applications. With an integrated design, the consolidated A/R master file is updated immediately, thus eliminating the need for either the invoice or the receipts A/R summary files.

Sizable benefits can be derived from an online accounts receivable application. Besides direct dollar savings resulting from lower interest payments, companies benefit from improved customer service and collection procedures. Customers are made to feel that a business fully understands its billing activities.

KEY WORDS

Accounts receivable

Current assets

Balance-only A/R system

Balance-forward A/R system

Open-item A/R system

Aging buckets

Dunning letters

Consolidated A/R master file

Customer monthly statement

Cycle billing

Account cycle time

Accounts receivable register

Deleted-invoice report

Cutoff point

Credit adjustment

Debit adjustment

Receivable aging schedule

Aged trial balance

Automatic cash application

Month-end closing

Average collection period

Integrated accounts receivable system

EXERCISES

1. Suppose you decide to add a dunning-letter feature to the accounts receivable application. With the new feature in place, letters would be sent to customers with long-overdue accounts.

    (a) How would the preparing of dunning letters change the design described in this chapter?

    (b) Compared to monthly statements, when would dunning letters be printed and mailed to customers?

2. Prepare the systems flowcharts required by an integrated accounts receivable system for the five programs shown below. Use standard symbols in preparing

each flowchart. Two flowcharts will fit on each $8\frac{1}{2}$-by-11-inch sheet of paper. Briefly describe each program.

(a) *Enter invoice transactions*

(b) *Enter cash receipts transactions*

(c) *Print invoice register*

(d) *Print deleted-invoice report*

(e) *Print aging schedule*

3. Suppose a new program called *Post A/R transactions* is added to the integrated A/R design. Prepare a systems flowchart for this new program. Use your experience with 4-in-1 in preparing the design.

4. Using Figure 6–4 as a guide, describe how the accounts receivable master file would be designed for a balance-only A/R system. In your design, show which data elements would be stored for each invoice, customer credit, and customer payment.

5. Using Figures 6–1 and 6–4 as guides, describe how the accounts receivable file would be designed for a balance-forward A/R system. Assume that a finance charge of 1.38 percent per month is to be added to a balance outstanding by more than 90 days.

DISCUSSION QUESTIONS

1. Why are there different A/R designs when a single standard design might do? If you were starting a business, which A/R system would you select? What factors would be important in making this decision?

2. Select a monthly statement you receive and describe what you like and dislike about the statement. How should information be presented on a monthly statement?

3. Why is it important to be able to display and examine customer accounts? Suggest several reasons.

4. Why is it important to be able to display an aged A/R account? Suggest several reasons.

5. Why is it sometimes advantageous for a company to print monthly statements daily? Weekly? Only at month end?

4-IN-1 CASE STUDY—PRODUCING MONTHLY STATEMENTS

For this 4-in-1 lesson, you are once again asked to do several things. These are the following:

- View a customer account.
- Print a customer account list.

- Print an aged accounts receivable summary.
- Print a customer (monthly) statement.
- Bring forward customer accounts.
- Document new account totals.

Viewing a Customer Account

With 4-in-1, you can display (view) a customer account at any time — before and after processing an invoice as well as before and after processing a cash receipt. To display an account, do the following:

1. Log on and enter a date of **012597**.

2. Type **10** from the main menu and press ENTER.

3. Type **1** and press ENTER from the view or print customer accounts menu.

4. Type **LAWNS** and press ENTER to display the LAWNS-ARE-GREEN account.

5. Press ENTER when asked, *Right customer?*

6. Press F1 when asked for earliest transaction.

7. Press F2 for customer totals.

8. Press TAB for next customer.

9. Press TAB to return to the view or print customer accounts menu.

Printing a Customer Account List

Besides displaying a customer account, you can also print a customer account list for review. To print an account, do the following:

10. Type **2** and press ENTER from the view or print customer accounts menu.

11. Press ENTER to place each customer account on a new page.

12. Press ENTER when asked, *Bring balance forward?* When you bring a balance forward, all account entries dated on or before the ending date (to be entered below) are brought together and are summarized into one "balance-forward transaction." Thus, *do not type "yes"* at this time.

13. Press F1 for the starting customer.

14. Press F1 for the ending customer.

15. Press F1 when asked for the starting date.

16. Press F1 when asked for the ending date.

17. Press ENTER when asked, *Print inactive accounts?*

18. Press ENTER when asked, *Field number to change?*

19. Press ENTER when asked, *Display this report?* This leads to the printing of the customer accounts listing.

20. Press TAB to return to the view or print customer accounts menu.

21. Press TAB to return to the main menu.

Printing the Aged A/R Summary

Besides printing a customer accounts listing, 4-in-1 allows you to age each customer account. To age an account, do the following:

22. Type **11** and press ENTER from the main menu.

23. Press F1 for the first customer.

24. Press F1 for the last customer.

25. Press ENTER to use 012597 as the statement cutoff date.

26. Press F1 to print the report for all salespersons. When the aged A/R summary report is printed, it is printed in salesperson order. This gives each salesperson an aging report for his or her customers.

27. Press ENTER when asked, *Field number to change?*

28. Press ENTER when asked, *Display this report?* At this time the aged A/R summary will be printed.

29. Press TAB twice to return to the main menu.

Printing Customer (Monthly) Statements

To print customer month-end statements, do the following:

30. Type **12** and press ENTER from the main menu.

31. Press ENTER for the statement cutoff date of 012597.

32. Press F1 for the first customer on file.

33. Press F1 for the last customer on file.

34. Press ENTER when asked to assign a statement frequency to the customer record.

35. Type **Y** and press ENTER when asked if you want to print a reference for each transaction.

36. Press ENTER when asked, *Print zero balance customers?*

37. Press ENTER when asked, *Field number to change?*

38. Type **DONE** and press ENTER to indicate that the printer has been prepared to handle custom forms (even though you can print on computer stock paper).

39. Press ENTER when asked, *Print form alignment?* At this point, the monthly statements will print.

40. Press TAB once all statements have been printed.

41. Type **DONE** and press ENTER to indicate that custom forms have been removed from the printer (even though you printed on computer stock paper) and the printer is reset with stock paper.

Bringing Customer Balances Forward

Once customer statements are printed, customer account balances can be brought forward. This requires you to repeat the steps to print customer accounts. Do the following:

42. Type **10** and press ENTER from the main menu.

43. Type **2** and press ENTER from the view or print customer accounts menu.

44. Press ENTER to place each customer account on a new page.

45. Type **Y** when asked, *Bring balance forward?* This step summarizes all account entries dated on or before the ending date (to be entered below).

46. Press F1 for the starting customer.

47. Press F1 for the ending customer.

48. Press F1 when asked for the starting date.

49. Press F1 when asked for the ending date.

50. Press ENTER when asked, *Print inactive accounts?*

51. Press ENTER when asked, *Field number to change?*

52. This leads to the printing of the customer accounts listing.

53. Press TAB to return to the view or print customer accounts menu.

Documenting Balance-forward Results

To document the effects of the balance-forward procedure, do the following:

54. Type **2** and press ENTER from the view or print customer accounts menu.

55. Press ENTER to place each customer account on a new page.

56. Type **Y** when asked, *Bring balance forward?*

57. Press F1 for the starting customer.

58. Press F1 for the ending customer.

59. Press F1 when asked for the starting date.

60. Press F1 when asked for the ending date.

61. Press ENTER when asked, *Print inactive accounts?*

62. Press ENTER when asked, *Field number to change?*

63. This leads to the printing of the customer accounts listing.

64. Press TAB to return to the view or print customer accounts menu.

65. Press TAB to return to the main menu.

66. Press TAB to log off.

QUESTIONS

1. When you view a customer account using 4-in-1, what information is displayed? How does it differ from information shown on the customer account list?

2. What happens when you bring a balance forward? What would happen if you brought a balance forward before you printed a monthly statement? Using 4-in-1, how would you correct this mistake?

3. Why might it be more appropriate to send the aged A/R to the sales force rather than to the collections department of a business? If you decided to send accounts to different collections personnel, how could you do this with 4-in-1?

4. Examine the beginning balance for the two customer accounts before and after the account balances are brought forward. What could you do differently in your installation of 4-in-1 to record the initial beginning balances accurately?

5. Is 4-in-1 an integrated A/R system? If so, how does it differ from the integrated A/R system discussed in the text?

PART

□□□

PAYABLES APPLICATIONS

Most businesses expect to be carried "on account" by their suppliers and, to a lesser extent, by their employees, much like they carry their customers on account. In this part of the text we will examine three more accounting applications, all of which relate to the payment and processing of a firm's bills. As we will show in the accounts payable application, Chapter 7, bills from suppliers can be paid and processed in different ways. A firm may decide to pay its bills promptly or to pay slowly; either approach has certain advantages and disadvantages. Chapter 8, which deals with fixed assets, reminds us that some bills, even though they are paid in full, cannot be deducted fully by a business as an expense. Instead a percentage of the bill must be applied as a business expense (deduction) to each of several years. These yearly deductions are made until the entire amount has been written off. Chapter 9, dealing with the payment of employees, explains a situation in which payment choices are much more limited: businesses must either pay their employees promptly or face the consequences.

7

Accounts Payable

A business can expect the delivery of a vendor invoice soon after goods are shipped by a supplier. When the supplier is efficient, the invoice will reach a business even before merchandise is recorded as being received. Once invoices are in the hands of a business, that firm must make several decisions: when to pay, what amount to pay, whether to challenge the invoice total, and whether to take the cash discount (if one is available). Such decisions must be built into the design of the accounts payable application.

Accounts payable processing may be viewed as the inverse of accounts receivable processing. With receivables, a firm must keep records of legal claims against customers for amounts due. Since the assets of a company include what is owed to the company, these amounts due can be defined as current assets. With payables, a firm must keep records of the legal claims against the business by its suppliers. These claims result from the supplier's decision to supply the business with goods on credit. An amount to be paid is defined as a *liability*, as opposed to an asset. Because business firms are expected to pay their bills within a short period of time (less than one year), this type of liability is better known as a *current liability*.

Two primary objectives of accounts payable processing are to keep credit balances with suppliers within reason and to pay vendor invoices promptly. These practices protect the credit rating of the business and also take advantage of favorable credit terms and cash discounts. The *credit rating* of a business is an indicator of its financial soundness. Very financially sound business firms may receive preferential *credit terms*. The credit extended to a B-rated firm must be 1 percent 10, net 20, for example, whereas the credit to an A-rated firm might be 2 percent 10, net 30. The length of credit terms determines the extent to which *trade credit* may be used as a source of short-term financing. Consider what will happen if these two firms make average purchases of $2,000 each day. Terms of net 20 mean that trade credit for the first is limited to $40,000 (20 days times $2,000); terms of net 30, however, lead to trade credit of $60,000 (30 days times $2,000) for the second.

Another important objective of accounts payable processing is improved control of all cash payments. In this regard, processing controls are vital. Because the accounts payable application specifies whom to pay and in what amount, there are ever-present risks of embarrassing financial mistakes, such as paying a vendor when goods were never received, and of employee embezzlement and fraud. Some accounts payable designs almost encourage employees to embezzle by making it so easy. The only mischief required is to instruct the computer to write a company check to a fictitious vendor and, later on. to delete from computer files any evidence that the check was ever written and processed.

7-1   PRELIMINARY OVERVIEW OF PROCESSING

Because the accounts payable application is fairly complex, tight financial controls are difficult to prepare. As Figure 7–1 shows, several sources and sinks are associated with the accounts-payable (A/P) system. Initially, the system is triggered by the receipt of a vendor invoice. The amount shown by the vendor as due and payable must then be matched against the total shown by the receipts summary, as recorded by purchasing and receiving. If the match is made, the amount due and payable is correct, and cash on hand is sufficient to pay the invoice, a vendor voucher-check can be printed and mailed to the vendor. Finally, accounts payable dollar amounts affect other systems in various ways. *Payables to capitalize* becomes a main input to the fixed-assets computer application (see Chapter 8); *payables distribution information* is sent to departmental managers and is a vital input to the general ledger computer application.

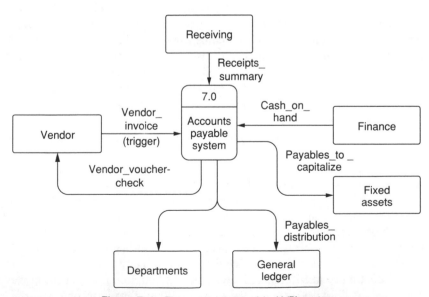

Figure 7–1   The accounts payable (A/P) system

The processing of accounts-payable information can be separated into four major functions: *Enter vendor payables*, *Enter payment instructions*, *Process payables (this period)*, and *Process payables summaries*.

1. *Enter vendor payables* (see Figure 7–2) adds vendor invoice information to the system. This function determines if incoming charges shown on an invoice are legitimate and, if so, adds all approved invoices to a consolidated payables file.

2. *Enter payment instructions* (see Figure 7–3) determines which vendor invoices to pay and in what amount and which invoices to hold until another billing period. Most firms make payments on approved invoices two to three times each month. Much like individuals, they must decide which bills to pay and which bills to hold. With accounts payable processing, invoices to pay are written to a *payables-this-period* file; invoices not to pay are written to a *payables-held-over* file. This second file becomes the new consolidated-payables file once all payables summaries have been processed.

3. *Process payables this period* (see Figure 7–3) produces the formal *vendor voucher-check*, updates a *pending check this period* file, and sends payables-to-capitalize information to the fixed-assets system. This function sets into motion several subsequent processing steps that are not shown: processing of the vendor voucher-check by the supplier, processing of checks returned by the bank, and processing of payables to capitalize by the fixed-assets system.

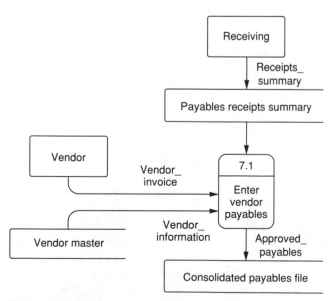

Figure 7–2 Entering vendor payables and adding them to the consolidated payables file

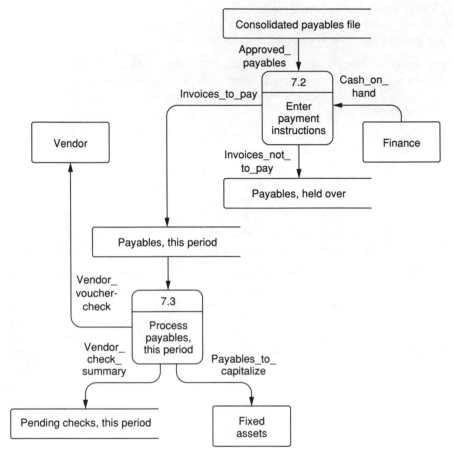

Figure 7–3   Entering payment instructions and processing invoices to be paid

4. *Process payables summaries* (see Figure 7–4) produces a variety of reports, including the A/P check register, the A/P general ledger distribution, and departmental expense reports. This information is important to the general ledger system and, following this, to the budget- and profit-planning computer applications (see Chapters 13 and 14).

Inputs to Processing

The three main inputs to accounts payable processing are the vendor invoice, the vendor master file, and the payables receipts summary file. The *vendor invoice* contains the same types of information as the customer invoice (see Chapter 4). Besides showing which goods are shipped, the vendor invoice shows the dollar charges for each line item shipped, terms of payment, and the total invoice charge before the cash discount is applied.

The *vendor master file* contains records to describe each vendor. Stored information includes the vendor's name and address, terms of payment, and vendor

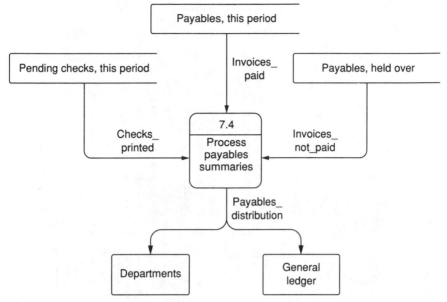

Figure 7–4 Processing payables summaries

product and background information. In processing, a vendor number is keyed and matched against the corresponding number stored on file. Figure 7–5, for example, shows the data-entry requirements associated with processing a vendor invoice. After a record code has been keyed (to indicate a charge or credit), the vendor number is transmitted. The matching of the two vendor numbers serves to add vendor information to the payables transaction.

Figure 7–5 shows that other information must be keyed beside the record code and vendor number. This information includes purchase order (P.O.) number, vendor invoice number, date of the invoice, invoice due date, dollar total of the invoice, cash discount (if one is possible), the pay code (the terms of payment), and the general-ledger codes and amounts. Initially, the pay code must be verified. If, for example, the vendor has permitted a 2 percent cash discount in the past but none this time, the invoice should be questioned. Typically, it is flagged for later review. Next, the history segment of the vendor record can be updated, by changing the totals for current monthly sales and year-to-date (YTD) sales. Third, the general ledger (G/L) distribution is made. The *general ledger distribution* shows how expenses are related to major activities of a business. If, for example, the vendor invoice shows the charges for 50 units of product 6453, this charge would be coded as a *direct cost*: the cost that can be traced to a single business activity, such as the sale of product line XYZ. If a company distributes direct charges for products by product line, an even finer distribution can be made. For example, if product 6453 is required only by product line E, then the entire charge can be posted to the chart of accounts number assigned to this product line. If, however, the invoice shows charges for legal or accounting fees—costs that cannot be traced to a single business activity—these would be coded as an *indirect cost*. By separating costs

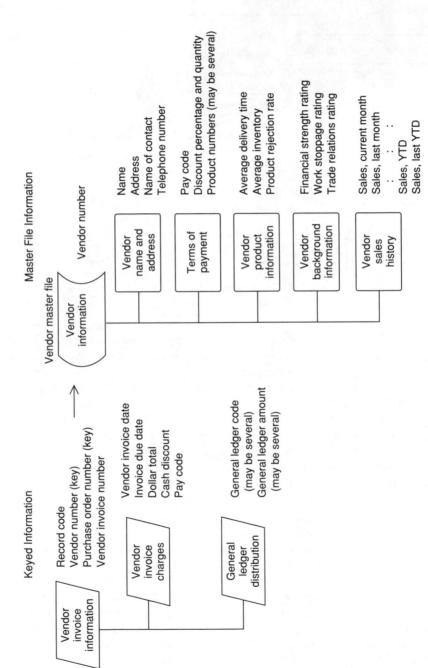

Figure 7–5   Relationships between payables data sets

in this way, a business is able to determine the expenses associated with each of its major functions or activities.

The *payables receipts summary* file, the third type of input, stores records that show the quantities received and approved and their estimated cost, compared with the quantity ordered, for each purchase order, by vendor. Before a vendor invoice is paid, the estimated cost of purchase should be compared with the vendor billed-for cost. If the difference between the two cost figures is significant, such as greater than 10 percent, the payables staff should closely inspect the vendor invoice using a cost verification display (see Figure 7–6). By comparing company information stored in the summary file (P.O. number, date of P.O., product number, description, quantity approved by the receiving department, and estimated cost) with information keyed or transferred into processing (vendor invoice number, date of invoice, vendor name and address, quantity billed, and invoice cost), the staff can determine what factors led to cost differences. In the case shown in Figure 7–6, a cost difference of $30.00 resulted from the vendor's cost being much greater than the estimated cost. The payables staff must now determine which cost is correct: the unit cost of .055 dollars per foot, stored in the product master file, or the vendor's unit cost of .085 dollars per foot.

Figure 7–6 should help clarify some of the difficulties associated with comparing purchasing and receiving information with vendor invoice information. The best way to verify the correctness of vendor charges is always to key the quantity billed for and the billed-for cost, line item by line item. Many firms do not require this extra data-entry work, however (see Figure 7–5). Instead, only the total invoice charge is keyed. Although it is much easier to enter only the total charge into processing, there is some risk with this practice.

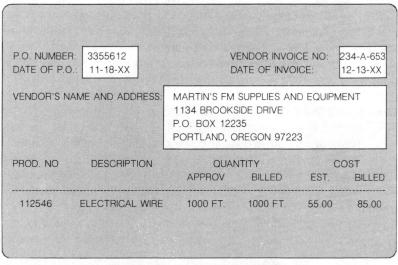

| P.O. NUMBER: 3355612 | VENDOR INVOICE NO: 234-A-653 |
| DATE OF P.O.: 11-18-XX | DATE OF INVOICE: 12-13-XX |

VENDOR'S NAME AND ADDRESS: MARTIN'S FM SUPPLIES AND EQUIPMENT
1134 BROOKSIDE DRIVE
P.O. BOX 12235
PORTLAND, OREGON 97223

| PROD. NO | DESCRIPTION | QUANTITY | | COST | |
		APPROV	BILLED	EST.	BILLED
112546	ELECTRICAL WIRE	1000 FT.	1000 FT.	55.00	85.00

Figure 7–6 Cost-verification display

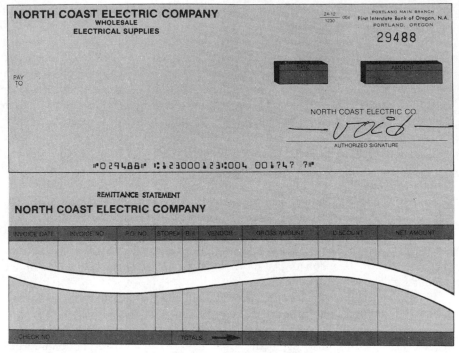

Figure 7-7   Vendor voucher-check

Outputs from Processing

The main products produced by accounts payable processing are vendor voucher-checks and payables summary reports. A *vendor voucher-check* is a two-part form, the lower portion of which (the voucher) contains information to help the vendor process the check (see Figure 7–7). The voucher provides space for printing the vendor invoice date, invoice number, purchase order (P.O.) number, and so on, as well as the discount taken and amount paid. The upper portion, the check, is negotiable. It shows the amount paid, that is, the amount to be taken to the bank for deposit.

Although several reports can be printed as products of processing, two reports, the payables check register and the general ledger distribution, are the most common. The *payables check register* shows which outstanding invoices are to be paid by the check-printing run. The register in Figure 7–8 shows, for example, that a payment of $484.00 to vendor 6612 will pay two outstanding invoices, numbers 654214 and 654412, in full. It also indicates that a discount of $6.00 is to be taken.

The check register illustrates one often-overlooked feature of payables processing. In processing, a business must assign its own reference, or *voucher number*, to each vendor invoice. In most designs this number is assigned by the com-

```
THUR. JUL. 23, 199X                    ACCOUNTS PAYABLE CHECK REGISTER
```

CHECK NO.	CHECK DATE	VENDOR NO.	NAME	VOUCH NO.	P.O. NO.	INVOICE NO.	INVOICE DATE	AMOUNT PAID	DISCOUNT TAKEN	CHECK AMOUNT
122000	07/16/9X	006612	DEXTER OFFICE SUPPLIES	001511	MM-9034	654214	06/15/9X	165.00	0.00	165.00
				001556	MM-8994	654412	06/22/9X	125.00	0.00	125.00
				001584	MM-8994		06/28/9X	200.00	6.00	194.00
							TOTALS----490.00		6.00	484.00
122001	07/16/9X	004413	WESTERN TELEPHONE CO.	001433		5566-7	06/25/9X	325.00	0.00	325.00
.	.		.	.	.	.	TOTALS----325.00	.	0.00	325.00
.	.	.		.	.	.	.	.	.	.
.	.	.		.	.	.	.	.	.	.

Figure 7–8 Payables check register

puter. Should the vendor later question the payment by a business, the specific transaction is traced using the voucher number. A *check number* is also assigned to each computer-printed check. This numbering can also be done by the computer, or checks can be prenumbered. Businesses usually prefer to assign the number directly by computer, because it permits the check number to be stored on file, together with the voucher number. Both numbers simplify the tracing of questionable payables transactions.

The *general ledger distribution* is similar to the check register except that it summarizes expenses by general ledger (G/L) code (see Figure 7–9). As illustrated, a G/L distribution shows the amount expended for advertising expenses. This listing is prepared by posting each charge shown on the check register to a general ledger account. It shows such details as the voucher number, vendor number, date of the vendor invoice, and amount distributed.

```
THURSDAY  AUGUST 11, 199X
                    ACCOUNTS PAYABLE DISTRIBUTION TO GENERAL LEDGER REPORT
FOR THE PERIOD:   05/01/9X  TO  05/15/9X
```

ACCOUNT-NO.	DESCRIPTION	VOUCHER NO.	VENDOR NO.	INVOICE DATE	AMOUNT DISTRIBUTED
11500-00100	ADVERTISING EXP.	001110	001000	3/31/9X	65.00
		001111	000300	4/22/9X	15.00
		001113	000600	4/23/9X	345.00
		001321	000655	4/25/9X	400.15
		001355	000712	4/27/9X	425.00
		001359	000126	5/06/9X	89.52
	ACCOUNT TOTAL----------------------------				1339.67

Figure 7–9 General ledger distribution

REVIEW QUESTIONS

1. Explain why accounts payable processing is sometimes viewed as the inverse of accounts receivable processing.

2. What are the two primary objectives of payables processing?

3. How does trade credit differ from a cash credit?

4. What is the difference between the payables-this-period file and the payables-held-over file?

5. Briefly describe the three main inputs to accounts payable processing.

6. What is the difference between a direct cost and an indirect cost?

7. Why is the vendor voucher-check a two-part form?

8. Why is a voucher number assigned in processing? Why is a check number assigned?

9. What is the main difference between the check register and the general ledger distribution?

7-2   PAYABLES PROCESSING

Figure 7–10 illustrates the system organization chart associated with the accounts payable design; Figure 7–11 shows the corresponding payables processing menu. As with other designs, the interactive portion of processing requires one program to build the payables transaction file, two programs to update or adjust files, and three programs to display accounts or summary totals. Two interactive programs unique to payables processing are entitled *Enter payment instructions* and *Display cash requirements*.

The *Enter payment instructions* program permits payables staff members to decide how many vendor invoices to pay, when to hold a vendor invoice for payment, when to remove the hold placed on an invoice, and when to make a partial payment. It computes how to maximize cash discount allowances. If, for example, $50,000 is available to pay outstanding bills of $75,000, the computer will determine which bills to pay in order to receive the greatest discount. This program must be flexible, however, to permit the payables staff to override programmed decisions. If the materials shipped by a vendor are not satisfactory, for example, the payables staff must be able to override a payment decision by entering instructions to hold the invoice.

The *Display cash requirements* program permits payables staff to determine the dollar value of outstanding invoices. Most cash requirement programs feature several types of display listings and summaries. One commonly used display lists, in date sequence, the invoices to be paid to take advantage of all cash discounts; another lists invoices to be paid in order to meet invoice due dates when the cash discounts are not taken. In this second listing, an invoice received on the first day

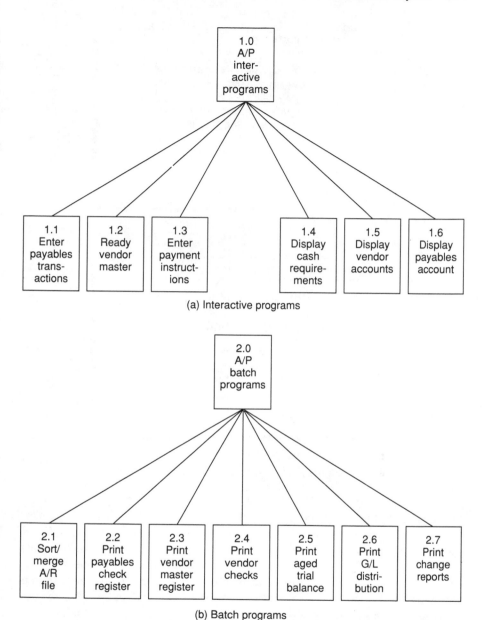

Figure 7–10 Accounts payable system organization chart

of the month with the terms 2 percent 20, net 30, would be listed after an invoice received on the fifth day of the month with the terms 2 percent 10, net 20.

The batch portion of the payables design is also similar to other applications. Besides vendor voucher-checks, products of processing include three registers, two or more processing summaries, and two file-change programs. The differences between the printed file registers and processing summaries produced by the

```
┌────────────────────────────────────────────────────┐
│ ┌─────────────────────────┐                         │
│ │ ACCOUNTS PAYABLE        │                         │
│ └─────────────────────────┘                         │
│                                                     │
│        ENTER PAYABLES TRANSACTIONS                  │
│        READY VENDOR MASTER                          │
│        ENTER PAYMENT INSTRUCTIONS                   │
│        DISPLAY VENDOR ACCOUNT                       │
│        DISPLAY PAYABLES ACCOUNT                     │
│                                                     │
│                                                     │
│                                                     │
│        RETURN                                       │
│                                                     │
└────────────────────────────────────────────────────┘
```

(a) Interactive menu choices

```
┌────────────────────────────────────────────────────┐
│ ┌─────────────────────────┐                         │
│ │ ACCOUNTS PAYABLE        │                         │
│ └─────────────────────────┘                         │
│                                                     │
│        PRINT PAYABLES CHECK REGISTER                │
│        PRINT VENDOR CHECKS                          │
│        PRINT G/L DISTRIBUTION                       │
│        PRINT A/P MASTER REGISTER                    │
│        PRINT A/P AGED TRIAL BALANCE                 │
│        PRINT VENDOR MASTER REGISTER                 │
│        PRINT CHANGE REPORTS                         │
│                                                     │
│        RETURN                                       │
│                                                     │
└────────────────────────────────────────────────────┘
```

(b) Batch menu choices

Figure 7–11   Payables processing menu

payables application are often minor. The payables check register and the general ledger distribution are both listings of invoices paid. In contrast, the *consolidated payables register* shows a complete listing of all invoices to be paid, whereas the *payables aged trial balance* places all outstanding invoices in one of several aging brackets, or buckets. With payables processing, aging is done to determine the current and future cash requirements. In most instances, aging computes how many invoices need to be paid within 10, 15, 20, 25, 30, and over 30 days.

The *Enter payables transactions* Program

The *Enter payables transactions* program is a multipurpose interactive processing routine. As Figure 7–12 shows, this interactive program is required to key vendor invoice and credit memo information to processing and to display vendor charges (or credits). In addition, the program creates or updates four online computer files: the vendor master file, the payables receipts summary file, the consolidated payables file, and the payables change file. The processing sequence is as follows.

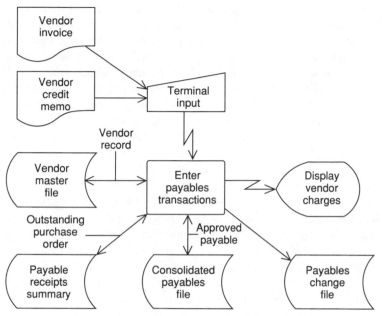

Figure 7–12   Entering payables information

First, the record code and vendor number are keyed. Following their transmission, the computer determines whether the vendor's record is stored on the vendor master file. If the record exists, vendor information is transferred into processing; the vendor's name and address are displayed for visual review. If the program determines that the vendor's record does not exist, a typical response is a message, such as, *The vendor's record cannot be located.* This message blocks further invoice information from entry into processing. The problem associated with the vendor number must be corrected before the invoice in question can be processed. Likewise, if the operator discovers that the vendor's name and address are different from the name and address displayed, processing should be stopped. In such a case, the operator should update the vendor master file before continuing with processing.

For the next step, the operator keys in the purchase order number, the entry of which (in combination with the vendor number) locates the outstanding purchase order stored on the payables receipts summary file. Once located, the record is read into processing. If the outstanding purchase order cannot be located, several possibilities exist: the order was placed, but the goods never arrived or are in transit; the order was not placed, and the invoice is in error; the order was placed, but was never entered into the purchasing and receiving application; or the purchase order number keyed to processing is in error. Regardless of which conditions exist, further processing of the vendor invoice must be stopped to permit investigation.

In the third step in processing, vendor invoice charges are entered (see Figure 7–5), after which the computer compares the billed-for charges and the estimated cost of the purchase. If the two costs are identical or are within a reasonable range, the decision to pay can be made. The trouble begins if the two costs are not within a reasonable range. In this instance, one of two actions can be taken, depending on the design of the interactive program. The operator can instruct the computer to move ahead, while placing a provisional "hold" on the vendor invoice. This hold indicates that the invoice is not to be paid and the hold must later be removed by an additional processing step. The other option is to block processing from moving ahead, which is safer than the first action but also requires more work. It means pulling copies of the original purchase order and receiving report from office files and comparing them with the vendor invoice to determine the reasons for any differences between the quantity ordered and the quantity received and between the estimated costs and the billed-for totals. Once the differences can be explained, it becomes safe to process the vendor invoice.

The fourth and final step entails keying of general ledger information (see Figure 7–5). This step requires display space to permit the entry of several G/L account codes and dollar amounts. Business firms must often break down each purchased item into two or more G/L categories; this breakdown is known as the *general ledger distribution*. It is common, for example, to separate the sales taxes paid from the cost of merchandise. Different codes are also required for different types of merchandise. Office furniture, for instance, requires one code; office supplies, another.

After the G/L distribution has been reconciled, the operator can make the final "go ahead" decision, which tells the computer to assign a voucher number to the invoice transaction and to perform three computer file updates: to update the payables receipts summary file by deleting the outstanding purchase order from the file; to update the consolidated payables file by adding the approved payable; and to update the vendor master file by adding sales history information. As a record of these updates, all information deleted from the summary file and all information added to the consolidated file is written to the payables change file.

The Consolidated Payables File

Each vendor invoice entered into processing adds an additional record to the consolidated payables file. As Figure 7–13 shows, this file consists of groups of outstanding payable vouchers within a vendor number. Grouping outstanding payables in this manner makes it easier to identify invoices for each supplier. It also allows a single check to be written for the entire amount due.

Three fields that require special attention are the pay code, the hold instruction code, and the dollar amount paid. The *pay code* refers to the vendor's stated terms of payment. For example, 1 percent 10, net 20, might be coded 11020; 2 percent 10, net 30, might be coded 21030. The *hold instruction code* is set by the payables staff to specify whether an invoice is to be paid and, if so, the dollar amount of payment. A code of 025M, for example, might indicate that a partial payment of 25 percent is to be paid by the end of the month. The *dollar amount paid* field stores any partial payment made on an outstanding invoice. A 50 percent partial payment on an outstanding invoice of $2,250 would be stored as $1,125 in the dollar amount paid field.

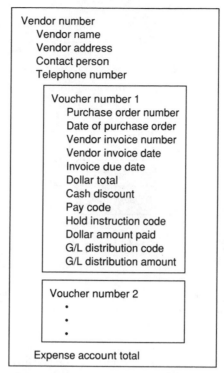

Figure 7–13   Consolidated payables file

The *Enter payment instructions* Program

Determining which vendor invoices to pay and which to hold is as difficult for a business as it is for most individuals. Under perfect conditions, a business pays all of its bills, receives the full benefit of all cash discounts, and meets the terms specified by all vendors. Usually, however, firms attempt to take advantage of cash discounts but find that there are times when the availability of cash falls short of outstanding payables. Then, too, some bills should be disputed, such as when a vendor bills for goods that were returned or for a purchase order that was canceled. Some vendors will intermix charges with credits improperly, which erroneously leads to the printing of an invoice instead of a credit memo. Still other bills should be negotiated. If a vendor has indicated that one set of terms is to be used yet places a different set on the invoice, it is necessary to contact the vendor and to work out a satisfactory solution.

To simplify the difficult task of deciding whom to pay, in what amount, and when, the *Enter payment instruction* program initially selects which invoices to pay using standard programmed decision rules. To begin processing, the operator must enter a *cutoff date* (see Figure 7–14), which the computer matches to invoice due dates (cash discount due dates or end-of-term due dates) in order to decide which invoices to pay. (In practice, as we will discuss in the next section, the availability of cash determines the most appropriate cutoff date.) When cash

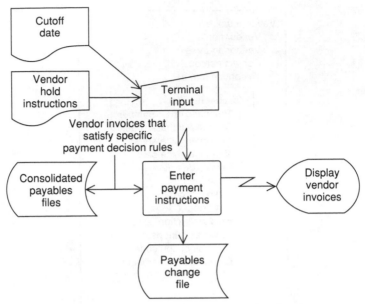

Figure 7–14 Payment instruction processing flowchart

becomes insufficient to cover all outstanding vendor invoices, the computer is programmed to indicate which vendor invoices to hold—even though their due dates are reached. This processing routine usually begins by instructing the computer to identify the largest invoice dollar amount outstanding combined with the smallest cash discount percentage. The invoice selected is flagged for later review, and the computer tests once again to determine if funds are now sufficient.

Besides using the computer to select invoices to be paid and to flag invoices to be held, the payment instruction program permits the payables staff to override these automated decisions. As Figure 7–15 shows, payment instruction displays permit the operator to hold payment (halt code), specify the amount of a partial payment, or stop payment altogether. Payment instruction programs also typically permit page-forward or -backward processing, which work as follows:

1. The operator makes a file selection, such as "display all invoices with an expected payment date of today."

2. The computer responds by displaying the first open invoice that meets this condition.

3. The operator transmits a page-forward message.

4. The computer displays the second open invoice that meets this condition.

5. The operator transmits a page-forward or -backward message.

6. The computer displays the third open invoice (page-forward) or the first open invoice (page-backward).

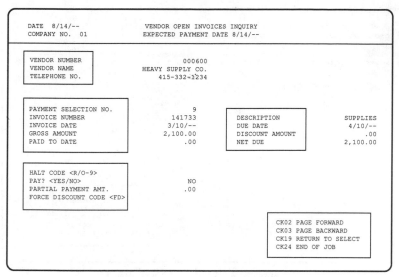

```
DATE   8/14/--                    VENDOR OPEN INVOICES INQUIRY
COMPANY NO.  01                   EXPECTED PAYMENT DATE 8/14/--


   VENDOR NUMBER                         000600
   VENDOR NAME                    HEAVY SUPPLY CO.
   TELEPHONE NO.                   415-332-1234


   PAYMENT SELECTION NO.                9
   INVOICE NUMBER                    141733         DESCRIPTION              SUPPLIES
   INVOICE DATE                     3/10/--          DUE DATE                 4/10/--
   GROSS AMOUNT                    2,100.00          DISCOUNT AMOUNT              .00
   PAID TO DATE                        .00           NET DUE                 2,100.00


   HALT CODE <R/0-9>
   PAY? <YES/NO>                        NO
   PARTIAL PAYMENT AMT.                .00
   FORCE DISCOUNT CODE <FD>

                                                   CK02 PAGE FORWARD
                                                   CK03 PAGE BACKWARD
                                                   CK19 RETURN TO SELECT
                                                   CK24 END OF JOB
```

Figure 7–15   Open invoices display

This combining of computer-based decisions with visual review, verification, and modification of these decisions by members of the payables staff is the underlying basis of the payables selection and payment process. In effect, individuals monitor the actions of the computer. When necessary, they override programmed decisions in need of adjustment.

The *Display cash requirements* Program

The program to display cash requirements is often selected prior to entering payment instructions. This interactive program shows how much cash is needed to pay all open invoices and how much cash is required to take full advantage of all cash discounts. For example, the aged-analysis of open invoices display helps to determine what cash will be needed to meet present and near-term financial obligations (see Figure 7–16). Typically, the cash requirements program provides several processing options. One option is to display the cash requirements for a single vendor, such as vendor number 0100. Another option is to display the cash requirements for all vendors. Still another option is to permit the payables staff to select different aging dates. One option built into more functional designs is to have the computer determine the effects of extending or reducing the cutoff date by one or two days. Another option is to show the cash discounts lost by extending the cutoff date or the discounts gained by reducing the date.

Printing Vendor Voucher-Checks

Once a firm cutoff date is established, the *check register* is printed (see Figure 7–8). As shown by Figure 7–17, this program requires a firm cutoff date as input. Once

```
DATE 8/14/--                          PAYABLE CASH REQUIREMENTS INQUIRY
COMPANY NO. 0100            ALL INVOICES BY DUE DATE - ALWAYS TAKE DISCOUNTS

----INVOICE------    DISC    --------------CASH REQUIREMENTS THROUGH--------------
NUMBER   DATE DUE     DUE     05/15/9X       05/20/9X       05/25/9X       FUTURE


0100   WESTERN TELEPHONE CO.
113-333  05/10/9X    05/20                   1350.00
114-675  05/10/9X    05/20                    680.00
114-777  04/10/9X    04/20     45.20
114-776  03/10/9X    03/20     15.60


                              --------       --------       --------       --------


*0100 TOTALS*                  60.80         2030.00


                                            ┌────────────────────────┐
                                            │ CK 02 PAGE FORWARD     │
                                            │ CK 03 PAGE BACKWARD    │
                                            │ CK 10 SINGLE VENDOR    │
                                            │ CK 12 ALL VENDORS      │
                                            │ CK 24 END OF JOB       │
                                            └────────────────────────┘
```

Figure 7–16   Aged-analysis display

specified, vendor invoices to be paid are written from the consolidated-payables file and added to the payables *pending-check file*. As shown earlier (see Figure 7–3), the payables pending-check file might be called the *payables-this-period* file (that is, it contains invoices to be paid this period). After deleting the invoices to be paid, the considerably smaller consolidated payables file is called the *payables-held-over* file. This smaller file now contains invoices to be paid at some later date.

Once the payables pending-check file is complete, the *payables check register* is printed. This valuable register lists each invoice to be paid; it must be carefully

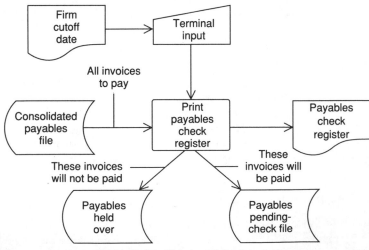

Figure 7–17   Check register flowchart

reviewed before vendor voucher-checks are printed. This review determines if vendor invoices deleted from the consolidated payables file were transferred to the pending-check file as specified, if cash discounts were processed correctly, and if the total dollar amount to be paid is consistent with the cash amount available.

Finally, printing of vendor voucher-checks begins after a check register is approved. Information that appears on the register also appears on the voucher portion of the check (see Figure 7–7). In printing the check, the only information not printed is the signature. Because of the risks associated with producing and storing continuous sheets of presigned checks, businesses use special equipment to add the signature to each check and to separate the sheets into individual checks.

Printing General Ledger Distributions

General ledger distributions, such as the distribution shown in Figure 7–9, are important products of accounts payable processing. Several different types of general ledger (G/L) distributions or summaries are prepared. These include the payables held-over G/L summary, the checks-written payables G/L summary, the checks-pending payables G/L summary, and the checks-canceled payables G/L summary. Although all these are similar, each is designed to show dollar totals at different stages in accounts payables processing:

- The *payables held-over G/L summary* shows the dollar amounts to be paid by account—such as for advertising, insurance, and office supplies—at some future date.

- The *checks-written payables G/L summary* shows the dollar amounts paid by G/L account for a specific check-printing run.

- The *checks-pending payables G/L summary* shows G/L account dollar amounts pending (that is, checks that have not been returned).

- The *checks-canceled payables G/L summary* shows the dollar amounts paid to vendors and reconciled (that is, checks that have been deposited by vendors, returned by the bank, and found to be correct by the business) by G/L account.

The final steps in payables processing take place after paid checks are returned from the bank. *Check reconciliation* programs determine if canceled check dollar amounts are in balance with the dollar amounts printed on the face of each vendor voucher-check. Through check reconciliation processing, canceled checks are deleted from the pending-check file; reconciliation change reports identify the checks deleted from the file.

REVIEW QUESTIONS

10. What is the purpose of the *Display cash requirements* program?

11. Name the four online files updated by the *Enter payables transaction* program.

12. How does the pay code field differ from the hold instruction field? From the dollar amount paid field?

13. What is a cutoff date? Why is such a date important to payables processing? Why are several cutoff dates tested before a firm date is established?

14. Of what value is a display of aged open invoices?

15. What four G/L distributions are important to payables processing?

16. How does check writing differ from check reconciliation?

7-3 FILE PROCESSING

Several file-processing activities must be carried out in conjunction with accounts payable processing. These include adjusting the vendor master file, the consolidated payables files, and the consolidated pending-check file. Additional programs are also needed to back up master, consolidated, and change files. Fortunately, most of these programs are simple in design.

Adjusting Computer Files

Before payables transactions are entered into processing, the vendor master file must be made current. Information closely monitored at this time includes any changes in vendor name and address and the pay code. When a change is noted, a vendor change slip is prepared; then the new vendor information is entered into processing and the master file is updated. As with other file updates, all changes must be initially displayed for review (see Figure 7–18). If the review indicates that the revised information is correct, the computer is instructed to update the file. To provide a permanent record of the update, the change is also written to the *vendor change file*.

The consolidated payables file must also be adjusted on those occasions when it becomes necessary to delete an invoice in error. If, for example, a vendor invoice is found to be in error and the vendor sends a corrected statement, the business receiving the correction must fill in an *adjusting entry slip* or a *credit memo*. In processing, the *Enter payables transactions* program must be capable of handling either type of transaction.

Finally, adjustments to the consolidated pending-check file must be made from time to time. These updates result when checks are not cashed by vendors—an unusual circumstance, but one that does occur. Consider the following situation: a check is returned by the postal service with a message printed on the envelope stating that the vendor has moved and left no forwarding address. In such cases, a business must be able to remove the pending check from the file. Otherwise, it will remain there forever.

File Backup and Reporting

File backup and reporting programs must be written in support of accounts payable processing. Each program creates a backup copy of a computer file and

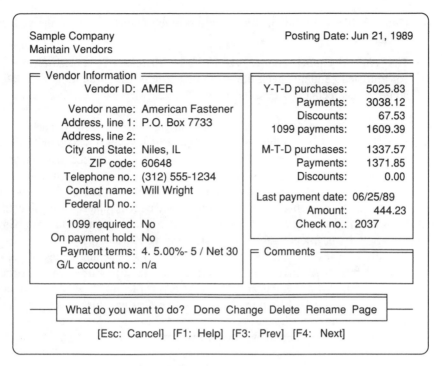

Figure 7–18 Maintain vendor display

prints a listing of the contents of the file. Besides the payables check register, three additional backup registers are printed: the vendor register, the consolidated accounts payable register, and the consolidated pending-check register.

- The *vendor register* lists all vendors contained on the vendor master file. This register is particularly helpful if a vendor account cannot be located.

- The *consolidated payables register* lists all invoices that remain to be paid. It is generally printed before and after the printing of the payables check register. Thus, the consolidated payables register shows invoices to be paid and invoices held over, whereas the check register shows invoices to be paid this period.

- The *consolidated pending-check register* lists all checks not yet cashed by vendors. This register is printed soon after checks returned from the bank have been posted against the consolidated pending-check file.

Besides these three registers, three change reports also back up processing.

- The *vendor change report* lists all changes to the vendor master file, including when a change was made (the time and date), by whom (the person), and what parts of the vendor record were altered (the content).

- The *payables change report* lists all vendor invoices added to the consolidated payables file and deleted from the payables receipts summary file (see

Figure 7–12). In addition, the report shows the updates made to the vendor master file.

- The *checks-pending change report* lists all checks deleted from the consolidated pending-check file. This listing tells when (the time and date) a check was reconciled by a business.

Collectively, these registers and reports provide an important backup to processing. Suppose, for example, that a company believes it has paid an invoice but that the vendor believes otherwise. To determine who is correct, the first step is to activate the *Display payables accounts* program to determine if an invoice has been paid and, if so, by which check number. As shown by Figure 7–19, when a payment is made, the check number used in payment is placed alongside the vendor invoice amount. This provides for a complete picture of how the company intends to apply its payment against an outstanding vendor charge.

Besides allowing invoice payments to be traced online, backup copies of computer files and reports are invaluable because they make it possible to reconstruct the entire accounts payable application, should entire files of data be lost or destroyed. Three files in particular provide a clear record of payables processing: the payables receipts summary file shows which vendor invoices are to be expected; the consolidated payables file shows which invoices were received and are yet to

```
Jun 21, 1989          *** DEMO VERSION OF BUSINESSWORKS ***          Page 1
3:25 pm                         Sample Company
                          Accounts Payable Detail Report

Invoice               Due                  Transaction   Original    Current
Number      Date      Date    Reference      Amount      Balance     Balance
=========  =========  ======= ============  ==========   ========   =========
AMER       American Fastener
2379       04/02/89   04/30   P.O. 2470                    49.40       49.40
2798       05/02/89   Close   Verbal                      498.23    CK002026
2979       05/10/89   Close   P.O. 2409                   429.39    CK002026
3076       06/04/89   Close   P.O. 2479                   489.23    CK002037
           06/12/89   Cr      return         -45.00
3128       06/23/89   07/22   P.O. 2483                   893.34      893.34
CK002026   06/10/89           Payment        927.62
CK002037   06/25/89           Payment        444.23     ----------  ----------

             Vendor Total                               2359.59      942.74
             Less Open Credits                                       -77.00
                                                        ----------  ----------
             Net Balance Due                                         865.74
─────────────────────────── [ (more) ] ────────────────────────────

     Report complete. Use ↑, ↓, PgUp, PgDn, Home or End to view
          [ ↵  or Esc: Finished with report]  [F1: Help]
```

Figure 7–19 Display showing how checks offset vendor invoices

be paid; and the consolidated pending-check file shows which checks were written but are yet to be returned. Because of their importance, copies of all three files should be stored off-site in fireproof vaults as insurance against unforeseen data center disasters.

7-4 PROCESSING CONTROLS

The design of a series of display screens, printed registers,- and change reports, showing before-and-after versions of payables files, is one method of securing control over processing. If a vendor, a member of the payables staff, or a financial officer of the business questions the status of an invoice, it should be possible to identify immediately an invoice as either being held and stored on file or to trace quickly an invoice that has been paid. In addition, transaction and batch control balances must be maintained. The design of these controls can be summarized by a major payables program.

The *Enter payables transactions* program maintains both transaction and batch controls. A transaction control balance is established during the checking of general ledger distributions. The sum of the general ledger entries is compared with the total invoice amount; if the sum differs from the total, the transaction is out of balance. Unless corrected, the transaction is blocked from further processing and cannot be added to the consolidated payables file.

Besides this internal balance, several batch control balances are maintained. The payables register must show that the dollars entered into processing equal the sum of the dollars stored on the payables change file, the dollars added to the consolidated payables file, the dollars added to the vendor master file, and the dollars subtracted from the payables receipts summary file (see Figure 7–12). In addition, the program must keep a separate accounting of the dollar total with and without cash discounts. The batch control equation is

Total discounted invoice total

$$= \text{Total invoice charge (net amount)} - \text{Cash discount available}$$

The *Print payables check register* program lowers the dollar amount stored on the consolidated payables file. When the decision is made to pay an invoice, dollars must be subtracted from the consolidated file and added to the payables pending-check file (see Figure 7–17). The equation maintained by this program is

$$\text{Total check amount} = \text{Total invoice charge (net amount)} - \text{Cash discounts taken}$$

Because it is important to review cash discounting carefully, most companies require cash discount percentages to be calculated. One ratio is

$$\text{Cash discount percentage} = \frac{\text{(Discounts available} - \text{Discounts taken)}}{\text{Discounts available}}$$

Unless this ratio is high, managers should question payment decisions.

The *Print vendor checks* program should compute and print the same amount as the total shown on the payables check register. Printed checks should not be signed and released unless the totals are identical.

The *Print general ledger distribution* program provides a final test of the accuracy of processing. A *trial balance* is obtained by matching expense account totals to the total check amount. If the totals do not agree, adjusting entries must be keyed to processing. Either a general ledger entry will have to be revised or a vendor invoice (debit or credit) adjustment will have to be made.

Manual audits should be conducted to supplement programmed controls. After checks are printed, a random sample of payables should be selected for audit. The check amount should be compared first with the total printed on the check register and next with the total printed on the consolidated payables register. As a further audit, the check amount should be compared with the amount shown on the original vendor invoice. Finally, a full test would trace the vendor charge back through purchasing and receiving.

7-5 MANAGEMENT IMPLICATIONS

An automated accounts payable application offers two main benefits. The first is obvious: prompt payment of vendor invoices. The computer helps determine when to pay, what amount to pay, whether to challenge the invoice total, and whether to take the cash discount. The second benefit, improved control of cash payments, is not so self-evident. Within large businesses, it becomes difficult to know whether all invoices submitted by vendors or all checks written to vendors are legitimate. The computer helps make this determination.

Substantial savings can result when a firm is able to process vendor invoices quickly. First, prompt payment enables a business to take the cash discount. When the terms 2/10, n/30 (2 percent ten days, net thirty days), are quoted, for example, the cost of credit is 36 percent if the cash discount is not taken. Promptness also often leads to more favorable terms of payment and to a resulting important improvement in *net trade credit*. For instance, if a business sells, on the average, $2,000 of goods per day, with an average collection period of forty days, outstanding accounts receivable will approximate $80,000. If the firm then buys $1,000 worth of goods from vendors per day, with an average payables period of ten days, accounts payable will approximate $10,000. The $70,000 difference between accounts receivable and accounts payable would thus indicate the *net trade credit amount*, or trade credit imbalance, that the business must finance. If the average payables period is extended from ten days to twenty-five days, however, the dollar amount of trade credit would be increased from $10,000 to $25,000 and the net trade credit amount would be reduced significantly—from $70,000 to $55,000.

The savings from improved control over processing are more difficult to document. The objective in design is to reduce the probability of employee embezzlement by providing for well-planned programmed controls and for scheduled and nonscheduled manual audits. Lacking the best of controls, payables processing is extremely vulnerable to embezzling. Shortages in cash can be hidden by writing checks to fictitious vendor accounts and then deleting all traces of the accounts. Some organizations are especially vulnerable to fraudulent vendor invoices. A large branch of the military, for example, makes little attempt to match vendor invoices to purchase orders or receiving documents. When an invoice is received, it is paid; not until several weeks later does the branch try to match the paid invoice to the original purchase order and to investigate if a match cannot be made. Unfortunately, this type of processing is not limited to a few instances. Far too many firms have weak payables controls.

A final savings to be realized through using the accounts payable application lies in being able to predict the cash required to pay current and future bills. Financial officers of a business need this information to help them estimate the demand for capital. With better understanding and enough time to make decisions, they are better able to minimize the cost of financing the net trade credit amount.

REVIEW QUESTIONS

17. Why must the consolidated payables file be adjusted from time to time?

18. What is the difference between the consolidated payables register and the consolidated pending-check register? Between the payables change report and the checks-pending change report?

19. Describe the transaction and batch control balances maintained by the *Enter payables transaction* program.

20. If control balance tests are working correctly, why are manual audits necessary?

21. What is a net trade credit amount? Why should a company be concerned about such an amount?

22. Explain how payables processing helps financial managers determine their cash-flow requirements.

REVIEW OF IMPORTANT IDEAS

Several decisions must be incorporated into the design of the accounts payable application. These include when to pay, what amount to pay, whether to challenge the invoice total, and whether to take the cash discount. Correct decisions help a business to attain two main objectives of payables processing: paying vendor invoices promptly and keeping vendor credit balances within reason.

Improved control of cash payments is another important objective of payables processing. Since this application specifies who to pay and in what amount, safeguards must be developed to reduce the risk of embezzlement and fraud.

Three processing runs are required by the payables application. The first run makes the vendor master file current and creates a file of approved payables. In creating such a file, vendor invoice information must be keyed and displayed. If the information is verified as correct, the program continues by updating four online computer files (the vendor master file, the payables receipts file, the consolidated payables file, and the payables change file).

The second processing run determines which vendor invoices to pay and which invoices to hold. In processing, one computer program applies a cutoff date to all open invoices in deciding which invoices to pay. When cash is insufficient to cover all open charges, the computer determines which invoices to hold, even though their due dates are reached. A separate program determines how much cash is needed to pay all open invoices and to take advantage of all cash discounts. This program assists financial officers in setting the cutoff date.

The third processing run splits the consolidated payables file and prints vendor voucher-checks, registers, and summary reports. Vendor voucher-checks contain a voucher portion to show why the check was written and a negotiable check portion. Prior to the printing of checks, a check register is prepared and reviewed. This register helps determine if vendor invoices have been processed correctly. After checks are printed, a general ledger distribution is produced. This distribution provides a further check on the accuracy of processing.

Vendor voucher-check information is written to a consolidated pending-check file. Here the information remains, awaiting the return of checks by the bank. A check reconciliation processing run deletes checks from the pending file and reports the results of processing.

Numerous registers and change reports are printed in addition to the check register and G/L distribution. The consolidated payables register and the consolidated pending-check register help track the status of vendor invoices. The vendor change report, the payables change report, and the check-pending change report show the results of updates and adjustments. Although the paperwork associated with payables processing may appear extreme, registers, reports, and G/L distributions permit the entire payables process to be reconstructed if files of data are lost or destroyed. This paper trail is required for a manual audit of processing. Audits supplement transaction and batch controls.

Substantial savings result from a well-designed payables application. Prompt payment of vendor invoices enables a business to improve its credit rating, take advantage of cash discounts, and reduce the net trade credit amount to be financed. Besides direct savings, indirect savings result from improved processing control and the ability to make better estimates of the demand for capital and its implications.

KEY WORDS

Credit rating

Trade credit

Consolidated payables file

Payables-this-period file

Vendor invoice

Vendor master file

Pay code

Hold-instruction code

Cutoff date

Pending-check file

Payables check register

Check reconciliation

Direct cost

Indirect cost

Vendor voucher-check

Voucher number

Check number

Vendor register

Trial balance

Net trade credit amount

General ledger (G/L) distribution

EXERCISES

1. A personal accounts payable system differs somewhat from an accounts payable system designed for a business. Personal income is often received in the form of a paycheck from an employer. Once deposited, the funds are used to pay monthly bills, which are received from stores and other businesses such as banks and utility companies.

    Design a personal accounts-payable system, using Figures 7–2 through 7–4 as guides. Assume that you would like to prepare a personal expense summary, which shows how your income was spent.

2. After the installation of a computer-based accounts payable system, a firm discovers that it is better able to pay its outstanding invoices on time. As a result, suppliers decide to offer more favorable terms of payment. The financial vice-president of the company estimates the following:

	BEFORE SYSTEM INSTALLED	AFTER SYSTEM INSTALLED
Sales/day	$1,800	$2,200
Average collection period	40 days	38 days
Purchases/day	$1,500	$1,900
Average payment period (to obtain discount)	15 days	20 days

    What is the net credit balance before and after the installation of the payables system? What conclusion can you draw? Assume that the cost of obtaining funds to finance accounts receivable is twelve percent per year.

3. Design a data-flow diagram for an online check reconciliation application. The program menu to be followed is shown below. Attach a short descriptive statement with each program to describe how processing is supposed to work.

    ```
    ENTER CANCELED CHECKS
    PRINT PAID CHECKS REGISTER
    PRINT OUTSTANDING CHECKS REGISTER
    PRINT G/L DISTRIBUTIONS (MAY BE SEVERAL)
    EXIT
    ```

4. There are several ways to create the payables pending-check file besides the way described and illustrated in this chapter (see Figure 7–17). Two options are the following:

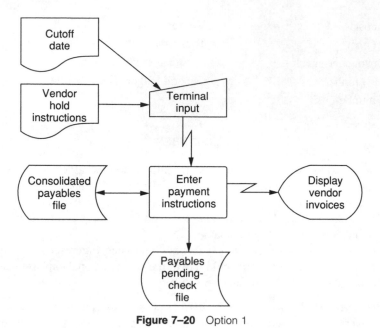

Figure 7–20   Option 1

Option 1: Create the file as part of the *Enter payment instruction* program. Use a cutoff date and vendor hold instructions to determine which payables are to be added to the payables file (see Figure 7–20).

Option 2: Create the file as part of the *Print payables check register* program. Update the consolidated payables file, however, instead of dividing it into two smaller files (see Figure 7–21).

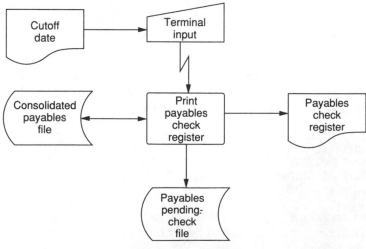

Figure 7–21   Option 2

Explain the advantages and disadvantages of each of these processing options compared with the design presented in the chapter.

5. It is necessary at times for a business to pay in advance for goods and services. For example, a vendor might require a cash down payment before agreeing to begin work on an order. Explain how the payables application would have to be modified to handle prepaid expenses.

6. Suppose a company is able to negotiate yearly installment plans with vendors. Under this agreement, the company would pay an outstanding balance in equal installments. How must the payables application be modified to support this requirement?

7. At times, a vendor invoice is received before purchased goods are received and accepted. How must the accounts payable design deal with this situation?

DISCUSSION QUESTIONS

1. Why must there be different types of decision rules written for the accounts payable application? List the decision rules you would include in an accounts payable design.

2. With many accounts payable designs, only the dollar amount of the vendor invoice is keyed to processing—the line-item detail is not keyed at any time in processing. How are quantity and cost totals verified if only the invoice total is key-entered?

3. Why is it important to be able to display and examine vendor accounts? Suggest several reasons.

4. Why is it important to be able to display the way a payment has been applied to an outstanding vendor charge? Suggest several reasons.

5. Why is it sometimes advantageous for a company to pay its bills daily? Weekly? Only at month end?

4-IN-1 CASE STUDY—ACCOUNTS PAYABLE

This lesson is much like the accounts receivable case study lesson. The main difference is that you will be asked to pay a vendor charge rather than to bill a customer. The following are the tasks you are asked to do:

- View a vendor's account.
- Add a vendor bill to pay.
- Print a bills payable edit list.
- Post the bills payable to the general ledger.
- Create a disbursement file.
- Print a disbursements edit list.

Viewing a Vendor Account

With 4-in-1 you can display (view) a vendor account at any time—before or after processing a vendor charge or before or after writing the check to offset the outstanding charge. To display a vendor account, do the following:

1. Log on and enter a date of **010597**. Press ENTER when asked, *Any change?*

2. Type **16** from the main menu and press ENTER.

3. When the view or print vendor accounts menu appears, type **1** and press ENTER to view accounts.

4. Press F1 to review the first vendor account. (Remember, this account was added as part of lesson 3.)

5. Press F1 again to view the second account.

6. Press F1 again to reach the end of file. Press ENTER to continue.

7. Press TAB twice to return to the main menu.

Adding a Vendor Charge

Both regular and recurring transactions can be processed using 4-in-1. In this chapter you are asked to process a *regular transaction*. This is the usual kind—once entered it becomes effective. A regular transaction can be a new bill, a debit memo, a credit memo, or a record of a vendor account balance brought forward. In the next chapter you will be asked to process a *recurring transaction*. This type occurs over and over again, as with a loan payment.

8. From the main menu, type **14**, *Process bills payable*.

9. When the transactions menu appears, type **1**, *Add transaction*.

10. Type **JXX** (in capital letters), and press ENTER when asked for the name of the vendor.

11. Press ENTER when asked if the JXX Tools and Supplies vendor is the right vendor.

12. Press ENTER to indicate that a bill is to be processed. The choices are B = bill, C = credit, D = debit memo, and F = balance forward.

13. Press ENTER to set the date as 010597.

14. Type **66995** and press ENTER to record the vendor invoice number.

15. Type **Hand tools** and press ENTER for the reference.

16. Type **369.50** and press ENTER for the amount.

17. Press ENTER when asked, *Credit A/P?* This indicates that you wish the dollar amount to be credited against the accounts payable general ledger number.

18. Press ENTER when asked, *Field number to change?*

19. You are asked to distribute the $369.50. Press F1 twice to apply the full amount to account 5020-00. This account was set up when the new vendor was added to the master vendor file (see Figure 3–19).

20. Press ENTER when asked, *Any change?*

21. Press TAB to enter another bill.

Adding a Second Vendor Bill

Figure 7–22 shows the billing information received from the A and P Chemical company. Enter this information into processing to process a second record to the bills payable file. When you are through, press TAB twice to return to the process bills payable menu.

Printing the Transaction Edit List

After all charges have been entered, the transaction edit list can be displayed or printed.

22. From the process bills payable submenu, type **4** and press ENTER.

23. Press ENTER when asked, *Display the report?* The bills payable edit list will be printed.

Posting the Accounts Payable Transaction

Bills payable must be posted before they alter vendor account balances or general ledger accounts.

24. From the process bills payable submenu, press **5**, *Post transactions*.

25. Type **Y** when asked, *Are bills payable transactions OK to post?* Print the register report and return to the main menu.

```
VENDOR                      A AND P CHEMICALS
INVOICE NUMBER              66996
INVOICE DATE                010597
REFERENCE                   Micro grow / additive
AMOUNT                      $1,890.00
CASH DISCOUNT               NONE

DISTRIBUTE FULL AMOUNT TO   ACCOUNT 5010–000

PAY FROM                    Checking account #1
```

Figure 7–22   A and P Chemical billing information

Creating a Disbursements File

The processing disbursements function is used to release cash to pay for outstanding bills. With 4-in-1 you must create a disbursement file before you can print a check. In adding transactions to this file, you must specify the type of disbursement you plan to make, given the following three options: you can print a check using the computer, specify that you wish to write a check by hand, or make a disbursement adjustment. In this section we ask you only to produce a disbursement register. In the next lesson you are asked to print a check using the computer.

26. From the main menu, type **15** and press ENTER.

27. Type **1**, *Add transaction*.

28. Type **JXX** (in capital letters), and press ENTER when asked for the payee.

29. Press ENTER when asked, *Right vendor?*

30. Press ENTER when asked for the type of check. The choices are *C* = computer check (the default), *H* = hand-written check, or *O* = other disbursement.

31. Press ENTER when asked if the bill was previously entered.

32. Type **012597** and press ENTER when asked for the transaction date.

33. Type **Hand tools** and press ENTER for the reference.

34. Type **362.11** and press ENTER for the amount paid.

35. Type **7.39** and press ENTER for the discount. This represents a 2 percent cash discount—a discount we have assumed to make this lesson more interesting.

36. Type **1** and press ENTER to pay from checking account #1.

37. Press ENTER to debit accounts payable.

38. Press ENTER when asked, *Field to change?*

39. When the disbursements processing screen appears, type **66995** and press ENTER to specify the invoice number. This information appears on the payables edit list.

40. Type **010597** and press ENTER for the invoice date.

41. Type **369.50** and press ENTER for the invoice amount.

42. Type **362.11** and press ENTER for the cash paid.

43. Type F1 to add the discount and the amount to credit.

44. Press ENTER when asked, *Any change?*

45. Press TAB to enter another transaction.

46. Post the A and P Chemical bill to the disbursements file. Use information

from the bills payable register to complete all entries. A and P does not give a cash discount. Instead, payment is due in full.

47. Press TAB twice to exit.

Printing the Transaction Edit List

After the disbursement file has been created, the disbursements edit list can be printed.

48. From the process disbursements menu, type **4** and press ENTER.

49. Press ENTER when asked *Display this report?* The disbursements edit list will be printed. Note the message on this list. In the next lesson you will be asked to post this transaction and print a company check.

QUESTIONS

1. With 4-in-1, to which general ledger accounts are bills payable posted? As shown by the disbursements edit report, how will this posting change after the check is written and the check total is posted?

2. Why is it important to keep disbursements separate from bills payable?

3. In creating a vendor account, a general ledger default was set. Why is this default important? How can it be overridden by 4-in-1?

4. Compare the 4-in-1 accounts payable procedure to the 4-in-1 customer invoice procedure. In what ways are they similar?

5. Edit lists were created for both bills payable processing and disbursement processing. Why are these lists important? What would happen if they were not built into the design?

CHAPTER

Fixed Assets

If a company acquires business property, such as a plant and equipment, that has a useful life of more than one year, it cannot by law deduct the cost of such property as an expense in a single year. Instead, the company must spread the cost over several years. This is called *depreciation* of business property. Because the dollar amount deducted each year for business expenses offsets taxable income, it is often referred to as a *tax write-off*.

Property is depreciable if it meets requirements specified by federal government law. Four such requirements are the following: first, the property must be used (or held) for the production of income; second, it must have a useful life of more than one year; third, it must be possible to determine the span of its useful life; and, fourth, it must be something that wears out or loses its value. For example, tangible property with a useful life of several years, such as equipment or machinery, is depreciable because it wears out. In contrast, real property, such as land, can never be depreciated because it does not wear out.

Property with a useful life of more than one year is also known as a *fixed asset*. It is fixed because it makes up the permanent part of a business. In processing fixed-assets information, procedures must be developed to do two things: to collect and record fixed-assets information and determine the depreciation schedule of the property and to maintain the depreciation schedule and determine the depreciation deduction (that is, the yearly tax write-off). In this chapter we examine both sets of activities.

8-1 FIXED-ASSETS ACCOUNTING SYSTEMS

One of the major difficulties associated with the design of fixed-assets accounting systems is that they are greatly affected by ever-changing federal and state tax legislation. Thus, before we examine the logical features of the fixed-assets system, the current status of methods of depreciation and the basic procedures of each method require study.

The Modified Accelerated Cost Recovery System (MACRS) is currently used by the federal government. It includes the General Depreciation System (GDS), the Alternative Depreciation System (ADS), and, for pre-1987 assets, the Accelerated Cost Recovery System (ACRS). For this chapter, we consider only the General Depreciation System. Under this system, assets must first be sorted by class life. As shown by Figure 8–1, each class life has a corresponding recovery period—the period of time in which the value of the asset can be depreciated.

As illustrated by Figure 8–2 (see step 13), the general depreciation system requires a firm to indicate the basis for depreciation, recovery period, convention, and method in order to compute the depreciation deduction. Each of these terms can be described briefly as follows:

Basis for depreciation is the dollar amount of the asset used for business purposes.

Recovery period is the number of years the asset is to be depreciated.

Convention determines the portion of the tax year for which the depreciation is allowable. This entry is optional.

Method indicates the applicable depreciation method used to determine the amount of depreciation. For three-, five-, seven-, and ten-year property, the applicable method is the 200 percent, or double, declining-balance method of depreciation. For fifteen- and twenty-year property and for property in a farming business, the applicable method is the 150 percent, or one-and-one-half, declining-balance method of depreciation. With either method, a switch to the straight-line method of depreciation is permitted in the first year that maximizes the depreciation allowance.

Before we continue, an introduction to the double and one-and-one-half declining methods and the straight-line method of depreciation is required. Of the three, the straight-line method is the easiest to understand.

Property that has a class life (in years) of	Is treated as
4 or less	3-year property
More than 4 but less than 10	5-year property
10 or more but less than 16	7-year property
16 or more but less than 20	10-year property
20 or more but less than 25	15-year property
25 or more	20-year property
In addition:	
Residential rental property	27.5 years
Nonresidential real property	31.5 years

Figure 8–1   Class-life categories of assets

Form **4562**		**Depreciation and Amortization**		OMB No. 1545-0172

Form **4562**

Department of the Treasury
Internal Revenue Service

Depreciation and Amortization

▶ See separate Instructions.
▶ Attach this form to your return.

OMB No. 1545-0172

1989

Attachment
Sequence No. **67**

Name(s) as shown on return

Identifying number

Business or activity to which this form relates

~~ciation *(Use Part III for automobiles, certain other vehicles, computers, and property used for entertainment,* ~~r amusement.)

Section A.—Election To Expense Depreciable Assets (Section 179)

		1	$10,000
~~e during the tax year (see instructions)		2	
~~ation		3	$200,000
	~ \	4	

8 Tenta~~~
9 Taxable income lim~~~
10 Carryover of disallowed deductio~ ..
11 Section 179 expense deduction (Enter the les~~.
12 Carryover of disallowed deduction to 1990 (Add lines 8 and 10, ~~~ ~~~

Section B.—MACRS Depreciation

(a) Classification of property	(b) Date placed in service	(c) Basis for depreciation (Business use only—see instructions)	(d) Recovery period	(e) Convention	(f) Method	(g) Depreciation deduction
13 General Depreciation System (GDS) (see instructions): *For assets placed in service ONLY during tax year beginning in 1989*						
a 3-year property						
b 5-year property		$10,000	5 yr		200 DB	$4000.00
c 7-year property						
d 10-year property						
e 15-year property						
f 20-year property						
~sidential rental property			27.5 yrs.	MM	S/L	
			27.5 yrs.	MM	S/L	
~ial real property			31.5 yrs.	MM	S/L	
			31.5 yrs.	MM	S/L	
~ System (ADS) (see instructions): *For assets placed in service ONLY during tax year beginning in 1989*					S/L	
~~			12 yrs.		S/L	
17 Property su~.			40 yrs.	MM	S/L	
18 ACRS and/or oth~						

			15	
~~uctions)			16	

19 Total (Add deductions on line 1~ ~
your return (Partnerships and S corporatio~~

20 For assets shown above and placed in service during the cu~~
of the basis attributable to section 263A costs (see instructions). . . . .

For Paperwork Reduction Act Notice. see page 1 of the separate instructions.

Form **4562** (1989)

Figure 8–2   Tax depreciation report

The Straight-Line Method of Depreciation

A *straight-line method* of depreciation permits the same percentage (or dollar amount) to be deducted each year. The deduction is calculated as follows:

$$\text{Straight-line depreciation (in dollars)} = \frac{(\text{Investment} - \text{Salvage value})}{\text{Useful life of asset}}$$

Suppose, for example, that a business buys (invests in) a used machine for $2,000. If the machine has a useful life of ten years and will have no salvage value (meaning that it cannot be sold as salvage ten years from now and thus has no residual value), the straight-line depreciation for the machine is $200 ($2,000 ÷ 10 years). In other words, $200 can be deducted as depreciation each year for ten years.

The Double (200 Percent) Declining-Balance Method of Depreciation

The *double declining-balance method* of depreciation is more complex than the straight-line method. Several steps are required in calculating yearly depreciation.

1. The *straight-line rate of depreciation* must first be determined by dividing the number 1 by the useful life of the investment. Returning to the example above, we can calculate the straight-line rate as 10 percent (1 ÷ 10 years).

2. The *accelerated rate of depreciation* must be determined by multiplying the straight-line rate (in percent) times the *declining-balance factor* (for example, 10 percent × 2 = 20 percent).

3. The first-year depreciation is calculated by multiplying the fixed investment times the accelerated rate of depreciation. In our example, first-year depreciation is $400 (.20 × $2,000).

4. The second-year depreciation is calculated by subtracting the previous depreciation from the investment and multiplying the balance times the accelerated rate of depreciation. The second-year depreciation for our $2,000 example investment would thus be $320 [($2,000 − $400 first-year depreciation) × .20 = $320].

5. The third-year depreciation is calculated in the same way as the second year. All previous depreciations ($400 + $320) must be subtracted before the balance is multiplied by the accelerated rate of depreciation. In our example, the third year of depreciation is $256.

The 150 Percent Declining-Balance Method of Depreciation

The 150 percent declining-balance method of depreciation is computed much like the double declining method.

1. The *straight-line rate* of depreciation must be determined first. In our preceding example, the straight-line rate is 10 percent.

2. The *accelerated rate of depreciation* is determined by multiplying the straight-line rate times the *declining-balance factor*, or 15 percent.

3. The first-year depreciation is calculated as follows: $2,000 × .15 = $300.00.

4. The second-year depreciation then becomes ($2,000 − $300) × .15 = $255.00.

5. Third-year depreciation is ($2,000 − $300 − $225) × .15 = $221.25.

Straight-line				
Year	Investment	Rate	Deduction	Reserve Dec. 31
First	$10,000	20%	$2,000	$ 2,000
Second	10,000	20%	2,000	4,000
Third	10,000	20%	2,000	6,000
Fourth	10,000	20%	2,000	8,000
Fifth	10,000	20%	2,000	10,000

200 percent declining-balance				
Year	Remaining Investment Jan. 1	Rate	Deduction	Reserve Dec. 31
First	$10,000	40%	$4,000	$4,000
Second	6,000	40%	2,400	6,400
Third	3,600	40%	1,440	7,840
Fourth	2,160	40%	864	8,704
Fifth	1,296	40%	518	9,222

150 percent declining-balance				
Year	Remaining Investment Jan. 1	Rate	Deduction	Reserve Dec. 31
First	$10,000	30%	$3,000	$3,000
Second	7,000	30%	2,100	5,100
Third	4,900	30%	1,470	6,570
Fourth	3,430	30%	1,029	7,599
Fifth	2,401	30%	720	8,319

Figure 8–3 Comparing methods of depreciation

The tables presented in Figure 8–3 compare the three methods of depreciation for a new machine costing $10,000. The machine has a useful life of five years and no salvage value. With the straight-line method, the deduction of 20 percent remains the same for each of the five years. The double declining and the one-and-one-half declining methods feature accelerated rates. For the first year the percentage rate for double declining balance is 40 percent, and the rate for one-and-one-half declining-balance is 30 percent. With both the double and the one-and-one-half methods, the straight-line depreciation exceeds the declining-balance methods in the third year. At this point, a switch can be made from declining balance to straight line for the remaining three years of the tax write-off.

Besides depreciation, businesses may elect to amortize certain capital expenses over a fixed period. *Amortization*, the process of gradually writing off the cost of an intangible asset during its useful life, applies to such things as reforestation costs, bond premiums, and construction-period interest and taxes. The term *intangible asset* describes an asset lacking in physical substance. It differs from a *tangible asset; tangible* denotes physical substance.

REVIEW QUESTIONS

1. Property is depreciable if it meets which federal requirements?

2. Explain the main advantage of the GDS system of depreciation.

3. Name the three main methods of calculating depreciation.

4. What is the difference between an intangible and a tangible asset?

8-2   PRELIMINARY OVERVIEW OF PROCESSING

In order for the computer to calculate the depreciation schedule for fixed assets, information describing each fixed asset must be entered into processing. As Figure 8–4 shows, fixed-assets *payables-to-capitalize* information is provided by the accounts payable application. This information must, in turn, be combined with *new property information*, information provided by the property control department of a company to show how property is to be identified and depreciated and where the property is to be located.

Two main outputs from the system are depreciation schedules and property-reporting information. A *depreciation schedule* shows how the dollar amount of an asset is to be written off over a specified period and how the amount was calculated. Most fixed-asset systems produce a number of schedules that include depreciation projections, asset retirements, and tax depreciations. *Property-reporting information* consists of labels or tags that are attached to fixed assets and a variety of property-control reports. These latter reports provide for an accounting of all fixed-assets inventory.

Figure 8–5 examines the main functions of the fixed-assets system. As shown, four main functions lead to the printing of depreciation schedules and property reports. Let's consider each of these steps.

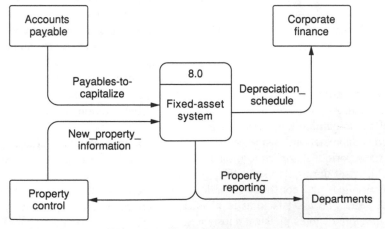

Figure 8–4   The fixed-assets system

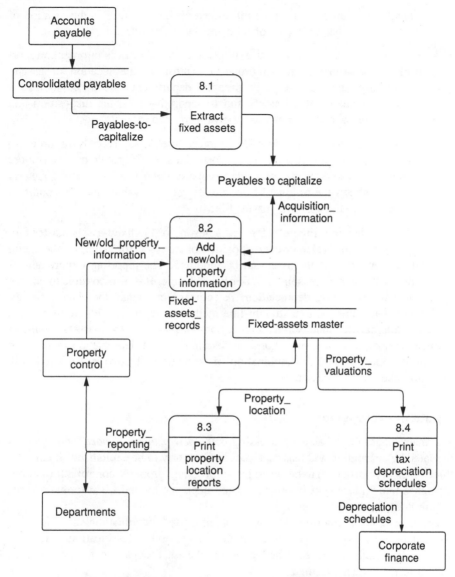

Figure 8–5 Four main functions of the fixed-assets system

1. *Extract fixed assets* is part of accounts payable processing. Assets to be depreciated are extracted from the consolidated payables file and are written to the payables-to-capitalize file. This output file contains information on all new company acquisitions.

2. *Add new/old property information* is responsible for updating the *fixed-assets master file.* For new acquisitions, new property information is combined with payables information to provide a complete description of the asset. For existing property (old property), property-control information is important.

Changes in depreciation, in the retirement of the assets, or in the location of the asset are other examples of adjustments to existing assets.

3. *Print property location reports* extracts fixed-asset records in order to report back to departments and to property control on the location of assets. Periodically, such as every six months, departments are asked to take a physical inventory of all assets and to report back on the disposition and condition of each item shown on the property report.

4. *Print tax depreciation schedules* extracts fixed-asset records in order to provide depreciation schedules to corporate finance. Corporate finance is more interested in property valuation than property control information. *Property valuation* shows the original value, the depreciated value, and the condition of each asset stored on the master file.

One step not shown in Figure 8–5 is the adjusting of the fixed-assets master file. If changes occur in the value or the disposition of an asset, for example, the useful life and salvage value of the asset can be modified. The reporting requirement is that there must be a clear reason for making the change. It is also possible to change the method of computing depreciation. A company can make the change from a declining-balance method to a straight-line method at any time without permission from the Internal Revenue Service. As a consequence, the fixed-assets computer application should include provisions for testing different depreciation methods to determine which method or combination of methods will provide a desired cash flow over the life of an asset.

Inputs to Processing

The main input to fixed-assets processing is the *new property report*. This report is prepared by accounting and lists each piece of property to be capitalized. It contains three types of information to be keyed into processing: property-control information, insurance and replacement information, and depreciation and tax information (see Figure 8–6).

Property-control information provides property identification and location particulars. Each asset is assigned a unique number and a classification code; each asset is also briefly described. The location of the asset (department, room number, and so forth) is then specified.

Insurance and replacement information provides depreciation, replacement, and maintenance information. Included in this category are the useful life (for tax-reporting purposes) and the retirement life of an asset. For example, for tax-reporting purposes, the useful life of an asset might be five years, even though the asset might actually be kept in service for seven years.

Besides different lives, the insurable value of an asset is stored. New property is generally valued at cost, whereas used property is assigned an appraised value. Both types of entries protect a business against unforeseen loss and damage to its assets.

Maintenance and appraisal schedules are stored. The maintenance schedule shows how and when the property is to be maintained; the appraisal schedule shows

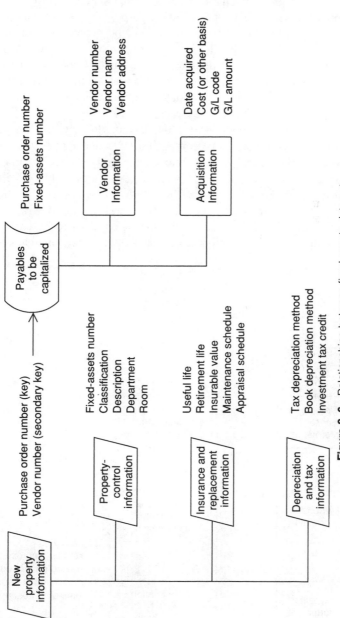

Figure 8-6 Relationships between fixed-assets data sets

how often the property is to be inspected. With inspection, it must be determined whether either the retirement life or the insurable value needs to be modified.

Department and tax information shows how the property is to be depreciated. Both tax and book depreciation methods are specified. The *tax depreciation method* indicates how the asset will be depreciated for purposes of tax reporting. The *book depreciation method* indicates how the asset will be depreciated for purposes of company-asset reporting. Under IRS rules, for example, a building can be fully depreciated in twenty-seven and one-half years, but this does not mean that the building has zero value for its owners. For this reason, the *book value* typically provides a more accurate property valuation. Consequently, both tax and book depreciation rates must be stored.

Depreciation and tax information may also include dollar values for tax credits. An *investment tax credit* is a direct credit against taxes that applies when a business acquires property. In the fiscal years that tax credits apply, the credit can range from 7 to 11.5 percent of the cost of the property and is applied in filing the tax forms for the year in which the asset was acquired.

To create fixed-asset records, keyed information is combined with information extracted from payables and stored on the file of payables to be capitalized. As Figure 8–7 shows, information important to fixed-assets processing includes vendor

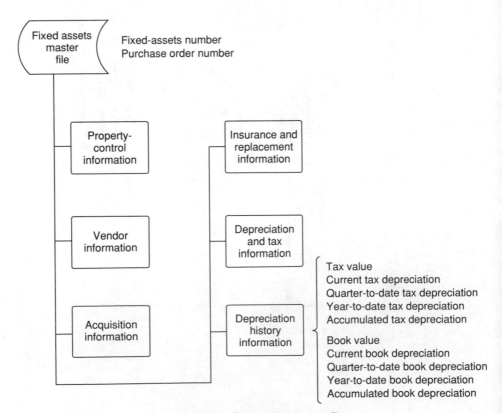

Figure 8–7   Fixed-assets master file

and acquisition information. *Vendor information* (number, name, and address) shows where the property was acquired. *Acquisition information* (the date acquired, the cost of the property, and general ledger assignments) shows the details of purchasing. These facts substantiate the investment in fixed assets by year and month of acquisition.

Outputs from Processing

Outputs produced by the fixed-assets computer application include the fixed-assets master file; online displays showing the status of fixed-asset accounts, depreciation projections, and tax write-off totals; printed property identification labels; and printed reports showing new property acquisitions, tax depreciation schedules, depreciation projections, and property and insurance schedules.

Figure 8–7 shows the structure of a fixed-assets master record. A fixed-assets number identifies a particular piece of property, and the purchase order number permits the property to be traced back to the initial requisition. Each file record is made up of property-control, vendor, acquisition, insurance and replacement, depreciation and tax information, and depreciation history information. In this final segment, current and year-to-date values are stored for both tax and book depreciation.

A variety of reports and displays can be prepared after new property information has been added to the fixed-assets master file and depreciation totals have been calculated. As an example, Figure 8–8 illustrates a *tax depreciation expense report*, which provides a comprehensive summary of the current, year-to-date, and cumulative depreciation for each asset stored on the fixed-assets master file. It also provides the user with totals: for example, the current depreciation for the Atlanta plant is $137,522.91.

With an online design, the fixed-assets information appearing on a report can also be displayed. Figure 8–9, for instance, shows how book value might be compared with tax value for a fixed asset. Here the tax value is less than the book value. This difference results from using different methods of depreciation: a straight-line method for calculating book value and a one-and-one-half declining-balance method for calculating tax value.

```
CORP 001   ABEL CORPORATION                    TAX  DEPRECIATION              REL 5.02 PAGE 2
FA050-A    FINANCIAL BOOK                  FROM 7-8 THRU 1-8 FOR 6 PERIODS     REPT DATE 7-13-


REGION          PLANT         DEPT
                ATLANTA       SHP0012


ITEM                     BEGIN ASSET DEPR   INSTALLED - - - - DEPRECIATION - - - -  SALVAGE   REMAINING
NUMBER        DESCRIPT   DEPR  LIFE  METH     COST   CUMULATIVE YEAR TO DATE CURRENT  VALUE     VALUE

1003235 CUTTING MACHINE  03-9X 05-00  5 GDS  1,465.13    764.80    276.90    138.45   146.51     700.33
1003610 STACKER-LINE       ******RETIRED*******                  1,887.84
1003643 YARDER           11-9X 13-10 15 GDS 45,000.00 15,600.00  2,800.00  1,400.00 5,000.00  29,400.00
1003693 PLANT BUILDING   04-9X 18-01 18 GDS 20,000.00  3,600.00  1,800.00    900.00     0.00  16,400.00

PLANT ATLANTA               ***TOTAL***     66,465.13 19,964.80  6,764.74  2,438.45 5,146.51  46,500.23
```

Figure 8–8 Tax depreciation expense report

```
┌─────────────────────────────────────────────────────────────────────────┐
│                                                                           │
│  FIXED-ASSET NUMBER:   34521              P.O. NUMBER:        984361       │
│                                                                           │
│  CLASS:    00.12                 DESCRIPTION:       OPTICAL READER         │
│  DATE ACQUIRED:   12-14-9X       DEPT.:   B12         ROOM:    468         │
│                                                                           │
│                                       VALUE                               │
│                                   BOOK          TAX                        │
│  LIFE                             10 YEAR       8 YEAR                     │
│  DEPRECIATION METHOD              S/L           1.5 DB                     │
│  DATE OF LAST UPDATE              1-15-9X       1-15-9X                    │
│                                                                           │
│  INSTALLED COST                   $5,800        $5,800                     │
│  SALVAGE VALUE                      800           800                      │
│  CURRENT DEPRECIATION               500         583.30                     │
│  ACCUMULATED DEPRECIATION         2,000       3,272.32                     │
│  REMAINING VALUE                  3,800       2,527.68                     │
│                                                                           │
└─────────────────────────────────────────────────────────────────────────┘
```

Figure 8–9   Comparing book and tax values

Displays showing different groups of assets (such as groups arranged by asset class, department, or general ledger code) are also part of a fixed-assets design. Like the display in Figure 8–9, these displays also compare book and tax values. They provide financial officers with the capability to page through the fixed assets of a company. Thus, at any point in time financial officers can determine the dollar value of major classes of business investments.

Other information produced by the fixed-assets application includes a variety of registers, tax depreciation reports, and accounting summaries. Four printed registers are the *new property register*, which lists all new property added to the fixed-assets master file; the *assets retirement register*, which lists all property retired (depreciated fully) but still stored on the fixed-assets-master file; the *fixed-assets master register*, which includes all properties stored on the fixed-assets master file; and the *fixed-assets change register*, which enumerates all changes (changes to the useful life, salvage value, and so forth) to properties stored on the fixed-assets master file.

Still other outputs include a variety of tax reports, the formats of which are largely determined by federal reporting requirements. Two of these are the *tax depreciation report* (Form 4562), which lists tax depreciation by type of asset for a fiscal year (see Figure 8–2), and the *Employee Business Expense Form* (Form 2106), which is used to show how automobiles are depreciated.

Depreciation projections, annual depreciation summaries, and insurance value and replacement cost analyses are important byproducts of this application. *Depreciation projections* show year-by-year depreciation totals for individual assets, for different classes of assets, and for the company as a whole. These projections and annual summaries are useful in budgeting and profit planning (see Chapter 14) and in planning future acquisitions. *Insurance-value analysis* shows the current and replacement costs of fixed assets. This information is used to determine how much insurance should be carried by a business. *Current-value cost*, the book value of the asset, is stored in the master file and can be reported with little difficulty. *Replacement-value cost*, the cost of replacing an asset, is more difficult to compute. Either a replacement-cost field must be added to the fixed-asset record to provide for an itemized reporting of the replacement value or replacement costs must be projected generally for an entire class of assets.

REVIEW QUESTIONS

5. What information is stored on the file of payables to be capitalized? On the fixed-assets master file?

6. What three types of information are contained on the new property report?

7. What is the difference between book depreciation and tax depreciation? Between book value and tax value?

8. What information is contained in the tax depreciation expense report?

9. Why are depreciation-projection capabilities built into the fixed-assets design?

8-3   FIXED-ASSETS PROCESSING

The flowchart in Figure 8–10 shows a modified accounts payables processing design, in which a *payables-to-be-capitalized* file is created. The extraction of

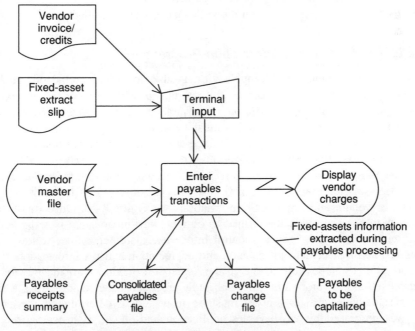

Figure 8–10 Modified payables processing

fixed-assets information to make up the file is simple and straightforward. Prior to processing, a *fixed-assets extract slip* is prepared and attached to the vendor invoice (or acquisition slip). Information recorded on the slip includes a fixed-assets identification number and the dollar total to be capitalized. The fixed-assets number permits the property to be identified later on during fixed-assets processing. The dollar total is required to allow the new file to be audited. Routine checks must be made to determine if the dollar amount extracted from accounts payable is consistent with the dollar amount held in the file of payables to be capitalized.

After fixed-assets information has been extracted, fixed-assets processing begins. As parts (a) and (b) of Figure 8–11 show, the design of the fixed-assets application is complex. Of the six interactive programs, three new programs are needed. The three programs enter new property information, adjust property information, and perform end-of-month depreciation calculations.

Besides these three update programs, three display programs allow individual account information and book and tax depreciation schedules to be reviewed. This capability to review fixed-asset information in different ways helps managers formulate equipment-replacement plans and policies based on up-to-date plant and equipment book and tax values.

Parts (a) and (b) of Figure 8–12 show the processing menus for fixed-assets processing. There is a close correspondence between the interactive and the batch programs. For example, the program to enter new property information creates a *property-change file*, which consists of new property records added to the fixed-assets master file; these records are required to print the *new property report* and *property identification labels*. The program to adjust property information modifies the *change file* to show changes to the fixed-assets master file other than the addition of new property; these change records show which fixed assets have been retired and how the book and tax values have been modified.

The *Enter new property information* Program

Although the accounts payable application is able to provide some of the data needed to describe new property, it does not provide all of the necessary information. Property-control information, insurance and replacement information, and depreciation and tax information must be keyed into processing. Once this material is keyed, it is merged with the fixed-assets information previously written to the file of payables to be capitalized.

Figure 8–13 shows the systems flow associated with adding information to the fixed-assets master file. Multiple keys are built into the design to allow for the transfer of vendor and acquisition information (see Figure 8–6). Once transferred information has been visually verified as correct, information that is to be added to processing is keyed. Property-control information is entered first, followed by insurance and replacement information and depreciation and tax information.

If it becomes impossible to merge the keyed information with the previously stored fixed-assets information, special audit procedures are required. As a first step, the payables master register must be inspected to determine if the property was processed by the payables application and, if so, if it was coded as

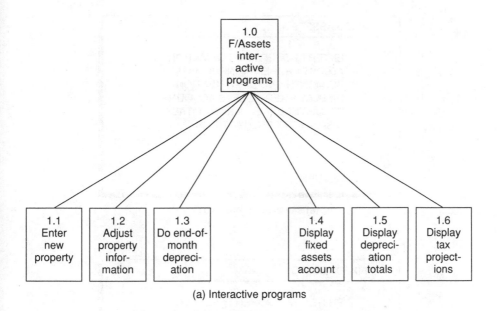

(a) Interactive programs

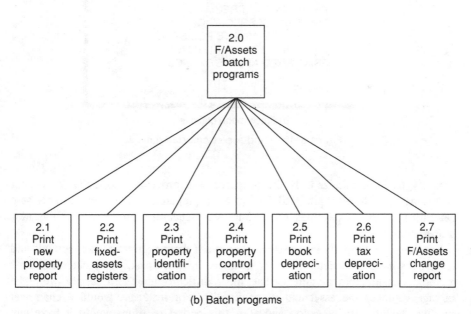

(b) Batch programs

Figure 8–11   A fixed-assets application

```
┌─────────────────────────────────────────────┐
│ ┌─────────────────────────┐                  │
│ │ FIXED ASSETS            │                   │
│ └─────────────────────────┘                  │
│                                              │
│       ENTER PROPERTY INFORMATION             │
│       ADJUST PROPERTY INFORMATION            │
│       DO MONTH-END DEPRECIATION              │
│       DISPLAY FIXED-ASSETS ACCOUNT           │
│       PROJECT DEPRECIATION TOTALS            │
│       DISPLAY TAX PROJECTIONS                │
│                                              │
│                                              │
│       RETURN                                 │
│                                              │
└─────────────────────────────────────────────┘
```

(a) Interactive menu choices

```
┌─────────────────────────────────────────────┐
│ ┌─────────────────────────┐                  │
│ │ FIXED ASSETS            │                   │
│ └─────────────────────────┘                  │
│                                              │
│       PRINT NEW PROPERTY REPORT              │
│       PRINT PROPERTY ID LABELS               │
│       PRINT PROPERTY-CONTROL REPORTS         │
│       PRINT BOOK DEPRECIATION                │
│       PRINT TAX DEPRECIATION                 │
│       PRINT FIXED-ASSETS REGISTER            │
│       PRINT RETIREMENT REGISTER              │
│       PRINT FIXED-ASSETS CHANGE              │
│                                              │
│       RETURN                                 │
│                                              │
└─────────────────────────────────────────────┘
```

(b) Batch menu choices

Figure 8–12   Fixed-assets processing menu

property to be capitalized. If the property was processed correctly, a register of the payables-to-be-capitalized file must be prepared and inspected. This step determines whether payables processing was successful in extracting the new property information.

Entering new property information is simple if depreciation and tax methods and tax credits have been determined in advance. In times past, these determinations required considerable judgment. The most difficult figures to supply were the salvage value of the asset and its useful life. For instance, would a chair last for five, ten, or fifteen years, and after this period of time, would it have any residual value?

Fortunately, federal depreciation laws have simplified requirements for reporting new property. A chair is presently classified as a seven-year property, for example. This means that 21 percent of the chair can be written off during the first year and 17 percent can be written off the second year, using the one-and-one-half declining-balance method of depreciation.

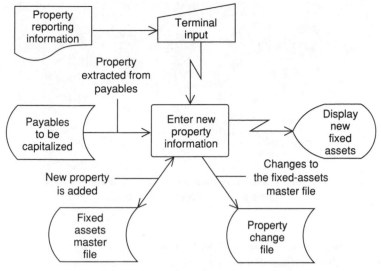

Figure 8–13 Adding new property records

Certain complexities remain, however. Some state tax-depreciation regulations differ from the federal requirements, which means that companies must keep different sets of records—those that satisfy federal reporting requirements and those that satisfy state (one or more) reporting requirements. Thus, 21 percent of the chair might be written off during the first year to meet federal reporting requirements; however, only 15 percent might be written off during the first year to meet state reporting requirements.

Following the verification of keyed information, including federal and state depreciation and tax values, the completed property record is written to the fixed-assets master file, with a copy of the change written to the property-change file.

The *Adjust property information* Program

Several types of adjustments to property records are required after property has been added to the fixed-assets master file. These adjustments follow from decisions to switch from one method of depreciation to another, to change fixed-assets retirement values, to retire fixed assets, to alter maintenance schedules, or to move property from one location to another. Each of these decisions leads to different computer-processing requirements.

To illustrate such a comparison, we will imagine a situation in which a company acquires a piece of property at a cost of $80,000. The property has an expected life of eight years; after this time, it will have a salvage value of $40,000. Because of higher-than-expected profits, the company wants a large tax write-off during the first year of the investment, followed by a more gradual tax write-off. By comparing straight-line and double declining-balance methods of depreciation for our hypothetical transaction (see Figure 8–14), we can see that the straight-line method provides a small but level write-off for all years, while the double

| | METHOD OF DEPRECIATION | | |
YEAR	STRAIGHT LINE	DECLINING BALANCE	DIFFERENCE
1	5000	20000	15000
2	5000	15000	10000
3	5000	5000	0
4	5000	0	−5000
5	5000	0	−5000
6	5000	0	−5000
7	5000	0	−5000
8	5000	0	−5000

Figure 8–14 Tax depreciation display

declining-balance method provides very large write-offs during the initial years but no additional depreciation after the third year. (At that time the remaining value of the asset would be equal to the salvage value.)

The kind of tax depreciation display shown in Figure 8–14 helps financial officers of a company decide how best to depreciate property. In our example, the company's officers might very well choose a third alternative: they might use double declining-balance for the first year only and straight line for the following years. This solution would provide a tax write-off of $20,000 for the first year and $2,858.00 for the second through the eighth years. Such a switch from one method of depreciation to another would be accomplished through the file-adjustment process. New reports must be prepared because of adjustments. The decision to change methods of depreciation would be placed on a *depreciation change report*. A decision to show how property was moved from one location to another, for example, would be placed on a *transfer-of-property report*.

Adjusting the property information leads to the update of the fixed-assets master file and the property-change file. The change file in this instance is the same file as the change file shown earlier (see Figure 8–13). A single file works well, provided the various types of transactions are properly coded. A transaction code of N indicates *new property*, for example, whereas a transaction code of R means *retired property*.

Property Identification and Reporting

Property-identification labels must be prepared for all new property. Before they are printed, however, two reports are required: a *new property register* and a *property change report*. This new property register lists all new additions and where the property is to be located. Property-control officers are responsible for checking this list and for matching it against new property reports prepared by the traffic division of a company. The property change report, produced from the property change file, lists all intra- and interdivision moves of property. This second list is also matched against property reports prepared by the traffic division.

Printing identification labels follows successful verification of both property registers. The labels themselves are either ordinary gummed labels or special-purpose metallic labels. Once printed, they are delivered to the property-control department, whose staff is responsible for affixing all labels to company property. Figure 8–15 illustrates a bar-coded label. Bar coding allows hand-held scanners to be used in taking a physical inventory. Scanners make physical inventory easier to accomplish, and they lead to fewer reporting errors.

Various reports are required by property-control personnel to control the movement of property in a firm. These documents include the new property report, the fixed-assets retirement report, the fixed-assets change report (showing the transfer of property from one location to another) and a special type of register called the *property-control report*. This last report is a register of all fixed assets arranged by asset number and location, usually by department. Other than this feature, the report by location is similar to other fixed-assets registers (see Figure 8–16). Each item listed, for example, is briefly described, and the values used in calculating depreciation are given. These values include the useful life of the property, the capitalized and the salvage values, and the date of acquisition. Book and tax depreciation values are compared. Total, net, and year-to-date figures are shown for both book and tax depreciation.

Property-control reports are necessary for conducting physical audits and inspections of properties. Most companies schedule continual audits so that all property is inspected at least twice a year. The purpose of these audits is twofold: to determine the condition of the property and to verify its location. The condition of the property often determines whether it should be replaced or returned to the vendor for repairs. If the property is deteriorating at a faster-than-expected rate, it is often possible to write-off any remaining depreciation; likewise, if the property is holding up better than expected, it is advisable to slow the rate of book depreciation. The location of the property should be the same as the location specified by the property-control report; however, an audit is required to verify this assumption. If property cannot be located, an investigation should be made to determine whether property has been transferred to another department (without authorization), was improperly labeled, or is missing.

If a firm is using inadequate controls, theft of company property can become a serious problem. Items such as calculators, typewriters, and even office furniture can disappear if the movement of property from one location to another goes unchecked. In many instances, locks and permanent mountings must be installed

Figure 8–15   Property identification label

```
RUN DATE:  APR. 08, 19XX - 16:36:52        M.C.P.A. DEMONSTRATION FURNITURE COMPANY                        PAGE 0001
                                          F I X E D   A S S E T   R E G I S T E R
DEPRECIATED AS OF   1/31      '*' BESIDE DEPR METHOD MEANS ITEM HAS BEEN SWITCHED TO STRAIGHT LINE


A ACTIVITY CODE     1=ACTIVE          2=FULLY DEPREC     3=NON DEPRECIABLE  4=EXPENDED        5=RETIRED        6=OTHER
C ASSET CATEGORY    1=GROUP ONE       2=GROUP TWO        3=GROUP THREE      4=R & D USE       5=DISTRIBUTION   6=SALES
                                                                           7=OTHER:  PFC 100 8=OTHER:  PFC 200 5=NOT DEPRECIATED
T ASSET TYPE        1=NEW             2=USED             3=GROUPED          4=SEPARATED       5=LEVEL          6=LEASED
O DEPR. METHOD      1=STRAIGHT LINE   2=1.25 DECLIN BAL  3=1.5 DECLIN BAL   4=DOUBLE DECLINE  5=DBLE DECL TO SL 6=SUM OF YRS DIGS
                    7=UNIT OF PRODUC  8=ACC CST RFC SYS  9=SL WITH HALF YR
```

ASSET-# DV LOC A C T	G/L D-TX	DATE-CAP	UNIT-DEP	EX-AMT-TX	CAP-VALUE	TOT-TX-DP	NET-BK-VAL(TX)	YTD-TX-DP
— — —DESCRIPTION— — —	COD D-BK	LF-TX-LF-BK	LIFE-UNT	FX-AMT-BK	SAL-VALUE	TOT-BK-DP	NET-BK-VAL(BK)	YTD-BK-DP
01978-00000 6 7564 1 3 1	22 5	1/01/		2,000.00	8,000.00	200.00	7,800.00	200.00
AUTOMOBILE	6 5	5		2,000.00	2,000.00	111.11	7,888.89	111.11
(VEHICLE # 1)								
01978-00001 6 7564 1 3 1	22 5	1/13/		.00	8,000.00	6,345.92	1,654.08	71.92
AUTOMOBILE	6 5	5		.00	2,000.00	4,866.67	3,133.33	66.67
(VEHICLE # 1)								
01979-00001 5 91020 5 4 1	13 4	2/13/		.00	30,000.00	18,600.00	11,400.00	.00
EXPERIMENTAL WIDGET BURNISHER	1 5	5		.00	5,000.00	9,583.00	20,417.00	.00
01979-00002 10 91020 1 2 1	21 4	3/12/		.00	300.00	173.08	126.92	4.08
STORAGE CABINET	1 7	7		.00	.00	82.57	217.43	3.57
01979-00003 13 91020 1 1 3	11 4	4/05/		.00	1,500.00	922.22	577.78	22.22
2 TYPEWRITERS	1 6	6		.00	420.00	330.00	1,170.00	15.00
01980-00001 10 400 1 6 1	12 4	10/13/	15,250	.00	9,000.00	1,500.00	7,500.00	375.00
AUTOMOBILE	4	4	100,000	.00	3,000.00	912.00	8,088.00	12.00
				.00	850.00	20.84	829.43	20.84
				.00	100.00	21.26	829.01	21.26
				.14	8,500.00	.00	8,500.54	.00
					500.00	.00	8,500.54	.00
					.00	.00	25,400.50	.00

Figure 8–16   Fixed-assets register

to keep certain types of equipment safe from theft. Physical audits of property help determine whether these special safeguards are required.

Depreciation Projections and Reporting

Besides reporting on the location of property, the fixed-assets computer application must report on book and tax depreciation write-offs. Both types of depreciation are computed monthly. At a prescribed time, the program to update end-of-month depreciation totals is activated (see Figure 8–17). This program calculates current depreciation totals and updates (resets) the quarter-to-date, year-to-date, and total-to-date depreciation totals. It writes the revised totals to a new fixed-assets master file and sends the old and the new reset totals to the property change file. Another update also takes place at this time—the update of general ledger accounts. As Figure 8–18 illustrates, there is a set of accumulated depreciation accounts separate from fixed-asset accounts. At month-end, these accumulated depreciation accounts are updated and used directly in reporting deductions for depreciation.

Once new depreciation totals are available, tax depreciation schedules can be printed. Most business firms must pay taxes quarterly, so a quarterly report showing depreciation by asset class is generally prepared. This report should be put together with care on custom forms and be saved for several years to provide evi-

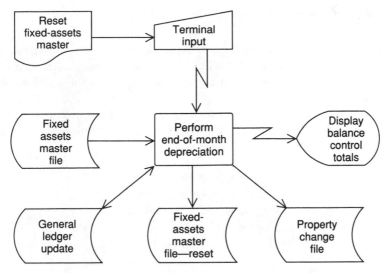

Figure 8–17 Updating end-of-month depreciation totals

dence in case of federal, state, or local tax audits. In addition to quarterly reports, most firms prepare monthly book and tax depreciation schedules that serve as supporting documents to the month-end financial statements. When the company books are audited by an external accounting group, the listings of depreciated assets must show where each asset can be located so that individual assets can be visually inspected if necessary. Likewise, month-end reporting of depreciation must be available to verify the correctness of processing. One method of verification is to calculate depreciation totals by hand and to compare these results with computer-based calculations. A small sample is used to determine whether the logic followed in programming is correct.

The projection of depreciation amounts is another important feature of the fixed-assets computer application. For example, the computer can be instructed to process all records stored on the fixed-asset master file in order to total the allowable depreciation (the tax write-off) for the current fiscal year, quarter by quarter, and to display the results.

1600	Computer equipment
1620	Furniture and equipment
1640	Vehicles
1660	Building
1680	Land
1700	Accum depr—computer equip
1720	Accum depr—furniture and equip
1740	Accum depr—vehicles
1760	Accum depr—building

Figure 8–18 Fixed-asset general ledger accounts

8-4   PROCESSING CONTROLS

Both financial and physical controls are required in the auditing of fixed assets. Besides keeping a detailed record of all fixed-asset dollar amounts, property-control reports describe the physical location and, at times, condition of fixed-asset properties.

The batch-balance control equations important to fixed-assets processing include equations for both tax and book depreciation. For tax depreciation, the control equation is

> Total fixed-assets dollar amount =
>> Last fixed-asset dollar amount
>> + New property additions dollar amount
>> − Tax depreciation dollar amount
>> ± Fixed-asset adjustment dollar amount

For book depreciation, the control equation is the same, except that book value dollar amounts are maintained.

As might be expected, the total fixed-asset dollar amount increases throughout the month or until the program to update end-of-month depreciation totals is activated. At that point the total fixed-asset dollar amount is sharply reduced. More important, the difference between the old and the new fixed-asset amount should equal the "tax-depreciation–taken dollar amount" plus (or minus) any special depreciation that has been coded as an adjustment.

Financial audits are more difficult when various types of adjustments are made. If, for example, an asset has been completely destroyed, any remaining fixed-asset tax or book value can be written off. The *Adjust property information* program must be designed to handle the adjustment to retire an asset. In processing, it is possible to delete the fixed-asset record from the master file and to record this change on the property change file. A sort of the change file by retirement code would then show the dollar value of this and all other retired assets.

This method of processing is admittedly quite feasible, but it is not recommended. Such procedures greatly confuse the audit trail. Rather than deleting the fixed-asset record from the master file at the same time that the record is written to the property change file, it is much safer to flag the fixed-asset record stored on the master file to show that it will be retired by the next run of the program to update end-of-month depreciation totals and to delete the asset from the fixed-assets master file during this end-of-month run. This procedure of flagging the record preserves the audit trail. During end-of-month processing the dollar value of assets retired from the fixed-assets master file is compared with the dollar value of assets retired as shown on property change reports. For processing to be correct, the two dollar totals should be identical.

The adjustments that cause the most confusion result from assets thought to be lost and later recovered. Although several factors account for this circumstance, the most important one is the failure to report the transfer of property from one location to another. If this practice is widespread, property-control reports will be highly inaccurate; property misplaced will be reported as destroyed, missing, or stolen.

When property is believed to be missing, the normal business practice is to flag the property record as missing and record the date and to continue to depreciate the property, following normal end-of-month processing instructions. This procedure continues until a complete physical inventory cycle has been completed. If the missing property has not been found by this time, the asset is retired and depreciation totals are adjusted, as required.

8-5 MANAGEMENT IMPLICATIONS

Financial managers of a business tend to rely heavily on the fixed-assets computer application once it is installed. Two immediate uses of the application are in the control of business property and in the preparation of federal and state tax reports. Many companies benefit simply from knowing where property is located and whether it is in service. This information permits equipment not in use in one department to be transferred to another department where it is needed. Expenditures for duplicate equipment are avoided when such transfers are successful.

Keeping accurate fixed-assets records and preparing numerous federal and state tax reports is another major reason for automating fixed-assets processing. Management quickly discovers that an online approach can save hundreds of hours of clerical and managerial time. With direct inquiry and updating capabilities, for example, records can be retrieved and modified instantly; complicated summary reports can be prepared in minutes. This application replaces the age-old procedure of manually attempting to locate a record in massive fixed-asset storage files, delivering the record to the financial department, adding new information to the record, recording the details of processing on a summary log, and returning the record to the file. Later on, the summary details would be consolidated for reporting purposes.

Two additional reasons for implementing the fixed-assets application are that it helps financial officers determine depreciation patterns and establish equipment-replacement policies. As Figure 8–19 shows, the projections of depreciation can be arranged by asset class or by asset class within each division of the company. This type of projection helps the financial officers of a business pinpoint when and where depreciation totals will turn down sharply. In Figure 8–19, for example, depreciation totals are quite level during the first and second quarters. During the third and fourth quarters, however, there is a downward drop in the depreciation totals caused by reduced allowable depreciation for machinery. Further inspection of the situation would reveal that three large pieces of equipment will be fully depreciated by the third quarter of the year.

When combined with projected acquisitions of plant and equipment, fixed-assets depreciation projections take on special importance. They help financial officers determine what funds will be available to acquire new plants and equipment, what types of assets are aging faster than others, and what effects new acquisitions will have on depreciation totals. These projected depreciation totals are vital to budget

| ASSET | QUARTER | | | |
CLASS	FIRST	SECOND	THIRD	FOURTH
BUILDING	326,000	320,000	314,000	308,000
FURNITURE	195,600	188,600	185,400	182,614
TRANSPORTATION	118,456	109,214	101,942	93,114
MACHINERY	532,496	512,331	424,431	416,210
OTHER	156,090	151,612	147,314	143,110
TOTAL	1,328,642	1,281,757	1,173,087	1,143,048

Figure 8–19 Tax depreciation projection

and profit planning. It can be shown, for example, that unless carefully planned, the expense known as depreciation can confuse corporate earnings. Highly cyclical earnings may be caused in large part by highly cyclical depreciation dollar totals.

REVIEW QUESTIONS

10. How is the property change file used in processing?

11. List the main types of adjustments that are made to records stored on the fixed-assets master file.

12. What must be done before property identification labels are printed?

13. What are property-control reports and why are they needed?

14. What processing functions are accomplished by the program to update end-of-month depreciation totals?

15. Explain how adjustments to processing complicate the process of financial auditing.

16. How should fixed-assets records be treated when property is reported as missing?

17. How can the fixed-assets application indirectly reduce duplicate equipment expenditures?

REVIEW OF IMPORTANT IDEAS

Properties with a fixed life of more than one year must be capitalized and depreciated. These properties are called fixed assets.

The fixed-assets computer application is greatly affected by federal and state tax legislation. The Modified Accelerated Cost Recovery System (MACRS) simplifies the reporting of depreciation by organizing different types of assets by class life. Assets acquired before 1987 are depreciated using the Accelerated Cost Recovery System (ACRS).

Preliminary processing of fixed-assets records must be designed into the accounts payable computer application. Fixed-asset information is extracted from other payables at this time and is written to a file of payables to be capitalized.

The program to enter new property information adds three types of information needed to describe fixed assets fully: property-control, insurance and replacement, and depreciation and tax information. This new information is merged with information extracted from payables processing. The completed fixed-assets record is written to the fixed-assets master file.

Records placed on the master file are used in a variety of ways. Several reports and displays provide comprehensive summaries of current, year-to-date, and cumulative depreciation for each asset stored on file. A complete set of registers and a variety of tax reports are also produced. Depreciation projections, annual summaries, and analyses of insurance value and replacement costs are printed.

From time to time it is necessary to make adjustments to property records. An important adjustment is to switch from one method of depreciation to another in order to improve the cash-flow position of a business.

Property labels and property-control reports are important products of processing. If adequate controls are in place, the theft of company property becomes more difficult. Property-control reports simplify physical audits and inspections.

End-of-month processing of fixed-assets records must be done with great care. The main processing control equations are designed to account for all tax and book depreciation dollar amounts. Adjustments must be treated differently. Records stored on the master file are flagged as well as written to the property change file. When flagged records are deleted from the master file their dollar totals are cross-checked against totals written to the change file.

Financial managers rely heavily on the fixed-assets application. It helps them manage property records and produce numerous book and tax depreciation reports. Managers use the application to determine depreciation patterns and to establish which types of assets to replace; they depend heavily on this application to produce required federal and state government reports.

KEY WORDS

Depreciation

Tax write-off

Fixed asset

Modified Accelerated Cost Recovery System

Straight-line method

Declining-balance method

One-and-one-half declining-balance method

Depreciation schedule

Amortization

Tax depreciation

Book depreciation

Insurance-value analyses

Extract slip

Property identification label

New property register

Property change report

Property-control report

Fixed-assets master file

EXERCISES

1. Figure 8–20 illustrates a more direct way of updating the fixed-assets master file. Instead of using the intermediate step of writing records to the file of payables to be capitalized, new fixed-assets records can be added as part of payables processing.

   (a) Explain the advantages of this more direct design.

   (b) Explain the disadvantages of this design.

   (c) Explain which design you prefer and the reasons for your choice.

2. Modify the data-flow diagram for accounts payable (see Figure 7–2) to show the change in design illustrated by Figure 8–20.

3. Compute the first, second, and third years' depreciation on a $160,000 piece of equipment using each of the following methods of depreciation. (Assume that the property has a useful life of five years and that after this period will have no salvage value.)

   (a) straight-line method

   (b) 1.5 declining-balance method

   (c) 2.0 declining-balance method

4. You are asked to provide additional information about the GDS method of depreciation. Suppose a fixed asset with a recovery period of ten years is to be entered and processed by the fixed-assets system.

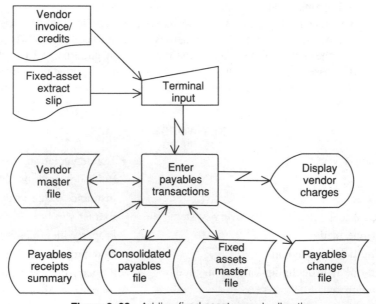

Figure 8–20 Adding fixed-asset records directly

(a) What GDS information must be keyed to processing? (Limit your answer to information required by GDS processing.)

(b) Compared to the straight-line method of depreciation, what, if any, formulas are required in processing GDS information?

(c) Which fixed-asset computer program is designed to calculate GDS depreciation? How does this process work? (Describe the steps required in performing GDS calculations.)

5. Suppose replacement costs are to be added to fixed-asset records. How must the fixed-assets design be modified to handle this requirement? Why is replacement cost important to a business? Where would a company find replacement-cost information?

6. How are routine checks made to determine whether the dollar amount extracted from payables is consistent with the dollar amount held in the file of payables to be capitalized?

DISCUSSION QUESTIONS

1. Name several reasons for implementing the fixed-assets computer application.

2. Some companies write off office equipment in seven years, for tax purposes, but depreciate office equipment over 40 years, for book value purposes. Is this practice wise? Discuss.

3. Some companies always try to depreciate fixed assets as quickly as possible. When might this practice be wise? Give several reasons.

4. Why is it important to be able to display a single fixed-assets account? Suggest several reasons.

5. Some fixed assets have a negative salvage value—it costs the company to sell or remove an asset. Should this factor be entered into the fixed-assets application? Why or why not?

4-IN-1 CASE STUDY—FIXED ASSETS

The 4-in-1 application does not provide a direct facility for processing fixed assets; however, it explains, in part, how fixed assets serve as an extension to accounts payable. In this lesson, you are asked to purchase a computer at a cost of $10,000. The computer is to be posted to the general ledger as an asset, belonging to classification 1600-000, Office equipment and furniture. Accumulated depreciation for the computer is accounted for by general ledger number 1700-000—the number reserved for all 1600-000 expenditures.

This lesson asks you to do the following:

- Add a new vendor account and a vendor charge.
- Post the charge to a fixed-asset account.

- Add a recurring disbursement to payables.
- Print disbursement checks.
- Post disbursements to the general ledger.

Adding a Vendor and Vendor Charge

1. Log on and enter a date of **011097**. Press ENTER when asked, *Any change?*

2. Type **14** from the main menu and press ENTER.

3. Type **1**, *Add transaction*, and press ENTER.

4. For the vendor name, type **Complex Computers**. Press ENTER.

5. Type **Y** when asked if you wish to add a new vendor.

6. Type the vendor information shown in Figure 8–21.

7. When you return to the process bills payable screen, press ENTER when asked *Right vendor?*

8. Press ENTER for B = Bill.

9. Press ENTER for the date 011097.

10. Type **16000** and press ENTER for the invoice number.

11. Type **New computer** and press ENTER for the reference.

12. Type **10000** and press ENTER for the amount.

13. Press ENTER to credit accounts payable.

14. Press ENTER when asked, *Field number to change?*

15. Press F1 to default to account 1600-000.

16. Press F1 to distribute the entire amount to this account.

17. Press ENTER when asked, *Any change?*

18. Press TAB twice to return to the process bills payable submenu.

1. Name	Complex computers
2. Address-1	346 Olive Street
3. Address-2	San Mateo
4. Address-3	CA 94403-7600
5. Contact	
6. Phone number	415-345-5576
7. First date	01/10/97
8. Comment	
9. Default exp acct	1600-000 Office equip & furniture

Figure 8–21 Adding vendor information

Posting the Transaction

19. Type **5** from the process bills payable submenu to indicate that you wish to post the new transaction.

20. To print, type **Y** when asked, *Are bills payable ready to post?*

21. Press END to return to the main menu.

Processing a Recurring Disbursement

22. Type **15** from the main menu and press ENTER.

23. Press F1 to add selection 7 to the process disbursements submenu. This selection will allow you to process a recurring disbursement, namely, a bill that will be paid monthly.

24. Type **7** and press ENTER.

25. Select **1** and press ENTER to add a recurring disbursement.

26. When the process disbursements screen appears, type **Complex** for the payee and press ENTER twice.

27. Press ENTER to produce a computer check.

28. Press ENTER to indicate that you plan to make monthly payments.

29. Type **012597** for the next payment date and press ENTER.

30. Press ENTER to indicate that you do not want to be notified in advance of this recurring disbursement.

31. Type **New computer** for the reference and press ENTER.

32. Type **200** to specify the amount of the monthly payment. Press ENTER.

33. Press ENTER for discount.

34. Press ENTER for checking account 1.

35. Press ENTER for field number to change.

36. Press TAB to return to the process recurring disbursements submenu.

37. Type **4** and press ENTER twice to print the recurring disbursements list.

38. Exit to log off 4-in-1. The next step asks you to log on again in order to print checks.

Processing Disbursement Checks

39. Log on again and enter a date of **012597**. Press ENTER when asked, *Any change?*

40. Type **15**, *Process disbursements*, and press ENTER.

41. Type **4** and press ENTER.

42. Press ENTER to print the disbursements edit list. Save this list to compare against the disbursements register.

43. Return to the process disbursements screen and type **5**, *Print disbursement checks*. Press ENTER.

44. Type **L** to list the checks to be printed. Press ENTER.

45. Type **1** for checking account 1.

46. Press F1 for first and F1 for last.

47. Press ENTER to print the list of checks. You can compare this list against the checks to be printed next.

48. Return to the print disbursement checks screen again and type **c** to print the checks. Press ENTER.

49. Type **2000** for the first check number.

50. Press F1 twice again. Press ENTER when asked, *Any change?*

51. Type **done** to indicate that you are ready to print check. Checks can be printed on stock paper as well as customer forms.

52. Press ENTER when asked *Print form alignment?*

53. Press TAB after checks are printed.

54. Type **done** again and press ENTER.

Posting the Disbursements

55. Type **6** to post the transactions. Note that checks must be printed before they can be posted. Press ENTER.

56. Type **Y** when asked, *Ready to post?* This leads to the printing of the disbursements register.

QUESTIONS

1. When you print the bills payable register, to which account is the 10,000 credited? To which account is the 10,000 debited? What do these two postings reveal?

2. Why must checks be printed for transactions before posting is allowed?

3. What is the value of the disbursements edit list? Of the check list?

4. How does the final disbursements register differ from the disbursements edit list? Of the two documents, which one is the most important? Explain why.

5. This lesson indicated how a recurring disbursement would be processed and suggested in part how a fixed asset would be processed by a company. The

lesson did not show how the purchased computer would be depreciated, however, nor how tax and book value would be determined. Based on your knowledge of accounting, what additional steps are required to depreciate the asset? Review the chart of accounts printed for the second lesson as the basis for your explanation.

CHAPTER

Employee Payroll

The employee payroll is often one of the first computer applications developed by a business. Historically, the reasons for automating payroll processing have included the following: faster processing of payroll checks and payroll reports, more accurate processing of payroll records, improved capability to meet governmental reporting requirements, and improved capability to analyze employee payroll data. More often than not, a batch design was used for payroll processing. The advantages of batch processing—at least several years ago—were that the payroll application was relatively easy to install and to maintain and that it was consistently able to accomplish its purpose, namely, placing employee paychecks in the hands of employees on or before the scheduled date of payment.

Although batch designs of payroll processing continue to be popular, there are special reasons for installing an interactive design. Interactive processing simplifies the maintenance of this application. Interactive steps simplify the adjusting of employee records, the entry and verification of hours-worked information, the retrieval of data stored on computer files, the adding of new employees to the system, and the routine checking of processing controls.

Central to the design of the employee payroll application is the *employee master file*. As with other master files, the employee master file contains a record for every employee. A unique feature of this master file is that it usually contains both personal and payroll data elements. *Personal elements* describe individual attributes, such as the person's name, date of birth, race, and sex. *Payroll elements* describe the terms and condition of payment. This part of the employee's record contains such items as wage or salary, payroll deductions, current earnings, and year-to-date (YTD) earnings.

Placing both personal and payroll information on a single record simplifies the employee payroll processing design; however, it complicates maintenance of the employee master file. Traditionally, the personnel department of a business has been responsible for gathering and feeding personal information into processing, and the payroll department has been responsible for wage and salary information. With batch processing, this division of labor often meant that two separate runs were required to update the master file: one to add personnel-related information and one to add payroll-related information. The alternative was to use a single update change form and to pass the form from one department to another.

Several problems arose with such an approach to processing. For example, when the payroll-edit report needed to be reviewed by staff in both the personnel and payroll departments, security and privacy problems resulted, the review took considerable time, and interdepartmental conflicts often occurred. One department, for example, would believe that the other department was responsible for making the majority of the errors.

With interactive processing, the problems associated with departmental conflicts have largely been eliminated. Separate file-updating selections, for example, keep personnel and payroll data-entry activities quite distinct. People in one department are not allowed to review the information entered into processing by the other or to see the errors made by people in another department. With an interactive design, the time required to enter and edit payroll updates has been reduced. All in all, an interactive design makes the process of payroll processing less stressful and more routine.

9-1   PRELIMINARY OVERVIEW OF PROCESSING

Figure 9–1 provides a preliminary processing overview of the employee-payroll computer application. The system is triggered by the receipt of time-keeping information from the employee. Once this information is received, the employee's record is brought into processing and updated with new hours-worked and dollars-paid totals. Besides the updated record, other major outputs of processing include the hours-worked register, the payroll register, and the employee paycheck.

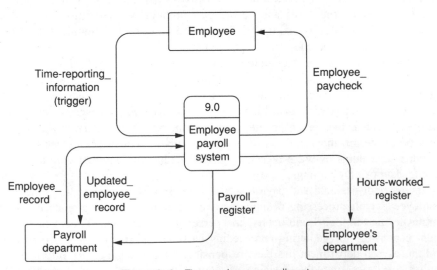

Figure 9–1   The employee payroll system

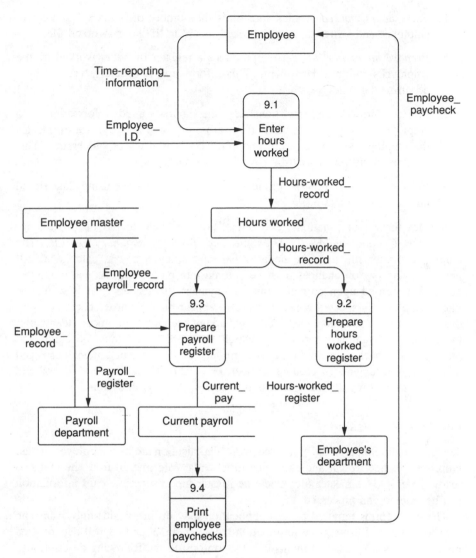

Figure 9–2 Main functions of the employee payroll system

As might be expected, the *hours-worked register* documents the number of hours worked. This information is verified by the employee's department. The *payroll register* documents employees' hours worked, gross pay, deductions from gross pay, and net pay (take-home pay). The contents of the payroll register must be verified by the staff of the payroll department. The *employee paycheck* is much like a vendor voucher-check (see Chapter 7): It contains a negotiable portion and a voucher portion. The voucher explains the calculations used in arriving at gross and net pay.

Figure 9–2 shows how the payroll system functions. The four steps can be summarized as follows:

1. *Enter hours worked* verifies and totals the number of hours worked by an employee and writes the hours-worked record to the hours-worked file.

2. *Prepare hours-worked register* produces a register of hours worked by the employees within a department. This information is generally verified by a departmental supervisor.

3. *Prepare payroll register* translates the hours-worked information into employee gross pay, deductions from gross pay, and net pay; it also updates the employee's payroll record and produces a register of processing. This information is verified by the payroll department.

4. *Print employee paychecks* produces employee paychecks using data stored on the current payroll file.

Besides these four functions, two others are important to payroll processing. These are *Update employee master file* and *Produce summary reports*. The employee master file must be updated *before* employee pay is calculated. All personnel and payroll changes must be entered into processing, so that employee pay will be based upon current terms of payment. (Consider what it would be like if employees expected a pay increase to appear on their next checks, only to discover that the update to increase the pay had not been made in time.) Meanwhile, the printing of summary reports, of which there are many, must be completed *after* payroll checks are produced. A summary of departmental labor costs and labor-cost breakdowns (by product, project, or work order) and several federal and state government reports are valued byproducts of the payroll system.

Inputs to Processing

The three main inputs to the employee payroll application are new employee forms, employee change forms, and employee time cards. Information from the first two ready the employee master file. Once the master file is set, time card information can be entered and processed.

The input forms required by this application may differ considerably from one firm to another. If firms place information from personnel and payroll departments on a single form, the keyed inputs usually conform to the following descriptions.

New employee forms are custom-printed data-entry sheets that are used to create an employee record. They are completed, in part, by the employee. Items such as employee name, address, Social Security number, and home telephone number are supplied by the individual. Besides personal information, job and wage information is placed on the form. Supplied either by the personnel or payroll department, this information includes the job or position number, the department, the hourly rate of pay (or salary), the overtime rate (if special), and the deductions to be taken from gross pay.

Employee change forms are also custom printed. They are similar to new employee forms, except that they show the changes to be made to an existing employee record. The most common types of changes concern an employee's status (active, inactive, terminated), mailing address, wage or salary, marital status, number of dependents, federal and state withholding, deduction withholding (usually several types), and method of payment (take, mail, or direct deposit). This list of changes suggests the organization of the employee master file processing menu, including, for example, change status, change address, and so forth. Interactive changes can be made by menu selection or by placing the employee change form on the terminal screen and keying in changes directly.

Employee time cards (or time records) document hours worked, generally by employee number and by department number, project number, and job or work-order number. As Figure 9–3 shows, time cards include some preprinted information, such as the name of the employee, employee number, department, and date. The hours worked are then itemized, by day of week, and totaled. Space is provided on the card for different types of overhead. Last, regular and overtime hours worked are generally recorded and totaled separately.

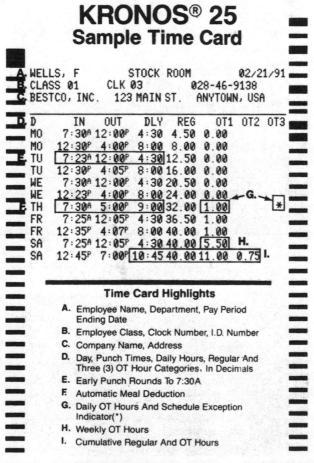

Figure 9–3 Employee time card

Once the employee master file is updated, it becomes the main input to processing. Figure 9–4 shows the file segments and the data elements associated with each segment for a single employee record. It also shows the relationship between time-reporting information, which is keyed into processing, and information stored on the master file. As illustrated, the number of stored items is considerable, compared with the key-entry requirements.

Keyed time-reporting information begins with the entry of the payroll number (keyed once for all employees), a record code, and the employee number. The *payroll number* is especially critical when a company prepares different types of payrolls (weekly, biweekly, bimonthly, and monthly). If, for example, an employee questions a paycheck, the three reference numbers important to tracing the transaction are the payroll number, the department number (or project or workorder number), and the employee number. The *record code* is needed to reverse data erroneously entered into processing. For instance, eight hours of sick leave might have been entered instead of eight hours of vacation time. The *employee number* is unique (one for each employee) and is required to locate an employee's record. A special number is required to make it possible to identify only one employee.

Because of the importance of the employee master file to processing, we need to be aware of how the file is organized. The six record segments illustrated by Figure 9–4 are as follows:

- The *employee name and address* segment contains the employee's name and home and work addresses (for the latter, the plant, department, or office). This segment also includes one or more telephone numbers.

- The *personnel information* segment stores Affirmative Action information (sex, age, handicaps) and date of employment. Date of birth is stored rather than age to simplify file maintenance. With date of birth, retirement profiles can be produced and birthdays can be recognized. This section can also contain information about the employee's educational history and work history.

- The *wage and salary information* segment specifies whether an employee is to be paid a salary or an hourly wage and whether the employee is exempt from overtime pay. The segment may also include the actual salary to be paid or a salary rate, the wage rate, the earned income credit (E.I.C.) rate (for employees who earn less than $11,000), and the overtime rate. Three accumulation rates are also stored in this segment of the file: vacation, sick leave, and pension rates. Finally, the number of tax exemptions and the various types of voluntary deductions must be stored. Voluntary deductions are based either on a percentage of gross pay, such as deductions for some professional dues, or on a fixed amount, such as $50.00 per month for an Individual Retirement Account (IRA).

- The *leave and pension history* segment contains accumulated vacation, sick leave, and pension amounts and year-to-date totals for vacation and sick leave used. The accumulated totals are revised monthly, prior to preparing the payroll register. If either sick leave or vacation time is used, the amounts must be keyed to processing.

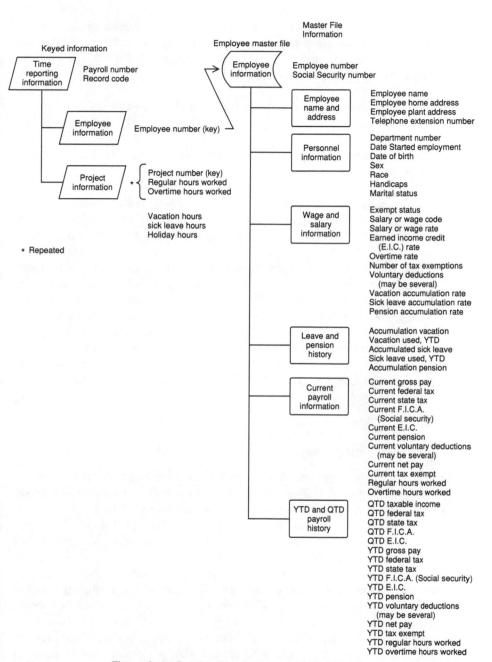

Figure 9–4 Relationships between payroll data sets

- The *current payroll information* segment includes current gross pay, all deductions from gross pay, and current net pay. In addition, regular and overtime hours are stored. These hours are required for determining current gross pay, according to this formula:

Current gross pay = Regular hours × Hourly wage rate
+Overtime hours × Overtime wage rate

By comparison (provided the employee is not eligible for an E.I.C. payment), the equation used in determining net pay is

Current net pay = Current gross pay − Current tax exempt
−Current federal tax − Current state tax − Current FICA
−Current pension − Current voluntary deductions

- The *YTD and QTD payroll history* segment consists of accumulated year-to-date (YTD) and quarter-to-date (QTD) payroll totals. QTD totals are generally limited to taxable income, federal and state tax withheld, Social Security (FICA) withheld, and E.I.C. advances paid. These totals must be reset after producing federal and state quarterly payroll reports. YTD totals are kept for two reasons: for showing employees how dollars have been allocated throughout the calendar year and for reporting year-end information to federal and state governments. YTD totals must be reset after producing year-end payroll reports and W-2 federal and state tax-reporting forms.

Outputs from Processing

The employee payroll application often produces a wide range of reports, such as those shown in Figure 9–5. Three essential printed outputs are the payroll register, employee paychecks, and the payroll journal (a summary report).

The *payroll register* lists the information to be placed on employee voucher-checks; control totals are also listed. As the register presented in Figure 9–6 shows, three lines per employee are required to list all pertinent payroll information. The first line begins with the department number and continues with the employee number, type, salary, and YTD payroll totals. The second line continues with the employee name, weeks worked, and current payroll totals. The third line shows the employee Social Security number and any supplemental pay totals. Notice too that payroll control totals (by department) are placed at the bottom of the register. The difference between YTD figures before and after processing must be equal to current payroll totals. That is,

YTD gross·amount out = YTD gross amount in + Current gross amount

Or, as shown for department 1000,

$$\$78,257.85 = \$68,246.60 + \$10,011.25$$

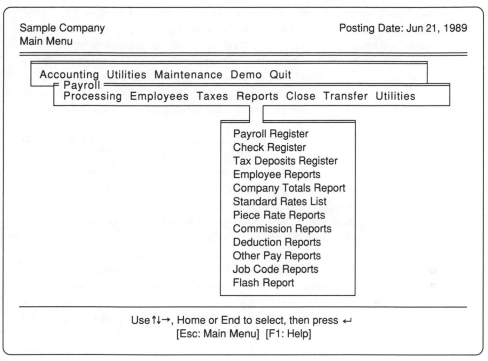

Figure 9–5 Types of payroll reports

```
WED. SEP 23, 199-                    M.C.B.A. Demonstration Furniture Company                     PAGE 0001
3:29 PM                                    P A Y R O L L   R E G I S T E R

FOR DEPARTMENT: 1000
FOR THE PAY PERIOD ENDING 07/14/9-   EMPLOYEE TYPES:  H = HOURLY  S= SALARY   CHECK TYPES:  R = REGULAR  V = VACATION
FREQUENCIES USED ON THIS RUN:   THIS PAY PERIOD:  ALL
VACATION CHECK 1:  NONE     VACATION CHECK 2:  NONE     VACATION CHECK 3: NONE      VACATION CHECK 4:  NONE

DEPT# EMP# EMP-TYP CHK-TYP SALARY REG-PAY   HOL-PAY YTD-GROSS YTD-TX-GRS YTD-FICA YTD-FWT YTD-SWT YTD-OST YTD-CWT OTH-DED
NAME       SOC-SEC-#       WKS-WRK OVT-PAY  SICK-PAY     GROSS TXBL-GROSS     FICA     FWT     SWT     OST     CWT NET-PAY
                           SUP-PAY VAC-PAY  SPEC-PAY
1000 100000        R       450.00     .00       .00 10,236.85  9,712.00   811.67 1,761.02  520.00   16.96     .00   27.50
Whittenhaus, Robert W.       1.00     .00       .00    475.00    475.00    29.69    76.54      .00    2.38     .00  338.89
     324-58-4201             .00      .00       .00

           OTHER EARNINGS         25.00 PRFTSHR TXBL
     300000  H     R         .00   300.00       .00  8,946.00  8,540.00   327.49   929.45  130.00   12.21     .00   73.52
Jones, Phillip               1.00    51.25      .00    351.25    351.25    21.95    65.50      .00    1.76     .00  188.52
     654-63-5464             .00      .00       .00

     500000  S     R 1,500.00        .00       .00 50,700.00 44,000.00 2,400.00 11,569.04 4,250.00     .00     .00 1,071.42
Hall, Frederick J.           1.00     .00       .00  1,500.00  1,500.00      .00   428.58      .00     .00     .00      .00
     346-41-6354             .00      .00       .00

ONE OR MORE DEDUCTIONS COULD NOT BE TAKEN ON THE ABOVE CHECK BECAUSE THE NET PAY WAS ZERO

     600000  H     R         .00 7,450.00       .00  8,375.00  8,375.00   523.44 2,236.03      .00   30.00     .00 1,017.49
Marianias, Markos           13.00     .00       .00  7,685.00  7,685.00   480.31 2,032.45      .00   26.55     .00 4,128.20
     654-75-6558             .00      .00    145.00

THE ABOVE CHECK HAD ONE OR MORE CALCULATIONS WHICH EXCEEDED THE ALLOWABLE MAXIMUM

           4 CHECKS TO BE PRINTED      4 REGULAR       0 VACATION
DEPARTMENT TOTALS:                               YTD-IN    THIS PERIOD    YTD-OUT
                  SAL-PAY:  1,950.00   GROSS:  68,246.60    10,011.25   78,257.85
                  REG-PAY:  7,840.00   TX-GRS: 60,615.75    10,011.25   70,627.00
                  OVT-PAY:     51.25   FICA:    3,530.65       531.95    4,062.60
                  VAC-PAY:      .00    FWT:    13,912.47     2,603.07   16,515.54
                  HOL-PAY:      .00    EIC:         .00          .00         .00
                  SICK-PAY:     .00    SWT:     4,900.00          .00    4,900.00
                  SPEC-PAY:  145.00    OST:        28.48        30.69       59.17
                  SUPP-PAY:     .00    CWT:         .00          .00         .00
                                       NET:                  4,655.61
                  PRFTSHR     25.00
DEPARTMENT TOTAL: EMPLOYER FICA LIABILITY                      531.95
```

Figure 9–6 Payroll register

These totals help verify the correctness of accumulated totals, including the federal withholding total (FWT) and the state withholding total (SWT).

Problems or errors in processing are printed on the payroll register. As Figure 9–6 shows, one or more deductions could not be taken for Federick J. Hall because net pay (for the period) was zero. Likewise, one or more calculations for Markos Marianias exceeded the maximum. Observe that regular pay for Marianias is $7,540.00. On inspection, it was discovered that the regular pay should have been $754.00.

Employee paychecks are printed following the review and approval of the payroll register, provided, of course, that all identified errors have been corrected. As Figure 9–7 shows, an employee voucher-check is a two-part form. The voucher portion provides an earnings record showing the dollar amounts leading to gross pay and the dollar amounts subtracted from gross pay to arrive at net pay. The check portion provides banking information. The printed face amount of the check is equal to the net-pay amount printed on the check-voucher.

A *payroll journal* is prepared to summarize payroll costs by department, job class, budget number, general ledger number, project number, or some other classification important to a company. These journals feature a summary page and detail pages. As Figure 9–8 shows, the summary page of a labor-cost-by-budget-number journal provides a breakdown of payroll costs by

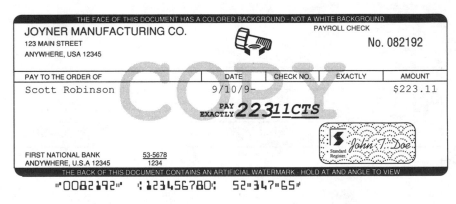

Figure 9–7   Employee voucher-check

```
Payroll Journal-Budget Number Breakdowns
Pay Period 42                                          Payroll Period 11/6/


    Budget      Dollar
    Number      Amount      Description

    501-006   $24,713.60    Direct Labor
    502-011    19,726.54    Indirect Labor
    503-141     8,911.14    Overtime Premium
    506-008    19,600.18    Salaries-Direct
    507-057    24,101.14    Salaries-Indirect
    724-211     7,278.95    FICA Withheld
    724-215    15,043.15    Federal Tax Withheld
    724-221     5,823.12    StateTax Withheld
    724-225     1,941.05    Federal Unemployment
    724-231       680.42    State Unemployment
    724-542     6.793.60    ERISA
```

Figure 9–8 Payroll journal summary totals

major expense category (salaries-direct, FICA withheld, and so on). The detail supporting page is then attached. A typical detail page prints individual employee totals by budget number, by department. If the summary figures look unusual (if they are either too high or too low), individual employee payments are inspected to determine whether the figures appearing on the journal differ from the employee-hours-worked figures initially sent to payroll for processing.

One of the real values of an interactive approach is that individual payroll records can be displayed and examined rather than printed. As Figure 9–9 shows, employee displays provide personal, wage and salary, and tax information. The display of John Anderson's record, for example, tells us that he is paid $10.00 per hour, is single, and has no exemptions or tax credits. If we want to review other parts of John Anderson's record, this design indicates that we can click on the Personal or Earnings buttons. As shown in Figure 9–10, the earnings history tells us that John has earned $2,000 and that his net pay to date is $1518.20. For this display, a click on the hours box would reveal that John has worked 200 regular hours.

Ad hoc displays are also extremely useful. As Figure 9–11 shows, an *ad hoc display* requires the user to specify the type of information required, using worded (rather than number-coded) inquiry commands, such as

```
FIND PERSONNEL WITH NAME = DAVENPORT OR ALEXANDER
    AND AGE = 30 THRU 45
    CONTROL ON NAME AND ACCUM SALARY
```

Following the entry of an inquiry command, reporting requirements are specified. In the display in Figure 9–11 the user instructs the computer to

```
DISPLAY FIRST-NAME NAME AGE SEX SALARY.
```

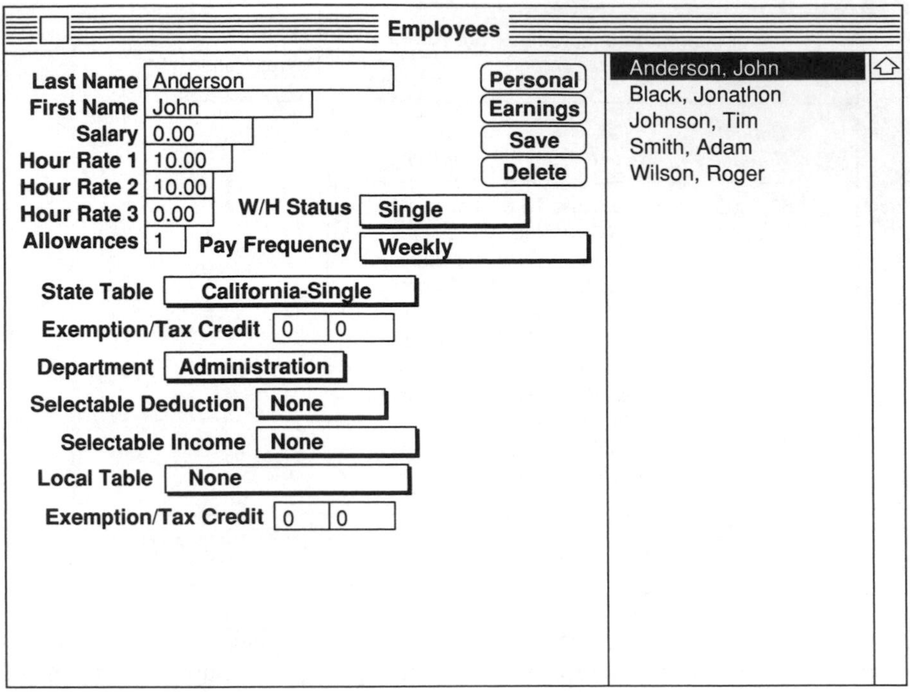

Figure 9–9 Employee payroll display

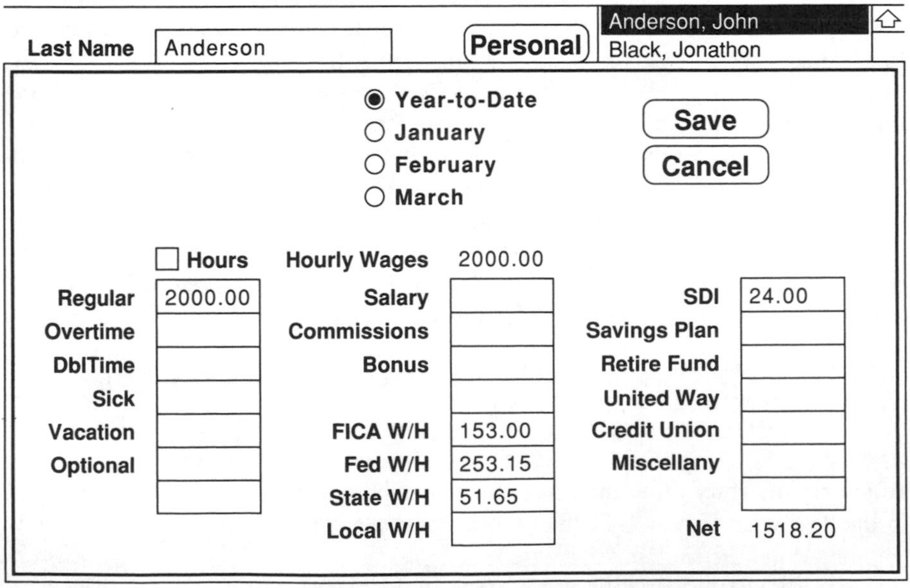

Figure 9–10 Employee personal earnings display

```
FIND PERSONNEL WITH NAME = DAVENPORT OR ALEXANDER
     AND AGE = 30 THRU 45
     CONTROL ON NAME AND ACCUM SALARY.
DISPLAY FIRST-NAME NAME AGE SEX SALARY.
ACCEPTED
7 RECORDS FOUND


                              LAST-NAME            A    S    FIXED
                                                   G    E    SALARY
                                                   E    X

   HENRY                      ALEXANDER            30   M    $22,500
   HOLLY                      ALEXANDER            40   F    $36,000
   CHARLY                     ALEXANDER            33   M    $20,960
   HELEN                      ALEXANDER            42   F    $25,000

                              4 *                              $104,460


   ANN                        DAVENPORT            38   F    $19,200
   GRETA                      DAVENPORT            42   F    $13,125
   VIRGINIA                   DAVENPORT            45   F    $23,800

                              3 *                              $56,125

                              7 *                              $160,585

END OF REPORT          7 RECORDS FOUND
```

Figure 9–11   Ad hoc inquiry and reporting

The computer responds with the word *Accepted* and displays the number of records that satisfy the conditions specified by the inquiry command. As illustrated here, the computer reports *7 records found*; the computer lists these records, showing each employee's name, age, sex, and accumulated salary.

REVIEW QUESTIONS

1.   What are the special reasons for installing an online employee payroll design?

2.   What are the three main inputs to the employee payroll application? How do they differ?

3.   What is the difference between the payroll number and the employee number? Between the project number and the employee number?

4.   Identify the main segments of an employee master file record.

5.   What are the three main outputs produced in processing? How do they differ from ad hoc displays?

6.   How does the payroll register differ from a payroll journal?

9-2   PAYROLL PROCESSING

Parts (a) and (b) of Figure 9–12 show the systems organization chart for the employee payroll computer application; Figures 9–13 (a) and (b) illustrate the corresponding program-processing menu. Of the five interactive programs, three are required to update the employee master file. The first of these, *Ready*

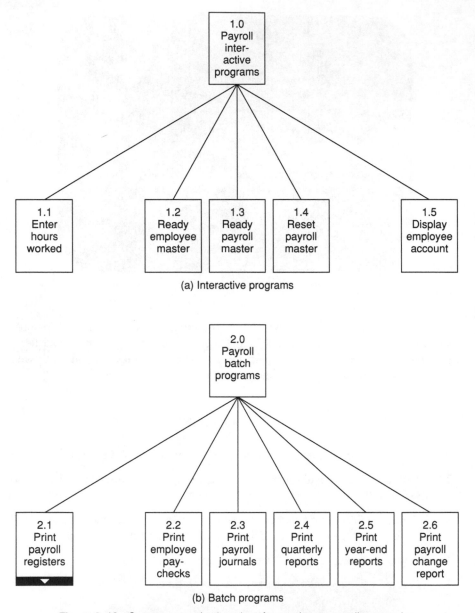

(a) Interactive programs

(b) Batch programs

Figure 9–12   Systems organization chart for employee payroll processing

employee master, is designed to add, change, or delete employee name and address information and other personnel information (see file segments one and two in Figure 9–4). The second, *Ready payroll master,* is designed to add, change, or delete wage and salary, leave and pension, current payroll, and QTD and YTD payroll history information (see file segments three through six in Figure 9–4). The third, *Reset payroll master* differs in function from the other two. This update

```
┌─────────────────────────────────────────────┐
│ ┌──────────────────────────┐                │
│ │ EMPLOYEE PAYROLL         │                │
│ └──────────────────────────┘                │
│                                             │
│      ENTER HOURS WORKED                     │
│      READY EMPLOYEE MASTER FILE             │
│      READY PAYROLL MASTER FILE              │
│      RESET PAYROLL MASTER                   │
│      DISPLAY EMPLOYEE ACCOUNT               │
│                                             │
│                                             │
│                                             │
│      RETURN                                 │
│                                             │
└─────────────────────────────────────────────┘
```

(a) Interactive menu choices

```
┌─────────────────────────────────────────────┐
│ ┌──────────────────────────┐                │
│ │ EMPLOYEE PAYROLL         │                │
│ └──────────────────────────┘                │
│                                             │
│      PRINT PAYROLL REGISTER                 │
│      PRINT HOURS-WORKED REGISTER            │
│      PRINT EMPLOYEE PAYCHECKS               │
│      PRINT PAYROLL JOURNALS                 │
│      PRINT QUARTERLY REPORTS                │
│      PRINT YEAR-END REPORTS                 │
│      PRINT EMPLOYEE REGISTER                │
│      PRINT CHANGE REPORT                    │
│                                             │
│      RETURN                                 │
│                                             │
└─────────────────────────────────────────────┘
```

(b) Batch menu choices

Figure 9–13   Program-processing menu

program is designed to reset selected payroll totals to zero, making the master file ready for the next payroll-processing period.

The single display program illustrated in Figure 9–12a generally leads to a secondary menu showing various types of display options. One display might be restricted to personnel information for an employee; another might be restricted to the employee's name and payroll information. Then, in addition, a series of summary displays is generally available. An operator might, for example, instruct the computer to display departmental payroll costs. In this instance, the name, hours worked, and gross pay for each employee assigned to a department would be listed. Other summary displays show payroll costs by plant (where there are several plants), payroll costs by labor class, and payroll costs by work order.

The batch portion of payroll processing includes programs designed to produce and summarize the current payroll and programs designed to prepare quarterly and year-end statements and listings. Current payroll programs include the printing of the hours-worked register, the payroll register, employee paychecks, and payroll journals. Current backup programs produce the master register and the employee change report. Quarterly and year-end programs for this design include one program to print quarterly reports, such as withheld income and Social Security tax reports, and one to print year-end reports, such as employee wage and tax statements, including the printing of W-2 forms.

Update employee master file Programs

Before time cards are processed by a company, the personnel and payroll departments must collect and enter into processing all employee changes. Personnel processing begins once an *employee change form* is received. This form provides space to record name-and-address and other personnel information. Payroll processing begins once the *payroll change form* has been received. Payroll changes occur with greater frequency than do personnel changes. Every time a company decides to promote, transfer, grant a pay increase to, lay off, terminate, or hire a person, a payroll change slip must be filled out.

Computer processing of either payroll or personnel change forms is greatly simplified with interactive programs. After selecting the option to alter personnel information, for example, the user might be presented with a file-change menu such as that shown in the top section of Figure 9–14. Following the display of the employee number and name, the computer asks

        DO YOU WISH TO CHANGE:
            1. EMPLOYEE NUMBER?
            2. SOCIAL SECURITY NUMBER?
            3. EMPLOYEE NAME?

and so on. The user responds by entering the number of the appropriate question—a **3**, for example, if a name change is required—in the designated *Enter changes* area of the display. After all changes have been indicated by number, a **12** (exit) is entered. This tells the computer to begin processing the file changes indicated and to exit once the last change has been made.

Suppose for the moment that this menu is presented and that only a name change is required. The user simply enters **3** and then **12**. Next, a name-change display screen is presented, like that shown in the bottom section of Figure 9–14. After the name change is made, the employee name currently stored on file and the revised name are both displayed. This practice permits the user to verify the newly keyed information visually. The computer asks

        IS THIS NAME CORRECT?

If the user indicates **no** instead of **yes**, the computer responds with one or more questions, such as

        DO YOU WISH TO ENTER A DIFFERENT NAME?

or

        DO YOU WISH TO EXIT?

```
EMPLOYEE NUMBER:  | 52314 |              NAME:  | JOHNSON, SILVIA ANN |


DO YOU WICH TO CHANGE:


1. EMPLOYEE NUMBER?                    7. DATE STARTED EMPLOYMENT?
2. SOCIAL SECURITY NUMBER?             8. SEX?
3. EMPLOYEE NAME?                      9. RACE?
4. EMPLOYEE HOME ADDRESS?             10. HANDICAPS?
5. EMPLOYEE PLANT ADDRESS?           11. MARITAL STATUS?
6. TELEPHONE EXTENSION NUMBER?       ⟨12.⟩ EXIT

ENTER CHANGES:   | FIRST:  _____ |
                 | NEXT:   _____ |
                 | NEXT:   _____ |
```

```
                     EMPLOYEE NAME CHANGE
THE EMPLOYEE NAME STORED ON FILE IS:

LAST NAME        | JOHNSON |
FIRST NAME       | SILVIA  |
MIDDLE NAME      | ANN     |

THE NAME SHOULD BE CHANGED TO (IF NO CHANGE PRESS RETURN):

LAST NAME        | PORTER  |
FIRST NAME       |         |
MIDDLE NAME      |         |

THE REVISED EMPLOYEE NAME IS:  | PORTER, SILVIA ANN |
IS THIS CORRECT?
```

Figure 9–14 Entering a name change

One change file, the employee change file, is built by the two programs to update the master file. With a single change file it becomes possible to determine when both personnel and payroll changes are made to an employee's record. Before the contents of the file are listed, all changes are sorted by employee number (or by employee number within department number). Once this is done the changes can be printed in employee-number sequence.

Another update master file program, *Reset payroll master* (see Figure 9–12a), is activated after all payroll reports have been printed. This program resets the current payroll totals to zero while retaining all QTD and YTD totals and all other employee-master-file detail. As a general rule, a new employee master file is created by this step in processing; the old master file is saved as a backup to processing.

The *Enter hours worked* Program

This program can be designed in two ways. With an integrated design, the program edits hours-worked information entered into processing, computes gross and net pay, updates the employee master file, and writes all time-keeping and payroll information to the hours-worked (and to be paid) file. Such an integration combines the two functional steps described earlier (see Figure 9–2). The systems flowchart in Figure 9–15 illustrates the steps important to processing. As indicated, the employee master file and the project master file are updated by processing; the single output-only file stores hours-worked and payroll information. The steps important to the design are as follows:

1. The employee number is verified first, followed by project number and hours-worked totals.

2. If all numbers are acceptable, current payroll information is calculated; this includes gross pay, deductions from gross pay, net pay, and so on.

3. Following pay calculations, the three payroll segments of the employee master file—leave and pension, current payroll, and YTD and QTD payroll history—are updated.

4. Hours worked and labor costs are transferred to update the project master file.

5. Hours worked and current payroll costs are written to the hours-worked file.

There are good reasons for updating both the employee master and the project master files at the same time. This design step blocks data in error from being posted incorrectly to work activities such as projects, work orders, or work centers. In processing, two keys must be initially verified: the employee number and the project

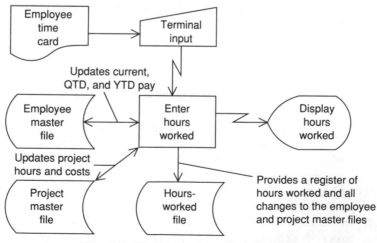

Figure 9–15   Entering hours-worked details

number. If either is incorrect—the right employee working on an invalid project or the wrong employee working on a correct project—it becomes impossible to add labor hours into processing.

In a second design of this program, firms replace time-reporting cards with employee-identification badges and require their employees to enter their times directly into processing using one-way data collection terminals. (With this design, the functions *Enter hours worked* and *Calculate employee pay* are kept separate.) To record the start time of work, the employee inserts his or her badge into the terminal, which allows the employee number printed on the badge to be read and transmitted to processing. Once the employee number has been received, the computer adds the employee number to the department number and enters the time of day (the start time). These three pieces of information are stored on the employee time-keeping file. Similarly, to record the stop time of work, the employee inserts the badge once again, logging the employee number, the department number, and the time of day. By matching these two sets of data for an employee, the computer determines the difference between the start and stop times and stores this difference on the employee timekeeping file. At the end of a designated period, such as a work day or a work week, timekeeping files are sorted by employee number to produce an hours-worked register, which lists both the total hours worked by each employee, by work area, and the combined total of the hours worked for all employees, by work area. The employee timekeeping file is also input to the employee payroll computer application, where it is used to produce the payroll register. First, however, the file must be adjusted. Any sick leave or vacation time, for example, must be key-entered and verified. Likewise, if an employee is to be paid for work done while away from a department, this too must be entered and verified.

Employee Payroll Registers

After hours-worked information has been successfully entered into processing, the employee master file is closed from further modification and the *payroll register* is printed. As shown earlier, this register provides a breakdown of employee earnings and deductions from earnings. It also provides control totals to help verify the correctness of processing and serves as a legal document suitable for longer-term storage. It fully documents the voucher portion of employee paychecks. These vouchers and actual paychecks are printed after the register is reviewed and approved.

Two additional registers, besides the payroll register, document the results of payroll processing (see Figure 9–16). The first of these, the *hours-worked register,* is printed following a sort of the hours-worked file, which is a combined transaction and change file. This file stores all information keyed to processing and all corresponding changes to the employee and project master files. The hours-worked register contains considerably more detail than is shown on the payroll register. It shows what data were keyed to processing and how these data were converted to dollars-paid totals. It shows if any adjusting entries were keyed and processed, and it shows dollar control totals. The dollars posted both to the employee master

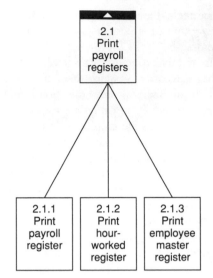

Figure 9-16   Three types of payroll registers

file and to the project master file are listed separately. These totals must equal the control totals printed on the payroll register.

The *employee master register* also contains considerably more detail than does the payroll register. This register lists the entire contents of the employee master file. Besides current and YTD payroll totals, the register prints all personnel information contained within employee records. This final register is produced for two reasons: to provide a backup listing to processing and to cross-check the accuracy of payroll processing. As with other master-file backup procedures, a tape copy of the master file is made at the same time as the listing. These materials serve as insurance should the employee master file somehow be lost or destroyed.

The *Print employee paychecks* Program

Employee paychecks can be printed immediately after the payroll register has been approved. Since the employee master file is sequenced by employee number, employee voucher-checks are printed in this sequence. If a different order is desired, such as alphabetical order, a sort of the employee master file is required. This sort, however, should not take place immediately prior to printing paychecks but should instead be scheduled just prior to the printing of the payroll register. In addition, the employee master file should not be sorted by employee name because it will only be resorted later to its initial order—by employee number. A better alternative is to create a current payroll file, using the master file, and to sort this new file before printing the register.

Keeping checks properly aligned is the biggest problem associated with running the employee paychecks program. *Check alignment* refers to printing information in the spaces provided, or *in registration*. One way around this problem is to process several voided checks initially, examining each and adjusting printer alignment as necessary. Once the alignment is correct, the total batch of checks can be printed.

As with the checks processed by the accounts-payable application, printed checks should not be signed by the computer. This practice is far too dangerous because of the possibility of fraud. As a safety measure, all checks should be endorsed after they are printed. An off-line signature die, controlled by the treasurer of a company, is used to add a company signature to each paycheck.

Payroll Reports

Besides payroll registers, several types of reports must be prepared to document payroll-processing activities fully and to comply with external audit and governmental guidelines and regulations. As illustrated earlier (see Figure 9–8), the summary page of a payroll journal shows payroll totals by major account, such as direct labor costs, indirect labor costs, FICA withheld, and federal tax withheld. In addition to major summaries, payroll journals are designed to show the details of processing, should summary totals be questioned. Figure 9–17, for example, illustrates a tax-withholding control proof page. The employee accounts appearing on this page are sequenced first by home department and second by employee number. The control proof provides a detailed listing of federal and state taxes and FICA withheld.

Control proofs, such as the tax-withheld control proof, are used in two ways. First, the company totals shown at the bottom of the proof are compared with the totals shown on the summary page of the payroll journal. The two sets of totals must be the same. Second, individual employee accounts are selected by company auditors and subjected to manual testing. If, for example, the H. T. Andrews account is selected (see line item 1 of Figure 9–17), the checkers will note that since Andrews is single (S) and has no dependents, the single-person federal and state tax tables should be used to determine if the income tax dollars deducted from gross pay are correct. Likewise, the FICA deduction is checked by multiplying gross pay times the FICA withholding rate percentage.

A quarterly report formatted to fit federal form 941 is the *Employer's Quarterly Federal Tax Return* (see Figure 9–18). The summary totals printed include total wages subject to withholding (entry 2), income tax withheld (entry 3), taxable FICA wages times the employer's rate (entries 6 and 7), and federal and state unemployment taxes due (entry 13). Besides a summary page, detailed supporting pages must be supplied. Federal form 941a, for example, lists taxable FICA wages by employee. The employee's Social Security number and name are both shown on this supporting page with the employee's taxable FICA wages.

Besides fulfilling quarterly report requirements, companies must schedule year-end payroll-processing runs. At year end, federal and state governments require business firms to print W-2 reporting statements, which are delivered to all employees who were active, at one time or another, during the calendar year. Figure 9–19 shows the different types of information placed on the W-2 form. The employer identification number and the employee's Social Security number are shown together with year-end totals of gross income and federal and state taxes withheld. The dollar amount of FICA withheld is also printed on the statement.

PAY150   J & L MARINA MFG. CORP.   PAY PERIOD ENDING 11/03/--

PAY PERIOD 07   TAX WITHHOLDING CONTROL PROOF   PAGE 1

HOME DEPT	EMPLOYEE NUMBER	EMPLOYEE NAME	TOTAL HOURS	GROSS PAY	M S	DEP	FEDERAL W/TAX	FICA	DEP AL	STATE W/TAX	SDI	FIRST NET
308	042150	H T ANDREWS	.000	850.00	S		195.50	61.66		21.25	.00	571.59
308	362350	A N HILL	.000	650.00	M	2	89.96	47.16		14.17	.00	498.71
308	487553	L L KELLY	.000	650.00	M	2	83.46	47.16		14.17	.00	505.21
308	501957	I E KOPECK	.000	450.00	M	1	48.88	32.66		10.21	.00	358.25
308	535153	P LUCAS	.000	650.00	M	2	83.46	47.16		14.17	.00	505.21
308	544056	P MAHONEY	.000	900.00	M	2	147.58	65.31		20.42	.00	666.69
308	649350	S OLIVER	.000	900.00	M	3	138.83	65.31		19.38	.00	676.48
308	755959	M ROOT	15.000	67.50	S	1	.00	12.72		.65	.00	54.13
308	815159	J STEWART	112.000	558.00	M	2	63.22	42.40		11.87	.00	440.51
310	191056	G DOUGLAS	88.000	528.00	M	3	70.37	43.46		13.20	.00	400.97
310	285957	T FLETCHER	58.000	315.00	M	3	13.50	28.66		4.75	.00	268.09
310	285957	T FLETCHER	40.000	200.00	M	3	.00	12.10		1.88	.00	186.02
310	292953	G FREEMAN	88.000	528.00	M	1	63.49	43.46		12.16	.00	408.89
310	302752	W GALLOW	20.000	100.00	M	2	20.00	5.85		2.00	1.00	71.15 VCHR
310	353359	K HEATH	.000	900.00	M	2	147.58	65.31		20.42	.00	666.69
310	379057	D HUDSON	88.000	539.00	S		96.92	44.13		13.48	.00	384.47
310	460857	J JENKINS	88.000	543.40	M	1	66.88	44.40		12.54	.00	419.58
310	496059	G A KIRK	80.000	900.00	M	3	147.54	65.31	1	18.89	.00	668.26
310	540252	V LYONS	88.000	528.00	M	1	63.49	43.46		12.16	.00	408.89
310	651158	C OLSON	10.000	60.00	M	1	.00	15.15		.46	.00	44.39
310	666750	L OSGOOD	.000	12.00	M	2	.00	8.64		.00	.00	3.36
310	698357	C PENDELL	88.000	396.00	M	1	39.16	32.60		8.86	.00	315.38
310	758250	L ROSS	12.000	72.00	M		.00	15.88		1.80	.00	54.32
316	151852	A COLLINS	74.000	259.00	M	1	14.50	22.39		5.43	.00	216.68
316	288951	L FORDE	98.000	360.50	M	1	32.77	28.53		7.97	.00	291.23
316	357657	G HENRY	90.000	332.50	M	2	22.10	26.84		6.23	.00	277.33
316	539858	Z LYNCH	10.000	35.00	M	1	.00	8.84		.00	.00	26.16
316	605154	P NEWTON	88.000	453.20	M	2	43.83	37.02		9.25	.00	363.10
316	612457	A NORTON	90.000	318.50	M	2	19.58	25.99		5.88	.00	267.05
316	689257	E PALMER	88.000	308.00	M	1	23.32	25.35		6.66	.00	252.67
316	710152	D PLATT	.000	900.00	M	2	147.58	65.31		20.42	.00	666.69
316	852053	J TRACY	.000	900.00	M	2	147.58	65.31		20.42	.00	666.69
324	124255	J M CALDWELL	.000	850.00	M	2	133.58	61.66		19.17	.00	635.59
324	155556	A COOPER	.000	900.00	M	2	147.58	65.31		20.42	.00	666.69
324	233557	M ELLIS	.000	900.00	M	2	147.58	65.31		20.42	.00	666.69
324	278853	E M FERGUSON	.000	1,600.00	M	2	241.04	107.03		35.83	.00	1,216.10
324	290957	J FOWLER	.000	900.00	M	3	138.83	65.31		19.38	.00	676.48
324	319459	M T GOLDSMITH	.000	850.00	M	3	133.58	61.66		19.17	.00	635.59
324	342352	H HAMMOND	.000	900.00	M	3	138.83	65.31		19.38	.00	676.48
324	346056	G C HARDING	.000	850.00	M	2	133.58	61.66		19.17	.00	635.59
324	494054	G KING	.000	900.00	M	2	213.50	65.31		22.50	.00	598.69
324	895979	J M VANDER	.000	900.00	S	1	202.25	65.31		21.46	.00	610.98
COMPANY TOTAL			1,413.000	24,713.60			3,661.43	1,879.40		548.05	1.00	18,623.72

Figure 9–17 Withholding control proof

```
FORM 941          EMPLOYERS QUARTERLY FEDERAL TAX RETURN          199-

                         ┌─────────────────────────────┐
                         │   QUARTER ENDED 02/04/9-     │
                         │        41-1234567           │
                         └─────────────────────────────┘

  2.  TOTAL WAGES & TIPS SUBJECT TO WITHHOLDING                23325.54
  3.  AMOUNT OF INCOME TAX WITHHELD                             4435.21
  4.  ADJUSTMENTS FOR PRECEEDING QUARTERS OF CALENDAR YEAR
  5.  ADJUSTED TOTAL OF INCOME TAX WITHHELD                     4435.21
  6.  TAXABLE FICA WAGES   23325.54 TIMES  15.3% = TAX OF       3568.81
  7.  TAXABLE TIPS          0.00 TIMES  15.3% = TAX OF             0.00
  8.  TOTAL FICA TAXES                                          3568.81
  9.  ADJUSTMENT
 10.  ADJUSTED TOTAL                                            3568.81
 11.  TOTAL TAXES                                               8004.02
      ADVANCE EARNED INCOME CREDIT PAYMENTS                        0.00
 12.  TOTAL DEPOSITS FOR QUARTER AND OVERPAYMENT
      FROM PREVIOUS QUARTER

 13.  UNDEPOSITED TAXES DUE. PAY TO IRS

 FEDERAL TAXABLE UNEMPLOYMENT WAGES     23325.54
 TIMES   0.80% =    186.60

 STATE TAXABLE UNEMPLOYMENT WAGES       23325.54
 TIMES   1.90% =    443.19
 TOTAL STATE INCOME TAX WITHHELD         1620.04
```

Figure 9–18   Quarterly 941 summary

1 Control number	22222		

2 Employer's name, address, and ZIP code	3 Employer's identification number	4 Employer's State number
ABC MANUFACTURING COMPANY 906 NE 6TH ST MINNEAPOLIS, MN 55414 L	41-6666666	4567890

	5 State employee □ De-ceased □ Pension plan □ Legal rep. □ 942 emp. □ Sub. total □ Cor-rection □ Void □
	6 *	7 Advance EIC payment 0.00

8 Employer's social security number	9 Federal income tax withheld	10 Wages, tips, other compensation	11 FICA tax withheld
444-55-6666	427.95	2250.00	149.60

12 Employee's name (first, middle, last)	13 FICA wages	14 FICA tips
EDWARD PETERSON	2250.00	0.00

	16 Employer's use
RT 5 BOX 764 ANYTOWN, MN 55333	

17 State income tax	18 State Wages, tips, etc.	19 Name of State
155.85	2250.00	MN
20 Local income tax	21 Local wages, tips, etc.	22 Name of locality

15 Employee's address and ZIP code

Form **W-2 Wage and Tax Statement 199--**   Copy A For Social Security Administration • See Instructions for Forms W-2 and W-2P   Dept. of the Treasury I.R.S
IRS App. 0000 13-2678063

Do NOT Cut or Separate Forms on This Page 16-lb. Paper

Figure 9–19   W-2 statement

Printing W-2 statements for all employees who were and are active during the calendar year poses special processing problems. Instead of deleting employees from the employee master file following their terminations, a year-end record must be maintained of the total dollars paid to employees regardless of whether they are still employed. One solution to this situation is to *transfer and save* records when processing employee terminations. In this instance, all inactive employees are deleted from the employee master file and placed on a special year-end payroll-reporting file. Another solution is to *flag* employees as inactive and to continue to store all inactive records on the employee master file. The flag blocks future payments to the employee. After year-end reports are printed, all records containing these special flags are removed. A batch program reads each employee record stored on file to delete inactive employees.

REVIEW QUESTIONS

7. Why are three interactive programs used in this application to update the employee master file?

8. What processing steps are important to the *Enter hours worked* program?

9. Why must adjustments be made when badge readers are used to enter employee times into processing?

10. What is the difference between the payroll register and the hours-worked register? Between the payroll register and the employee master register?

11. What is the biggest problem associated with running the employee paychecks program?

12. Why are control proofs important to processing?

13. Explain why printing W-2 statements poses special data-retention problems.

9-3 LABOR DISTRIBUTION

An important product of payroll processing is the analysis of payroll costs. One type of analysis is commonly known as *labor distribution:* the breakdown of labor costs by department, project, product, work center, or some other measurable type of company work activity. Input to labor-distribution reporting is a work-activity master file, such as the project master file shown in Figure 9–15. This file is updated as hours-worked information is keyed and added to the employee master file. For example, the update procedure for adding project information to the project master file is as follows.

1. A project number is keyed into processing and matched with the same project number stored on file.

2. Once matched, a new record is added to the project. This record contains the employee number, regular hours worked, overtime hours worked, and payroll costs (the cost of regular hours worked and of overtime hours worked).

3. After the new record is added, a second project number is keyed into processing and matched, which leads to the creation of another project record. It may be for the same employee (if the employee worked on more than one project) or for another employee. In only the latter case must a new employee number be keyed into processing. This cycle of matching project numbers and of adding project time and cost information to the project master file continues until all project information for each employee has been successfully transferred.

Following the transfer of work activity information, the analysis of labor times and costs can begin. This analysis can take place in several ways. Most labor distribution reports can be printed directly using the times and costs now stored on file. These reports are designed to compare current hours worked and costs with those for the previous month, with YTD hours worked and costs, or with hours worked and costs for the previous month a year ago. Most labor distribution reports show percentage differences between one period and another. Still other reports show whether differences between periods are significant.

Labor-distribution results are often displayed rather than printed. As the display illustrated in Figure 9–20 makes clear, a substantial amount of detail can be shown on a single display screen. In this example, the computer was initially instructed to

FIND THE DEPARTMENTS WHERE SORTING TOOK PLACE.

LABOR-DISTRIBUTION ANALYSIS: | SORTING |

| DEPARTMENT | THIS MONTH | TOTAL HOURS WORKED | | |
		LAST MONTH	DIFFERENCE	PERCENT
18	635	512	123	24
24	1400	1262	138	11
62	419	592	107	34
79	672		80	14
TOTAL	3216	2678	448	17

Figure 9–20 Labor distribution reporting

Once the departments were found, the computer was told to

COMPARE THIS MONTH'S HOURS-WORKED TOTAL TO LAST
MONTH'S HOURS-WORKED TOTAL AND SHOW THE DIFFERENCE
IN HOURS AND AS A PERCENT.

Finally, the computer was instructed to

HIGHLIGHT BY DEPARTMENT WHERE THE PERCENTAGE DIFFER-
ENCE WAS SIGNIFICANT.

As illustrated, departments 18 and 62 show much higher levels of activity measured on a percentage basis.

Labor distribution displays and reports are prepared by companies for several reasons. They are helpful in preparing departmental staffing tables—month-by-month comparisons of hours worked by department, by type of work performed, that help managers determine how many employees, by department, will be needed to complete the work at hand. Second, they are helpful in projecting costs for various work activities and in controlling areas of high cost. If, for instance, the cost of operations is increasing while production is holding constant, the question of whether labor costs are responsible for this increase can be asked. Third, labor distribution reporting helps in identifying areas of high and low worker productivity. For example, standard hours and costs can be compared to actual hours and costs. If the standard time to produce 1000 pieces is 15.60 hours and actual time takes 16.00 hours, the difference from standard is 2.6 percent. Percentage differences above 5 percent may be critical, requiring the attention of management. Standard times are generally set by industrial engineers. They are based on the rated speed of the equipment required by an operation or on the speed of an average worker assigned to an operation.

9-4 JOB COSTING

Some companies integrate job costing with the employee-payroll application. *Job costing,* the posting of labor, equipment, and material costs to each job undertaken by a company or department, requires that three types of data be entered into processing. These are

- regular and overtime hours worked, by employee, by job number
- equipment hours used, by machine, by employee, by job number
- material consumed, by item or material number, by employee, by job number

Because hours-used totals for equipment and quantity-used totals for materials are entered at the same time as hours-worked information is entered into processing, the computer is able to transform these figures into dollars, by job. In so doing, the ongoing and actual costs of a job can be summarized.

Figure 9–21 shows the heart of the job-costing system. As indicated, seven data stores are required for this system, including the employee master data store. The design of the system must initially verify an employee number entered into processing. Following this, the first job number is verified by matching it against the number stored on the job-costing master file. Following job verification, the regular hours worked and overtime hours worked are entered and employee pay is calculated.

Second, if equipment hours are reported for the job number, the machine number and the hours used are entered. As this is done, machine rates are used to calculate the cost of the equipment.

Third, if material usage is reported for the job number, the material number and the quantity used are entered. This leads to the use of material cost rates to calculate the cost of the material.

An example of the job-costing data structure is as follows:

> Employee number
> Job number 1
>> Machine number 1
>>> Material number 1
>>> Material number 2
> Job number 2
>> Machine number 2
> Job number 3
>> Machine number 3
>>> Material number 3

The rules followed in processing are as follows. Each employee number leads to one or more job numbers and each job number leads (a) to zero, (b) to one or more machine numbers, or (c) to one or more material numbers. Machine numbers are generally followed by material numbers.

A variety of reports can be prepared as products of the job-costing application.

- *Job ledgers* show the charges for an individual job, including labor, material, equipment costs, and in some instances estimated overhead charges.

- *Material usage reports* show the cost of materials required by different jobs. Each entry on this report typically contains the material number, material description, date used, unit cost of the material, quantity consumed, and extended cost (unit cost × quantity consumed). The extended cost can be shown by material number, but it is generally listed by job number, employee number, or machine number.

- *Equipment usage reports* show the cost of equipment required by different jobs. Each entry on this report typically contains the machine number, machine description, date used, hourly cost of the machine, hours used, and extended cost (hourly cost × hours used). The extended cost can be shown by machine number or by job or employee number.

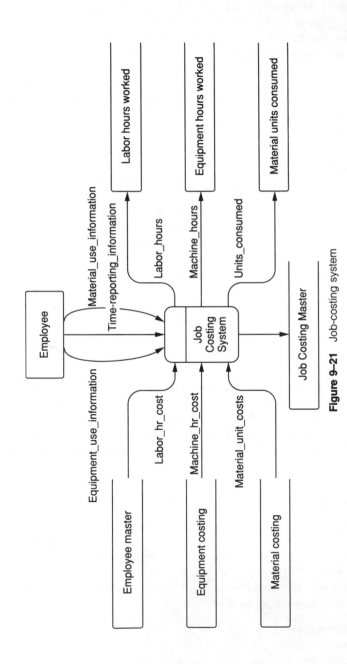

Figure 9–21 Job-costing system

- *Labor-hour usage reports* show the cost of labor required by different jobs. Each entry on this report typically contains the employee number, employee name, date of work, regular pay rate, overtime pay rate, regular hours worked, overtime hours worked, and extended cost (pay rate × hours worked). The extended cost can be shown by employee number or by job or machine number.

Collectively, these reports help managers isolate the costs of doing business. They show areas where costs are higher than expected and permit faster response to cost-related problems.

9-5 PROCESSING CONTROLS

As with other online business computer applications, both transaction and batch controls are required in processing employee payroll records. A transaction-based control procedure might work as follows. Employees fill out weekly time cards, showing regular and overtime hours worked each day, vacation and sick leave taken, and total hours worked during the week. In processing these cards, data-entry personnel key the weekly total of hours worked, followed by the number of hours worked per day and the vacation and sick leave taken. After the last daily entry, the computer sums the daily hours to arrive at the weekly total and compares this summed total with the keyed weekly total. The two figures must be the same.

A better way to ensure correct entry of hours-worked information is to automate the keeping of employee time. Modern electronic time-keeping equipment eliminates the hand calculation of employee hours worked per day and per week. Some time-keeping equipment keeps both employee totals and balances and departmental totals and balances. This practice permits the total hours worked by department also to be carried forward in data processing.

A strict set of batch controls is required following the posting of hours-worked information to the employee master file. The control equations are

$$\text{Total hours worked} = \text{Regular hours} + \text{Overtime hours}$$

$$\text{Total hours paid} = \text{Total hours worked} + \text{Approved leave hours}$$

These two hourly totals are changed each time new hours-worked information is accepted by the computer. They are critical in the control of the employee payroll.

Because the computer converts total hours paid to total dollars paid, it is rather difficult to verify the accuracy of all paychecks. Control procedures used to guard against higher-(or lower-) than-normal paychecks include subjecting hours-worked and dollars-paid totals to a series of range and comparison tests and checking payroll figures by hand to determine if they are correct. A typical range test is to flag any paycheck that falls above an upper (dollar) limit and to print this information on the employee payroll register. The upper limit for an hourly employee, for example, might be $3,000. Any monthly check for an amount greater than $3,000 would be flagged for inspection. Another range test is to flag all hours worked totals that seem unusual—overtime hours that total more than an established upper (hourly) limit, for example, or a combination of overtime hours to be paid and regular hours that falls below an established lower limit.

Payroll comparison tests are useful for pointing out unusual or incorrect situations. One comparison is to divide the dollars paid by the hours worked for a pay period, do the same for the last pay period, and match the two resulting figures (which should normally be identical). If this comparison reveals instead that dollars paid per hour worked for the first period are significantly different than those for the last period (say, plus or minus 5 percent), the reasons for the difference must be explained. Another test pits departmental pay averages for one period against departmental pay averages of the last period. Here again, any significant difference must be explained.

With interactive processing it is possible to decentralize the visual review of payroll records and totals. Following the computation of departmental payroll costs, departmental supervisors can display, review, and either approve or disapprove all hours-worked, hours-paid, and dollars-paid totals. If totals look unusual, it is possible to question an employee directly. This can determine whether the hours-worked totals stored on file agree with the totals that were initially submitted by the employee.

Last, manual calculations must be made to verify the correctness of payroll. A workable procedure is to select a small random sample, such as 1 percent of all employees, each payroll period and to determine by hand the payments to be made to each employee included in the sample. In each case the hours worked, the hours paid, the gross dollars paid, and the net dollars paid must agree with the figures determined by the computer.

9-6   MANAGEMENT IMPLICATIONS

Companies must exercise special caution in designing employee payroll computer systems. This is the one application in which mistakes in processing cannot be tolerated and the reliability of processing cannot be questioned. Timeliness in processing is critical. It is not acceptable to distribute checks late or as soon as computer programs are fixed. Nor is it acceptable to print all but a few paychecks. In these instances, work will spread that there are problems with the computer. When this occurs, people begin to question the company's ability not only to process their pay but also to conduct business generally.

In the design of this application, special attention must be given to the appearance of employee paychecks. The paycheck and voucher reflect a company's professionalism and responsibility to its employees. The voucher, in particular, should be easy to read and to understand; employees should not have to question how deductions were made. If some items appearing on the voucher need to be abbreviated, such as Earned Income Credit (EIC), the meaning of the abbreviation should be defined, perhaps on the reverse side of the voucher.

Besides appearance, special attention should be given to the distribution of signed paychecks. Many companies require that supervisors distribute paychecks at a designated time and place each week. This practice gives recognition to the importance of the paycheck. It provides supervisors with an opportunity to say thanks to their people for a job well done. It also provides employees the opportunity to examine their paychecks. If problems are discovered, they can be reported immediately.

More recently, many employees have indicated a preference for the direct deposit of their paychecks, to avoid trips to the bank and to ensure the timely deposit of check amounts. With this processing option, however, the check voucher must still be printed and distributed to the employee. The voucher tells the employee how gross pay and net pay were calculated and what amount was deposited.

After payroll processing is running smoothly, there may be some pressure to expand the application into a much larger, integrated, personnel-planning, payroll-processing design. These larger designs entail certain dangers, however. They tend to be more difficult to control and maintain, and, unless costed properly, they can make payroll processing overly expensive. A larger design means that more people are typically allowed online access to employee records. When this occurs, there is increased danger that some records will be incorrectly modified and that, as a consequence, some employees will not be paid.

With minor modifications to the design, several valuable by-products can be produced. Besides paychecks and payroll reports, several types of managerial summaries can be prepared. These summaries include labor-distribution breakdowns—labor costs by department, by plant, by type of position, by project, and so forth. Other summaries include wage and salary analyses—analyses of regular pay, overtime pay, sick leave, and vacation leave. Affirmative action reports can be produced from this application, as can seniority profiles. Collectively, these summaries and reports help explain how wages and salaries are increasing or decreasing, how labor costs are shifting (say, from one product line to another), how employee leave patterns are changing, and how employee productivity patterns are changing. These types of information help managers plan and control a most precious resource—the people employed by a business.

REVIEW QUESTIONS

14. What is labor distribution reporting? Why are labor distribution displays and reports prepared by a company?

15. What is job costing? Why is job costing a more complicated extension of payroll processing than labor distribution?

16. Describe one range test that is built into the program to enter hours worked. Describe one comparison test.

17. What advantages are associated with decentralized payroll processing?

18.   Why must companies exercise special caution when designing the employee payroll computer application?

REVIEW OF IMPORTANT IDEAS

There are special reasons for developing an online employee payroll computer application. Interactive steps simplify the adjustment of employee records, the entry and verification of hours-worked information, the retrieval of data stored on the employee master file, the addition of new employees to the master file, and the routine checking of processing controls. Interactive processing reduces interdepartmental conflicts—personnel and payroll staff groups become directly responsible for entering and verifying data related to their operations.

The employee master file must be fully updated prior to the entry of hours-worked information and the printing of employee paychecks. For new employees, personnel and payroll information must be added to the file. For existing employees, all personal, job, and pay changes must be made to employee records currently stored on file. This preliminary processing of the master file typically requires two interactive programs: one to ready the personnel portion of the file and another to ready the payroll portion of the file.

Hours-worked information must be entered into processing for each payroll run. The number of hours worked is either printed on time cards or entered directly into processing with badge-reading equipment. After hours-worked totals are verified, computer processing determines current employee gross pay, deductions from gross pay, net (take-home) pay, and YTD employee earnings and adds this information to an employee's record. The results of processing are printed on the payroll register, which shows net pay and how it was determined as well as the YTD totals updated by processing.

Employee paychecks, payroll journals, and periodic payroll reports are important products of this application. Employee paychecks are two-part forms showing net pay and how net pay was calculated. Payroll journals summarize payroll costs by department, job class, budget number, general ledger number, project number, or some other classification important to a company. Periodic reports include quarterly and year-end federal and state tax reports.

Labor distribution includes the analysis of hours-worked and payroll cost information. A labor distribution file, such as a project labor distribution file, is updated each time hours-worked and dollars-paid totals are approved. This secondary update provides a company with an accurate measurement of the hours required for different types of work activities. It helps determine if the costs of operations are increasing or decreasing relative to rates of production.

Job costing is the posting of labor hours and costs, machine hours and costs, and materials used and costs to a job-costing file. This extension of payroll processing helps managers identify total costs of each job undertaken. It permits faster response to cost-related problems.

Control of payroll processing is complicated because hours-worked totals must be transformed into dollars paid. Range and comparison testing and hand-checking of payroll totals are required for successful verification of the correctness of payroll processing.

KEY WORDS

Employee master file

Employee time cards

Payroll number

Employee number

Payroll register

Payroll journal

Leave and pension history

Ad hoc display

Employee change form

New employee forms

Payroll change form

Hours-worked register

Employee master register

Control proofs

Labor distribution

Job costing

EXERCISES

1. Suppose a company decides to stop printing paychecks and chooses instead to deposit all payroll funds directly into employee checking accounts. To activate the system, the employee leaves a blank deposit slip with the employer; the employer then uses the slip to append the bank deposit code to the employee number and to instruct the bank about the forthcoming direct deposit.

    (a) How does a direct-deposit system change the employee payroll system? (Modify Figure 9–1 in answering this question.)

    (b) Which computer programs are affected by a direct-deposit approach to processing? (See Figure 9–12.) Describe these changes.

    (c) What are the advantages and disadvantages of the direct-deposit employee payroll system?

2. Revise the data-flow diagram in Figure 9–2 to show how payroll is processed when employee identification badges are used to enter hours-worked information into processing.

3. Prepare a flowchart showing the steps associated with entering employee times directly into processing, using one-way data collection terminals. Show all inputs and outputs to processing, including all reference files and files updated directly. Then explain how a processing design would handle the following situations:

    (a) An employee enters a start time of work but fails to enter a stop time.

    (b) An employee works in an area lacking a data collection terminal.

    (c) A data collection terminal breaks down after several start times have been recorded.

    (d) A badge is too dirty to be read.

4. Prepare a flowchart showing the steps needed to reset the employee master file. Three different flowcharts are to be prepared. These should show

   (a) how the current portion of the payroll master file is reset to zero;

   (b) how the quarter-to-date portion of the payroll master file is reset to zero; and

   (c) how the year-to-date portion of the payroll master file is reset to zero.

   What reports must be prepared either before or after the file is reset?

5. You are asked to provide further information regarding the job-costing application.

   (a) Show how the following computer files are organized (list the data elements): equipment costing, material costing, labor hours worked, equipment hours worked, material units consumed, and job-costing master.

   (b) Design a job ledger display screen.

   (c) Design a job ledger printed report.

6. The Earned Income Credit (EIC) permits employees to receive additional income payments from their employers if their adjusted gross income is less than a prescribed ceiling. The EIC payment does not affect either the amount of income tax or the Social Security insurance paid by the employee, and it is not subject to any form of payroll tax. Finally, even though the EIC is paid to the employee by the employer, the federal government pays for the credit. In filing tax-withholding quarterly statements, employers subtract all EIC payments from total income tax and Social Security withheld.

   (a) How do EIC payments affect the employee payroll system? Trace through the system as described in the chapter to answer this question.

   (b) A set of tables supplied by the federal government is used in calculating EIC payments. For example, if a married employee is paid monthly and the amount of wages (before deducting for withholding allowances) is less than $454.00, the advance EIC payment is $39.00 less 10 percent of wages in excess of $454.00. There are separate tables for weekly, biweekly, semimonthly, quarterly, semiannual, and annual payroll periods. Each table contains single and married categories. Where would these tables be required in payroll processing?

DISCUSSION QUESTIONS

1. The development of the employee payroll application provides little, if any, cost savings. Even so, it is one of the first applications developed by a business. Explain why managers decide to implement this application early on in the development of computer-based applications. Give several reasons.

2. Why is it important to be able to display an employee's account? Give several reasons.

3. Select a local company and explain how that company can make use of labor distribution reporting.

4. Select another local company and explain how that company can make use of the job-costing application.

5. Show how the employee master file should be designed so that it can be used to prepare a weekly, bimonthly, and monthly payroll for a company. Would separate files be easier to manage? Discuss.

4-IN-1 CASE STUDY—EMPLOYEE PAYROLL

In this set of exercises using 4-in-1, you are asked to do several types of payroll processing tasks. These include the following:

- adding employees to the employee file
- printing the employee list
- processing the employee payroll
- printing the process employee transaction list
- printing employee paychecks
- posting payroll charges
- printing quarterly reports
- printing W-2 forms

Adding Employees to the Employee File

1. Log on and enter a date of **010197**. Press ENTER when asked, *Any change?*

2. From the main menu, type **18** and press ENTER.

3. When the maintain employee data submenu appears, type **1**, *Add employees*, and press ENTER.

4. Use the data shown in Figure 9–22 to complete the data-entry requirements. For the first employee, Ardith Monroe, type the name, address-1 and address-2, social security number, employee type (the choices are E = regular, N = non-employee, and T = terminated), and the W2 state. Next, accept the state ID number (the number assigned by the state to the employer) and the W2 local code (generally a city). Indicate that the company provides a pension and record the annual premium amount paid by the company for employee term life insurance. Finally, add the general ledger wage account number.

5. Press ENTER when asked, *Field number to change?*

```
┌─────────────────────────────────────────────────────────────┐
│                 A and J Enterprises Employee List             │
│    1  Employee name      Ardith Monroe         Frank Numashi   │
│                                                                │
│    2  Address-1          1655 Pearl St.        1403 Ridgeline Dr. │
│    3  Address-2          Springway OR 97000    Springway OR 97000 │
│                                                                │
│    4  Soc sec #          470-70-7777           570-60-6666      │
│                                                                │
│    5  Emp type           E                     E               │
│                                                                │
│    6  W2 state           OR                    OR              │
│    7  State ID #         95-555                95-555          │
│    8  W2 local code      7777                  7777            │
│    9  W2 pension         Y                     Y               │
│   10  W2 term prem       200                   200             │
│                                                                │
│   11  Wage acct #        8000-000              8200-000        │
└─────────────────────────────────────────────────────────────┘
```

Figure 9–22   New employee information

6. When the quarter-to-date (QTD) and year-to-date (YTD) screen appears, press F1 to set all totals to zero.

7. Press ENTER when asked, *Field number to change?*

8. Repeat steps 5 through 7 to add the second employee, Frank Numaski, to the employee file. Then return to the maintain employee submenu.

Printing the Employee List

With 4-in-1, an employee list can be printed to verify all employees on file.

9. From the maintain employee submenu, type **4** and press ENTER.

10. Press F1 twice and ENTER four times to complete the print instructions. Press ENTER when asked, *Field number to change?*

11. Press ENTER to print the report. Return to the main menu.

Processing the Employee Payroll

Once employees are added to the file, they can be paid.

12. From the main menu, type **19** and press ENTER to begin processing the payroll.

13. When the process payroll submenu appears, type **1** and press ENTER.

14. Press ENTER when asked to enter the checking account number. Press ENTER when payroll appears and you are asked, *Any change?*

15. Press F1 for the first employee. Press ENTER when asked, *Right employee?*

16. Type **C** for computer check and press ENTER.

17. Use the payroll information shown in Figure 9–23 to serve as a guide in completing the next twenty steps. Press ENTER after each step.

    a. Type **011597** for the check date.

    b. Type **1325** for the check amount.

Date 01/01/97   A and J Enterprises, Inc.   #0029 Page 0001
                    P A Y R O L L   T R A N S A C T I O N   E D I T   L I S T
Types: C = computer check   H = hand-written check   N = non-G/L   (historical only)

Employee-name			Soc-sec-#	Reference	
Check-#	Check-date	Type	Check-amt	PR-checking-acct	

Ardith Monroe			470-70-7777		
	01/15/97	C	1,325.00	PAYROLL	
Gross-pay	1,925.00	Tips	.00	SUI	100.00
Txbl-grs	1,925.00	Tip-cr	.00	SWT	100.00
FICA-grs	1,925.00	EIC	.00	OST	.00
FUI-grs	1,925.00	FWT	150.00	CWT	.00
SUI-grs	1,925.00	FICA	150.00	Othr-ded	200.00
OST-grs	.00	FUI	150.00		

Distributions: 8000-000   Sales & marketing wages   1,925.00
               6250-000   Employee Benefits   200.00

*** No check has been printed for this transaction***

Frank Numashi			570-60-6666		
	01/15/97	C	1,175.00	PAYROLL	
Gross-pay	1,600.00	Tips	.00	SUI	75.00
Txbl-grs	1,600.00	Tip-cr	.00	SWT	75.00
FICA-grs	1,600.00	EIC	.00	OST	.00
FUI-grs	1,600.00	FWT	125.00	CWT	.00
SUI-grs	1,600.00	FICA	125.00	Othr-ded	100.00
OST-grs	.00	FUI	75.00		

Distributions: 8200-000   Warehouse & shipping wages   1,600.00
               6250-000   Employee Benefits   100.00

*** No check has been printed for this transaction***

2 Transactions	Totals:	Check-amt	2,500.00	EIC	.00
		Gross-pay	3,525.00	FWT	275.00
		Txbl-grs	3,525.00	FICA	275.00
		FICA-grs	3,525.00	FUI	225.00
		FUI-grs	3,525.00	SUI	175.00
		SUI-grs	3,525.00	SWT	175.00
		OST-grs	.00	OST	.00
		Tips	.00	CWT	.00
		Tip-cr	.00	Othr-ded	300.00

Figure 9–23 Payroll information for two employees

c. Press ENTER for reference.

d. Type **1925** for gross pay.

e. Press F1 for taxable gross pay.

f. Press F1 for taxable FICA (social security).

g. Press F1 for taxable state unemployment.

h. Press F1 for taxable federal unemployment insurance.

i. Type **0** for other state tax.

j. Type **0** for tips.

k. Type **0** for tip credits.

l. Type **0** for EIC.

m. Type **150** for federal withholding tax.

n. Type **150** for FICA.

o. Type **150** for federal unemployment tax (the amount paid by the company).

p. Type **100** for state unemployment tax (the amount paid by the company).

q. Type **100** for state withholding tax.

r. Type **0** for other state taxes.

s. Type **0** for city withholding tax.

t. Type **200** for other deductions.

18. Press ENTER when asked, *Any change?*

19. When asked to distribute wages, type **w** for wages and press F1 twice to distribute the entire wage to sales and marketing. Press ENTER when asked, *Any change?*

20. Type **d** to distribute deductions.

21. Type **6250** for the general ledger account. Press F1 to distribute the full amount.

22. Press ENTER when asked, *Any change?* Press TAB to exit.

23. Press F1 to begin the processing of Frank Numashi's check. Use the payroll data in Figure 9–23 to complete this transaction. When you have finished, press TAB to return to the process payroll submenu.

Printing the Process Payroll Transaction List

Figure 9–23 shows the first page of the payroll transaction list.

24. Type **4** and press ENTER from the process payroll submenu.

25. Press ENTER when asked *Display this report?*

Printing Employee Paychecks

With 4-in-1, paychecks can be printed on custom forms or on regular paper (even if they appear incomplete).

26. Type **5** and press ENTER from the process payroll submenu to print payroll checks.

27. Press ENTER for checking account 2.

28. Type **1000** and press ENTER for the starting check number.

29. Press F1 twice. Press ENTER when asked, *Field to change?*

30. Type **done** and press ENTER. Press ENTER when asked *Print form alignment?* After this step, checks will be printed.

31. Type **done** again and press ENTER after checks are printed.

32. Press TAB until you log off 4-in-1. After logging off, you are asked to log on again using a new date.

Posting Payroll Charges

33. Log on and enter a date of **011597**. Press ENTER when asked *Any change?*

34. Type **19** and press ENTER.

35. When the process payroll submenu appears, type **6** and press ENTER to post transactions.

36. Make sure your printer is turned on. Type **y** when asked, *OK to post?* The payroll transaction register will be printed.

37. Press TAB to return to the main menu.

Printing Quarterly Reports

Even though this is not the quarter end, 4-in-1 can produce quarterly payroll reports.

38. Type **21** from the main menu.

39. When the quarter-end payroll procedures menu appears, type **1**, *Print quarterly payroll report*. Press ENTER.

40. For state ID, press F1. Press ENTER when asked, *Any change?*

41. Press ENTER to print the report.

Printing W-2 Forms

Even though this is not year end, 4-in-1 can be used to print W-2 reports.

42. Type **3** from the quarter-end payroll procedures submenu.

43. Press ENTER twice to select the defaults on the W2 submenu display. Press ENTER when asked, *Field number to change?*

44. Type **done** even though you plan to use computer stock paper.

45. Make sure your printer is turned on. Press ENTER when asked, *Print form alignment?* The W-2 slips will be printed.

46. Type **y** followed by **done** to complete this procedure.

47. Type TAB twice to exit.

QUESTIONS

1. What is the value of the employee list?

2. Compare the payroll transaction edit list to the payroll transaction register. In what ways are they similar? How do they differ?

3. Examine the quarterly payroll report. What is the purpose of this document?

4. What is the purpose of the W-2 slip?

5. This application requires the user to undertake considerable work before entering payroll figures into processing. Even then, the computer is very valuable. Summarize the value of this application.

PART

IV

MATERIALS CONTROL
APPLICATIONS

In this three-chapter section, we will examine applications that stress ways to improve materials management. We begin with the order entry application, an application designed to process and speed the filling of customer orders. An important objective of this application is to provide fast response to customer orders for goods and services. Next, we look at an inventory control application developed, in part, to keep track of all goods stored in inventory and, in part, to help determine proper inventory stocking levels. We then finish this section with a two-stage purchasing and receiving application. This application is designed to process purchase orders and to verify the receipt of goods from suppliers. The objective in this instance is the development of formal processing procedures for reordering and accepting goods into stock.

Of the three materials control applications, we will examine the second, finished-goods inventory, in most detail. It is this application that must balance the demand for inventory (which is recorded by the processing of customer orders) with its supply (which is regulated by the purchasing of additional goods from suppliers). This application most clearly demonstrates the value of improved materials control.

10

Customer Order Entry

Customer order entry is an application that businesses use to reduce the time between the receipt of a customer order, the processing and filling of the order, and the shipment of goods. By quickly translating a customer's order for goods and services into instructions for filling the order from stock, the application provides the capability to improve order turnaround. Businesses have come to rely on fast turnaround as an important part of their customer service programs. With help from the order-entry application, they are able to promise the customer same day service in filling requests for goods and services. Because the application deals in large part with the filling of customer orders, it is often called *order filling*. The name is somewhat misleading, however, because order entry actually includes three types of processing activities: order processing, order filling, and order packing and shipping.

- *Order processing* checks the correctness of the customer order, including the verification of each customer's credit. It requires maintaining the customer master file.

- *Order filling* shows how the items ordered are to be picked from inventory. It requires maintaining the product master file and verifying that stock is carried in inventory.

- *Order packing and shipping* leads to the printing of packing slips and bills of lading. It creates summary file records required in billing customers for goods shipped.

These three sets of activities make customer order entry a complex data-processing application. Fortunately, it is also one of the more valuable applications developed for business.

Online customer order entry is required by companies that process hundreds of customer orders daily and warehouse and distribute large quantities of stock carried in *finished-goods inventory* (inventory that is ready for sale). These companies often must stock thousands of items and maintain thousands of square feet of warehouse space. Very large distributors, for example, with a large customer base, might sell to 20,000 customers, carry 50,000 products in stock, and maintain 100,000 square feet of warehouse space. From an administrative point of view, the key to managing this complex environment is an automated system that moves orders in and goods out as accurately and efficiently as possible. With online processing, for instance, orders received before two o'clock in the afternoon can be packed and shipped before five o'clock the same day. In addition to prompt service, the order is filled and shipped correctly: the customer receives the correct quantity, size runs, and colors, and the merchandise is shipped to the correct customer and the correct address.

There are other reasons for developing this application besides providing faster and more accurate customer order processing. Three of these reasons follow:

- Order entry simplifies order processing. One of the most difficult aspects of processing customer orders is keeping track of all orders, customers, and products—each order to be filled, each filled order, each customer account, each product account, each product location, and the stock carried at each location. With online processing, the computer keeps track of all of this information.

- Order entry standardizes customer and product inventory records. With standard records, it becomes possible to undertake different types of customer and product analyses. *Customer analyses* deal with the study of customer buying habits, whereas *product analyses* deal with the study of product demand. Understanding the characteristics of both is vital to the management of business firms.

- Order entry integrates administrative and operational groups in an organization. An administrative group—the group of people who keep the records and process the paperwork in a business—is commonly referred to as a "white collar group." An operations group—the people who run the machines and operate the warehouse or plant—represents a "blue collar" group. For this application, order processing is performed by an administrative group, and order filling and shipping are performed by an operations group. With online processing, the computer is better able to integrate the work of both groups.

Compared to a batch design, an online design of processing offers a number of important advantages. It can simplify edit and file-update procedures, improve account inquiry capabilities, reduce clerical costs, improve processing controls, and decentralize data-processing activities. Like the receivables design, an online design builds checks and balances into the interactive portion of processing. These help verify that each customer order is processed correctly.

10-1   PRELIMINARY OVERVIEW OF PROCESSING

Figure 10–1 provides a preliminary overview of order-entry processing. The processing cycle begins with a customer order. Once the order is approved (that is, it is found to be acceptable), a picking slip is printed and sent to the warehouse. A *picking slip* shows what items are ordered, where they are located in the warehouse, and in which sequence the items should be picked from stock. Once the items shown on the picking slip have been successfully picked, the results are fed back into the order-entry system. The system is required to produce three types of output: a packing slip, a bill of lading, and a shipping summary. As with invoicing, a packing slip and a bill of lading show what items were ordered, packed, and shipped. Shipping summary information provides the same information, but in a form that can be directly used by the customer-invoicing application.

Figure 10–2 shows the two main parts of the order entry system. The first part is *Process customer order*. Once an order is approved, it is placed on a customer order transaction file. The file contains *current orders*, that is, orders to be filled next in the order-processing system. The other possibility is to place the order on a future order and back order file. A *future order* is one held to be filled at a later date, as specified by the customer. A *back order* is one that cannot be filled because of insufficient stock. Both future and back orders are known as *pending orders*: they will become current orders pending some future instruction.

The second part of the system, *Ship customer order*, is triggered by the receipt of picked results, recorded on a picking slip. Once received, the normal procedure is to remove the current order from the customer order transaction file and then to print the packing slip, the bill of lading, and the shipping summary. An exception procedure occurs when only part of the order can be filled (even though picking instructions stated that the entire order was to be filled). In this instance, the current order is removed from the customer order transaction file, and shipping documents

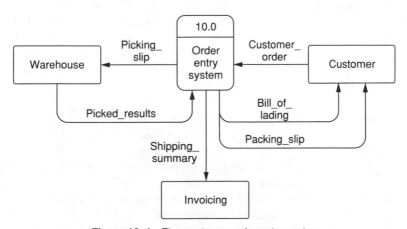

Figure 10–1   The customer order-entry system

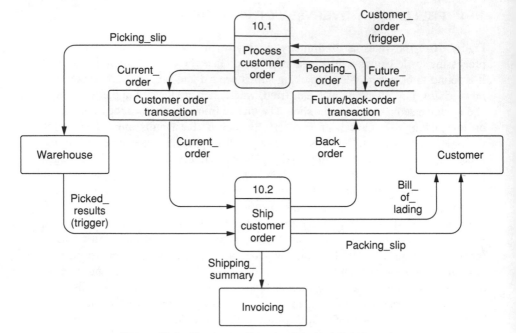

Figure 10–2   The two main parts of the order-entry system

are produced for goods picked. For goods that cannot be picked, a back order must be created and stored on the future/back order transaction file.

Processing Customer Orders

As shown in Figure 10–3, the first step in processing customer orders is the function *Enter customer orders*. This function records what items are ordered by a customer, determines if each line item contained on the order can be filled from stock, and determines how best to pick the items from stock. The main input is the customer order. As Figure 10–4 illustrates, a *customer order* can look quite different from either a customer invoice or a shipping document. Close inspection shows, however, that the customer order form contains the same types of information as a customer invoice.

- *Order information* identifies the customer account number (if one exists), the customer P.O. number (when appropriate), the date, and the method of payment.
- *Packing information* identifies each product or catalog number, the quantity ordered, and the method of shipment.
- *Billing information* provides the customer name and address and (when appropriate) the salesperson/distributor codes.
- *Product information* provides the product name, product description, and pricing and discount information.

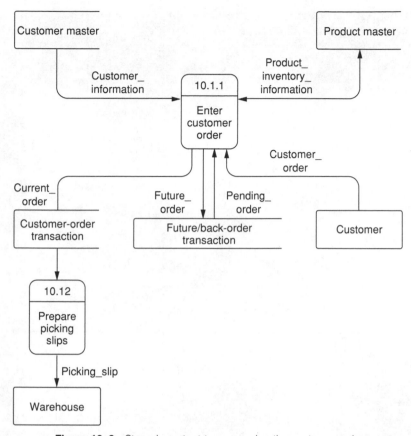

Figure 10–3   Steps important to processing the customer order

With these four types, the only other information needed is *business order information*, namely the number assigned by a business to a customer's order.

Figure 10–5 shows how these types of data are brought together in processing and how a customer order is entered into processing. Keyed data consist of the assigned business order number and record code, order information, and packing information. Data-entry requirements are thus similar but not identical to those for invoicing. With order entry, a business determines the method of payment *prior* to the actual shipment of goods. Likewise, the order fill date allows the customer to specify in advance when goods should be packed and shipped: today, as soon as possible (ASAP), and so forth.

Information stored on master files and brought into processing consist of customer and product details. As Figure 10-5 shows, customer records for order entry are the same as customer records for invoicing. Product records, in contrast, must be enlarged by the addition of two new record segments: product inventory and product location. The *product inventory segment* is required to store four types of counts and the "estimated date of delivery of new stock." The difference between these four counts of inventory can be explained as follows:

PLEASE FILL OUT THIS ORDER FORM CAREFULLY.
ERRORS WILL CAUSE A DELAY IN PROCESSING YOUR ORDER.

IN A HURRY? PHONE IN
YOUR ORDER - 800/258-1710

Customer Contact
ALAN L. ELIASON

Phone Number
345 - 2005

Date
JUNE 21, 19XX

BILLING ADDRESS:

COMPANY: ELIASON and ASSOCIATES
DEPT/ATTN: SOFTWARE DEVELOPMENT
STREET: 2520 CHARNELTON
CITY: EUGENE   STATE: OR   ZIP: 97405

Purchase Order No.
9432

Partial Shipment Allowed?
☒ YES   ☐ NO

SHIPPING ADDRESS:

COMPANY: ELIASON and ASSOCIATES
DEPT/ATTN: BILLING DEPARTMENT
STREET: 2520 CHARNELTON
CITY: EUGENE   STATE: OR   ZIP: 97405

Special Instructions:

Taxable: ☐ YES   ☐ NO
Tax Bond or
Exempt No. (if applicable):

Delivery Requirement:
☒ ASAP

☐ Not Before:

Digital Intransit Insurance?
(50¢ per $100 Order Value)
☒ YES   ☐ NO

Order Item No.	DECdirect Ordering No.	Page Number	Quantity	Unit Price	Extended Amount
1	F- VT 18X – AC	64	1	2,400.00	2,400.00
2	F- QV001 – C2	64	1	250.00	250.00
3	F-				
4	F-				
5	F-				
6	F-				
7	F-				

Sub-Total 2,650.00
Discount −132.50
Tax —
Total 2,517.50

METHOD OF PAYMENT
Cash/Money Order or Charge Card required on all orders less than $35.00*.

Make checks payable to DIGITAL EQUIPMENT CORP.

Invoice upon shipment __X__
Check/Money Order with order _____
Master Card _____ Visa _____
    Charge Card Account No _____
    Card Assignee _____
    Expiration Date _____

MAIL ORDER TO:
DIGITAL EQUIPMENT CORP.
P.O. BOX CS2008
NASHUA, NH 03061

By executing this order, I acknowledge that I have read, understood and accept the terms and conditions on the reverse side of this order form.

Alan L. Eliason
Authorized Signature   Date

← Please Sign Here

*Puerto Rico customers: Orders less than $35.00 must be placed at the Digital facility (809) 754-7575.

Figure 10–4 Customer order form

- *Quantity on hand* is the count (the quantity) of finished goods carried in stock (on hand) and available for sale.
- *Quantity on order* is the count of stock previously ordered by a business but not yet delivered.
- *Quantity on back order* is the count of stock needed to fill customer orders that for lack of stock were not filled earlier.
- *Quantity on future order* is the count of stock needed to fill customer orders that specify delivery at a future date.

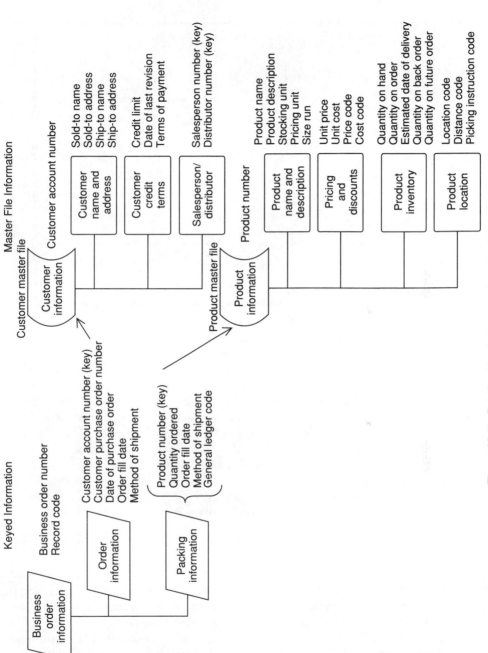

Figure 10–5 Relationships between order-entry data sets

XYZ Company

PICKING TICKET

| Order-#: | 102 | Order-date: 03/10/99 | | Warehouse: 1 Main |

| Sold-to: | Neptune Underwater Supply
345 Fisherman's Pier
Santa Marina, CA 91100 | | Ship-to: | Neptune Underwater Supply
1550 S. Coastline Blvd.
Refugio Beach, CA
91809 |

| Cust-#: 100 | P.O.#: 10537 | Terms: Net 30 | | Sales rep: 23 |

| Ship-via: Air freight | Date-to-ship: 03/16/99 | | Date-shipped: _____ |

| Loc
Line-# | Item-#
Description-1
Description-2 | | Qty
Ordered | Unit | Qty
To-ship | Qty
Shipped |

| 21
001 | 4
Saw, 2hp 7 1/4" Circular | | 10 EACH | | 10 _____ |

| 1 Line item | | Total quantity: | | 10 _____ |

Figure 10–6   A picking slip

The *product location segment* stores codes to tell where stock is located in the warehouse and provides picking instructions. For example, B-6543, a bin location code, means that stock is located in row B, bin number 6543. A distance code of D83-954 states that bin B-6543 is 83 feet from a main traffic aisle, which, in turn, is 954 feet from the main packing area. Last, a packing instruction code tells order pickers how stock is to be drawn. Code AAA might indicate that a package in a bin cannot be opened, whereas code AAP might mean just the reverse.

Once the current order is completed and added to the customer order transaction file, picking slips can be prepared (see Figure 10–6). *Picking slips* (or *tickets*) tell the warehouse crew what items have been ordered, the quantity ordered, where it is located in the warehouse, and in what sequence it should be picked from stock.

Shipping Customer Orders

Figure 10–7 depicts the steps in processing once the customer order is received from the warehouse. The two inputs to processing are items picked and items short. This second input represents items that could not be picked because of a shortage of stock. When items are short, the customer order must be adjusted, which is a two-step update. First, the current order stored on the customer order transaction file must be modified to show the difference between the quantity ordered and the quantity picked. Second, the future/back order transaction file must be modified. This time the difference between the quantity ordered and the quantity shipped must be added as a back order.

Once all adjustments are made, the normal outputs of processing, the packing slips, bill of lading, and the shipping summary, can be prepared. As Figure 10–7 shows, inputs are limited to items-picked information and the current order.

Although the customer invoice could also be produced during step 10.2.2, there are several reasons why it is not. First, invoices are always sent to the sold-to address, not the ship-to address. With larger businesses, these two addresses often differ. Second, packing slips and bills of lading often become soiled in the course of a shipment's movement through the warehouse and the loading dock. It might be acceptable for these documents to be difficult to read, but it is not acceptable for an invoice to be difficult to read. Third, many business firms enclose merchandising literature with their invoices. An insert describing a special sale of office supplies might be included with a bill, for example. It is assumed that the people paying the bill will be interested in "special sale" literature or will pass it to the appropriate people in their organization.

Printed outputs other than those shown on the data-flow diagrams include three registers, three change reports, and a variety of processing summaries. The register of most interest is the *open-order register*, which lists all orders to be filled. The *daily order-filling report*, in contrast, lists all orders filled during the day. Open-order information is combined with orders-filled information to calculate the *order-fill rate*, which is computed as follows:

$$\text{Order-fill rate} = \frac{\text{Orders filled}}{\text{Open orders}}$$

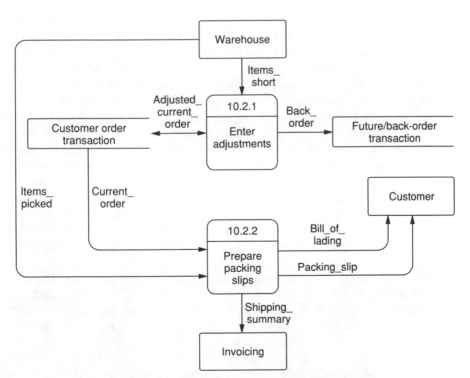

Figure 10–7   Steps important to shipping the customer order

Accurate and efficient order processing leads to order-fill rates in excess of 95 percent. This means that if 100 orders are open during the day, ninety-five or more will be filled and shipped the same day.

REVIEW QUESTIONS

1. What are the main reasons for developing the customer order-entry application?

2. What are the benefits of an interactive approach to processing?

3. What are the main inputs to the customer order-entry application? What are the main outputs?

4. Which file links the process customer order section of the order-entry system with the ship customer order section?

5. How does the product master file differ from customer invoicing in terms of makeup?

6. What is the order-fill rate? Why is a high rate desired?

10-2   ORDER-ENTRY PROCESSING

Parts (a) and (b) of Figure 10–8 show the system organization chart for customer order entry. The *Enter customer orders* program builds a *customer-order transaction file*, transaction by transaction. Three interactive programs also update or adjust computer files. They ready the customer master file and the product master file and adjust the orders stored on the customer order and the future/back order file. The need to update and adjust results from a variety of situations (for example, the customer decides to cancel an order, to increase the quantity to order, to change the ship-to location, or to change the order-fill date). Likewise, internal business adjustments, such as changing the quantity-shipped total, canceling a line item on an order, or substituting one product for another, must be made. Finally, three display programs are indicated. The *Display customer order* program permits a company to track each unfilled order. Should a customer question whether an order has been filled, the answer can be determined in seconds. The *Display customer account* program provides direct access to each customer account. The *Display product account* program also permits direct access. This display permits the status of each product carried in inventory to be reviewed.

The batch portion of the application consists of eleven print programs. The print requirements for registers and change reports show what types of online files are maintained in processing. For example, since the records of the customer master file can be modified online, a copy of the file (the customer master file register) and all changes made to the file (the customer change report) must be printed. In addition to registers and change reports, the two transaction documents printed are picking slips and packing slips. Several processing summaries are also included in

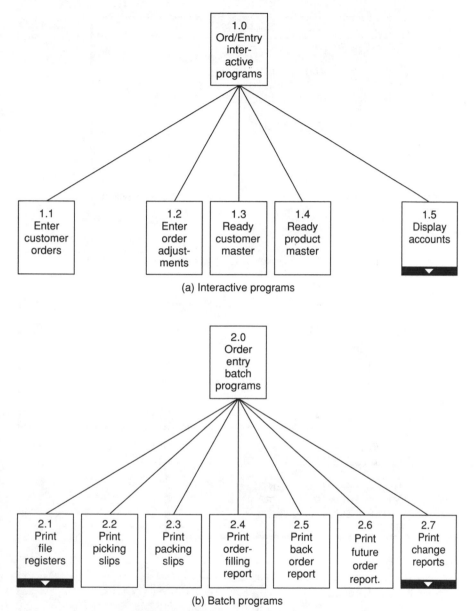

(a) Interactive programs

(b) Batch programs

Figure 10–8 Systems organization chart

the design. These lead to a future order report, a back order report, and a daily order-filling report.

Figure 10–9(a) and (b) show the program menus that follow from the chart of organization. The seven interactive and eleven batch programs make order entry one of the larger computer applications.

```
┌──────────────────────────────────────┐
│  CUSTOMER ORDER ENTRY        │        │
│                              └────────│
│        ENTER CUSTOMER ORDERS          │
│        READY CUSTOMER MASTER          │
│        READY PRODUCT MASTER           │
│        DISPLAY CUSTOMER ACCOUNT        │
│        DISPLAY PRODUCT ACCOUNT         │
│        DISPLAY CUSTOMER ORDER          │
│                                        │
│                                        │
│        RETURN                          │
└──────────────────────────────────────┘
```

(a) Interactive menu choices

```
┌──────────────────────────────────────┐
│     CUSTOMER ORDER ENTRY     │        │
│                              └────────│
│          PRINT PICKING SLIPS          │
│          PRINT PACKING SLIPS          │
│          PRINT ORDER-FILLING REPORT   │
│          PRINT BACK-ORDER REPORT      │
│          PRINT FUTURE-ORDER REPORT    │
│          PRINT REGISTERS              │
│          PRINT CHANGE REPORTS         │
│          RETURN                       │
│                                        │
└──────────────────────────────────────┘
```

```
┌──────────────────────────────────────┐
│ CUSTOMER ORDER ENTRY          │       │
│                               └───────│
│      PRINT ORDER ADJUSTMENTS          │
│      PRINT CUSTOMER CHANGES           │
│      PRINT PRODUCT CHANGES            │
│      RETURN                           │
└──────────────────────────────────────┘
```

```
┌──────────────────────────────────────┐
│     CUSTOMER ORDER ENTRY      │       │
│                               └───────│
│        PRINT OPEN-ORDER REGISTER      │
│        PRINT CUSTOMER REGISTER        │
│        PRINT PRODUCT REGISTER         │
│        RETURN                         │
└──────────────────────────────────────┘
```

(b) Batch menu choices

Figure 10–9   Program menus

The *Ready customer master file* Program

Before customer orders can be processed, both the customer and the product master files must be current. The source documents used in updating the customer master file are the new customer form and the customer change form. The *new customer form* is completed in large part by the customer or the salesperson assigned to the customer's account. An important field completed by the credit department of a business is the customer's credit rating. Two or more credit references are generally obtained, one from the customer's bank and one from a credit-rating service such as Dun and Bradstreet. A credit-rating service estimates the financial strength of a customer and provides a composite credit appraisal. When the credit rating for a customer is low, credit managers usually require a more detailed credit report that documents specific financial activities, such as the customer's payment history.

The *customer change display* contains less information than the new customer form. It is used to revise information stored on file about the customer. Figure 10–10 illustrates a display page for revising a customer's account. To begin processing, the operator must enter the customer account number. Following input, the computer locates the customer's account and displays the customer name and stored record. After visual verification of the name, the operator enters the number of a field to be changed. If the number five is entered, for example, the cursor moves to the credit limit field. Directional keys are also used to move from one field to another.

Often changes made to the customer master file are made immediately before the entry of the customer's order. Consider the following example. Instead of sending an order by mail, a customer decides to place a direct order by telephone. On receiving the call, the order taker asks for the customer's account number, and the customer responds, "612554." The order taker keys in the account number to display the sold-to and ship-to names and addresses and asks the customer to verify each name and address. The customer replies, "We have made a change in our sold-to street address. Our new address is 3564 Cardinalle Road."

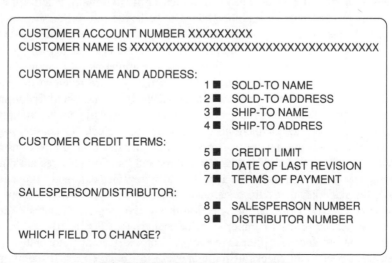

```
CUSTOMER ACCOUNT NUMBER XXXXXXXXX
CUSTOMER NAME IS XXXXXXXXXXXXXXXXXXXXXXXXXXXXXXXXXXXXXX

CUSTOMER NAME AND ADDRESS:
                                 1 ■   SOLD-TO NAME
                                 2 ■   SOLD-TO ADDRESS
                                 3 ■   SHIP-TO NAME
                                 4 ■   SHIP-TO ADDRES
CUSTOMER CREDIT TERMS:
                                 5 ■   CREDIT LIMIT
                                 6 ■   DATE OF LAST REVISION
                                 7 ■   TERMS OF PAYMENT
SALESPERSON/DISTRIBUTOR:
                                 8 ■   SALESPERSON NUMBER
                                 9 ■   DISTRIBUTOR NUMBER
WHICH FIELD TO CHANGE?
```

Figure 10–10   Customer change display

In such a situation, one interactive program rather than two could be used to change the customer master and to process the details of the customer order. There are two good reasons for using separate programs, however. First, any change to the customer master file must be carefully documented. All changes to the customer master file, for example, are written to a customer change file; later, the contents of the change file are printed to produce a customer change register. Second, using separate programs means that changes to the customer master file can be made in advance of processing the customer order. Most companies ask their customers to record name-and-address changes on customer order forms. This change information must be processed before beginning to key-enter the customer's order.

The *Ready product master file* Program

The product master file must also be made ready in advance of order processing. Although this procedure resembles that used to ready the customer file, it is not identical. The documents used to record changes to the product master file are the new product form and product change forms. New product forms are required for all new or improved products carried in inventory. An improved product, for example, might be the second edition of a textbook. This product would be assigned a unique product number. Considerably more new products are added to inventory than most people expect: it is not unusual for a business to replace 20 to 25 percent of the items carried in stock each year with new or improved items. For each addition, a product number must be assigned. Following this, product name and description, pricing and discounts, product inventory, and product location information must be keyed into processing.

Product change forms, in contrast to the new product form, generally contain a minimal amount of information. They are used to show new product prices and discounts, additions to inventory, and changes in product location. Figure 10–11 illustrates a "notice of cost change" form. This form, like many others, provides room for the product number and the change to be keyed into processing.

Product changes must always be completed before customer order processing begins. The objective is to make the product master file consistent with the latest changes in the warehouse. As might be expected, completing all changes on time tends to be difficult when large shipments of new stock are received or when a major reorganization of the warehouse is undertaken. It is common to find terminal operators making changes to the product master file as early as six o'clock in the morning, in order to complete all changes by ten o'clock. Generally, pricing and discount changes are entered into processing first. Later, after stock has been received, counted, and stored, product inventory and location changes are made.

Making changes of one kind, one after another, simplifies data-entry procedures. Suppose, for example, that only price changes are to be made. After the operator selects "price change" from the file selection menu, the program displays a *change table*, which lists by product number all price changes (see Figure 10–12). In some cases, both the old and new prices are shown to provide the operator with a point of reference. Special edit checks help the operator to isolate errors. If the old price is $6.99 and the new price is $79.90, the computer will respond with:

NOTICE OF COST CHANGE

BRANCH _____WESTFIR_____

DATE _____04 - 08 - 9X_____

_____Martin A. Mitchell_____
Signed

_____Helen Matthews_____
Approved

PRODUCT NUMBER	NEW COST
22222	7.90
36859	11.46
89734	19.13

Figure 10–11   A product change form: notice of cost change

THE PRICE DIFFERENCE IS TOO GREAT.
    PLEASE VERIFY.

Entering the different types of changes separately makes it easier to spot and correct input errors and clerical mistakes. For example, since all changes to the product master file are displayed, a visual review can be made easily. Only after

PRODUCT NUMBER	NEW PRICE	OLD PRICE
22222	8.99	8.49
36859	12.22	11.98
89734	44.46	24.46

THE PRICE DIFFERENCE IS TOO GREAT.
.PLEASE VERIFY.

Figure 10–12   Price change table

changes are visually reviewed and approved is the file updated, with changes written to the product change file. This change file must be sorted by type of change before the change report is printed; otherwise, the report will list the first change entered into processing, the second change entered into processing, and so forth, regardless of the type of change (price, cost, quantity, or location). The way around this problem is to enter all price changes at one time, followed by all cost changes, and so on. In this way, the change report will list all price changes followed by all cost changes.

The *Enter customer orders* Program

After all customer and product changes have been completed, customer order information is entered into processing (see Figure 10–13). As with invoicing, the customer master file serves as a reference file. Customer information, such as sold-to and ship-to addresses, is read into processing and added to the customer order record. The product master file, in addition to serving as a reference file, is updated by processing. The actual update is simple: the field for on-hand quantity is changed to correspond to the quantity ordered by the customer. If, for example, the on-hand field shows 100 units and the customer orders 10, then 10 units are transferred to the customer order record and the on-hand field is reduced to show a remaining balance of 90 units.

Inputs to customer order processing include customer returns as well as new and pending orders. As a general rule, all customer returns are processed before orders because returns add units to quantity-on-hand totals. Following the processing of customer returns, different types of customer orders are processed; these include preshipped orders, future orders, back orders, and current orders.

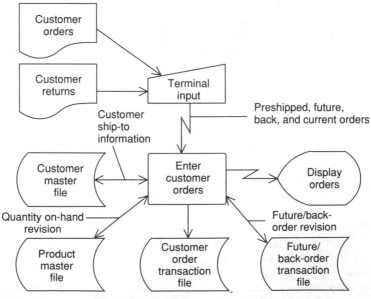

Figure 10–13   Enter customer orders

Preshipped orders consist of orders for which stock has been picked from inventory in advance of processing. Such orders are ill-advised in an automated order-entry system: every preshipment violates the objective of keeping the product master file accurate. There are times, however, when preshipped orders cannot be avoided. Suppose the president of the company decides to give away six dozen shirts or a rush order is received while the computer is being serviced. These situations lead to preshipped orders.

Future orders consist of orders that have been held to be filled according to a customer's request for a shipment on a specific future date. Processing future orders requires that a file be checked daily to determine which ones should be filled. As Figure 10–13 shows, future orders are stored in the future/back order transaction file. In processing, each order-fill date is compared with the current date; if the dates match and adequate stock is on hand, the order is scheduled for picking.

Back orders are also reviewed daily to determine which orders, if any, can be filled. The computer is instructed to compare back order requirements to the latest version of the product master file. If an order can be filled, it is written to the customer order file. The back order, in turn, is deleted from the back order file.

Current orders are orders received for the first time. Generally, they are filled after preshipped, future, and back orders have been processed. In processing, the customer account is initially verified and customer information is added to the customer order transaction. Following customer verification, the order-fill date is checked to determine if the order (or some part of the order) should be filled as soon as possible or at some future date. When the order is to be filled as soon as possible, product information is verified, the field for on-hand quantity of the product record is updated, product information is transferred to the customer order file, and the completed transaction is written to the customer order file. When the order is to be filled at some future date, product information is verified and transferred; however, the product master file is not updated. Instead, the now-verified order is written to the future/back order transaction file. Back orders work much the same. If the order cannot be filled, product information is verified and transferred; however, the product file is not updated. Rather, the order is written to the future/back order transaction file as a verified back order.

The *Print picking document* Program

Picking slips are printed following the entry of customer orders into processing. As Figure 10–14 shows, the program to print packing slips may be preceded by a sort program that sequences the items in each customer order by bin (or warehouse) location code. Suppose, for example, that business order 6345 contains three items. If the order were not properly sequenced, an order picker might walk to the back of the warehouse to pick the first item, then to the front to pick the second item, then again to the back to pick the third item. To avoid such an inefficient situation, the computer sequences the items to be picked to *minimize travel time*. Thus, in our example, a computer sort would sequence the order so that the first and third items located at the back of the warehouse would be picked first, followed by the second item at the front of the building.

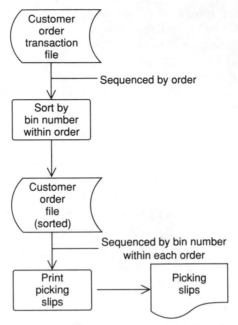

Figure 10–14   The program to print picking slips

A time-consuming sort of the entire customer order file can be avoided if the picking order is sequenced before writing the order to the customer order file. The program to enter customer orders is designed to manage a table of the items to be ordered and their locations. After the final item is entered, the computer identifies the most efficient picking route and, following this route, writes the order—line item by line item—to the customer order file.

The *Customer order adjustments* Program

Adjustments must be made to the customer order file to resolve any differences between items indicated by the computer as held in stock and items actually picked. The flowchart in Figure 10–15 shows this interactive routine. Typically, a member of the warehouse office staff prepares adjustment slips and enters adjustment data into processing; this practice avoids sending all paperwork to a centralized order-entry staff. The entry of adjustments updates the customer order and future/back order file directly. As with other interactive programs, all changes are recorded on a separate file for later printing and review.

Only limited types of adjustments are permitted at this late stage in processing. It is possible, for example, to change the quantity-picked figure or to adjust the shipping and insurance charges. Other adjustments, however, such as entering different product account numbers, product location codes, on-hand quantities, and so forth, are never made part of the adjustment program. Problems such as an incorrect count of inventory require different business procedures. (In the next

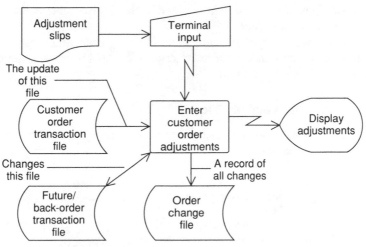

Figure 10–15   Enter customer order adjustments

chapter we will examine the online application to assist in the management and control of inventory.)

Before a quantity-picked adjustment is made, the decision of whether to back order or cancel the difference must be made. If the difference is canceled, processing is straightforward: the customer order is revised. If the difference is to be treated as a back order, however, processing becomes more complex. In this case, the customer order must be revised, and the back order file must be updated. As might be expected, there are alternate ways of handling back orders. The back order file can be updated as part of the adjustments program, or it can be updated during the printing of the order-change report.

The adjustments program performs one more task other than changing order-picked totals: it posts shipping weight and charges and insurance charges to the customer order file. This information cannot be determined until goods are packed and made ready for shipment. Whenever possible, however, tables of shipping and insurance charges should be built into the adjustments program. Then only the actual shipping weight remains to be keyed into processing; table look-up procedures determine actual shipping and insurance costs.

The *Print packing slip* Program

After the customer-order transaction file is adjusted, packing slips are printed and summary information needed to bill the customer is written to an invoice transaction file. As with the entry of adjustments, processing is monitored by a member of the warehouse staff, who loads a remote printer with packing slips and initiates printing. The adjusting of orders and the printing of packing slips close to the area where they are needed illustrate two key features of online systems: the ability of individuals to communicate directly with the computer from remote locations and the capability to distribute the authority for processing. These concepts of *remote job entry* and *distributed data processing* are highly visible in the customer order-entry computer application.

It should be clear that the packing slip program does little more than use the contents of the customer order transaction file. At this point in processing, adjustments should not be required.

Customer Order Transaction File

The actual layout of the customer order transaction file is highly similar to the layout of the customer invoice transaction file produced by the packing-slip program. As

```
Business order number (invoice number)
Record code
Date of business order
Customer account number
       Customer sold-to name
       Customer sold-to address
       Customer ship-to name
       Customer ship-to address
       Credit limit
       Date of last revision
       Terms of payment
       Salesperson number
       Distributor number
Customer purchase order number
Date of purchase order
Method of payment

    Product number (1)
           Product name
           Product description
           Unit of measure
           Size run
           Unit price
           Unit cost
           Quantity discount
           Location code
           Distance from packing room
           Packing-instruction code
    Quantity ordered
    Quantity shipped
    Quantity back ordered
    Quantity canceled

Order-fill date
Date of shipment
Method of shipment
Shipping weight
Freight charge
Insurance charge
General ledger number
```

Figure 10–16 Customer order transaction file

Figure 10–16 shows, each record in the file contains business order, customer, product, and packing and shipping information. Indeed, the order transaction file differs from the invoice transaction file only in the following ways:

- Each customer order transaction record begins with a business order number.

- Each record contains product location data (bin location, picking instructions, and so forth) that are not needed when processing the customer invoice.

- Each record contains an order-fill date and the method of shipment desired by the customer—items that may or may not be placed on the invoice. Records *do not* contain line item charges or the total invoice charge. These financial totals are computed during the processing of invoices.

Because these differences are minor, the customer order and the customer invoice transaction files should be designed at the same time, even if only one application is to be implemented. Suppose, for example, that a business decides first to design a customer-invoicing computer application, to be followed by the more complicated order-entry application. The chances are that if a business designs the invoicing file without considering the layout of the customer order file, it will be forced to redesign the invoicing file when thinking about order entry.

Even though order transaction records vary in length, an indexed sequential or relational method of file organization is recommended. The organization should permit direct access to customer orders so that orders can be examined and, if necessary, adjusted. Business order numbers are the primary keys when the file is organized to permit direct access. In addition, some order-entry systems maintain secondary key indexes to permit the retrieval of records by customer or by product number. Multikey retrieval simplifies locating a record on the customer order transaction file.

REVIEW QUESTIONS

7. Why must master files be current before customer orders are processed?

8. Why is one computer program required for changing the customer master file and another required for processing a customer order when all processing could be done using a single computer program?

9. Why are change tables recommended in making changes to the product master file?

10. What are the differences between preshipped orders, future orders, back orders, and current orders?

11. What objective is sought by programming the computer to specify how orders should be picked from stock?

12. What information may be changed by the customer order adjustments program? What information should not be changed at this time?

13. Why is direct access recommended for the customer order transaction file?

10-3 PROCESSING SUMMARIES AND REGISTERS

Besides printing picking and packing slips, the order-entry computer application produces important summary reports and several file registers. The summary reports of greatest interest are those that are used to summarize order-entry performance and show order-filling requirements for back orders and future orders. The *daily order-filling report*, for instance, lists all orders filled during the day to show several performance measures. We have already discussed one of these measures, the order-fill rate (the number of orders filled divided by the number of open orders). Other performance measures include the following:

$$\text{Distance traveled per order} = \frac{\text{Total distance traveled}}{\text{Number of orders filled}}$$

$$\text{Items per customer order} = \frac{\text{Number of line items ordered}}{\text{Number of orders filled}}$$

$$\text{Value of average order} = \frac{\text{Dollar value of orders filled}}{\text{Number of orders filled}}$$

$$\text{Weight of average order} = \frac{\text{Total weight of orders filled}}{\text{Number of orders filled}}$$

$$\text{Quantity shipped of average order} = \frac{\text{Total quantity shipped}}{\text{Number of orders filled}}$$

The reports of back orders and future orders are similar in design to the daily order-filling report. The *back order report* lists all orders that cannot be filled and provides several kinds of performance measures, including the back order percentage (the number of line items back ordered divided by the number of line items filled) and the back order fill rate (the number of back orders filled divided by the number of back orders to be filled). The flowchart in Figure 10–17 shows the steps required in printing the back order report. If back orders are not written to the back order file during the online adjustment of orders, then a back order file update must take place. Consider the alternative design illustrated. If company policy is to back order the difference between the quantity ordered and the quantity shipped, this difference will be written to the order change file. As now illustrated, processing the change file is required to update the future/back order file and to provide a printed record of all customer order changes. This printed record, the *customer order adjustments report*, must be carefully reviewed. If adjustments

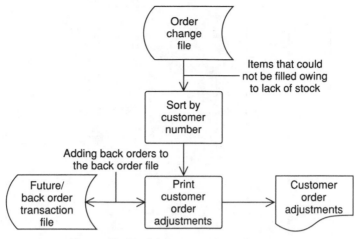

Figure 10–17   Printing customer adjustments

leading to back orders appear to be overly high, members of the warehouse crew are dispatched to doublecheck inventory stock counts. After the customer order adjustments report is approved, the back order report is printed (see Figure 10–18), usually in the sequence of customer account numbers or product or item numbers. Figure 10–19 shows a back-order-by-item report. A third alternative is to sequence back orders by business order number; the difficulty with this choice, however, is that it fails to group multiple back orders for either customers or products.

The *future order report* is usually printed after the back order report and is identical to it in format. Because both reports list orders to be filled at some future date, some firms see little need to keep the two reports separate. In other firms, the back order report is used by the warehouse staff, and the future order report is used by the sales staff. Hence two reports are needed.

Still another processing summary often prepared at this time is the *sales-analysis summary report*. By now it should be evident that customer order entry, combined with customer invoicing, captures valuable sales information. Besides showing

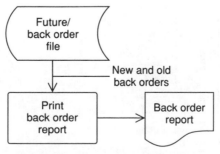

Figure 10–18   Printing back orders

```
WED, MAR 25, 199-            M C B A   Demonstration Furniture Company                    PAGE 0001
8:56 AM                         BACK ORDERS BY ITEM

ITEM NO  DESCRIPTION         CUST    NAME                    ORDER   ORDER        QTY    UNIT     DIS
                             NO                              NO      DATE         B/O    PRICE    %

300      EXECUTIVE CHAIR     000100  Sunnyside Furniture     10030   03/25/9-      1     151.00    5
                             000200  21st. Century Enterprises  10016   03/09/9-     11     188.00    5

                                             ITEM TOTALS:           2  ORDERS      12

400      SECRETARIAL CHAIR, METAL  000100  Sunnyside Furniture   10021   03/06/9-    150     32.50    5
                                   500000  Fieldings Office Emporium  10012   03/05/9-      9     32.50    5

                                             ITEM TOTALS:           2  ORDERS     159

DP600    DESK PAD, EXECUTIVE TYPE  500000  Fieldings Office Emporium  10012   03/05/9-     16     28.91    5
         PEN & PENCIL SET

                                             ITEM TOTALS:           1  ORDERS      16

       3 ITEMS ON B/O   TOTAL UNIT QTY ON B/O -   187   TOTAL SALE VALUE OF ALL B/O ITEMS -   7,456.61
```

Figure 10–19 Back-order-by-item report

sales by customer and by product, the profit and percentage of profit by customer order, by customer, by salesperson, by distributor, by product, and by product line can all be determined. The sales analysis computer application is made possible by the order-entry and customer-invoicing applications. Chapter 15 explores the subject of sales and profit analysis.

The order-entry application produces several file registers in addition to processing summaries. Three of these are the open-order register, the customer master register, and the product master register. The *open-order register*, which lists the contents of the customer order transaction file *before* goods are picked, is printed infrequently. It becomes important whenever there is some question about the accuracy of the file, such as questions arising when file-balance controls are inaccurate or when problems occur with computing equipment. The other two registers should be familiar by now. The *customer master register* lists all customer accounts stored on the customer master file. If there are questions regarding the accuracy and completeness of customer information, the register provides a point of reference. The *product master register* shows what information is stored in the product master file. Like the customer register, the product register is printed to provide a reference, if stored information is questioned.

10-4 INTERACTIVE DISPLAY PROGRAMS

An important design objective of customer order entry is the development of a responsive system capable of handling several types of inquiries. If, for example, a customer wants to know the status of a particular order, it should be possible to conduct a search to answer this question in seconds. Or suppose a member of the sales force asks, "Do we have in stock 50 Halon 1211 fire extinguishers?" Direct inquiry should return a response almost immediately.

Generally, an interactive order-entry design provides, at a minimum, three interactive display programs: the customer order, customer account, and product account display programs (see Figure 10–20). The *customer order display program*, by far the most complex of the three, is designed to provide fast response to inquiries about the location of a particular order. Imagine a large, 1,000-order-per-day warehousing facility that sometimes has difficulty filling orders. Customers soon begin to call, asking for the latest information. The problem with locating a single order, however, is that it may be stored in one of several locations—for example, in the customer order transaction file (if it is scheduled to be filled), the future/back order transaction file (if it is waiting to be filled), or the invoice transaction file (if it has been filled). There are other possibilities: the order may not have been received, or, if received, it might be held by the credit department.

To make it easier to locate customer orders, order-entry computer applications often feature an *order status file*, the contents of which are limited to the order status code and three or four data elements (business order number, customer account number, and customer P.O. number). This code may be as simple as

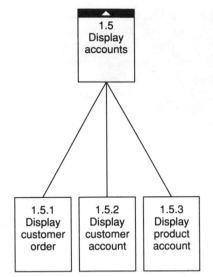

Figure 10–20   Order-entry display programs

1 = customer order file

2 = future/back order file

3 = invoice transaction file

4 = received, but held by the credit department

After a request is received, the status file is searched. Once the order status is known, several actions can take place: the customer can be told that the order was shipped, the customer's call can be transferred to the credit department, or the stored details of the order can be displayed and reviewed directly.

Customer and product display programs also provide other valuable information. Suppose a customer asks: "Do you have our correct address?" This information can be checked in seconds. Product account displays are equally important. Since the on-hand amount of inventory is now stored in the product master records, the question of whether an order can be filled can be answered directly. No longer is it necessary to dispatch a member of the warehouse crew to find and bring back a count of the stock available for sale.

10-5   PROCESSING CONTROLS

The use of an order status file represents a different approach to establishing processing controls. By maintaining such a file, a business keeps an account of all transactions internal and external to processing. Transactions that have been held for review, for example, and transactions that have been transferred to the customer invoicing application represent counts external to processing. The *master control equation* developed to explain this accounting is as follows:

$$\begin{aligned}
\text{Total orders} = \;& \text{Orders, customer order transaction file} \\
& + \;\text{Orders, future/back order transaction file} \\
& + \;\text{Orders, invoice transaction file} \\
& + \;\text{Orders, held}
\end{aligned}$$

As with other control equations, these counts must be revised daily. In addition, parts of the master control equation are made up of several smaller equations. The "orders held" component, for instance, must be changed as decisions are made to delay new orders or to release orders from the "orders held" category. The equation describing this activity is

$$\text{Orders held} = \text{Orders held, yesterday} + \text{Additions} - \text{Deletions}$$

Similar types of equations control the count of orders stored in the future/back order transaction file.

The count of orders in the customer order file will vary throughout the day. Each time an order is entered successfully into processing, the count is increased by one. The count continues to increase until the file is closed and packing slips are printed. Later on, the count is modified by the enter adjustments program—as problems are discovered, it may be necessary to place some orders in the back order category. Next, the count is reduced to zero, as filled orders are written to the invoice transaction file. Reducing this count to zero is offset, however, by increasing the count of records stored in the invoice transaction file by the same amount.

To complicate matters, it is sometimes necessary to process more than one customer order transaction file during the day. Suppose the daily order file is closed at two o'clock in the afternoon. Orders received after two can still be entered into processing if they are written to a new customer order transaction file. This second file is often kept open until the next day. To establish processing controls for two or more files with the same name, each file must be numbered in a way that allows counts to be kept separate. One method of numbering, for example, might list 875 orders for customer order transaction file #206 and 116 orders for customer order transaction file #207. Provided that the open-order file is always assigned the next larger number, these counts mean that file #206 is a closed file because file #207 exists.

Besides tracking the count of orders, processing controls must balance quantity totals to ensure that no quantity ordered is lost. This control total is the same as the control required in customer invoicing, with minor modifications. The control equation is

$$\begin{aligned}
\text{Quantity ordered} = \;& \text{Quantity shipped} + \text{Quantity, future ordered} \\
& + \;\text{Quantity, backordered} + \text{Quantity, canceled} + \text{Quantity, held}
\end{aligned}$$

Unless this equation is in balance, there is a serious problem with computer processing.

Last, in addition to keeping control totals for customer orders, processing controls must be kept for the customer and product master files. At the very minimum, a record count must be maintained for the customer master file. Processing controls for the product master file require more attention. Besides a count of all records, the count of the on-hand quantity of inventory must be carefully monitored. This activity is discussed in the next chapter.

10-6   MANAGEMENT IMPLICATIONS

Even though the order-entry application is difficult to design and implement, management is rarely disappointed with the results that follow from it. Improved customer service is a major benefit: less than a twenty-four-hour turnaround between the receipt of an order and its shipment, for example, impresses customers. Such fast service indicates that a business is responsive to the needs of its customers. Two closely related benefits are the ability to track customer orders and to provide greater accuracy in filling orders. In a large order-entry facility, a major headache is keeping track of customer orders. With inaccurate processing procedures, some companies lose orders; others pack and ship the correct amount but send it to the wrong customer. With an automated approach, the details of processing are directed, in large part, by the computer. If an adjustment to an order is made, for instance, the computer is programmed to respond as follows:

> IS THE DIFFERENCE TO BE
> 1. BACK ORDERED?
> 2. CANCELED?

A computer-based order-entry application often permits better use of human and material resources. Worker productivity is improved all along the line, for example, because less time is needed to pick goods from stock, to respond to customer inquiries, to process an order, to make adjustments to an order, and to enter customer and product changes. The interactive features of the design contribute to other improvements in worker productivity. Because work can be distributed much more easily, the people who are most familiar with the particular aspects of processing are able to make needed changes. For example, sales representatives familiar with processing orders for a designated regional sales area can be assigned this responsibility. Likewise, representatives who discover that adjustments to an order are required can be responsible for entering these adjustments.

Savings in material resources also result. As discussed in the next chapter, proper controls on inventory help lower the total quantity of stock carried. Controls also lead to less pilferage and other types of stock losses.

Performance reporting is an important product of the order-entry application. By tracking order-fill rates, back order and future order percentages, order adjustment rates, and the like, management is able to determine whether the order-entry system is working smoothly. Equipped with appropriate tracking measurements, management can take corrective action before problems become serious.

REVIEW QUESTIONS

14. Besides the order-fill rate, what are other order-entry performance measures?

15. Why should the order-entry application include easy-to-use interactive display programs?

16. How does an order-status file simplify the search for a customer's order?

17. What is the master control equation for this application? Why is it important?

18. How does an order-entry application help improve worker productivity?

19. Why is distributed data processing an important consideration in the design of this application?

REVIEW OF IMPORTANT IDEAS

The customer order-entry computer application contains three types of processing activities: order processing, order filling, and order packing and shipping. The main input to processing is the customer order. After the details of an order have been successfully entered, the computer determines whether the order can be filled. The filling of an order reduces the count of stock and produces a picking slip showing where stock is located and how many items to pick from each location. Order packing and shipping follows order filling. Packing slips show what items were shipped compared with what items were ordered.

Before customer orders are processed, the customer and product master files must be as accurate as possible. Customer changes generally consist of name and address changes and new customers added to the customer master file. Product changes show all changes in the warehouse, including receipt of new merchandise, movements of goods from one location to another, price and cost changes, and stock adjustments. Change tables are used to simplify these numerous changes.

After preshipped orders, future orders, and back orders have been processed, current orders are filled. This type of scheduling helps to ensure that all customers are treated fairly.

Even though the computer indicates that stock is on hand, there will be times when computer-printed information is wrong. Thus, adjustments must be made to quantity-picked figures. The difference between the quantity ordered and the quantity actually picked must be canceled or back ordered.

Besides picking and packing slips, the customer order-entry application produces a number of processing summaries, registers, and change reports. The three processing summaries of special interest are the daily order-filling report and the reports listing back orders and the future orders.

A well-designed order-entry application contains easy-to-use display programs that help identify the status of a customer's order and information stored on the customer and product master files. A major benefit is the ability to track customer orders.

Maintaining control of order-entry processing is simplified by the use of a single master control equation. The parts of this equation are made up of several smaller control equations.

KEY WORDS

Order entry

Order filling

Finished-goods inventory

Customer order

Quantity on hand

Quantity on order

Quantity on back order

Quantity on future order

Picking slip

Product change form

Customer change form

Pending order

Open-order register

Order-fill rate

Customer order transaction file

Preshipped orders

Future orders

Back orders

Daily order-filling report

Order status file

Master control equation

EXERCISES

1. Suppose a company decides to adopt a policy to cancel rather than back order any differences between items specified by the computer as to be picked and items actually picked for a selected number of items. Suppose further that the company wants a register of all items canceled. How would the order-entry system be modified to handle this policy decision?

2. A merchandising manager indicates that she would like the following activities incorporated into the order-entry application. At the time the warehouse picking list is prepared, the computer should prepare a postcard for mailing to the customer. For filled orders, the postcard should thank the customer and indicate when shipment will be made. For orders that cannot be completely filled, the postcard should thank the customer and indicate what is shipped and what will be shipped at a later date. Explain the design implications of this processing requirement.

3. Some business firms practice what might be called a "best customer rule." The rule states that orders received from best customers are filled before all others (including future orders and back orders). How would this policy decision be incorporated into an order-entry design?

4. A standard customer purchase agreement involves shipping a predetermined quantity of stock to customers on a scheduled basis, such as 500 units every 30 days. Explain how this variation would be included in an order-entry design.

5. Explain where, when, and how the following ratios would be computed by the order-entry application described in this chapter:

    a.   order-fill rate

    b.   distance traveled per order

    c.   items per customer order

    d.   value of average order

    e.   weight of average order

    f.   quantity shipped of average order

6.   Suppose you decide to add customer invoicing (see Chapter 4) to the order-entry computer application.

    (a)   Which new interactive programs, if any, need to be written and added to the system organization chart?

    (b)   Which new batch programs, if any, need to be written and added to the system organization chart?

    (c)   Explain how the new integrated system works.

7.   Using the master control equation as a guide, design the processing control equations to control the count of future orders and back orders stored on the future/back order transaction file.

DISCUSSION QUESTIONS

1. What happens if the customer and product master files are not updated in advance of processing? What happens if their contents are not accurate?

2. Some people argue that the packing slip and the picking slip can be the same item and that this slip can be printed before orders are sent to the warehouse. What are the problems with this approach?

3. Suppose that when new goods are received on the shipping dock, the quantity received is immediately added to the product master file. What are the problems with this approach?

4. Suppose that customer demand is very heavy and that not all orders processed can be picked and shipped on the same day. How should the order-entry system be adjusted to resolve this imbalance?

5. You are faced with a decision: you must determine whether to implement the customer invoicing application or the order-entry application first. Explain the steps important to making this decision.

4-IN-1 CASE STUDY—CUSTOMER ORDER ENTRY

The 4-in-1 software does not provide for the customer order-entry, finished goods inventory, or purchasing and receiving computer applications. However, this absence provides an opportunity to add additional sales and payables transactions into processing and to review the processing features important to each. For this specific lesson you are asked to

- review a customer account to determine outstanding receivables balances
- enter new sales transactions into processing for sales accounts 4010-000, 4020-000, and 4030-000.
- add a third customer to the customer file
- print a sales edit list

Reviewing customer accounts

The 4-in-1 application allows you to review a customer account at any time.

1. Log on and enter a date of **012597**. Press ENTER when asked, *Any change?*

2. From the main menu, type **10** and press ENTER.

3. Type **1** and press ENTER to review an account.

4. Press F1 to display FARMERS-COOP. Press ENTER when asked, *Right Customer?*

5. Press F1 for earliest.

6. Press F2 for totals. Examine this account. Remember, this customer started with a beginning balance and made a cash payment.

7. Press TAB for the next account.

8. Press F1 to display LAWNS-ARE-GREEN. Press ENTER when asked, *Right Customer?*

9. Press F1 for earliest, followed by F2 for totals. Examine this account. Remember that this customer received a credit.

10. Press TAB until you return to the main menu.

Entering Eight Sales Transactions

This lesson asks you to add eight new sales transactions. Figure 10–21 shows the edit listing you are asked to produce following the entry of these new sales totals.

11. Type **8** from the main menu. Press ENTER.

12. Type **1** to add a transaction. Press ENTER.

13. Type **LAWNS** (in capital letters), and press ENTER. Press ENTER again when asked, *Right customer?*

14. Enter the following:

S	for sale
012597	for transaction date
(blank)	for document number
412.50	for amount
Microgrow	for reference

```
Date 01/25/97              A and J Enterprises, Inc.           #0037 Page 0001
                           S A L E S   E D I T   L I S T
- - - - - - - - - - - - - - - - - - - - - - - - - - - - - - - - - - - - - - - -
Customer-name                 Trans-date    Doc-#    Debited-to  Trans-amt
Trans-type          Invoice?  Reference                         Credited-to
- - - - - - - - - - - - - - - - - - - - - - - - - - - - - - - - - - - - - - - -
ANGEL'S GARDENS               01/25/97                 A/R        1,200.00
Sale                No        Garden tools                        1,200.00
  Distributions:    4020-000  Sales—product   B

ANGEL'S GARDENS               01/25/97                 A/R           50.00
Sale                No                                              50.00
  Distributions:    4020-000  Sales—product   B

ANGEL'S GARDENS               01/25/97                 A/R          100.00
Sale                No        Building supplies                    100.00
  Distributions:    4030-000  Sales—product   C

FARMERS-COOP                  01/25/97                 A/R          550.00
Sale                No        Tools                               512.50
  Distributions:    4020-000  Sales—product   B                    37.50
                    2450-000  State sales tax payable

FARMERS-COOP                  01/25/97                 A/R          700.00
Sale                No        Building supplies                   655.00
  Distributions:    4030-000  Sales—product   C                    45.00
                    2450-000  State sales tax payable

FARMERS-COOP                  01/25/97                 A/R        1,400.00
Sale                No        Building supplies                   1,310.00
  Distributions:    4030-000  Sales—product   C                    90.00
                    2450-000  State sales tax payable

LAWNS-ARE-GREEN               01/25/97                 A/R          412.50
Sale                No        Microgrow                           390.00
  Distributions:    4010-000  Sales—product   A                    22.50
                    2450-000  State sales tax payable

LAWNS-ARE-GREEN               01/25/97                 A/R          300.00
Sale                No        Building supplies                   277.50
  Distributions:    4030-000  Sales—product   C                    22.50
                    2450-000  State sales tax payable

  8 Sales transactions                    Grand total:           4,712.50
```

Figure 10–21   Sales edit list

N	for payment with sale
Y	for *Debit A/R?*
(blank)	for field number to change
4010-000	for sales account number
390	for amount to distribute
N	for *Any change?*
2450-000	for next account number
F1	to apply balance

15. Press ENTER and press TAB to end the sales distribution.

16. Type **N** when asked if you want to prepare an invoice.

17. When asked for the next customer name, type **FARM** (in capital letters), and press ENTER. Press ENTER for right customer.

18. Enter the following sales information:

S	for sale
012597	for transaction date
(blank)	for document number
550	for amount
Tools	for reference
N	for payment with sale
Y	for *Debit A/R?*
(blank)	for field number to change
4020-000	for sales account number
512.50	for amount to distribute
N	for *Any change?*
2450-000	for next account number
37.50	for amount to distribute
N	for any change
TAB	for next account
N	for *Do you wish to prepare an invoice?*

Adding a New Customer

19. Type **ANGEL'S GARDENS** for the customer.

20. Type **Y** to add the new customer to the customer master file. Press ENTER.

21. Add the following address on lines 1 and 2:
    5506 Masonville Rd.
    Rice Hill, WA 97200

22. Type **Paul Pears** for contact.

23. Type **687-4431** for telephone number.

24. Press ENTER for first date.

25. Type **Large home sales chain** for comment.

26. Type **MMP** for salesperson.

27. Press ENTER for M (monthly) statement frequency.

28. Press ENTER when asked, *Field number to change?*

29. You will return to the sales transaction screen. After indicating **Y** for right customer, add the following:

S	for sale
012597	for transaction date
(blank)	for document number
1200	for amount
Garden tools	for reference
N	for payment with sale
Y	for *Debit A/R?*
(blank)	for field number to change
4020-000	for sales account number
1200	for amount to distribute
N	for *Any change?*
TAB	for next account
N	for *Do you wish to prepare an invoice?*

30. Enter another sale for ANGEL'S GARDENS as follows:

S	for sale
012597	for transaction date
(blank)	for document number
50	for amount
(blank)	for reference
N	for payment with sale
Y	for *Debit A/R?*
(blank)	for field number to change
4020-000	for sales account number
50	for amount to distribute
N	for *Any change?*
TAB	for next account
N	for *Do you wish to prepare an invoice?*

31. Add another sale for FARMERS-COOP as follows:

S	for sale
012597	for transaction date
(blank)	for document number
700	for amount
Building Supplies	for reference
N	for payment with sale
Y	for *Debit A/R?*
(blank)	for field number to change
4030-000	for sales account number
655	for amount to distribute
N	for *Any change?*
2450-000	for next account number
45	for amount to distribute

N	for any change
TAB	for next account
N	for *Do you wish to prepare an invoice?*

32. Add another sale for LAWNS-ARE-GREEN as follows:

S	for sale
012597	for transaction date
(blank)	for document number
300	for amount
Building Supplies	for reference
N	for payment with sale
Y	for *Debit A/R?*
(blank)	for field number to change
4030-000	for sales account number
277.50	for amount to distribute
N	for *Any change?*
2450-000	for next account number
22.50	for amount to distribute
N	for any change
TAB	for next account
N	for *Do you wish to prepare an invoice?*

33. Add another sale for FARMERS-COOP as follows:

S	for sale
012597	for transaction date
(blank)	for document number
1400	for amount
Building Supplies	for reference
N	for payment with sale
Y	for *Debit A/R?*
(blank)	for field number to change
4030-000	for sales account number
1310	for amount to distribute
N	for *Any change?*
2450-000	for next account number
90	for amount to distribute
N	for any change
TAB	for next account
N	for *Do you wish to prepare an invoice?*

34. Add a final sale for ANGEL'S GARDENS as follows:

| S | for sale |
| 012597 | for transaction date |

(blank)	for document number
100	for amount
Building Supplies	for reference
N	for payment with sale
Y	for *Debit A/R?*
(blank)	for field number to change
4030-000	for sales account number
100	for amount to distribute
N	for *Any change?*
TAB	for next account
N	for *Do you wish to prepare an invoice?*

35. Exit at this time. With the process sales and DR/CR memos submenu facing you, type **4** to print the sales edit list.

QUESTIONS

1. Are the totals correct for FARMERS-COOP and LAWNS-ARE-GREEN? How would you document that these totals are correct?

2. Two of the three customers were required to pay sales tax. Why was one customer excempt?

3. What does this lesson tell you about adding customers to a customer master file?

4. Suppose 500 sales transactions were processed during the day. What would the G/L account distribution totals (see page two of the sales edit list) tell you about daily sales?

CHAPTER

11

Finished-Goods Inventory

Closely related to the customer order-entry computer application is the application for finished-goods inventory. As discussed in the last chapter, an essential requirement for successful order-entry processing is an accurate, complete product master file. Lacking such a file, an order-entry system is bound to fail. In this chapter, we will more closely examine the design and maintenance of the product master file. In particular, we will show how to plan for and control onhand stocks of inventory. To simplify the subject as much as possible, we will focus on one business environment—warehousing—as in the last chapter.

In the finished-goods inventory application, the product master file, following its modification, is once again enlarged by the customer order-entry computer application. Besides showing the inventory on hand, the larger file shows when to order more stock (the *order frequency*), how much to order (the *order quantity*), and from whom to order (the *approved vendor*). These three decisions are fundamental to *inventory management*.

The finished-goods application differs from other applications in an important way: it is designed to maximize the return on capital invested in inventory. To realize this objective, management must carefully balance the demand for inventory with its supply. A common saying states that inventory management always tries to keep as little stock on hand as possible, to order new stock at the best possible prices, and never to run out of stock. In practice, it is difficult to do all three things at once.

One way to appreciate the objective of maximizing the return on capital invested in inventory is to examine the factors that contribute to a favorable return. The *return-on-investment* (R.O.I.) equation tells us, for example, that for a given profit margin on sales (percentage earned), the resulting R.O.I. is determined by turnover:

$$\text{R.O.I.} = \text{Percentage earned on sales} \times \text{Inventory turnover}$$

where

$$\text{Inventory turnover} = \text{Annual requirements} \div \text{Average inventory}$$

$$\text{percentage earned on sales} = \text{Earnings} \div \text{Sales}$$

As the equation shows, *inventory turnover* refers to the number of times the stock carried in inventory can be sold during the year. Suppose, for instance, that the percentage earned on sales is 15 percent and turnover is three times per year. The resulting R.O.I. would be 45 percent. This means that if every product carried in stock is turned three times during the year, every dollar invested in this product returns 45 cents. Clearly, if a firm can reduce its total investment in its average inventory, while holding sales and earnings constant, the benefits can be most dramatic. A chemical distributor, for example, discovered that a finished-goods inventory application greatly enhanced its ability to reduce its investment in inventory. A detailed cost comparison revealed that the application led to an overall investment reduction of $100,000. As another example, a small manufacturing company increased inventory turnover by 33 percent (from 2.9 to 3.8 times per year) and cut stocks by $500,000; in addition, the computer was found to be 99 percent accurate in reporting on-hand stocks. Such results are not uncommon and explain why online methods of inventory control have become so popular.

In addition to maximizing the return on invested capital, a well-designed finished-goods inventory application offers these six important advantages:

- Taking a *physical inventory*—the manual checking of stock—is simplified because manual counts can be verified by computer.

- Stockouts, the number of times a firm is out of stock, and stock losses can be reduced.

- Product prices and costs can be carefully managed.

- Warehouse-stocking procedures can be improved because space requirements and storage locations for stocks can more easily be determined.

- Management can spot interesting sales trends and areas of strong (and weak) customer demand and, as a consequence, can develop more realistic sales and product-stocking plans.

- Reliable sources of supply can be identified, and the supply of stock can be carefully monitored.

Finally, there are several more good reasons for designing an interactive finished-goods inventory application. Most important, maintaining the product master file is simplified because it is easier to add, change, or delete records stored on file. Second, inquiry capabilities are improved. No longer is it necessary to search through page after page of stock-keeping reports and registers. Various types of efficient search routines can be built in to perform product-inquiry tasks. Third, the study of an individual product or of a *product line* is simplified. This product status study can lead to dramatic improvements in inventory turnover as well as in product earnings and sales totals. Fourth, inventory management tasks can be better distributed. Members of the warehouse crew, for example, can be made responsible for making online adjustments to the count of stock on hand.

11-1   PRELIMINARY OVERVIEW OF PROCESSING

Figure 11–1 shows the context of the inventory system. As indicated, the system links the order-entry system with purchasing and receiving, warehouse operations, and inventory control. Order entry, in this case, represents the *actual demand* side of the system. The quantity of stock to release is determined by the customer orders received by a company. The amount of stock on hand represents the *actual supply* side of the system. The supply of stock is triggered initially by a *purchase requisition*, which shows what stock is to be replenished. New stock enters the system and is documented by *stock receipts*. Like a cash receipt, a stock receipt records the quantity and cost of the stock placed in inventory.

Besides dealing with actual supply and demand, the inventory system must show projected, or *estimated, demand*. Since the supply of stock must be determined in advance of customer orders, the demand for stock must be estimated. Inventory control staff members are responsible for this determination. They must set stock projections by estimating the quantity of stock to release for customer orders. Finally, warehouse staff members must make physical inventory counts and feed these to the system. Counts verify the correctness of the quantity-on-hand totals required by the system.

The main processing steps associated with the finished-goods inventory system are shown in Figure 11–2. The heart of processing is the update of the product master file, shown in the center of the figure. Because this update can occur in so many ways, it is best to examine each update procedure.

1. *Perform stock analysis* (procedure 11.1) monitors the status of a stock and determines whether stock should be ordered. Each stock-to-order decision is placed in a product reorder file. In addition, each stock-to-order decision updates the stock status of the product master file by showing the revised quantity-on-order figure.

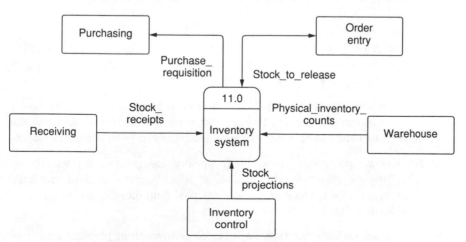

Figure 11–1   The finished-goods inventory system

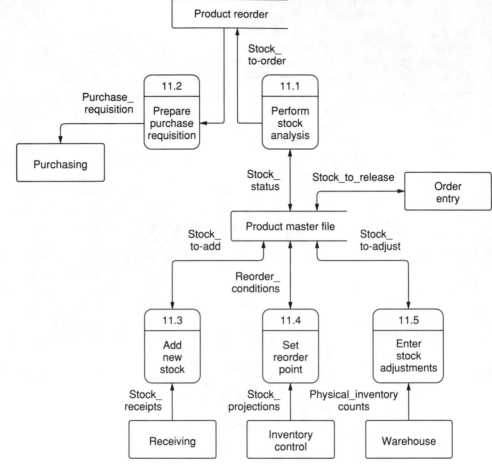

Figure 11–2 Main processing steps of the finished-goods inventory system

2. *Prepare purchase requisition* (procedure 11.2) draws information from the product reorder file to print the purchase requisition. The purchase requisition shows which stock to order, in what quantity, and when. Purchasing is responsible for determining from whom to order.

3. *Add new stock* (procedure 11.3) results from the receipt of stock. Once the quantity received is known, two product master fields can be updated: the quantity on hand can be increased, and the quantity on order can be decreased.

4. *Set reorder point* (procedure 11.4) updates the product master file by specifying the on-hand quantity level at which stock should be reordered (the *reorder point*). Stock projections coupled with other inventory stocking considerations lead to *reorder conditions*.

5. *Enter stock adjustments* (procedure 11.5) follows from physical inventory counts by the warehouse crew. When shorts are discovered, the on-hand

quantity must be decreased. If longs are found—too much stock compared to the stock shown on file—the on-hand quantity must be increased.

Besides the updates controlled by the finished-goods inventory system, the product master file is also updated by the order-entry system. As Figure 11–2 shows, stock is released as a result of the order-entry system.

The Product Master File

The product master file, which is used in customer invoicing and customer order entry, is enlarged once again by the finished-goods inventory system. Figure 11–3 shows this modified file; the shaded areas show data elements used previously. To simplify this rather complex data structure, think of this file as storing three main types of information:

1. *Stock-keeping information* describes each product stored on file and includes the product name and description, pricing and discount, product inventory, and product location segments. Most of this information is required by the order-entry system. For the finished-goods application, stock-keeping information is essential in checking the status of products. Unless the quantity on hand and on order are known, duplicate reorders for stock will be placed. Likewise, it is essential to know the difference between beginning and ending inventory, which is calculated as follows:

   Beginning inventory + Moves in − Moves out = Ending inventory

   If the physical count of inventory does not equal the computed ending-inventory total, *inventory shrinkage* has occurred. Shrinkage (or shorts) can result from a variety of factors, including waste or loss, improper reporting of parts added to inventory, physical inventory errors, and pilferage. Regardless of the cause, managers must keep a watchful eye on any differences between stock thought to be available for sale and stock actually available for sale.

2. *Product requirements information* includes product forecast and sales history segments. The product forecast segment establishes the demand for a product for a specified time period, such as next month, next two months, or next six months. It often uses an *ABC code* to indicate whether a product is classified as high-value (A), medium-value (B), or low-value (C). Other data important for determining product requirements are product forecast coefficients and historical sales figures. Sales history information is usually kept for an entire calendar year (although some firms insist that sales data be stored for five years). Historical data is valuable because it permits individuals to study actual figures showing how demand changes.

3. *Stock replenishment information* includes product reorder and product performance segments. The amount to be ordered (the order quantity) and the

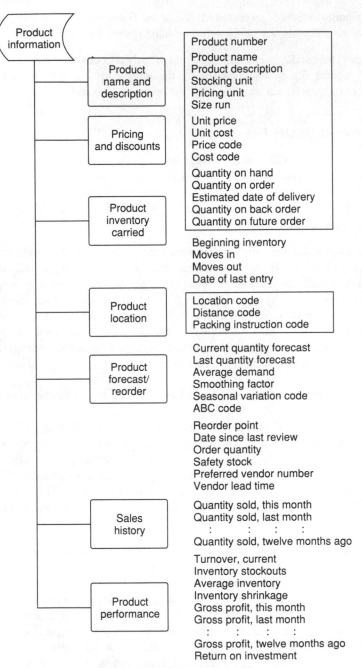

Figure 11–3   Product master file

point at which stock is to be ordered (the reorder point) describe conditions under which stock is to be replenished. Product performance data help show whether product reorder decisions are correct. By tracking inventory turnover, stockouts, average inventory, inventory shrinkage, product profitability and return on investment, managers are able to determine how well a particular product or product line is controlled.

Reports and Displays

A wide variety of displays and printed reports can be designed for the finished-goods inventory application. These displays and reports are used to verify stock-keeping information and to fine-tune stock replenishment decisions. Suppose, for example, that an inventory planner wants to list all product accounts for which no demand is shown over the past six months. To process this request, the date-of-last-entry field is compared to the current date. If the comparison leads to a period of more than six months, the stock carried in inventory under this number could be classified as *obsolete inventory*. A list of all such numbers could be displayed or printed to document the inventory value of obsolete goods (see Figure 11–4). Most obsolete-inventory reports break down summary counts to show on-hand and on-order amounts. The on-order amounts, in particular, need to be questioned. For example, Figure 11–4 shows an on-order amount of 1,000 units of item number 97791. This order, if possible, should be canceled because the product is obsolete. An ABC analysis, to itemize inventory amounts by class, is also printed. This helps the inventory planner visualize the impact of removing obsolete items from stock.

The most common types of output are displays or reports designed to show the status of goods held in stock and to indicate what items are due to be reviewed for

| | Obsolete Inventory | | | 10/20/ XX | |
Planner: A4				Page 10	
Item Number	Inv. Class	Unit Cost	Date Last Activity	On Hand	On Order
07518	B	8.50	3/15/ XX	23,600	
97791	B	27.50	5/01/ XX	18,400	1,000
05687	C	4.30	2/03/ XX	15,000	
32702	C	12.00	10/01/ XX	9,000	
				267,700	22,100
Summary	A			98,000	12,100
By	B			100,700	1,000
Category	C			69,000	9,000

Figure 11–4 Obsolete inventory report

PURCHASE ADVICE

ITEM NO.	PRODUCT DESCRIPTION	ON HAND	ON ORDER	RE ORDER	ORDER SIZE	ITEM COST
65349	TRAIL FUEL PACKS	82	0	85	160	$ 5.63
44361	SWITCHING LIGHTS	22	16	25	16	$211.15

Figure 11–5 Purchase advice display

reorder. *Stock status reports* permit inventory planners to review information stored in the product master file and, as a result of the review, to solidify inventory plans. *Purchase-advice displays* are used to specify how items should be reordered. As Figure 11–5 shows, a purchase advice clarifies which products carried in inventory are at a stock level lower than the reorder point. As indicated, the reorder point for product 65349 is 85, whereas the quantity on hand is 82. Thus, an order for 160 additional items should be placed. The on-hand quantity for item number 44361 is also less than the reorder point. The purchase advice shows that the on-order field is already set to 16, however, so no reorder is required.

REVIEW QUESTIONS

1. In balancing the demand for inventory with the supply to inventory, what three decisions are fundamental?

2. Explain how return on investment (R.O.I.) is related to inventory management.

3. What are the primary reasons for developing the finished-goods inventory application? What are important secondary reasons?

4. What are the three main types of information contained in the product master file.

5. What is an ABC code?

6. What information is contained on the purchase advice display?

11-2 FINISHED-GOODS INVENTORY PROCESSING

Figure 11–6 (a) and (b) show the systems organization chart for the finished-goods inventory application; Figure 11–7 (a) and 11–7 (b) show the corresponding

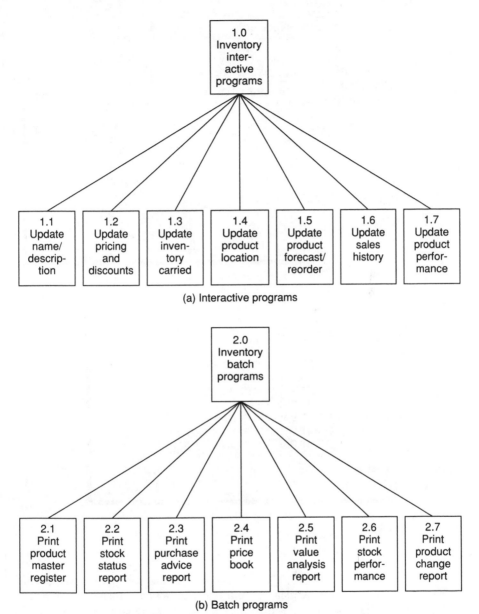

(a) Interactive programs

(b) Batch programs

Figure 11–6   Systems organization chart

program-processing menu. The interactive part of processing shows how product update routines have been subdivided into specific file-processing tasks. One task updates product location information; another updates product forecast/reorder information. Each update program is matched by a display program. If an update is not required (or permitted), the same segment of the product master file can be displayed for review.

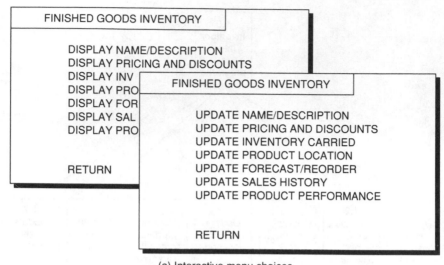

FINISHED GOODS INVENTORY

DISPLAY NAME/DESCRIPTION
DISPLAY PRICING AND DISCOUNTS
DISPLAY INV
DISPLAY PRO
DISPLAY FOR
DISPLAY SAL
DISPLAY PRO

RETURN

FINISHED GOODS INVENTORY

UPDATE NAME/DESCRIPTION
UPDATE PRICING AND DISCOUNTS
UPDATE INVENTORY CARRIED
UPDATE PRODUCT LOCATION
UPDATE FORECAST/REORDER
UPDATE SALES HISTORY
UPDATE PRODUCT PERFORMANCE

RETURN

(a) Interactive menu choices

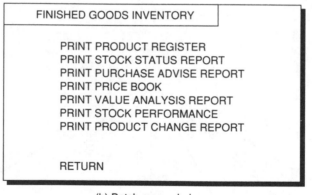

FINISHED GOODS INVENTORY

PRINT PRODUCT REGISTER
PRINT STOCK STATUS REPORT
PRINT PURCHASE ADVISE REPORT
PRINT PRICE BOOK
PRINT VALUE ANALYSIS REPORT
PRINT STOCK PERFORMANCE
PRINT PRODUCT CHANGE REPORT

RETURN

(b) Batch menu choices

Figure 11–7   Program-processing menu

The batch portion of processing is more straightforward than the interactive portion. As Figure 11–6 (b) shows, processing summaries make up the main part of the design. Of these, the *stock status report*, the *purchase advice report*, and the *price book* are hard-copy printings of information stored on file. The *inventory value analysis* shows the dollar value of stock carried in inventory. Financial planners use this information in determining cash requirements for inventory. *Stock performance reports*, of which there are several, show facts and figures about obsolete inventory, month's supply of inventory, turnover rates, inventory stockouts, return on investment, distance traveled, space requirements, and inventory shrinkage. These reports are important guides for inventory management.

Adding Stock-Keeping Information

Typically, fifty or more pieces of information must be kept for each item stored in inventory. In an effort to streamline the entering and maintenance of product information, some inventory designs combine file-processing menus with data-input display screens (see Figure 11–8). The particular display entitled *Add a new part* permits different types of inventory information to be entered when a new part is added to inventory. Besides the number and description for the part, information concerning its location, product line, part status, ABC code, and order policy are entered using a single screen. The menu appearing at the top of the screen shows what additional tasks can be performed. For example, the operator might choose to change the description of the part or to delete the part from the file.

Although adding stock-keeping information to the product master file is time-consuming, it is not difficult. Inputs to processing consist of new or change notification sheets, such as the item-change notification sheets or inventory mark-down sheets. Efficiency of data entry can be greatly improved by entering changes of the same kind one after another. Easy-to-follow change notification sheets, such as price change sheets, also simplify the design of processing controls.

Revising Product Requirements Information

From a systems designer's viewpoint, a difficult part of processing is the construction of a set of displays that will help managers review inventory plans and, if necessary, adjust product reorder decisions. To aid in this process, the computer is used initially to forecast future product sales. Managers must review these forecasts to decide if they are realistic—that is, if they are consistent with sales promotion programs and expected changes in market demand.

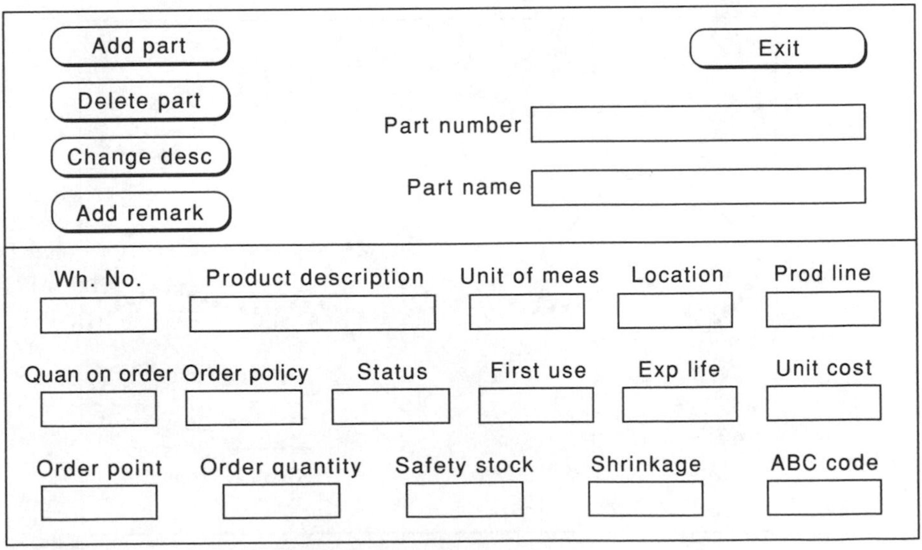

Figure 11–8 Combined menu and data-entry display

Both extrinsic and intrinsic product forecasts can be prepared by the computer. An *extrinsic forecast* assumes that a correlation exists between an external event, such as housing starts or birth rates, and internal company sales. By knowing what is happening outside the firm, planners are better able to predict how internal sales will be affected.

An *intrinsic forecast* assumes that the best way to forecast the demand for a product is to examine past sales trends. This historical data-analysis approach is appropriate when attempting to determine the demand for a single product, such as a down-filled sleeping bag. To begin the forecasting process, inventory planners generally classify products by demand pattern (see Figure 11–9). Of the three basic patterns—constant, trend, and seasonal—the first is the easiest to calculate (and also the least common). The following equation is used to prepare a forecast for a *constant-demand* pattern.

$$F_n = F_{n-1}$$

where

$$F_n = \text{Forecast in period } n$$

$$F_{n-1} = \text{Last forecast in period } n$$

Thus, if period n were July, its forecast would be the same as the forecast for June (period $n - 1$).

Trend analysis is used to forecast sales when demand is either increasing or decreasing. Two popular mathematical approaches used frequently in tracking

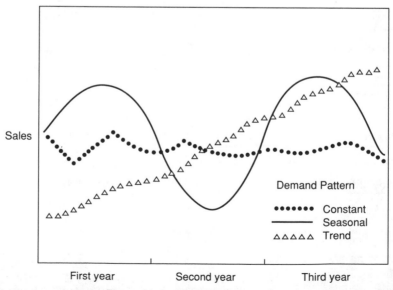

First year   Second year   Third year

Figure 11–9 Three demand patterns

trend-demand patterns are *least squares regression analysis*, which yields a straight line of "best fit," and *exponential smoothing*, which produces a forecast trend line and is preferred in setting forecasts based on historical sales trends. Of the two, we will briefly consider exponential smoothing.

Exponential smoothing is a weighted-average approach to forecasting in which some weight (known as alpha) is applied to the latest actual demand information and another weight (known as one minus alpha) is applied to the last forecast information. The exponential smoothing formula is as follows:

$$F_n = \alpha D_{n-1} + (1 - \alpha)F_{n-1}$$

where

$$F_n = \text{New forecast, in units}$$

$$F_{n-1} = \text{Last forecast, in units}$$

$$D_{n-1} = \text{Last demand, in units}$$

$$\alpha = \text{Smoothing factor}$$

Assume, for example, that sales in March for down-filled sleeping bags were 1,050 units, compared with the sales forecast for March of 1,100 units. When alpha (α) is set at .10, the new April forecast can be set:

$$F_{\text{April}} = (.10)(1,050) + (.90)(1,100) = 1,095 \text{ units}$$

Stating the equation somewhat differently, we can see that exponential smoothing is a weighted average.

$$F_n = 105 + 990 = 1,095 \text{ units}$$

where 105 is the weight given to the last actual demand (10 percent) ánd 990 is the weight given to the last product forecast (90 percent).

The advantage of exponential smoothing over other weighted-average forecasting methods is that little historical sales information needs to be retained and stored on the product master file—only the last quantity forecast and current demand (quantity sold this month). This storage advantage is not necessarily a managerial advantage, however. Many managers are uncomfortable examining sales data unless they have several sales periods to consider. For this reason, twelve or more months of historical data are usually kept for each product carried in inventory.

Adjusting Stock Replenishment Information

Estimating the demand for each product carried in stock is one part of the inventory planning and control puzzle. Other parts involve stock replenishment considerations: determining when to reorder (the reorder point), how much to order (the order quantity), how much extra inventory to carry in stock (the safety stock), from whom to order (the preferred vendor), and when to expect a new shipment (the vendor lead time). Designing a system to enable managers to make these stock replenishment decisions is not an easy matter. A brief overview of how the quantity to order and the reorder point are determined will illustrate some of the mathematical complexity involved.

The quantity to order can be expressed as

Quantity to order = (Estimated quantity to be sold)
$$-(\text{Quantity on hand} + \text{Quantity on order})$$

Suppose 1,260 sleeping bags are estimated to be sold; the quantity on hand is 500 and the quantity on order is 300. We determine that the quantity to order would be 460 bags (1,260 − 500 − 300). In actuality, however, if the manufacturer of the bags is offering a 25 percent reduction of the cost per unit for orders of 500 or more, this quantity to order would require adjustment. It would make more sense to order 500 sleeping bags rather than 460. To account for such conditions, inventory managers use analytic expressions to help them determine the most economic order quantity. The most familiar expression for the *economic order quantity* (E.O.Q.) is

$$\text{E.O.Q.}(\hat{Q}) = \sqrt{2(R)(S) \div (C)(I)}$$

where

$$R = \text{Annual demand, in units}$$
$$S = \text{Purchase order cost, in dollars}$$
$$C = \text{Cost per unit, in dollars}$$
$$I = \text{Cost of capital, in percent}$$
$$\text{E.O.Q.}(\hat{Q}) = \text{Quantity to order, in units}$$

This formula is designed to minimize the cost associated with purchasing and carrying stock in inventory.

When price breaks are permitted, such as those shown in Figure 11–10, the calculation of order quantity must take into consideration three factors: the cost of

Quantity Purchase	Unit Price	Discount
1 – 11	$1.00	none
12 – 23	.90	10 percent
24 – 47	.75	25 percent
48 and above	.60	40 percent

Figure 11–10 Quantity price breaks

purchasing, the cost of carrying stock in inventory, and the changing unit cost of the item. The total cost equation must recognize all of these variable costs:

$$T = R(C) + [S(R) \div Q] + [C(I) \times (\frac{Q}{2})]$$

where

T = Total cost

Q = Quantity to order

$R(C)$ = Annual demand times the cost per item

$S(R) \div Q$ = Total purchase order cost

$C(I) \times (Q/2)$ = Total inventory carrying cost

To determine the most appropriate order quantity, the computer must compute the total inventory cost at several quantity levels. Typically, this involves determining the E.O.Q. and then calculating the total cost at this quantity level ($\hat{Q}$) and at all discount breaks higher than this level.

Once the most appropriate order quantity has been determined, the reorder point can be set. Expressed in units, the *reorder point* (R.O.P.) is equal to the vendor lead time (the time in days that it takes a vendor to fill an order) times average daily demand, plus safety stock (the stock held in reserve to offset higher-than-normal demand):

R.O.P. = (Vendor lead time)(Average daily demand) + Safety stock

Suppose, for example, that it takes 30 days to receive new sleeping bags and that 200 bags are carried in inventory as safety stock. The reorder point is determined by first calculating the average demand, which is equal to the forecasted demand divided by the number of days in the month.

Average daily demand = $F_n \div$ Days in the month

Assume that average demand is 42 bags per day. Inserting this value into the R.O.P. equation shows that the point at which stock should be reordered is 1,460 bags (30 days × 42 bags per day + 200 bags carried as safety stock = 1,460 bags). When the on-hand and the on-order stock are reduced to this quantity level, the stock status report will indicate that a new order should be placed with a vendor.

Setting Reorder Cycles

In setting reorder conditions, some business firms calculate the order frequency instead of the reorder point. The *order frequency* states in days rather than in units when the stock status of an item should be reviewed. Determining the order frequency requires that the E.O.Q. ($\hat{Q}$) be determined first so that the number of orders to be placed during the year can be determined.

$$\text{Number of orders} = \text{Annual demand} \div \hat{Q}$$

Once the number of orders is known, the order frequency is determined by dividing the number of working days by the number of orders

$$\text{Order frequency} = \text{Annual working days} \div \text{Number of orders}$$

For instance, assume annual demand is 10,000 units and the E.O.Q. ($\hat{Q}$) is 800 units. At this order quantity, the number of orders per year would be 12.5 (10,000 ÷ 800). When the number of working days per year is 250, the order frequency is every 20 days (250 working days per year ÷ 12.5 orders per year = 20 days between orders). Thus, the level of stock should be checked by a member of the warehouse crew every twenty days. Checking involves comparing the quantity on hand and on order to the quantity needed during the next twenty days. The quantity-to-order decision then follows as before.

Cycle buying follows from the calculation of order frequency periods. With cycle buying, stock analysis is performed by the computer as follows. First, the computer checks each item stored on file and computes the days since the last review (the difference in days between the date of the last review and the current date). Second, this computed period is compared to the order frequency. When the period since the last review is equal to or greater than the order frequency, product-review information is written to an output file. This small file typically contains the number and name of the product, its location in inventory, and the quantity on hand and on order. The printed report shows the products to review at this time and their location.

Cycle buying is advantageous for a variety of reasons. Consider the following. It combines the taking of a physical inventory with the reordering of stock. If a manual check reveals a difference between the actual and computer-predicted amount on hand, adjustments to the product master file can be made. It helps control inventory shrinkage. A stock-loss tolerance standard can be set for each product carried in inventory. If losses are greater than the standard, steps can be taken to determine what is wrong. It permits higher-valued items to be reviewed more often than lower-valued items. In this instance, the usage value of the product is calculated to determine how often the product should be reviewed. *Usage value*, in dollars, is simply the average demand for the product times its unit cost:

$$\text{Usage value} = \text{Average demand} \times \text{Unit cost}$$

Figure 11–11 shows the results of a stock review based on usage value, when cycle buying is implemented. As illustrated, all A items are scheduled for review weekly because they are the most highly valued stock items carried in inventory. All C items, in contrast, are reviewed only twice a year because the cost of reviewing C items is more than the cost associated with running out of stock. Because B items

Item Category	No. of Items	Count Frequency	Items Each Week
A	2000	Weekly	2000
B	6000	Monthly	1500
C	12000	Semi annually	500
Total	20000		4000

Figure 11–11   Results of cycle buying

are of medium value, they are reviewed more frequently than C items, but less frequently than A items.

Reporting Stock Status and Reorder Information

Stock status and purchase advice displays and reports provide inventory managers with a recap of stock-keeping information and of decisions about product demand and reordering. With several online display screens, an inventory manager is able to review the actions taken by the computer or the effects of override decisions in regulating the quantity to carry in inventory. One display, for example, shows how the product forecast was determined. Another display screen shows how re-order decisions were made. Still another display screen permits inventory planners to study the sales history for a product. Figure 11–12 for example, illustrates the sales trend for a single item over the past twelve months. As indicated, sales of

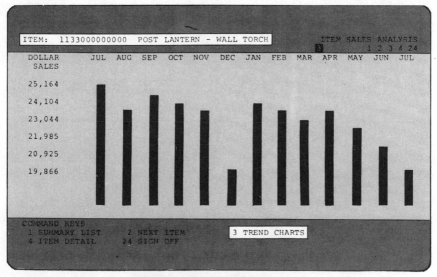

Figure 11–12   Sales history display

this post lantern reveal a downward trend, but they also show a six- to seven-month cycle.

The *stock status report* provides a summary of inventory activity for the current period (see Figure 11–13). Although this report contains several types of product information, its main use is to show the quantity on hand and on order, the quantity on hand that has been allocated, the remaining quantity available for sale, the average unit cost, and the on-hand cost of the item.

The stock status display is similar to the stock status report (see Figure 11–14). This particular display shows inventory location by warehouse and stocking information including quantity on hand, on order, on reserve (meaning serving as safety stock), and on back order.

```
GATEWAY MFG CO          PERIOD END INVENTORY STOCK STATUS    DATE 12/11/   TIME 13.46.17   PAGE 1   AM16C

ALL WAREHOUSES                      SEQUENCE BY ITEM

               ITEMS FROM 27002          TO 27006-80

                        ALL CLASSES
                        ALL VENDORS
```

ITEM CLASS	ITEM NUMBER	ITEM TYPE	ITEM DESCRIPTION			ITEM INVENTORY					
WHSE NO.	ITEM NUMBER	— — PERIOD TO DATE — — ISS / SALE RECEIPTS		ADJ.	QTY ON-HAND	QTY ON-ORDER	QTY ALLOC.	QTY AVAIL.	AVERAGE UNIT COST	ON HAND COST
70	27002-01	4 ADAPTER PLATE			EA					
1	036657	3042	0	0	3256	9000	225	11031	.2400	781.44
20	27003-20	1 PUMP ASSEMBLY			EA					
1		3125	3334	0	267	250	225	292	27.9500	7,452.65
50	27004-01	2 HANDLE			EA					
1		3034	4099	0	316	0	0	316	2.6000	821.60
	27005-A	1 PUMPING UNIT			EA					
A		0	0	0	13	0	0	13	37.7368	490.57
1		3042	4105	0	144	225	0	369	38.0150	5,474.16
		12243	11538	0	3996	8475	450	12021		15,030.42
	27006-F2	F TANK SIZE FEATURE			EA					
A		0	0	0	0	0	0	0	.0000	.00
1		0	0	0	0	0	0	0	.0000	.00
		0	0	0	0	0	0	0		.00
	27006-00	2 TANK TOP 8 INCHES			EA					
A		0	0	0	12	0	0	12	2.4316	29.17
B		0	0	0	187	0	0	187	2.4316	454.70
1		1575	1602	0	216	0	2200	1984-	2.3905	516.34
		1575	1602	0	415	0	2200	1785-		1,000.21
50	27006-10	2 TANK TOP 10 INCHES			EA					
1		2419	920	0	1392-	0	0	1392-	3.0050	4,182.96-
50	27006-20	2 TANK TOP 12 INCHES			EA					
1		656	660	0	99	0	1000	901-	4.7200	467.28
	27006-70	2 TANK BOTTOM 8 INCHES			EA					
A		0	0	0	0	0	0	0	1.5103	.00
B		0	0	0	0	0	0	0	1.5103	.00
1		1575	1591	0	209	0	2200	1991-	2.0102	420.13
		4650	3171	0	1084-	0	3200	4284-		3,295.55-
50	27006-80	2 TANK BOTTOM 10 INCHES			EA					
1		2417	918	0	1393-	0	0	1393-	1.6005	2,229.49-

```
                                                              REPORT TOTAL   10,505.59
```

Figure 11–13 Stock status report

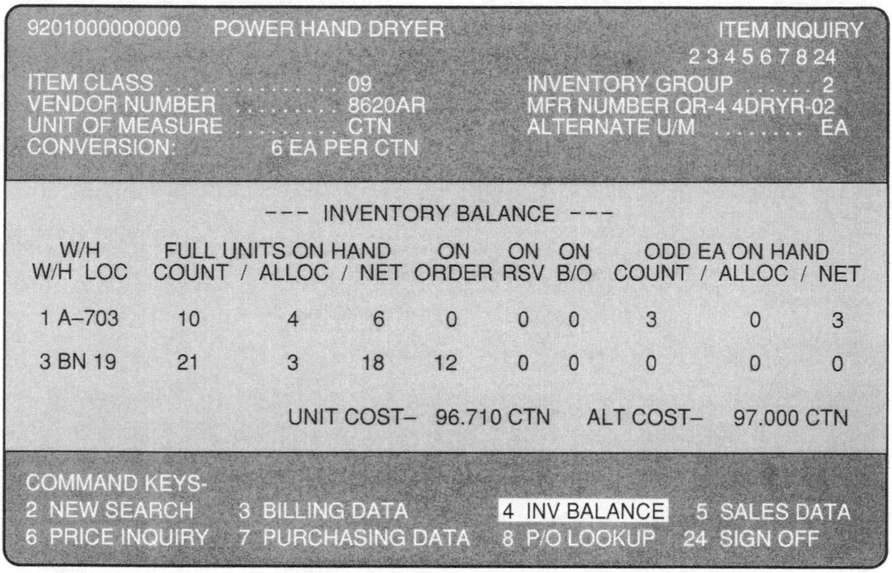

```
9201000000000   POWER HAND DRYER                          ITEM INQUIRY
                                                        2 3 4 5 6 7 8 24
ITEM CLASS .................. 09        INVENTORY GROUP ...... 2
VENDOR NUMBER ........... 8620AR        MFR NUMBER QR-4 4DRYR-02
UNIT OF MEASURE .......... CTN          ALTERNATE U/M ......... EA
CONVERSION:        6 EA PER CTN
```

--- INVENTORY BALANCE ---

W/H W/H LOC	FULL UNITS ON HAND COUNT / ALLOC / NET			ON ORDER	ON RSV	ON B/O	ODD EA ON HAND COUNT / ALLOC / NET		
1 A–703	10	4	6	0	0	0	3	0	3
3 BN 19	21	3	18	12	0	0	0	0	0

```
            UNIT COST– 96.710 CTN    ALT COST–  97.000 CTN
```

```
COMMAND KEYS-
2 NEW SEARCH      3 BILLING DATA      4 INV BALANCE   5 SALES DATA
6 PRICE INQUIRY   7 PURCHASING DATA   8 P/O LOOKUP    24 SIGN OFF
```

Figure 11–14   Stock status display

Figure 11–15 shows a *purchase advice report*. This more detailed report fully describes reorder decisions: the quantity available, the order point, the E.O.Q., the safety stock, and vendor lead time. This report is designed for use by purchasing agents and is available on request. Inventory managers also use this report to review product reorder decisions for a warehouse, a class of products, or a range of vendors.

REVIEW QUESTIONS

7. How many master files are updated by the finished-goods application?

8. Explain the difference between extrinsic and intrinsic forecasts.

9. Explain the exponential smoothing formula.

10. What is the E.O.Q.$(\hat{Q})$? How is it calculated?

11. What is a reorder point? How is it calculated?

12. What is the order frequency? How is it calculated?

13. What is cycle buying? What are its main advantages?

14. How is usage value calculated? For what is it used?

15. Which items from the product master file are printed on the purchase advice report?

GATEWAY MFG CO   INVENTORY REORDER REPORT DATE 12/11/ TIME 8.42.07 PAGE 1 AM12M

SEQUENCE BY VENDOR

VENDORS FROM 001011 TO 096267

DESCRIPTION

VENDOR ITEM NUMBER CLASS	ITEM NUMBER	WH NO	U/M	QTY ON-HAND	QTY ON-ORDER	QTY ALLOCATED	QTY AVAILABLE	ORDER POINT	E.O.Q.	SAFETY STOCK	LEAD TIME	L/T ADJ	AVERAGE PERIOD USE
NUT													
001011 80	07243	1	EA	5,087	0	0	5,087	7,000 *	10,182 *	0	030P	02	665
PLATED CYLINDER 12 IN													
006592 30	99239-RM	1	EA	1,017	0	0	1,017	2,500 *	109 *	0	120P	10	76
CASTING													
015772 30	99990-RM	1	EA	11,247	0	0	11,247	15,000 *	414 *	0	150P	10	357
HINGE WASHER													
018834 80	03587	1	EA	12,631	0	0	12,631	72,000 *	6,961 *	0	015P	02	665
HINGE WASHER													
018334 80	03640	1	EA	4,871	0	0	4,871	6,000 *	12,000 *	0	015P	02	665
ROUND STOCK 5/8 DIA -CRS													
024775 30	99544-RM	1	FT	5,327	0	0	5,327	8,000 *	1,476 *	0	030P	02	712
1/8 SHEET METAL													
...775 30	99750-RM	1	SF	10,851	0	0	10,851	20,000 *	1,435 *	0	060P	02	1,201
...4 IN - HRS													
0247...	...0-RM	1	LB	6,445	0	0	6,445	10,000 *	902 *	0	060P	02	567
BAR STOCK POT													
024775 30	99950				0	0	1,261	15,000 *	1,209 *	0	090P	02	526
VALVE													
030716 80	03021	1	EA	93			93-	1,063 *	9,000 *	0	060P	02	332
CONTROL BOX													
042598 70	33480-A	1	EA	4,898	0	225		6,000 *	544 *	308	060P	05	342
WRENCH													
072303 80	03385	1	EA	7,927	0	0	7,927		1,208 *	0	030P	02	337
RUBBER TUBE 1 x 3													
096267 80	34180-A	1	EA	3,143	0	0	3,143	6,000 *	*	0	030X	05	332
RUBBER TUBE 314 x 2													
096267 80	34180-B	1	EA	3,267	0	0	3,267	6,000 *	3,220		030X	02	332
RUBBER TUBE 1/4 x 4													
096267 80	46800-C	1	EA	5,232	0	0	5,232	7,000 *	2,629 *	0		02	332

TOTAL NUMBER OF RECORDS SELECTED   15

NOTE-   *   -MANUALLY ENTERED
        M   -LEAD TIME MANUFACTURING
        P   -LEAD TIME PURCHASING
        X   -OTHER LEAD TIME

Figure 11–15 Purchase advice report

11-3 METHODS OF COSTING FINISHED-GOODS INVENTORY

A critical factor in setting up the finished-goods inventory application is selecting the method of costing inventory. Because the cost of goods often varies from one reorder decision to the next, a method is needed to determine what cost to apply. Four methods of costing inventory are the average cost method; the standard cost method; the first-in, first-out (FIFO) method; and the last-in, first-out (LIFO) method.

Average Cost Method

The average cost method assumes that the cost of inventory is the total cost of goods on hand divided by the total quantity on hand. Figure 11–16 illustrates how this method works. The important steps are as follows:

1. Determine the average unit cost. This is the total on-hand cost divided by the total on-hand quantity and includes the cost and count of the beginning inventory.

Dec. 1	Beginning Inventory	100 units @ $1.00 = $100.00
Dec. 7	Purchase	200 units @ $1.20 = $240.00
Dec. 19	Purchase	200 units @ $1.15 = $230.00
		500 $570.00

Average cost $570/500   = $1.14 per unit

Ending inventory:
  Beginning inventory   = 100 units +
  Moves in   400 units −
  Moves out   450 units = 50 units

Cost of Ending
   inventory = 50 units x $1.14 per unit = $57.00

Cost of goods available for sale	$570.00
Less: Ending inventory	57.00
Cost of goods sold	$513.00

Figure 11–16   Average cost method of costing inventory

2. Based on the average cost, determine the cost of the ending inventory.

3. Determine the cost of goods sold (the cost of goods available for sale less the cost of the ending inventory).

Standard Cost Method

The standard cost method uses a cost set by management. Let's suppose the standard cost for our last example is set at $1.15 per unit. As shown by Figure 11–17, the standard cost yields a positive or negative variance unless the standard cost is exactly the same as the actual cost. Managers often use this method to set a price target for the purchasing department. For example, in this example, the purchasing

Dec. 1	Beginning Inventory	100 units @ $1.00 = $100.00
Dec. 7	Purchase	200 units @ $1.20 = $240.00
Dec. 19	Purchase	200 units @ $1.15 = $230.00
		500 $570.00

Actual cost	= $570.00
Standard cost (500 units x $1.15 per unit)	= 575.00
Cost Variance	$ 5.00

Cost of goods sold (450 x $1.15)	$517.50
Less: Average cost of goods sold	513.00
Cost Variance	$ 3.50

Figure 11–17   Standard cost method of costing inventory

Dec. 1	Beginning Inventory	100 units @ $1.00 = $100.00
Dec. 7	Purchase	200 units @ $1.20 = $240.00
Dec. 19	Purchase	200 units @ $1.15 = $230.00
		500 $570.00

December Sales   450 units

Cost of goods sold:
            100 units @ $1.00 = $100.00
            200 units @ $1.20 = $240.00
            150 units @ $1.15 = $172.50
                              $512.50

Closing inventory:
            50 units @ $1.15 = $ 57.50

Figure 11–18   First-in, First-out (FIFO) method of costing inventory

managers should be able to purchase additional stock items for less than $1.15 per unit. As illustrated, they were able to do this.

First-in, First-out (FIFO) Method

This method is based on the assumption that the oldest item placed in inventory (first in) will be sold first (first out). Figure 11–18 illustrates how this method works. As indicated, the oldest units purchased at a cost of $1.00 each are sold first. The units acquired the most recently are accounted for in a future period.

Last-in, First-out (LIFO) Method

This method is the reverse of FIFO and is based on the assumption that the last item placed in inventory (last in) will be sold first (first out). Figure 11–19 illustrates

Dec. 1	Beginning Inventory	100 units @ $1.00 = $100.00
Dec. 7	Purchase	200 units @ $1.20 = $240.00
Dec. 19	Purchase	200 units @ $1.15 = $230.00
		500 $570.00

December Sales   450 units

Cost of goods sold:
            200 units @ $1.15 = $230.00
            200 units @ $1.20 = $240.00
            50 units @ $2.00 = $100.00
                              $570.00

Closing inventory:
            50 units @ $1.00 = $ 50.00

Figure 11–19   Last-in, first-out (LIFO) method of costing inventory

	Average cost	Standard cost	FIFO	LIFO
Sales	$585.00	$585.00	$585.00	$585.00
Less:				
Cost of goods sold	$513.00	$517.50	$512.50	$520.00
Gross profit	$ 72.00	$ 67.50	$ 72.50	$ 65.00

Figure 11-20   Comparison of inventory costing methods

how this method works. In this instance, the newest units purchased at $1.15 each are sold first; it may take considerable time before the oldest units purchased at $1.00 each are charged against the cost of goods sold.

Comparison of Methods

A comparison of these four methods reveals that selecting the method of costing inventory affects gross profit totals. Figure 11-20 provides such a comparison. In preparing this table, it was assumed that each unit was sold at $1.30. What do these differences mean? During a period of rapid inflation, LIFO will result in the lowest gross profit and FIFO the highest. The standard and average cost methods usually fall in between these highest and lowest profit totals. The average cost method, for example, levels out the effects of cost increases and decreases. The standard cost method is also compared with average cost.

In terms of their complexity, FIFO and the average cost methods are the easiest to audit and review. Both methods have advantages: FIFO keeps inventory cost close to its replacement value, and the average cost method saves disk space. LIFO and the standard cost method also have key advantages, even though they are more complicated to audit and review. LIFO prevents paying taxes on fictitious profit during times of rising prices, and the standard method isolates cost variance better than any other method.

11-4   FINISHED-GOODS INVENTORY ANALYSIS

Besides reviewing items held in stock to determine whether to reorder and how to cost inventory, inventory planners must carefully evaluate overall inventory performance. When a program of evaluation is combined with stock review, a company is better able to meet its inventory management and order-filling objectives.

Inventory-Value Analysis

Inventory-value analysis supports an ABC approach to inventory control. In this type of analysis, the initial step in processing is to determine the usage value (average demand times unit price) for each item carried in inventory. Returning to an earlier example, suppose that the average annual demand for down-filled sleeping bags is 840 and that each bags sells for $50.00. The usage value for down-filled bags is thus $42,000. Now suppose that the average demand for polyester-filled bags is 1,760 and that each of these bags costs $25.00. The usage value would be $44,000, or approximately the same as that for down-filled bags, even though demand is more than twice as great.

After usage value has been determined, the next step in inventory value analysis is to rank all products from highest to lowest usage value and then to calculate the cumulative cost associated with this ranking. As Figure 11–21 shows, this procedure leads to a *value-analysis report*—a listing of all items carried in stock, ranked in order of their usage value. This report often reveals interesting findings. It is common, for example, to discover that 20 percent of all items stored make up 80 percent of the cumulative usage value!

The final step in inventory value analysis is to assign an A code to the items of highest value, a B code to items of medium value, and a C code to those of lowest value. As Figure 11–21 reveals, A items account for less than 22 percent of all items, yet they have a cumulative usage value percentage of 79.4 percent. C items, in contrast, account for over 53 percent of all items, but have a cumulative usage value percentage of 4.8 percent. Finally, B items fall in between A and C items. These account for 25 percent of all items and have a cumulative usage value of 15.8 percent.

The value-analysis report helps the controller (the chief financial officer) of a company project inventory cash requirements. If, for example, the cumulative cost of inventory is increasing by 5 percent a month, this increase can be used in estimating future cash requirements. This report is also valuable in setting the value of inventory for insurance purposes. By comparing the value of inventory with the dollar amount of insured coverage, a business is able to determine if it is adequately protected.

Inventory Investment Analysis

Inventory investment analysis examines the performance of stock items to determine whether the supply of stock appears high, whether the turnover of stock appears low, and whether the return on investment (R.O.I.) is acceptable. To answer the first question—whether the supply of stock appears high—the month's supply of stock must be calculated as follows:

$$\text{Month's supply} = \text{Current inventory} \div \text{Average demand}$$

(If, for example, the average demand is 1,000 units and 6,500 units are stored in inventory, the month's supply is 6.5). Inventory investment, measured by month's supply, is shown on the *month's supply report* (see Figure 11–22). This report permits inventory managers to evaluate all stock items with a high month's supply. For example, the month's supply for product 8300003-21 is well above the average. To reduce the stock on hand, the reorder point can be lowered and the order quantity can be reduced in size.

ITEM NUMBER	DESCRIPTION	ITEM COUNT	%	ANNUAL USAGE QTY	UNIT COST	ANNUAL USAGE VALUE	CUMULATIVE COST	%
8300007-80	PUMP ASSM	1	.9	6,250	185.90	1,161,875	1,161,875	9.4
8300004-81	TANK ASSM	2	1.9	5,107	224.73	1,147,696	2,309,571	18.7
07085	HOUSING ASSM	3	2.8	10,000	97.74	977,400	3,286,971	26.6
8300005-20	PUMPING UNIT	4	3.7	3,762	216.93	816,090	4,103,061	33.1
8300005-23	PUMPING UNIT	5	4.6	2,488	210.63	524,047	4,627,108	37.4
8300005-21	PUMPING UNIT	6	5.6	2,045	233.07	476,628	5,103,736	41.2
8300004-80	TANK ASSM	7	6.5	2,493	182.23	454,299	5,558,035	44.9
8300004-01	TANK TOP	8	7.4	5,819	77.05	448,353	6,006,388	48.5
8300007-81	PUMP ASSM	9	8.3	2,045	202.04	413,171	6,419,559	51.9
8300005-22	PUMPING-UNIT	10	9.3	1,705	241.39	411,569	6,831,128	55.9
8300007-8	PUMP ASSM	11	10.2	1,705	210.36	358,663	7,189,791	58.1
A7685	COVER ASSM	12	11.1	10,200	32.49	331,398	7,521,189	60.8
07106	PUMP SHAFT	13	12.0	10,200	28.00	285,600	7,806,789	63.1
07087	DISCHARGE FERRULE	14	13.0	10,000	28.18	281,800	8,088,589	65.3
8300004-83	TANK ASSM	15	13.9	1,431	180.87	258,824	8,347,413	67.4
8300004-84	TANK ASSM	16	14.8	1,003	223.37	224,040	8,571,453	69.2
8300004-20	TANK BOTTOM	17	15.7	7,512	28.60	214,843	8,786,296	71.0
07685	COVER	18	16.7	10,200	20.41	208,182	8,994,478	72.7
8300004-00	TANK TOP	19	17.6	3,737	50.39	188,307	9,182,785	74.2
07730	MOTOR	20	18.5	6,250	28.45	177,812	9,360,597	75.6
8300003-80	FRAME	21	19.4	4,601	35.00	161,035	9,521,632	76.9
A7666	STAND PIPE ASSM	22	20.4	10,000	16.00	160,000	9,681,632	78.2
A7761	PROBE	23	21.3	7,512	20.30	152,493	9,834,125	79.4
07086	SHELL	24	22.2	10,000	12.50	125,000	9,959,125	80.5
07682-2	STAND	25	23.1	5,819	20.52	119,405	10,078,530	81.4
07686-2	TREADLE ASSM	26	24.1	5,819	19.53	112,597	10,191,127	82.3
8300006-01	HANDLE	27	25.0	10,100	10.69	107,696	10,298,823	83.2
07090	SEALING PLATE	28	25.9	11,000	9.63	105,930	10,404,753	84.1
8300003-21	BASE	29	26.9	1,649	57.16	95,256	10,500,009	84.8
07730-1	MOTOR	30	27.7	2,045	44.59	91,186	10,591,195	85.6
A7696	CLAMP	31	28.7	10,000	9.06	90,600	10,681,795	86.3
07730-2	MOTOR	32	29.6	1,705	52.91	90,211	10,772,006	87.0
8300003-22	BASE	33	30.6	1,487	56.00	84,640	10,856,646	87.7
	CONECTION	34	31.5	10,000			56,646	88.3
	TREADLE ASSM	35	32.4					88.9
								89.4
8300004-83				179	200.39	35,869	11,682,000	
07510	IO		44.4	14,582	2.36	34,413	11,716,845	
A7762	CONTROL BOX	49	45.4	2,488	210.63	34,160	11,751,005	
07688-2	LEVER ARM	50	46.3	14,548	2.29	33,314	11,784,319	935
8300003-23	BASE	51	47.2	558	58.16	32,453	11,816,772	95.5
07690	HINGE BASKET	52	48.1	10,500	2.91	30,555	11,847,327	95.7
A7641	FILTER SLEEVE	53	49.1	10,000	3.00	30,000	11,877,327	96.0
07725	WRENCH	54	50.0	10,000	3.00	30,000	11,907,327	96.2
8300003-25	BASE	55	50.9	502	58.16	29,196	11,936,523	96.4
8300004-02	TANK TOP	56	51.9	444	62.70	27,838	11,964,361	96.7
07186	TUBE	57	52.8	10,000	2.69	26,900	11,991,261	96.9
07198	ADAPTOR PLATE	58	53.7	10,000	2.62	26,200	12,017,461	97.1
8300008-01	ADAPTOR PLATE	59	54.6	10,000	2.62	26,200	12,043,661	97.5
07693	WHEEL BOLT	60	55.6	21,000	1.12	23,520	12,067,181	97.5
7105	WEARING COLLAR	61	56.5	10,000	2.08	20		
8300003-85	FRAME	62	57.4	558	36.60		12,372,185	100.0
	DRIVING COLLAR	63	58.3	10,000		1,000	12,373,185	100.0
	LEVER ARM	64	59.3	9.3			12,374,185	100.0
A760		65	60.3		.10	1,000		
07108					.09	918	12,375,103	100.0
21896				20,000	.04	800	12,375,903	100.0
12102	WASHER		97.2	70,000	.01	700	12,376,603	100.0
07109	SET SCREW	106	98.1	10,000	.07	700	12,377,303	100.0
06478	WHELL WASHER	107	99.1	40,000	.01	400	12,377,703	100.0
07460	HINGE WASHER	108	100.0	20,000	.01	200	12,377,903	100.0

Figure 11–21   Value-analysis report

Inventory Investment – Month's Supply 10/01/XX				
Finished Goods				
Part Number	ABC Code	Current Inventory	Unit Cost	Month's Supply
8300007-80	A	$ 500,600	$ 185.90	6.6
8300004-81	A	23,000	224.73	6.2
8300003-21	B	44,560	57.16	6.0
No. Items – 375		$1,939,500	Average	2.7
Summary by Category	A B C	$ 755,000 500,000 864,000		5.6 2.9 1.8

Figure 11–22 Month's supply report

Inventory turnover analysis is similar to month's supply analysis. The summary produced, the *inventory turnover report*, provides a ranking of inventory turnover ratios (see Figure 11–23). Each ratio is calculated as follows:

$$\text{Inventory turnover} = \text{Annual requirements} \div \text{Average inventory}$$

Inventory Investment – Turns per Year 10/01/XX						
Fabricated Parts:						
Part Number	ABC Code	Order Policy	Order Quantity	Average Inventory	Annual Reqmts	Turnover Ratio
07688-1	C	Fixed	1000	1850	1110	0.6
07682-1	C	Fixed	700	555	444	0.8
8300004-85	B	Period	30 days	163	179	1.1
8300003-25	C	Period	180 days	418	502	1.2
No. Items – 5,164					Average	2.8
Summary by Category	A B C					4.8 2.6 1.1

Figure 11–23 Inventory-turnover report

Inventory Investment — Return Investment					10/ 1/ XX
Finished Goods					
Part Number	ABC Code	Total Sales	Turnover Ratio	Percent Earned	Return on Investment
0893167	C	5000	1.1	.034	.0374
0996524	B	40000	2.6	.045	.1170
0439621	A	160000	4.8	.055	.2640
Number of Items	4316			Average	.1524
Summary	A Items				.3236
	B Items				.1564
	C Items				.0451

Figure 11–24 Return-on-investment report

Thus, for part number 07688-1, the annual requirement of 1,110 would be divided by the average inventory, 1,850, to yield a turnover ratio of 0.6.

The inventory turnover report helps inventory planners to review the order policy and order quantity decisions set for products. Typically, if order quantities are too high, turnover will be too low. Suppose, for example, that following review it is determined that the order quantity for part number 07688-1 must be reduced to 500 units. This action increases the turnover rate by 0.5 (from 0.6 to 1.1). As Figure 11–23 shows, a turnover ratio of 1.1 is the average rate for C items.

Return-on-investment analysis determines which product returns are higher or lower than average. This information is printed on a *return-on-investment report* (see Figure 11–24). R.O.I. is determined by multiplying the turnover ratio times the percent earned on a product. As the figure shows, part number 0893167, a C item, provides a small return of .0374 (3.74 percent on sales), whereas part number 0439621, an A item, provides a much higher return of .2640 (26.4 percent on sales). In addition, even though R.O.I. is high for part number 0439621, it is low compared with the average for all A items (32.36 percent on sales).

Analyses such as month's supply, inventory turnover, and return on investment help inventory managers visualize the performance characteristics of products carried in inventory. They isolate products that are above and below average. Careful review of these products combined with corrective action, when necessary, is the basis underlying the concept of *inventory control*. A vital objective is to maximize the return on investment in inventory in a way that is consistent with the prompt delivery of goods and services to customers.

Inventory Location Analysis

Inventory location analysis examines the location of items in inventory to determine if they should be relocated to save travel time, to consolidate stock stored in multiple locations, to free inventory space, or to reduce inventory shrinkage. Several types of reports help inventory planners make these determinations. For example, travel-time

Inventory Locaton – Bin Location					10/ 1/ XX
		Finished Goods			
Part Number	ABC Code	Total Sales	Total Orders	Distance Each Trip	Distance Traveled
064100	C	5000	75	850	12.07
095450	B	18000	380	85	6.12
069340	B	10000	212.5	112	4.51
069086	A	46000	35	512	3.42

Number of Items	2354		Average	3.8
Summary A Items				2.4
B Items				3.3
C Items				5.4

Figure 11–25   Distance-traveled report

figures are printed on a *distance-traveled report* (see Figure 11–25), which shows the cumulative distance traveled by the warehouse crew in stocking parts and in filling customer orders. The total distance-traveled time is arrived at by using the following equation:

Distance traveled = Distance each trip × (Number of stock receipts
+ Number of orders picked)

Suppose, for instance, that the annual demand for product number 069340 (see Figure 11–25) is 10,000 units, the quantity to order is 800 units, and the average customer order is 50 units. If the warehouse crew must walk 112 feet to stock this product or to fill a customer order, the total distance traveled is determined as follows:

$$N_1 = \text{Number of stock receipts} = \text{Annual demand} \div \hat{Q}$$
$$= 10{,}000 \div 800 = 12.5$$

$$N_2 = \text{Number of orders picked} = \text{Annual demand} \div \text{Average sale}$$
$$= 10{,}000 \div 50 = 200$$

$$\text{Distance traveled} = 112 \text{ ft} \times (12.5 + 200) = 23{,}800 \text{ ft}$$
$$= 23{,}800 \text{ ft.} \div 5{,}280 \text{ ft. per mile} = 4.51 \text{ miles}$$

Information printed on the distance-traveled report isolates cases in which total travel time appears to be much higher than normal. To equalize travel time, inventory planners must make tradeoffs: the distance associated with high order counts (high N_1 and N_2) is reduced, and the distance associated with low order counts (low N_1 and N_2) is increased. By coordinating changes in bin location, inventory planners attempt to minimize overall travel time.

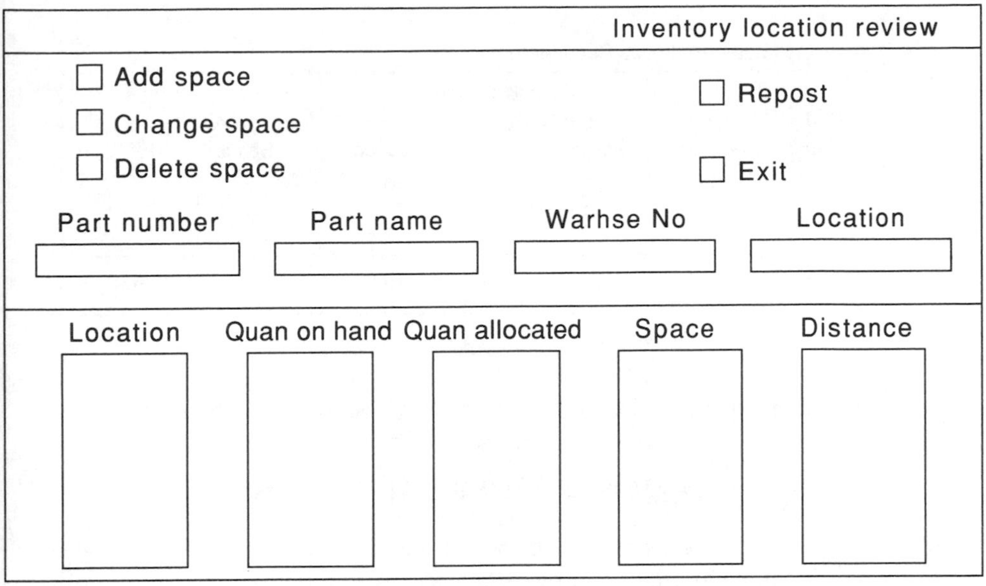

```
┌─────────────────────────────────────────────────────────────────────┐
│                                        Inventory location review      │
├─────────────────────────────────────────────────────────────────────┤
│   ☐ Add space                              ☐ Repost                    │
│   ☐ Change space                                                      │
│   ☐ Delete space                           ☐ Exit                     │
│                                                                       │
│   Part number        Part name        Warhse No        Location       │
│   [          ]       [          ]     [          ]     [          ]   │
├─────────────────────────────────────────────────────────────────────┤
│   Location    Quan on hand Quan allocated    Space       Distance     │
│   ┌──────┐   ┌──────┐  ┌──────┐        ┌──────┐      ┌──────┐        │
│   │      │   │      │  │      │        │      │      │      │        │
│   │      │   │      │  │      │        │      │      │      │        │
│   │      │   │      │  │      │        │      │      │      │        │
│   └──────┘   └──────┘  └──────┘        └──────┘      └──────┘        │
└─────────────────────────────────────────────────────────────────────┘
```

Figure 11–26 Inventory location review

Reducing the number of stock items stored in multiple locations is often accomplished by reducing the space requirements of slower-moving items and giving this space to faster-moving items. This solution addresses what is sometimes called the "grocery shelving" problem: shelf space is constant, but product demand is variable. The objective of managing shelf space is to increase the amount of space for faster-selling items to maximize sales, to avoid running out of stock, and to avoid multiple stock locations. Because space is limited, this increase must be achieved either by eliminating slower-moving items or by reducing the shelf space previously assigned to them. Juggling a fixed amount of inventory space is especially difficult when a firm maintains several warehouse locations. With several locations, stored-product location data must be expanded and online displays must be designed to show the various storage locations. A display must show the quantity stored at each location and whether the quantity can be used to fill customer orders (see Figure 11–26).

Multiple stock locations can be avoided, although not completely eliminated—unless, of course, a business has excess storage space. To maximize the use of available space, inventory managers must conduct space-analysis studies. The report needed for these studies is the *space requirements report*. As Figure 11–27 shows, this report compares the space assigned with the space required by products carried in inventory. Suppose, for example, that product 30008 is stored in three locations and measures 5 by 5 by 5 inches, or 125 cubic inches. At most, 160 of these items will be carried in stock. The space required (in cubic feet) is calculated as follows:

Inventory Locaton – Space Requirements						10/ 1/ XX
			Finished Goods			
Part Number	Part Location	Maximum Stock	Cubic Inch	Assigned Space	Required Space	Diff
30008	7433			3.0		
	96147			4.0		
	43444			3.5		
Total		160	125	10.5	11.57	(1.07)

Figure 11–27   Space-requirements report

Space required = (Maximum inventory) (Cubic inch requirements)
÷ 1,728 cubic inches per cubic foot

= (160)(125) ÷ 1,728 = 11.57 cubic feet

If the stock cannot be consolidated, there will be times when the space provided by the existing three locations will be inadequate. With too little space, stock will have to remain in receiving or in another temporary location until sufficient units are sold.

The final type of inventory location analysis common to business deals with tracking inventory shrinkage. Shrinkage can result from a number of factors, such as pilferage or errors in physical inventory. The formula used in determining shrinkage is as follows:

Shrinkage = Beginning inventory + Moves in
− Moves out − Ending inventory

Thus, if beginning inventory for an item is 500 units, ending inventory is 650 units, 600 units move in, and 400 units move out, the shrinkage during the month would be 50 units (500 + 600 − 400 − 650).

Figure 11–28 illustrates an inventory shrinkage report. A unique feature of shrinkage is that it can be positive as well as negative. As shown, part number

Inventory Locaton – Shrinkage Analysis						10/ 1/ XX
			Finished Goods			
Part Number	Part Location	Begin Invt	Moves In	Moves Out	End Invt	Shrinkage
31124	85AJ	500	600	400	650	(50)
43694	54BP	900	100	300	500	(200)
93214	654R	1820	850	1240	1500	70
93241	896J	625	70	225	400	(70)

Figure 11–28   Inventory-shrinkage report

93214 reveals a surplus of 70 units. The typical reason for such a surplus is that 70 units were stocked incorrectly—in the wrong bin location. Inspection of all accounts often shows that surplus items can be matched against outstanding losses. As the figure shows, product number 93214 has a surplus of 70 items, whereas product number 93241 has a reported short of 70 items. Because these two counts are the same and one account number can be transformed into the other, the odds are high that the two products were switched.

11-5 MANAGEMENT IMPLICATIONS

Finished-goods inventory is a popular computer application because it provides inventory planners with a wealth of record-keeping and stock performance information. Another review of the contents of the product master file (see Figure 11–3) illustrates that this single application is able to describe, locate, and provide an accounting for each product carried in inventory. This capability is much more important than it might initially appear. If, for example, a business attempts to keep in stock 10,000 or more items, some automated method must be found to assist in record keeping and in making routine inventory decisions. Otherwise the task of inventory management is enormous.

Besides its benefits for record keeping, this computer application is extremely popular because it allows inventory planners to monitor computer-based decisions, substituting, where appropriate, programmed decisions with their own. Still another benefit is that inventory management can be decentralized. People familiar with the characteristics of items carried in inventory are able to rule on inventory decisions. Online designs also simplify file-update procedures and improve processing controls so that people familiar with the types of updates required are responsible for making these updates. Through visual review of all updates, processing control can be markedly improved.

The concept of "just in time" can be implemented with a computer-based system of managing inventory. This concept means that new stock arrives just as it is needed to fill new orders. A just-in-time approach requires careful coordination of order entry, inventory management, and purchasing and receiving. We will discuss this concept more in the next chapter.

Producing various types of displays and reports represents a major managerial benefit of an automated approach to inventory management. By closely monitoring stock value, month's supply, turnover, return on investment, distance traveled, multiple inventory locations, space requirements, and inventory shrinkage, inventory planners are better able to make more objective inventory plans. Combining these studies, business firms discover that they are able to carry smaller quantities of stock while increasing sales volume and overall product profitability. This ability to operate at higher leverage (less investment in relation to sales) can dramatically improve the financial well-being of a business. Reducing the funds needed for inventory permits funds to be released for use in more profitable operations.

REVIEW QUESTIONS

16. Explain the difference between LIFO and FIFO.

17. What is the standard cost method of costing inventory?

18. Explain the difference between usage value and value analysis.

19. Name three types of inventory investment analysis reports.

20. Define the term "inventory control."

21. How does inventory location analysis differ from inventory investment analysis?

22. What types of information are contained on the space requirements report?

23. Name three types of inventory location studies.

24. What advantage is gained by a decentralized finished-goods inventory design?

REVIEW OF IMPORTANT IDEAS

The finished-goods inventory application must provide product inventory counts (quantity on hand, on order, on back order, and so forth) and show all product-reorder decisions (when to order, how much to order, and from whom to order). Careful review of both types of information leads to better understanding of how to make inventory decisions.

This application is designed to maximize the return on capital invested in inventory. By improving inventory turnover while holding the percentage earned on sales constant, companies are able to increase their return on invested capital dramatically.

The design of the application is straightforward. The heart of processing is the update of the product master file. Once updated, the file is used in a variety of ways. Two common products of processing are stock status and purchase advice reports and displays. Stock status reports show the current status of items held in stock relative to future supply and demand for these items. Purchase advice reports show product reorder decisions: which products to order (or review), the quantity to order, and, in some instances, the preferred source of supply.

Planners can determine which products to order by studying computer-calculated reorder points or order frequencies. Cycle buying follows from the calculation of order frequencies. With cycle buying, taking a periodic physical inventory is combined with ordering stock. Cycle buying permits high-valued items to be checked more frequently than lower-valued items.

A key decision to be made by inventory managers is the choice of the best method of costing inventory. The average and standard methods level out the effects of cost increases and decreases. LIFO and FIFO require an exact accounting of the costs of goods that move in and out of inventory.

Inventory value analysis, investment analysis, and location analysis are vital parts in an overall inventory management plan. Inventory value analysis assigns A, B, and C codes to items carried in stock. Inventory investment analysis examines the supply of stock, product turnover rates, and product returns on capital invested in inventory. Inventory location analysis determines more economical ways to store products in company warehouse facilities. Collectively, these different types of analysis permit inventory planners to monitor carefully and adjust inventory management decisions. In so doing, a business firm is better able to achieve its objective of maximizing the return on capital invested in inventory.

KEY WORDS

Order frequency	Economic order quantity
Inventory management	Reorder point
Return on investment	Cycle buying
Inventory turnover	Average Costing
Physical inventory	Standard Costing
Stockout	FIFO
Inventory shrinkage	LIFO
ABC code	Usage value
Stock status report	Value analysis
Purchase advice	Inventory control
Extrinsic forecast	Month's supply report
Intrinsic forecast	Distance-traveled report
Trend analysis	Space requirements report
Exponential smoothing	

EXERCISES

1. Suppose the economic order quantity for a product is 700 units, the vendor lead time (the time to reorder) is twenty days, the average daily demand is forty units, and the safety stock is 125 units.

   (a) What is the reorder point for this product?

   (b) How much stock will be on hand when the new order arrives?

   (c) How much stock will be on hand when the new order arrives if the average demand is forty-two units and it takes twenty-two days to receive the new order?

2. Suppose product sales and the product sales forecasts from June through October for product number 64521, Golden Wire Baskets, are as follows:

MONTH	PRODUCT FORECAST	PRODUCT SALES
June	900	920
July	904	950
August	913	935
September	917	960
October	926	945
November	?	

(a) When alpha (α) equals 0.2, what is the product forecast for November?

(b) Compute the November forecast once again, but set the value of alpha (α) at 0.3 instead of 0.2. After adjusting, the product forecast should read as follows: forecast for June equals 900, forecast for July equals 906, forecast for August equals 919, and so forth.

(c) Compare the two product forecasts. Based on this comparison, what can you say about setting the correct value of alpha? Would you change your view if the actual product sales for November were 900 units?

3. The following information is known about a product carried in inventory:

Annual demand	40,000 units
Purchase order cost	$20.15
Cost per unit	$10.00
Cost of capital	10 percent
Annual working days	250 days
Percent earned on sales	4 percent
Average inventory	2,000

Based on this information, calculate the

(a) economic order quantity

(b) order frequency

(c) usage value

(d) return on investment

4. The following information is known about the space requirements for three products.

PART NUMBER	PART LOCATION	MAXIMUM STOCK (IN UNITS)	CUBIC FEET PER UNIT	ASSIGNED SPACE (CUBIC FEET)
112	A	3000	.003	5.0
118	B	5000	.005	40.0
120	C	2000	.006	14.0
120	D	4000	.006	25.0

Based on this information,

(a) show what further information would be placed on the space-requirements report, and

(b) show how multiple-stock locations for part number 120 would be eliminated and reported on a revised space requirements report.

(c) Show how the table can be adjusted one more time to provide sufficient space for part number 112.

5. Suppose we know the total annual sales, total orders, dollars earned per order, maximum stock, and average inventory for products 112, 118, and 120 (see Exercise 4).

PART NUMBER	TOTAL ANNUAL SALES (IN UNITS)	TOTAL ORDERS	DOLLARS EARNED PER ORDER	MAXIMUM STOCK (IN UNITS)	AVERAGE INVEN- TORY (IN UNITS)
112	24,000	120	$8.00	3000	2000
118	44,000	400	4.00	5000	2200
120	60,000	300	6.00	6000	3000

(a) Based on this information, calculate the return on investment for each product.

(b) If the minimal return is set at 50 percent and above, what can you conclude from your analysis?

(c) If the business decides to base product price on percent earned per unit of product sold rather than on dollars earned per order, what percent would be required for all three products to have a return on investment of exactly 50 percent?

6. Examine the stock status report shown on Figure 11–13.

(a) Write the equation used to calculate the quantity available.

(b) Write the equation for determining the on-hand cost.

(c) In three instances, the quantity on hand is shown as negative. How could this happen?

7. Suppose we know that 600 units of a product were sold during the month of June and that the beginning inventory and the units moved in for the product during the month were as follows:

June 1	Beginning Inventory	300 units @ 6.00
June 5	Purchase	100 units @ 5.95
June 8	Purchase	100 units @ 6.15
June 18	Purchase	200 units @ 5.90
June 29	Purchase	100 units @ 6.10

(a)   What is the average cost and the cost of goods sold when the average cost method is used in costing inventory?

(b)   If the standard cost is $5.95, what is the cost of goods sold and the cost variance when the standard cost method is used in costing inventory?

(c)   Using FIFO, determine the cost of goods sold.

(d)   Use LIFO to estimate the cost of goods sold.

(e)   With these four cost-of-goods-sold figures, what conclusion can you draw about which method of costing is best?

DISCUSSION QUESTIONS

1. Some companies state that the quantity ordered is equal to the quantity on hand plus the quantity on order minus the quantity allocated (see Figure 11–13). What are the advantages and disadvantages of defining the quantity available in this manner?

2. Some managers might think that the computer can be used to make reorder decisions for all categories of inventory (A, B, and C) and that rarely, if ever, should a computer-based decision be overruled. Discuss the dangers of this view.

3. Which type of manager might find inventory value analysis the most important? Inventory location analysis? Inventory investment analysis?

4. The standard cost method is often viewed as the best method of costing inventory and the most difficult to implement. Why is this true?

4-IN-1 CASE STUDY—FINISHED-GOODS INVENTORY

This 4-in-1 software does not provide for an accounting of finished-goods inventory. In its place, inventory managers must rely on the sales register to review the release of products from inventory and the accounts payable register to review additions to inventory. In addition, they would be required to keep manual track of moves in and moves out of inventory and to determine reorder points and the quantity to reorder.

For this lesson you are asked to

- Post the sales transactions entered into processing for lesson 10.
- Print another sales register.
- Print the purchase activity for a vendor's account.
- Determine, by hand, inventory balances.

Printing the Sales Register

1. Log on and enter a date of **013097**. Press ENTER when asked, *Any change?*

2. Type **8** from the main menu and press ENTER.

3. Type **6** from the process sales and DR/CR memos menu to post sales. Press ENTER.

4. Type **Y** when asked *Are transactions ready to post*? This produces the sales register showing the last eight sales transactions entered into processing.

5. Press TAB to END.

Printing a Vendor Account

6. From the main menu, type **16** and press ENTER.

7. Type **2** to print a vendor's account. Press ENTER.

8. Press ENTER when asked, *Print on separate pages*?

9. Press ENTER when asked, *Bring balance forward*?

10. Type **A AND P CHEMICALS** for the starting vendor.

11. Type **A AND P CHEMICALS** for the ending vendor.

12. Press F1 for earliest.

13. Press F1 for latest.

14. Press ENTER for *Print inactive accounts*?

15. Press ENTER when asked, *Field number to change*?

16. Press ENTER when asked *Display the report*? This prints the A AND P CHEMICALS account for the month of January.

17. Press TAB three times to exit.

QUESTIONS

1. If each unit of Microgrow costs $5.00, how many units were added to inventory in January?

2. Examine the sales register from lesson 4 and this lesson. If Microgrow sells for $10.00 per unit (and if there were no freight charges associated with the second purchase of the product by LAWNS-ARE-GREEN), how many units of Microgrow were removed from inventory in January?

3. If Microgrow sales are not expected to increase over the next few months, how many months supply are on hand beginning February 1?

4. If sales for Microgrow are expected to increase fivefold during February (meaning 5 times January sales) and the reorder point for Microgrow is 150 units, will another order need to be placed?

Complete the following table to prove you answer. You can assume that January's beginning inventory is zero and that any new shipment would arrive in March:

	JANUARY	FEBRUARY
Beginning inventory		
Moves in		
Moves out		
Ending inventory		

12

Purchasing and Receiving

Purchasing and receiving is an integral part of materials management. The purchasing department of a business buys material in amounts authorized by purchase requisitions it receives from warehouse and inventory managers. Purchasing is responsible for four basic activities: selecting suppliers, or vendors; expediting delivery from suppliers; coordinating communications between suppliers and the departments within the company; and identifying new vendor products and services that contribute to company profits.

These activities help to clarify why purchase orders should not be printed directly as part of an inventory computer application. Selecting suppliers, for example, includes identifying vendors who are best able to deliver needed products, negotiating the most advantageous terms of purchase, and issuing the necessary purchase agreements, which take the form of *purchase orders*. The computer is able to accomplish only the last of these tasks once the terms of a purchase have been entered into processing. Terms of purchase must be negotiated in advance; they must be determined for each purchase order rather than set arbitrarily by the computer.

The receiving department of a business, in contrast to purchasing, receives goods previously ordered. This department is responsible for checking vendor shipments for correctness and for moving goods from receiving areas to warehouse locations. If goods are found to be unacceptable, the department notifies members of the purchasing staff, who in turn must notify the vendor and work out the problems associated with the faulty material.

As with purchasing, there are four main types of receiving activities: verifying the correctness of vendor shipments, inspecting incoming material, informing the purchasing department about materials that do not conform to company standards, and telling members of the warehouse crew where to stock newly received material. In effect, receiving unites a company's purchasing, inventory control, and accounts payable activities. By accepting products and moving them to warehouse locations, a company is able to verify that an outstanding purchase order has been filled, an on-order quantity has been received, and a vendor invoice can be paid. Likewise, once merchandise is accepted (not returned), the vendor knows that payment of the vendor invoice should be forthcoming.

There are several good reasons for developing an online purchasing and receiving application. This application can provide a firm with (1) faster and more accurate processing of purchase requisitions and receiving reports, (2) improved inquiry capabilities, (3) improved vendor relationships,(4) better control of materials inventory, and (5) better control of accounts payable. Besides these more obvious benefits, the purchasing and receiving application helps inventory management. In a "just-in-time" environment, business firms realize that the supply of incoming materials must be carefully managed. Otherwise a smooth flow of production or order-entry processing will be disrupted. Clearly, even the best order-entry system will look inadequate if stock is not available. Instead of filling orders, a firm must place incoming requests for stock on back order.

12-1   PRELIMINARY OVERVIEW OF PROCESSING

Figure 12–1 provides an overview of the purchasing and receiving subsystems. The system is activated by the receipt of a purchase requisition prepared by the inventory system. Once received, the purchasing department must identify the sources of supply, select the best vendor, print the purchase order, and store the details of the order on a *pending purchase order file*. This file stores all outstanding, or open, purchase orders. In practice, the pending purchase order file serves a dual

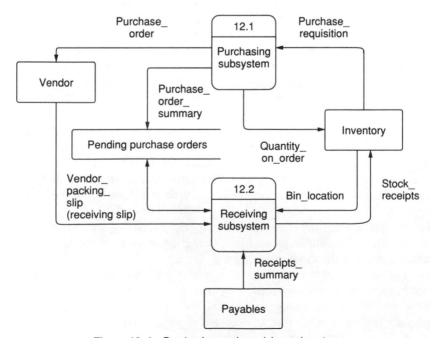

Figure 12–1 Purchasing and receiving subsystems

purpose: it provides a link to the receiving subsystem and to the accounts payable system (not shown).

The receiving subsystem is activated by the receipt of the vendor packing slip placed inside a shipped package. The receiving staff must compare the quantity of goods shipped with the quantity shown as on order. The two outputs from processing are stock receipts to be added to inventory and a receipts summary showing the charges resulting from the purchase. This summary is a second important input to the accounts payable application.

Figure 12–2 breaks down the purchasing subsystem into two main steps: *Enter purchase requirements* and *Print purchase orders*. Initially, purchase requirements are entered into processing, establishing what items to order, from whom, at what price, and when delivery can be expected. The main output is the current purchase order, which is stored on the purchase order transaction file. Second, after all purchase order transactions are stored, purchase orders are printed and sent to vendors. The results of processing are written to the pending purchase order file.

The receiving subsystem is somewhat more complex than the purchasing subsystem. As Figure 12–3 shows, three steps are important: *Enter new stock receipts, Print receiving report,* and *Print stock tickets.* The first step enters

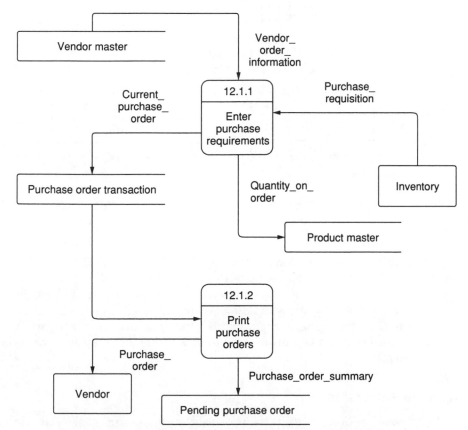

Figure 12–2   Two main steps in processing purchase orders

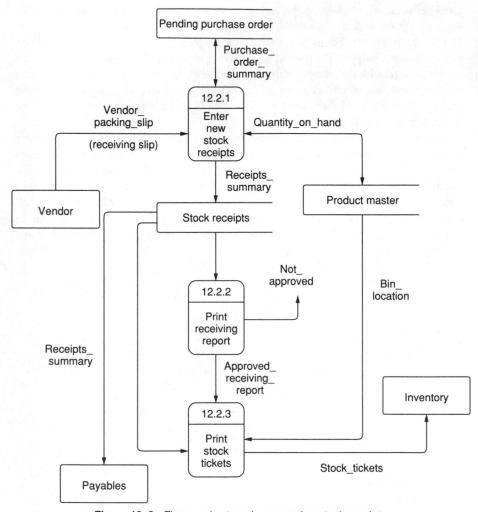

Figure 12–3 Three main steps in processing stock receipts

new stock receipt totals into processing, removes the purchase order from the pending–purchase order file, updates the quantity-on-hand field of the product master file, writes the receipts summary to the stock receipts file. The second step produces the receiving report, to show which shipments were received and the status of each shipment: quantity ordered, quantity received, quantity accepted, and so forth. Once the register is approved, the printing of stock tickets begins. A *stock ticket* documents the quantity of stock to be added to inventory and the new stock location.

Inputs To Processing

In this divided application, there are two main inputs to processing: purchase requisitions and receiving slips. A *purchase requisition* provides the authority to issue purchase orders to outside suppliers. It describes the product to be ordered, by number (if possible) and by name, and states the quantity desired and the desired date of delivery. To this information, the purchasing agent must usually add or modify the name of the vendor, the product price and terms of purchase, and the terms of shipment. In setting the terms of shipment (when goods are to be shipped by the vendor and how), the purchasing agent must factor in a number of lead times—for example, the time required by the vendor to receive and fill an order, the time required by the shipper to deliver it, and the time required by receiving to inspect and put it away. In more complicated situations, the agent must also estimate the time required to negotiate the price and terms of payment.

A *receiving slip* shows goods delivered by suppliers and provides the authority to print stock tickets. The slip is a summary of the vendor's packing slip, showing the quantity received and the results of the inspection of the shipment (the quantity actually packed, the quantity short, the quantity long, the quantity rejected, and the quantity of items to be reworked).

Outputs from Processing

Valued outputs produced by the purchasing and receiving application include two different transaction documents (purchase orders and stock tickets), two or more types of processing summaries, and three important summary files (the purchase order pending file, the encumbrance summary file, and the payables receipts summary file). Collectively, these documents, summaries, and files define all new purchase orders, purchase orders "let" but not received, and all new material receipts. This information is vital in attempting to determine the status of quantities on order; it is even more vital in deciding whether or not to pay a vendor invoice.

Figure 12–4 illustrates a typical business purchase order. This transaction document is similar to the customer invoice. It must provide space for the purchase order number, the date, the vendor number, the name and address of the vendor, product information (product number, quantity desired, product description, and price), and shipping information (ship via and by what date). The two numbers of special importance are the purchase order number and the vendor number. The *purchase order number* should be unique so that it identifies a single purchasing agreement. This number is also used by the vendor in referring to an order. Typically, the vendor prints the purchase order number on the packing slip and vendor invoice, so that goods ordered can be matched against goods billed for and received.

Like the purchase order number, the *vendor number* should be unique. Each vendor number should refer to a single source of supply. By using a unique vendor number and a unique purchase order number, a company is able to trace an outstanding order in one of two ways. By entering a purchase order number, for example, an outstanding order can be displayed directly. Likewise, by entering a vendor number, a listing can be produced of all purchase order numbers placed with that vendor.

Besides purchase orders, the purchasing portion of the application prints a *new order register* to document which orders have been let and a *purchase order encumbrance summary* to show what funds should be set aside to cover

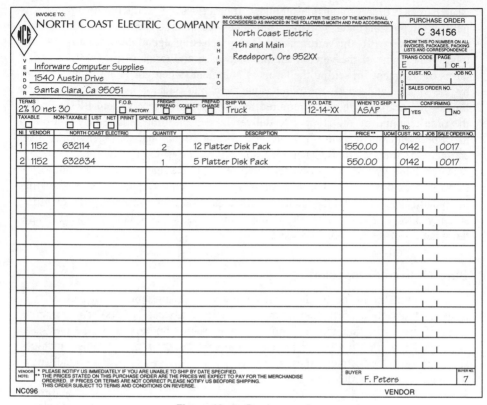

Figure 12–4   Purchase order

outstanding purchases. The need to encumber funds is widely recognized in business and government. By setting aside funds to cover authorized pending purchases, companies are better able to keep expenses within their yearly budgets.

The receiving portion of the application produces a receiving report and stock tickets or labels to document stock receipts. The *receiving report* shows the quantity of materials received from the vendor and the disposition of these materials (see Figure 12–5). For example, of the 1,500 snap plate blocks ordered, 1,400 were accepted from lot 1, 109 were accepted from lot 2, and none were accepted from lot 3. Receiving reports may also contain several disposition codes, such as *Release to inventory, Return to vendor, Rework in our plant,* and *Scrap.* Release means that goods have passed inspection and can be made ready to transport to a warehouse location. Prior to transport, a *stock ticket* is prepared. This ticket generally contains the product number, descriptive information, and the bin location number. The ticket is attached to each shipment to indicate clearly where goods are to be placed in the warehouse.

Other products produced by receiving include a report of overdue purchase orders and a payables receipts summary. The *overdue purchase order report* lists all purchase orders that should have been received at an earlier date. Equipped with this information, purchasing agents are able to contact vendors directly to determine

```
CORPORATION 01-777 BOYD, RESEARCH GROUP                   RECEIVING REPORT                                        PAGE    1
P1X100-C                                              FOR 14 DAYS BEFORE 8/14/9-              RUN    FRIDAY   8/14/9- AT  21.26

      BUYER CODE - BH                       BUYER NAME - FAWLTY     ALBERT
  P.O.                        LN  SB  RCPT                              ORDERED         UNIT  RECEIVED   RECEIVED    DUE    EARLY  P
 NUMBER  __VENDOR_NAME__      IT  LN  _NBR_  PART_NUMBER DESCRIPTION_ QUANTITY U/M PRICE QUANTITY  _DATE_   DATE  _/LATE_  C
 CJ4298  BASTALLIO            01      LOT01  82108602-001 SNAP PLATE, BLK  1,500 EA 42.98    1,400  8/30/9-  8/30/9-            N
                                      LOT02                                                   109  8/30/9-  8/30/9-
                                      LOT03                                             UNACCEPTD  8/30/9-  8/30/9-

                             02      LOT04  82109206-308 CASING, PLASTIC  1,500 EA 25.12    2,000  8/30/9-  8/30/9-            N

 BH4901  ELECTROL, INC.      01      LOT01  43168999-001 BLOWER, HISPEED    800 EA 26.25      400  8/01/9-  8/15/9-   14E     N
                                      LOT02                                                   400  8/27/9-  8/15/9-   12L

                             02      LOT01  43168900-001 BLOWER,LOPWR       800 EA 26.25 UNACCEPTD  8/01/9-  8/15/9-   14E     N
                                      LOT02                                                   200  8/15/9-  8/15/9-
                                      LOT03                                                   200  8/15/9-  8/15/9-

 BT4900  MOTO DIRECT SALES   01      LOT01  60069555-001 GATE ARRAY         800 EA 64.40      400  8/01/9-  8/15/9-   14E     N
                                      LOT02                                                   400  8/15/9-  8/15/9-
 BT3009  TEXAS               01  06  BS006  70940118-122 TRANSISTOR       1,000 EA  1.59    1,000  7/31/9-  7/24/8-            N
```

Figure 12–5   Receiving report

why shipments are late. The *payables receipts summary* shows the status of received materials. This information is required to verify the charges shown on the vendor invoice.

REVIEW QUESTIONS

1. Name the four basic purchasing activities. Name the four basic receiving activities.

2. What are the main reasons for developing an online purchasing and receiving application?

3. What is stored on the pending purchase order file?

4. Name the two main types of input for this divided application.

5. Why should purchase order numbers and the vendor numbers be unique?

6. What information is printed on the receiving report?

12-2   PURCHASE ORDER PROCESSING

Parts (a) and (b) of Figure 12–6 show the organization of the purchasing computer application. Six interactive programs are featured: one of these creates transaction files, two update master files, and three display accounts on purchase orders. Batch programs are also required. These produce registers, a transaction document, processing summaries, and change reports.

Figure 12–7 (a) and (b) show the purchasing processing menu. Interactive programs are used to enter purchase requirements, to ready vendor and product master files, to display product and vendor accounts, and to display pending purchase orders. After purchase requirements have been successfully entered into processing, batch programs are needed to print the new order register and purchase orders. The remaining batch programs produce processing summaries, product and vendor registers, and change reports.

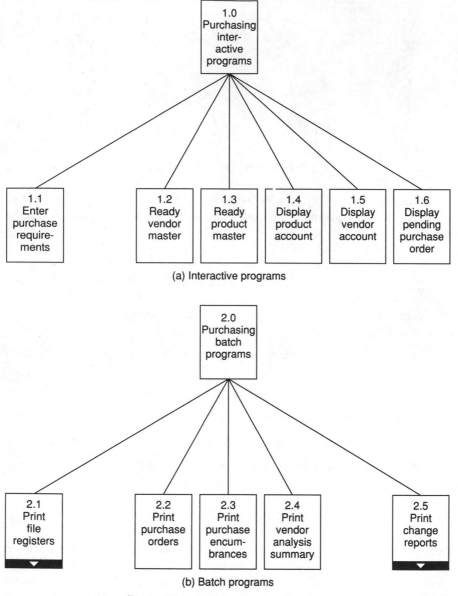

(a) Interactive programs

(b) Batch programs

Figure 12–6   Systems organization chart

The *Enter purchase requirements* Program

Three types of purchase requirements information must be either be keyed or read
to processing from computer files: purchase order information, vendor information, and product information. As Figure 12–8 shows, keyed information can be
kept to a minimum, if vendor and product master files are available. Following
the entry of the purchase order number, the current date, and the required date of

```
PURCHASING

        ENTER PURCHASE REQUIREMENTS
        READY VENDOR MASTER
        READY PRODUCT MASTER
        DISPLAY PRODUCT ACCOUNT
        DISPLAY VENDOR ACCOUNT
        DISPLAY PENDING PURCHASE ORDER


        RETURN
```

(a) Interactive menu choices

```
PURCHASING

            PRINT PURCHASE ORDERS
            PRINT PURCHASE ENCUMBRANCES
            PRINT VENDOR ANALYSIS

            RETURN
```

```
PURCHASING

        PRINT ORDER CHANGES
        PRINT VENDOR CHANGES
        PRINT PRODUCT CHANGES

        RETURN
```

```
PURCHASING

            PRINT NEW ORDER REGISTER
            PRINT VENDOR REGISTER
            PRINT PRODUCT REGISTER

            RETURN
```

(b) Batch menu choices

Figure 12–7 Purchasing processing menu

Keyed information

Master File
Information

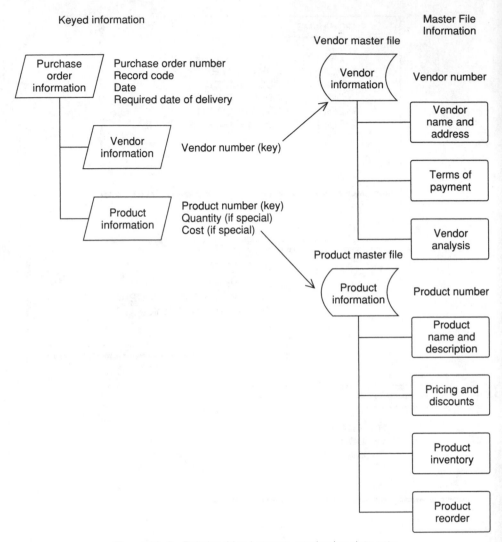

Figure 12–8   Relationships between purchasing data sets

delivery, the vendor number is keyed. This step transfers vendor name and address into processing for visual verification. Next, the first product number, quantity to be ordered, and unit cost are keyed. This step transfers product name and description, pricing and discounts, and reorder information into processing. After product information has been verified, the computer responds by asking for the next product number. Data entry continues until all product line items have been successfully brought into processing.

The design of the *Enter purchase requirements* program must allow for the override of programmed decisions. For example, if the quantity to be ordered and the unit cost are the same as the computer-determined order quantity and unit

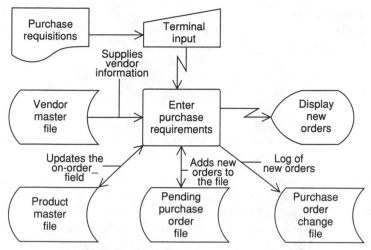

Figure 12–9   Entering purchase order requirements

cost, only the product number is keyed and transmitted. If either the quantity to be ordered or the unit price is changed, however (perhaps due to a special purchase agreement), the totals displayed must be replaced with the new figures, which override the amount or price stored on file.

A number of separate actions take place during the entry of purchase order requirements (see Figure 12–9). After purchase order information has been entered, vendor information is transferred from the vendor master file. Next, product information is transferred, and after the number is verified, the product master file is updated: the on-order field is increased by the quantity ordered. Last, the completed order is written to the pending purchase order file because this file stores all open purchase orders. Changes to the pending file are also written to the purchase order change file to provide a record of all new purchase orders.

Readying Master Files

Before purchase order information can be successfully processed by the computer, the vendor and product master files must be current. If, for example, a new supplier is identified, vendor information must be collected and entered prior to entering purchase requirements. Vendor information consists of three of more segments, including name and address, terms of payment, and vendor analysis. The contents of each can be summarized as follows:

- *Vendor name and address.* This segment is limited to the vendor's name for ordering and billing, vendor address (street, city, state, postal code), the name of the person to contact, and telephone number.

- *Terms of payment.* This segment may store specific information such as the following:

Product number   3210
Product   Type I ribbons
Price schedule   5.75   1 to 11
                    5.30   12 to 35
                    4.95   over 35
Terms   5% prepaid, net 30

It may instead be limited to general information, such as 5 percent prepaid, net 30, catalog number R962. The number R962, in this instance, indicates where the item is listed in the vendor's catalog.

- *Vendor analysis.* This section contains both product and background information. *Vendor product information* specifies product delivery and quality performance averages. Important fields include the vendor's average delivery time (the time between the receipt of the purchase order and the shipment of goods), the average inventory carried by the vendor, and the product rejection rate. *Vendor background information* is more subjective than product information. It includes the financial strength of the vendor (AAA, BB, B), the work stoppage rating, and a trade relations rating.

Entering new product information is more complicated than entering new vendor information. Each of the seven record segments discussed in the last chapter must be completed; variable fields such as the on-hand quantity must be set to their current value. Four segments are especially vital in purchasing: product name and description, pricing and discounts, product inventory, and product forecast. For example, the product name and description is used to explain to the vendor the product being ordered and the number assigned to that product by the business. Pricing and discount information stores the average cost of the product. If, in ordering, the unit cost indicated on the purchase order is significantly higher than the unit cost stored on file (such as 10 percent or more), this information should be reviewed. Inventory information shows the quantity on hand, the quantity on order, and the expected date of delivery. When an order is placed with a vendor, these last two fields must be updated. Finally, forecast information includes the preferred vendor number and the vendor lead time. When several sources of supply are to be maintained, a separate file is often used to store vendor numbers and lead times. Storing several numbers is acceptable because some vendors are able to deliver materials faster but at a slightly higher price.

Printing and Reviewing Purchase Orders

After the vendor and product master files have been updated and purchase requirements have been successfully entered into processing, purchase orders are printed. Printing is a two-step batch process. Prior to printing purchase orders, a new-order register is produced. This register lists all new orders contained on the purchase order pending file; it shows processing control totals to verify that the file is in balance.

Information shown on the new-order register can also be visually reviewed. By calling the *Display purchase order* program and by keying in the purchase order number, an open order can be examined (see Figure 12–10). There are several advantages in displaying an order. A vendor might call, for example, to request that a specific order be reviewed. Once the order number is known, the purchasing agent can inquire directly. Notice, however, what occurs without online inquiry capabilities. The vendor might ask: "Did you receive 100 units of part number 300000 on your order number P00053?" Without online inquiry capabilities, a search by hand through a tub file or a search through a batch-produced printout is required. With online inquiry, the purchasing agent enters the purchase order number to retrieve the pending order and answers the question directly.

Direct status reporting is possible because the pending purchase order file always shows the latest information of all open orders. Sometimes this information is invaluable. As Figure 12–10 shows, two quantities of part number 300000 were ordered, each with a different due date. Moreover, the vendor was able to ship 100 units well in advance of the first due date. This split shipment indicates that three or more shipments will be received and that at least two of these can be expected at some future date.

After the new-order register is approved and all necessary changes have been made, purchase orders are printed. Usually, this processing job is easy, even with a large number of orders. One difficulty occurs when purchase orders are placed by telephone in advance of the printed purchase order. When this occurs, *Written confirmation of telephone order* or a similar message must be printed on the order. This provision avoids possible double filling and billing of the order by the vendor; the printed purchase order continues to provide written confirmation of a verbal commitment to buy.

PURCHASE ORDER REVIEW

   ○ Change order   ○ Add receipts   ○ Print   ○ Exit

Vendor number	Vendor name	Order number	Date of order
22345	Martins, Inc.	456333	9/10/9x

No	Product no	Qty Ordered	Quan rec	Receipt date	Date due
1	300000	200	100	09/09/9x	9/15/9x
2	300000	800			9/20/9x
3	300000	200			9/24/9x

Figure 12–10 Open-order display

Purchase Commitments				10/20/XX
				Page
Vendor No.	Vendor Name	Delivery Week	No. of Deliveries	Value
A 11678	Allen Bradley	42 10/21	16	$ 33,250
		43 10/28	21	47,500
		44 11/04	11	26,110
		45 11/11	4	580
				$ 107,440

Figure 12–11 Current purchase commitments

The *Print purchase order encumbrance* Program

A valuable summary produced by the purchasing application is the *purchase order encumbrance summary*. Because the cost of purchased goods is known (the quantity ordered times the unit cost equals the cost of purchased goods), it is possible to predict accurately the dollar amount to be encumbered. This information can be printed in sequence by purchase order or by vendor number sequence, or, as we will show in the chapter on budgeting, by department or by general ledger number.

A variation of the encumbrance summary is a listing of purchase commitments by vendor. As Figure 12–11 shows, this report summarizes the open purchase orders held by each vendor. It can be combined with a report of planned purchase commitments by vendor (see Figure 12–12). This purchase projection is produced using product forecast information stored in the product master file. Product forecasts combined with cycle times serve to estimate the value of purchase orders

Planned Purchase Commitments			10/20/XX
			Page
Vendor No.	Vendor Name	Planned Week	Receipt Value
A 11678	Allen Bradley	44 11/04	$ 8,900
		45 11/11	20,600
		46 11/18	15,750
		47 11/25	28,300
		48 12/02	12,000
		49 12/09	8,070
			$ 190,400

Figure 12–12 Planned purchase commitments

to be let. Financial officers of a company find the reports of current and planned purchase commitments extremely valuable. These reports show the dollar amount needed to cover current purchases as well as the projected dollar amount necessary to cover purchases over the next two- to three-month period. As such, they simplify the difficult task of planning cash flow resulting from company purchases.

12-3   MATERIAL RECEIPTS PROCESSING

After stock is received from a vendor, a company must have procedures to verify that the products received are the same as the products ordered, that the quantity received is the same as the quantity ordered, that the quality of the products is acceptable, and that the purchase order, product, and vendor numbers recorded by the vendor are accurate. Some of these comparisons must be performed by hand. For example, a physical examination and count of items received must be done to verify that the product quality is acceptable and to determine the "actual" number of items received. Computer processing is used, however, to compare the actual count with the quantity ordered.

Figure 12–13 (a) and (b) show the receiving processing menu. Compared with the purchasing menu (see Figure 12–7), the interactive and batch programs are highly similar. Some programs, as indicated, are the same. With receiving, the *Enter new material receipts* program is the only new interactive part of the purchasing and receiving design. Four new batch programs—*Print receiving report, Print stock tickets, Print payables receipts summary,* and *Print overdue purchase order report*—are required, however. These batch programs document new materials received, their disposition and their expected cost to the business, and new materials that should have been received and are overdue.

The *Enter new material receipts* Program

After materials have been counted and inspected, products can be released from the receiving area in a company. Just prior to this release, new material receipts are processed. As Figure 12–14 shows, five types of information must be keyed: receiving slip, purchase order, vendor, product, and product inspection information. *Receiving slip information* includes a receiving slip number assigned by the company, a record code (debit or credit), the vendor's packing slip number, and the date of the new material receipt. Should the need arise to question the vendor about a particular order, the packing slip number provides an immediate point of reference. Some companies keep several date fields instead of one. They store the shipment arrival date, the shipment release date, and the material restocking date. If it takes several days to inspect incoming products and to transfer and restock goods in the warehouse, different dates must be kept to estimate product reorder lead times.

Figure 12–14 shows that four keys are entered into processing. Each key locates data stored on computer files. For instance, the purchase order number is entered to locate the open order stored on the file of pending purchase orders. The ven-

RECEIVING

ENTER NEW MATERIAL RECEIPTS
READY VENDOR MASTER
READY PRODUCT MASTER
DISPLAY PRODUCT ACCOUNT
DISPLAY VENDOR ACCOUNT
DISPLAY PENDING PURCHASE ORDER

RETURN

(a) Interactive menu choices

RECEIVING

PRINT RECEIVING REPORT
PRINT STOCK TICKETS
PRINT RECEIPTS SUMMARY
PRINT OVERDUE PURCHASE ORDERS
RETURN

RECEIVING

PRINT ORDER CHANGES
PRINT VENDOR CHANGES
PRINT PRODUCT CHANGES

RETURN

RECEIVING

PRINT VENDOR REGISTER
PRINT PRODUCT REGISTER

RETURN

(b) Batch menu choices

Figure 12–13   The receiving processing menu

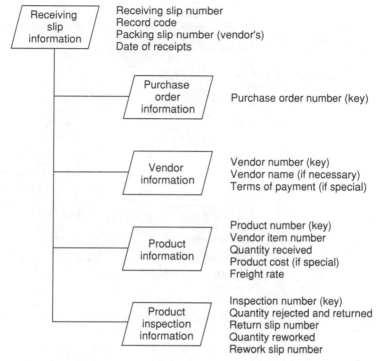

Figure 12–14   Receiving data-entry requirements

dor and product numbers identify accounts stored on the vendor and product master files. If an inspection file is maintained, entering an inspection number leads to the transfer of totals for the quantity rejected for return and the quantity rejected for rework.

Figure 12–15 illustrates the separate actions required in processing new material receipts. Initially, receipts information is posted against the vendor and product master files. This step verifies the correctness of the vendor's number and name and each product number and description. Following verification, several file updates are performed. These updates (1) remove open purchase orders from the pending file; (2) revise the quantity on hand, the quantity on order, and the moves-in totals for a product account; and (3) revise the average delivery time (vendor lead time) and product rejection rate (yield) for a vendor account.

Each file update procedure must be carefully designed. Suppose, for example, that 200 items were ordered and a partial shipment of 100 was received. In this case, an open order cannot be deleted from the pending file. Instead, the amount received must be added to the record of open purchase orders. This permits the quantity ordered and the quantity "left to receive" to be displayed (see Figure 12–10).

The design of the procedure to update the product master file must consider the timing of events. If the quantity on hand is increased by the quantity released—"in advance" of restocking the items in the warehouse—the product master file will be incorrect, at least temporarily. If the on-hand and on-order fields are changed

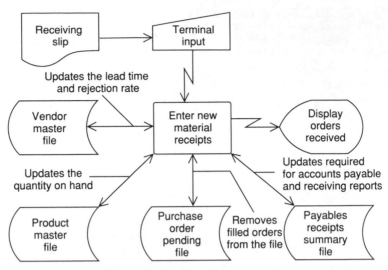

Figure 12–15   Entering new receipts

following restocking, however, the product file records will also be incorrect. In this situation, products will be shown to be on order when, in fact, they have been received and are awaiting someone's attention in either the receiving or the warehouse area of a company. The key in this situation is to minimize the time required for restocking.

Besides file updates, the new material receipts program must calculate any differences between purchase orders and new receipts, such as the difference between the quantity ordered and the quantity received, and must write this information together with all file updates to the payables receipts summary file. This file is used for a variety of purposes: it is carried over to accounts payable processing to test the validity of vendor claims for payment and is used to print the receiving report and new stock tickets.

Readying Master Files

As with the purchasing portion of the application, the vendor and product master files may need to be revised before the entry of any new receipts information. Several vendor changes might have occurred, for example, between the placement of the order and the receipt of new materials: the name of the vendor, the address, the contact person, or the telephone number might be different. Likewise, the vendor might report a more favorable price schedule than before, extending the new prices to all incoming orders. Still other possibilities include different terms of payment and different catalog numbers. Regardless of the type of change, each must be noted and entered into processing to keep the vendor master file current.

Changes to the product master file are required if the vendor decides to change the product description, such as the unit of measure, the size run of the product, the color, or the unit cost. In rare cases, the vendor might change the product name.

Printing Stock Tickets

Once the purchasing order change file is complete, batch programs to prepare stock tickets can be scheduled. Figure 12–16 shows that the printing of stock tickets is a two-step process. Prior to printing stock tickets, the receiving report is printed. This report documents the complete status of each purchase order. It compares items ordered with items received, states the disposition of split shipments, and reports whether any items were damaged. The receiving report might show *extended cost totals*. These dollar totals provide an estimate of the dollar amount due on the vendor invoice.

Stock tickets can take a variety of shapes and formats. Typically, a stock ticket contains product description and location information (product number, description, and bin location number). However, some business firms view the stock ticket as a multipurpose document (see Figure 12–17). It is designed as a receiving and order-entry document. By perforating the ticket and attaching several ticket stubs or

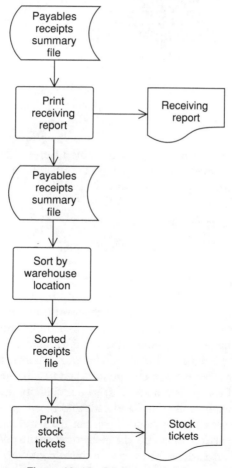

Figure 12–16   Printing stock tickets

Figure 12–17   Stock ticket

coupons, the ticket can be used in order-entry processing. When an order is picked from stock, a stub or coupon is detached from the stock ticket. Each stub or coupon contains detailed bar-coded information about the product, such as product number, packing and shipping requirements, insurance cost, and product weight. Scanning the bar codes prior to packing the product helps to ensure that the correct item has been picked from stock. This procedure simplifies the paperwork processing associated with preparing the order for shipment.

The *Payables receipts summary* Program

The *payables receipts summary*, a valuable summary produced by the receiving application, is in many ways similar to the purchase order encumbrance summary and, in fact, may adhere to the same reporting format. The payables receipts summary, in contrast, shows the quantities received and their estimated cost, compared with the quantities ordered and their estimated cost. Since the revised estimated cost is usually less than or equal to the dollar amount shown on the purchase order encumbrance summary, the receipts summary permits previously encumbered funds to be released for additional expenditures. More important, the final estimate of costs is required by the accounts payable application for comparing the quantity received and its estimated cost to the quantity billed for, as recorded on the vendor invoice. If there is a significant difference, payment of the vendor invoice is delayed. Instead of payment, a copy of the purchase order is pulled and compared against receiving slips and the receiving report. When a trace reveals that the invoice is in error, direct contact with the vendor is required to resolve the outstanding bill.

REVIEW QUESTIONS

7. What is meant by "an override set of instructions"?

8. What master files are required by the purchasing and receiving application?

9. Explain the difference between vendor product information and vendor background information, the two types of information stored on the vendor analysis section of the vendor master file.

10. Why is it important to be able to display the status of an open order?

11. Why do financial officers find the reports of current and planned purchase commitments valuable?

12. After stock is received, what must be verified by the staff of the receiving department?

13. What file updates are performed by the *Enter new material receipts* program?

14. What information is stored on the payables receipt summary file? How is this file used in processing?

15. Why do business firms print stock tickets?

12-4 PROCESSING CONTROLS

The design of processing controls for the purchasing and receiving application is similar to the design of controls for the customer invoice application. For each, a strict accounting of quantity and cost totals must be maintained. The following summary outlines the processing control steps built into the purchasing application.

1. The program *Enter purchase requirements* must sum the "new purchase order quantity," which is the same as the total determined by the finished-goods computer application, unless modifications have been keyed into processing. It must also revise the pending purchase order quantity and cost totals to reflect the new purchase order quantity and cost. The pending purchase order (P/O) formulas in each case are:

   Pending P/O quantity = Old pending P/O quantity ± New P/O quantity

   Pending P/O expense = Old pending P/O expense ± New P/O expense

2. The *Print new-order register* program must report both pending P/O quantity and expense totals and show how each total was reached. This permits verification to be completed prior to the printing of purchase orders.

3. The *Print purchase order encumbrance* program must print both quantity and expense totals. From this point, the totals can be brought across to other applications to show the financial impact of outstanding purchases.

The receiving application continues to modify the pending purchase order quantity and cost totals. Once goods are received and inspected, the differences between the quantity ordered and the quantity received must be entered into the processing control formulas, as follows:

1. The *Enter new material receipts* program must sum the total quantity received, the total quantity accepted, the total quantity rejected and returned, and the total quantity reworked. Each of these totals leads to a control equation. The quantity-received total, for example, changes the pending P/O formulas as shown. Unlike purchasing, the quantity and expense totals are subtracted from the pending totals.

   Pending P/O quantity = Old pending P/O quantity − Quantity received
   − Quantity canceled by vendor

   Pending P/O expense = Old pending P/O expense
   − Quantity-received estimated expense

   The program also calculates quantity and cost differences, as shown in the following four variance equations. What do these variances mean? The quantity-received variance shows the difference between what was ordered and what was received; the quantity-accepted variance shows the difference between what was received and what passed inspection. The last two equations deal only with expense differences. The quantity-received expense variance and the encumbered funds variance equations are meaningful if the costs are different than estimated. The encumbered-funds variance is especially important because the firm must adjust to funds set aside to pay for received goods.

   Quantity-received variance = Quantity ordered − Quantity received

   Quantity-accepted variance = Quantity received − Quantity accepted

   Quantity-received expense variance
   = P/O estimated expense − Receiving estimated expense

   Encumbered funds variance
   = P/0 estimated expense − Estimate expense of accepted goods

2. The *Print receiving report* program must be designed to show both revised pending P/O quantity counts and dollar amounts; quantity-ordered, quantity-received, quantity-rejected and returned, and quantity-reworked totals; and quantity and expense variance totals. Each of these equations must be in balance prior to printing stock tickets.

3. The *Print payables receipts summary* program is designed to print the total quantity and expense of new material receipts. These totals are brought across to the accounts payable application. They help control the release of funds from a business.

12-5   MANAGEMENT IMPLICATIONS

There are several good reasons for developing the purchasing and receiving application besides using it to keep a strict accounting of the quantities ordered and received and their estimated costs. Some of the more obvious reasons are faster and more accurate processing of purchase requisitions and receiving slips, improved vendor information, and better file inquiry procedures. With interactive programs a clear advantage is the improved edit and update of new purchase and material receipts transactions. The less obvious but equally important reasons include the capability to take advantage of special sales or discounts offered by vendors, to evaluate vendors, and to control the quality of incoming materials. These less obvious reasons are better known as vendor analysis programs: supplier selection, vendor evaluation, and quality assurance programs.

Supplier selection programs are designed to select the best source of supply—the vendor capable of providing the highest quality products for the lowest cost and the shortest delivery time (vendor lead time). Objectives such as these are difficult to achieve by one vendor. As a consequence, the supplier selection program requires that the three dimensions of quality, cost, and lead time be weighted so that different scores for vendors can be compared. When fully developed, supplier selection programs permit purchasing agents to ask direct questions such as the following:

VENDOR 65332 HAS QUOTED A 49.99 PRICE FOR MOISTURE-FREE PARKAS. IS THIS A GOOD PRICE?

The computer will respond to this question by calculating the weighted score for moisture-free parkas supplied by vendor number 65332, comparing this weighted score with that for other firms that supply moisture-free parkas, and displaying the findings.

Vendor evaluation programs compare the quality, cost, and lead time associated with the purchase of items. These programs calculate and store a wide variety of vendor performance ratios and statistics, including the actual vendor lead time (difference between date of purchase and date of receipt); the product delivery fill rate (quantity received divided by the quantity ordered), the product acceptance rate (quantity accepted divided by quantity received); and the product cost change (differences between current and last vendor unit price). These ratios are helpful in selecting vendors. They are important in helping purchasing agents interpret market conditions. The analysis of product cost change, for example, helps determine how inflation affects the product lines carried by a business. Suppose unit costs are found to be increasing by .08 percent a month. This means that either product prices must be increased to cover the cost of inflation or profit margins will be lower. In either case, vendor evaluation determines the base figures from which to make pricing decisions.

Quality assurance programs compare product quality and reliability standards to actual figures to determine if incoming materials meet or exceed these standards. One standard, for example, might be 30 or fewer defective parts in lot sizes of 1,540. Taking a small sample from the large lot, such as a sample of 50 in a lot of

2,000, and noting the number of defects in the sample can determine whether the entire large lot should be accepted or rejected. In cases such as these, the computer stores the quality standard and the required sampling plan. It accepts as input the percent defective and decides if the entire lot of material is acceptable. Finally, it updates the change in vendor quality compared with previous shipments.

Many firms have developed elaborate vendor quality comparison tests in their attempts to select vendors capable of supplying high-quality products. Although testing was also done in precomputer days, the results of several quality tests were seldom updated and compared. Today, the computer makes quality comparison testing both possible and practical.

REVIEW QUESTIONS

16. What types of processing controls must be maintained to ensure that pending purchase order file totals are correct?

17. What is the difference between the quantity-received expense variance and the encumbered-funds variance? Why are both variances important?

18. What benefits to the firm result from well-conceived supplier selection programs? From vendor evaluation programs? From quality assurance programs?

REVIEW OF IMPORTANT IDEAS

Four basic activities are associated with purchasing: selecting suppliers, expediting delivery from suppliers, coordinating communications between suppliers and departments within a company, and identifying new vendor products and services that will contribute to company profits. In addition, four activities are associated with receiving: verifying the correctness of vendor shipments, inspecting vendor materials, informing the purchasing department of materials failing to conform to company standards, and telling members of the warehouse crew where to stock new merchandise. The purchasing and receiving application helps standardize these two sets of activities. Besides permitting faster and more accurate processing of purchase requirements and receiving slips, the application leads to better control of materials into the firm.

Purchasing begins with the processing of purchase requisitions. Following careful verification, all processed requisitions are placed on the pending purchase order file. This file stores all open orders until they are filled—that is, until goods shipped by the vendor are received and approved by the firm. The file is used to print the new-order register and vendor purchase orders.

Receiving begins with the processing of receiving slips. Through processing, the open orders stored on the pending files are removed and transferred to the payables-receipt summary file. Processing also updates the product master file (to show the addition of new material) and the vendor master file (to show new delivery times and product rejection rates).

The receiving stock report and stock tickets are printed after receiving slips are processed. The receiving report documents the complete status of each product by comparing the quantity ordered with the quantity received and approved. Stock tickets show product description and location information.

Two important summary reports produced in processing are the purchase order encumbrance summary and the payables receipts summary. The encumbrance summary lists purchase commitments by vendor in order to show the dollars necessary to cover purchases. The payables receipts summary is similar. It lists purchase commitments by vendor in order to show the dollars necessary to cover the cost of accepted merchandise.

A strict accounting of quantity and cost totals is maintained by the purchasing and receiving application. These controls help determine that the quantity ordered is the same as the quantity billed for and the quantity received.

Improved supplier selection programs, vendor evaluation programs, and quality assurance programs are important parts of a well-designed purchasing and receiving application. With computer assistance it becomes easier to determine the best source of supply and to identify which vendors satisfy quality and reliability standards.

KEY WORDS

Purchasing department

Receiving department

Pending purchase order file

Purchase requisition

Receiving slip

Purchase order

New order register

Purchase order encumbrance summary

Receiving report

Stock ticket

Payables receipts summary

Vendor analysis

Supplier selection program

Vendor evaluation program

Quality assurance program

EXERCISES

1. Draw the context diagram for the purchasing and receiving system.

2. A manager questions: "Why do we need a purchasing and receiving application when we already have a finished-goods application?" He adds: "Let's have the computer tell us how much to order, from whom, and print the purchase order automatically."

   What is wrong with this approach? Explain why the purchasing and receiving application should allow purchasing agents to override computer-set reorder decisions.

3. Companies often contract with vendors to make split shipments. Rather than sending the entire order at one time, a vendor might agree the ship one-third immediately, one-third two months from now, and one-third four months from now. How would split shipments be accommodated by the purchasing and receiving application?

4. Suppose a company decides to centralize all purchasing activities and to decentralize receiving activities. Draw the level-0 data-flow diagram for this revised design.

5. Some vendors ship a quantity slightly higher than the quantity ordered to compensate for defective items. How would this practice be handled by the control equations for this application?

6. During the entry of purchase order requirements and receiving slip processing, the product master file is updated. However, as shown by Figures 12–9 and 12–15 no product change file is available to store these changes. Does this mean that changes to the product master file cannot be traced? Explain your answer.

7. A suggested output of the receiving application is an inspection report showing items reworked and items rejected. How would such a report be produced?

DISCUSSION QUESTIONS

1. Besides the keeping of a strict accounting of quantities ordered and received and their costs, what are several good reasons for developing the purchasing and receiving application?

2. Many vendor analysis programs are limited to showing how much business a vendor does with a company. What is the value of this type of analysis? Why are analyses such as supplier selection, vendor evaluation, and quality assurance not found on many purchase and receiving application designs? Consider several reasons and then question whether these reasons are sound.

3. Some companies employ standing purchase orders that instruct vendors on one purchase order to ship daily over a 30- to 60-day period. What is the value in this approach? What are the dangers? Is this method consistent with the just-in-time concept?

4. Some people believe that purchasing and receiving is one of the least creative business computer applications. What are its most creative aspects?

4-IN-1 CASE STUDY—PURCHASING AND RECEIVING

Because 4-in-1 software does not provide a purchasing and receiving component, we use this lesson to purchase additional items and post them to the general ledger. For this lesson, you are asked to do the following:

- Adjust a vendor account
- Enter new purchase transactions for purchase accounts 5020-000 and 5030-000.
- Add a fourth vendor to the vendor file.
- Print a bills payable edit list and a bills payable register.

Adjusting a Vendor Account

4-in-1 allows you to review and adjust a vendor account at any time.

1. Log on and enter a date of **010697**. Press ENTER when asked, *Any change?*

2. From the main menu, type **13** and press ENTER.

3. Type **2** and press ENTER to change vendors.

4. Press F1 three times to reach the vendor named JXX Tools and Supplies.

5. Type **8** when asked, *Field number to change?*

6. Type **Tools/building supplies** for the new comment.

7. Press ENTER and TAB twice to return to the main menu.

Entering Additional Purchases

At this time, we ask you to add three additional purchases. Figure 12–18 shows the edit listing you will produce after entering purchase order information.

```
01/06/97              A and J Enterprises, Inc.          #0040 Page 0001
                  B I L L S   P A Y A B L E   E D I T   L I S T
- - - - - - - - - - - - - - - - - - - - - - - - - - - - - - - - - - - - -
Vendor-name                    Trans-date      Credited-to       Trans-amt
Invoice-#          Trans-type   Reference                        Debited-to
- - - - - - - - - - - - - - - - - - - - - - - - - - - - - - - - - - - - -
BUILDING SUPPLY, INC.          01/06/97         A/P               1,500.00
                   Bill        Building supplies
Distributions: 5030-000        Purchases - product C    1,500.00

BUILDING SUPPLY, INC.          01/06/97         A/P                 500.00
98486              Bill        Tools
Distributions: 5020-000        Purchases - product B      500.00

JXX TOOLS AND SUPPLIES         01/06/97         A/P                 800.00
70621              Bill        Tools/building supplies
Distributions: 5020-000        Purchases - product B      300.00
               5030-000        Purchases - product C      500.00

        3 Bills payable transactions             Grand total: 2,800.00
```

Figure 12–18   Bills payable edit listing

8. Type **14** from the main menu and press ENTER.

9. Type **1** to add a purchase order transaction. Press ENTER.

10. Type **JXX** for the vendor name and press ENTER. Press ENTER again for *Right vendor?*

11. Enter the following purchase order information:

B	for bill
010697	for transaction date
70621	for invoice number
Tools/building supplies	for reference
800	for amount
Y	for *credit A/P?*
(blank)	for field number to change
5020-000	for purchase account number
300	for amount to distribute
(blank)	for *Any change?*
5030-000	for amount to distribute
(blank)	for *Any change?*
TAB	to exit

Adding a New Vendor

12. Type **BUILDING SUPPLY, INC.** for the next vendor. Press ENTER.

13. Type **Y** to add the new vendor. Press ENTER.

14. Press ENTER for name.

15. Type the following address on Address-1 and Address-2:
    5246 Wishbone Lane
    Beaver Valley, CA 95060

16. Type **Fred Rogers** for contact.

17. Type **415-642-3000** for phone number.

18. Press ENTER for the first date.

19. Type **Full Supplier** for comment.

20. Type **5030-000** for default expense account.

21. Press ENTER when asked, *Field number to change?* Press ENTER again for *Right vendor?*

22. Enter the following purchase order information:

B	for bill
010697	for transaction date
98431	for invoice number

Building supplies	for reference
1500	for amount
Y	for *credit A/P?*
(blank)	for field number to change
F1	for default account number
F1	for amount to distribute
(blank)	for *Any change?*
TAB	to exit

23. Type **BUILD** for the next vendor. Press ENTER. Press ENTER again for *Right vendor?*

24. Enter the following purchase order information:

B	for bill
010697	for transaction date
98486	for invoice number
Tools	for reference
500	for amount
Y	for *credit A/P?*
(blank)	for field number to change
5020-000	for tools account number
F1	for amount to distribute
(blank)	for *Any change?*
TAB	to exit

25. Press TAB to return to the process bills payable submenu.

Printing the Transaction Edit List

26. Type **4** and press ENTER.

27. Press ENTER when asked, *Display this report?* The bills payable edit list will be printed (see Figure 12–18).

Posting the Transactions

28. From the process bills payable submenu, type **5** and press ENTER.

29. Type **Y** when asked, *Are bills payable transactions OK to post?* The bills payable register will be printed.

30. Exit to end this lesson.

QUESTIONS

1. Why was it necessary to distribute the purchase order cost to two G/L accounts when adding the first new transaction?

2.. What does this lesson tell you about adding vendors to the vendor master file?

3. What does the bills payable register tell you that the bills payable edit list does not?

4. Why are bills payable for a "brand new" business typically greater than sales? What are the implications of this imbalance?

PART

FINANCIAL AND MARKETING APPLICATIONS

As we have observed throughout the earlier chapters, information produced by one application is often passed on to another application. In this final section, we observe this passage of information on a much larger scale. The general ledger application, for example, is designed to process all financial details passed to it from financial applications. Such a transfer is necessary to prepare month- and year-end companywide financial reports; it is essential in comparing actual financial totals to planned totals, as considered by the budget- and profit-planning applications. The last applications considered in this section, the sales analysis and market planning applications, rely on sales details saved from customer invoicing (or customer order entry). These must be transferred in order to begin processing. This transfer makes it possible to calculate, summarize, and provide different views of sales performance—by customer, product, or salesperson.

In these last three chapters our attention will shift from transaction- to transform-based applications. As we study processing that transforms information provided by other applications, we begin to see differences between higher- and lower-order business computer applications. Lower-order applications focus largely on processing specific types of business transactions. With higher-order applications, this interest disappears. The new focus is one of transforming detailed information into different summary forms and, in so doing, providing timely, reliable, and complete information to management.

13

General Ledger

A most important business computer application is the comprehensive financial application known as the general ledger. As stated in chapter 2, this application (with its corresponding term, *general ledger*) consolidates all financial transactions of a business in order to summarize financial activity by account number, changes to assets and liabilities, and to profit and net worth. It is the application from which financial statements are prepared. One of these, the *balance sheet*, compares business assets (what is owned) with business liabilities (what is owed) to determine the net worth of a company (the difference between what is owned and what is owed). Another important statement, the *profit-and-loss statement*, shows the revenues, expenses, and profits or losses of a business for an accounting period (such as a period of one month). A third statement, the *cash flow statement*, shows the flow of funds (cash) to and from a business, with its corresponding increase or decrease in cash for an accounting period.

13-1 MASTER CHART OF ACCOUNTS

The design of the general ledger computer application initially requires the preparing of a *master chart of accounts*. This master chart codes different types of assets, liabilities, revenues, and expenses. Figure 13–1 illustrates a simplified personal chart of accounts that has been designed to summarize a person's wealth and financial health. As shown, two sets of account numbers define major types of personal assets (1XX-XX) and other longer-term assets (2XX-XX); two sets of numbers define personal liabilities (3XX-XX and 4XX-XX). The subheadings attached to each account number further define account categories. Expense account 740-XX, for instance, might subdivide insurance expenses as follows:

740-10   Home insurance
740-20   Life insurance

CURRENT ASSETS		INCOME	
100-XX	Cash	600-XX	Salary
110-XX	Marketable securities	610-XX	Interest and dividends
120-XX	Inventory	620-XX	Other income

OTHER ASSETS		EXPENSES	
200-XX	Real estate	700-XX	Housing
210-XX	Automobile	710-XX	Food
220-XX	Furniture and fixtures	720-XX	Medical
		730-XX	Automobile

CURRENT LIABILITIES		740-XX	Insurance
		750-XX	Taxes
300-XX	Accounts payable	760-XX	Contributions
310-XX	Taxes payable	770-XX	Education
		780-XX	Repairs

LONG-TERM LIABILITIES		790-XX	Clothing
		800-XX	Entertainment
400-XX	Banks loans	810-XX	Other expenses
410-XX	Finance company loans		

PERSONAL EQUITY		PROFIT (OR LOSS)	
500-XX	Equity	900-XX	Current earnings

Figure 13–1   Personal chart of accounts

740-30	Automobile insurance
740-40	Health insurance
740-50	Dental insurance

The various relationships between the master chart of accounts and the financial statements produced by a business include:

1. The company balance sheet. This statement consists of the accounts labeled assets, liabilities, and owner's equity. It is called a balance sheet because business assets must equal, or balance, business liabilities plus owner's equity.

$$\text{Assets} = \text{Liabilities} + \text{Owner's equity}$$

In accounting for certain pieces of property, it is common to find multiple entries for one piece of property on different parts of the balance sheet. For example, if a business buys a building for $75,000 but owes the bank $65,000, the business would record assets of $75,000, an outstanding liability of $65,000, and equity of $10,000—the difference between assets and liabilities.

2. The company profit-and-loss statement. This statement consists of accounts labeled income (or revenues), expenses, and current earnings (net income). In this instance, current earnings equals income minus expenses.

$$\text{Earnings} = \text{Income} - \text{Expenses}$$

3. The general ledger general journal report. This report balances debits and credits to general ledger accounts. For example, in accounting for business expenses, charges posted to the profit-and-loss statement must be reflected on the balance sheet. Suppose a $1,000 check is written to pay a single building mortgage payment. Suppose further that $950 of the $1,000 will pay the outstanding interest on the mortgage, and $50 will be applied to reduce the amount of the loan. In recording this payment, several entries must be made. First, the $1,000 must be entered as an expense. Second, the $1,000 must usually be subdivided. Expense account 700-10 might show interest expense of $950, whereas expense account 700-20 might show principal expense of $50 (see Figure 13–1). Third, long-term liability must be reduced by $50, since the payment reduced the principal of the loan. Fourth, owner's equity must be increased by $50, since the payment increased the difference between assets and liabilities.

REVIEW QUESTIONS

1. What is the main purpose of the general ledger application?

2. What information is printed on the company balance sheet? On the profit-and-loss statement?

3. What is a master chart of accounts?

4. Two equations, one for the balance sheet and the other for the profit-and-loss statement, must be in balance. Show these two equations.

13-2 PRELIMINARY OVERVIEW OF PROCESSING

General ledger processing is different from all of the applications discussed thus far. In review, the required input to processing is the chart of accounts, defined by accounting in advance (see Figure 13–2). The chart of accounts establishes the codes against which all income and expenses are to be charged. A second input is the general journal. The *general journal* is used to debit and credit financial amounts that fall outside the general ledger summaries prepared by other computer applications.

Once inputs are fed to processing, the general ledger acts as a transformer, taking G/L details and converting them to a set of aggregated accounts. Four functions are important to the G/L design (see Figure 13–3):

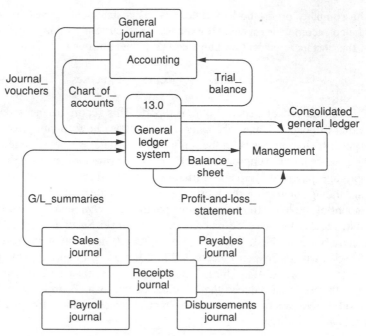

Figure 13–2   The general ledger system

1. *Enter general journal vouchers* enters and verifies G/L account information recorded on journal vouchers and posts this information to the *consolidated general ledger master file*.

2. *Post G/L summary files* transfers G/L account totals from subsidiary G/L transaction files to the consolidated G/L master file.

3. *Print trial balance* processes information stored on the consolidated G/L master file following all postings, to determine if all account totals are in balance—such that debits equal credits.

4. *Print financial statements* produces a set of financial statements once all posted information is in balance.

As this functional view shows, the heart of the G/L system is the consolidated G/L master file. This file stores both current and year-to-date (YTD) financial totals by account, where accounts are defined by the master chart of accounts. Once the master file is updated, the first trial balance test is conducted. If, in testing, debits do not equal credits, for example, adjustments must be made. Following this, a second trial and, where necessary, a third, fourth, and so on must be performed until the consolidated G/L master file is in balance.

Inputs to Processing

The main inputs to the consolidated G/L master file are G/L distribution totals created by the processing of various types of business transactions, using the applications we have discussed in previous chapters. These totals are placed

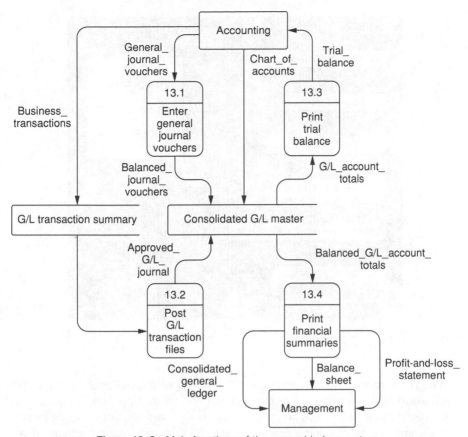

Figure 13–3 Main functions of the general ledger system

in summary files for posting to the general ledger. As we will see from the following review, five major registers or journals are produced by other computer applications to document dollars posted to the general ledger (see Figure 13–4). These are: the sales journal, the receipts journal, the payables journal, the disbursements journal, and the payroll journal.

The *sales journal* is prepared as a by-product of customer invoicing. When posting takes place at the end of invoice processing, posted amounts, printed on the invoice A/R summary report, represent the G/L sales journal for a company. In producing this document, G/L posting must credit sales amounts and debit accounts receivable, much like the following:

		DEBITS	CREDITS
1100	Accounts receivable	1,800.00	
2200	Sales tax payable		50.00
4100	Sales—store 1		1,000.00
4200	Sales—store 2		750.00
	Totals	1,800.00	1,800.00

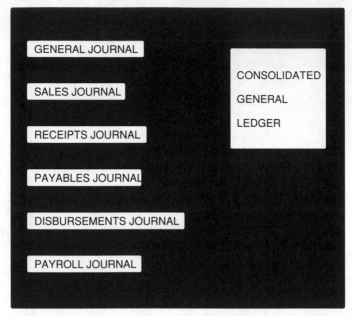

Figure 13–4 The main journals that support the building of the consolidated general ledger.

The *receipts journal* is prepared as a by-product of the customer cash receipts application. When posting takes place at the end of receipts processing, posted amounts, printed on the receipts A/R summary, represent the G/L receipts journal for a company. In producing this document, G/L posting must credit accounts receivable and debit cash in the bank, much like the following:

		DEBITS	CREDITS
1010	Cash in bank	290.00	
1100	Accounts receivable		300.00
4700	Sales discounts	10.00	
	Totals	300.00	300.00

These opposing A/R credits indicate how the accounts receivable balance is determined. The equation is

Beginning A/R balance + Receipts credits − Sales debits = Ending A/R balance

The *payables journal* is prepared as a by-product of the accounts payable computer application. When posting takes place as part of producing the payables summary, the posted listing represents the G/L payables journal for a company. In this document, G/L posting must credit accounts payable and debit those accounts where bills were incurred and need to be paid (for example, inventory, delivery and freight, and legal and accounting fees). Consider the following:

		DEBITS	CREDITS
1400	Inventory	1,000.00	
2100	Accounts payable		1,500.00
5500	Delivery and freight	25.00	
6900	Legal and accounting fees	475.00	
	Totals	1,500.00	1,500.00

The *disbursements journal*, the first of two check-related G/L listings, is prepared as a by-product of the accounts payable check-writing program. Posted amounts, printed on the payables check register, represent the G/L disbursements journal for a company. In producing this document, G/L posting must credit cash in the bank and debit those accounts where cash was spent (for example, accounts payable or equipment), as in the following:

		DEBITS	CREDITS
1010	Cash in bank		1,100.00
1600	Computer equipment	600.00	
2100	Accounts payable	500.00	
	Totals	1,100.00	1,100.00

The *payroll journal*, the second check-related G/L listing, is prepared by the payroll check-writing program. Posting in this instance is more complex than previous postings. The G/L listing must credit cash in the bank and accounts that will need to be paid to state and federal governments. Debits, meanwhile, consist of wages paid and other employee expenses paid by the company. A typical listing of debits and credits might appear as follows:

		DEBITS	CREDITS
1020	Cash in bank		3,525.00
2320	FICA W/H payable		275.00
2330	Employer FICA payable		250.00
2340	Fed unemployment payable		225.00
2370	State unemployment payable		175.00
6250	Other employee benefits		200.00
6200	Employer FICA paid	250.00	
6210	Fed unemployment paid	225.00	
6220	State unemployment paid	175.00	
8000	Wages	4,000.00	
	Totals	4,650.00	4,650.00

Observe that, in this case, the cash required to pay employee wages is less than the wages amount. The balance of $650.00 in this example would be paid at a later date.

Besides these five major journals, other postings to the general ledger require use of the general journal or G/L journals from other business applications, such as fixed assets. Interactive processing is used to process general journal vouchers (see Figure 13–5). In processing a *general journal voucher*, one or more accounts must be credited, and one or more accounts must be debited. As illustrated, account 1720, accumulated depreciation for furniture and equipment, is debited; the offsetting credit is account 6400, depreciation expense.

This review of inputs to G/L processing underscores some of the complexities of this application. Additional complexity results when accounts are not in balance. As an example, suppose the finished-goods inventory equation will not balance, where

$$\text{Beginning inventory} + \text{Moves in} - \text{Moves out} > \text{Ending inventory}$$

When this occurs (and it often does in practice), an adjustment is required to balance the equation. The modified equation becomes:

$$\text{Beginning inventory} + \text{Moves in} - \text{Moves out} - \text{Inventory write-off} = \text{Ending inventory}$$

The scope of the G/L application explains in large part why general ledger posting should be carried out by a number of online applications. The advantages include spreading the work of G/L processing more evenly over an accounting period, editing all G/L distributions and totals and trapping errors at their source,

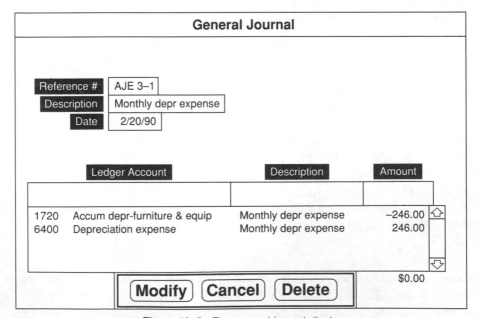

Figure 13–5 The general journal display

and reducing the number of summary files to be carried forward in processing for month-end posting to the general ledger. Improved speed in the balancing of the general ledger master file and fewer numbers of general journal transactions are further benefits.

Outputs from Processing

The main outputs from G/L processing are the general ledger trial balance, the consolidated general ledger, and several types of financial statements. Figure 13–6 shows that a trial balance can span several time periods and include or exclude zero balances (that is, accounts with no activity). With an online application, the trial balance can be viewed or printed.

Figure 13–7 illustrates a printed *general-ledger trail balance report*. As shown, current financial totals are added to opening balance totals to provide the consolidated closing balance. Both prime account and subsidiary account totals are shown on this report. *Cash in bank and on hand* is a prime account, for example,

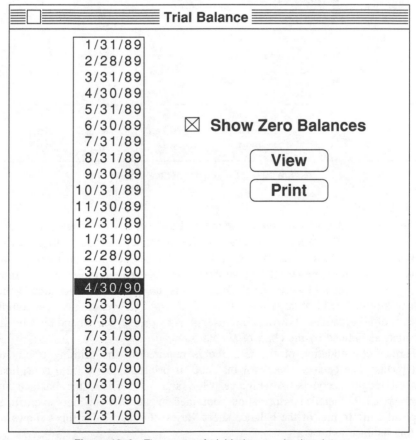

Figure 13–6   The range of trial balance selection dates

```
THE ALPHABET SOUP COMPANY          A C C O U N T I N G   I V                      PAGE 1
                          G E N E R A L   L E D G E R   T R I A L   B A L A N C E      REPORT # RE-254
                                              OCT. 19                                 PROCESSED 11/4/--


 LOC.   PRIME   SUB        DESCRIPTION        OPENING BALANCE      CURRENT MONTH      CLOSING BALANCE
  01     101    CASH IN BANK AND ON HAND
                001  DEPOSIT - CHASE MANHATTAN   1,727,413.91        509,462.94CR       1,217,950.97
                002  GWF - MANUFACTR HANOVER     2,429,504.74CR    1,105,932.58         1,323,572.16CR
                005  IMPREST - ONEIDA NAT BANK     294,298.06         16,660.12CR         277,637.94
                006  DISABILITY FUND                  568.99            134.38              703.37
                007  PETTY CASH                    25,320.00                             25,320.00
                008  CASH -RESEARCH BUILDING        2,025.00                              2,025.00
                009  P/R FUNDS -ONEIDA NAT         124,621.63            438.97CR         124,182.66
                010  CASH IN TRANSIT
                PRIME ACCOUNT 101 TOTAL           255,257.15CR        579,504.93          324,247.78


  01     121    NOTES RECEIVABLE
                026  NOTES RECEIVABLE               2,349.00             13.00CR           2,336.00
                PRIME ACCOUNT 121 TOTAL             2,349.00             13.00CR           2,336.00


  01     122    ACCOUNTS RECEIVABLE - CUSTOM
                025  A/R CONSUMER PRODUCTS         403,385.11         165,745.57          569,130.68
                027  ACCOUNTS RECEIVABLE-CUST.   28,819,642.54        375,701.06       29,195,343.60
                030  ACCT RECEIVABLE-OTHER          10,302.14          3,925.00CR           6,377.14
                PRIME ACCOUNT 122 TOTAL        29,233,329.79         537,521.63       29,770,851.42


  01     123    ACCOUNTS RECEIVABLE - FACTOR
                028  ACCOUNTS RECEIVABLE-FACTORED 7,460,578.13        784,022.01        8,244,600.14
                PRIME ACCOUNT 123 TOTAL          7,460,578.13        784,022.01        8,244,600.14


  01     124    ACCOUNTS RECEIVABLE - OFFICE
                030  LOANS TO EMPLOYEES             6,241.96            899.00CR           5,342.96
                032  PAYROLLL ADJUSTMENTS          23,994.78          7,632.93CR          16,361.85
                033  A/R/ - SALES OF RESIDENTS      1,319.92             50.00CR           1,269.92
                034  ACCTS REC-PERMANENT ADV.       9,050.00            100.00CR           8,950.00
                PRIME ACCOUNT 124 TOTAL            40,606.66          8,681.93CR          31,924.73


  01     129    RESERVES ON ACCOUNTS RECEIVABLE
                042  RESERVE FOR DISPUTED INVO.    275,000.00CR                          275,000.00CR
                043  RESERVE FOR DOUBTFUL ACCT      75,117.30CR        3,400.90CR          78,518.20CR
                045  RESERVE FOR ALLOWANCES        131,593.05CR        8,323.90CR         139,916.95CR
                047  RESERVE FOR DEDUCTIONS        397,000.00CR                          397,000.00CR
                194  CUSTOMER DEPOSITS-RETURNED        19.80                                  19.80



                          FINAL TOTAL                * * *

                            INCOME/EXPENSE    7,090,169.62CR       45,343.31CR        7,135,512.93CR

                          ASSETS/LIABILITIES   7,090,169.62        45,343.31          7,135,512.93
```

Figure 13–7   General-ledger trial balance

whereas *Petty cash* is a subsidiary account. Last, control totals are placed at the bottom of the trial balance, as checks to make sure that all accounts are in balance.

With G/L processing, debits must equal credits before financial reports can be printed. With an online design, the general journal is required to enter adjustments into processing to achieve balance. Once this is done, the final in-balance general ledger is printed. This final version, the *consolidated general ledger*, is a complete register of all accounts, showing all transactions by prime account and by subsidiary account, as defined by the chart of accounts.

Further consolidation of the G/L file is required in the printing of financial statements. The balance sheet, for instance, is printed directly from consolidated general ledger accounts. As Figures 13–8 and 13–9 show, the balance sheet summarizes the detailed information contained in the G/L accounts even further. Typically, the format of the balance sheet varies; this particular sheet shows only ending balance figures.

```
┌─────────────────────────────────────────────────────────────┐
│                      Service Type                             │
│                  An Oregon Corporation                        │
│              See Accountant's Compilaton Report               │
├──────────────────────┬───────────────────┬──────────────────┤
│                      │  Balance Sheet     │                  │
│                      │  As of 02/28/9X    │                  │
│                      │                    │                  │
│                      │     Assets         │                  │
│                                                               │
│   ┌─────────────────┐                                        │
│   │ Current Assets: │                                        │
│   └─────────────────┘                                        │
│   Cash on Hand                    $   883.85                  │
│   Returned Checks                     135.78                  │
│   Cash in Bank — Bank of the N.W.     670.86                  │
│   Cash in Bank — Valley State Bank    631.34                  │
│   Money Market Certificates         1,000.00                  │
│   Accounts Receivable               3,773.63                  │
│   Prepaid Insurance                   367.59                  │
│                                                               │
│      Total Current Assets                      $  7,463.05    │
│                                                               │
│   ┌──────────────┐                                           │
│   │ Fixed Assets:│                                           │
│   └──────────────┘                                           │
│   Leasehold Improvements          $ 4,764.92                  │
│   Accum. Depr. —Leasehold Impr.      (153.02)                │
│                                   $ 4,611.90                  │
│      Net Value Leasehold Impr.                               │
│                                                               │
│   Fixtures & Equipment            $ 1,618.74                  │
│   Accum. Depr. —Fixtures & Equip.    (584.20)                │
│                                   $ 1,034.54                  │
│      Net Value Fixtures  & Equip.                            │
│                                                               │
│   Vehicles                        $ 6,987.50                  │
│   Accum.Depr. —Vehicles            (1,001.23)                │
│                                   $ 5,986.27                  │
│      Net Value Vehicles                                      │
│                                                               │
│      Net Value Depreciable Assets              $ 11,632.71   │
│                                                               │
│   ┌──────────────┐                                           │
│   │ Other Assets:│                                           │
│   └──────────────┘                                           │
│   Deposits                        $   310.00                 │
│                                                               │
│      Total Other Assets                        $    310.00   │
│                                                               │
│      Total Assets                              $ 19,405.76   │
└─────────────────────────────────────────────────────────────┘
```

Figure 13–8   Balance sheet—assets

The balance sheet is used to determine the financial health of a business. The organization presented in the balance sheet shown in Figures 13–8 and 13–9, for example, is representative of a business facing financial difficulties. Applying financial tests to these companywide data leads to several conclusions. First, current assets are lower than current liabilities ($7,463.05 versus $8,155.02). A financially healthy firm would show current assets to be approximately twice as large as current liabilities. Second, total debt to equity is approximately 250 percent ($13,826 divided by $5,579). This disparity is dangerous—total debt should be approximately

```
┌─────────────────────────────────────────────────────────────┐
│                        Service Type                          │
│                     An Oregon Corporation                    │
│               See Accountant's Compilation Report            │
│              ┌──────────────────────────────┐                │
│              │        Balance Sheet         │                │
│              │       As of 02/28/9X         │                │
│              │                              │                │
│              │         Liabilities          │                │
│              └──────────────────────────────┘                │
```

Current Liabilities:		
Accounts Payable — Trade	$ 2,618.22	
Accounts Payable — Other	1,017.66	
Note Payable — Bank of the N.W.	1,611.03	
Accrued Wages Payable	572.28	
Accrued State Withholding	68.63	
Accrued Federal Withholding	55.38	
Accrued FICA Tax	209.01	
Accrued State Unemployment	548.24	
Accrued Federal Unemployment	318.72	
Estimated Federal Income Tax.	175.85	
Curr Portion Long Term Liab.	960.00	
Total Current Liabilities		$ 8,155.02
Long Term Liabilities:		
Contract Payable —Bank of the N.W.	3,631.00	
Loan Payable —Bank of the N.W.	3,000.00	
Curr Portion Long Term Liab.	(960.00)	
Total Long Term Liabilities		$ 5,671.00
Total Liabilities		$13,826.02
Equity:		
Common Stock	$ 1,000.00	
Paid In Capital/Excess of Par	2,705.50	
Retained Earnings	1,015.66	
Net Profit (or Loss)	858.58	
Total Equity		$ 5,579.74
Total Liabilities & Equity		$19,405.76

Figure 13–9   Balance sheet—liabilities

equal to owner's equity. Last, current liabilities are approximately 150 percent of total equity ($8,155 divided by $5,579). Once again there is a problem: a financially healthy firm would show a ratio of less than 50 percent.

Figure 13–10, the profit-and-loss statement for the same firm, is more positive than the company balance sheet. As shown, net income, after taxes, is close to 17 percent of total income (sales). This percentage is quite high. Likewise, if net income continues to average better that $429 ($858.58 divided by 2, since the statement reflects the first two months of the year) per month, the yearly return on

	Service Type An Oregon Corporation See Accountant's Compilation Report			
	Income Statement For the Period 01/01/9X to 02/28/9X			
	Current -period		*Year-To-Date*	
	Amount	*Ratio*	*Ratio*	*Amount*
Income				
Sales—Class A	$ 1,232.87	36.36	35.48	$ 2,258.45
Sales—Class B	2,158.19	63.64	64.52	4,106.20
Total Income	$ 3,391.06	100.00	100.00	$ 6,364.65
Expenses				
Advertising	$ 62.58	1.85	2.13	$ 135.80
Auto Expense	102.98	3.04	4.45	283.33
Bank Charges	5.12	.15	.15	9.24
Depreciation	135.73	4.00	4.26	270.84
General Expense	42.12	1.24	1.03	65.59
Insurance	27.00	.80	.85	54.00
Legal & Accounting	231.72	6.83	5.50	350.14
Office Expense	57.66	1.70	1.58	100.31
Rent	320.72	9.46	10.08	641.44
Repairs & Maintenance	61.14	1.80	1.81	114.93
Telephone	60.17	1.77	1.78	113.04
Utilities	72.09	2.13	1.96	124.93
Wages —Sales	1,138.87	33.58	32.92	2,095.16
Payroll Taxes	389.98	11.50	15.26	971.47
Total Expenses	$ 2,707.88	79.85	83.76	$ 5,330.22
Taxable Income	$ 683.18	20.15	16.24	$ 1,034.43
Estimated Income Tax	116.14	3.42	2.76	175.85
Total Estimated Income Tax	$ 116.14	3.42	2.76	$ 175.85
Net Income(or Loss)	$ 567.04	16.73	13.48	$ 858.58

Figure 13–10   Profit-and-loss statement

net worth will approximate 92 percent ($429 times 12 divided by $5,579). This return is spectacular.

Some business firms have a tendency to consider only the bottom line on the profit-and-loss statement. By now it should be clear that profit alone does not necessarily mean financial well-being. For example, if sales lead to ever-increasing current liabilities that cannot be adequately offset by current assets, a company is in financial trouble. The high interest expense associated with short-term loans becomes increasingly difficult to offset. And if short-term requirements become too large, further credit extensions must be refused. Thus, instead of reviewing only the profit-and-loss statement, business firms must study changes to assets and liabilities *in relation to* changes in profits and losses. This principle explains in large part why the general ledger application is so valuable: it produces both balance sheets and profit-and-loss statements, and, more important, it allows both statements to be studied individually and in relation to each other.

REVIEW QUESTIONS

5. What is a trial balance? Of what importance is a trial balance to the general ledger system?

6. What journals are the main sources of input to the consolidated G/L master file?

7. What types of information are recorded on a general journal voucher?

8. What are the advantages of updating the general ledger directly (as part of other business computer applications, such as customer invoicing or accounts payable)?

9. Name the main reports produced by general ledger processing.

13-3   GENERAL LEDGER PROCESSING

Figure 13–11(a) and (b) shows the structure of the G/L computer application; Figure 13–12(a) and (b) shows the corresponding G/L menus. For this application, all new transactions are produced by the *Enter general journal vouchers* interactive program. Another interactive program, called *Perform G/L trial balance*, attempts to balance all general ledger accounts. The program *Perform end-of-month closing* is used to reset the G/L master file. This program sets all current-balance totals to zero; the closing balance becomes the opening balance for the next accounting period.

As shown by Figure 13–11(b), the batch portion of processing is used to print the trial balance, the consolidated G/L, the balance sheet and profit-and-loss statement, and supporting schedules (such as G/L details for a specific account, the G/L trial balance for a set of accounts, and the G/L audit report). Another program option is the capability to post G/L transactions contained in summary files, such as the transactions leading to the sales journal.

A number of other programs could be added to either the interactive or the batch part of processing to perform special types of financial analyses desired by managers. These include analyses of cash sources and uses (cash flow statement), of sales and purchases, and of current versus historical financial ratios. For example, in the detailed breakdown of sales and cost of sales of an automotive dealership, shown in Figure 13–13, over 60 codes are required to classify sales information. This breakdown serves to classify sources of income. As indicated, income is grouped by new passenger vehicles, used passenger vehicles, general service,

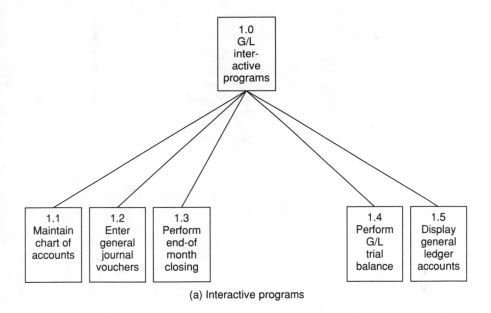

(a) Interactive programs

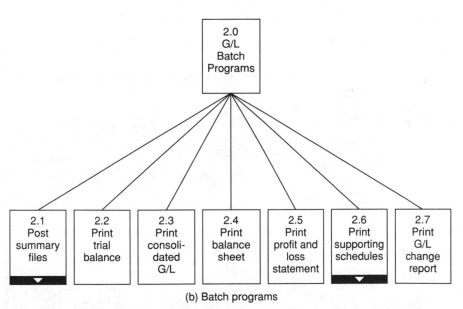

(b) Batch programs

Figure 13–11   General ledger systems organization

```
GENERAL LEDGER

      MAINTAIN CHART OF ACCOUNTS
      ENTER GENERAL JOURNAL VOUCHERS
      PERFORM E-O-M CLOSING
      PERFORM G/L TRIAL BALANCE
      DISPLAY GENERAL LEDGER ACCOUNTS



      RETURN
```

(a) Interactive menu choices

```
GENERAL LEDGER

         POST SUMMARY FILES
         PRINT TRIAL BALANCE
         PRINT CONSOLIDATED G/L
         PRINT BALANCE SHEET
         PRINT P AND L STATEMENT
         PRINT SUPPORTING SCHEDULES
         PRINT G/L CHANGE REPORT

         RETURN
```

```
SUPPORTING SCHEDUALS

      PRINT G/L DETAIL ACCOUNT
      PRINT G/L TRIAL BALANCE ACCOUNT
      PRINT AUDIT REPORT

      RETURN
```

```
POST SUMMARY FILES

         PRINT SALES JOURNAL
         PRINT RECEIPTS JOURNAL
         PRINT BILLS PAYABLE JOURNAL
         PRINT DISBURSEMENTS JOURNAL
         PRINT PAYABLES JOURNAL


         RETURN
```

(b) Batch menu choices

Figure 13–12 General ledger program menu

```
                                      SALES
                                  COST OF SALES

Acct. Number
Sales Cost

5100   6100   ┌─────────────────── NEW VEHICLES ──────────────────
5101   6101   │ Passenger - Sedan - Type 1409
5102          │ Passenger - Sedan - Type 1409 Discount
5104   6104   │ Passenger - Sports Coupe
5105          │ Passenger - Sports Coupe Discount
5111   6111   │ Passenger - Fastback
5112          │ Passenger - Fastback Discount
5114   6114   │ Passenger - Hatchback - Type XC14
5115          │ Passenger - Hatchback - Type XC14 Discount
5121   6121   │ Passenger - Wagon
5122          │ Passenger - Wagon Discount
5141   6141   │ Truck - Shortbed - Type 2
5142          │ Truck - Shortbed - Type 2 Discount
5144   6144   │ Passenger - Sedan - Type 1500Y
5145          │ Passenger - Sedan - Type 1500Y Discount
5147   6147   │ Passenger - Coupe - Type1505Z
5148          │ Passenger - Coupe - Type1505Z Discount
5161   6161   │ Passenger - Fleet and Employee
5162          │ Passenger - Fleet and Employee Discount
5171   6171   │ Demonstrator
5172          │ Demonstrator - Discount
5181   6181   │ Other Makes
5182          │ Other Makes - Discount
5191   6191   │ Dealer Installed Accessories
       6192   │ Dealer Installed Accessories - Cost
       6193   │ Dealer Installed Accessories - Labor

5200   6200   ┌─────────────────── USED VEHICLES ─────────────────
5201   6201   │ Dealer Makes - Retail
       6203   │ Dealer Makes - Reconditioning
5251   6251   │ Other Makes - Retail
       6253   │ Other Makes - Reconditioning
5281   6281   │ Wholesale
       6283   │ Inventory Adjustments

5400   6400   ┌─────────────────── SERVICE - GENERAL ─────────────
5401          │ Shop Labor Mechanical - Customer Sales
5402          │ Shop Labor Mechanical - Factory Warranty Sales
5404          │ Shop Labor Mechanical - Intern Sales
       6405   │ Cost of Labor - Genaral Shop
5411          │ Other Shop Labor and Material - Customer Sales
5412          │ Other Shop Labor and Material - Internal Sales
       6415   │ Cost of Labor and Material - Other Shop
5421   6421   │ Gas, Oil, and Grease
5441   6441   │ Sales Repairs - General

5500   6500   ┌─────────────── SERVICE - PAINT AND BODY ──────────
5501          │ Shop Labor - Customer Sales
5502          │ Shop Labor - Factory Warranty Sales
5504          │ Shop Labor - Internal Sales
       6505   │ Cost of Labor - Paint and  Body
5511   6511   │ Paint and Supplies
5531   6531   │ Contract Paint and Body

5700   6700   ┌─────────────── PARTS AND ACCESSORIES ─────────────
5701   6701   │ General Repair Order - Customer Sales
5702   6702   │ General Repair Order - Factory Warranty Sales
5704   6704   │ General Repair Order - Internal Sales
5711   6711   │ Other Makes  General Repair Order
5721   6721   │ Paint and Body Repair Order - Customer Sales
5722   6722   │ Paint and Body Repair Order - Factory Warranty
5724   6724   │ Paint and Body Repair Order - Internal Sales
5741   6741   │ Over the Counter - Retail
5742   6742   │ Over the Counter - Wholesale
5744   6744   │ Over the Counter - Paint and Body Shops
5771   6771   │ Other Parts and Accessories
       6772   │ Inventory Adjustment - Parts
       6774   │ Inventory Adjustment - Accessories
       6776   │ Inventory Adjustment - Other
```

Figure 13–13   Detailed sales and cost of sales account breakdown

paint and body service, parts and accessories, and so on. If the company later decides to add new and used truck vehicles to its product line and to track both types of truck income, additional chart of account codes must be added.

Organizing the General Ledger Master File

The organization of the general ledger master file requires special attention in the design of the G/L application. As Figure 13–14 shows, the file is organized by chart of account number, which serves as the primary key. This number often consists of ten or more digits for multidivision companies and contains several parts. Figure 13–15 uses a twelve-digit classification scheme, for example. The terms used in this scheme are the same as those shown on the organization of the G/L master file.

- Digits 1 and 2 separate the different divisions, plants, or parts of a company, such as Division 1, Foods, and Division 2, Feed and Seed.

- Digits 3, 4, and 5 indicate major (prime) account groupings, such as gross sales, accounts receivable, accounts payable, and gross salaries.

- Digits 6, 7, and 8 identify subsidiary accounts within each major account, such as subsidiary checking accounts within the major account, cash in bank.

- Digits 9, 10, 11, and 12 define the department or the cost center responsible for the account, such as the controller's office or the data-processing department.

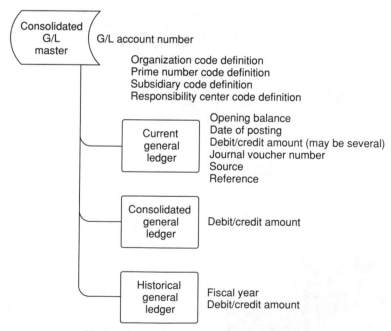

Figure 13–14   Organization of G/L master file

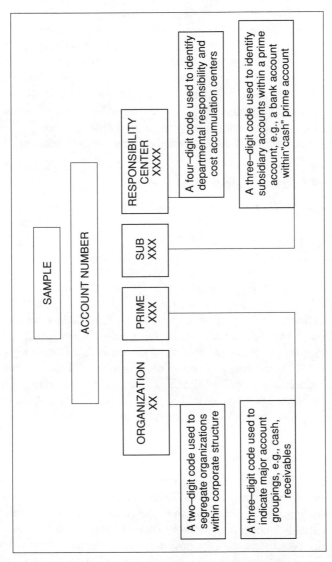

Figure 13–15 Corporate chart-of-accounts classification scheme

Such a chart of accounts is often necessary to define fully the financial activities of a business and to specify which managers are responsible for the control of various expenses and revenues. A fully specified chart of accounts is especially required by large organizations. In larger institutions, individual units (divisions, plants, areas, departments) are responsible for evaluating the financial soundness of their operations.

The three file segments shown in Figure 13–14 separate the current, consolidated, and historical general ledgers. The *current general ledger* stores information for a designated accounting period, such as the current month. This segment provides a detailed record of each posting to each general ledger account number. The *consolidated general ledger* is much simpler in design. This segment is usually limited to one field for each account, for each accounting period, showing the dollars posted during the period. The *historical general ledger* contains data to permit year-to-year comparisons. Here, too, information is limited. The segment stores the date plus the dollars posted to the account for each accounting period.

Balancing the General Ledger Master File

Once all financial totals have been entered or posted, the trial balance program can be run. As Figure 13–11(a) and (b) shows, either an interactive or a batch program can be used to perform the trial balance. In practice, the interactive program is used first; the batch program is held in reserve and used later to print *general ledger worksheets* for use in attempting to determine what must be done to balance the file or as the final vault copy of the general ledger trial balance report.

Two popular processing strategies are followed to balance general ledger files. The first is to balance only the current portion of the file, holding off the update of the consolidated, YTD portion until the current portion is in balance. The second is to balance portions of the current portion of the file before attempting to achieve a final balance. This latter strategy features the posting of G/L debits and credits at the time they are initially processed. For example, all payroll-related G/L activity would be posted and balanced at the end of each payroll run. The balanced payroll journal is kept separate from all other general ledger postings.

Printing Financial Summaries

Once the current position of the general ledger is in balance and the consolidated YTD portion is updated, financial summaries can be printed. This is one of the easiest steps in processing, since printing the profit-and-loss statement follows directly from the balanced consolidated general ledger master file. Prior to processing, print parameters must be specified (for example, *Print current profit and loss only* or *Print and compare current and YTD profit and loss totals*). Moreover, if historical month-by-month general ledger totals are kept on file, it is possible to specify such comparisons as current profit this year to profit for same month last year, or profit this YTD to profit last YTD.

Besides printing common types of financial summaries, online general ledger applications are designed to produce various types of financial performance

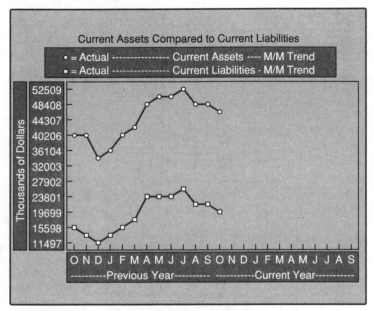

Figure 13–16 Comparing current assets with current liabilities

summaries and comparisons. Figure 13–16, for instance, graphs current assets to current liabilities to show differences in their respective trends. Figure 13–17 compares revenues to net income and presents the corresponding trend. This graph might be prepared for the company as a whole, or several graphs might be prepared to show the performance of various divisions of the company. Finally, Figure 13–18 shows expenditures by department over a twenty-six–week period. This *composite bar chart* illustrates the proportional differences in expenditures; the attached table shows the columns of figures used in preparing the bar chart.

Graphs of general ledger dollar comparisons should not be viewed as rare examples of general-ledger outputs or of things to come. With the dynamic increase in the development of online graphic display devices, color pictures of financial performance are quite common. More important, recent technological innovations suggest that pictures and tables of financial performance are replacing detailed listings of financial results—at least for portraying financial-performance summaries.

13-4   PROCESSING CONTROLS

The general ledger application clarifies why processing controls are vital to all business computer applications. Companies have discovered that the key to balancing the general ledger lies not within the general ledger application itself, but rather within transaction-based applications such as customer invoicing and

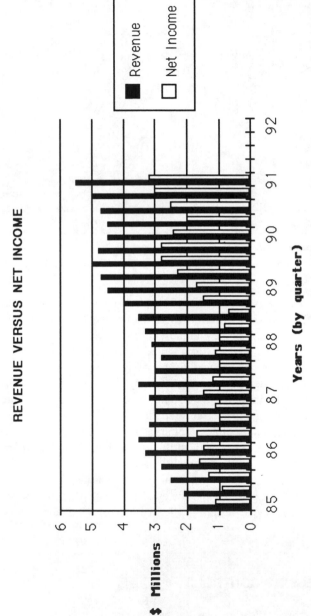

Figure 13–17   Comparing revenue with net income

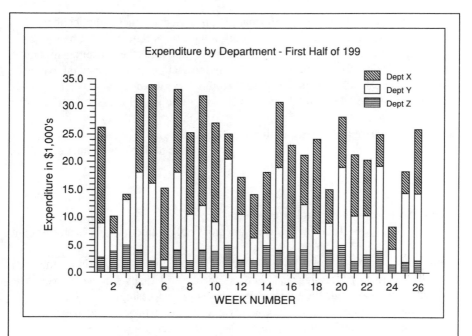

WEEK	DEPT A	DEPT B	DEPT C	TOTAL
1	17,103	6,227	2,696	26,026
2	2,889	3,210	3,851	9,950
3	963	8,282	4,815	14,060
4	13,996	14,124	3,916	32,036
5	17,912	14,065	1,990	33,967
6	12,904	1,284	899	15,087
7	14,894	14,058	4,045	32,997
8	14,766	8,346	2,054	25,166
9	19,902	8,089	3,978	31,969
10	17,912	5,265	3,786	26,963
11	4,622	15,410	5,008	25,040
12	6,805	8,282	2,119	17,206
13	7,832	4,173	2,055	14,060
14	10,914	2,311	4,879	18,104
15	11,877	15,023	3,916	30,816
16	16,820	2,440	3,788	23,048
17	8,988	8,217	3,981	21,186
18	16,949	6,099	1,027	24,075
19	5,842	4,943	4,045	14,830
20	9,052	14,188	4,815	28,055
21	10,850	8,206	2,086	21,142
22	9,951	7,190	3,082	20,223
23	5,906	15,248	3,820	24,974
24	3,853	3,017	1,284	8,154
25	3,916	12,391	1,862	18,169
26	11,745	12,242	1,926	25,913

Figure 13–18   Comparing departmental expenses

accounts payable. If summary information processed by these applications is in balance prior to G/L posting, the balancing adjustments required will be minimal.

A brief review of the processing controls required by the customer-invoicing application shows the relationship between transaction-based financial balances and the totals carried forward and posted to the general ledger. The batch controls required for invoice dollar totals are expressed by two equations (see Section 4-5):

$$\text{Total invoice charge} = \text{Sales dollars} + \text{Tax dollars} + \text{Freight dollars} + \text{Insurance dollars}$$

and

$$\text{Total invoice receipts (net dollar amount)} = \text{Total invoice charge (gross dollar amount)} - \text{Cash discount}$$

These dollar amounts must be in balance if processing is to continue; they are carried forward in processing and serve as the control totals for the invoice A/R summary file—the input file to accounts receivable processing.

What was not stated earlier is that invoice-control balances and their various subtotals are also carried forward to the general ledger. That is, the total invoice charge is posted to the accounts receivable G/L account, the sales dollars subtotal is posted to a second G/L account, the tax dollars subtotal is posted to a third G/L account, and so forth. This posting is done transaction by transaction, whenever invoices are prepared. At the end of the month, month-end summaries are produced for each account. The sum of the dollars posted to accounts receivable must equal the sums posted to sales dollars, tax dollars, freight dollars, and insurance dollars.

The importance of this procedure should be obvious: the month-end summation should always be in balance, provided that the daily totals posted to the general ledger were in balance. A second, more important aspect of this procedure—one not as obvious—is that a clear audit trail is preserved in processing. For example, an auditor can begin with the general ledger and trace an account entry back to a subsidiary journal, such as the sales journal. Likewise, the totals appearing on the journal can be traced. Individual entries can be traced back to daily batch balance figures and, eventually, to figures appearing on shipping documents and customer order–filling slips. This path, from general ledger totals, to subsidiary journals, to batch balance–control totals, to individual source documents, constitutes the audit trail required by business. Should financial totals appear suspect, it must be possible to retrace the steps in processing to determine whether each step is accurate.

13-5   MANAGEMENT IMPLICATIONS

The general ledger application, more than any other, shows that business data processing must consist of a well-devised data structure. This application clarifies why summary data must be collected at various points in processing; it shows the relationships that must exist between the general ledger and subsidiary ledgers, such as summary journals and detailed registers. The general ledger application also helps better clarify two other concepts important to online systems design: it specifies how the company audit trail is constructed from individual, to daily, to monthly processing activity; it begins to explain how company audits of computer-based processing are conducted.

Because of the importance of the general ledger application in relation to other applications, some companies believe that a simplified version of the application should be implemented prior to the development of any other transaction-based application, such as customer invoicing, accounts payable, or employee payroll. There is considerable merit to this *top-down approach* to design. Clearly, a well-defined and complete master chart of accounts must be developed in advance. Designers must know when and where account codes will be required; the entries that are to appear on the consolidated G/L ledger must be specified. Without such a master chart, summary data will not be in correct format, and it will be especially difficult to tie together different types of business information.

Besides consolidating business information, the general ledger application provides managers with timely and meaningful financial summary information. Without an online design, the general ledger is often a historical document, arriving too late (such as one to two months after an accounting period) to do much good. With an online design, the general ledger should be in final form within one week following the end of an accounting period. If, for example, the books are closed on the fifteenth of each month, upper management should be able to review general ledger summaries within seven days and thus determine before the end of the month whether company performance is acceptable. Moreover, the general ledger makes possible a far-reaching and complete analysis, addressing not only questions of profit or loss but also financial conditions and trends. Provided with a number of special reporting options, managers are able to come up with a clearer, more comprehensive picture of the financial well-being of the organization.

REVIEW QUESTIONS

10. What is the difference between the current and the consolidated general ledger? Between the consolidated and the historical general ledger?

11. Name the two popular processing strategies followed in balancing the general ledger file.

12. What is the key to balancing the general ledger? Explain why processing controls are vital to all transaction-based applications.

13. What is the difference between the general ledger and a subsidiary journal? Between a subsidiary journal and a batch control?

14. Why must the master chart of accounts be defined in advance? What occurs if it is not properly defined in advance?

REVIEW OF IMPORTANT IDEAS

The general ledger application consolidates the financial transactions of a business in order to summarize, by account, changes to assets and liabilities and to profit and net worth. Various types of financial data are integrated by the use of a master chart of accounts. Such a chart defines the major financial activities of a business and shows how these activities are tied together.

The preliminary processing of the general ledger application consists of updating and balancing the current G/L master file. The file can be updated in one of two ways: financial summary totals can be recorded on journal vouchers, from which they must be keyed to processing; or account totals can be posted directly by using summary files created by other online applications. The master file can also be balanced in one of two ways: either an interactive or a batch program can be used to determine whether the various financial totals are in balance. In practice, the batch program is only chosen when a printed copy of the entire master file is desired or when worksheets are needed to fix out-of-balance conditions.

The general ledger journals produced by transaction-based computer applications, such as accounts receivable and accounts payable, serve as inputs to general ledger processing. The age-old practice of double-entry bookkeeping is built into the general ledger design. In all instances, inputs to the general ledger must be in balance. Debits must be offset by credits in order to properly post summary totals.

The main outputs from general ledger processing are the general ledger trial balance report, the consolidated general ledger, and several financial statements, including the balance sheet and the profit-and-loss statement. Most online applications feature various types of financial performance display summaries and comparisons.

The general ledger application clarifies why processing controls are vital to all business computer applications. The key to balancing the general ledger (and thus the books of a business) can be traced to transaction-based processing systems. If the summary totals produced by these lower-level systems are in balance prior to their posting, the balancing of G/L master file is greatly simplified.

The general ledger application shows the value of a top-down design. Systems designers must specify early on in the design process what types of summary data are to be prepared. This must be done to tie together successfully the many different types of general ledger information produced by transaction-based computer applications.

KEY WORDS

General ledger

Balance sheet

Profit-and-loss statement

Master chart of accounts

Debit

Credit

Double-entry bookkeeping

General journal voucher

Consolidated G/L master file

General ledger trial balance input

Consolidated general ledger

Current general ledger

Subsidiary journals

Composite bar chart

EXERCISES

1. Suppose a student's expenses exceed his or her income each month. Suppose further that the student in question is not concerned. The student comments: "Before I started my studies, I worked out a method of financing it, without asking for help from my parents."

   Using the general ledger accounts shown in Figure 13–1, explain the student's financial strategy.

2. Consider the following: "We keep making a profit each month according to our profit-and-loss statement; however, our owner's equity continues to be lower each month. How could this be happening?" asked the puzzled store owner.

   Using the general ledger accounts shown in Figure 13–1, explain the situation faced by the store owner.

3. Suppose that the direct update of the G/L master file is to be designed into the customer-invoicing computer application.

   (a) Using a data flow diagram, show where and when the posing of G/L accounts would take place.

   (b) Explain how debits and credits would be balanced in processing.

   (c) Explain how control would be maintained in processing.

   (d) Discuss the advantages and disadvantages of such a direct posting.

4. You have decided to design a personal general ledger system to help you track your personal assets, liabilities, income, and expenses. The entry of data to processing will consist of using a limited number of source documents. These are the voucher portion of your paycheck, your personal checkbook check register, bank statements mailed to your home, monthly bills, and cash register receipts for such items as entertainment expenses, lunches, transportation, and educational supplies. Using Figure 13–1 as a guide, explain how data entered from each source document will change general ledger account totals.

5. Suppose you work as a salesperson for the dealer that uses the detailed sales and cost of sales account breakdown shown in Figure 13–13. Suppose next that a point-of-sale system is used in entering sales transactions. How would the detailed set of codes be used on a daily basis? Propose a method to simplify the entry of general ledger data into processing (Refer to Chapter 5 to answer this question.)

DISCUSSION QUESTIONS

1. How can the online general ledger application contribute to greater profits in a company? List several ways.

2. Some people argue that financial statements, such as the profit-and-loss statement, offer little more than a means of keeping score (that is, they show how much money was won or lost). Do you agree with this statement? If so, why? If not, why?

3. Suppose the sales, receipts, payables, disbursements, and payroll journals were not processed by a company and that the only online application installed was the general ledger application. Discuss the implications of this situation.

4. Company A, the takeover company, merges with company B. Both firms have developed online G/L applications. What possible actions might company A take to produce a single balance sheet and profit-and-loss statement for the two companies? Discuss several design strategies. Consider the strengths and weaknesses of each strategy.

4-IN-1 CASE STUDY—GENERAL LEDGER

The 4-in-1 software provides a complete general ledger component. As demonstrated in Chapter 3, this component permits users to maintain a chart of accounts, process the general journal, view G/L account activity, and print the trial balance and financial statements. In this lesson, we begin by asking you to use the general journal to enter transactions. A general ledger transaction is entered as a debit or credit amount, referenced by chart of account number. Much like an accounts payable or sales transaction, a general ledger transaction can be either regular or recurring. Once entered and posted, a regular transaction becomes effective. A recurring transaction, in contrast, occurs over and over again at a specified point in time.

The objective of this lesson is to introduce you to the process of combining accounts into month-end financial reports. The first report, the *trial balance*, shows each G/L account beginning balance, total debits and credits, and ending balance for the time period selected. The second report, the *profit-and-loss statement*, shows the income resulting from the sales and expenses of A and J Enterprises. The third report, the *balance sheet*, shows the assets, liabilities, and stockholder's equity of A and J Enterprises. The tasks you are asked to do include:

- Enter a transaction to add cash to the business.
- Make an adjusting entry.
- Print a general journal transaction edit list.
- Post all transactions.
- Print a trial balance report.
- Print a balance sheet.
- Change the layout of a report.
- Print a profit-and-loss sheet.

Adding Cash to the Business

The first transaction you are to make is the addition of cash to the business. Up to now, you have probably wondered how checks could be written before money was deposited in the bank. We will correct this problem. Assume that $50,000 is added to cash, this being offset by $30,000 in capital stock and $20,000 of long-term debt.

1. Log on and enter a date of 010197. Press ENTER when asked, *Any change?*

2. From the main menu, type **2** and press ENTER.

3. When the process general journal submenu appears, type **1**, *Add transactions*. Press ENTER.

4. Press ENTER when asked, *Any change to current period?*

5. When the add transaction submenu appears, type **1010** and press ENTER twice. This indicates that you plan to debit cash receipts for checking account #1.

6. Press ENTER for the transaction date.

7. Type **25000** for the debit amount and press ENTER.

8. For reference, type **Funds for payables** and press ENTER.

9. Press ENTER when asked, *Field number of change?*

10. When the process general journal screen appears the second time, type the following:

1020	for checking account number 2, and press ENTER twice
ENTER	for the transaction date
25000	for the debit amount
Funds for payroll	for the reference
ENTER	when asked, *Field number to change?*

11. When the process general journal screen appears the third time, type the following:

3000	for capital stock, and press ENTER twice
ENTER	for the transaction date
30000	for the credit amount
Startup funds	for the reference
ENTER	when asked, *Field number to change?*

12. When the process general journal screen appears the fourth time, type the following:

2650	for other long-term debt, and press ENTER twice
ENTER	for the transaction date
20000	for the credit amount
Startup loan	for the reference
ENTER	when asked, *Field number to change?*

13. Press TAB to quit at this time. Do not press ENTER.

14. Log off at this time.

Adjusting the LAWNS-ARE-GREEN Sale

When the first LAWNS-ARE-GREEN sale was made in Chapter 4, the sales tax was treated as a sales revenue, when it should have been posted as a sales tax payable (account 2450). To correct for this error, do the following:

15. Log on and enter a date of **013097**. Press ENTER when asked, *Any change?*

16. From the main menu, type **2** and press ENTER.

17. When the process general journal submenu appears, type **1**, *Add transactions*. Press ENTER.

18. Press ENTER when asked, *Any change to current period?*

19. When the add transaction submenu appears, type **4010** and press ENTER twice.

20. Press ENTER for the transaction date.

21. For the credit amount, type ENTER. This allows you to debit sales.

22. For the debit amount, type **5.25** and press ENTER.

23. For reference, type **Correct incorrect posting** and press ENTER.

24. Press ENTER when asked, *Field number of change?*

25. When the process general journal screen appears the second time, type the following:

2450	For state sales tax payable press ENTER twice
ENTER	for the transaction date
5.25	for the credit amount
Correct incorrect posting	for the reference
ENTER	when asked, *Field number to change?*

Adjusting for Depreciation

Another transaction required at month-end are adjustments for depreciation.

26. When the add transaction submenu appears, type **1600** and press ENTER twice.

27. Press ENTER for the transaction date.

28. For the credit amount, type ENTER. This allows you to credit office equipment.

29. For the credit amount, type **200** and press ENTER.

30. For reference, type **Reduce for depreciation** and press ENTER.

31. Press ENTER when asked, *Field number of change?*

32. When the process general journal screen appears the second time, type the following:

1700	for accumulated depreciation—office equipment (press ENTER twice)
ENTER	for the transaction date
200	for the debit amount
Depreciation expense	for the reference
ENTER	when asked, *Field number to change?*

33. Press TAB to exit.

Printing the General Journal Edit List

The general journal edit list can be printed at any time.

34. Type **4** from the process general journal submenu. Press ENTER.

35. Type **Y** when asked, *Are general journal transactions ready to print?* The edit report will be printed.

36. Press END to exit.

Posting Transactions

37. Type **5** form the process general journal submenu. Press ENTER.

38. Type **Y** when asked, *Are general ledger transactions ready to post?* The general journal register will be printed.

39. Press END to exit to the main menu.

Printing the Trial Balance

40. Type **4** form the main menu. Press ENTER.

41. Press F1 for first and F1 for last.

42. Press ENTER for start date and ENTER for stop date.

43. Press ENTER for show detail.

44. Press F1 for all.

45. Press ENTER when asked, *Field number to change?*

46. Press ENTER to print the report. The trial balance will be printed.

47. Press TAB to exit to the main menu.

Printing the Balance Sheet

To print the balance sheet, do the following:

48. Type **5** from the main menu and press ENTER.

49. Type **2** to print statements. Press ENTER.

50. Type **1** for layout number. Press ENTER.

51. Press ENTER for ending period date.

52. Type F1 for profit centers.

53. Press ENTER for one copy.

54. Press ENTER when asked, *Field number to change?*

55. Press ENTER to print the balance sheet.

56. Press TAB to exit to the print financial statements submenu.

Changing the Layout of a Report

Figure 13–19 shows the revised profit-and-loss statement. To change the layout of this statement, do the following:

57. Type **1** to change the financial sheet layout. Press ENTER.

58. Type **2** to change a layout. Press ENTER.

59. Type **2** for layout number.

60. Press ENTER to change the layout of the profit-and-loss statement.

61. Type **0080** under seq# to specify the line number you wish to change.

62. Type **Y** when asked, *Any change?*

63. Type **4030** and press ENTER.

64. Type **000** and press ENTER.

65. Type **P** to indicate that sales for product C are to be printed.

66. Press ENTER when asked, *Any change?*

67. Press F1 twice to display the next two pages.

68. Type **0285** and press ENTER.

69. Type **5030** and press ENTER. Type **000** and press ENTER.

```
                  Your Company Name Here
                     Income Statement
               For the period:  01/01 97 to 01/31/

                                    Current-period
                                      Amount

Sales — product A                 $    472.25
Sales — product B                    1,762.50
Sales — product C                    2,342.50              2,342.50
    Total product sales           $  4,577.25          $  4,577.25


    Total misc. & other sales     $       .00          $       .00
                                  =========            =========
    NET SALES                     $  4,577.25          $  4,577.25

Purchases — product A             $  1,890.00          $  1,890.00
Purchases — product B                1,169.50             1,169.50
Purchases — product C                2,000.00             2,000.00
Inventory purch discounts               (7.39)               (7.39)

    Cost of goods sold

Sales & marketing wages              1,925.00             1,925.00
Warehse & shipping wages             1,600.00             1,600.00

    Selling costs

Employer FICA paid                     264.38               264.38
Fed unemployment paid                  225.00               225.00
State unemployment paid                175.00               175.00
Employee Benefits                     (300.00)             (300.00)

    Total gen'l & admin costs     $  8,941.49          $  8,941.49

       OPERATING EXPENSES         $  8,941.49          $  8,941.49

       OPERATING INCOME           $ (4,364.24)         $ (4,364.24)
                                  =========            =========

    Other income (expense)        $       .00          $       .00
                                  =========            =========
       INCOME BEFORE TAXES        $ (4,364.24)         $ (4,364.24)

    Federal & state income tax    $       .00          $       .00

       NET INCOME                 $ (4,364.24)         $ (4,364.24)
                                  =========            =========
```

Figure 13–19   Revised profit-and-loss statement

70. Type **P** to display the purchases for product C.

71. Type TAB three times to exit.

Printing the Profit-and-Loss Statement

To print the profit-and-loss statement, do the following:

72. With the print financial statements submenu facing you, type **2** and press ENTER.

73. Type **N** for print ratios. Press ENTER.

74. Press ENTER for start date and ENTER for stop date.

75. Press F1 for all.

76. Type **1** for number of copies.

77. Press ENTER twice to print this report.

78. Press TAB to exit once the profit-and-loss statement is printed.

QUESTIONS

1. What is the primary purpose of the general journal?

2. Why is it important to be able to enter adjustments into processing?

3. Assets do not equal liabilities and net worth on the balance sheet; the difference is $4,364.24. Where did this figure come from? What must be done to balance the balance sheet?

4. Why is it important to be able to change the layout of a financial report?

14

Budget and Profit Planning

Two financial planning computer applications can be implemented in conjunction with the development of the general ledger application. The first of these, the *budget planning application*, is designed to compare budgeted to actual business expenses. This application requires departments and divisions of a company to estimate the amount of money they will need to cover their expenses over a specified period. Once these estimates are approved by upper management, funds can be allocated to various divisions and departments. This process of deciding on what level to approve is known as *budgeting*. Funds allocated to departments signify the dollars included in a *budget*, a formal business planning document showing what amount of money has been allocated to pay for departmental expenses. As this chapter illustrates, budgeting combines both planning and control. Planning estimates what level of funding is needed and determines the amount of money to be included in a budget; control monitors the actual expenditure of funds to determine if the budgeted amount was realistic.

Besides the budget planning application, this chapter also examines the *profit planning application*. Profit planning compares planned business profits with actual profits. Profit planning requires departments and divisions to estimate their expenses at different stages of production. These estimates are compared against actual cost-per-unit figures.

14-1 BUDGET PLANNING OVERVIEW

There are several reasons for developing an online budget planning computer application. This application can enhance a business's ability to understand and plan for anticipated business expenses; it can improve budget allocation procedures, tracking of planned versus actual business expenditures, and financial reporting. In addition, an online budget planning computer application enables management to ask a variety of "what if" questions about company finances, such as: "What if personnel costs were increased by 10 percent?" In this instance, management would like to know the financial implications of a 10 percent increase in labor costs.

The online budget planning application is usually designed to deal with fixed or variable budgeting. A *fixed budget* does not change as production or sales volumes increase or decrease. Instead, each department or cost center is allocated a fixed dollar amount to cover its expenses. If this amount proves to be inadequate—due to higher-than-expected company activities—the budgeted amount must be adjusted upward to provide for additional funding for operations. Likewise, lower-than-expected company activities require that budgeted amounts be adjusted downward. Typically, these adjustments are made either quarterly or yearly, rather than month by month. With a fixed budget, departments must learn to live with the level of funding made available.

A *variable budget* does change as volumes vary. For example, the budget for running a machine for 2,000 hours is different from the budget for running the same machine for 5,000 hours. To account for differences in volume, a standard rate, such as the cost per hour or the cost per unit, is established for different work centers. This rate is multiplied by production forecast or *activity figures* expressed as either the total number of machine hours required, the number of labor hours required, or the number of units to be produced. Budget totals are based on formulas such as the following:

> Budget total = Machine hour rate (standard) ×
> Number of machine hours (estimated)

> Budget total = Labor hour rate (standard) ×
> Number of labor hours (estimated)

> Budget total = Cost per unit (standard) ×
> Number of units produced (estimated)

Regardless of which type of budgeting is adopted—fixed, variable, or some combination thereof—budgeted expenses must be compared with actual expenses. As discussed in the last chapter, actual expenses are summarized by the current and YTD portions of the consolidated G/L master file.

As shown by Figure 14–1, the budget-planning system involves departments and the budget office (or some high-level decision-making group in an organization). The first major function is a *planning function*: budget requests and budget decisions lead to budget allocations for departments and budgeted expenses for the company as a whole. All budgeted expenses are stored on a budget master file. The second major function is a *control function*: budgeted expenses are compared against actual expenses stored on the consolidated G/L master file. This comparison leads to a number of budget control reports known as *budget variance reports*. These show such figures as the difference between budgeted expense and actual expense for the current period, and the amount of money remaining to cover actual expenses for the remainder of a budgeted period.

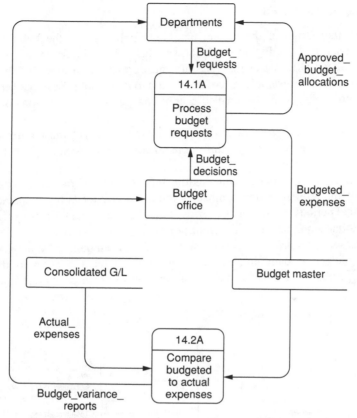

Figure 14–1   The budget planning system

The inputs and outputs shown in Figure 14–1 can be summarized as follows:

1. *Budget requests* consist of entering into processing the total dollars estimated as being needed by various company divisions and departments.

2. *Budget decisions* consist of entering into processing the total dollars budgeted to various divisions and departments.

3. *Approved budget allocations* produce the documents showing how funds have been budgeted.

4. *Budget variance reports* produce the reports and displays showing the differences between budgeted and actual company expenses.

Typically, *budget requests* (the requests for dollars to be placed in the budget) are larger than *budget allocations* (the actual dollars placed in the budget). Since the different divisions and departments of a company almost always have financial needs greater than what can supported, budget cuts must be made by the budget office. These cuts entail reducing requested dollars until they reach a level that can be supported.

The Budget Master File

Central to the design of the budget planning application is the building of the *budget master file*. As Figure 14–2 shows, this file is similar in some ways to the consolidated G/L master file. The file must contain a *master chart of budget accounts* section, for example, to control access to processing. Each budget number keyed to processing must be verified before changes to other sections of the file can be made.

Besides the master chart of budget accounts, the budget master file contains budget request, budget appropriation, consolidated budget control, and historical budget control sections.

The *budget request* section contains the total amount of money requested and the date of the request. Many companies require dollar totals to be spread across several fiscal periods. As shown, quarterly, first-, second-, and third-period requests indicate dollar requirements at different points in each fiscal year.

The *budget appropriations* section stores the total amount of money set aside for each budget account number, as well as the total allocation to date, the period-by-period breakdown of the allocation, and the date of appropriation. It is

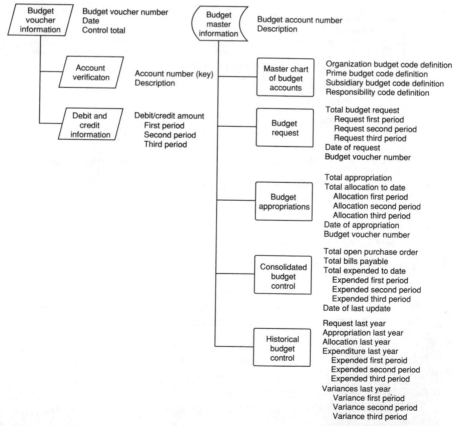

Figure 14–2   Relationships between budget master-file data sets

common to appropriate (budget for a department) one dollar amount and to allocate a smaller amount. The dollar difference is held in reserve. For example, $50,000 might be appropriated to cover material expenses, but $45,000 might be allocated. The remaining $5,000 would be held in reserve to cover higher-than-expected material costs. This money is allocated once the actual need for funds is better known.

The *consolidated budget control* section holds both expended and encumbered expense totals. As Figure 14–2 shows, two encumbered expense totals are stored: the total open purchase order and the total bills payable. These dollar amounts are transferred from the general ledger during the update of the budget control section. In addition, the total dollars expended is stored in this section of the file. This total, also broken down by period, is compared against the budget allocation total to determine the budget variance.

The *historical budget control* section contains one or more years of budget planning totals and one or more years of actual expense and budget variance totals. Historical budget information is useful for making comparisons such as examining the difference between previous budget requests and budget allocations, or the difference between the current and last year's budget appropriations.

Inputs to Processing

Four types of input are required to ready the budget master file: budget account change slips, budget request worksheets, budget appropriation worksheets, and budget change slips.

The *budget account change slip* adds new budget accounts to the budget master file, changes an existing budget account number, or deletes an old number from the chart of budget accounts.

The *budget request worksheet* itemizes the types of funds required, by account number, period by period, for a division or department. The worksheet is a planning document. In some cases it shows how fixed budget requests were determined; in other cases it indicates how estimated activity units were determined. Once completed, the worksheet shows the total and itemized funds needed to cover the expenses of a division or department.

The *budget appropriation worksheet* itemizes the funds to be allocated, by account number, period by period, for a division or department. Appropriated totals (either dollars or a percentage of requested dollars) must be keyed to processing, much like budget request totals. Once keyed, the difference between the total dollars requested and the total dollars appropriated can be reconciled.

The *budget change slip* modifies appropriation totals when there is a need to adjust these totals during a fiscal year. Suppose department A loses an employee, for example, and management decides not to fill the position (replace the person). Suppose further that management decides to add another staff position to department B, with the understanding that a budget change will be processed to transfer salary funds. In this instance, a budget change slip would be completed to show that funds will be transferred from the salary account for department A to the salary account for department B.

In making up budget request and appropriation worksheets, budget planners find it helpful if they can review their previous worksheets online and make changes to these sheets as required. This practice avoids the need to hand-copy all budget entries; it avoids the totaling of budget rows and columns. Such online capabilities are often referred to as *spreadsheet software*: they feature online entry of data into rows and columns, followed by the summation of worksheet entries, as specified by the data-entry operator.

A final input to the budget planning application is the *flow-of-funds forecast*. This forecast is based on sales estimates and production requirements for the company as a whole. It shows how many dollars can be appropriated, period by period. Figure 14–3 shows a flow-of-funds forecast for a real estate firm for a fiscal year. As shown, revenues from rent (cash inflow) are less than adequate to cover uses of cash (cash outflow) for the first and second quarters; however, the third and fourth quarters lead to a positive net cash flow. A spreadsheet such as this is required in budgeting operating expenses for the year. As another example, suppose the sales forecast indicates that 100,000 units of 4-inch liners for potted plants will be sold during the next fiscal period. From cost accounting data, unit cost data for these liners show that production costs will be approximately $0.30 per unit, with selling

```
                        Projected Flow of Funds



                              1Q          2Q          3Q          4Q
   ┌─────────┐
   │ Sources │
   └─────────┘
   Revenues                    $           $           $           $
      Rent..................200.0       300.0       400.0       400.0
      Loans..................  0.0         0.0         0.0         0.0

   Cash inflow..............200.0       300.0       400.0       400.0
   ┌──────┐
   │ Uses │
   └──────┘
   Asset purchases
      Land................... 0.0         0.0         0.0         0.0
      Building............... 0.0         0.0         0.0         0.0
                              0.0         0.0         0.0         0.0

   Expenses
      Operating expense....150.0       200.0       209.0       218.4
      Real estate taxes.... 70.0        70.0        70.0        70.0
                           220.0       270.0       279.0       288.4

      Federal Taxes........-65.8       -40.3         4.8         1.7
      Interest.............. 73.2        72.4        71.4        70.4
      Principle reductions.. 9.0         9.8        10.8        11.8

   Cash outflow.............236.4       311.9       366.0       372.3
   ┌──────────────────────────┐
   │ Working capital changes  │
   └──────────────────────────┘
   Sale of property.......... 0.0         0.0         0.0         0.0
   ┌───────────────┐
   │ Net cash flow │ .........-36.4      -11.9        34.0        27.7
   └───────────────┘
```

Figure 14–3   Flow of funds forecast

costs of approximately $0.08 per unit and administrative and all other costs totaling approximately $0.08 per unit. From these per-unit figures and the sales estimate, it can be determined that the production budget should be $30,000, the sales budget $8,000, and the administrative budget also $8,000. Such individual-item sales and budget figures are combined with the sales and budget figures for all other products to compose the flow-of-funds forecast. Collectively, they forecast the amount of money that can be appropriated during a fiscal period.

Outputs from Processing

Two main products from the budget planning application are annual budget materials and budget control reports. Figure 14–4 illustrates the annual budget for a single cost center in plant A. As shown, two variable cost rates are set for direct labor; one variable cost rate and one fixed cost rate are set for indirect labor.

					Annual Activity Units			
					Machine Hours			4,000
					Labor Hours			10,000
					Days			250

Acct. #	Account Description	Rates			Amounts			
		Var. #1	Var. #2	Fixed	Var. #1	Var. #2	Fixed	Total
501-006	Direct Labor	5.85000	2.39000		23,400	23,900		47,300
502-017	Indirect Labor	1.67500		38.40	6,700		9,600	16,300
503-141	Overtime Premium	.40000	.12000		1,600	1,200		2,800
724-211	Payroll Taxes & Fringe	1.58500	.50200	6.68	6,340	5,020	1,920	13,280
	TOTAL PAYROLL EXPENSE	9.51000	3.01200	46.08	38,040	30,120	11,520	79,680
579-018	Solvent S46B		.06000			600		600
579-040	Other Operating Supplies	.70000	.03000	2.00	2,800	300	500	3,600
581-007	Maintenance Parts	3.00000		1.00	12,000		250	12,250
637-001	Travel Expense			4.00			1,000	1,000
	TOTAL OTHER EXPENSE	3.70000	.09000	7.00	14,800	900	1,750	17,450
711-107	Maint. Labor & Overhead	1.87500		9.00	7,500		2,250	9,750
575-018	Electricity -	1.20000		2.80	4,800		700	5,500
580-016	Depreciation			86.00			21,500	21,500
	TOTAL DIST. EXPENSE	3.07500		97.80	12,300		24,450	36,750
714-700	General Plant Expense			88.00			22,000	22,000
716-711	Taxes & Insurance			12.80			3,200	3,200
	TOTAL ALLOCATED EXPENSE			100.80			25,200	25,200
	COST CENTER TOTALS	16.28500	3.10200	251.68	65,140	31,020	62,920	159,080

Figure 14–4   Annual budget

The two variable rates represent the cost per machine hour and the cost per labor hour. They are applied against the estimated machine and labor hours printed in the right-hand corner of the budget sheet. The dollar amount placed in the budget for direct labor is calculated by multiplying the variable rates by the estimated number of required hours. Thus, the total direct labor cost of $47,300 is determined as follows:

Direct labor costs (based on required machine hours)
$$= \$23,400 \ (\$5.85000 \text{ per machine hour} \times 4,000 \text{ hours})$$

Direct labor costs (based on required man hours)
$$= \$23,900 \ (\$2.39000 \text{ per labor hour} \times 10,000 \text{ hours})$$

The fixed cost rate does not vary with the number of hours required. Instead, it represents the cost per day regardless of the number of hours worked, machine hours used, or units produced. This can be seen by observing how the $16,300 total for indirect labor is computed (see Figure 14-4).

Indirect labor costs (based on required machine hours)
$$= \$6,700 \ (\$1.67500 \times 4,000 \text{ hours})$$

Indirect labor costs (based on fixed cost per day)
$$= \$9,600 \ (\$38.40 \times 250 \text{ days per year})$$

An interesting feature of a combined variable-fixed cost budget is that cost center rates are also set for cost center totals. The last line of Figure 14-4 shows variable rates are $16.285 per machine hour and $3.102 per labor hour; the fixed cost rate is $251.68 per day. Likewise, the activity units (see upper right-hand corner) are set at 4,000 machine hours, 10,000 labor hours, and 250 days. Given these two sets of figures, the annual budget of $159,080 can be determined.

The monthly budget is determined using the activity rates supplied by the annual budget (see Figure 14-5). Notice that the variable rates for the cost center totals continue to be set at $16.285 and $3.102; the fixed rate remains at $251.68. These rates are held constant, while activity rates are allowed to vary. Thus, machine hours are now shown to be 368, labor hours are set at 381, and 21 days are indicated.

Annual and monthly budgets are important products of processing—they specify how many dollars are available to be spent and, if based on standard rates, show how the dollars were arrived at. Even so, the reason for developing the online budget planning application can most often be traced to the preparation of *budget variance* or *budget control reports*. Figure 14-6 illustrates one type of budget control report. This particular report compares actual monthly expenses against a monthly budget and YTD expenses against last year's YTD expenses. For each comparison, the variance is shown. Thus, account G, *Total—all expenses*, shows an actual expenditure this month of $2,467 versus a budgeted amount of $3,174. The budget variance of $707 is simply the difference between the two cost figures ($3,174 − $2,467 = $707). Likewise, YTD expenses for this account are $4,942.

		Monthly Activity Units						
		Machine Hours 368						
		Labor Hours 381						
		Days 23						

Acct. #	Account Description	Rates			Amounts			
		Var. #1	Var. #2	-Fixed	Var. #1	Var. #2	Fixed	Total
501-006	Direct Labor	5.85000	2.39000		2,153	911		3,064
502-017	Indirect Labor	1.67500		38.40	616		883	1,499
503-141	Overtime Premium	.40000	.12000		147	46		193
724-211	Payroll Taxes & Fringe	1.58500	.50200	7.68	583	191	177	951
	TOTAL PAYROLL EXPENSE	9.51000	3.01200	46.08	3,499	1,148	1,060	5,707
579-018	Solvent S46B		.06000			23		23
579-040	Other Operating Supplies	.70000	.03000	2.00	258	11	46	315
581-007	Maintenance Parts	3.00000		1.00	1,104		23	1,127
633-001	Travel Expense			4.00			92	92
	TOTAL OTHER EXPENSE	3.70000	.09000	7.00	1,362	34	161	1,557
711-107	Maint. Labor & Overhead	1.87500		9.00	690		207	897
575-018	Electricity	1.20000		2.80	442		64	506
580-016	Depreciation			86.00			1,978	1,978
	TOTAL DIST. EXPENSE	3.07500		97.80	1,132		2,249	3,381
714-700	General Plant Expense			88.00			2,024	2,024
716-711	Taxes & Insurance			12.80			294	294
	TOTAL ALLOCATED EXPENSE			100.80			2,318	2,318
	COST CENTER TOTALS	16.28500	3.10200	251.68	5,993	1,182	5,788	12,963

Figure 14–5 Monthly budget

These are much lower than the expenses for a year ago, which are shown as $9,775. The difference between the two, $4,833, is recorded as the YTD variance.

Most budget control systems feature several budget reporting options. Six reports concerning fixed budgets compare (1) the fixed monthly budget against current monthly expenses, (2) the fixed YTD monthly budget against YTD monthly expenses, (3) the fixed twelve-month budget (last twelve months) against the last twelve months' expenses, (4) the fixed averaged annual budget (annual budget ÷ 12) against current monthly expenses, (5) the averaged YTD monthly budget (YTD budget ÷ months YTD) against monthly expenses, and (6) the fixed annual budget against the YTD budget. Besides fixed-budget comparisons, a number of reporting options must also be provided for variable budgets.

Somewhat more complicated budget comparisons determine budget-to-expenses percentages. One such comparison is based on the following ratio:

$$\text{Budget variance percentage} = \frac{\text{YTD expenses} - \text{YTD monthly budget}}{\text{Annual budget}}$$

DEPARTMENT 192   BUDGET CONTROL REPORT FOR JUNE 19XX - BUSINESS PLANNING DIVISION   PAGE 1

ACCT	DESCRIPTION	THIS MONTH TRANS	THIS MONTH $AMOUNT	THIS MONTH PERCENT	YEAR-TO-DATE TRANS	YEAR-TO-DATE $AMOUNT	YEAR-TO-DATE PERCENT	BUDGET MONTHLY	BUDGET VARIANCE	Y-T-D	Y-T-D VARIANCE
010	SALARY	2	1200.00	48.6	4	2400.00	48.6	1300.00	100.00	2800.00	400.00
012	OTHER PAYROLL EXPENSE	2	200.00	8.1	4	375.00	7.5	175.00	25.00-	450.00	75.00
--A--	PAYROLL	4	1400.00	56.7	8	2775.00	56.1	1475.00	75.00	3250.00	475.00
020	ELECTRICITY	1	50.00	2.0	2	120.00	2.4	75.00	25.00	110.00	10.00-
022	GAS	1	46.00	1.9	1	46.00	.9	50.00	4.00	65.00	19.00
024	TELEPHONE	1	38.00	1.5	2	85.00	1.7	60.00	22.00	75.00	10.00-
025	WATER	1	32.00	1.4	2	64.00	1.3	40.00	8.00	59.00	5.00-
026	GARBAGE				2	48.00	1.0	25.00	25.00	38.00	10.00-
027	OTHER	1	58.00	2.3	1	58.00	1.2	24.00	34.00-	22.00	36.00-
--B--	UTILITIES	5	224.00	9.1	9	421.00	8.5	274.00	50.00	360.00	52.00-
030	OFFICE SUPPLIES	2	80.00	3.2	3	130.00	2.6	100.00	20.00	110.00	20.00-
032	CLEANING	1	40.00	1.6	1	40.00	.8	50.00	10.00	40.00	.00
034	LAUNDRY	2	30.00	1.3	2	30.00	.7	30.00	0.00	25.00	5.00-
--C--	SUPPLIES	5	150.00	6.1	6	200.00	4.1	180.00	30.00	175.00	25.00-
040	ADVERTISING				1	80.00	1.6	100.00	100.00	200.00	120.00
042	PRINTING	1	58.00	2.4	1	58.00	1.2	120.00	62.00	250.00	192.00
044	PHOTOGRAPHY				1	135.00	2.7	100.00	100.00	250.00	192.00
046	GRAPHICS	1	200.00	8.1	2	295.00	6.0	150.00	50.00-	300.00	5.00
048	MISC. EXPENSE				1	35.00	.7	25.00	25.00	50.00	15.00
--D--	GENERAL EXPENSES	2	258.00	10.5	6	603.00	12.2	495.00	237.00	1050.00	447.00-
050	MORTGAGE	1	350.00	14.2	2	700.00	14.2	350.00	0.00	700.00	0.00
052	TAXES				0	0.00	.0	100.00	100.00	200.00	200.00
053	INSURANCE				0	0.00	.0	25.00	25.00	50.00	50.00-
--E--	REAL ESTATE EXP	1	350.00	14.2	2	700.00	14.2	475.00	125.00	950.00	250.00
060	REPAIRS - BUILDING				0	0.00	.0	75.00	75.00	3331.00	3331.00
062	EQUIPMENT	1	85.00	3.4	1	85.00	1.7	100.00	15.00	50.00	35.00-
063	FURN. AND FIXTURES				0	0.00	.0	50.00	50.00	300.00	300.00
065	SPECIAL EXPENSES				2	110.00	2.2	30.00	30.00	300.00	300.00
065	UNCLASSIFIED				1	48.00	1.0	20.00	20.00	300.00	48.00-
--F--	BUILDING EXPENSE	1	85.00	3.4	4	243.00	4.9	275.00	190.00	3981.00	3738.00
--G--	TOTAL--ALL EXPENSES	18	2467.00	100.0	35	4942.00	100.0	3174.00	707.00	9775.00	4833.00

Figure 14-6 Budget control report

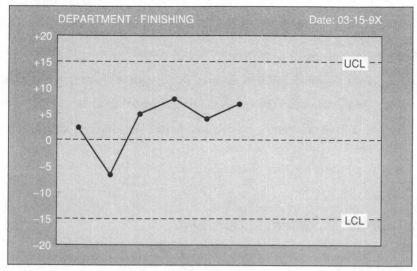

Figure 14–7   Control chart

As an example, suppose the annual fixed budget for a department is $50,000, that expenses thus far (YTD) are $38,500, and that the YTD monthly budget (the sum of the monthly budget totals from the first month of the budget to the current month) is $35,000. Use of these figures yields a budget variance of 7 percent:

Budget variance = ($38,500 − $35,000) ÷ $50,000 = .07 × 100 = 7 percent

Budget variance percentages, such as the 7 percent figure, become especially useful when they are plotted to permit month-by-month comparisons. Figure 14–7 illustrates one type of variance graph based on percentages. As shown, actual variance percentages are compared against upper and lower control limits, set at plus and minus 15 percent, respectively. Whenever the budget variance falls above the upper control limit (above +15) or below the lower control limit (below −15), the budget is said to be out of control. An out-of-control situation calls for corrective action. If expenses are high, cost reductions are required to bring them back in line with the YTD monthly budget. Should expenses appear to be too low, a study must determine how a department is able to delay its anticipated expenditures.

REVIEW QUESTIONS

1. How does the budget planning application combine both planning and control?

2. Why do companies develop the online budget planning application?

3. What is the difference between a fixed budget and a variable budget?

4. What is a budget variance report?

5. How does a budget request differ from a budget appropriation?

6. What segments make up the budget master file?

7. How is the flow-of-funds forecast used in the budget planning application?

8. What are the two main outputs of the budget planning application?

9. What is a fixed cost rate? A variable cost rate? How are cost center budgets determined?

10. How is a budget variance percentage calculated?

14-2   BUDGET PLANNING PROCESSING

Figures 14–8 (a), (b) and (c) illustrate the budget planning systems organization chart; Figures 14–9 (a) and (b) show the corresponding program processing menu. These figures reveal that the budget planning application is similar to the general ledger application in many ways. For instance, several interactive programs are required to update the budget master file. Likewise, budget totals and comparisons can be either printed or displayed. Interactive processing designs typically permit budget requests and appropriations to be both displayed and reviewed. Some designs may include a variety of budget variance display options,

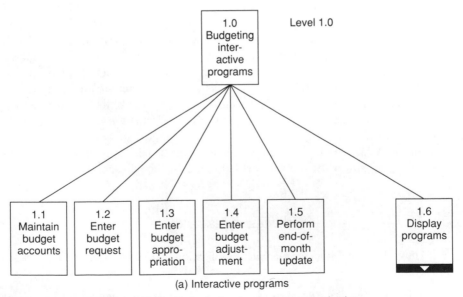

(a) Interactive programs

Figure 14–8   Budget planning systems organization

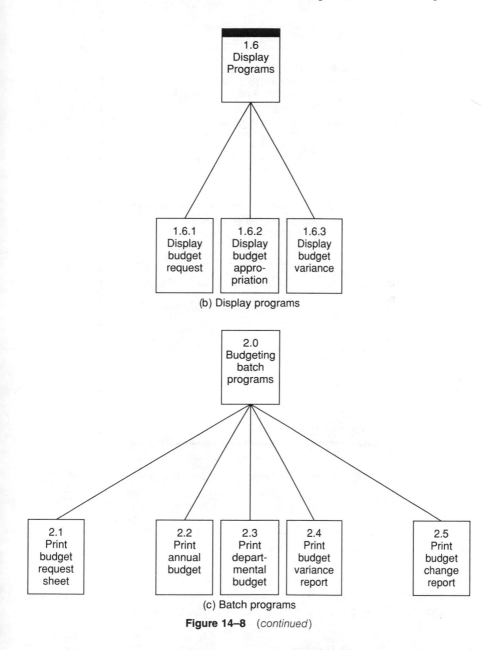

(b) Display programs

(c) Batch programs

Figure 14–8   (*continued*)

such as department-by-department comparisons and expense-to-budget account comparisons.

The batch portion of processing produces budget worksheets, a variety of processing summaries, and the budget change report. The *budget request worksheet* is a dual-purpose document. Besides listing information stored on the budget master file, it is used in preparing new budget requests. Current budget figures,

```
BUDGET PLANNING

        MAINTAIN BUDGET ACCOUNTS
        ENTER BUDGET REQUEST
        ENTER BUDGET APPROPRIATION
        ENTER BUDGET ADJUSTMENT
        PERFORM END-OF-MONTH UPDATE
        DISPLAY BUDGET REQUEST
        DISPLAY BUDGET APPROPRIATION
        DISPLAY BUDGET VARIANCE

        RETURN
```

(a) Interactive menu choices

```
BUDGET PLANNING

        PRINT ANNUAL REQUEST WORKSHEET
        PRINT ANNUAL BUDGET
        PRINT DEPARTMENTAL BUDGET
        PRINT BUDGET VARIANCE REPORT
        PRINT BUDGET CHANGE REPORT




        RETURN
```

(b) Batch menu choices

Figure 14–9   Budget planning program menu

for example, are often very helpful in determining new budget request figures. The *annual budget* and *departmental budget summaries* are also dual-purpose documents. These documents provide a register of the contents of the budget master file; they show the makeup of the monthly and annual budget in its final form. The *budget change report*, in contrast, is much like other file-change reports. It traces how interactive processing alters the contents of the budget master file.

Updating the Budget Master File

Figure 14–8(a) shows that five interactive programs update portions of the budget master file or perform specific update functions. Each of the programs will now be briefly reviewed.

The *Maintain budget accounts* program permits budget account numbers to be added to, changed in, or deleted from the master budget account section of

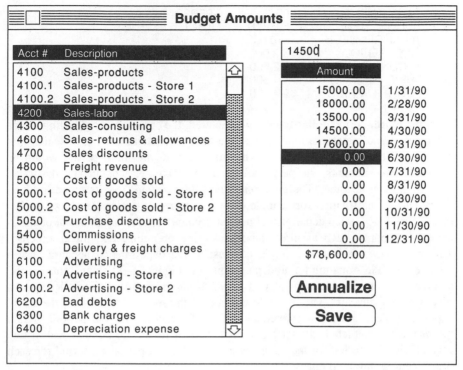

Figure 14–10   Entering budget amounts into processing accounts

the budget master file. In building the budget chart of accounts, care should be taken to make budget account numbers similar to general ledger account numbers. This practice permits budget-to-expense comparisons to be made directly. If, for example, the general ledger chart-of-account code for office supplies is 6600-000 and the budget chart-of-account code for travel expense is 56600-000, a direct comparison between the two codes is easily made, because the internal part of the general ledger code 6600-000 is identical to the budget code.

The *Enter budget request* program allows direct entry and editing of budget request dollar totals. As Figure 14–10 shows, budget amounts can be entered into processing accounts by account and month by month.

Unfortunately, the budget request program is not as simple as it appears. For each budget amount requested, two or more postings to the budget master file must be made, and all changes must be written to the budget change file. The reason for double posting (updating more than one account) is to permit business expense budget totals by budget item to be isolated from departmental and cost center budget totals. An example will help clarify the difference between these two types of totals.

Suppose department 09, the personnel department, entered into processing a travel budget request for $10,000. The request is entered as follows:

```
DEPARTMENT:          09           PERSONNEL
BUDGET ITEM:         637-001      TRAVEL EXPENSE
TOTAL REQUEST:       $10,000
FIRST PERIOD:        $ 2,000
SECOND PERIOD:       $ 2,500
THIRD PERIOD:        $ 1,500
FOURTH PERIOD:       $ 4,000
```

After the fourth-period dollar amount was entered, the computer would sum periods 1 through 4 and match the total against the total request. Following this, the total request and the funds requested for the first, second, and third period would be posted to two accounts: the personnel department budget account and the travel expense budget account. The *departmental budget account*, as its name implies, stores budget information for a single department or cost center. As shown earlier (see Figure 14–5), each departmental budget account contains a number of business expense accounts, such as direct labor, overtime premium, and travel expense. The *travel expense budget item*, in contrast to the departmental account, stores travel expense information for all departments. As Figure 14–11 shows, this second posting serves to complete an entry in a *budget-planning matrix*. Each department within a company makes up a single column of the matrix. As shown, the travel expense for department 9 is entered and totaled for each of the four periods. When the matrix is completed, the total request for travel funds can be analyzed in two ways: period by period for the company as a whole, and period by period for each department within a company.

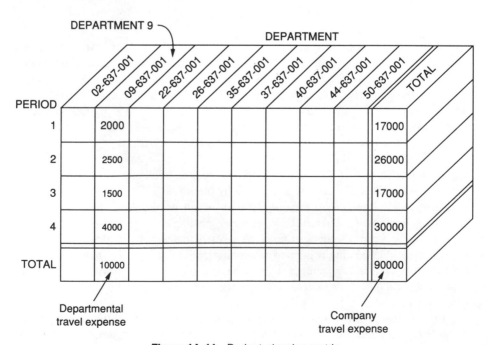

Figure 14–11 Budget-planning matrix

The *Enter budget appropriation* program features direct entry and editing of budget appropriation totals. Input to the program follows from two types of source documents: the *budget appropriation worksheet*, a master planning document that specifies the dollar amount to be appropriated and allocated, and the *activity* (or production) *forecast*, which indicates by cost center the number of machine hours required, labor hours required, and work days for each period. The budget appropriation worksheet itemizes the fixed portion of a departmental budget. Under the heading *direct advertising*, for example, the number of dollars to be allocated for advertising would be listed. The activity forecast itemizes the variable portion of the budget. Within the forecast, units to be produced must be translated by the computer into machine and labor hours. For instance, if 10,000 units are to be produced over a 30-day period, and each unit requires .035 hours of machine time and .16 hours of a person's time, this production estimate (10,000 units) and these standard hourly rates (time required per unit) would be translated by the computer as 350 machine hours and 1,600 labor hours during the next 30-day period. (Try these calculations to see if you agree.)

Much like the *Enter budget request* program, the *Enter budget appropriation* program posts appropriated dollars to both departmental budget accounts and to business expense budget items. Figure 14–12, continuing our previous example, displays the appropriation and allocation of travel expense funds for department 09, the personnel department. As indicated, 80 percent of the budget request was funded; 70 percent of the total appropriation was allocated. These appropriation and allocation figures are posted to the personnel department budget account (an 09 account) and to the travel expense budget item account (a 637 account). Once figures are posted, it is also possible to display and review and revise them, if necessary. Later in the year, when more is known about the financing required for the fourth period, the dollars appropriated but not allocated will be either released to the personnel department or transferred to another department to meet an emergency funding situation.

```
DEPARTMENT: 09              PERSONNEL
BUDGET ITEM:  637-001       TRAVEL EXPENSE
DATE OF REQUEST:   11-15-9X  OF APPROPRIATION:  12-14-9X

                 REQUEST    APPROPRIATION  /  ALLOCATION

TOTAL            $10,000    $8,000            $7,000

1ST PERIOD       2,000      1,500             1,500
2ND PERIOD       2,500      2,000             2,000
3RD PERIOD       1,500      1,500             1,500
4TH PERIOD       4,000      3,000             2,000

LEVEL         APPROPRIATED: 80%       ALLOCATED: 70%
```

Figure 14–12 Budget appropriation display

A great deal of work takes place before budget appropriation decisions are made. Budget officers must work with several top-level managerial groups to arrive at the final activity (production) forecast and to establish companywide budget funding limits. Once this is done, the task of balancing budget requests with available funds begins. Suppose, for example, that $90,000 is available for travel expense for an entire fiscal year and that requests for travel total $160,000. The computer could be used to make a direct percentage travel allocation of 56.3 percent ($90,000 ÷ $160,000) to each department; however, budgeting is not as easy as this. In fact, most budgetary decisions follow from top-level management committee meetings. Managers at the top of an organization must decide on how many dollars to allocate for specific business activities (budget items) and then decide on how to divide the total allocation among departments.

The *Enter budget adjustment* program is similar in many ways to the *enter budget appropriation* program. Each time an adjustment in a departmental budget is to be made, a change slip must be prepared and processed. The several types of budget adjustments include releasing previously appropriated but never allocated budget funds, transferring funds from one department to another, and increasing or decreasing the total budget. This last adjustment might follow from a revised activity forecast—thus changing activity units such as machine and labor hours required—or from an administrative decision to reduce business overhead expenses, such as administrative and selling expenses, if sales have been lower than expected. Other factors such as new wage and salary settlements, increases in raw material prices, or increases in the cost of energy also lead to changes in budgeted totals.

The *Perform end-of-month update* program is one of the more important budget planning update programs. As in general ledger processing, the end-of-month program must ready the master file for next month's processing. With budgeting, this requires shifting the current month's budget totals to last month's totals, resetting the current budget variance totals to zero, and shifting next month's budget totals to this month's budget totals. After the shifts are performed, the old file is generally written to magnetic tape and stored. As with general ledger processing, this procedure makes it possible to restore the budget master file.

The budget perform end-of-month update program also differs from the end-of-month general ledger update program. As Figure 14–13 shows, the interactive program merges and transfers information from the old budget master and the consolidated G/L master file to a new budget master file. By merging, actual expense information is combined with budgeted expense information. In addition, the consolidated budget-control section of the file is revised (see Figure 14–2). At month-end, current expense totals are added to expended to-date totals; total purchase order encumbrances and total bills payable encumbrances are revised. At year-end, the update is expanded to include the revision of the historical budget control section of the file. In this instance, the total expended to-date figures are shifted, period by period, to the historical part of the file. In addition, the budget variance per period is also computed and shifted. Finally, the total dollar amount requested and the total allocated are shifted and thus preserved for future budget planning sessions.

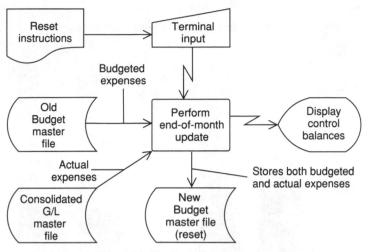

Figure 14–13 End-of-period update

Comparing Budgeted Expenses Against Actual Expenses

Figure 14–14 shows a budget variance display resulting from comparing budgeted travel dollars against travel dollar expenses. As illustrated, the allocated total is compared with the expended and the encumbered dollar totals. The running balance shown on the right-hand side indicates that the department was under budget by $500 for the first period and that the department remained at this level during the second period. It also shows that expenditures in the third period were much higher than expected. Currently, the department is over budget by $1,500. To the trained eye, this display shows a dangerous budget situation. Unless the budgeted amount is increased to the appropriated level, the department will have problems

```
DEPARTMENT:  09                    PERSONNEL
BUDGET ITEM:  637-001               TRAVEL EXPENSE
DATE OF UPDATE:  8-15-9X            OF APPROPRIATION:  12-14-9X

               ALLOCATION  EXPENDED   ENCUMBERED    BALANCE

TOTAL           $7,000      $3,500     $3,000       $ 500

1ST PERIOD       1,500       1,000                   500
2ND PERIOD       2,000       2,000                   500
3RD PERIOD       1,500         500      3,000       (1,500)
4TH PERIOD       2,000

LEVEL   APPROPRIATED: 80%   ALLOCATED: 70%   EXPENDED: 93%/70%
```

Figure 14–14 Budget variance display

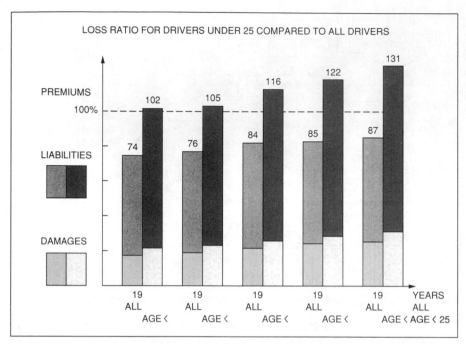

Figure 14–15   Bar chart

remaining under budget. As indicated, 93 percent of the yearly allocation has been either expended or encumbered. Even if the additional $1,000 is released (from appropriated to allocated status, as shown in Figure 14–12), 81 percent of the yearly appropriation will have been expended or encumbered.

Because different people like to see budget variance information presented and interpreted in different ways, it is common to find a number of display options built into the interactive portion of the budget planning application. One option features a series of budget request, appropriation, and variance tables. Another option provides planning and control charts for selected budget accounts, such as the chart shown in Figure 14–7, or budget planning matrices for business expense accounts (see Figure 14–11). There are still other options. Bar charts, for example, are especially helpful in comparing budgeted against actual expenses. The bar chart in Figure 14–15 compares liabilities and damages for all drivers to drivers under 25. As indicated, expenses (liabilities and damages) exceed budgeted amounts (premiums) for drivers under 25 compared to all drivers. What is even more serious is that the loss ratio (the ratio of expenses to budgeted amounts) is increasing for all age groups.

REVIEW QUESTIONS

11.   Why should budget and general ledger account numbers be similar?

12.   Explain why budget totals must be double-posted.

13. What is a budget planning matrix? Why is it important in processing budget request information? In processing budget appropriation information?

14. What is the difference between appropriated and allocated budget dollars?

15. What are budget adjustments? Explain different types of adjustments required by the budget planning application.

16. Why are computer graphics important in budget planning and control?

14-3 PROFIT PLANNING

Figure 14–16 provides a preliminary overview of the profit planning system. A comparison of this overview with the budget planning overview (see Figure 14–1) indicates that with profit planning, revenue projections and budget requests (expenses) must be determined in advance. *Revenue projections* signify estimates of sales volumes, expressed in dollars rather than units. These projections or forecasts are generally made for each product or for each major product line carried in

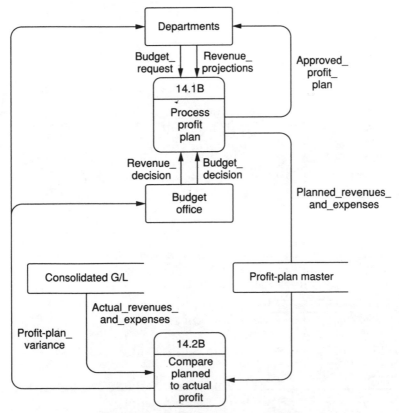

Figure 14–16 The profit-planning system

inventory. Following the entry of departmental information, the first major function of the profit planning system is to process the profit plan. A *profit plan* combines revenue with budget projections. These plans yield projected income for each major stage of manufacturing in a business. As shown, the processing of such a plan involves adjusting revenue and budget figures by means of revenue and budget decisions. The end result is an approved profit plan, which is distributed to departments and filed on the profit plan master file.

The second major function of the profit-planning system is a control function. As shown by Figure 14–16, planned revenues and expenses are compared against actual revenues and expenses. The purpose of this comparison is to produce a wide variety of profit planning variance reports.

The most difficult aspect of the profit planning system is the setting of revenue and expense projections, especially when sales are seasonal. Figure 14–17 shows a seasonal profit plan worksheet for store 14 of the Mason Electric Supply Com-

```
                          MASON ELECTRIC SUPPLY
                  SEASONALITY PROFIT PLAN WORKSHEET:   STORE 14
                            FOR THE YEAR 199X
                            (000'S OMITTED)
```

	JAN	FEB	MAR	APR	MAY	JUN	JUL	AUG	SEP	OCT	NOV	DEC	YTD$
NET SALES:													
RESIDENTIAL	8.4%	8.1%	7.9%	8.0%	8.1%	8.3%	8.4%	8.5%	8.2%	8.6%	8.8%	8.9%	4,768
COMMERCIAL AND INDUSTRIAL	6.2	6.2	6.2	8.3	8.3	8.3	8.3	8.3	8.3	10.4	10.4	10.4	480
RETAIL STORES SALES	8.1	7.5	7.1	7.1	7.5	7.9	8.1	8.1	8.7	9.1	10.0	10.6	492
TOTAL SALES	8.2%	7.9%	7.7%	7.9%	8.0%	8.3%	8.4%	8.4%	8.2%	8.8%	9.0%	9.2%	5,740
COST OF SALES:													
RESIDENTIAL	8.4%	8.1%	7.9%	8.0%	8.1%	8.3%	8.4%	8.5%	8.2%	8.6%	8.8%	8.9%	2,861
COMMERCIAL AND INDUSTRIAL	6.0	6.0	6.0	8.5	8.5	8.5	8.5.	8.5	8.5	10.3	10.3	10.3	117
RETAIL STORE SALES	8.1	7.5	7.1	7.1	7.5	7.9	8.1	8.1	8.7	9.1	10.0	10.6	492
DISTRIBUTION EXPENSE	8.3	8.3	8.3	8.3	8.3	8.3	8.3	8.3	8.3	8.3	8.3	8.3	120
TOTAL COST OF SALES	8.3%	7.9%	7.7%	7.9%	8.0%	8.2%	8.4%	8.4%	8.3%	8.7%	9.0%	.9.2%	3,590
OPERATING INCOME	8.0%	7.8%	7.6%	8.0%	8.1%	8.3%	8.4%	8.4%	8.2%	9.0%	9.1%	9.2%	2,150
OPERATING EXPENSES:													
CONTACTS OFFICE	8.3%	8.3%	8.3%	8.3%	8.3%	8.3%	8.3%	8.3%	8.3%	8.3%	8.3%	8.3%	240
MARKETING	8.4	8.1	7.9	8.1	8.1	8.2	8.4	8.4	8.2	8.6	8.8	8.9	571
PURCHASING	8.3	8.3	8.3	8.3	8.3	8.3	8.3	8.3	8.3	8.3	8.3	8.3	300
ADMINISTRATION	8.3	8.3	8.3	8.3	8.3	8.3	8.3	8.3	8.3	8.3	8.3	8.3	108
TOTAL OPERATING EXPENSES	8.4%	8.2%	8.1%	8.2%	8.2%	8.3%	8.4%	8.4%	8.3%	8.4%	8.5%	8.6%	1,219
INCOME BEFORE INTEREST DEDUCTION:													
SHORT-TERM INTEREST	8.3%	8.3%	8.3%	8.3%	8.3%	8.3%	8.3%	8.3%	8.3%	8.3%	8.3%	8.3%	(144)
OTHER INTEREST	0.0	0.0	0.0	0.0	0.0	0.0	0.0	0.0	0.0	0.0	0.0	0.0	0
INCOME BEFORE TAXES	7.5%	7.0%	6.6%	7.6%	7.9%	8.3%	8.3%	8.5%	8.0%	9.9%	10.0%	10.3%	787
INCOME TAX PROVISION	7.4	6.9	6.6	7.7	8.0	8.2	8.5	8.5	8.0	9.8	10.1	10.3	377
NET INCOME	7.6%	7.1%	6.6%	7.6%	7.8%	8.3%	8.3%	8.5%	8.0%	10.0%	10.0%	10.2%	410

Figure 14–17 Seasonality report

pany. As indicated, dollar amounts for both sales and expenses are set for the year; however, month-by-month breakdowns are estimated not by dollar amount but by percent of annual sales and expenses. Percent-by-month totals are often easier to estimate than are totals of unit or dollar volumes per month. This worksheet shows clearly how the annual figures are expected to be realized, as well as the sales variation expected during the year. As estimated, sales reach their peak in December (9.2 percent) and their low point in March (7.7 percent). This small variation of 1.5 percent (9.2 − 7.7) nevertheless leads to important variations in net earnings. As shown, earnings are much higher at the end of the year than at the first of the year. The last three months account for 30.2 percent of net earnings, whereas the first three months account for but 21.3 percent.

Profit planning is especially useful in appraising company performance. When properly designed, profit planning evaluates companywide performance in comparison with the company's plans, programs, and profit objectives.

The profit planning application becomes easier to design and implement once the budget planning application becomes automated. In budget planning, for example, standard rates are required to "cost out" the charges associated with different volumes of production. In the profit planning application, these standard rates take on additional meaning. Here, too, different volumes mean different things. With low volumes and high fixed-cost rates, the profitability of a department or profit center will be low. At higher volumes, however, which reduce fixed cost significantly, profits will be higher.

Figure 14–18 illustrates a comparison of cost per unit to price per unit. At low volumes, the cost per unit is high, as shown by cost curve C. Tracing this curve shows that dollars per unit decrease as volume increases. The price curve, P,

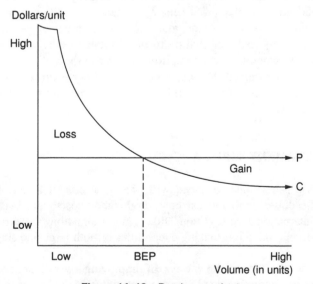

Figure 14–18 Break-even chart

meanwhile, is held constant for all levels of volume. Finally, the *break-even point* (BEP) indicates the volume at which the unit price equals the unit cost. Before this volume is reached, unit cost exceeds unit price (and thus there is a loss). Beyond the BEP, unit price exceeds unit cost, and so profits begin to be realized.

Prices such as the price P shown in Figure 14–18 are typically not the figures quoted to customers. Instead, they represent *value-added* or *transfer prices*. The concept of value added, as suggested earlier, results from the addition of value to a product by the manufacturing process. When, for example, a product is finished by a manufacturing process, it is said to be worth more (to have a higher value) than before it was finished. Similar to prices, the profit resulting from the profit planning application does not mean the profit obtained from the sale of a product to a customer. Once again, profit is associated with the value added to the product. Suppose a product enters manufacturing and has a value of $8.98, incurs a manufacturing cost of $3.24, and has a value-added price of $12.61. Thus, the value-added profit per unit resulting from this operation is $0.39 per unit ($12.61 − $8.98 − $3.24). Once computed, the new value-added price is transferred to the next department, that is, to the next stage of manufacture. At this point, the $12.61 price becomes the new "value of (the) product before manufacturing."

Setting the value-added rates at each stage of manufacturing is the most difficult part of the profit planning application. It involves estimating *profitability standards*, much like the cost standards required for budgeting. In the preceding example, the profitability standard rate entered into processing would be $0.39 ($12.61 − $3.24 − $8.98). This rate is stored with the budgeted cost rate of $3.24 on the profit planning master file.

Once the value-added rates are determined, the profit planning application closely resembles the budget planning application. Besides displaying profit center rates and plans, the application must be designed to compare actual profit center totals against projected totals and to display profit center variance. In addition, actual profit for each product line, store, or division must be broken down by profit center and compared against projected contribution to profit totals (see Figure 14–19). If the comparison is not favorable, the assumptions leading to the setting the profitability standards must be questioned. Finally, a variety of *profit control reports* must be built into this application. These permit managers to review projected to actual profit in several ways.

14-4   MANAGEMENT IMPLICATIONS

Most business organizations are faced with the same crucial financial problems: inflation of the dollar, high interest cost, high labor costs, and ever-increasing national and international competition. Taken in combination, these problems are severely challenging the profit-making capabilities of both large and small business firms.

In times past, there were three ways of improving overall profitability: raising product prices, increasing employee productivity (thereby lowering the costs of

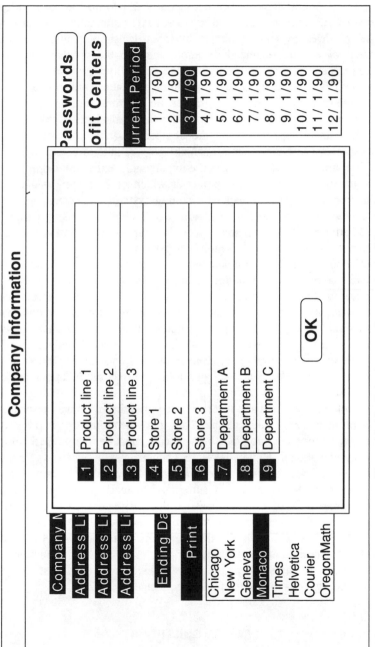

Figure 14–19 Selecting a profit center from a list of choices

operations), and improving the management of existing financial resources. Today, these three alternatives are not all necessarily feasible. It is impractical, for example, to set prices higher when competitors fail to do the same. Moreover, improvements in employee productivity are never automatic, and productivity cannot be improved by making simple business decisions. Thus, improving the management of existing financial resources may be the only avenue open for improving profitability. This reasoning helps explain why many firms are beginning to rely so heavily on budget and profit planning computer applications.

Several important managerial advantages result from well-designed financial planning systems. Managers are able to determine the actual expenditures for a single department, a division, or the company as a whole, and to compare these totals against budgeted commitments. They are able to determine the points at which departmental, divisional, or companywide expenses *begin* to exceed budgeted amounts, as well as the points at which profit centers *begin* to return lower-than-expected profits. Financial planning systems enable managers to gain a better appreciation of financial conditions and problems by using current rather than dated financial information and by examining this information in several ways, using different display formats, to highlight particular features.

Viewed in combination, the implementation and proper use of financial planning systems can lead to major savings for a company. For example, one large industrial firm discovered that they could improve their overall profit margins by more than 2 percent following the installation of an integrated online budget planning application. By tracking and evaluating budget plans in relation to actual and encumbered expenditures, they were able to make selected budget cuts, where necessary, to stay within tightly set companywide budget plans. More important, they were able to make the cuts that had minimum effect on the operations of their business.

Other companies have realized that there are initial disadvantages associated with budget or profit planning applications. They have determined that these systems cannot simply be dropped into place but, instead, must be finely tuned before they become fully operational. Hundreds of rate changes may be required, for instance, before value-added rates begin to represent standard conditions. However, once this phase is past, the full advantages of automated financial planning systems begin to become apparent. Managers soon realize that they can react to changes in the marketplace much faster than before, since they are especially sensitive to changes in the cost of labor and materials. While other firms are trying to find out what types of expenditures are eroding their profit margins, those firms with computer-based financial planning systems can pinpoint the financial impact of cost changes and take the necessary steps to control for these changes.

REVIEW QUESTIONS

17.   What are the two main functions of the profit planning system?

18.   What is the most difficult aspect of profit planning?

19. What is a break-even point?

20. What are value-added prices?

REVIEW OF IMPORTANT IDEAS

The budget planning application is designed to compare estimated against actual business expenses. The profit-planning application is an extension of budget planning. With profit planning, standard profits are compared against actual profits.

The budget planning application must be designed to handle both fixed and variable budgeting. A fixed budget does not vary with changes in production or sales; a variable budget does vary with these types of changes.

Budget requests provide an estimate of the dollars needed by department. Budget appropriations are the actual dollars placed in a budget. Whereas requests, appropriations, and allocations are stored on the budget master file, only allocations are compared against actual expenses. The transfer of actual expense data to the budget master file is performed after the update of the consolidated G/L master file.

The budget master file stores the master chart of budget accounts and consolidated and historical budget-control items, in addition to budget requests and budget appropriations. Budget variances are determined by comparing actual and encumbered expenses against budget allocations.

Annual and departmental budgets are important products of the budget planning application. Even so, a major reason for developing the application is the preparing of budget control reports. Because individuals like to see information presented in different ways, most budget control systems feature a variety of reporting options.

Five interactive programs are necessary to update the budget master file. Three of these maintain the master chart of budget accounts, enter budget request information into processing, and enter budget appropriation information into processing. The fourth processes budget adjustments, and the fifth performs an end-of-month update. This final program transfers actual expense information from the consolidated G/L master file to the budget master file.

Substantial work is necessary to prepare budget requests and budget appropriations. Companywide budget amounts must be established before attempts are made to balance requests with available funds. To simplify this time-consuming task as much as possible, flow-of-funds forecasts and budget planning matrices are computed. Budget matrices show both departmental budget accounts and companywide budget item totals.

The profit planning application is designed to handle variable revenues and expenditures. This application requires forecasts to specify the levels of activity in upcoming periods. The two forecasts required are the revenue and budget forecasts.

Profit planning is especially useful in appraising company performance. By comparing estimated against actual profit, a company can determine if performance is consistent with plans, programs, and profit objectives.

The concept of value added is essential to profit planning. For profit planning to be successful, value-added profitability rates, expressed in dollars, must be set for each stage of manufacturing. Determining these rates is the most difficult aspect of this computer application.

KEY WORDS

Budget planning

Budgeting

Budget

Profit planning

Fixed budget

Variable budget

Budget variance report

Budget request

Budget appropriatoin

Budget master file

Master chart of budget accounts

Spreadsheet software

Flow-of-funds forecast

Budget control report

Departmental budget account

Budget planning matrix

Activity forecast

Revenue projections

Break-even point

Value-added prices

Profitability standard rate

Profit control report

EXERCISES

1. Suppose the number of days worked for plant A (see Figure 14–4) is reduced to 230, and the percent of machine hours and labor hours is reduced by alike amount. What is the revised annual budget? How many dollars must be set aside to cover machine hour costs, labor hour cost, and fixed costs?

2. With the number of days worked remaining at 250, suppose labor costs for plant A (see Figures 14–4 and 14–5) are increased by 20 percent for all labor categories (direct labor, indirect labor, overtime premiums, payroll taxes and fringe benefits, and maintenance labor and overhead).

   Suppose further that this increase is to apply to both variable and fixed rates. What is the new annual budget? What is the new monthly budget?

3. The *Perform end-of-month update* program does three things: it resets current totals to zero, it revises the consolidated budget-control portion of the file, and it updates the historical budget-control section of the file. Using Figure 4–13 as a guide, explain

   (a) how the reset instruction would be designed for the three types of updates;

   (b) what control balances would be displayed for the three types of updates;

   (c) why control balances are important to processing;

   (d) what steps would be taken if the control totals show an accounting imbalance; and

   (e) what types of printed reports are necessary as backups to processing.

4. Since the profit planning application is similar to the budget planning application in many ways, it can be designed with these similarities in mind. Using Figures 14–8 and 14–9 as guides,

   (a) design the profit planning program menu;

   (b) describe the functions to be performed by each program shown on the menu; and

   (c) explain how your design differs from the budget planning menu.

5. Suppose you were assigned the task of developing budget and profit planning reporting display options for management.

   (a) Explain how you would determine which options would be needed.

   (b) List and explain several types of variable-budget reporting options.

   (c) List and explain several types of profit planning reporting options.

6. The budget planning and profit planning systems are similar to other types of planning and control systems. Consider the following: Rogers Information Processing, Inc., needs to design a project planning and control system. Neil Rogers explains, "We need a system that will allow us to make project forecasts and to compare these forecasts against actual project times to determine project variance. Inputs to the making of project forecasts will be project time projections, supplied to us by our project managers. My brother and I will modify these projections if they are too optimistic (or pessimistic). We will let each manager know his or her approved project schedule."

   Ron Rogers, Neil's brother, asked, "Where will we get actual project times?"

   Neil answered, "From our payroll processing system."

   Describe this project planning and control system by drawing a data flow diagram similar to the DFDs drawn for the budget planning and profit planning systems.

DISCUSSION QUESTIONS

1. How can financial planning systems, such as the budget and profit planning applications, lead to major savings to a company? List several ways.

2. Many individuals have difficulty holding onto their money. However, when they are required to budget carefully, they often discover their money is sufficient to pay off outstanding bills. Why does budgeting help so much?

3. Why is a variable yearly budget much more difficult to implement than a fixed yearly budget? What new tasks must be performed by managers in determining a variable yearly budget?

4. Would a budget planning system work without a fully defined general ledger application? Why or why not?

4-IN-1 CASE STUDY—BUDGET AND PROFIT PLANNING

The 4-in-1 software does not provide for a separate budget or profit planning function. However, by allowing the user to place ratios alongside the profit-and-loss statement, changes in percentage can be observed. For this lesson, we ask you to print a second profit-and-loss statement, showing current period ratios.

1. Log on and enter a date of **013197**. Press ENTER to indicate no change.

2. Type **5**, *Print financial statements*, from the main menu.

3. Type **2** to print a statement.

4. Type **2** for the layout.

5. Press ENTER for ratios.

6. Press ENTER for start and press ENTER for stop dates.

7. Press F1 for profit centers.

8. Press ENTER to print one copy.

9. Press ENTER when asked, *Field number to change?*

10. Press ENTER to print.

11. Press TAB to end this lesson.

QUESTIONS

1. What is the value in knowing the ratio of sales for products A, B, and C to net sales? What is the value of knowing the ratio of purchases for A, B, and C to cost of goods sold?

2. How do ratios such as those shown on the profit-and-loss statement help in planning next month's budget?

3. How do ratios help in profit planning?

15

Sales Analysis and Market Planning

Implementing the customer-invoice, order-entry, and finished-goods computer applications does more than permit rapid processing of customer and product transactions. These applications create and maintain valuable master and summary computer files. As this chapter will show, information placed in these files permits the design of two management reporting applications: sales analysis and market planning. The sales analysis application evaluates sales performance in order to provide managers with a better understanding of factors important for improving the sales volume and profitability of sales. The market planning application compares internal company sales with external economic indicators and corresponding market conditions in order to identify factors important for improving the market share of a business. In this chapter, we will begin with the sales analysis application because it is the easier of the two to understand. We will then modify this design in describing the market planning application.

15-1 SALES ANALYSIS OVERVIEW

Sales analysis has different meanings for different companies. To some, it means an *analysis of net sales volume*, that is, the study of sales transactions leading to total income shown on the profit-and-loss statement. To others, it concerns *profitability analysis*, the study of the profitability of market territories, products, customer groups, or other sales control units. Of the two, profitability analysis is the wiser choice, because studies of sales volume are often misleading. Large sales volume for old-line product groups, for example, might contribute very little to company profits compared with lower sales volume for new-line product groups. Finally, to still others, sales analysis means an analysis of *sales force performance*. This type of study examines the activities of members of the sales force to determine which performance patterns contribute to high dollar sales.

Before sales-analysis information can be processed, the customer-invoicing computer application must be modified so that it can ready the computer files for four different types of sales analysis: daily sales analysis, customer sales analysis, product sales analysis, and sales force sales analysis. The invoicing application is actually a logical starting point because it captures both net sales volume (sales less returns) and net sales income. In addition, it can be modified to update a sales force master file as sales transactions are processed.

Figure 15–1 provides an overview of the sales analysis system. Before sales analysis reports are produced, four files must be readied: daily sales by region, customer sales recap, product sales recap, and sales forces sales recap.

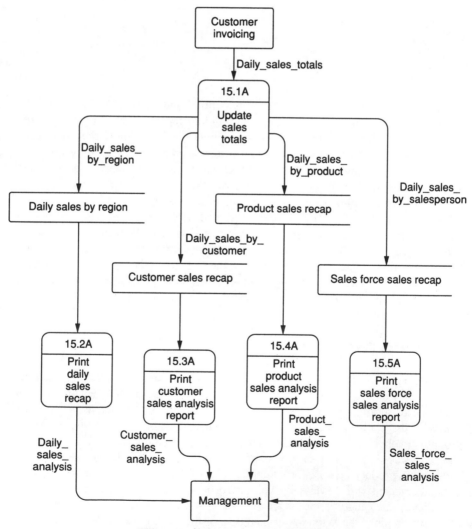

Figure 15–1   The sales analysis system

The *daily sales by region* file stores the sales receipts (and customer returns) for a business day (see Figure 15–2). This file is used to produce a daily record of sales activity by invoice for each customer, store location, or other business account, such as by salesperson name. The contents of this daily file are similar to the contents of the invoice A/R summary file; differences include the addition of the salesperson number and name and the product cost. The salesperson number permits records to be grouped on the file according to that number. Knowing the product cost, in addition to the total invoice charge, permits the gross profit (contribution to profit) to be calculated for each customer order.

The *customer sales recap* file stores facts about each customer. For the sales analysis application, sales recap information is stored on a separate file or is added to the customer master file as two new segments: sales history and customer profitability (see Figure 15–3). The sales history segment stores historical sales volume totals (quantity sold this month, quantity sold last month, and so on). This information permits customer sales trends to be displayed. The customer profitability segment stores historical customer profit totals. This information allows current and year-to-date totals to be displayed and customer profit trends to be plotted.

The *product sales recap* file stores facts to describe each product carried in inventory by a business. Like the customer sales recap, product recap information can be stored on a separate file or added to the product master file (see Figure 15–4). Unlike the customer master file, no new segments need to be added to the product master file, provided the product sales history and product profitability record segments exist. These two segments allow for a direct comparison of product sales volumes and profitability totals.

The *sales force sales recap* file stores facts to describe each member of the sales force. As Figure 15–5 shows, this recap file (or sales force master file) consists

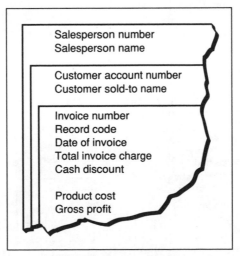

Figure 15–2 Daily sales file

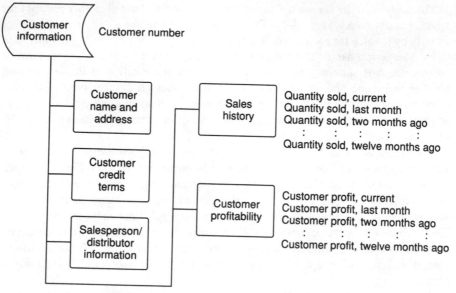

Figure 15–3   Expanded customer master file

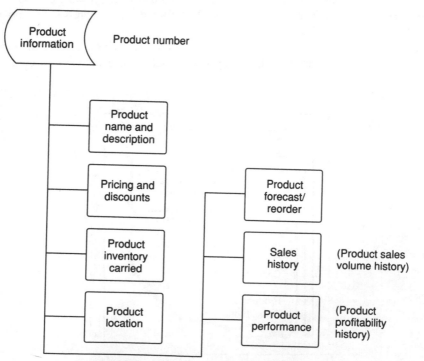

Figure 15–4   Product master file segments

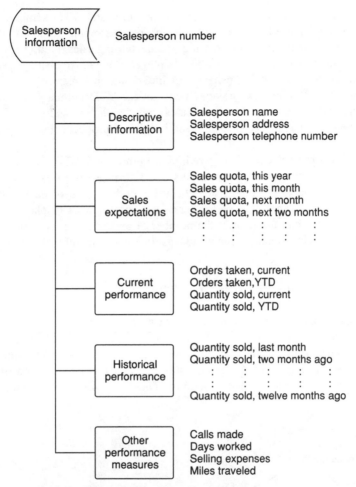

Figure 15–5 Sales force sales recap

of records that contain five or more record segments: *descriptive information*, which includes each salesperson's name and location; *sales expectations*, which stores the sales volume each salesperson is expected to attain (his or her sales quota), both this month and over the coming months; *current performance*, which holds totals of orders taken and quantity sold for the current period and for the year to date (YTD); *historical performance*, which shows quantity-sold totals for the fiscal or calendar year; and *other performance measures*, such as the number of customer calls made and the number of days worked.

Figure 15–1 shows that after the daily sales files and the customer, product, and sales force recap files are readied, a variety of reports can be produced. The four reports illustrated and the purpose of each can be described as follows:

The *daily sales analysis* provides a daily accounting of sales activity by invoice, for each member of the sales force. Sales managers use this report to identify areas of marginal sales productivity and profitability.

The *customer sales analysis* provides a monthly and YTD summary of sales activity, by customer. Sales managers depend on this report to identify customers whose sales volumes show an increasing or a decreasing sales trend. The sales trend line can be inspected more closely when displayed. Interactive displays permit sales managers to study the buying behavior of individual customers.

The *product sales analysis* provides a current and YTD summary of sales activity by product, within each product line. Sales, merchandising, and product managers use this report to identify product-line and individual product sales and profitability trends.

The *sales force sales analysis* provides a current and YTD summary of sales activity by salesperson. Sales managers need this report to evaluate the sales coverage provided to customers and the sales performance of each salesperson. Current, historical, and other performance measures can be displayed as well as printed. For example, the ratio of the number of customer orders to the number of customer calls helps isolate the most and least productive members of the sales force.

15-2   SALES ANALYSIS PROCESSING

Before sales analysis information can be printed or displayed, computer files required in processing must either be prepared or updated. Fortunately, all processing requirements can be accomplished during the entry of customer invoice transactions. As Figure 15–6 shows, sales analysis files are updated directly by the program to enter invoice transactions. These updates include adding current

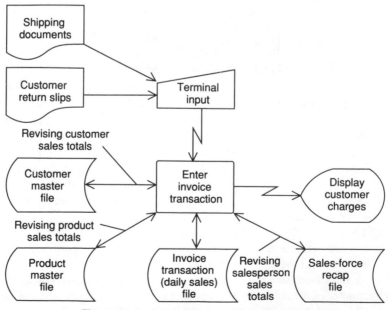

Figure 15–6   Sales analysis systems flowchart

sales and profit totals to the customer master file, for each customer order; adding current sales and profit totals to the product master file, for each line item of a customer order; and adding current sales and profit totals to the sales force recap file, for each customer order. These updates include changing current and YTD sales and profit totals and, in the case of the sales recap file, changing current sales force performance information. With the exception of sales force performance information, no new information needs to be keyed into processing. The initial keying of the customer number, for example, leads to the update of the customer master file; the keying of the product number leads to the update of the product master file. The entry of the salesperson number is avoided by storing the number in each customer record, provided only one member of the sales force is permitted to contact a customer. If several members of the sales force contact the same customer, the number of the appropriate salesperson must be keyed for each order.

To make the sales analysis system fully operational, it should be possible to display all before-and-after results of sales analysis updates to the customer and product master files and to the sales force recap file. As Figure 15–7 (a) and (b)

```
 _____
|  _____         |
| | SALES ANALYSIS                 |        |
| |_____|        |
|                                           |
|        DISPLAY CUSTOMER ACCOUNT           |
|        DISPLAY PRODUCT ACCOUNT            |
|        DISPLAY SALES FORCE ACCOUNT        |
|        DISPLAY SALES COMPARISONS          |
|        CLOSE END-OF-MONTH TOTALS          |
|                                           |
|                                           |
|                                           |
|        RETURN                             |
|_____|
```

(a) Interactive menu choices

```
 _____
|  _____         |
| | SALES ANALYSIS                 |        |
| |_____|        |
|                                           |
|        PRINT DAILY SALES ANALYSIS         |
|        PRINT CUSTOMER ANALYSIS            |
|        PRINT PRODUCT ANALYSIS             |
|        PRINT SALES FORCE ANALYSIS         |
|                                           |
|                                           |
|                                           |
|        RETURN                             |
|_____|
```

(b) Batch menu choices

Figure 15–7 Sales analysis processing menu

```
                              ┌─────────────────────┐
                              │ ITEM SALES ANALYSIS │
                              └─────────────────────┘
    ┌──────┐              ┌──────┐
    │ LINE:│ 15           │ ITEM:│ ALL
    └──────┘              └──────┘
      CLASS 15      LAB SUPPLIES                       SALES -- MAY 19       APR 19

    1   39548349      EVEN ARM BALANCE                    1,148        908      126 %
    2   40233987      BUNSEN BURNER                          86        121       71 %
    3   42315155      FUNNEL SUPPORT                         26         41       63 %
    4   44352096      BEAKER TONGS                           56         37      151 %
    5   46548349      TEST TUBE CLAMP                       137        146       94 %
    6   48645987      ALCOHOL LAMP                          322        301      107 %
    7   51794520      LABORATORY TONGS                       18         45       40 %
    8   56903585      TISSUE CULTURE TUBE RACK              186        170      109 %
    9   56905498      SINGLE BURNER STOVE                   125        211       59 %
   10   57060669      PLASTIC GOGGLES                       161         44      366 %
   11   60117701      RUBBER TUBING                         262        190      138 %
   12   61212821      TEST TUBE BRUSH                        49         41      120 %
                                                         ─────      ─────
                                                         2,550      2,255      113 %

    COMMAND KEYS
     1   START OVER        2   NEXT PAGE        3   PAGE BACK
     4   SALES             5   PROFIT           6   QUANTITY      24   SIGN OFF
```

Figure 15–8   Sales-comparison display

show, the sales analysis processing menu features five interactive programs, three of which allow for direct examination of records stored on the customer, product, and sales force files. The fourth program permits information stored on these files to be compared and sales histories to be plotted. *Sales comparison displays* are typically designed to compare current sales against last month's sales or against last year's sales. One such comparison is shown in Figure 15–8. As illustrated, May sales are compared with April sales for items in class 15, Lab supplies. *Sales trend displays* are designed to plot or chart yearly sales (see Figure 15–9). These displays help sales managers visualize increasing and decreasing sales volume trends, seasonality associated with a customer's purchases, and unusual customer buying characteristics, such as large purchases every other month. Finally, the fifth interactive program is designed to reset end-of-month sales figures for customer, product, and sales force accounts. End-of-month performance reporting must be scheduled just prior to activating this program.

The *Print Daily Sales Analysis* Program

A valued sales management report is the *daily sales analysis*. Prior to the printing of this report, the daily sales file is sorted by customer number, within salesperson number. Once sequenced, the report is printed directly. Figure 15–10 illustrates one version of the daily sales analysis report. Each invoice processed is listed in customer number sequence, within salesperson number. Thus, all sales for salesperson 01, Archer, are listed before all sales for salesperson 02, Ballard. The details printed for each invoice include the invoice number, amount, cash

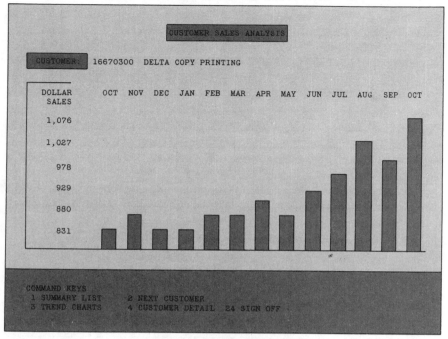

Figure 15–9   Sales trend display

discount, net sales amount (invoice amount less cash discount), invoice cost, gross profit (net sales less invoice cost), and profit percentage (gross profit divided by net sales amount).

Designers of this print program generally specify that exceptions to profitability standards be flagged for management review. A special flag would be placed alongside invoices for which the percentage of gross profit is either too high (say, above 40 percent) or too low (say, below 10 percent). Lower-than-acceptable profit percentages may occur, for example, if salespersons are imprudent in offering price concessions, overriding product prices stored on file. Sales managers need to know where and when this occurs. Likewise, if a salesperson sets a price too high—to make a hit-and-run sale—this should be brought to the attention of the sales manager.

Besides sales managers, financial managers also depend on the daily sales analysis to make sure that cash discounts have been computed properly. If company policy is not to allow discounts to some accounts (for example, see account number 11100000, listed under Archer), this situation can be reviewed. If company policy is to allow up to 3 percent for fast-paying accounts, the computer can be programmed to flag any account thought to be abnormal. A customer account with a reported discount of 4 percent, for example, would be flagged.

A display of individual sales force performance should also be possible with the sales analysis design. As shown by Figure 15–11, it should be possible to determine rate of commission, sales totals, and gross margin totals. To select from

```
 5/03/                              DAILY SALES RECAP                       PAGE 1
                                      DMAS CORP.

 SALESMAN / CUSTOMER       INVOICE  INVOICE  INVOICE   CASH    NET SALES   INVOICE   GROSS   PROFIT
        NO/ NAME             NO      DATE    AMOUNT  DISCOUNT   AMOUNT      COST    PROFIT  PERCENT

  01        ARCHER
 10100000 ABBOTT BEAUTY CORP.   776003   5/03/    67.01     .63     66.55     43.95    22.60      34
 11100000 BAINTREE APPLIANCE CENTER 776001  5/03/ 1,886.89           1,965.51  1,380.55  584.96      30

          TOTAL-ARCHER                         1,953.90     .63   2,032.06  1,424.50   607.56      30
```

```
 5/03/                              DAILY SALES RECAP                       PAGE 2
                                      DMAS CORP.

 SALESMAN / CUSTOMER       INVOICE  INVOICE  INVOICE   CASH    NET SALES   INVOICE   GROSS   PROFIT
        NO/ NAME             NO      DATE    AMOUNT  DISCOUNT   AMOUNT      COST    PROFIT  PERCENT

  02        BALLARD
 20100000 QUINN & ASSOCIATES    775079   5/03/  736.59-   12.89-    767.28    546.70-   220.58-     29
 25000020 UNIVERSITY CONTRACTORS 776000  5/03/  642.67    11.07     638.64    487.57    151.07      24
        - APTOS
          TOTAL-BALLARD                          93.92-    1.82-    128.64-    59.13-    69.51-      54
```

```
 5/03/                              DAILY SALES RECAP                       PAGE 3
                                      DMAS CORP.

 SALESMAN / CUSTOMER       INVOICE  INVOICE  INVOICE   CASH    NET SALES   INVOICE   GROSS   PROFIT
        NO/ NAME             NO      DATE    AMOUNT  DISCOUNT   AMOUNT      COST    PROFIT  PERCENT

  04        JACKSON
 20000040  POWER PLUMBING       776002   5/03/   479.81     8.40    499.80    394.90    104.90      21
        - SUNNYVALE
          TOTAL-JACKSON                         479.81     8.40    499.80    394.90    104.90      21
```

```
 5/03/                              DAILY SALES RECAP                       PAGE 3
                                      DMAS CORP.

 SALESMAN / CUSTOMER       INVOICE  INVOICE  INVOICE   CASH    NET SALES   INVOICE   GROSS   PROFIT
        NO/ NAME             NO      DATE    AMOUNT  DISCOUNT   AMOUNT      COST    PROFIT  PERCENT

      FINAL TOTALS                            2,339.79     7.21   2,403.22  1,760.27   642.95      27
```

Figure 15–10   Daily sales analysis

this display, all the manager must do is to select the salesperson from the list presented, using the mouse. The scroll bar allows the manager to select from a list of people greater than ten.

Customer Sales Analysis

At the end of the month, the customer master file is readied to print the *customer sales analysis report*. Since the file contains all the information needed, arranged by customer number, processing of the file requires no intermediate steps. Figure 15–12 shows one version of this report. The current and YTD sales volume, gross

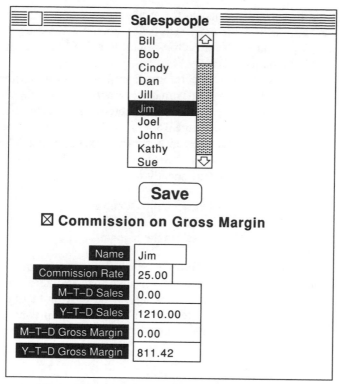

Figure 15–11   Display of individual sales performance

4/29/ AS OF 4/29/		CUSTOMER SALES ANALYSIS DMAS CORP					PAGE 1

CUSTOMER NAME	SALES AMOUNT		GROSS PROFIT		PROFIT PERCENT		DROP-SHIP SALES AMOUNT	DROP-SHIP PROFIT
	CUR	*YTD*	*CUR*	*YTD*	*CUR*	*YTD*	*YTD*	*YTD*
10100000 ABBOTT BEAUTY CORP.	143.06	1,075.85	48.01	419.56	34	39	.00	.00
10300000 ALEXANDERS' HOSPITAL SUPPLIES	171.34	1,435.77	58.84	552.78	34	39	.00	.00
10800010 A & S RESTAURANT	388.73	2,650.68	134.86	945.29	35	36	.00	.00
10800020 DEW-DROP-INN	422.78	2,733.24	147.63	992.04	35	36	.00	.00
11100000 BAINTREE APPLIANCE CENTER	4,051.89	10,303.30	1,193.67	3,125.76	29	30	.00	.00
11300000 CALDWELL INDUSTRIAL SUPPLY CO.	206.05	9,760.52	45.90	1,972.18	22	20	.00	.00
11380010 ROWE ELECTRONICS	178.29	5,145.97	47.96	1,467.12	27	29	.00	.00
27000000 WADDELL & SIMPSON	565.72	3,846.75	202.64	1,471.55	36	38	.00	.00
27300000 WENTZEL BROS.	1,299.14	11,959.71	395.55	3,578.49	30	30	.00	.00
28000000 XAVIER HARDWARE & PAINT	341.60	9,865.65	101.70	3,523.10	30	36	.00	.00
29000000 YOUNG & STRICKLAND SUPPLY	208.53	8,839.37	65.07	2,395.43	31	27	.00	.00
FINAL TOTALS-	26,167.05		7,666.45		29			
NO. RECORDS- 32		202,852.91		62,518.55		31	1,702.89	495.02

Figure 15–12   Customer sales analysis report

profit, and profit percentage are shown for each customer of a firm. In addition, special columns such as average order size (sales amount divided by the number of orders), customer returns volume, drop-shipment volume, and split-shipment volume can be placed on the report.

Interactive displays supplement the information shown on the customer sales analysis report. For example, if the sales manager wants to know the current-year sales for a customer, it should be possible to scroll through a customer list, stopping at the account that is desired (see Figure 15–13). If the customer master file can also be accessed by a database management software package, it should be possible to produce other customer summaries, such as the names of the most profitable customers. The instructions submitted directly might be

> SELECT the top ten customers
> FROM the customer master file
> WHERE sales are the highest

Although the special types of customer analysis are numerous, the most commonplace include the identification of accounts that are the most profitable and the least profitable, and accounts showing the greatest profit improvement, the poorest profit improvement, and the greatest customer return volume. Studies of this type are performed interactively, using specially designed file-processing menus.

Current Year Sales

A Sample Company
Current Year Sales
3/31/90

Customer	Date	Document		Amount
DayStar Inc	1/11/90	12	150.00	
				150.00
F & C Services	1/11/90	10588	1,060.45	
	2/ 1/90	10591	1,076.25	2,136.70
Gray, Bill	1/11/90	11	100.00	100.00
Hunt and Walters Co	2/ 1/90	13	100.00	100.00
Jim Carrol Consulting	2/ 1/90	14	687.34	687.34
O'Neil, Gregory	1/11/90	10590	31.50	31.50
Wyatt & Felling	1/11/90	10589	200.00	200.00
				3,405.54

Figure 15–13 Interactive display of customer sales

Product Sales Analysis

As with customer sales analysis, the program to print product analysis can be scheduled as soon as possible after month-end closing. Since this file is arranged by product number, no preliminary processing should be required, except when products need to be arranged by product number within product class. In this instance a computer sort is required to achieve the desired report-writing sequence.

Figure 15–14 illustrates a typical product sales analysis report. This report with subtotals summarizes the current and YTD sales history for each product within each major product class. For example, sales of basketballs are compared to sales of skis under product class Sporting/recreational. The history includes totals for quantity sold, sales volume, gross profit, profit percent, and number of orders.

Interactive displays supplement reports. With displays, it is possible to page through different product classes, selecting different reporting formats, in order to quickly spot weaknesses in product sales. As Figure 15–15 shows, interactive displays make it relatively easy to spot low and high product performance. For example, in a July-to-June sales comparison, sales of chrome fluorescent fixtures decreased to 27 percent of June sales; however, sales of two-light wall mounts increased to 121 percent of June sales. The sales comparisons are calculated as the current month's sales divided by the previous month's, rounded to whole numbers.

Interactive display menus generally allow individuals to review several types of product sales volume totals. These include comparing this month's product sales with product sales for the same month last year, with average sales for the previous twelve months, and with current quarter-to-date (QTD) sales. Besides product sales volume displays, individuals like to review several types of profitability and

```
4/29                                    ITEM CLASS SALES ANALYSIS                                   PAGE   3
AS OF 4/29/                                    DMAS CORP.


                                                                             PROFIT
                                       QTY SOLD      SALES AMOUNT       GROSS PROFIT        PERCENT     NO. ORDERS
    ITEM NC       ITEM DESCRIPTION    *CUR*  *YTD*  *CUR*     *YTD*     *CUR*     *YTD*    *CUR*YTD    *CUR* *YTD*

9391000000000-1  PINBALL MACHINE       5    137    112.89    3,903.19    38.94  1,066.96    30   30     1     6
9502000000000-1  ROBOT - 3FT          32    382    411.30    4,909.87   122.02  1,456.59    34   31     2    11
9581000000000-1  TALKING PHONE         5     95     26.70      483.67     9.20    151.17    31   32     1     5

10  * TOYS *              CLASS TOTAL-             851.56              266.33               31          7
                                                          12,554.10           4,019.39         32          38


CLASS-11         *  SPORTING/RECREATIONAL  *

9701000000000-1  CAMPER TIRE 7.00-15 *TUBE  10   86   303.85   2,638.41    93.85    832.41    31   32     2     8
9710000000000-1  OUTBOARD MOTOR        4     27    507.00    3,416.84   175.00  1,175.84    35   34     1     6
9737000000000-1  BICYCLE - 26IN        6     28    625.80    3,322.70   212.10  1,392.10    34   42     2    10
9742000000000-1  POOL TABLE            0     22       .00    5,127.82      .00  1,294.32     0   25     0     4
9773000000000-1  BASKETBALL - R/W/B   12    226    546.00   11,087.05   186.00  4,307.05    34   39     2    11
9796000000000-1  SKIS - 180 CM         8     52  1,229.20    8,099.55   349.20  2,379.55    28   29     1     5

11  *  SPORTING/RECREATIONAL  *CLASS TOTAL-       3,211.85            1,016.15               32          8
                                                          33,692.37           11,381.27         34          44


FINAL TOTAL-                                    26,167.05            7,666.45               29
                                                          202,852.91          62,518.00         31

NO. RECORDS-    7C
```

Figure 15–14 Product sales analysis report

```
                         ┌─────────────────────┐
                         │  ITEM SALES ANALYSIS │
                         └─────────────────────┘

        ┌──────────┐                    ┌───────┐
        │ LINE:  5 │                    │ ITEM: │  ALL
        └──────────┘                    └───────┘


     CLASS 01    *   INDUSTRIAL   *               SALES -- JUL 19--   JUN 19--


      1   0000000002650  FLUORESCENT FIXTURE CHROME           480       1,800       27 %
      2   1103000000000  TWO-LIGHT WALL MOUNT               1,667       1,380      121 %
      3   1111000000000  OUTDOOR LANTERN - WALL             2,780       2,998       93 %
      4   1127000000000  OUTDOOR LANTERN - HANGING          3,814       3,915       97 %
      5   1133000000000  POST LANTERN - WALL TORCH         20,167      21,732       93 %
      6   1143000000000  POST LANTERN - STEEL FRAME         1,778       1,668      107 %
      7   1178000000000  FIXTURE HANGER                     3,770       3,495      108 %
      8   1180000000000  CHANDELIER CRYSTAL                   600         620       97 %
      9   1194000000000  FLOOD LIGHT - 14IN/500W            3,525       4,935       71 %
     10   1210000000000  OPAL GLASS - 12IN                  1,300       1,625       80 %
     11   1216000000000  MODULE LIGHTS - POPPY RED            598         754       79 %
     12   1232000000000  LIGHT REFLECTOR - 14 1/2              21          82       26 %
     13   1250000000000  SLIP JOINT PLIERS - 6 3/4          1,335       1,275      105 %
     14   2206000000000  LONG CHAIN NOSE PLIERS - 7 1/2       519         505      103 %
     15   2222000000000  TUBE EXTRACTOR                     3,950       4,063       97 %
     16   2235000000000  U-BOLT FOOT MOUNT                    192         222       86 %


     COMMAND KEYS
       1   START OVER          2   NEXT PAGE         4   SALES
       5   PROFIT             6   QUANTITY          24   SIGN OFF
```

Figure 15–15   Item sales analysis interactive display

quantity-sold totals, for example, to compare this month's contribution to profit with that for the same month last year, and this month's quantity sold with the current YTD total. With such a wide variety of display formats available, individuals are generally able to tailor the process of product analysis to suit their particular needs.

Sales Force Sales Analysis

The sales analysis important to sales managers is the month-end summary of sales force activity. By way of illustration, Figure 15–16 shows a comparative *salesperson sales analysis report*. Like the daily sales analysis, this month-end report includes current and YTD sales and cost amounts, gross profit and profit percentage totals, and the number of orders taken. The difference between the two reports is that no supporting invoice detail is placed on the month-end summary. As such, the analysis provides a consolidated summary of the information shown earlier.

With interactive displays, the analysis of salesperson performance becomes easier to interpret. If information about sales expectations and historical sales performance is stored in the sales force recap file, it becomes possible to plot and compare expected sales trends with actual trends. Likewise, if other performance measures such as calls made, orders taken, and miles traveled are stored, different types of salesperson performance ratios can be calculated, compared with sales force

```
4/29/                          SALESFORCE SALES ANALYSIS                    PAGE   1
MONTH-END                           OMAS CORP.

        SALESPERSON            SALES        COST        GROSS      PROFIT      NUMBER
        NO / NAME              AMOUNT       AMOUNT      PROFIT     PERCENT     ORDERS

01   ARCHER      *CUR*       10,475.57     7,366.57    3,109.00      30         12
                 *YTD*       64,316.91    45,226.94   19,089.97      30         56

02   BALLARC     *CUR*       10,107.97     7,224.22    2,883.75      29         15
                 *YTD*       87,678.73    59,879.60   27,799.13      32         73

03   BROWN       *CUR*        2,166.40     1,488.92      677.48      31          8
                 *YTD*       28,935.02    20,508.83    8,426.19      29         45

04   JACKSON     *CUR*        2,651.16     1,873.12      788.04      29          6
                 *YTD*       15,228.32    10,049.24    5,179.08      34         30

05   LEVITRE     *CUR*          765.95       547.77      218.18      28          4
                 *YTD*        6,693.93     4,669.75    2,024.18      30         22

DELETED TOTALS   *CUR*            .00          .00          .00       0          0
                 *YTD*            .00          .00          .00       0          0

FINAL TOTALS     *CUR*       26,167.05    18,500.60    7,666.45      29         45
                 *YTD*      202,852.91   140,334.36   62,518.55      31        226
```

Figure 15–16 Salesperson sales analysis report

averages, and displayed (see Figure 15–17). Ratios of particular interest include orders per call, average order size, calls per day, selling expense to total sales dollars, miles traveled between calls, and percentage of sales quota realized. As illustrated, Archer records high sales performance compared with sales force averages. On inspection, the only ratio that might give cause for some concern is Archer's calls per day (3.4 YTD versus the sales force average of 4.8). Even then, this lower ratio can be explained by Archer's higher-than-average ratio of miles per call. It is considerably higher than the sales force average.

MONTH-END JULY, 19XX

SALESPERSON NO/NAME	PERFORMANCE RATIO	SALESPERSON AVERAGE		SALES FORCE AVERAGE	
0001 ARCHER		CUR	YTD	CUR	YTD
	ORDERS PER CALL	.844	.667	.352	.344
	AVERAGE ORDER	582	612	418	396
	CALLS PER DAY	3.5	3.4	4.2	4.8
	EXPENSES PER SALES DOLLAR	.041	.045	.067	.065
	MILES PER CALL	35.4	36.8	12.2	12.5
	PERCENT OF QUOTA	108	122	96	98
MARKET POTENTIAL $ 1,500,000					

Figure 15–17 Salesperson performance ratios

REVIEW QUESTIONS

1. What is sales analysis?

2. How is the customer invoice application used in the design of the sales analysis application?

3. What four files are required in the design of the sales analysis computer application?

4. How does the customer sales analysis report differ from the product sales analysis report? How does it differ from the salesperson sales analysis report?

5. What is the difference between a sales comparison display and a sales trend display?

6. In the printing of the daily sales recap, why should exceptions to profitability norms be flagged?

7. What types of interactive displays are designed for customer sales analysis? For product sales analysis?

8. What is a salesperson performance ratio? How are performance ratios used in the sales force sales analysis?

15-3 MARKET PLANNING OVERVIEW

Market planning begins with the setting of market and sales potentials. Once these are established, management can make a sales forecast, define its sales territories, set sales budgets, and assign sales quotas. This is the planning part of the market planning system. The control part is comparing planned with actual sales information. This comparison shows whether market plans represent realistic estimates of potential markets, of competitive behaviors, and of economic and social trends.

Market planning terminology is different from sales analysis. The important terms are the following:

Market potential: the expected sales of a product, good, or service for an entire industry

Sales potential: the share of market potential that a company might expect to achieve

Sales forecast: the estimated sales of a company, showing the difference, if any, between sales potential and sales projections

Sales quotas: the expected sales performance set for each member of the sales force

Sales potential is a percentage of market potential. If the market potential is a million dollars and the sales potential is a hundred thousand dollars, the company can be expected to capture 10 percent of the entire market (that is, Sales potential = Market potential × Market share, or Market share = Sales potential ÷ Market potential). Perhaps surprisingly, the sales forecast is often less than the sales potential. Inadequate production, lack of trained employees, or insufficient numbers of retail outlets can prohibit a company from realizing its expected market share. Finally, sales quotas are also related to expected market share. For example, if the sales potential in the southwest territory is 5 percent of the total company sales potential, then 5 percent of the sales forecast would be set as the salesperson's sales quota.

Figure 15–18 illustrates the market planning system. Since market planning involves establishing forecasts and quotas, followed by comparing these totals against actual sales totals, a two-stage planning and control design is advised. The first stage, *Ready sales forecast*, is primarily concerned with adjusting sales

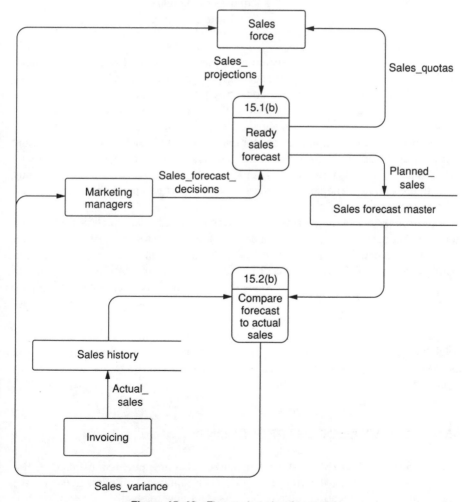

Figure 15–18 The market planning system

projections by making sales forecast decisions. Once sales forecasts are firm, sales quotas can be set for market territories and for individual sales personnel. The results of these forecast decisions are stored as planned sales on the *sales forecast master file*.

The second stage of the system, *Compare forecast to actual sales*, serves as the control function. This stage compares planned sales performance, as stored on the sales forecast master file, to actual sales, processed by the customer invoice application and stored on a sales history file. Sales history data must follow the same format as sales forecast data. For example, both the planned sales and the actual sales summary would be stored by product line as follows:

> product line number
> product line name
> > actual sales, YTD
> > > actual sales, January
> > > actual sales, February
> > > . . .

A variety of reports can be prepared once planned sales and actual sales data are consolidated. A brief summary of four such reports is as follows:

The *market performance report* compares projected sales totals against actual totals and shows percentage differences. This general report examines the extent to which a company is able to achieve its sales forecast and sales potential.

The *customer performance report* compares projected sales totals against actual totals by customer class. Sales managers use this report to determine the accuracy of customer surveys. With surveys, customers indicate what they intend to buy over future periods. The customer performance report compares these results with what customers actually buy.

The *product performance report* compares projected sales totals against actual totals by product class. Sales managers use this report to verify the accuracy of product inventory forecasts. Product forecast information itself consists of sales predictions for established and new products. Of the two, forecasts for new products are generally given more attention. Since there is limited historical sales information stored on the product master file (less than one year), sales managers must use considerable judgment in projecting sales figures for new products.

The *sales force performance report* compares sales quotas against actual sales totals for each member of the sales force. The difference between actual sales and the sales quota represents the degree to which salespersons are able to perform as expected.

15-4   MARKET PLANNING PROCESSING

Figure 15–19 (a) and (b) illustrate the market planning processing menu. Compared to sales analysis, the choice of processing options is similar; however, the market planning application contains an important new interactive program entitled *Enter market forecast*. Another difference is that the market planning application

```
┌─────────────────────────────────────┬──┐
│  MARKET ANALYSIS                     │  │
│                              ────────┘  │
│                                         │
│        ENTER MARKET FORECAST            │
│        DISPLAY CUSTOMER ACCOUNT         │
│        DISPLAY PRODUCT ACCOUNT          │
│        DISPLAY SALES FORCE ACCOUNT      │
│        DISPLAY MARKET COMPARISONS       │
│        PERFORM END-OF-MONTH UPDATE      │
│                                         │
│                                         │
│        RETURN                           │
│                                         │
└─────────────────────────────────────────┘
```

(a) Interactive menu choices

```
┌─────────────────────────────────────┬──┐
│  MARKET ANALYSIS                     │  │
│                              ────────┘  │
│                                         │
│        PRINT MARKET PERFORMANCE         │
│        PRINT CUSTOMER PERFORMANCE       │
│        PRINT PRODUCT PERFORMANCE        │
│        PRINT SALES FORCE PERFORMANCE    │
│        PRINT FORECAST CHANGE REPORT     │
│                                         │
│                                         │
│        RETURN                           │
│                                         │
└─────────────────────────────────────────┘
```

(b) Batch menu choices

Figure 15-19   The market planning processing menu

compares planned sales performance against actual performance; the sales analysis application is limited to the analysis of actual sales totals.

The most difficult part of the market planning application is determining the market potential and sales potential for a product or line of products. Setting the market potential calls for an estimate of product demand. Most market potential studies make use of broad-based external market factors, such as population, housing, and income statistics. By comparing the trends of external market factors against industry sales (the product sales for the entire industry), a company is able to determine the correlation between the two. For example, a very high correlation, such as +.898, indicates that by knowing one trend, a planner can predict with accuracy the corresponding trend.

Attempting to correlate sales data is not as easy as it may appear, however. Consider the following: Suppose a business sells kitchen and bathroom fixtures. Suppose further that the marketing manager of the company believes that there is a high correlation between new housing starts and the sales of fixtures. After limited study, the manager rejects this idea: a plot of housing starts against the sales of fixtures shows little correlation.

Suppose next that the decision is made to lag housing-starts statistics by six months and to compare this trend with the sales of fixtures. This comparison leads to a very high correlation. Once this discovery is made, the reason for this relationship becomes clear: general contractors place orders for fixtures approximately six months after they have received the approval to begin work on a new home.

The *Enter Market Forecast* Program

The first processing step in the market planning application is to enter sales forecast totals into processing. As Figure 15–20 shows, the entry of product and customer forecasts leads to the updating of several files. These updates include adding sales forecast totals to the customer master file, to record estimated sales within customer class, and to the product master file, to record estimated sales by product or by product line. Besides customer and product data, sales quotas must be added to the sales force recap file to revise the sales expectations segment. Last, in addition to these three updates, a record of all forecast changes must be written to the forecast change file.

Unlike the sales analysis application, the file updates called for by the market planning application must be carefully balanced against previously stored sales forecasts. As an example, sales forecast totals might be initially compared with product inventory forecasts to determine if forecast totals are in agreement. As you will remember, product inventory forecasts—one for each product—are set and maintained by the finished-goods inventory application.

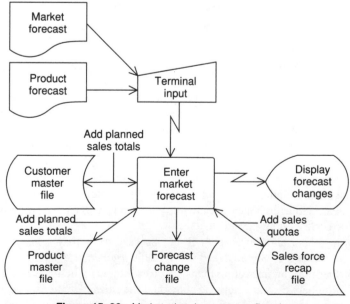

Figure 15–20   Market planning systems flowchart

SUMMARY PAGE
PRODUCT SALES FORECAST

PRODUCT LINE	SALES FORECAST	INVENTORY FORECAST	VARIANCE DOLLARS	PERCENT
BINDERS	55,000	50,000	5,000	1.10
CASSETTES	38,000	30,000	8,000	1.27
LABELS	15,000	18,000	(3,000)	.83
RIBBONS	46,000	38,000	8,000	1.21
TAPES	340,000	300,000	40,000	1.13
TOTAL	494,000	436,000	58,000	1.13

Figure 15–21 Comparing the sales and inventory forecasts

Continuing this example, Figure 15–21 illustrates what might occur during an actual comparison of two sets of forecast data—product forecast data and sales forecast data. In this example, the sales forecast is higher than the product inventory forecast for four of the five product lines. The overall difference is 13 percent. This difference is especially high for two lines, cassettes and ribbons. These differences are 27 and 21 percent, respectively.

Differences in forecast totals suggest that either the sales forecast is too optimistic, sales managers are predicting heretofore unanticipated changes in the market, or product inventory forecasts are incorrect. In any case, forecasted data must be revised so that both the sales and the product inventory forecasts are similar. Figure 15–22 shows the effect of modifying the sales forecast by making

PAGE 1: REVISED SALES FORECAST
PRODUCT SALES FORECAST

PRODUCT LINE	REVISED SALES FORECAST	INVENTORY FORECAST	VARIANCE DOLLARS	PERCENT
BINDERS	50,000	50,000	0	.00
CASSETTES	33,000	30,000	3,000	1.10
LABELS	15,000	18,000	(3,000)	.83
RIBBONS	42,000	38,000	4,000	1.11
TAPES	310,000	300,000	10,000	1.03
TOTAL	450,000	436,000	14,000	1.13

Figure 15–22 Revising the sales forecast

it more pessimistic. As shown, the forecast for the sale of binders is brought into line with the inventory forecast; however, because of improved market conditions, sales managers also show that the product inventory forecast for cassettes, ribbons, and tapes requires an upward adjustment. Last, the inventory forecast for labels is believed to be set too high. As a result, sales managers hold to their estimate for this item.

Product-line sales forecasts are added to the product master file once sales and product inventory forecasts have been reconciled. The actual update occurs in either of two ways: both individual product and product-line forecasts are revised, or only product-line forecasts are revised. The more common method is to update only product-line forecasts. When this option is selected, forecast totals are placed in a *market planning table*. This table is designed to store actual as well as sales forecast totals. In processing, the market planning application initially loads the table; the customer invoice application updates it by adding actual sales totals. The market planning table rather than individual product records is used in preparing month-end performance reports. If the table is kept small, month-end performance can be displayed as well as printed.

Revising the sales forecast to fit product inventory forecasts leads to changes in customer and sales force forecasts as well. Figure 15–23 illustrates a revised customer forecast. The summary display of customer sales forecasted for the next period is reduced by $44,000. Instead of store sales of $16,000, the forecast is lowered to $15,000. Likewise, sales to wholesales (W/SALE) have been reduced by $15,000 (from $135,000 to $120,000).

Once the customer forecast has been adjusted, the revised forecast totals are added to the customer master file. Like product-line forecasts, customer sales forecast information is summarized by class of customers, rather than by individual customer. Accordingly, forecast totals are stored at the front of the file (or in a

SUMMARY PAGE
CUSTOMER SALES FORECAST

CUSTOMER CLASS	SALES FORECAST		REDUCTION	
	INITIAL	REVISED	DOLLARS	PERCENT
STORE	16,000	15,000	1,000	.06
W/ SALE	135,000	120,000	15,000	.11
MANF	33,000	29,000	4,000	.12
DIRECT	185,000	175,000	10,000	.05
DIST	125,000	111,000	14,000	.11
TOTAL	494,000	450,000	44,000	.09

Figure 15–23   Revising the customer forecast

```
SUMMARY PAGE
SALES-FORCE QUOTAS
```

| PERSON/ | SALES QUOTA | | REDUCTION | |
TYPE OF SALE	INITIAL	REVISED	DOLLARS	PERCENT
STORE	16,000	15,000	1,000	.06
DIRECT	185,000	175,000	10,000	.05
ARCHER	65,000	58,000	7,000	.11
BALLARD	70,000	62,000	8,000	.11
BROWN	42,000	38,000	4,000	.10
JACKSON	68,000	62,000	6,000	.09
LEVITRE	48,000	40,000	8,000	.17
TOTAL	494,000	450,000	44,000	.09

Figure 15–24   Revising sales quotas

separate file) in a market planning table. Later these forecast totals are compared with actual customer sales supplied by the customer invoice application.

Figure 15–24 shows the final step in entering market planning forecasts into processing. As illustrated, the total sales force quota must be the same as the revised product and customer sales forecast totals. An alternative to setting sales volume totals is to set both volume and profit totals. With a profit quota to work toward, members of the sales force strive to sell their more profitable products. This approach differs from quotas based on volume, where the objective is to maximize total sales dollars.

The market planning application must be designed to update the sales force master file differently than the update of the product and customer master files. In this instance, revised sales quotas are added to each salesperson record. This sets the level of planned sales for the coming sales period. Later these planned sales are compared with actual sales totals supplied by the customer invoice application.

Market Performance Analysis

The addition of market planning information to the product, customer, and sales force master files shows how sales information can be analyzed in managerial terms. With market planning studies, the extent to which market plans are accurate and the degree to which a company is able to achieve its sales potential can be reported.

The performance reports displayed or printed as products of the market planning application compare the expected and actual performance data for four areas: the sales supported by a particular market, the sales of a particular product or product line, the sales made to individual customers—what they were expected to buy versus what they actually bought—and the sales produced by salespersons, both individually and as a group. Market performance analysis permits each of these

```
SUMMARY PAGE
SALES-FORCE PERFORMANCE
```

| PERSON/ | SALES | | VARIANCE | |
TYPE OF SALE	QUOTA	ACTUAL	DOLLARS	PERCENT
STORE	16,000	17,000	2,000	1.13
DIRECT	175,000	162,000	(13,000)	.93
ARCHER	58,000	60,000	2,000	1.03
BALLARD	62,000	61,500	(500)	.99
BROWN	38,000	41,000	3,000	1.08
JACKSON	62,000	52,500	(9,500)	.85
LEVITRE	40,000	36,000	(4,000)	.90
TOTAL	450,000	430,000	(20,000)	.09

Figure 15–25 Sales-force performance summary

situations to be examined in detail. It is not enough to know that forecasted sales were $450,000 and actual sales were $430,000. Differences must then be studied to discover why and where sales totals were lower than anticipated.

Figures 15–25 and 15–26 illustrate how sales differences are displayed. In Figure 15–25, actual sales were lower than forecasted sales for more than one reason: direct-mail sales combined with Jackson's and Levitre's disappointing performance led to more of the poor showing. This summary of sales force performance does little besides point the finger at strong and weak parties, however. Figure 15–26 provides more insight. As shown, weakness in three product lines—labels, ribbons,

```
PAGE 2:  CUSTOMER CLASS: DIRECT MAIL SALES
··············································PRODUCT PERFORMANCE···········································
```

| PRODUCT | SALES | | VARIANCE | |
LINE	QUOTA	ACTUAL	DOLLARS	PERCENT
BINDERS	20,000	21,500	1,500	1.08
CASSETTES	18,000	17,500	(500)	.97
LABELS	5,000	3,000	(2,000)	.60
RIBBONS	12,000	8,000	(4,000)	.67
TAPES	120,000	112,000	(8,000)	.93
TOTAL	175,000	162,000	(13,000)	.93

Figure 15–26 Direct-mail performance summary

and tapes—indicates a softening in demand. Such market conditions suggest the presence of much stronger competition or of a dramatic shift in the consumer's willingness to buy. In either case, the interactive displays help to define the nature of the problem. The specific reasons for the downturn in demand must then be determined by sales managers and product managers.

15-5 MANAGEMENT IMPLICATIONS

Providing management with an organized series of interactive displays illustrates once again why online computer applications are so important to business. With a series of consolidated summaries, managers are able to review and analyze the market's reaction to overall market plans as well as to individual selling plans. Moreover, these summaries permit managers to investigate factors contributing to better- (or poorer-) than-expected sales showings. Without computers, comprehensive studies such as sales and market analysis are seldom done; it simply takes too long to consolidate and prepare the sales summaries needed. With computers, however, information stored on easy-to-access market planning tables can be accessed in seconds.

There are associated dangers with fingertip access to sales information. Managers can be subjected to too much information: page after page of sales figures begin to look alike if a person is bombarded with all details at once. Likewise, fingertip access to information can lead some managers to overreact. They tend to forget that markets are often cyclical and show both highs and lows. Suppose that 50,000 units of cassettes are forecasted to be sold during the month of August and that, as of August 15, only 15,000 units have been sold. A sales manager might take this information and begin to lash out at members of the sales force, blaming them for poor performance. Later the manager may well discover that although product sales per day are always low during the first half of the month, they normally become extremely heavy toward month-end, reaching levels as high as 5,000 units per day.

Once an interactive approach to sales analysis and market planning is properly understood, situations such as overreacting to changes in the marketplace become less common. With understanding, the true value of the sales analysis and market planning applications become clear. The next two examples show the impact of these two applications on organizations.

Example 1. An extensive sales analysis was recently undertaken by a large gasoline conglomerate. By careful tracking of sales volumes and profitability, the company was able to identify and eliminate 2,000 of its least profitable service stations. The investigation also led to improved control over product inventory and coordination of complex supply and distribution channels.

Example 2. A medium-sized publisher was able to develop more efficient market analysis procedures for targeting its sales efforts. By collecting, storing, and displaying a variety of school-district market factors (size, socioeconomic conditions, ethnic variability, median IQ, and so forth), managers were able to predict what magazines would sell well in different school districts.

Examples such as these show that marketing and sales organizations are relying more on computers to assist them in organizing sales and market information. With interactive capabilities, computers are being used to compare and plot sales totals as well as to predict where goods will be sold, by whom, and for what purpose. Sales managers report that the ability to display sales information in different forms is critical to sales and market planning. They state that displays help them organize their thoughts and improve the clarity of their thinking.

REVIEW QUESTIONS

9. What is market planning, and how does it differ from sales analysis?

10. What is the difference between market potential and sales potential?

11. Name the four types of performance reports produced by the market planning computer application.

12. What is the most difficult part of the market-planning application? Explain why it is difficult.

13. What types of forecasts are inputs to the *Enter market forecast* Program?

14. What is a market planning table? How is it used?

15. What dangers can be associated with fingertip access to sales and market information?

16. Why are interactive displays important to the design of the sales analysis and market planning applications?

REVIEW OF IMPORTANT IDEAS

The sales analysis computer application evaluates past sales performance in order to provide sales managers with a better understanding of factors important to sales volume and profitability. Market planning, in contrast, compares internal company sales with external market conditions. This second application provides sales managers with a better understanding of factors important to achieving a desired market share.

The sales analysis application is relatively easy to design, provided the customer invoice computer application can be modified to ready the files required in processing. Besides a daily sales file, the customer, product, and sales force files must be updated by the invoice application. The design calls for the retrieval of records from these three files for display purposes.

A variety of sales management displays and reports are produced by the sales analysis application. The sales analysis report provides an accounting of daily sales activity by invoice, for each member of the sales force. The customer, product, and sales force analysis reports provide a current and YTD summary of sales activity by customer, product, and salesperson, respectively.

The market planning application is an extension of the sales analysis application. It compares actual sales totals to planned sales totals. Unlike the sales analysis application, preliminary processing is required to add forecast information to the customer, product, and sales force files. These forecasts show the estimated sales of a company, indicating the differences, if any, between sales potential and expected company sales.

Estimating future sales is the most difficult part of the market planning application. An analysis of product demand often involves attempting to correlate external market factors with internal sales trends.

Following the entry of forecasts into processing, the market planning application compares estimated sales with actual sales. As in the sales analysis application, actual sales totals are supplied by the customer invoice application. By comparing estimated and actual sales, sales managers are able to determine the accuracy of their plans and the degree to which the company is able to achieve its sales potential.

A series of interactive displays is critical to the design of both the sales analysis and market planning applications. These displays permit managers to discover the strengths and weaknesses of product lines, customer classes, market territories, and individual members of the sales force. A major benefit of interactive displays is that they help managers organize their thinking.

KEY WORDS

Sales analysis

Profitability analysis

Sales force performance analysis

Sales force recap file

Sales comparison display

Sales trend display

Daily sales analysis report

Customer sales analysis report

Product sales analysis report

Salesperson sales analysis report

Market planning

Market potential

Sales potential

Sales forecast

Sales quota

Market planning table

EXERCISES

1. Besides storing product-line information, the sales forecast master file stores market territory and customer class summary information.

    (a) What fields make up the customer class section of the sales forecast master file? (Use Figure 15–23 as a guide in answering this question.)

    (b) What fields make up the market territory summary section of the master file?

    (c) Suppose a new section called *store sales summary* is added to the master file. What fields would make up the *store sales summary* section of the master file?

2. Using Figure 15–16 as a guide, design a summary report for sales force performance. The report should compare sales quotas with actual sales for the current period and YTD, for each member of the sales force. In addition, it should show the gross profit and the profit percentage on actual sales and compare this with the total estimated gross profit and profit percentage to be realized once the sales quota totals are achieved.

    Fill in your report for the salesperson named Archer, using some of the data shown in Figure 15–16. Besides these actual sales totals, you have been provided the following estimated totals: April sales quota of $13,000, YTD sales quota (January through April) of $68,000; April estimate of profit of $4,190 and YTD estimate of profit (January through April) of $19,200.

    What can be said about Archer's sales performance for the first four months of the year?

3. Suppose a company wants to calculate and display the salesperson performance ratios shown in Figure 15–17. Suppose further that you are the systems designer responsible for this project. Your manager gives you the following two-part assignment.

    (a) Provide answers to these questions: What types of information must be keyed into processing? Who would prepare this information? When would the information be prepared? What information would be entered as a batch, for the entire sales force, and what information would be entered interactively, for one salesperson at a time?

    (b) Show how the sales analysis application would be modified to handle this additional processing requirement.

    • Prepare the revised sales analysis processing menu (see Figure 15–7).
    • List the revised contents of the sales force master file (see Figure 15–5). Expand the *other performance measures* record segment, as needed.

4. Most business firms must set up special record-keeping procedures to account for the transfer of merchandise within different units of the same division of a company. Because each unit is treated as a profit center, any transfer of goods between units must be recorded as a special type of sale. In processing intradivision sales, personnel are instructed to do two things: to cooperate with other units of the company and to protect the unit's profit margins. Consider the following situation: Suppose store 1 has only two 165 × 13 tires in stock, but needs four to complete a customer sale. Suppose next that store 1 discovers that nearby store 2 has two 165 × 13 tires in stock and is willing to send them over immediately.

    (a) Design a systems flowchart showing how the results of this intradivision transfer would be handled. Show which files are updated and which files are read- or write-only files.

    (b) Show the contents of the sales transaction file created in part (a). How will gross profit be calculated from these stored facts?

5. Suppose a company wants to set up an integrated sales analysis–market planning application. Prepare the application menus for this integrated application. Explain how your design will work.

6. Modify the display screen shown in Figure 15–11 to include market planning information. Do not change the sales analysis information shown or add additional sales analysis information.

7. Using Figure 15–13 as a guide, design an interactive display for current-year market plan versus actual sales. Explain how your design would work.

DISCUSSION QUESTIONS

1. The sales analysis application is much less difficult to design than the market planning application. Why is this so? Give several reasons.

2. Would a sales analysis–market planning application work if a large percentage of sales were cash sales? Explain how this design would differ from the one presented in the chapter.

3. How can a sales analysis–market planning application lead to major savings in a company? Give several reasons.

4. Would a sales analysis–market planning application indicate where and when to add new members to the sales force? Explain how your design would be modified to incorporate this requirement.

4-IN-1 CASE STUDY—SALES ANALYSIS AND MARKET PLANNING

4-in-1 does not provide for a separate sales analysis or profit planning application. It can be used, however, to provide different types of customer, product, and salesperson information. In this lesson you are asked to:

- Display the sales of an individual customer.
- Display the sales of a single product.
- Display the sales for an individual salesperson.

Displaying the Sales of a Customer

1. Log on and enter a date of **020597**. Press ENTER when asked, *Any change*?

2. Type **10** from the main menu and press ENTER.

3. Type **2** to print customer accounts. Press ENTER.

4. Press ENTER to type on separate pages.

5. Type **Y** to bring the customer's balance forward.

6. For starting customer, type **ANGEL** to display the account ANGEL'S GARDENS.

7. Press ENTER for ending customer.

8. Press F1 for both starting and ending dates.

9. Press ENTER for inactive accounts.

10. Press ENTER when asked, *Any change?*

11. Print the report. When finished, return to the main menu.

Displaying the Sale of a Product

12. From the main menu, type **3** to view a general ledger account.

13. Type **4010** and press ENTER.

14. Type **000** and press ENTER.

15. Press ENTER for the earliest date.

16. Type **020597** for the latest date.

17. Press ENTER when asked, *Field number to change?*

18. Examine the display screen. Then press TAB to return to the main menu.

Displaying the Sales of a Salesperson

19. From the main menu, type **11**. Press ENTER.

20. Press F1 for the starting customer.

21. Press F1 for the ending customer.

22. Press ENTER for cutoff date.

23. Type **JPR** for salesperson.

24. Press ENTER for field number to change.

25. Press ENTER to print the report.

26. Press TAB to end this lesson.

QUESTIONS

1. Why is it important to be able to determine both current and aged accounts receivable for each customer? For each salesperson? How does this help in sales and market planning?

2. Why is it important to be able to display the sales for each product or product line sold by a company? How does this help in sales and market planning?

Glossary/Index

2391188

Transaction-based applications (*cont.*) to process a specific type of business transaction and to describe facts important to processing, 35 (*See also* Business computer application; Management-based applications)

Transaction-control procedure: A processing control procedure designed to verify that the counts and amounts within the data for a transaction are in balance, 86–87 (*Contrast with* Batch-control procedures)

Transaction file: A physical file or files containing relatively temporary records that describe the details of an event, 38, 39 (*Contrast with* Master file)

Transaction processing: A method of processing in which a single transaction is entered into processing and worked on as it is received by the CPU, 10 (*Contrast with* Batch processing)

Transfer of property report, 258

Transposition error, 43

Travel time, to minimize, 331

Trend analysis: A forecasting methodology that attempts to predict the rate of increase or decrease of product sales, based on historical sales data, 364

Trial balance: A balancing process in which the dollar total shown for a series of transactions is matched against the distribution (brought about by aging of accounts or by assignment to general ledger accounts) of the same dollar total, 426

Two-way communications, 19

Update program: A type of computer program that is designed either to create (add) records to be stored on computer files or to modify (change or delete) records that have been previously stored on computer files, 44

Usage value: The dollar value of stock based on the quantity sold times the unit cost, 368

User, 1

Value-added: The unit value (measured in dollars) added to a product by a manufacturing process, 480

Value-analysis report: A report produced by the finished-goods inventory application that lists all items carried in stock, ranked in order of their usage value, 376, 377 (*See also* Usage value)

Variable budget: A budgeted amount that changes as production or sales volumes

increase or decrease, 458 (*See also* Fixed budget)

Vendor analysis: The section of the vendor master file that contains vendor product and background information and supports the analysis of vendor accounts, 402

Vendor-analysis record segment, 400, 402

Vendor background information, 402

Vendor change file, 226

Vendor-evaluation program: A program designed for the purchasing and receiving application to compare the quality, cost, and lead time associated with the purchase of items, 413

Vendor invoice: A billing statement prepared by a vendor that informs a business of the charges for goods and services supplied to them and specifies when payment is due, 210

Vendor master file: The master file that contains information on every vendor that conducts business with a company in accounts payable, 210 in purchasing and receiving, 400, 401–02, 408

Vendor name-and-address record segment, 212, 400, 401

Vendor number/code, 400

Vendor product information, 402

Vendor register: A printed register that lists the contents of the vendor master file, 227

Vendor voucher check: A two-part formal business document that contains a payment amount (which can be taken to a bank for deposit) and a description of payment (what the payment is for and how the payment amount was calculated), 209, 214, 230, 231–35

Video display design, 66–68

Video-screen report layouts, 47

Visual table of contents (VTOC), 84

Voided check, 89

Voucher number: The reference number assigned to a vendor invoice to keep each invoice unique, 214–15

W-2 statement, 293, 295

Wage and salary information segment, 278, 279

Window: A viewport or opening within a video-display screen that permits the user to display one view of a system using a portion of the screen. Windows are used in conjunction with frame-based systems, 68

YTD and QTD payroll history segment, 278, 279